Seventh Edition

Corporate Financial Analysis

In a Global Environment

Diana R. Harrington

Distinguished Professor, Finance · Babson College

THOMSON

SOUTH-WESTERN

Australia · Canada · Mexico · Singapore · Spain · United Kingdom · United States

THOMSON
SOUTH-WESTERN

Corporate Financial Analysis in a Global Environment, 7/e
Diana R. Harrington

VP/Editorial Director:
Jack W. Calhoun

VP/Editor-in-Chief:
Michael P. Roche

Executive Editor:
Michael R. Reynolds

Developmental Editor:
Joe Squance

Marketing Manager:
Charlie Stutesman

Production Editor:
Margaret M. Bril

Media Developmental Editor:
John Barans

Sr. Media Production Editor:
Mark Sears

Manufacturing Coordinator:
Sandee Milewski

Production House:
Cover to Cover Publishing, Inc.

Printer:
Transcontinental Printing
Louiseville, Quebec,
Canada

Design Project Manager:
Bethany Casey

Internal Designer:
Bethany Casey

Cover Designer:
Bethany Casey

Cover Images:
PhotoDisc, Inc.,
MapArt™/Cartesia
Software

Internal Image:
PhotoDisc, Inc.

The auhor would like to dedicate this book to her daughter Maya Anna Maria del Carmen Harrington and her Papa.

Preface

Corporate Financial Analysis was written with the objective of discussing financial analysis as it relates to managerial decision making. The goal of the manager is to enhance the value of the company. Managers can create value through the financial decisions they make, and good financial analysis can assist the manager in making better decisions—decisions that enhance the value of the firm. Value creation, and the role that good analysis can play in helping the manager to make value-enhancing decisions, is the topic of this book.

This book takes a practical orientation toward value. Thus, it does not present abstract financial theory or rigorous mathematical proofs; rather, it explains how the tools, concepts, and theories of finance can be used to improve decision making. Current examples of actual business situations are used throughout the book to illustrate the application of modern financial theories and techniques. In acknowledgment of our shrinking world and the multinational character of the financial arena students will enter, this seventh edition also contains explanations of commonly needed concepts in international finance.

Using This Book

This book was written for three different groups of readers. First, the book is intended to be used by students studying finance. Although written as a companion reference for students taking finance case courses, the book also has been, and will continue to be, useful for students who want a basic supplement to a more advanced textbook, or for instructors who wish to discuss the applications or concepts presented in more theoretical finance courses.

Second, the book is useful for executive management education in courses where basic techniques of financial analysis are needed or used. Experience in teaching executives suggests that a straightforward, pragmatic approach is required in such courses, and this book was written and revised with this requirement in mind.

Third, the book can serve as a useful reference for the practicing manager who wants a review of financial concepts and techniques. Thus, the book can be used effectively as a stand-alone reference.

Since managers and students of management can best develop the ability to apply techniques and concepts of financial decision making through practice, problems are included at the end of each chapter. The reader is encouraged to work through these problems and refer to the solutions in the appendix at the end of the book.

Acknowledgments

The book is a compilation of ideas and materials developed during the past few years at Babson College, the Darden Graduate School of Business at the University of Virginia, the Kellogg School of Management at Northwestern University, and by my previous author, Brent Wilson, now Dean at Brigham Young University, Hawaii. The material has benefited from the responses of colleagues and students in undergraduate and MBA classes and has been refined through the comments of executives attending executive management courses.

Many people have directly or indirectly contributed to the quality of the material in this book. Brent Wilson co-authored the first three editions. Colleagues, students, and business executives not only encouraged the writing of each edition, but have made helpful suggestions for improving the presentation of the concepts and ideas. For this edition, Linda Stoller, Mike Fetters, and James Parrino of Babson College, gave considerable assistance.

Diana R. Harrington

Contents

4 | Valuation 1: Capital Budgeting

5 | Valuation 2: Company Valuation, Acquisitions, Divestitures, and Mergers

Chapter One

Analyzing Corporate Performance

Over the past two decades, our world has changed more profoundly and more rapidly than we could ever have dreamed. Not only have political systems been challenged and changed, but many of the basic notions on which we have based personal and corporate financial decisions have been contested, rewritten, and even discarded. Companies now compete with others from all over the world for customers and for suppliers of labor, goods, and capital. The markets for goods and capital have become increasingly integrated, and will continue to do so.[1] At the same time, the Internet has added both challenges to existing systems for doing business and opportunities to create totally new ways to market, sell, manage, communicate, and inform. Information that was once privately held or held only by experts now is widely available with the click of a computer mouse, and communications between people and companies are virtually instantaneous. The Internet has made business truly global, and we have just begun to understand the possibilities and implications for doing business using it. What is certain is that managers of companies have to be flexible, creative, and pay close attention to the world around them.[2]

These changes have affected all our lives as citizens, customers, employees, and shareholders. Thus it is important that corporate managers, shareholders, lenders, customers, and suppliers understand the past performance and the forces that will affect the future performance of the companies upon which they rely. All those who depend on a company for products, services, or a job must be informed about the company's ability

---

[1] In much of Europe we already have seen the power of reduced intercountry barriers and a common currency, the euro. The eventual impact of Euro Zone on U.S. and world trade patterns is part of the evolving future that managers must include in their strategies and analyses.

[2] In fact, one of the changes managers must face is the rapid introduction of substitute products and methods of delivery created by the Internet.

to meet their demands now and over time as the world changes and businesses adapt.[3]

This chapter's purpose is to provide the basic tools any individual can use to begin an analysis of business performance and strength. These tools are often mathematical and are simple to calculate, but they require some experience to use well. Your skill in using them will increase with experience.

I. Who Needs to Analyze an Enterprise's Performance?

Many different groups of people need insight into business performance:

Customers: The company's customers are concerned with its viability as a vendor of goods or services. Qualified vendors are able to fulfill both their contractual obligations and the customers' needs, and will be able to provide product innovations and future service for their products. Those that are fragile may not.

Suppliers: Suppliers provide the resources that a company uses:

Goods and services: Individuals and companies that provide goods and/or services to a company are concerned with whether the company can pay its obligations on time and whether it will continue to be a customer.

Capital: Money is a good that is provided to businesses by lenders and by shareholders. Lenders are concerned with the company's ability to pay the interest, repay the loan, and abide by the loan covenants (the requirements) during the time that the loan is outstanding. Shareholders (the company's owners and potential owners) are interested in evaluating the skill of the company's management and in determining the financial strength of a company as they think about the company's future and its value.

Employees: Employees are a special group of suppliers. They supply the labor needed by the company, and because of their intimate relationship with the company, need to better understand the forces affecting it. The future of their company, the industry, and their jobs depends upon understanding the company's potential and contributing to its innovation.[4]

---

[3] Enron is one of the stories that propels us to understand the business of companies: long considered to be a financial innovator, its demise impacted its employees, their families, the company's suppliers, customers, shareholders, and bondholders, the U.S. government, and the very market for its products worldwide.

[4] In the last three decades a significant number of the largest U.S. companies with publicly traded stock changed ownership. Many of these ownership changes also resulted in serious reductions in their workforces. From the late 1990s the increasing number of cross-border mergers had serious implications for employees in many countries, and, following the end of the Internet-driven stock market bubble, corporate rationalizations and failures, particularly in the technology and Internet sectors, have had a chilling impact on workers who lost their jobs. Finally, the 2001–2003 economic slowdown and corporate malaise have resulted in reduced workforces at many major companies.

To understand a company, you must speak its language. Companies present their histories in many forms, but the most powerful and concise is shown in its financial reports. To understand this history first we will introduce you to the basic financial statements provided by companies. Since financial statements are expressed in currency, and we need ways to understand the magnitude and import of the numbers, our second step will be to interpret the statements. To do this we will show you how to calculate and interpret ratios created from information contained in the company's financial statements. Finally, using four simple ratios, you will see how to relate corporate financial performance to the shareholders' response to past and anticipated performance.

As interesting as past performance may be, managers and business analysts are more interested in what will happen in the future. We know that past performance of a company, as shown in its financial statements, may help predict future performance. Chapter 2 will describe how historical statements and analysis of those statements can be used to help forecast the future.

To start the analysis of a company's performance let's look first at the raw material we have to work with: the various financial statements that most companies provide to their internal and external analysts. We will use information from an actual company operating in the United States to help us understand and interpret the financial statements. The appendix to this chapter shows you how to extend this analysis to companies operating in different countries.[5]

II. Financial Statements

The types of financial information published in financial statements vary by country, each of which has different requirements for the disclosure of financial information. Most industrialized countries require that financial statements disclose sufficient data to allow a meaningful analysis of performance. Regulations in the United States, the United Kingdom, other Commonwealth countries, and the European Union require the most complete disclosure.[6] The growing trend of major international companies to raise funds in foreign capital markets has meant that these multinational companies provide at least the minimum level of financial information expected by investors in the countries where they are raising capital.

---

[5] In this chapter we will use U.S. companies for our analysis because many of you are based in the United States or deal with U.S.-based companies and are more familiar with U.S. accounting principles. A truly useful and comprehensive analysis of a company should include the performance of its worldwide components and competitors. For that, knowledge of other countries' accounting standards is needed. A brief discussion of that topic appears in the appendix to this chapter.

[6] U.S. accounting standards required transparency, a clear picture of a company's revenues, expenses, assets, and liabilities. However, the accounting problems of many companies, notably Enron, WorldCom, and others, suggest that U.S. companies have not been transparent and are not immune to accounting manipulation and obfuscation.

In all countries public disclosure requirements apply only to publicly owned companies.[7] Privately owned companies—companies owned by an individual or small group, such as a family—may not be required to disclose any financial information to the public. However, even with privately held companies some groups, such as lenders or private investors, often have or require access to their financial statements.

In the United States, publicly owned companies are required to prepare four financial statements: statements of earnings, financial position, cash flows, and changes in shareholders' equity. Typically, these statements are prepared quarterly and annually.

1. Statement of Earnings

The **statement of earnings**, also known as the **income statement, statement of operations**, or **profit and loss statement**, shows the total revenues earned by a company and the total expenses incurred to generate those revenues during a specific period of time. The difference between revenues and expenses is termed **net income** (also known as net earnings, profit, or margin) or **net loss** for the period.

The statement of earnings summarizes all revenue or expense transactions during a specified period of time, the reporting period. A **quarterly report** includes the transactions made during a three-month reporting period. An **annual report** includes all income and expense items for a year.[8]

Exhibit 1-1 is an example of an annual statement of earnings.[9] It is the 2001 statement for Target Corporation, a U.S. retailer.[10] Note that Target Corporation's fiscal year ends the first business day of February and thus is not the same as the calendar year. Because of this, the reporting date for fiscal year 2001 is February 2, 2002. This can be somewhat confusing, but is a normal complication when the fiscal and calendar years are not the same.

Target Corporation operates over 1,300 department stores under three different names: Target, a chain of 1,000 discount stores including SuperTarget and Target Greatland located in most states; Mervyn's, a group of midrange stores in the 14 Midwestern states; and Marshall

---

[7] Publicly held companies are those whose equity (common stock) is traded in the capital markets.

[8] For many companies the year end coincides with the end of the calendar year. For others, the year end is chosen to coincide with an appropriate time in its business cycle. For example, the year end for a seasonal business might be when inventories and accounts receivable are at their lowest.

[9] Note that expenses, or negative numbers, can be identified by parentheses, brackets, or red type. In other statements they are not highlighted by brackets or colors: the reader is expected to know that expenses are deductions. As a reader of financial statements you will become accustomed to a variety of reporting schemes.

[10] Note that many financial statements use the term *consolidated*. This means that subsidiaries owned by the company are operated and treated as if they were fully integrated into the company's activities. In some cases ownership in another company may be treated as and shown as an equity investment and not consolidated. This is done when the company owns a relatively small part of the company.

Exhibit 1-1 Target Corporation

Consolidated Results of Operations

(millions, except per share data)

	2001	2000	1999
Sales	$39,176	$36,362	$33,212
Net credit revenues	712	541	490
Total revenues	39,888	36,903	33,702
Cost of sales	27,246	25,295	23,029
Selling, general and administrative expense	8,420	7,900	7,231
Credit expense	463	290	259
Depreciation and amortization	1,079	940	854
Interest expense	464	425	393
Earnings before income taxes and extraordinary items	2,216	2,053	1,936
Provision for income taxes	842	789	751
Net earnings before extraordinary items	1,374	1,264	1,185
Extraordinary charges from purchase and redemption of debt, net of tax	(6)	—	(41)
Net earnings	$ 1,368	$ 1,264	$ 1,144

Field's, a group of 64 upscale stores located in 8 upper Midwestern states. It also owns a catalog retailer and apparel supplier. Over 80 percent of Target's sales come from the Target stores. These stores are known for more upscale and fashionable merchandise than its main rivals, Kmart and Wal-Mart.

2. Statement of Financial Position

The **statement of financial position** is also referred to as the **balance sheet**. This statement reports the corporation's assets, liabilities, and owners' equity at a particular date in time, typically the end of the reporting period. The corporation's assets must equal or balance the funds used to purchase the assets (hence the term balance sheet).[11] Funds provided by lenders are recorded on the balance sheet as liabilities; funds provided by shareholders are recorded as owners' equity or shareholders' equity for publicly held corporations. Target calls shareholders' equity shareholders' investment.

The statement of financial position differs from the statement of earnings in that it reports the firm's status at a point in time, the end of the

---

[11] A formula is used to represent this relationship:

$$\text{Assets} = \text{Liabilities} + \text{Owners' Equity}$$

reporting period. Whereas the statement of earnings reports on the flow of transactions or funds, the statement of financial position reports on the resulting financial status. Thus a quarterly balance sheet, called a statement of financial position by Target, specifies the status of the assets, liabilities, and owners' equity at the end of a quarter; an annual report indicates status at the conclusion of the reporting year. Target's statements of financial position, or balance sheets, for fiscal years 2001 and 2000 are presented in Exhibit 1-2.

3. Statement of Cash Flows

A company generates new financial assets in several ways: by borrowing additional funds, issuing new owners' equity, retaining the period's earnings, and/or decreasing assets (for instance, selling excess equipment). The resources thus generated can be used to increase assets by purchasing new equipment, decrease liabilities by paying off loans, or decrease owners' equity by paying a dividend or repurchasing outstanding shares. Previously known as the **statement of changes in financial position** or **funds flow statement**, the **statement of cash flows** reports the amounts of cash generated by the company during the period, as well as the disposition of cash. The difference between the sum of the sources of cash and the sum of its uses is typically reported as a net change in cash and cash equivalents, as used by Target, or as a change in net working capital. **Net working capital** is current assets minus current liabilities. Cash equivalents are assets that can rapidly be converted into cash, such as short-term capital market investments. The cash flow statements for 2000 and 2001 from the 2001 Target Corporation's Annual Report are shown in Exhibit 1-3.

The cash flow statement shows that Target has been investing heavily in property and equipment as it expanded to new locations. In addition, Target expanded its accounts receivable. Most of these investments were made using the company's earnings and by borrowing.

4. Statement of Changes in Shareholders' Equity

This report is called the **statement of changes in shareholders' equity, statement of shareholders' investment,** or **statement of retained earnings**. This statement provides additional details on the composition of the owners' equity accounts for the company and shows how much the company earned in the period, how much of it was paid out, and how much was retained on the shareholders' behalf. This statement also shows any shares repurchased, reports any new shares the company issued, and reports on the impact of exercised options.[12]

The purpose of this statement is to highlight changes in owners' equity or retained earnings that have occurred during the reporting period.

---

[12] **Options** are rights to purchase shares at a predetermined price at a time or within a time period. In general these rights are given to management for performance or as a part of their employment contract. We will discuss these in more detail later in the book.

Exhibit 1-2   Target Corporation

Consolidated Statements of Financial Position

(millions)

Assets	February 2, 2002	February 3, 2001
Cash and cash equivalents	$ 499	$ 356
Accounts receivable		
(net of $261 million allowance)	3,831	1,941
Receivable-backed securities		
Inventory	4,449	4,248
Other	869	759
Total current assets	9,648	7,304
Property and equipment		
Land	2,833	2,467
Buildings and improvements	10,103	8,596
Fixtures and equipment	4,290	3,848
Construction-in-progress	1,216	848
Accumulated depreciation	(4,909)	(4,341)
Property and equipment, net	13,533	11,418
Other	973	768
Total assets	$24,154	$19,490

Liabilities and shareholders' investment

	February 2, 2002	February 3, 2001
Accounts payable	$ 4,160	$ 3,576
Accrued liabilities	1,566	1,507
Income taxes payable	423	361
Current portion of long-term		
debt and notes payable	905	857
Total current liabilities	7,054	6,301
Long-term debt	8,088	5,634
Deferred income taxes and other	1,152	1,036
Shareholders' investment		
Common stock	75	75
Additional paid-in capital	1,098	902
Retained earnings	6,687	5,542
Total shareholders' investment	7,860	6,519
Total liabilities and shareholders' investment	$24,154	$19,490

Exhibit 1-3   Target Corporation

Consolidated Statements of Cash Flows

(millions)	2001	2000	1999
Operating activities			
Net earnings before extraordinary items	**$ 1,374**	$ 1,264	$ 1,185
Reconciliation to cash flow:			
Depreciation and amortization	**1,079**	940	854
Deferred tax provision	**49**	1	75
Other non-cash items affecting earnings	**211**	237	163
Changes in operating accounts providing/(requiring) cash:			
Accounts receivable	**(963)**	—	—
Inventory	**(201)**	(450)	(323)
Other current assets	**(91)**	(9)	(54)
Other assets	**(207)**	13	(65)
Accounts payable	**584**	62	364
Accrued liabilities	**29**	(23)	100
Income taxes payable	**128**	87	166
Cash flow provided by operations	**1,992**	2,122	2,465
Investing activities			
Expenditures for property and equipment	**(3,163)**	(2,528)	(1,918)
Increase in receivable-backed securities	**(174)**	(217)	(184)
Proceeds from disposals of property and equipment	**32**	57	126
Other	**(5)**	(4)	(15)
Cash flow required for investing activities	**(3,310)**	(2,692)	(1,991)
Net financing (requirements)/sources	**(1,318)**	(570)	474
Financing activities			
(Decrease)/increase in notes payable, net	**(808)**	245	564
Additions to long-term debt	**3,250**	2,000	285
Reductions of long-term debt	**(802)**	(806)	(600)
Dividends paid	**(203)**	(190)	(195)
Repurchase of stock	**(20)**	(585)	(581)
Other	**44**	42	18
Cash flow provided by/(used for) financing activities	**1,461**	706	(509)
Net increase/(decrease) in cash and cash equivalents	**143**	136	(35)
Cash and cash equivalents at beginning of year	**356**	220	255
Cash and cash equivalents at end of year	**$ 499**	$ 356	$ 220

Amounts presented herein are on a cash basis and therefore may differ from those shown in other sections of this Annual Report. Cash paid for income taxes was $666 million, $700 million and $575 million during 2001, 2000 and 1999, respectively. Cash paid for interest (including interest capitalized) was $446 million, $420 million and $405 million during 2001, 2000 and 1999, respectively.

This statement is similar to the cash flow statement; however, it focuses specifically on changes within the owners' equity segment of the balance sheet. In the statement there are several columns reporting the annual changes in various equity accounts.

- **Common stock.** This is the number of shares issued and held by the company's shareholders, its owners. The shares are recorded on the balance sheet at a **par value,** or face value, of the stock. The face value may be the value for which the share was sold when it was first issued or some nominal amount, for example, $1.00. Target's common stock has a par value of $0.083.[13]
- **Additional paid-in capital.** This is the amount above par value the shareholders paid for their shares when the company first issued them.[14]
- **Retained earnings.** This is the sum of the income kept (retained) by the company after all dividends are paid. The balance sheet retained earnings account is the sum of all previous earnings retained. Investors expect that a company will put this income to use for their future benefit.[15]
- **Preferred stock.** Preferred stock is stock that typically has a predetermined dividend that must be paid before any common shareholders receive dividends. Normally the owners of the shares have no voting rights. Preferred stock also has a par value. Target's preferred stock has a par value of $0.01. The preferred stock of Target is convertible into common stock.
- **Treasury stock.** These are shares that the company is authorized to issue but has not sold to current or potential shareholders. These may also be shares that have been sold and repurchased by the company.

Other companies may show different accounts in the equity section of the balance sheet.[16] If there are unusual accounts, you should read the footnotes to the financial statements to determine what they represent.

Exhibit 1-4 shows the statement of changes in shareholders' equity for Target Corporation from its 2001 Annual Report.

---

[13] When the stock is first issued, or sold, it is sold for a price set by the company and its investment bankers. If new stock is issued several times over the company's life, the issue price is likely to be different each time. The par value typically remains the same.

[14] Once the stock is issued in the capital markets, it trades in the markets for whatever shareholders' believe is its value. The company does not trade the issued stock, but its actions and success influence the price for which shareholders will sell their shares to others and the price nonshareholders are willing to pay.

[15] Later in this book we will discuss how management and a company's board decide the proportion of the annual net income to retain and to send to shareholders in the form of dividends.

[16] For example, there may be purchase rights: the right to purchase stock, usually preferred, and usually at a set price and/or time. These rights may be issued in conjunction with a financing arrangement or merger.

Exhibit 1-4   Target Corporation

Consolidated Statements of Shareholders' Investment

(millions)	Common Stock Shares	Convertible Preferred Stock	Common Stock	Additional Paid-in Capital	Retained Earnings	Total
January 30, 1999	884	$ 268	$74	$ 286	$4,683	$5,311
Consolidated net earnings					1,144	1,144
Dividends declared					(191)	(191)
Repurchase of stock	(19)		(1)		(580)	(581)
Issuance of stock for ESOP	3			81		81
Conversion of preferred stock	41	(268)	3	289		24
Stock options and awards:						
Tax benefit				29		29
Proceeds received, net	4			45		45
January 29, 2000	912	—	76	730	5,056	5,862
Consolidated net earnings					1,264	1,264
Dividends declared					(194)	(194)
Repurchase of stock	(21)		(1)		(584)	(585)
Issuance of stock for ESOP	2			86		86
Stock options and awards:						
Tax benefit				44		44
Proceeds received, net	5			42		42
February 3, 2001	898	—	75	902	5,542	6,519
Consolidated net earnings					1,368	1,368
Dividends declared					(203)	(203)
Repurchase of stock	(1)				(20)	(20)
Issuance of stock for ESOP	3			89		89
Stock options and awards:						
Tax benefit				63		63
Proceeds received, net	5			44		44
February 2, 2002	905	$ —	$75	$1,098	$6,687	$7,860

5. Financial Statement Footnotes

In addition to the data contained in the financial statements, companies also include significant financial information in notes to the statements. These footnotes typically contain more detailed information about the items on the balance sheet and income statement. Most companies provide further information about taxes, details about debt, contingent liabilities, leases, nonconsolidated subsidiaries, the impact of foreign exchange on accounts and transactions, employee benefit plans, options, and depreciation schedules for property, plant, and equipment. To give you an example from the Target statements, Target reports how its revenues are recognized (at the time of sale), how its accounts receivable are managed (through a special purpose subsidiary), and whether its advertising costs are expensed or capitalized (they were expensed). In addition to describing the conventions used in the accounting, most unusual items in the statements also are described in the footnotes.

Because specific accounting policies can have a significant impact on the performance reported in financial statements, companies usually include in the footnotes an explanation of the major accounting procedures used in preparing the statements. For example, in 1998 the U.S. Accounting Standards Board, the group that determines accounting policies in the United States, required that software developed by a company for its own use be capitalized and depreciated. In the past these costs had been shown as an expense when the money was spent.[17] At present, companies and the Financial Accounting Standards Board (FASB) are wrestling with how to handle the costs of incentive options.

Some footnoted items can be very important. Stock analysts spend considerable time in trying to understand and value the impact of un- or underreported items. For example, it was not until late 1992 that U.S. companies were required to report the present value of the cost of providing nonpension-related post-retirement benefits, such as health care, for their employees. Previously, U.S. companies reported the costs of these benefits as they were paid or when the employee retired, not as they were earned during the employee's career. This accounting change had a significant impact on the earnings of many U.S. companies at the time. Canny stock analysts had estimated the size of the earnings impacts on companies most affected and determined how it would impact the value of the company. Based on their revised information, stock analysts made buy and sell recommendations for stocks.

---

[17] Expensing means that the full cost is reported on the income statement in the period when the expense is incurred. Capitalizing the expense means that the cost is turned into an asset on the balance sheet and depreciated or amortized (reported as an expense) on the income statement over a period of years. Changing from an expense to a capitalized and depreciated asset reduces the reported expenses in the year in which the asset is purchased or created (and thus increases income and taxes) and spreads out the expenses, income, and tax reduction over several years. As you will see later in this book, the time value of money makes a current tax reduction more valuable than an equivalent tax reduction in the future.

Controversies continue about how to value options and how to account for an acquisition, among other things.[18] This is a changing and dynamic area. Many expect major changes in accounting rules and scrutiny will be forthcoming as a result of the accounting revelations and restatements of such companies as Tyco, Enron, WorldCom, and Merck in the spring and summer of 2002.

Included in the notes to the financial statements of all companies in countries that abide by international accounting standards is information about their accounting standards and policies. For purposes of brevity, the notes to the Target Corporation financial statements have not been reproduced here.[19]

III. Analysis of Financial Statements

When analyzing financial statements, keep in mind the purpose of the analysis: to better understand the company's performance. Because different analysts are interested in different aspects of a company's performance, no single type of analysis is appropriate for all situations. However, there are several general factors the analyst should bear in mind when reviewing data on financial statements:

1. All financial statement data are historical.
2. Historical data are collected and reported on the basis of the particular accounting principles allowed in the country and used by the company.
3. The variability of seasonal funds flows and requirements in some companies make the timing of reporting important.

First, all financial statement data are historical. Although one may make projections based on such data, the accuracy of projections depends both on the forecaster's ability and the continued pertinence of the historical relationships to current or future operations and to industry and economic conditions.

Second, historical data are collected and reported on the basis of the particular accounting principles used by the company. These accounting principles and rules vary from country to country. Even within a country

---

[18] A recent and rather bitter controversy has erupted over how best to value an acquisition of another company. There are two choices. The first is a **pooling-of-interests** in which the tax and accounting principles of the two companies are maintained as they had been before the acquisition. As an example, depreciation for fixed assets would remain the same. The alternative, the **purchase method**, requires that the assets of the acquired company be revalued to their fair market value and depreciated. However, any amount that was paid for the company above its asset value must be shown as goodwill on the balance sheet and be used as an offset to future earnings.

[19] To see the full financial report you may log onto a company's web site, or obtain it in the form of the 10-K, the company's annual report to the Securities and Exchange Commission, through the SEC's document search engine, EDGAR, at http://www.sec.gov. The SEC can also be reached via links from many financial web sites. Some of these sites are listed at the end of this and other chapters.

or an industry several approaches to specific issues may be allowed at one time, and these approaches may change over time. One example of such discretion is the price at which a company can transfer an item out of inventory (reported on the balance sheet) into cost of goods sold (reported on the income statement) when a product is sold. Exhibit 1-5 shows the inventory balance that would be reported on the balance sheet and the expense in cost of goods sold as well as the resulting income and taxes from using three different inventory methods. The inventory methods are descriptively named FIFO, LIFO, and average cost. Each of these indicates the price at which inventory is transferred out of inventory into cost of goods sold when goods are made and sold. FIFO transfers goods at the first price (first-in, first-out), LIFO at the price of the last purchase (last-in, first-out), and average cost at the average cost of the items in inventory. To understand the difference the choice of methods can have on the balance sheet and income statement items, including taxes and profits, you need only look at Exhibit 1-5. From this exhibit you can see that the choice of inventory method can make quite a difference, and can distort comparisons between companies using different methods. You need look only at the inventory balance and net income figures to see the magnitude of the differences that come from the different inventory accounting

Exhibit 1-5

Inventory Methods and the Impact on Earnings

		Inventory Method		
Balance Sheet Impacts		First-In, First-Out (FIFO)	Last-In, First-Out (LIFO)	Average Cost
Date	Action			
Jan. 1	Buy 10 units at $10 each	$ 100	$ 100	$ 100
Jan. 15	Buy 10 units at $15 each	150	150	150
Jan. 15	Inventory value	250	250	250
Jan. 16	Use 10 units in manufacturing, sell item and move inventory cost to cost of goods sold	(100)	(150)	(125)
Jan. 16	Inventory balance	$ 150	$ 100	$ 125
Income Statement Jan. 1–Jan. 16				
Revenues from sale of 10 units at $25		$ 250	$ 250	$ 250
Cost of goods sold		(100)	(150)	(125)
Operating income		150	100	125
Other expenses		(75)	(75)	(75)
Net income before taxes		75	25	50
Taxes (@ 34%)		(26)	(9)	(17)
Net income		$ 50	$ 17	$ 33

methods. Over time the cumulative results are identical regardless of the method chosen. However, at any point in time they are not.

We have chosen to show the impact on results of different inventory valuation methods. Perhaps even more important to financial results is revenue recognition. It certainly has been a source of great controversy in 2002 as companies had to revise their earnings, sometimes quite substantially as a result of strange choices or outright fraudulent reporting. The issue is the point at which revenue from a sale is recognized. This recognition issue becomes quite difficult with longer-term contracts and bundled products, for example a machine, a service contract, and service delivery.

It is important to know what principles are being used before drawing conclusions about any company's performance over time. This is even more important when comparing companies, even those within an industry, as each company may use different accounting practices. Even more difficult is the comparison of companies operating in different countries since no single set of accounting standards exists worldwide. In fact, information on the accounting principles in other countries can be difficult to obtain and tedious to absorb and understand. To show how important the differences can be we have included an appendix to this chapter, "Cross-Border Ratio Analysis," to aid the reader. In addition, there are sources for accounting standards in various countries listed at the end of the appendix.

Third, because of the variability of seasonal funds flows and requirements in some businesses, the analyst should be aware of the timing of the reporting. For some companies in highly seasonal or cyclical industries, comparisons of results from different reporting periods should be approached cautiously.[20]

Despite these concerns, an analyst can develop an insightful examination of a corporation's financial performance. The most common method of analyzing financial statements is through the use of ratios. These ratios are simple mathematical relationships between various items on financial statements. In this chapter we will describe the most commonly used ratios. In addition to the commonly used ratios described and demonstrated in this chapter, most analysts develop and use specialized ratios to examine specific companies or industries. While you need to be able to compute the ratios, the important analytical skill is in determining which ratios to use in each case and interpreting the results; the ratios, by themselves, are relatively meaningless. Only by comparing ratios over time and between companies—and by understanding the underlying causes of the differences among them—does ratio analysis help the shareholder, lender, employee, analyst, portfolio manager, or manager gain insight into corporate performance.

---

[20] After understanding the nature of the company's business, the analyst can compare ratios at the same time from year to year or can adjust the numbers for seasonal peaks and troughs. In addition, while using year end figures is typical, the analyst may gain more insight using averages.

The key ratios commonly used for analyzing the internal performance of a company can be categorized into four groups: (1) profitability ratios, (2) asset utilization or efficiency ratios, (3) capitalization or financial leverage ratios, and (4) capital market ratios. For each group there is a key ratio that summarizes the company's performance in that area. To look at the ratios, let's first turn to the company's profits, and how to gauge them.

1. Profitability Analysis Using Ratios

Analysts use a number of methods to determine the relative profitability of a company. The key ratio is called the **return on sales** (ROS). This ratio relates a company's net earnings or income to its sales or revenues.[21] This ratio is also referred to as **net profit ratio** or **profit margin**. Using data from the Target Corporation's annual financial statements, this ratio is calculated as follows.[22]

$$\text{Return on sales} = \frac{\text{Net income}}{\text{Net sales}}$$

$$= \frac{\$1,368}{\$39,888}$$

$$= 0.0343 \text{ or } 3.43\%$$

This ratio tells us what percentage of each dollar of revenue is available for the owners (the shareholders) after all the expenses are paid to other suppliers. For Target the net income is $0.0343 for every $1.00 of revenue.

Within every industry there is variation: some companies are more profitable than others; some industry segments have superior earnings; some countries provide better profit environments than do others. In an industry that is domestic and international, and consists of small, large, and specialized retailers, Target operates as a large U.S. retailer. Target's ROS of 3.4 percent is better than the 3.3 percent return for its large rival Wal-Mart, and well above the losing performance of Kmart. Interestingly, Wal-Mart's Mexican company, Wal-Mart de Mexico, outperformed all three companies. By the way, these differences were not only for 2001.

The differences between companies in different industries are even more dramatic. Exhibit 1-6 shows the ROS averages for companies in a

---

[21] Net sales are generally net of discounts, returns, and allowances to customers. If no net sales figure is reported, the analyst will use total sales or revenues. For Target we used total revenue, which includes credit revenues. Whether to use total sales or total revenues is up to the analyst. In addition we used net income after extraordinary items. In most cases, particularly when the company usually has extraordinary items and/or they are small, this is appropriate. However, if the extraordinary items are large and/or infrequent we should use net earnings before extraordinary items. This ratio can then be compared to the ratios from other years.

[22] Target Corporation's financial data is used in the remainder of this chapter to illustrate the calculation of the ratios. Because Target's financial statements report performance in millions of dollars, all the numbers are in millions, unless otherwise noted.

Exhibit 1-6

Return on Sales—Various U.S. Industries, 2001

Number of Companies	Industry	Return on Sales
8	Advertising	11.1%
8	Biotech	7.4%
15	Computer systems	−0.6%
7	Consultants	3.7%
19	Department stores	1.4%
66	Electric utilities	6.0%
8	Employment	1.2%
20	Finance	16.1%
32	Food manufacturing	4.2%
10	Furniture manufacturing	4.7%
10	Grocers	1.6%
9	Jewelers	−0.7%
22	Paper producers	3.6%
8	Software	−4.4%
19	Steel	−0.6%
7	Wireless communications	−26.4%

number of industries in the United States in 2001.[23] As you can see, there is a wide range of profit margins among industries operating in the United States. The profitability of companies differs among industry groups and depends on their competitive situations. For example, grocers operate with very low profit margins because competition in this industry tends to be based on low prices.[24] On the other hand, profit margins in industries with highly differentiated products, such as jewelry, are generally much higher, and the volume of sales of each item can be much lower.

In addition to the differences in ROS among industries, profitability can change for any company or industry over time. Target (and most discount retailers) has a relatively steady ROS over time: over the last 5 years Target's ROS rose continuously, albeit slowly, from 2.7 percent in 1997 to a high of 3.4 percent in 2001.

Cyclical companies usually have much lower returns on sales at the bottom of a business cycle when costs tend to be high, but prices have been kept low in an effort to lure the few buyers that exist. At the top of a cycle, companies are able to raise or maintain their prices and, since they

---

[23] These are industry averages. There are companies that outperform the averages and those that under perform. However, the average is illustrative of the different performance from industry to industry.

[24] To cover all costs, and market a profit for shareholders, high volume is typical in this industry.

are operating close to capacity, fixed costs per unit tend to be low.[25] The automobile industry is an example of a cyclical industry. Exhibit 1-7 shows the profits of one of its major participants, General Motors, for 10 years beginning in 1991. The impact of the business cycle on the profitability of this company is clear and extends throughout the industry. This example simply serves to show how important it is for the analyst to know and understand the nature of a company's business to properly interpret ratios.

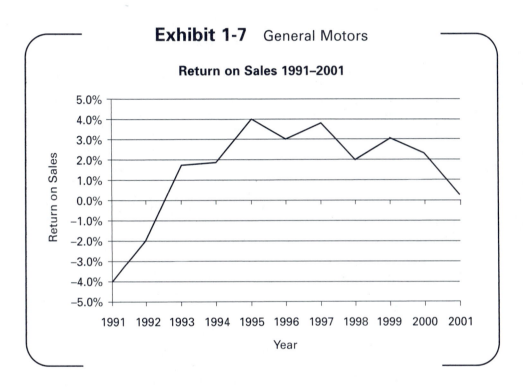

Exhibit 1-7   General Motors

Return on Sales 1991–2001

The return on sales is the key profitability ratio. This ratio tells the analyst what proportion of the revenues remain after all expenses are met. However, when the analyst sees significant changes in the ROS over time or relative to other companies, more information is needed; the analyst needs to examine what contributed to the return on sales. Looking at the expenses can do this.

Companies make and sell products in many ways. Companies with low profit margins may have high costs of production; high marketing,

---

[25] To examine the relationship between fixed and variable costs we use break-even analysis. This analysis shows at what level of sales revenues the company's fixed and variable costs are fully covered with no profit. The formula for accounting breakeven is:

$$\text{Break-Even Sales} = \frac{(\text{Fixed costs} + \text{Depreciation}) \times (1 - \text{Tax rate})}{(\text{Sales price} - \text{Variable costs}) \times (1 - \text{Tax rate})}$$

selling, or research expenses; or a combination of these. Changes in profitability reflect changes in some or all of these costs. Thus, as a first step in understanding the sources of profitability, many analysts look at the profit a company earns after direct costs of production. This profitability ratio is called the **gross margin** or **gross profit**. While Target does not, most companies report the gross profit. We can easily calculate it; the gross margin or profit is simply revenues minus cost of goods sold.

$$\text{Gross margin} = \frac{\text{Gross profit}}{\text{Total revenues}}$$

$$= \frac{\$12,642}{\$39,888}$$

$$= 0.317 \text{ or } 31.7\%$$

For Target the gross margin was 31.7 percent. This means that 68.3 percent of every dollar of revenue Target earned was used to cover the direct costs of producing or obtaining the products it sold. Because the net profit margin was 3.4 percent, the rest of the company's profits, 28.3 percent, went to cover all other expenses such as the costs of administration, including interest on debt, research and development, and taxes.

Another ratio can be used to determine the relative profitability of a company after all costs except taxes: **operating profit/sales**. Operating profit or margin is gross profit minus all operating expenses such as selling, general, and administrative expenses.

$$\text{Operating profit/Sales} = \frac{\text{Operating profit}}{\text{Net sales}}$$

$$= \frac{\$2,216}{\$39,888}$$

$$= 0.0556 \text{ or } 5.56\%$$

Target's gross margin or profit was 31.7 percent; the operating margin was 5.6 percent. The difference between the two, 26.1 percent, was the portion of net sales that Target spent on nonproduction-related expenses. This portion can vary substantially over time and among companies. How much a company spends on nonproduction-related expenses depends, among other things, on the importance of new product development and the efficiency of corporate headquarters.

Analysts who want to know how profitably a company produces and markets its goods, not how inexpensively it finances itself, may calculate yet another ratio, **EBIT/sales**. **EBIT** stands for earnings before interest and taxes. Since Target reports its earnings before taxes *but* after interest, we simply add back interest to obtain the EBIT number.

$$\text{EBIT/Sales} = \frac{\text{Earnings before interest and taxes}}{\text{Net sales}}$$

$$= \frac{\$2,680}{\$39,888}$$

$$= 0.0672 \text{ or } 6.72\%$$

You will note that Target's EBIT/sales is not the same as its operating profit/sales ratio because Target paid interest on its debt. That interest expense was included in the operating expenses, but not included in this ratio. This ratio is particularly useful for those determining whether a company can pay its interest expenses and with what degree of safety.

The final profitability ratio that is in widespread use, particularly among stock analysts, is **EBITDA**. Actually the ratio is **EBITDA/sales** or EBITDA/revenues, with EBITDA standing for earnings before interest, taxes, depreciation, and amortization. Using this ratio the analyst attempts to eliminate all the outside influences (interest) and timing effects (depreciation) on the company's profitability figure. Thus financing costs, interest, depreciation, timing of the capital expenses as dictated by tax authorities, and taxes are ignored in calculating EBITDA. For Target, operating profit was $2,680, but this included depreciation expenses of $1,079.[26] The EBITDA was the sum of the two, $3,759. Remember all numbers are in millions.

$$\text{EBITDA/Sales} = \frac{\text{EBITDA}}{\text{Sales}}$$

$$= \frac{\$2,680 + \$1,079}{\$39,888}$$

$$= \frac{\$3,759}{\$39,888}$$

$$= 0.0942 \text{ or } 9.42\%$$

The EBITDA ratio is one that has gained widespread acceptance among financial analysts, particularly investment analysts, as they attempt to find a ratio that represents real cash earnings, earnings not impacted by such things as the differences in tax treatment of assets.[27] It is also believed that this ratio is more comparable for companies using different accounting practices or when comparing companies that use different accounting systems. In an increasingly global world where analysts follow industries with companies operating under different accounting and tax rules, a ratio that reduces the tax/accounting-induced differences is a valuable tool.[28]

2. Profitability Analysis Using Common-Size Statements

Another approach to understanding the profitability and expenses of a company is called the **component percentage analysis**. The results of this

---

[26] The EBIT (earnings before interest and taxes) figure comes from the income statement shown in Exhibit 1-1. Depreciation will either come from the income statement or, if not reported on the income statement, from the consolidated statement of cash flows.

[27] This ratio often is used as a proxy for cash earnings. This is similar to the cash flow figure we will discuss extensively in Chapters 4, 5, and 7.

[28] Few analysts will know all of the different accounting and tax rules in every country where they may research companies. While an analyst with accounting/tax rule knowledge may understand the business performance of a company better or uncover hidden liabilities or assets, the fact is that quick comparisons are important and EBITDA helps the global analyst do the job better.

analysis are called **common-size statements**. To calculate component percentages, the analyst simply relates each cost or profit reported on the income statement to that period's revenues or sales.[29] Such an analysis is useful when looking at the company's performance over time. A component analysis of Target's income statements for 1999 to 2001 is shown in Exhibit 1-8. While ratios may tell an interesting story, this analysis shows in detail the cost-revenue relationships for the company. This analysis shows that the relationship between Target's revenues and expenses are incredibly stable. To say the least, such stability is very unusual.

3. Profitability Using Growth Rates

Of great interest to those looking at a company's financial performance is how rapidly various items are growing, in particular revenues and profits. Indeed, these particular growth rates have their own names: top-line growth for revenues, and bottom-line growth for profits. Like the common-size statements we can look at the growth of the revenues and profits and at each of the expense items as well.[30] In Exhibit 1-9 you can see the result of the growth rate analysis for Target over the past two years.

A growth rate analysis can show how well the company is progressing, and how well it is keeping the expense and profit items in line with each other. You can also look at the growth rate of asset and liability accounts using this same type of analysis. As you can see, Target's growth rates have been positive and growing, with a slight drop off in revenue and earnings growth rates in 2001. Credit expense has grown dramatically.

Growth rate analysis is quite telling, and is particularly useful when we use the past as a basis for forecasting the future. We will do this in Chapter 2. However, you must take care. The growth rate analysis can be misleading; various outside influences can dramatically impact the growth rates and lull the unsuspecting analyst into a false sense of robust or diminished growth. Of all the external influences there are two that are worth noting: growth by expansion or acquisition, and inflation.

Growth by acquisition or expansion can mask natural growth—growth that comes as a result of growing sales alone. For example, can we tell how well Target was actually growing in sales at its existing locations from the data in Exhibit 1-9? Perhaps some or all of the growth came from the purchase or opening of new stores. It is often difficult to tell. But creative analysts were not deterred. They have used a variety of ways to determine the rate of natural growth. Two that have been widely used and reported are sales per square foot and same-store sales. **Same-store sales**, sales from stores owned in both periods, has become a widely used way to discuss this natural growth independent of expansion and acquisition. Let's look at Target's revenue growth on a same-store, thus comparable, basis.

---

[29] This form of ratio analysis also can be used to examine the composition of various items on the balance sheet. The comparison is of each asset, liability, and equity account to total assets. The balance sheet items can also be compared to revenues.

[30] This is particularly easy using a computer spreadsheet program.

Exhibit 1-8   Target Corporation

Percentage Components for Income Statements

(dollars in millions)

Income Statement Items	2001 Dollars	2001 Percentage	2000 Dollars	2000 Percentage	1999 Dollars	1999 Percentage
Sales	$39,176	98.2%	$36,362	98.5%	$33,212	98.5%
Net credit revenues	712	1.8%	541	1.5%	490	1.5%
Total revenues	39,888	100.0%	36,903	100.0%	33,702	100.0%
Cost of sales	27,246	68.3%	25,295	68.5%	23,029	68.3%
Selling, general and administrative expense	8,420	21.1%	7,900	21.4%	7,231	21.5%
Credit expense	463	1.2%	290	0.8%	259	0.8%
Depreciation and amortization	1,079	2.7%	940	2.5%	854	2.5%
Interest expense	464	1.2%	425	1.2%	393	1.2%
Earnings before income taxes and extraordinary items	2,216	5.6%	2,053	5.6%	1,936	5.7%
Provision for income taxes	842	2.1%	789	2.1%	751	2.2%
Net earnings before extraordinary items	1,374	3.4%	1,264	3.4%	1,185	3.5%
Extraordinary charges from purchase and redemption of debt, net of tax	(6)	0.0%	0	0.0%	(41)	-0.1%
Net earnings	$ 1,368	3.4%	$ 1,264	3.4%	$ 1,144	3.4%

Note: Some percentages totals may not add due to rounding.

Exhibit 1-9   Target Corporation

Growth Rates of Various Income Statement Items

	2001	2000	1999	1998	1996
Growth rates:					
Revenues	8.09%	9.50%	9.91%	11.55%	9.54%
Basic earnings per share	8.57%	9.37%	22.35%	24.50%	62.20%
Cost of sales	7.71%	9.84%			
Selling, general and administrative expense	6.58%	9.25%			
Credit expense	59.66%	11.97%			
Interest expense	9.18%	8.14%			
Net earnings	8.23%	10.49%			

While Target's revenue growth declined from over 9 percent in 1999 and 2000 to just over 8 percent in 2001, square footage rose. Comparable-store sales rose 4.1 percent at Target stores in 2001, but were negative for Mervyn's and Marshall Field's.[31] Now we can see that new stores contributed to the positive revenue growth rate in 2001 for the company in all three divisions. This was true in 2000 as well.[32]

Let's take one last look at Target's growth rates. Target's management kept expenses in line with or below the growth in revenues except for credit and interest expenses. Target's credit expense came from marketing, operating, and managing its own credit cards. Although it is a small expense (it rose from 0.8 in 2000 to 1.2 percent of sales in 2001), it is still important for the analyst to understand what occurred and why. The period covered was a recession, a time when the demand for credit usually grows. As for the other expense that rose, interest expense, we must look at both Target and the economy. The interest expense is *net* interest expense; debt costs (interest expenses) are offset by any returns from the investment of cash in marketable securities, called cash equivalents by Target. Declining interest rates on marketable securities characterized 2001, and that decline affected all companies that held such securities. That drop was not offset by a comparable drop in the cost of Target's debt.

One other insidious problem that can mask an understanding of growth is inflation. Inflation comes when the amount of money in circulation rises but the value of goods and services does not. Thus the value of the currency declines—it takes more currency to buy the same goods.

[31] Square footage rose by 8.1 percent in 2001 and by 7.5 and 6.5 percent in the previous two years. Square footage increases were in the Target Stores Division, not Marshall Field's or Mervyn's.
[32] If a company shows growth in sales by adding new stores, growth can decline dramatically when expansion ceases or slows.

One problem with inflation is that it distorts financial history. Let's demonstrate what inflation can do to a simple financial analysis and its interpretation. Exhibit 1-10 shows the income statement for a company with and without inflation's impacts exposed. The figures with inflation are called **nominal**; those without inflation are **real**. To determine the real rates we subtract the inflation rate from the nominal growth rate. The resulting real growth rates are shown in the bottom half of Exhibit 1-10.

Exhibit 1-10 Hypothetical Company

Growth Analysis with and Without Inflation

In Currency	2002	2001	2000	1999	1998
Revenues	293	266	242	220	200
Cost of goods sold	(190)	(173)	(157)	(143)	(130)
Gross income	103	93	85	77	70
Selling, general, and administrative expenses	(73)	(67)	(61)	(55)	(50)
Operating income	30	26	24	22	20
Taxes	(12)	(11)	(10)	(9)	(8)
Net income	18	15	14	13	12

Nominal Growth Rate	2002	2001	2000	1999	
Revenues	10%	10%	10%	10%	
Cost of goods sold	10%	10%	10%	10%	
Gross income	10%	10%	10%	10%	
Selling, general, and administrative expenses	10%	10%	10%	10%	
Operating income	10%	10%	10%	10%	
Taxes	10%	10%	10%	10%	
Net income	10%	10%	10%	10%	

Real Growth Rates					
Revenues	−2%	0%	3%	5%	
Cost of goods sold	−2%	0%	3%	5%	
Gross income	−2%	0%	3%	5%	
Selling, general, and administrative expenses	−2%	0%	3%	5%	
Operating income	−2%	0%	3%	5%	
Taxes	−2%	0%	3%	5%	
Net income	−2%	0%	3%	5%	
Rate of Inflation	**12%**	**10%**	**7%**	**5%**	

Factoring out inflation-driven growth gives us quite a different view of a company's real growth over a period. If we had not included the impacts of inflation, we might have believed the company shown in Exhibit 1-10 was growing at a steady 10 percent. However, it was not. The numbers masked deterioration in all the categories. After inflation is removed, our hypothetical company actually declined in real terms in the final year of our example. As you can see, it is critical to know how inflation impacts performance, or perceived performance. If we had not done the analysis in real terms, we would have seen a different picture of this company's results.

How extensive should be an analysis of real growth? It depends, in part, on how the analyst will use the results and how extreme the conditions were. In 2002, when U.S. inflation had been at record low levels for some time, such an analysis seems extraneous. However, the United States is not the world, and high inflation does exist in some countries, and may exist in the United States in the future.

General inflation, inflation that impacts all expenses and revenues equally, is not the only inflation of concern. Even when general inflation in a country is low, inflation in such things as wages may be high. While inflation is not so interesting at the moment in the United States, economic conditions change and the literate analyst will take it into consideration.

4. Asset Utilization Ratios

Once the analyst has examined the company's expenses and profits, the next area of interest is assets. Most companies acquire assets to produce sales revenues and ultimately, profits. **Asset utilization ratios** indicate how effectively or efficiently a company uses its assets. These asset utilization ratios also are called **efficiency** (how well the company uses assets to generate sales) or **turnover ratios** (how many times the asset value is replicated in sales each year). The information needed to calculate these ratios is taken from both the statement of earnings, or income statement, and the statement of financial position, or balance sheet. We can look at individual asset accounts and/or the total assets of the company.

The ratio used to look at how efficiently a company uses all its assets is the **total asset turnover ratio** (TATO).

$$\text{Total asset turnover} = \frac{\text{Net sales}}{\text{Assets}}$$

$$= \frac{\$39,888}{\$24,154}$$

$$= 1.65 \text{ times or } 165\%[33]$$

Target's sales were 1.65 times or 165 percent of its year-end 2001 assets.

---

[33] We report this and all ratios, except the price earnings ratio, as a multiple and a percentage. You may see it reported either way. Be consistent in your analysis and aware of how ratios are reported when using data from your's or another source.

For the rookie analyst, a little care must be taken in calculating this ratio. For example, if the company has had a large increase or decrease in its assets during the year, average assets might be a better figure to use than period-end total assets. For Target the 2001 TATO is 2.05 based on beginning assets and 1.82 based on the average assets for the year. While there is a difference for Target, for some companies the difference is far more dramatic. One important note of caution when making comparisons in this or any other ratio: be certain that the ratios are calculated in a similar fashion when comparing data provided by others and/or over time. While a consistent use of average assets is preferable in most cases, most reported ratios are based on the year-end asset figure.

Using the total asset turnover ratio alone does not lead the analyst to any firm conclusions about a company's efficiency. However, when the information about asset efficiency is joined with information about the nature of the business, the industry, and economic conditions, the skilled analyst can gain real insight.[34]

Industries can be very different from one another: some are capital intensive and others are labor intensive. **Capital intensity** is the degree to which capital goods—property, plant, and equipment—are used to produce products. If products are produced with a high level of labor and relatively little capital investment, the production process is called **labor intensive**. You can see the dramatic differences in capital in the different industries shown in Exhibit 1-11. As dramatic as the differences are they are not surprising. Manufacturers using considerable assets to produce their products are capital intensive—they have low TATOs. The wireless communications industry has very high capital intensity with its major investments in communications infrastructure.[35] Grocers, on the other hand, have a high TATO, meaning they are quite asset efficient.

Total asset turnover is used to indicate a company's degree of operating leverage. **Operating leverage** is a measure of the degree to which a company's costs are fixed (for example, depreciation on plant and equipment) rather than variable (for example, expenses for materials and labor). A company with high operating leverage (considerable fixed costs) has much higher increases in EBIT once all its fixed expenses have been covered—it has reached breakeven. Later we will discuss financial leverage.

While the analyst must be thoughtful in calculating and interpreting TATO, the ratio has another useful property: by multiplying TATO by ROS, we can calculate a third ratio, the **return on assets** (ROA).

$$\text{Return on assets} = \text{Return on sales} \times \text{Total asset turnover}$$

$$= \frac{\text{Net income}}{\text{Net sales}} \times \frac{\text{Net sales}}{\text{Assets}}$$

$$= \frac{\text{Net income}}{\text{Assets}}$$

---

[34] Target's financial performance will be compared across time and with others in its industry later in this chapter.

[35] Non-wireless telecommunications companies are very capital intense, but their ROS is much higher.

Exhibit 1-11   Various U.S. Industries

Total Asset Turnover, 2001

Industry	Return on Sales	Total Asset Turnover	Return on Assets
Advertising	11.1%	68%	7.5%
Biotech	7.4%	52%	3.8%
Computer systems	−0.6%	115%	−0.7%
Consultants	3.7%	180%	6.7%
Department stores	1.4%	170%	2.4%
Electric utilities	6.0%	52%	3.1%
Employment	1.2%	239%	2.9%
Finance	16.1%	7%	1.1%
Food manufacturing	4.2%	103%	4.3%
Furniture manufacturing	4.7%	146%	6.9%
Grocers	1.6%	250%	4.0%
Jewelers	−0.7%	5.3%	−3.7%
Paper producers	3.6%	72%	2.6%
Software	−4.4%	53%	−2.3%
Steel	−0.6%	95%	−0.6%
Wireless communications	−26.4%	32%	−8.4%

Using this relationship for Target, the ROA is calculated as follows:

$$\text{ROA} = \text{ROS} \times \text{TATO}$$
$$= 0.0343 \times 1.65$$
$$= 0.0566 \text{ or } 5.66\%$$

One can, of course, calculate the ROA directly:

$$\text{ROA} = \frac{\text{Net income}}{\text{Assets}}$$
$$= \frac{\$1,368}{\$24,154}$$
$$= 0.0566 \text{ or } 5.66\%$$

By understanding this relationship, you can see why capital-intensive companies have lower returns on assets, all other things being equal, than do service companies with fewer assets. The asset efficiencies and the returns on assets for various industries were shown in Exhibit 1-11. You can see the impact of operating leverage. For example, grocers have low ROS but their TATO (sale per dollar of assets) is high. This operating leverage increases from 1.6 ROS to 4.0 percent ROA. Paper producers, on the other hand, decrease the return from a ROS of 3.6 to an ROA of 2.6 percent because of the considerable investment in assets.

After examining the overall asset efficiency of a company, you, or any analyst, will probably want to delve into the way the company uses some or all of its assets.[36] This is particularly true if you find the asset efficiency to be different from what was expected or has changed over time. If it is different, what should be the logical next step? The next step is to look at the assets themselves. Let's start with the biggest assets.

For most companies, especially manufacturers and retailers, inventory is a very large asset. The ratio that will help you understand how the company has used its inventory is the **inventory turnover ratio**.

$$\text{Inventory turnover} = \frac{\text{Cost of sales}}{\text{Inventory}}$$

$$= \frac{\$27,246}{\$4,449}$$

$$= 6.12 \text{ times or } 612\%$$

This ratio indicates the times Target's inventory that was sold and replaced during the reporting period, in this case one year. Remember, we report the ratio as a multiple and a percentage because both are reported in various sources. Since Target is a discount retailer chain we would expect the inventory turnover to be rapid, and it is. Other industries are typified by long inventory turnovers. You can think of why jewelry stores, with their high-value, infrequently sold inventory, and liquor producers, with their long maturation process, might have very slow inventory turnovers. The important thing is to determine whether the turnover is out of line with the company's own history or is abnormal relative to others in the industry.

As with every ratio there are some nuances. First, like the total asset turnover ratio, if inventory grew substantially during the year, average inventory may be a more accurate denominator for the ratio. Second, the numerator should be cost of sales rather than net sales; cost of sales, also called cost of goods sold, does not include the profit portion of net sales and leaves only the production costs.[37] Third, you may want to look beyond a total inventory analysis. Finally, it is important to remember that the quality of the information contained in this ratio depends on how the company values its inventory.

Let's look a bit more closely at two of these nuances. First, let's look beyond the total inventory, the figure reported by Target. Other companies, like manufacturers, report their inventories at each stage of the production process: raw materials, work-in-process, and finished goods.[38] An

---

[36] All this analysis is like detective work. When you find a clue you are urged to dig deeper. Some analysts say it is like peeling an onion: the more layers you remove the more there are, until you are crying.

[37] If net sales were used and the company had high prices relative to costs, the ratio would be higher than actual turnover.

[38] Target is not a manufacturer and thus reports only total inventory. However, Target does have three very different divisions and the analyst with access to the information may choose to look at the inventory turnover in each division. In this case we have only revenue information for the divisions, not cost of sales, to make the calculations shown on the following page.

analysis of these stages can be instructive. If finished goods rose it could come from falling sales or an inventory buildup before a seasonal peak. Stockpiling in advance of potential shortages or price increases or an overabundance of obsolete inventory can cause raw material increases. Analyzing only the total inventory may mask these rapid and significant changes.

The second inventory-related item to take into account is the way in which inventory is valued. Every company must choose a way to value its inventory. You might think this is easy and inconsequential, but it is not. The choice can make quite a difference in the company's performance. In Exhibit 1-5 you saw the impact of different inventory methods on net income and taxes. While the example is for a static environment over a short period of time, imagine the same inventory valuations with rapidly changing costs when goods are kept in inventory for a long time. Clearly, the method of inventory valuation is important in times of high or rapidly changing rates of inflation and deflation, and when there are changes in the prices of raw materials due to changes in technology or supplier power.

Keeping these caveats in mind, a high inventory turnover ratio indicates that the company is using its financial resources efficiently by maintaining low inventories. Target's inventory turnover is relatively quick. The nature of some companies' production processes—for example, aircraft manufacturers—makes achieving a high inventory turnover ratio impossible, while others, like grocery stores, deal in more perishable items and thus would be expected to have a rapid turnover of inventory.

The inventory turnover ratio also can be expressed in terms of the number of days goods are held in inventory:

$$\text{Days' inventory} = \frac{\text{Inventory}}{\text{Cost of sales}} \times 365[39]$$

$$= \frac{\$4,449}{\$27,246} \times 365$$

$$= 59.6 \text{ days}$$

This analysis can be done for each of the different kinds of inventory a company may have.

Because Target has a TATO ratio that is lower than its inventory turnover ratio, we will want to look at how efficiently other assets are

Divisional Information	Revenues	Inventory	Inventory Turnover (times)
Target	$32,588	$3,090	10.55
Mervyn's	4,038	561	7.20
Marshall Field's	2,829	396	7.14
Other	433	402	1.08
Corporation	$39,888	$4,449	8.97

[39] We use 365 days as the calendar year. While some analysts choose to reduce the year to 360 days to account for the five legal U.S. holidays, since assets are held for all 365 days for the year regardless of the work habits of the employees, 365 is the appropriate number.

being utilized by the company. For example, it would make sense to look at the **accounts receivable**, the sales made for credit for which payment has not been received. The ratio of **accounts receivable to net sales** indicates the relative proportion of the company's sales made on credit and still outstanding at the end of the reporting period.

$$\text{Accounts receivable/Net sales} = \frac{\text{Accounts receivable}}{\text{Net sales}}$$

$$= \frac{\$3,831}{\$39,176}$$

$$= 0.0978 \text{ or } 9.78\%$$

Note for Target that we used sales, not total revenue, since total revenue includes the revenues from credit card operations.

As you can see, of the sales made by Target in 2001, 9.8 percent remained unpaid at the end of the year.[40] This is more than we would have expected from a discount retail chain where virtually all sales are made for cash or paid for with credit or debit cards.

Creative analysts developed a variation of this ratio that converts the percentage of sales into the length of time the average account receivable is unpaid or outstanding. Many find **days' sales outstanding** or the **receivables collection period** easier to interpret and more informative than the accounts receivable/net sales ratio. To calculate the days in receivables, simply multiply the accounts receivable/net sales ratio by the number of days in the year.

$$\text{Days' sales outstanding} = \frac{\text{Accounts receivable}}{\text{Net sales}} \times 365$$

$$= \frac{\$3,831}{\$39,176} \times 365$$

$$= 35.7 \text{ days}$$

Obviously, companies that sell their products on credit, such as furniture manufacturers, will have long collection periods. Grocery chains, which offer little or no credit, will have low receivables and very short collection periods. Target's customers paid their bills in an average of 36 days, the largest portion of which was attributable to Target's Stores and Target's Visa card. On the basis of this information, a curious analyst would want to look at the company's trend in accounts receivable over time and how the company is doing relative to others in the industry.[41]

---

[40] Had we wanted to know the average accounts receivable outstanding over the year, we could have used average accounts receivable in the ratio. The average figure is especially important when significant changes have occurred.

[41] The analyst should also determine the normal credit terms for the company and the industry. Most companies that offer credit have standard credit terms such as 2/10 net 30. This means that there is a 2 percent discount for accounts paid in 10 days, but the full amount is due in 30 days. Credit card customers have terms that include no discount for early payment but a penalty for late payments. When credit policies exist, the actual accounts receivable should be compared to the terms that are offered by the company.

Management and lenders may want to look closely at the receivables. In some companies most customers pay on time, but others are slow to clear their obligations. This is especially true with problem companies or in problem economies. To understand such problems lenders and management may want to look at an **aging of accounts receivable**: the accounts receivable are broken into groups by the length of time the account has been overdue. This is a particularly useful way to understand abnormally long collection periods when the ratio is skewed by a single large account that has been overdue for a long time. This analysis requires internal information, so it is best used by corporate analysts or lenders with considerable inside information.

Any asset or liability may be scrutinized by an analyst. Not only are assets of interest, but the analyst may be interested in the efficiency with which the company manages its short-term liabilities. For example, the company's suppliers might wonder how much the company owes to its suppliers in relation to what it purchased from them.[42] To determine this, the **accounts payable to purchases ratio** would be used. Since most external analysts do not have access to the amount the company purchases over any period, the ratio of **accounts payable to cost of sales** is substituted.

$$\text{Accounts payable/Cost of sales} = \frac{\text{Accounts payable}}{\text{Cost of sales}}$$

$$= \frac{\$4,160}{\$27,246}$$

$$= 0.1527 \text{ or } 15.27\%$$

This may also be calculated in days. This ratio is called the **payables payment period**.

$$\text{Payables payment period} = \frac{\text{Accounts payable}}{\text{Cost of sales}} \times 365$$

$$= \frac{\$4,160}{\$27,246} \times 365$$

$$= 55.7 \text{ days}$$

Target pays its suppliers more slowly than its customers pay Target. Companies that use their suppliers as a source of funding, such as Target, will have longer payables payment periods.[43]

For companies with seasonal sales, care must be taken when calculating this ratio as well as when calculating days' sales outstanding and the inventory turnover ratio. When a company's sales have grown substan-

---

[42] Some analysts consider this a measure of financial leverage—a measure of how much debt the company uses to finance its assets.

[43] In Chapter 2 we discuss the working capital cycle. This cycle include the disparity between the payment from customers and to suppliers as a source of working capital for a company. The difference between accounts payable and accounts receivable days for Target is 20 days.

tially over a period or the company has seasonal sales, using the annual cost of sales may inflate or deflate the ratios and provide an unrealistic look at the actual patterns experienced by the company. In such situations an analyst may calculate monthly ratios based on the cost of sales for that month, or an average for several months during the same season, rather than using the annual figure.[44] In addition to, or in place of, these ratios, the analyst may perform a **component percentage analysis** of the company's balance sheet. In this analysis, also known as a common-size statement, each asset, liability, and equity account balance is compared with the total assets figure.[45] This analysis is especially useful for comparing changes over time. Such a component analysis is shown in Exhibit 1-12, and by looking at it you can see that accounts receivable and long-term debt are the two items where there has been significant change for Target. Other years could be added to the analysis if there had been major business or economic changes over the time.

Now that we have investigated the profitability and asset efficiency of Target, the next step is to see how the company has financed its assets. In the common-size balance sheet we saw some changes in the way the company was financed.

5. Capitalization Ratios

Capitalization or **financial leverage ratios** provide information about the sources the company has used to finance its investment in assets. The term **financial leverage** is used to indicate the impact debt financing has on the returns of the company to its owners, the shareholders. When the income generated by investment in assets is greater than the cost of debt, the equity holders will benefit from financing an increased amount of assets through borrowing. This is called leverage or, in some countries, particularly the United Kingdom, **gearing**. Later we will see how financial leverage or gearing affects the shareholders' return, the return on equity. First, let's see how we measure a company's financial leverage.

The majority of the financial leverage ratios are based on information from a company's balance sheet. Of primary interest to a company's owners is how much of the company they have financed. To measure this we can use the **assets to equity ratio** also called leverage or financial leverage. Because we want to know the company's position at the end of the year, we do not use averages of the accounts over the year. Instead, we use the balance at the end of the year.[46] For Target, this ratio is calculated as shown on page 33.

---

[44] This can be especially important in an environment with high and changing inflation rates.

[45] A variation of this component-sized analysis is to compare each asset and liability account to total revenues. This can expose the relationships that exist between assets and liabilities, and revenues and revenue growth.

[46] Once again, if the equity and/or assets have changed dramatically over the year or at any point in the year, we may need to calculate averages to the ratio itself at several points during the year to fully understand the situation.

Exhibit 1-12   Target Corporation

Component Balance Sheet Items as a Percentage of Assets

(dollars in millions)	February 2, 2002		February 3, 2001	
	Dollars	**Percentages**	**Dollars**	**Percentages**
Assets				
Cash and cash equivalents	$ 499	2.1%	$ 356	1.8%
Accounts receivable (net of $261 million allowance)	3,831	15.9%	1,941	10.0%
Receivable-backed securities				
Inventory	4,449	18.4%	4,248	21.8%
Other	869	3.6%	759	3.9%
Total current assets	9,648	39.9%	7,304	37.5%
Property and equipment				
Land	2,833	11.7%	2,467	12.7%
Buildings and improvements	10,103	41.8%	8,596	44.1%
Fixtures and equipment	4,290	17.8%	3,848	19.7%
Construction-in-progress	1,216	5.0%	848	4.4%
Accumulated depreciation	(4,909)	−20.3%	(4,341)	−22.3%
Property and equipment, net	13,533	56.0%	11,418	58.6%
Other	973	4.0%	768	3.9%
Total assets	$24,154	100.0%	$19,490	100.0%
Liabilities and shareholders' investment				
Accounts payable	$ 4,160	17.2%	$ 3,576	18.3%
Accrued liabilities	1,566	6.5%	1,507	7.7%
Income taxes payable	423	1.8%	361	1.9%
Current portion of long-term debt and notes payable	905	3.7%	857	4.4%
Total current liabilities	7,054	29.2%	6,301	32.3%
Long-term debt	8,088	33.5%	5,634	28.9%
Deferred income taxes and other	1,152	4.8%	1,036	5.3%
Shareholders' investment				
Common stock	75	0.3%	75	0.4%
Additional paid-in-capital	1,098	4.5%	902	4.6%
Retained earnings	6,687	27.7%	5,542	28.4%
Total shareholders' investment	7,860	32.5%	6,519	33.4%
Total liabilities and shareholders' investment	$24,154	100.0%	$19,490	100.0%

Note: Some percentages totals may not add due to rounding.

$$\frac{\text{Assets to equity or}}{\text{financial leverage}} = \frac{\text{Assets}}{\text{Shareholders' equity}}$$

$$= \frac{\$24{,}154}{\$7{,}860}$$

$$= 3.07 \text{ times or } 307\%$$

If the assets to equity ratio were 100 percent, the company would be totally financed by its owners. A higher ratio shows that a company finances some of its assets with debt—it is leveraged. When this ratio is combined with ROA, we can find the return that shareholders earned on the book value of their investment in the company, the **return on equity** (ROE).[47]

$$\text{Return on equity} = \text{ROS} \times \text{TATO} \times \text{Financial leverage}$$

$$= \frac{\text{Net income}}{\text{Net sales}} \times \frac{\text{Net sales}}{\text{Assets}} \times \frac{\text{Assets}}{\text{Equity}}$$

This can be reduced to

$$= \text{ROA} \times \text{Leverage}$$

Or

$$= \frac{\text{Net income}}{\text{Assets}} \times \frac{\text{Assets}}{\text{Equity}}$$

Or

$$= \frac{\text{Net income}}{\text{Equity}}$$

For Target, the return on equity is calculated as follows:

$$\text{ROE} = \text{ROS} \times \text{TATO} \times \text{Leverage}$$

$$= 0.0343 \times 1.65 \times 3.07$$

$$= 0.174 \text{ or } 17.4\%$$

You can, of course, calculate Target's ROE directly.

$$\text{ROE} = \frac{\text{Net income}}{\text{Equity}}$$

$$= \frac{\$1{,}368}{\$7{,}860}$$

$$= 0.174 \text{ or } 17.4\%$$

You can see how operating and financial leverage impact shareholders' return: from a return on sales of only 3.4 percent, asset efficiency and the use of debt result in a return on equity that is over 5 times the ROS.

---

[47] The book value is the value of the total equity reported on the statement of financial position, the balance sheet. Later we will also be using book value per share, the per-share value of the book value.

Importantly, we can use this set of ratios to test a potential change in operating or financial strategy. What if Target management had used even more debt in its financing—for example, its assets to equity ratio was 4 times or 400 percent? The resulting ROE would have been 22.6 percent, 1.3 times its current level.[48] If shareholders alone had financed the company, the return on equity would have been only 5.7 percent, exactly the same as the company's return on its assets. Finally, you can see that if the total asset turnover (TATO) and the assets to equity ratio both were 100 percent, the ROS, ROA, and ROE all would be the same—3.43 percent.[49] The obvious conclusion is that the fewer assets a company uses to generate sales, and the more debt it uses to finance those assets, the higher the return shareholders can earn.

Financial leverage is a powerful thing. Exhibit 1-13 shows the impact of leverage on shareholders' return. The exhibit graphs the return on equity with different asset/equity levels. The returns can vary from a positive to negative, and are dramatically changed by an increase in financial leverage: the higher the company's financial leverage, the more the return on equity can vary as the return on assets changes with company success or economic change.

Exhibit 1-13

Return on Equity at Different Degrees of Financial Leverage

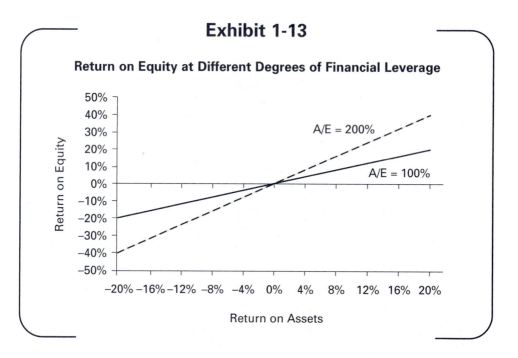

---

[48] This is calculated by multiplying product of the ROS of 3.43 and TATO of 1.65 times and by the asset/equity ratio of 4.0.

[49] You can test any combination of possible outcomes that may lie within the strategic possibilities for a company.

You also can see the impact of financial leverage on the various industries shown in Exhibit 1-14. For example, the grocers had a 1.6 percent return on sales, but a return on equity of 14.0 percent. This came as a result of the combined impacts of high operating leverage and very high financial leverage. In contrast, low operational and relatively low financial leverage kept the computer systems and software companies from experiencing greater losses.

Exhibit 1-14   Various U.S. Industries

Financial Leverage and ROE, 2001

Industry	Return on Sales	Total Asset Turnover	Return on Assets	Assets/ Equity	Return on Equity
Advertising	11.1%	68%	7.5%	209%	15.8%
Biotech	7.4%	52%	3.8%	140%	5.4%
Computer systems	−0.6%	115%	−0.7%	230%	−1.6%
Consultants	3.7%	180%	6.7%	243%	16.2%
Department stores	1.4%	170%	2.4%	254%	6.0%
Electric utilities	6.0%	52%	3.1%	470%	14.8%
Employment	1.2%	239%	2.9%	191%	5.5%
Finance	16.1%	7%	1.1%	2760%	30.7%
Food manufacturing	4.2%	103%	4.3%	334%	14.4%
Furniture manufacturing	4.7%	146%	6.9%	180%	12.4%
Grocers	1.6%	250%	4.0%	350%	14.0%
Jewelers	−0.7%	530%	−3.7%	240%	−8.9%
Paper producers	3.6%	72%	2.6%	360%	9.3%
Software	−4.4%	53%	−2.3%	220%	−5.2%
Steel	−0.6%	95%	−0.6%	350%	−2.0%
Wireless communications	−26.4%	32%	−8.4%	240%	−20.3%

Since Target's assets to equity ratio is 307 percent, it has significant debt—in fact, over $2.00 of debt for every dollar of equity. Is this too much debt? To determine whether this level of leverage is high, let's look at other capitalization ratios.

Shareholders are not the only ones interested in the way a company finances itself. Lenders, who may provide a large portion of the company's capital resources, are especially interested in the way the company is capitalized. While they could certainly deduce their position from the assets to equity ratio, they have developed ratios that show their position directly.[50] Two commonly used lender-perspective ratios are **long-term debt to equity** and **long-term debt to total assets**. For our Target example, the first is calculated as follows:

$$\text{Long-term debt to equity} = \frac{\text{Total long-term debt}}{\text{Equity}}$$

$$= \frac{\$8,993}{\$7,860}$$

$$= 1.1441 \text{ or } 114.41\%$$

And the second is calculated as follows:

$$\text{Long-term debt to assets} = \frac{\text{Total long-term debt}}{\text{Assets}}$$

$$= \frac{\$8,993}{\$24,154}$$

$$= 0.3723 \text{ or } 37.23\%$$

Note that both these ratios used as long-term debt the long-term and the current maturities of the debt.[51] In addition, Target includes capital leases and the current capital lease obligations in its long-term debt account. For some companies these are separate items. The capital leases are included because they constitute long-term, contractual obligations that have many of the same features and obligations of debt.[52] These are typically included in long-term debt, but may be shown as a separate item.

Some analysts use only the long-term debt and do not include either the capital leases or the current maturities of either the long-term debt or the capital leases. Others omit the current portions, but include both the long-term debt and capital leases. The decision of what to use is up to the analyst, and reflects both the analyst's concerns and the economic situation. It is critical with this ratio to observe how it is calculated when using others' data.

Another ratio looks only at the long-term debt, and does not include the current portion or debt-like accounts. The long-term debt could be compared to equity, but in this ratio it is compared to the total capital of the company. The **long-term debt to total capital ratio** uses as total

---

[50] Debt/Assets is $[1 - (\text{Equity}/\text{Assets})]$.

[51] Target lumps notes payables with the current maturities of the long-term debt. Without further information to separate the two items, we have added the sum of $905,000 to the long-term debt.

[52] In determining the long-term debt of a company, analysts often disagree about the items to include. The previous calculations included both current and noncurrent portions of the long-term debt. You also might choose to include deferred taxes, long-term contingent liabilities, or any other long-term liabilities. If these items are included, they must be included consistently throughout any analysis or comparisons. When using ratios from a commercially available source, it is important to know what data was used in making the calculations and how the calculations were performed. Not every source uses the same data or methodology.

capital the sum of the long-term debt and equity used to finance the business. The ratio for Target is calculated as follows:

$$\text{Long-term debt to total capital} = \frac{\text{Long-term debt}}{\text{Long-term debt + Equity}}$$

$$= \frac{\$8,088}{\$8,088 + \$7,860}$$

$$= 0.5071 \text{ or } 50.71\%$$

Debt is over 50 percent of all long-term capital for Target. This ratio is sometimes confused with the long-term debt to total assets ratio. Including all debt-like accounts, that ratio would be 37.23 percent.

The appropriate magnitude of capitalization ratios depends upon the perspective of the analyst, the nature of the company, and its situation. Lenders such as bondholders and bankers typically prefer low debt ratios because they provide greater security for their loans. Since equity investors' returns are improved by more leverage, shareholders generally prefer more leverage: this leverage provides a higher return on equity if the company is profitable.[53] Issues involved in determining the appropriate amount of debt—the appropriate capital structure—is discussed in Chapter 7.

Lenders and other sources of short-term capital—for example, suppliers of goods to the company—also want to know how the company will meet its obligations. For companies that use significant amounts of short-term debt to finance their operations three ratios have been found to be useful: total liabilities to assets, the current ratio, and the acid-test ratio.[54] For Target, the first of these, **total liabilities to assets**, is as follows:

$$\text{Total liabilities to assets} = \frac{\text{Total liabilities}}{\text{Total assets}}$$

$$= \frac{\$16,294}{\$24,154}$$

$$= 0.6746 \text{ or } 67.46\%$$

Over 67 percent of Target's assets have been financed by lenders, including trade creditors, rather than by its owners, the shareholders.

By any ratio we choose to use, Target is a leveraged, or geared, company. Before we draw any conclusions, let's see if the amount of debt and liabilities is of critical concern. One way to test the danger is to see

---

[53] High degrees of financial leverage also, in times of decreased revenues and profits, result in low or negative returns on equity. This is a dilemma. Lenders want less risk to preserve the principal; shareholders want more risk since their downside is limited to zero but their upside is theoretically limitless; managers want to do what is best for the owners, although not at the risk of their jobs. This is what economists call an agency problem: different interested parties have different interests. This type of agency problem was played out in a disastrous way in many U.S. companies in 2002.

[54] In this case we include the accounts payable as short-term debt. While these accounts are not interest bearing (the "lenders" do not charge interest), they are still obligations that the company has incurred and must pay. You may or may not include them.

if Target can pay off its most immediate obligations if it were forced to do so. We can use the **current** and **acid-test ratios** to measure the company's ability to pay its current liabilities using current assets, including cash and marketable securities.[55] These ratios, also called **liquidity ratios**, reflect the size of short-term obligations. Target's current ratio is calculated as follows:

$$\text{Current ratio} = \frac{\text{Current assets}}{\text{Current liabilities}}$$

$$= \frac{\$9,648}{\$7,504}$$

$$= 1.2857 \text{ or } 128.57\%$$

A current ratio of 1.0 describes a company where the current assets will just cover the current liabilities. A current ratio greater than one is preferable.

Companies with high liquidity ratios are considered more liquid than those with low liquidity ratios: their short-term assets are greater than their short-term liabilities. Being more liquid generally means that a company is better able to pay off its short-term obligations than is its less liquid peers. Target Corporation is somewhat liquid: its current ratio is 1.29 times or 129 percent. This means that Target could pay off its current liabilities using the proceeds from its current assets alone. There is one catch, however. Some current assets are not as easy to turn into the cash as others. The current asset that is often hardest to turn into cash is inventory, and Target's single largest current asset is inventory.

Since Target's single largest current asset is its inventory, we can use another ratio, the **acid-test ratio**, also called the **quick ratio**, to test its real liquidity. This ratio is like the current ratio, except it eliminates the assets that are not readily and rapidly turned into cash, such as inventory. In addition to eliminating the inventory, we can also exclude prepaid expenses and deferred income taxes since neither would be available to cover current liabilities. Target's quick or acid-test ratio is calculated as follows:

$$\text{Acid-test ratio} = \frac{\text{Cash and marketable securities} + \text{Accounts receivable}}{\text{Current liabilities}}$$

$$= \frac{\$499 + \$3,831}{\$7,054}$$

$$= 0.6138 \text{ or } 61.38\%$$

Note that Target calls its marketable securities cash equivalents.

An acid-test ratio of 61.38 percent tells us that Target has less easy-to-liquidate current assets than it has current liabilities. If Target had to pay

---

[55] Short-term investments can be investments in such things as marketable securities. Some analysts and companies call these "near cash" or "cash equivalents" since normally they are easily converted into cash in a very short period of time.

all its current liabilities simultaneously, it would have to rapidly liquidate its inventories or turn to other sources of financing. In Target's defense, its inventories are rather salable and hence a low quick or acid-test ratio is not as big a concern for management or Target's lenders. However, for companies where inventory turnover is slow, such as jewelers or liquor manufacturers, the acid-test ratio is more important than the current ratio in determining the company's short-term payment capacity. In understanding both the current and quick ratios, skill and insight are an analyst's best allies.

Determining what constitutes a high or low level of liquidity first depends on who is analyzing the current or acid-test ratios. A banker who has made a short-term loan would like both ratios to be high, because the banker believes they indicate that the company has sufficient current assets to pay all current liabilities, including the current portion of the bank's loan. On the other hand, the company's management might prefer a lower ratio in the belief that they show the company has minimized funds invested in current assets that may yield low returns.

An analysis of the ratios also must be viewed in the context of the industry in which the company operates and the company's practices. Companies with rapid turnovers of receivables and inventories generally need smaller liquidity cushions, and thus can have lower current and acid-test ratios than those with slower turnovers.

All these capitalization ratios show the relative ability of a company to repay the principal (what is owed) of its short- and long-term debt obligations. However, the ability to repay principal is only one of the concerns lenders have. In fact, it may be the lesser of two concerns: whether the company can repay the principal, and whether the company can pay the interest on the debt. Because the lender's product is loans, and to make a profit the product must be "sold," lenders are concerned less with actual repayment of the principal than with the company's ability to repay it if requested. Companies that have the ability to repay the debt make good candidates for loans, if they can pay the interest on the debt.

Lenders have developed **coverage ratios** to test the borrower's ability to pay interest. They test the company's ability to pay interest, interest and principal, or interest, principal, and other contractual obligations. These ratios are called **debt-service ratios** when the ratio measures the ability to pay interest plus principal payments.

Over the long term, interest must be paid out of funds generated by company operations. Since we are measuring the ability to pay interest, and interest is tax deductible, we will use earnings before interest and taxes in comparison to interest expense in a ratio called **EBIT coverage**. In most cases both the interest on the debt and capitalized interest on the leases are included in the interest expense figure. Target includes capitalized interest in its interest expense number. In some cases the analyst will have to use data from the annual report footnotes for capitalized lease interest expense.

$$\text{EBIT coverage} = \frac{\text{Earnings before interest and taxes}}{\text{Interest expense}}$$

$$= \frac{\$2,680}{\$464}$$

$$= 5.78 \text{ times or } 578\%$$

Note that Target's EBIT, not net income, was used in calculating this ratio. Both interest and its tax effect are deducted from EBIT in calculating net income. Since interest is a pretax expense EBIT is the appropriate figure for the numerator of this ratio. With a ratio of 578 percent, Target is able to meet its interest obligations easily.

Analysts use a number of variations on the coverage ratios to determine the ability of a company to meet its interest obligations. For example, an analyst might add depreciation, a noncash expense, to EBIT in estimating the coverage ratio.[56] This ratio is called the **cash flow coverage ratio**. The depreciation figure comes from Exhibit 1-1.

$$\text{Cash flow coverage} = \frac{\text{EBIT} + \text{Depreciation}}{\text{Interest expense}}$$

$$= \frac{\$2,680 + \$1,079}{\$464}$$

$$= 8.10 \text{ times or } 810\%$$

If a company has depreciation, the ratio for cash flow coverage will exceed that for EBIT coverage. In addition to depreciation, an analyst can add or subtract other cash flows from the EBIT to determine the cash available to pay interest expenses.

While interest coverage is of primary concern, lenders also require that principal payments be made to retire or reduce the debt principal. Unlike interest costs these payments are not deductible for tax purposes, so they must be paid with after-tax funds.[57] To determine the ability of the company to meet both interest and principal payments, the ratio of **debt-service coverage** is used. In this ratio principal repayments are adjusted to a before-tax basis to compensate for their lack of tax deductibility. The principal payment obligations and marginal tax rates for a company can be found in the notes to financial statements. Since Target has capital leases with required annual payments, these are included in the principal payments.

$$\text{Debt-service coverage} = \frac{\text{Earnings before interest and taxes}}{\text{Interest} + [\text{Principal payments}/(1 - \text{Tax rate})]}$$

$$= \frac{\$2,680}{\$464 + [(\$802)/(1 - 0.38)]}$$

$$= 1.52 \text{ times or } 152\%$$

---

[56] In case your accounting is hazy, depreciation is a way to spread the tax impact of capital asset investments, not the reflection of an actual cash expense in the year it is reported. Thus, while depreciation is shown as an expense, it does not reflect an outflow of cash.
[57] The tax rate is the rate paid by the company, not the statutory rate.

Note that for Target both the interest and debt-service coverage ratios are well above their logical minimums, 100 percent. In fact, even when principal payments, including capital lease obligations are included, the company can cover its obligations, at least its debt obligations, over 1.5 times.

These two basic ratios, interest coverage and debt-service coverage, can be adapted for other contractual or noncontractual obligations, such as preferred stock dividends, using either EBIT or cash flow in the numerator. Each variation of these two basic ratios gives a somewhat different view of the company's ability to meet its contractual and/or perceived obligations. It is up to the analyst to determine which ratio gives a better view, and to be certain that any comparisons are based on the same methodology.

Lenders and lessors like coverage ratios to be high. Shareholders, seeking higher returns, prefer the ratios to be low. The best level for each of the ratios depends on the nature of the business, the economic situation, and the willingness of the owners or managers to take risk. For Target, while the financial leverage ratios are relatively high, the company is well able to cover its interest and debt service, with room to spare. Its EBIT is not highly variable, and its business is stable. It does not appear as if the company is likely to sustain an unexpected or cyclical downturn, thus making the risk of missing payments quite low.[58] As a consequence, Target seems well able to manage its current level of debt. Lenders should take comfort in their position, while shareholders reap the benefits of leverage on their returns.

6. Sustainable Growth Rate

By combining return on sales, total asset turnover, and leverage, you saw that we shareholders' return on equity could be calculated. Whether the shareholders receive all the returns immediately or not depends upon the dividend payment policy of the company. As illustrated in Exhibit 1-15 some of the returns may be sent to the shareholders in the form of cash dividends, while the rest are retained by the company to fund future growth on behalf of the shareholders.[59]

To measure the proportion of the earnings paid out to shareholders we can use the **dividend payout ratio** (DPO). The amount of dividends

---

[58] It is important to note whether the interest rates on a company's debt are fixed (unchanging over the life of the debt) or floating (change in relation to some widely used rate). With variable rates, the rates can change as the economy strengthens or weakens, and thus these fixed coverage ratios have little value. In the case of variable rates, an analysis using alternative interest rate predictions would be used. We discuss probabilistic analysis in a later chapter.

[59] Indeed some may be used to repurchase shares, thus making the remaining shareholders' proportional share of the company increase. One note—some companies make share repurchases on a regular basis. Some stock analysts have begun including the share repurchases in a recalculated dividend yield called the "all-in-yield." They believe this better represents the true dividend-related return the company provides to its shareholders.

Exhibit 1-15

Disposition of Net Income to Shareholders

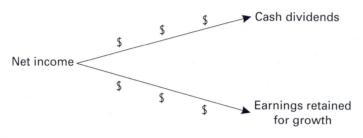

paid out to Target's common equity shareholders is shown in the statement of cash flows, Exhibit 1-3.

$$\text{Dividend payout} = \frac{\text{Dividends paid}}{\text{Net income}}$$

$$= \frac{\$203}{\$1,368}$$

$$= 0.1484 \text{ or } 14.84\%$$

The proportion of earnings retained for use by the firm, the **earnings retention ratio**, is simply the inverse of the payout ratio:

$$\text{Earnings retention} = \frac{\text{Net income} - \text{Dividends}}{\text{Net income}}$$

$$= \frac{\$1,368 - \$203}{\$1,368}$$

$$= 0.8516 \text{ or } 85.16\%$$

Or you can use the dividend payout ratio to calculate it:

$$\text{Earnings retention} = 1 - \text{Dividend payout ratio}$$

$$= 1 - 0.1484$$

$$= 0.8516 \text{ or } 85.16\%$$

A retention ratio of 85.16 percent means that of its 2001 earnings, Target kept slightly over 85 percent of its net income to reinvest for the shareholders' future benefit. The payout ratio is determined by company policy in the light of economic conditions and industry practice.

The retention ratio is interesting in itself since it tells us about the company, its age, the conditions in the industry, and its prospects for growth. Older, slower growing companies typically have higher payout ratios, and newer, faster growing companies pay little or no dividends.

The ratio has another use when combined with the ROS, TATO, and leverage ratios.[60] By multiplying them, we can determine the maximum rate at which the company can grow using internally generated funds. This rate is called the **sustainable growth rate** (SGR) or the **self-sustainable growth rate** (SSGR). In doing this analysis we must assume that the key ratios all stay the same; that is, as earnings are retained, they are matched with enough new debt to keep the ratio of assets to equity the same, and neither the TATO nor the ROS ratio changes. The SGR is calculated as follows:

$$SGR = ROS \times TATO \times Leverage \times Retention\ ratio$$

$$= \frac{Net\ income}{Sales} \times \frac{Sales}{Assets} \times \frac{Assets}{Equity} \times \frac{Earnings\ retained}{Net\ income}$$

$$= \frac{\$1,368}{\$39,888} \times \frac{\$39,888}{\$24,154} \times \frac{\$24,154}{\$7,860} \times \frac{\$1,165}{\$1,368}$$

$$= 0.0343 \times 1.65 \times 3.07 \times 0.8516$$

$$= 0.1479\ or\ 14.79\%$$

This ratio may also be calculated using the following shortcut:

$$SGR = ROE \times (1 - DPO)$$

$$= 0.1737 \times (1 - 0.1484)$$

$$= 0.1479\ or\ 14.79\%$$

The sustainable growth rate is just under 15 percent. This means that if Target's ratios stay the same in the future as they were in 2001, the company can grow at almost 15 percent per year: Target can grow its revenues, expenses, profits, assets, liabilities, and equity by 15 percent on the basis of its internally generated funds alone.

By segmenting the sustainable growth rate into the four sources of growth—profitability, asset efficiency, leverage, and profit retention, we can look at each of the four factors that affect the sustainable growth rate. This ratio segmentation approach provides for a clear diagnosis of past financial performance. In addition, understanding this concept and an analysis of the SGR components can allow an analyst or manager to determine what would happen if the company had followed a different strategy for any component. For example, if the sustainable growth rate turned out to be lower than expected or desired, management could review the various components to determine the areas in which the company had underperformed. Exhibit 1-16 shows the components and

---

[60] Most companies do not pay out more in dividends than they earn during a year. However, some companies have a policy of never cutting dividends. If management is faced with a year with depressed earnings or losses, it can either change the dividend policy or pay out more in dividends than the company earned. To pay out more dividends than its current year's earnings a company can do one or more of three things: borrow, sell assets, or sell new common stock.

Exhibit 1-16

Industry Average Financial Ratios and Self Sustainable Growth, 2001

Industry	Return on Sales	Total Asset Turnover	Return on Assets	Assets/ Equity	Return on Equity	Dividend Payout Ratio	Retention Ratio	Self-Sustainable Growth
Advertising	11.1%	68%	7.5%	209%	15.8%	6.4%	93.6%	14.8%
Biotech	7.4%	52%	3.8%	140%	5.4%	5.5%	94.5%	5.1%
Computer systems	-0.6%	115%	-0.7%	230%	-1.6%	0.0%	100.0%	-1.6%
Consultants	3.7%	180%	6.7%	243%	16.2%	0.0%	100.0%	16.2%
Department stores	1.4%	170%	2.4%	254%	6.0%	29.4%	70.6%	4.3%
Electric utilities	6.0%	52%	3.1%	470%	14.8%	62.8%	37.2%	5.5%
Employment	1.2%	239%	2.9%	191%	5.5%	2.4%	97.6%	5.3%
Finance	16.1%	7%	1.1%	2760%	30.7%	40.0%	60.0%	18.4%
Food manufacturing	4.2%	103%	4.3%	334%	14.4%	37.6%	62.4%	9.0%
Furniture manufacturing	4.7%	146%	6.9%	180%	12.4%	56.4%	43.6%	5.4%
Grocers	1.6%	250%	4.0%	350%	14.0%	31.5%	68.5%	9.6%
Jewelers	-0.7%	530%	-3.7%	240%	-8.9%	9.1%	90.9%	-8.0%
Paper producers	3.6%	72%	2.6%	360%	9.3%	85.0%	15.0%	1.4%
Software	-4.4%	53%	-2.3%	220%	-5.2%	1.0%	99.0%	-5.1%
Steel	-0.6%	95%	-0.6%	350%	-2.0%	25.6%	74.4%	-1.5%
Wireless communications	-26.4%	32%	-8.4%	240%	-20.3%	0.0%	100.0%	-20.3%

sustainable growth rates for several different industries. There is a wide range of sustainable growth rates. To understand how useful this information is, let's look specifically at Target.

Based only on its 2001 sustainable growth rate, Target could grow at a rate of approximately 15 percent per year, that is, it could grow its sales, assets, liabilities, dividends, and so forth.

If Target management wanted the company to grow at a faster rate it would have to change something. Management could use the ratios that underlie the sustainable growth rate to understand what it could change. The most obvious candidate for change would be to cut the dividend. If Target had cut its entire dividend in 2001, its sustainable growth rate would have been almost 17.5 percent, the same as the return on equity.[61] Changes could be made to the profit margin, the efficiency of its assets, or even its financial leverage.[62] Changing these usually takes considerable time and effort, even when the change is possible.

All the ratios we have looked at thus far concern the health of the company. What we have not looked at is how its owners have been faring. What have they gotten for owning a part of the company—the stock? What has been their return and what has happened to their share price?

7. Market Ratios

In addition to ratios that are calculated using only data from the company's financial statements, analysts often calculate ratios using information from the market for publicly owned companies' stock. These ratios facilitate analyzing the company's financial market performance because the company's internal performance should and will be reflected in the capital market's evaluation. Since the return on investment for an equity owner may come primarily from changes in the market price of the equity, these ratios are of particular interest to the shareholders of a company. Equity investors purchase shares of common stock in the company, thus most market ratios are calculated on a per-share basis. A typical starting point for market analysis is **earnings per share** (EPS). Target's basic earnings per share for 2001 was $1.52.[63]

---

[61] Cutting the dividend is an action taken with extreme reluctance by directors and management. The reason is that they believe that it signals to the marketplace (the current and potential security holders) that the company is in some difficulty. Evidence shows and managers believe that stock and bond prices will react negatively.

[62] In order to have a SSG of 17.5 percent, all other ratios staying the same, the ROS could rise to 4 percent by price increases or expense reductions, the asset efficiency to 193 percent by selling assets or increasing revenues, or the leverage to 362 percent by decreasing equity.

[63] There are many versions of earnings per share. What we have shown here is primary or basic earnings per share. We might also show EPS including extraordinary items, $1.50, or calendar year, not fiscal year, EPS. In addition we could report EPS for TTM, trailing twelve months, the 12 months from the reported date of the earnings. Finally, we could show the EPS as if all conversions of convertible debt and/or preferred stock were made and stocks options and performance shares were exercised.

$$\text{Earnings per share} = \frac{\text{Net income}}{\text{Number of common shares outstanding}}$$

$$= \frac{\$1,368}{901.5}$$

$$= \$1.52$$

Remember, all the Target numbers, including the number of shares, are in millions, except the per share numbers.

Other ratios are based on the market price for a share of common stock. In early January 2001, the share price for Target was $44.00. Using this price, several useful ratios can be calculated. The first is the **price/earnings** or **P/E ratio**.

$$\text{Price/Earnings} = \frac{\text{Market price per share}}{\text{Earnings per share}}$$

$$= \frac{\$44.00}{\$1.52}$$

$$= 28.95 \text{ times}$$

Note that the P/E ratio normally is not cited as a percentage but as a multiple: Target's price was over 28.95 times its earnings using the stock price that coincided with the company's year end.[64]

The P/E ratio can be used to evaluate the relative financial performance of the stock. Most analysts believe that it gives an indication of how much investors are willing to pay for a dollar of the company's earnings, and it provides a scaled measure that allows market value comparisons of companies with different earnings levels. Typically, investors are expecting companies with high P/E ratios to grow in the future, to have more rapid increases in future dividends because earnings retained will feed the company's growth. Additionally, companies with higher sustainable growth rates are expected to have higher P/E ratios, again presuming that the company will grow in the future. Low P/E companies are either companies with little expected growth or, remembering this is a ratio, with low earnings. For the most part, analysts find low P/E companies to be troubled or low-growth companies. The exception is cyclical companies at their cyclical earnings lows where the P/E will be high, or when earnings are high the P/E will be low. Exhibit 1-17 shows our industries and you can see for yourself whether there is a relationship between ROE and P/E.

Comparing stock price to earnings is the traditional way of relating the market price to the shareholders' return at any point in time. However, earnings are impacted by many things that have nothing to do directly with the operations of the company—for example, its financial structure or its taxes. To circumvent any misunderstandings that might come from

---

[64] In times of volatile stock prices the P/E can change rapidly, even over the period of hours as the stock price rises and falls. The P/E of Target at the end of its fiscal year is an example since it rose by $2.00 to $44.00 and then fell shortly thereafter. To compensate for rapid fluctuations we might use an average price in calculating the ratio.

Exhibit 1-17 Various Industries

Market Ratios, 2001

Industry	Return on Equity	Self-Sustainable Growth	Price/ Cash Flow	Price/ Sales	Price/ Earnings	Market/ Book Value
Advertising	15.8%	14.8%	24.6	2.8	23.1	5.7
Biotech	5.4%	5.1%	30.1	4.2	45	3.6
Computer systems	-1.6%	-1.6%	17.2	1.4	45	3.9
Consultants	16.2%	16.2%	20.5	1.2	30.1	5.4
Department stores	6.0%	4.3%	14.2	0.9	41.3	3.0
Electric utilities	14.8%	5.5%	11.2	0.8	21.1	1.7
Employment	5.5%	5.3%	9.8	0.8	49.9	2.3
Finance	30.7%	18.4%	NA	2.8	23.8	4.8
Food manufacturing	14.4%	9.0%	13	1.3	26	4.8
Furniture manufacturing	12.4%	5.4%	8.6	0.8	44.1	1.9
Grocers	14.0%	9.6%	7.9	0.3	23.3	3.4
Jewelers	-8.9%	-8.6%	NMF*	0.5	13.6	1.2
Paper producers	9.3%	1.4%	7.3	0.8	36.2	2.3
Software	-5.2%	-5.1%	48.5	3.6	78.8	4.7
Steel	-2.0%	-1.5%	14.2	0.5	29.8	1.2
Wireless communications	-20.3%	-20.3%	48.2	1.5	87.2	2.4

*NMF indicates there is no meaningful figure to report.

differences in financial structures between companies or over time, many analysts use a **market price/EBIT** multiple. The EBIT figure does not include interest or tax expenses.[65]

$$\text{Market Price/EBIT} = \frac{\text{Market price per share}}{\text{EBIT per share}}$$

$$= \frac{\$44.00}{\$2,680/901.5}$$

$$= 14.8 \text{ times}$$

Another ratio that is of increasingly widespread use is **market price/EBITDA**. Earlier in this chapter we discussed the EBITDA and you saw how it removed the timing impacts of depreciation as well as financing costs. That ratio for Target is:

$$\text{Market Price/EBITDA} = \frac{\text{Market price per share}}{\text{EBITDA per share}}$$

$$= \frac{\$44.00}{(\$2,680 + \$1,079)/901.5}$$

$$= 10.55 \text{ times}$$

Stock market analysts are increasingly relying on market price to EBITDA and revenues ratios as a way to level industry and country accounting differences.

Since accounting and tax requirements can impact earnings, analysts, particularly stock analysts, have found ways to look at the price being paid for a share relative to other features of corporate performance. Two of these are in widespread use. The first is the **market price/revenues** or **market price/sales ratio**. For Target, the market price is almost 100 percent of the revenues.

$$\text{Market Price/Sales} = \frac{\text{Market price per share}}{\text{Revenues per share}}$$

$$= \frac{\$44.00}{\$39,888/901.5}$$

$$= 0.994 \text{ times}$$

This ratio, or multiple, has seen a resurgence of use in valuing technology, especially Internet stocks, since most have no earnings. As we have seen, there are risks in using this ratio. Investors must believe that revenues will eventually generate earnings. It is a dangerous measure to use out of context. In particular, take care when revenues include funds unrelated to the company's business, such as interest income.

The second ratio is the **market price/cash flow ratio**. While cash flow can be defined in many ways, discussed in later chapters, most analysts use the simple approach of simply adding back to net income the noncash charges for the period. The most typical noncash charge is depreciation. Target's depreciation was $1,079 for 2001, or $1.20 per share.

---

[65] Often the word "market" is left out of market price in published information.

$$\text{Market Price/Cash Flow} = \frac{\text{Market price per share}}{\text{Earnings per share +}}$$
$$\text{Noncash charges per share}$$

$$= \frac{\$44.00}{\$1.52 + 1.20}$$

$$= 16.2 \text{ times}$$

For companies with significant noncash charges, analysts believe this ratio better reflects the true underlying earning power of the company. This particularly is true for companies with limited earnings, or companies in early stages of development. Exhibit 1-17 shows the price/earnings, price/revenues, and price/cash flow ratios for various industries. None of these ratios show whether shareholders have fared well—whether the company has created value for the shareholders. Only the market/book value ratio can help answer that question.

To determine whether management has created and is expected to create value for its shareholders we can use the **market-to-book value ratio**. This ratio relates the market value (market price) per share of common stock to the book value or net worth per share. A market-to-book value ratio greater than 100 percent indicates that shareholders are willing to pay a premium over the book value of their equity. The book value per share of a company is calculated by dividing shareholders' equity on the statement of financial position or balance sheet by the number of shares outstanding. The book value of the equity is the combination of what the shareholders paid for their shares when they were first issued and the earnings the company has retained over time for the shareholders' benefit.

$$\text{Market-to-book value} = \frac{\text{Market value per share}}{\text{Book value per share}}$$

$$= \frac{\$44.00}{\$7,860/901.5}$$

$$= \frac{\$44.00}{\$8.72}$$

$$= 5.0 \text{ times}$$

As you can see, Target's shareholders are happy about how management has used their investment, since they place a publicly traded value on their equity 5 times the capital they invested. Had they believed that management had squandered what it had been given, the market-to-book value ratio might well have been below 1.0, or 100 percent. Market-to-book values, price/earnings ratios, and returns on equity for a number of industries are shown in Exhibit 1-17.[66] None of these industries show a ratio below parity, but let us keep in mind that 2000 and

---

[66] The analyst should keep in mind that book values result from specific accounting conventions that require the use of historical values for assets and retained earnings. When historical values do not reflect the current economic value or the earning potential of these accounts, the use of replacement cost or inflation-adjusted valuations may result in better information.

2001 were perceived to be market highs and, if true, these ratios would be at historically high levels.

Let's look for a moment at Exhibit 1-17. There are some interesting relationships to note. There are logical relationships for the most part. For example, steel manufacturers and jewelers have the lowest market price/book values and negative ROEs, while consultants and financial companies have some of the highest market price/book values and ROEs. However, wireless communications has a market/book value of 2.4 and has the most negative ROE of our industries. What is going on? Don't the shareholders recognize the negative ROE in this industry? In fact, these numbers force you to consider the future, which is just what the capital markets were doing. At the end of 2001 the markets saw a bright future for wireless communications companies. Typical of a bubble, this has since been reversed.

One other ratio used by stock analysts and investors is the **dividend yield**. This indicates the return on a share of stock provided by the current dividend payment.

$$\text{Dividend yield} = \frac{\text{Dividends per share}}{\text{Market price per share}}$$

$$= \frac{\$0.22}{\$44.00}$$

$$= 0.005 \text{ or } 0.5\%$$

Target's shareholders received less than a 1 percent dividend yield. By way of comparison, at that time a broad group of large U.S. company stocks, the Standard and Poor's 500, were yielding 1.4 percent.[67] Again, since the stock market was just coming off record highs, this yield was well below its long-term average.

The dividend policy of a company tends to be related to its industry, its maturity, and its need for future equity investments. Companies that are in mature industries, and thus have few needs for new investment, and those that need to have loyal shareholders tend to pay higher dividends. Those in new industries where there are significant needs for financing future opportunities rarely pay a dividend. Paying out a dividend should be and usually is related to the company's need for investment capital.

In recent times and for many companies the dividend yield has not fully reflected the full payout to shareholders. These companies buy back outstanding stock, thus allowing the investor who wants cash to sell some shares, rather than being forced to receive a dividend.[68] In the case of reg-

---

[67] At the same time the following were S&P 500 multiples:

	Market Price		
	Earnings	Book Value	Sales
Year-end 2001	36.7	4.8	2.4
5-Year average	30.5	4.9	3.1

[68] This is particularly useful when the tax rate on dividends is higher than that on capital gains.

ular share repurchase plans, stock analysts have combined the share re-purchase with actual dividends paid to create an "all-in-dividend yield" measure. For some companies, the share repurchases are the most significant cash source for shareholders, especially those who want regular cash payments from their shares.

Of course, dividends are only part of the return investors expect from their investment in common stock; the remainder comes from the potential growth in future dividends that results from wise investment of the profits retained by the company. Usually companies with higher dividend yields are expected to have lower growth in future dividends. Since they are paying more of their earnings out in the form of current dividends, these companies typically have growth rates lower than their sustainable growth rates. Companies with lower current dividends usually are retaining more of their profits for future growth. This is reflected in their sustainable growth rates.

8. Return Versus Risk Performance Ratios

There is another ratio that has gained widespread use. It is called the **spread**, a variation of which is called **economic value added**. This ratio is designed to give the analyst a measure of how well the company is doing without the distortions of accounting conventions, and taking the capital providers into account. While there are differences in the ways that this ratio is calculated, in general it is:

Spread = Return on equity − Required return on equity

To calculate the spread we must have an estimate of the investors' required ROE, also called the cost of equity and labeled R_e. For Target, the required ROE, the R_e, is 11.1 percent and the spread is a generous 6.3 percent.[69]

Spread = Return on equity − Required return on equity

= 17.4% − 11.1%

= 6.3%

Many analysts adjust the return on equity for transactions that affect accrual accounting earnings, such as depreciation, accounting adjustments, and investments. These adjustments will be discussed in Chapter 4. For Target, the analyst might add back to the net income of $1,368 the depreciation of $1,079 and adjust it by changes in such things as accounts receivable, inventories, accounts payable, and property, plant, and equipment. The result would be an adjusted ROE of over 25 percent, and a spread of 9.9 percent.

To show the usefulness of this ratio, we can compare the spread to the market-to-book value ratio. This comparison suggests that investors can

---

[69] We discuss how to calculate R_e in Chapter 6. In this case, since we compare the earned ROE with an expected ROE, R_e, we can call this a risk-adjusted return: the shareholders take risk into account in determining the required return.

see beyond accrual accounting to the real value being created by the company, and reflect this value in the stock price (as reflected in the market-to-book value ratio). Since Target's management, at least in 2001, had a very positive spread, we would expect investors to be pleased. The market-to-book value was 5.0 times or 500 percent. This shows that investors recognized the value that Target management had created, and were expecting more positive spreads in the future.

The average spreads for a variety of industries are shown in Exhibit 1-18. The first set of numbers that should catch any analyst's eye is those for the software industry. What is going on when the spread is so negative and the market value/book value is among the highest? Either the numbers are wrong or investors have high expectations for the future of this industry. It is high expectations: they must believe that the 2001 ROE does not reflect the future ROE. By mid 2001 expectations had dropped dramatically.

The electric utility industry stands in stark contrast: the ROE exceeds that which investors require but the market price of the stock is only 1.7 times the book value per share. Why? Prospects for increasing ROEs for this industry at the end of 2001 were, at best, unlikely. Steel is another industry worth noting. Investors did not like this industry (its market/book value is only 1.2 times), the spread was negative, and had been for years. This analysis of the spread and shareholders' expectations makes sense and, more importantly, provides insight into performance and shareholders' optimism about future performance.

Even better than numbers in Exhibit 1-18 is the graphic relationship that is shown in Exhibit 1-19. Here the spread and market/book value ratios of a number of U.S. industries are plotted. If there is a relationship between the returns generated by a company and investors' enthusiasm, we should find the higher the ROE spread, the higher the market value/book value ratio. To see if there is a relationship, beyond using a visual guess, we added a trend line.

As you can see, there is a relationship between market value/book value and the spread, even though there are exceptions. When thinking about this ratio remember the data is for one year and reflects, in the main, investors' optimism or pessimism about the future *at that point in time.* It is interesting to note that investors can use this kind of analysis to find and target over- and undervalued industries. The undervalued industry candidates are those below the diagonal line. Those above the line have high relative market values. To add perspective, remember that these industries do not contain all the companies in the industry, only those listed on the New York Stock Exchange. Thus, smaller and newer companies are excluded.

EVA® analysis is a conceptually similar but proprietary version of the spread analysis we just discussed. In this analysis a charge for capital costs, the cost of debt and equity, is subtracted from the net operating profit. As with the adjusted spread, EVA® seeks to estimate the economic profit above the capital investors' required minimum. To use this method, a variety of balance sheet and income statement items are adjusted to better reflect the surplus or residual income that remains after deducting the

Exhibit 1-18

Industry Average Market-to-Book Values, Price/Earnings Ratios, Sustainable Growth Rates, and Shareholder Spreads, 2001

Industry	Self-Sustainable Growth Rate	P/E	Market/ Book Value	Return on Equity	Required ROE	Spread
Advertising	14.8%	23.1	5.7	15.8%	8.9%	6.9%
Biotech	5.1%	45.0	3.6	5.4%	10.6%	-5.2%
Computer systems	-1.6%	45.0	3.9	-1.6%	10.0%	-11.6%
Consultants	16.2%	30.1	5.4	16.2%	12.9%	3.3%
Department stores	4.3%	41.3	3.0	6.0%	8.9%	-2.9%
Electric utilities	5.5%	21.1	1.7	14.8%	4.9%	9.9%
Employment	5.3%	49.9	2.3	5.5%	8.3%	-2.8%
Finance	18.4%	23.8	4.8	30.7%	11.1%	19.6%
Food manufacturing	9.0%	26.0	4.8	14.4%	6.6%	7.8%
Furniture manufacturing	5.4%	44.1	1.9	12.4%	8.9%	3.5%
Grocers	9.6%	23.3	3.4	14.0%	7.7%	6.3%
Jewelers	-8.6%	13.6	1.8	-8.9%	10.2%	-19.1%
Paper producers	1.4%	36.2	2.3	9.3%	8.3%	1.0%
Software	-5.1%	78.8	4.7	-5.2%	12.3%	-17.5%
Steel	-1.5%	29.8	1.2	-2.0%	10.6%	-12.6%
Wireless communications	-20.3%	87.2	2.4	-20.3%	14.6%	-34.9%

Exhibit 1-19

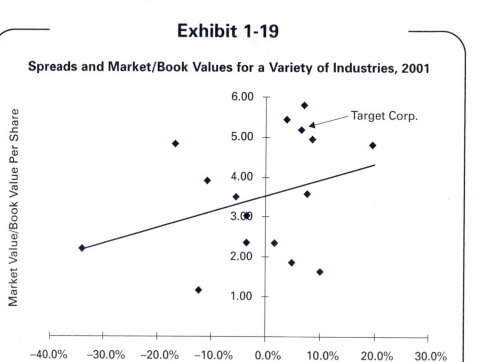

Spreads and Market/Book Values for a Variety of Industries, 2001

cost of borrowing or using shareholders' capital. The cost of the company's capital is also called the weighted average cost of capital, the WACC, a concept discussed in Chapter 7. In formula form the EVA® is

$$\text{EVA®} = \text{Invested capital} \times (\text{ROIC} \times \text{WACC})$$

Or

$$\text{EVA®} = \text{Invested capital} \times (\text{Return on invested capital} \times \text{Weighted average cost of capital})$$

Where:
ROIC = NOPLAT/Beginning of year invested capital × 100%
NOPLAT = Operating profits with taxes adjusted to a cash basis
WACC = Capital-structure weighted average marginal costs of debt and equity

NOPLAT earnings are earnings before interest charges and are adjusted for noncash charges—charges that have no impact on the economic, real earnings of the company in that period. Adjustments would be made for such things as the current value of future employees' benefits. The required return on capital is the return that capital providers require the company to earn on their investments. Exhibit 1-20 shows the spread, the ROE – R_e, and EVA® estimates. In some cases the differences between the spread and EVA® spread estimates are very small. In other

Exhibit 1-20

EVA® and Spreads for Selected Industries, 2001

| | Spread | EVA Spread® | |
	Return on Equity – Cost of Equity	Return on Capital – Cost of Capital	Difference
Advertising	–6.2%	–0.9%	5.3%
Banks	3.5%	12.8%	9.3%
Biotechnology	–9.6%	–1.3%	8.3%
Cement	2.5%	6.1%	3.6%
E-commerce	–42.4%	–22.3%	20.1%
Furniture	3.4%	6.5%	3.1%
Grocers	4.8%	6.5%	1.7%
Paper	–1.2%	4.2%	5.4%
Soft drinks	13.5%	12.1%	1.4%
Steel	–7.6%	1.5%	9.1%
Tobacco	27.5%	22.9%	4.6%
Wireless communications	–46.4%	–14.3%	32.1%

Data adapted from http://www.stern.nyu.edu/~adamodar/.

cases, for example, wireless communications and e-commerce, the differences are substantial.

This discussion of ratios is not intended to be all-inclusive. Rather, it is intended only to illustrate the types of ratios that may be calculated to provide the analyst or manager with insights into the performance of the corporation. Any number of ratios can be computed; the important thing is to determine what information is relevant to the problem at hand, and then to undertake the appropriate analysis.

IV. Comparative Ratio Analysis

While we have discussed many ways of looking at the performance of a company, actually calculating the ratios or percentages is relatively simple. The critical ingredient in a successful analysis is the analyst's interpretation of these figures. To interpret the ratios, analysts generally compare a company's performance to that (1) from various time periods, (2) of one or more companies in the same industry, (3) of the average performance of the industry, and even (4) of companies in other industries. To ensure comparability of the results, and to be able to explain the differences in performance among various time periods or companies, the analyst must thoroughly understand the company, its products, marketing techniques, organization, the industry, and the way the ratios were calculated. Furthermore, the financial statements used to prepare the various ratios must be based on comparable accounting procedures or properly adjusted statements. Using Target Corporation's financial statements as an example, we can see how much more we can discover about the company's performance by making such comparisons.

1. Historical Comparisons

The easiest first step in making historical comparisons is to do a full analysis of the components in the company's sustainable growth rate over time. This analysis, showing the five relevant ratios for Target from 1997 to 2001, is given in Exhibit 1-21. What you see is a company that has shown a steady increase in sustainable growth attributable primarily to increases in ROS. Another analysis will let us look at the source of the ROS increases.

Exhibit 1-21   Target Corporation

Key Ratios, 1997–2001

	2001	2000	1999	1998	1997
Return on sales	3.4%	3.4%	3.4%	3.0%	2.7%
Total asset turnover	1.65	1.89	1.97	1.97	1.96
Assets to equity	3.07	2.98	2.92	2.94	3.18
Earnings retention	85.2%	84.7%	83.3%	81.0%	78.0%
Sustainable growth rate	14.8%	16.4%	16.2%	14.2%	13.2%

Exhibit 1-22 extends the component percentage analysis of Target's income statement we showed in Exhibit 1-8 for 5 years. This comparison shows that while the cost of sales was the largest component of the company's expenses, it decreased in 2001. In addition, Target decreased its selling, general, and administrative costs. At first glance the increase in credit expenses is dramatic, a future analysis shows that credit revenues increased as well. It was the combination of these changes that improved the return on sales from a low of 2.7 percent in 1997 to 3.4 percent in 1999–2000. The experienced analyst would know that such steady numbers over 5 years of significant economic change is rather rare.

Another way to gain insight into the pattern of performance is to examine the growth in various accounts over the same periods. Since looking at the magnitude of raw data can mask the changes in various accounts **percentage change analysis** can be used to determine the relative change in an item (expense, income, asset, or liability) over time. The percentage changes can be compared with the changes in related items over the same time period. Exhibit 1-23 (page 58) shows this analysis for Target. As you can see, this analysis shows the change in each account each year. The most unstable items were those in credit revenues and expenses. This parallels the erratic history most credit card issuers have had.

Exhibit 1-22 Target Corporation

Common-Sized Income Statements, 1997–2001

| | Common-Sized Statements | | | | |
	2001	2000	1999	1998	1997
Sales	98.22%	98.53%	98.55%	99.1%	99.0%
Net credit revenues	1.78%	1.47%	1.45%	0.9%	1.0%
Total revenues	100.00%	100.00%	100.00%	100.0%	100.0%
Cost of sales	68.31%	68.54%	68.33%	73.1%	73.2%
Selling, general and administrative expense	21.11%	21.41%	21.46%	16.4%	16.3%
Credit expense	1.16%	0.79%	0.77%	1.6%	1.7%
Depreciation and amortization	2.71%	2.55%	2.53%	2.5%	2.5%
Interest expense	1.16%	1.15%	1.17%	1.3%	1.5%
Earnings before income taxes and extraordinary items	5.56%	5.56%	5.74%	5.0%	4.8%
Provision for income taxes	2.11%	2.14%	2.23%	1.9%	1.9%
Net earnings before extraordinary items	3.44%	3.43%	3.52%	3.1%	2.9%
Extraordinary charges from purchase and redemption of debt, net of tax	–0.02%	0.00%	–0.12%	–0.1%	–0.2%
Net earnings	3.43%	3.43%	3.39%	3.0%	2.7%

Note: Some percentage totals may not add due to rounding.

2. Comparisons to Other Companies

Looking at one company's ratios, even across time, gives us only a limited view into the company's performance. We need to see how the company has done in contrast to other companies. Because financial characteristics differ among industries, it is important that companies chosen for comparison first be limited to those within the same industry. Such an analysis is shown in Exhibit 1-24 (page 59). Data for Kmart and Wal-Mart, the other major companies in the same industry, are compared with the basic ratios for Target.

Let's compare Target and Wal-Mart first; Kmart has had difficulty of late. While the sustainable growth rates of the two companies are not very different, they achieved the result in different ways. Target used more financial leverage and Wal-Mart was more efficient in its total asset use. These differences should be of interest to management as well as potential investors. Without further analysis, the higher financial leverage makes

Exhibit 1-23   Target Corporation

Year-to-Year Income Statement Changes

	2001	2000	1999	1998
Sales	7.7%	9.5%	8.3%	11.6%
Net credit revenues	31.6%	10.4%	69.6%	7.0%
Total revenues	8.1%	9.5%	8.9%	11.5%
Cost of sales	7.7%	9.8%	1.7%	11.4%
Selling, general and administrative expense	6.6%	9.3%	42.4%	12.0%
Credit expense	59.7%	12.0%	−48.8%	7.7%
Depreciation and amortization	14.8%	10.1%	9.5%	12.6%
Interest expense	9.2%	8.1%	−1.3%	−4.3%
Earnings before income taxes and extraordinary items	7.9%	6.0%	24.4%	17.3%
Provision for income taxes	6.7%	5.1%	26.4%	13.4%
Net earnings before extraordinary items	8.7%	6.7%	23.2%	20.0%
Extraordinary charges from purchase and redemption of debt, net of tax	NA	NA	51.9%	−47.1%
Net earnings	8.2%	10.5%	22.4%	24.5%

Target potentially more vulnerable to economic downturns and company weaknesses. We will look at the positive and negative impacts of leverage in Chapters 7 and 8.

Of the three companies, Target had the best profit margins. Kmart had losses magnified by the fact that its operating efficiency was almost as high as that of Wal-Mart. Financial leverage was also high. The negative profit margin accompanied by high operating and financial leverage resulted, even in the absence of dividends, in a negative sustainable growth rate. Of the three, management, analysts, investors, lenders, suppliers, and customers should be concerned about Kmart, and they certainly were.

3. Comparisons with Others in the Industry

Comparisons can include several companies or all of those in the relevant industry. Typically, industry-wide comparisons are based on industry averages. These averages are available from several sources that collect and publish the data. Exhibit 1-25 (page 60) compares the 2001 Target data with five 2001 industry averages. Because of financial differences in companies in different segments, of different sizes, or operating in different regions of the country, analysts commonly select from the industry a sample of companies that correspond in size and sector with the company. In Exhibit 1-25 you see Target compared to others based on asset size, as well as those operating in the discount and nondiscount portions of industry.

Exhibit 1-24

Comparison of Target Corp. with Kmart and Wal-Mart, 2001

	Target	Wal-Mart	Kmart
Return on sales	3.4%	3.0%	−0.7%
Total asset turnover	1.65	2.63	2.5
Return on assets	5.6%	8.0%	−1.7%
Assets/Equity	3.07	2.37	2.9
Return on equity	17.4%	18.9%	−4.8%
Dividend payout ratio	14.8%	18.8%	0.0%
Retention ratio	85.2%	81.2%	100.0%
Sustainable growth rate	14.8%	15.3%	−4.8%

Target is one of the large companies. Target's discount retail division dominated the company's assets, returns, and revenues. As a consequence, Target should be compared to large and discount retail segments. However, the company has two higher-scale divisions, Marshall Field's and Mervyn's. This situation, and the situation for most multi-division companies, argues for a segment or divisional analysis. If the data is available that is the best analysis. For now, however, the point is to do comparisons that are relevant to Target Corporation.

An analysis of the data indicates that Target's performance compares favorably with that of the industry no matter how the industry is defined. Its costs were lower than the industry average, giving Target a higher after-tax profit margin of 3.4 percent as compared with just over 1 percent for the industry. Even more important in an industry where mergers were occurring, its ability to grow without as many demands on outside sources is superior to the averages, and to most of its larger competitors.

An analyst should assess a number of other things in looking at a company. If the performance being analyzed occurred over a period during which there was a significant change in industry or economic conditions (for example, inflation or global economic change), the analyst might want to look at the company's relative performance. The benchmark might be the industry as we have used here, or other retailers, or a widely used market index of companies like those on the New York Stock Exchange.[70]

V. Summary

Using the major external sources of financial information, the financial statements, an analyst can learn a great deal about the financial performance

---

[70] For comparison, Target Corporation's ROS was 8.2, ROA 5.7, ROE 16.8, P/E 1.2, P/Sales 0.39, and the Market/Book Value 1.2 times the averages for the companies in the Standard and Poor's 500.

Exhibit 1-25

Comparison of Target with Those in the U.S. Industry by Sector and Size

	Department Stores			Department Stores		
	Target	Discount	Non-discount	Large	Medium	Small
Return on sales	3.4%	1.6%	−5.0%	1.0%	1.0%	1.0%
Total asset turnover	1.65	2.1	1.23	1.9	1.5	1.9
Return on assets	5.6%	3.3%	−6.2%	1.9%	1.5%	1.9%
Assets/Equity	3.07	1.82	3.68	3.0	2.6	2.7
Return on equity	17.4%	6.0%	−22.6%	5.7%	3.9%	5.1%
Dividend payout ratio	14.8%	5.4%	33.7%	67.7%	17.6%	1.1%
Retention ratio	85.2%	94.6%	66.3%	32.3%	82.4%	98.9%
Sustainable growth rate	14.8%	5.1%	−15.0%	1.8%	3.2%	5.1%

of a company through comparative ratio analysis. Calculating a ratio is not difficult, it just takes a little practice. Understanding the ratios is not hard, it just takes a little experience. All the analysis is much like a detective searching for clues behind the raw data. These clues often require further digging. It is in the choice of ratios and the interpretation of the results where skill is required.

Proper interpretation requires an understanding of the company as well as of the environment. It is critical that the analysts understand and take into account the general economic conditions, the competitive situation, and the business and financial strategies of the company. All of these factors, individually and in combination, affect the financial results for the company and the value that will be earned by the company's owners, its shareholders.

Selected References

Sources of industry data and financial ratios are found in current issues of:

Dun & Bradstreet, *Industry Norms and Key Business Ratios.*

Robert Morris Associates, *Annual Statement Studies.*

Troy, Leo. *Almanac of Business and Industrial Financial Ratios.* Upper Saddle River, NJ: Prentice Hall.

The concept of sustainable growth is discussed in:

Copeland, Tom, Tim Koller, and Jack Murring. *Valuation: Measuring and Managing the Value of Companies.* New York: John Wiley & Sons, 1990.

Higgins, Robert C. "How Much Growth Can a Firm Afford?" *Financial Management,* Fall 1977, pp. 7–16.

Rappaport, Alfred. *Creating Shareholder Value.* New York: The Free Press, 1986.

Van Horne, James C. "Sustainable Growth Modeling," *Journal of Corporate Finance,* Winter 1987, pp. 19–25.

For information about spread and EVA® analysis, see:

Ehrbar, Al. *Stern Stewart's EVA: The Real Key to Creating Wealth.* New York: John Wiley & Sons, 1998.

Grant, James. "Foundations of EVA® for Investment Managers," *Journal of Portfolio Management,* Fall 1996, pp. 41–48.

Stern, Joel M., G. Bennett Stewart III, and Donald H. Chew, Jr. "The EVA® Financial Management System," *Journal of Applied Corporate Finance,* Summer 1995, pp. 32–47.

Stewart, G. Bennett III. *The Quest for Value.* New York: Stern Stewart & Co. with Harper Collins Publishers, Inc., 1998.

http://www.stern.nyu.edu/~adamodar/

For further information on ratio analysis, see:

Brealey, Richard A., and Stewart C. Myers. *Principles of Corporate Finance.* 7th ed. New York: McGraw-Hill, 2003, chap. 29.

Brigham, Eugene F., Louis C. Gapenski, and Michael Ehrhardt. *Financial Management.* 9th ed. Fort Worth, Texas: The Dryden Press, 1999, chaps. 2 and 3.

Fraser, Lyn M., and Eileen Ormiston. *Understanding Financial Statements.* 6th ed. Upper Saddle River, NJ: Prentice Hall, 2001.

Keown, Arthur J., John Martin, William Petty, and David Scott, *Financial Management: Principles and Applications.* 9th ed. Upper Saddle River, NJ: Pearson Education, 2002.

Ross, Steven A., Randolph W. Westerfield, and Jeffrey F. Jaffe. *Corporate Finance.* 6th ed. Homewood, Ill.: Irwin McGraw-Hill, 2002, chap. 2.

Web sites of interest:

Ratios on a variety of publicly traded companies as well as a source of company and industry profiles can be found on numerous web sites including: http://www.hoovers.com, http://www.bigcharts.com, http://www.morningstar.com, http://finance.yahoo.com, and http://moneycentral.msn.com/investor.

Corporate annual, quarterly reports and other filings with the Securities and Exchange Commission can be found at http://www.sec.gov.

In addition, many companies have their own web sites. These can be found through various search engines such as http://www.google.com and http://www.teoma.com.

Study Questions

1. Melissa Hampton was reviewing the recent performance of the EASY Chair Company, a company with a reputation for producing high-quality home furniture. Over the years, the name EASY had become synonymous with a kind of chair called a recliner. By 2002, the company was producing a variety of home furnishings, including reclining sofas, sleep sofas, living room cabinets, upholstered furniture, and solid-wood dining room furniture. In the past decade, the company had also entered the office furniture business by producing office systems and patient seating for clinics and hospitals. To determine the impact that diversification and expansion had on EASY, Ms. Hampton collected the following data for the company:

EASY Chair Company
Financial Data

(dollars in millions except per share)

	2002	2001	2000	1999	1998
Sales	$592.3	$553.2	$486.8	$420.0	$341.7
Net income	$28.3	$27.5	$26.5	$24.7	$23.0
Dividends per share	$0.50	$0.50	$0.40	$0.40	$0.40
Number of shares	17.9	17.9	18.3	18.4	18.3
Total assets	$361.9	$349.0	$336.6	$269.9	$233.0
Total equity	$214.6	$194.3	$178.8	$165.3	$147.0

    a. How had EASY's sustainable growth rate changed over time?
    b. What caused any changes you found?
    c. The home furniture industry had the following ratios over the same time. How did EASY compare with the industry?

Home Furniture Industry Ratios

	2002	2001	2000	1999
Return on equity	15.1%	15.5%	15.3%	15.7%
Retention ratio	71.0%	71.0%	71.0%	72.0%
Sustainable growth rate	10.7%	11.0%	10.9%	11.3%

2. Perplexed by the declining profit margin and the rate of growth of EASY's net income, Melissa Hampton pressed the company management for more detailed information. The management asks you, one of EASY's financial analysts, to compute component and percentage changes for the following statements and determine if there were any positive or negative trends.

EASY Chair Company
Income Statement

(in millions)	2002	2001	2000	1999
Net sales	$ 592	$ 553	$ 487	$ 420
Cost of sales	(430)	(398)	(352)	(290)
Gross profit	162	155	135	130
Selling, general, and administrative expenses	(112)	(107)	(91)	(86)
Income from operations	50	48	44	44
Interest expense	(7)	(8)	(4)	(2)
Other income	3	3	3	2
Income before taxes	46	43	43	44
Taxes	(18)	(15)	(16)	(19)
Net income	$ 28	$ 28	$ 27	$ 25

3. Ms. Hampton was not satisfied with EASY's performance. She believed that the company could achieve the following ratios:

EASY Chair Company
Ms. Hampton's Target Ratios

Dividend payout	45.0%
Market price	$15.00
Dividend yield	5.2%
Number of shares outstanding	18,000
Return on equity	13.7%
Long-term debt/equity	27.3%
Current ratio	551.0%
Acid-test ratio	407.3%
Profit margin	5.1%
Gross margin	27.6%
Return on assets	9.4%
Inventory turnover	733.3%
Operating profit	8.7%
Accounts receivable collection period	92.5 days
Accounts payable payment period	28.7 days
Tax rate	34.0%

Using Ms. Hampton's target ratios for EASY, complete the following financial statements:

EASY Chair Company
Ms. Hampton's Revised Financial Statements

Income Statement
Sales   _____
Cost of sales   _____
   Gross profit   _____
Selling, general, and administrative expenses   _____
   Operating profit   _____
Interest   _____
   Earnings before taxes   _____
Taxes   _____
   Net income   _____

Balance Sheet
Assets
Cash   _____
Accounts receivable   _____
Inventory   _____
   Total current assets   _____
Net property, plant, and equipment   _____
   Total assets   _____

Liabilities and Owners' Equity
Accounts payable   _____
Other current liabilities   _____
   Total current liabilities   _____
Long-term debt   _____
   Total liabilities   _____
Owners' equity   _____
   Total liabilities and owners' equity _____

Dividends per share   _____

4. As the new financial analyst for Peterson's Chemicals, you have been asked to analyze the profitability problems encountered during the last two years. Current financial statements and selected industry averages are as follows:

Peterson's Chemicals
Financial Statements

(dollars in millions)

Income Statement	2002	2001
Sales	$ 1,478	$ 1,435
Cost of goods sold	(1,182)	(1,076)
Gross profit	296	359
Selling and administrative expenses	(443)	(445)
Operating profit	(147)	(86)
Interest expense	(27)	(29)
Net income	$ (174)	$ (115)

Balance Sheet	2002	2001
Assets		
Cash and equivalent	$ 120	$ 76
Accounts receivable, net	432	437
Inventory	324	284
Other current assets	37	38
Total current assets	913	835
Plant, property, and equipment	300	375
Total assets	$ 1,213	$ 1,210
Liabilities and Owners' Equity		
Accounts payable	$ 500	$ 412
Other current liabilities	309	98
Total current liabilities	809	510
Long-term debt	178	300
Total liabilities	987	810
Owners' equity	226	400
Total liabilities and owners' equity	$ 1,213	$ 1,210

Using your analysis of the financial statements, how does Peterson's compare to the following industry averages?

Chemical Industry Averages

Current ratio	150%
Acid-test ratio	90%
Receivables collection period	65 days
Payables payment period	60 days
Debt/equity	110%
Return on assets	7%
Return on equity	19%

5. Peterson's management has decided to reexamine the company's short-term credit policies. The chief financial officer estimates that reducing the receivables collection period to 78 days would result in a sales decrease of 3 percent. The purchasing department reports that by reducing the payables period to 68.5 days, discounts would be available that would reduce the cost of goods by 9 percent. Initially the cash required to finance these changes would come from additional long-term debt, resulting in a debt to equity ratio of 100 percent. As an analyst:

   a. determine whether Peterson's Chemicals would have been profitable if management had made these changes at the beginning of 2002.
   b. determine how the ROE and ROA would have been affected.
   c. prepare new financial statements to reflect these changes.

6. Lacey Harmoniski had just moved to the Endura Republic as a part of a business school summer internship. His mentor and supervisor, Mr. Rickki, had handed him THE FASTNER CO. income statements and asked him to analyze them. His mentor was proud of the progress the company had made. Lacey knew that the analysis would show how well the joint fastener company had done over the past five years, and that his analysis was his introduction to a company of which his mentor was proud. Mr. Rickki had described the economic environment as one that was difficult: inflation had been high and variable. The company, he said, had coped with the inflation, and prospered.

   a. Calculate common-size statements for the income statements of THE FASTNER CO. On the basis of this analysis, determine how well the company did.

THE FASTNER CO.
Income Statements

(currency in millions)	2002	2001	2000	1999	1998
Volume (in units)	54,518	55,631	54,540	54,000	50,000
Revenues	10,119	8,294	6,480	4,800	4,000
Cost of goods sold:					
Labor	2,255	1,762	1,456	1,120	1,000
Material	4,588	3,584	2,636	1,856	1,600
Gross profit	3,276	2,948	2,388	1,824	1,400
Marketing expenses	873	715	559	414	345
Administrative expenses	539	435	334	244	200
Operating profit	1,864	1,798	1,495	1,166	855
Taxes	615	593	493	385	282
Net income	1,249	1,205	1,002	781	573

b. What was the price per unit of the goods being sold by THE FASTNER CO.?

c. Mr. Rickki has asked that Lacey calculate and comment on the growth rates of the various items on the income statement. Lacey asks that you draft the report. Please do so.

d. In spite of the fact that Mr. Rickki had not asked, Lacey decided to put one of the new business school tools to use: an analysis of real growth rates. In addition to the nominal growth rates of the various items, please help by calculating and commenting on the real growth rates the company has achieved over the past four years. Inflation over the four years was as follows:

	2002	2001	2000	1999
Inflation rate	28%	26%	40%	12%

e. Draft a report to Mr. Rickki stating your conclusions regarding how THE FASTNER CO. has performed in real and nominal terms.

Appendix One A

Cross-Border Ratio Analysis[1]

One problem that constantly arises in doing ratio analysis is comparability: ratios cannot be used to compare two companies or industries if the accounting principles used by one company are different from those used by another. This is true whether the accounting impacts the value of an asset, a liability, income, or expense, or the how and when revenue is recognized. Thus it is important to understand the accounting principles that are being used and to take those differences into account in analyzing financial statements.[2]

Understanding the general accounting principles U.S. firms use can be difficult, but once the accounting rules are learned and understood, the task of comparing companies is relatively straightforward. The accounting rules allow some discretion about how some items are valued, such as inventory. The accounting methods or principles being used must be described in the footnotes to the financial statements.[3] Thus differences between the rules used by different companies can be noted and taken into account.

---

[1] This appendix was prepared with James Parrino, Babson College, with assistance from Virginia Soybel, Babson College, Mike Fetters, Babson College, and Gary S. Schieneman, Smith New Court, New York.

[2] One other problem became clear during 2002. Not only can companies choose different, yet accepted, accounting principles, some managements have strained the principles and even abused them. Thus what we believed was accounting with transparency became accounting with suspicion. The U.S. Congress passed the Sarbanes-Oxley Act of 2002, which was designed to create more responsible corporate governance and accounting transparency. One of the important provisions of the act is that the chief operating and financial officers of the corporation must attest to "appropriateness of the financial statements and disclosures contained in the periodic report, and that those financial statements and disclosures fairly present, in all material respects, the operations and financial condition of the issuer."

[3] At the outset it is critical that the reader understand that there can be differences in the methods chosen for accounting within an industry and even for the same company over time. However, most of the principles are described in the footnotes to the financial statements.

When comparing the financial statements of companies from different countries, the analyst has a much harder job. Accounting standards vary widely from country to country and, until recently, companies in many countries were not even required to disclose the accounting principles on which their financial reports were created.

Various accounting groups around the world have attempted to harmonize the accounting rules and principles used around the world. The result of these efforts is the *International Accounting Standards,* published by the International Accounting Standards Committee.[4] The rules of the IASC are voluntary.[5] By 2003 there was a movement, as yet unsuccessful, to make accounting standards standard worldwide.

In making industry comparisons, analysts choose to deal with accounting differences in two ways. First, many analysts simply ignore companies that operate using accounting principles from another country. This, however, is a dangerous approach. As world commerce becomes increasingly global, the analyst can no longer ignore a major competitor, a significant industry participant, or a potentially interesting investment opportunity simply because of accounting differences.

The second approach is quite different: analysts examine the companies in an industry but ignore differences in the methods of accounting. This approach purports to give the analyst a view of the global industry but, as you will see, it can be a distorted view. The error in this approach is amply demonstrated by Exhibit 1A-1, which shows data from non-U.S. companies that have been adjusted to meet U.S. generally accepted accounting principles (GAAP).[6] This exhibit reveals how big an impact on reported performance a change in accounting principles can have.[7] While this data is rather old, the differences are no less dramatic today.

It is important to note that we do not suggest that one accounting system is superior to another. The point of this appendix is that different systems result in different reported performance, and the analyst must take these differences into account. This discussion is not intended as a criticism of any accounting system, only a demonstration of the dangers that await the unwary.

In this appendix we discuss the various ways in which a company can account for various items on its financial statements. The appendix is not

---

[4] For information about the Committee and the accounting standards it has developed and proposed, go to its web site at http://www.iasc.org.uk.

[5] These standards are being followed by companies in most countries and have resulted in disclosure of the accounting principles on which the statements are prepared. In addition, the IASC is generating common accounting principles. The rules set forth by the IASC do not meet the reporting standards of the U.S. Securities and Exchange Commission, and were rejected in late 1999 as incomplete by the U.S. Financial Accounting Standards Board.

[6] Generally accepted accounting principles (GAAP) means accepted by the accounting organization operating in that jurisdiction. It does not mean that any particular set of principles is generally accepted around the world.

[7] While this data is from the end of the 1980s, the same holds true today. This is one of the best comparisons that has been done, and dramatically points out the range of differences.

Exhibit 1A-1

Telecommunications Equipment Producers

Financial Statement Changes to Adjust to
U.S. Generally Accepted Accounting Principles, 1986

Company	Change in		Return on Assets		Return on Equity	
	Net Income	Equity	Reported	Adjusted	Reported	Adjusted
Mitel, Canada	7.4%	−20.1%	−10.0%	−9.4%	−22.6%	−21.1%
Bell, Canada	−15.3	−6.9	4.9	4.2	14.0	12.6
Sumitomo Electric	−5.9	−2.3	2.6	2.4	8.7	8.4
Siemens	40.1	30.7	2.8	4.0	11.1	12.6
Philips	−11.0	−12.4	1.9	1.8	6.3	6.2
Ericsson	16.2	17.9	1.5	1.8	8.2	8.1
British Telecom	14.9	−32.5	9.0	10.0	20.7	40.0
GEC	−1.0	2.0	8.4	8.3	16.6	16.2
Racal	−19.6	50.4	3.6	2.6	10.5	6.6
Standard Telephone and Cables	−27.1	60.1	8.4	4.8	22.0	9.4
NEC, U.S.	N.A.	N.A.	0.6	6.0	3.0	3.0

Source: Speech given by Gary S. Schieneman, Smith New Court, to Association for Investment Management and Research and the European Federation of Financial Analysts Societies, November 1991, London, England.

meant to be an exhaustive compilation of these differences, but to open the reader's mind to the world of global accounting and its implications for analyzing performance.

I. Accounting Principles Background

Why do differences in accounting principles exist? There are many reasons that differences exist, but the primary ones are:

1. **Culture.** Accounting standards reflect a society's attitude toward business. Countries that have a distrust of business will usually require strict disclosure, and companies will be given few choices about how to do their accounting. This factor has a major impact on the accounting standards.
2. **Level of economic development.** Accounting systems generally reflect the level of economic development in the economy.
3. **Legal requirements.** Accounting systems are developed to serve the needs of those who will use the financial statements. In general, accounting systems are either mandated by law or by an institution

that represents the accounting profession.[8] In countries with legally mandated systems, the government plays a dominant role in the development of the rules, and little or no differences exist between the financial and tax accounting systems. The goal is to control the corporation and collect taxes. Nonlegalistic systems are generally developed to serve groups interested in the company's performance, such as lenders and shareholders. The United States has a nonlegalistic system.[9]

The accounting principles used throughout the world are relatively few. Any accounting system must report a company's liabilities and assets, its expenses and revenues.[10] In addition, every accounting system must deal with problems created by foreign operations and inflation. Once an analyst understands the basic principles, understanding the rules for any country becomes manageable. There are many items that change from system to system. The major differences concern how to account for the value of research and development, investment securities, inventories, fixed assets, leases, deferred taxes, bad debts, and acquisitions and goodwill. In addition, asset valuation and the effects of inflation also will be discussed.[11] Let us begin by seeing how big the differences can be, and how the differences can impact performance. Let's look at research and development expenses.

II. Research and Development

If you are just becoming familiar with the accounting rules of one country, then how significant these accounting principle-based differences can be might not be obvious to you. As an example of how distortions can occur, let's look at a concrete example.

In most countries, all research and development costs, except for software, are expensed. However, that is not true in all countries. Some consider research and development an investment made in the company's future, and therefore treat it as an investment. Exhibit 1A-2 shows the ways research and development is treated in six countries.

---

[8] In the United States, that group is the American Institute of Certified Public Accountants, and its Financial Accounting Standards Board changes the rules. The International Accounting Standards Board is developing global standards. However, each country has its own rules. A detailed description of the accounting rules for each country can be obtained from the body that regulates accounting in that country.

[9] Some legalistic characteristics have been added by the Securities and Exchange Commission following the accounting scandals of 2002.

[10] The impact of depreciation on earnings and company value, as well as the particular changes that can occur in asset revaluation when there is very high inflation, are discussed in Chapters 2 and 4.

[11] As you read the rest of this appendix, remember that the differences in performance that come from using different accounting principles often are the result of differences in when a particular item (e.g., research and development) is reported and/or the actual value of what is being reported (e.g., how to translate foreign exchange or how to account for inflation).

Exhibit 1A-2

Methods for Accounting for Research and Development Expenses

	Canada	France	Germany	U.K.	Japan	U.S.
May be expensed in the year spent, but may be capitalized		X				
Expensed in the year spent, but may be capitalized					X	
Expensed in the year spent	X		X	X		X

As with any investment, research and development (R&D) can be capitalized by adding its cost to the balance in the long-term asset account and amortizing it over time or expensing it in the year it is spent. Panel A of Exhibit 1A-3 shows the impact on the financial statements of capitalizing and amortizing R&D, and the statements if R&D is expensed. Panel B shows the key ratios that result from the two sets of statements. The companies shown in this exhibit are identical, except that one expenses its $20,000 in R&D on its income statement and the other capitalizes it on its balance sheet. You will note that the key ratios are affected by this accounting principle difference. In fact, the impact is even felt in the sustainable growth rates: the company that expenses R&D has a very low sustainable growth rate, while it is higher for the capitalizing company. Remember, these companies are identical in every way except in the accounting for R&D.[12]

Obviously the difference between these two methods of accounting for R&D is the timing of the expenses for tax purposes—when the money spent is reported on the income statement. For the company that expenses R&D, it impacts the income statement in the year the R&D is done. The capitalizing company spreads out the impact over time. This difference in timing is at the root of most of the differences in accounting principles, and thus it is useful to keep in mind.

The R&D example also shows how big an impact on financial performance different accounting methods can have. To understand the relative performance of two companies operating under different accounting principles, we must adjust the statements to a common standard.

In our global world where a company of interest might be operated from a country other than the analyst's, it is important to know the accounting rules for that country. Accountants in a country know their own

---

[12] The question of whether they are identical depends on the tax code that impacts the amount of taxes that each would pay. Here we assumed the same rate of taxes.

Exhibit 1A-3

Impact of Expensing or Capitalizing Research and Development Expenses

Panel A (in units of currency):

	Expensed	Capitalized
Income Statement		
Revenues, net	100,000	100,000
Cost of sales	(45,000)	(45,000)
Gross margin	55,000	55,000
Other costs and expenses:		
General and administrative	(20,000)	(20,000)
Depreciation and amortization	(7,500)	(7,500)
Research and development	(20,000)	—
Total costs and expenses	7,500	27,500
Earnings before interest and taxes	7,500	27,500
Net interest	(1,000)	(1,000)
Earnings before taxes	6,500	26,500
Income taxes	(2,145)	(8,745)
Net income	4,355	17,755

(continued)

accounting rules and usually do a good job of keeping track of changes in them. Analysts unfamiliar with the accounting rules must understand in detail the accounting rules that govern the company they are analyzing. Sometimes the differences in accounting rules between countries can be difficult to discover.[13] For the analyst who wants to analyze the performance of an industry, memorizing the rules for each of several countries is a difficult task. For the novice, nonaccountant analyst, the task is impossible.

This is not to suggest that there is nothing to be done. There are some basic choices that must be made in creating an accounting system, and understanding those differences will help the analyst begin the task of analysis. In general, the main differences are in standards for valuing assets and liabilities and recording revenues and expenses. This appendix gives you some simple rules about differences in accounting principles

---

[13] Increasingly, the differences in accounting principles are available on web sites. For the particular country's accounting rules, try a query through http://www.teoma.com or http://www.google.com, or http://www.ifad.net.

Exhibit 1A-3

Impact of Expensing or Capitalizing
Research and Development Expenses *(continued)*

Panel A *(continued)*:

	Expensed	Capitalized
Balance Sheet		
Assets		
Cash and equivalents	10,000	10,000
Receivables, net	45,000	45,000
Inventories	35,000	35,000
Total current assets	90,000	90,000
Gross property, plant, and equipment	400,000	420,000
Accumulated depreciation	(150,000)	(150,000)
Net property, plant, and equipment	250,000	270,000
Total long-term assets	250,000	270,000
Total assets	340,000	360,000
Liabilities and Owners' Equity		
Accounts payable	75,000	75,000
Income taxes payable	10,000	10,000
Accruals	3,000	3,000
Total current liabilities	88,000	88,000
Long-term debt	125,000	125,000
Total liabilities	213,000	213,000
Common equity	127,000	147,000
Total net worth	127,000	147,000
Total liabilities and net worth	340,000	360,000
Other information:		
Number of shares	1,000	1,000
Dividends per share	2.50	2.50
Earnings per share	4.36	17.76
Panel B: Sustainable Growth Analysis		
Earnings/Revenue	4.4%	17.8%
Revenue/Assets	29.4	27.8
Return on assets	1.3	4.9
Assets/Equity	267.7	244.9
Return on equity	3.4	12.1
Dividend payout ratio	57.4	14.1
Sustainable growth rate	1.5	10.4

that will enable you to begin to analyze companies from different countries. However, the appendix is designed to give you only a basic introduction to the differences that exist. It will not make you an expert in any accounting system. For those whose company or clients depend upon the quality of the analysis, much more expertise is needed.

III. Consolidation

One of the first things that the analyst must determine is what is included in the financial statements. A financial statement can be **consolidated**, combining each of the accounts (such as balance sheets and income statements) from the company's various operations and subsidiaries, or not. When the subsidiaries' accounts are not consolidated, the ownership of the subsidiaries' operations is shown as an investment on the parent's balance sheet. The subsidiary investment shows the net value of the subsidiaries.

Consolidated statements can be confusing: by including in one statement financial data from different businesses, it can be hard to draw conclusions about the company's performance. For example, many U.S. auto manufacturers own both an auto production operation and a subsidiary that finances dealer inventory and consumer vehicle purchases.[14] Their statements are the merging of data from a production operation and a lending institution, and the resulting ratios resemble neither. Auto manufacturers are not the only companies with these diverse consolidated operations. Accounting rules in many countries do not allow consolidation. It is allowed and even required in the United States.

IV. Inventory

A company invests in all kinds of assets. One asset that can be accounted for in a number of different ways is inventory. If the cost of any item held in inventory (e.g., raw materials used in manufacturing a product awaiting sale) changes from the time it is purchased to the time it is used to produce the goods for sale, the method of inventory valuation impacts the financial statements.[15] There are several methods that can be used to value inventory.[16]

---

[14] For example, General Motors and GMAC, and Ford and Ford Motor Credit.

[15] All inventory accounting methods assign the same value to inventory when it is purchased and when it is transferred to cost of goods sold if no change has occurred in the cost of the items in inventory from the time of its purchase to the time of its sale.

[16] Several more exotic methods of inventory valuation are used in a limited number of countries, for instance, base stock, latest purchase price, and next-in, next-out. These methods are not as widely used, however, as those described in the text. The interested reader should consult the references listed at the end of this appendix for a further explanation and accounting rules for the country of interest.

- **Last-in, first-out (LIFO):** The cost attributed to the item removed from inventory is based on the cost of the most recently purchased item in inventory. LIFO is not permitted in most countries. Among large industrialized nations it may be used in the United States, Japan, and Germany. A variation of this is the lower-of-cost-or-market value. For many assets this latter method is used worldwide. These assets include many financial assets such as marketable securities and investments in other types of securities.
- **First-in, first-out (FIFO):** The cost attributed to the item removed from inventory is based on the cost of the oldest item in inventory.
- **Weighted-average cost:** The cost attributed to the item removed from inventory is based on the average cost of the items in inventory.
- **Specific identification:** The cost attributed to the item removed from inventory is the price paid for the specific item when it was purchased. This is the most accurate of the historically based methods, but it is expensive to maintain a record of prices. Thus it is used for very large and expensive items held in inventory.

Exhibit 1A-4 shows an example of how a company's cost of goods sold and inventory accounts would look at the end of its first year of operations under these different inventory accounting methods. For the analyst, the inventory method chosen determines the allocation of the inventory's

Exhibit 1A-4

Inventory Valuation Method's Impact on Inventory and Cost of Goods Sold

(as of December 31 in units of currency)

Method	Inventory Value	Cost of Goods Sold
LIFO	200	600
FIFO	100	700
Weighted average	115	685
Specific identification	150	650

Assuming:	Transaction
January 1	Purchase 200 units for 1.00.
April 1	Purchase 1,200 units for 0.50.
July 1	Sell 600 units.
October 1	Sell 600 units.
December 31	Market price for each new unit, 1.25.

value between the income statement (cost of goods sold) and the balance sheet (inventory). Furthermore, the method chosen impacts either the cost of goods sold or inventory. One is a more accurate reflection of its actual economic value. For example, when prices for an item have risen, LIFO attributes a realistic cost to the income statement's cost of goods sold, but leaves the balance sheet's inventory undervalued. When prices are declining, the reverse would be true.

The differences that can result in the inventory and cost of goods sold values are significant, and the problem for the analyst can be seen when looking at performance ratios. Using the financial statements in Exhibit 1A-5, the ratios are summarized in Exhibit 1A-6.

V. Inflation

Thus far the differences in the ratios are the result of differences in accounting methods. Inflation distorts both the financial information and the actual performance of a company. Let's use an example to see how the distortions can occur before discussing how the data might be adapted for comparability.

Exhibit 1A-5

Effects of Different Accounting Methods for Inventory*

(in units of currency)

	LIFO	FIFO	Weighted Average	Specific Identification
Income Statement				
Revenue	1,000	1,000	1,000	1,000
Cost of goods sold	(600)	(700)	(685)	(650)
Selling, general, and administrative expenses	(100)	(100)	(100)	(100)
Operating profit	300	200	215	250
Depreciation	(50)	(50)	(50)	(50)
Research and development	(50)	(50)	(50)	(50)
Earnings before income taxes	200	100	115	150
Interest	(50)	(50)	(50)	(50)
Earnings before tax	150	50	65	100
Taxes	(60)	(20)	(26)	(40)
Net income	90	30	39	60

* For simplicity, taxes for reporting purposes equal the actual tax liability. Differences in taxes are accounted for by changes in cash.

Exhibit 1A-5

Effects of Different Accounting Methods for Inventory *(continued)*

(in units of currency)

	LIFO	FIFO	Weighted Average	Specific Identification
Balance Sheet				
Assets				
Cash	50	90	84	70
Accounts receivable	250	250	250	250
Inventory	200	100	350	150
Property, plant, and equipment, net	400	400	400	400
Other assets	100	100	100	100
Total assets	1,000	940	949	970
Liabilities and Equity				
Accounts payable	250	250	250	250
Long-term debt	400	400	400	400
Deferred tax	0	0	0	0
Common equity	100	100	100	100
Retained Earnings:				
Beginning of year	160	160	160	160
Net income	90	30	39	60
Retained earnings, end of year	250	190	199	220
Total equity	350	290	299	320
Total liabilities and equity	1,000	940	949	970

Exhibit 1A-6

Ratios That Result from Different Methods of Inventory Valuation

Method	LIFO	FIFO	Weighted Average	Specific Identification
ROS	9.0%	3.0%	3.9%	6.0%
Sales/Assets	100.0%	106.4%	105.4%	103.1%
Assets/Equity	285.7%	324.1%	317.4%	303.1%
ROE	25.7%	10.3%	13.0%	18.8%

Exhibit 1A-7 shows the monthly income statements for a company operating in a world where inflation is 25 percent.[17] From an analysis of the company's performance you would conclude that the company's sales had grown. However, the unit volume of 10 units per month had not grown over the whole time. You might falsely conclude that the company had such market power that it sold 25 percent more each year, if you did not know that the company was in an inflationary environment. How fast has the company really grown? Inflation has distorted our view of the real performance.

We can compensate for the problem of inflation by thinking and forecasting in real (adjusted for inflation) terms instead of nominal (unadjusted for inflation) terms. To see how the company actually performed, the real and nominal statements are shown in the last two columns of Exhibit 1A-7. Revenues started at 100 and reached 1,455 by the end of the 12 months, in nominal terms. In real terms, however, there had been no change at all: the value of revenues is still 100.

This straightforward example assumes that revenues and all costs rise with inflation, but if this is true it is reflected only when the proper method for accounting for inventory is used.[18] Even when an appropriate method of inventory valuation is used the inventory account can be seriously misvalued. This example demonstrates that inflation can cause major distortions in reported financial performance. It is these distortions that the analyst must attempt to understand.[19]

Inflation can distort both the income statement and the balance sheet in a variety of ways, and accounting systems in different countries deal with the problem in different ways. Some ignore the problem, while others have developed sophisticated methods to correct for the distortions created by inflation.[20] The inflation-adjustment methods are, however, variations of two approaches: general price-level or specific price-level adjustments.

1. General Price-Level Adjustments

General price-level adjustments are also called constant dollar accounting. This method adjusts for decreases in the value of the currency that

---

[17] This is moderately high inflation, but by no means as high as inflation can be.

[18] Both LIFO and the latest-purchase methods are more likely to compensate for the problems created by inflation than either FIFO or weighted-average cost. This is because they transfer goods from inventory to cost of goods sold at more current prices, and the resulting income better represents what the company actually earned. However, the inventory is not valued realistically. If a company uses a method such as FIFO in a time of inflation, unless inventory is turned over very rapidly, the cost of inventory charged to cost of goods sold misstates its current cost and results in a misstatement of income.

[19] In spite of the fact that accountants like to believe that financial statements can be made to reflect financial performance, in times of high inflation financial statements do not provide reliable information. As an example of the problem consider how you might adapt revenues to real terms when inflation over a short time span is highly variable, for instance, 20 percent the first half of a month and 75 percent in the second half, and affects various revenue and expense items differently.

[20] In countries that have had high inflation for long periods of time, accountants have more sophisticated approaches to adjusting financial statements for inflation. Brazil, Israel, and Argentina, for example, have well-developed inflation accounting systems.

Exhibit 1A-7

Impact of Inflation on Revenues, Costs, and Unit Volume: Nominal Income Statements—25 Percent Inflation

(in units of currency)

						Nominal								Real
	0	1	2	3	4	5	6	7	8	9	10	11	12	12
Revenues	100	125	156	195	244	305	381	477	596	745	931	1,164	1,455	100
Costs	(50)	(62)	(78)	(97)	(122)	(152)	(191)	(239)	(298)	(372)	(465)	(582)	(727)	(50)
Gross income	50	63	78	98	122	153	190	238	298	373	466	582	728	50
Other costs	(20)	(25)	(31)	(39)	(49)	(61)	(76)	(95)	(119)	(149)	(186)	(233)	(291)	(20)
Earnings before taxes	30	38	47	59	73	92	114	143	179	224	280	349	437	30
Taxes	(15)	(19)	(23)	(29)	(37)	(46)	(57)	(72)	(89)	(112)	(140)	(175)	(218)	(15)
Net income	15	19	24	30	36	46	57	71	90	112	140	174	219	15
Unit volume	10	10	10	10	10	10	10	10	10	10	10	10	10	10
Real revenue	100	100	100	100	100	100	100	100	100	100	100	100	100	100

accompany inflation.[21] Conceptually, adjustments are made so that the revenues, expenses, assets, and liabilities are reported in units of the same purchasing power. **Purchasing power** reflects the units of currency needed to buy the same quantity of goods from one time to the next. This is an inflation-adjusted currency value. The first column of Exhibit 1A-8 shows the statements that would be reported in the absence of adjustments for inflation. Because the company shown in this exhibit experienced 20 percent inflation over the period, the ratios do not tell us the actual performance of the company in any useful way. Columns 2 and 3 provide general price-level-adjusted statements for the same period, the first adjusting the income statement and the second adjusting the balance sheet.

2. Specific Price-Level Adjustments

This method, also called **constant cost accounting**, focuses on specific asset values rather than a general change in purchasing power caused by inflation. Rather than using historical costs, the replacement value of the asset is used. This value can be determined by multiplying the historic value by an index reflecting subsequent inflation.[22] For example, the index used for fixed assets might be an appraisal or a construction-cost index that shows a gain in prices due to inflation. Any gain or loss as a result of the revaluation would be reported either as an inflation gain or loss on the income statement, or directly to the retained earnings account on the balance sheet. Exhibit 1A-8 Column 4 shows the result of specific price-level adjustments to the income statement and Column 5 the impact if the adjustments are reported to the balance sheet.

The general price-level adjustments can be quite different from those calculated using a general inflation index. Thus it captures the changes that specifically change the price of one asset or asset category. General price-level adjustments or specific price-level adjustments can be used separately or together, and can be used on some or all of the items on the financial statements. An analyst familiar with the two basic adjustment techniques is capable of interpreting the specific approach used in any country.

The problem that the accountant faces when there is inflation is how to adjust for inflation and how to do so in a way that can be understood.[23] This section has provided a particularly brief introduction to the problem of understanding performance at a time of inflation. You need to be wary of inflation since it can compromise the value of the information contained in the financial statements.

---

[21] The example in Exhibit 1A-7 shows the impact of inflation on the value of the currency.
[22] In general, this index will be a government-calculated index reflecting the changes in wholesale or consumer prices. Just how the index is calculated varies from country to country, and even can vary over time.
[23] If inflation is not taken into account, distortions in accounting occur that can result in real changes in managers' behavior. For instance, consider the United States in the late 1970s, when managers turned to more service-oriented operations rather than asset-based investments since the depreciation drag was considerable.

Exhibit 1A-8

Effect on Financial Statement of Different Accounting Methods for Inflation

(in units of currency)

Income Statement	No Adjustment	Constant Dollars Income Statement Adjustments*	Constant Dollars Balance Sheet Adjustments†	Specific Cost Income Statement Adjustments‡	Specific Cost Balance Sheet Adjustments**
Revenues, net	1,000	1,000	1,000	1,000	1,000
Cost of sales	(600)	(600)	(600)	(600)	(600)
Other	(100)	(100)	(100)	(100)	(100)
Gross margin	300	300	300	300	300
Depreciation and amortization	(50)	(60)	(60)	(53)	(53)
Research and development	(50)	(50)	(50)	(50)	(50)
Earnings before interest and taxes	200	190	190	197	197
Net interest	(50)	(50)	(50)	(50)	(50)
Earnings before taxes	150	140	140	147	147
Income taxes (@ 40%)	(60)	(56)	(56)	(59)	(59)
Inflation gains (losses)	—	100	—	40	—
Net income	90	184	84	128	88

(continued)

Exhibit 1A-8

Effect on Financial Statement of Different Accounting Methods for Inflation (continued)

(in units of currency)

Balance Sheet	No Adjustment	Constant Dollars Income Statement Adjustments*	Constant Dollars Balance Sheet Adjustments†	Specific Cost Income Statement Adjustments‡	Specific Cost Balance Sheet Adjustments**
Assets					
Cash and equivalents	50	54	54	51	51
Receivables, net	250	250	250	250	250
Inventories	200	200	200	200	200
Net property, plant, and equipment	400	470	470	417	417
Other assets	100	120	120	120	120
Total assets	1,000	1,094	1,094	1,038	1,038
Liabilities and Net Worth					
Accounts payable	250	250	250	250	250
Long-term debt	400	400	400	400	400
Common equity	100	100	100	100	100
Retained earnings:					
Beginning of year	160	160	160	160	160
Net income	90	184	84	128	88
Inflation adjustments			100		40
End of year	250	344	344	288	288
Total equity	350	444	444	388	388
Total liabilities and equity	1,000	1,094	1,094	1,038	1,038

Exhibit 1A-8

Effect on Financial Statement of Different Accounting Methods for Inflation *(continued)*

(in units of currency)

Ratios	No Adjustment	Constant Dollars Income Statement Adjustments*	Constant Dollars Balance Sheet Adjustments†	Specific Cost Income Statement Adjustments‡	Specific Cost Balance Sheet Adjustments**
Return on sales	9.0%	18.4%	8.4%	12.8%	8.8%
Sales/Assets	100.0	91.4	91.4	96.3	96.3
Return on assets	9.0	16.8	7.7	12.4	8.5
Assets/Equity	285.7	246.4	246.4	267.4	267.4
Return on equity	25.7	41.4	18.9	33.0	22.7

* Inflation constant dollar application to long-term assets, holding gains (losses) flow through income statement, general price index = 1.2, depreciation based on revalued assets (net PP&E = 400 × 1.2 minus the change in depreciation).

† Inflation constant dollar application to long-term assets, holding gains (losses) flow directly through to balance sheet, general price index = 1.2, depreciation based on revalued assets (net PP&E = 400 × 1.2 minus the change in depreciation).

‡ Inflation specific cost application to long-term assets, holding gains (losses) flow through income statement, general price index = 1.2, depreciation based on revalued assets, PP&E appraised at 417 (PP&E = 420 minus change in depreciation).

** Inflation specific cost application to long-term assets, holding gains (losses) flow directly through to balance sheet, general price index = 1.2, depreciation based on revalued assets, PP&E appraised at 417 (PP&E = 420 minus change in depreciation).

Note: For simplicity, financial taxes for reporting purposes (40%) equal the actual tax liability. Difference is taxes are accounted for by changes in cash.

Inflation not only changes the financial statements of the company, but can radically change the very way it conducts its business. In highly inflationary environments financial profits often become much more important than operating profits: production becomes the servant to speed, distribution methods may depend upon how and when the product is priced rather than the most efficient method of distribution; the work of the employees on pay day becomes how to preserve personal wealth rather than how to do their jobs. Inflation has fascinating consequences.

VI. The Impact on Statements of Nondomestic Transactions

Few companies operate solely in one country. Many buy supplies or sell products outside their domestic environments, and many hold assets or have liabilities in several countries. These transactions provide special challenges for accountants and particular problems in statement comparability for analysts. For assets and liabilities held outside the domestic environment, the problem is how to translate the value from the local currency into that in which the company's statements are reported: assets and liabilities held or owed in a foreign country must be reported in the company's home currency. For revenues and expenses, the problem is how to report transactions that occur outside the company's domestic environment into the company's home currency.[24] All foreign currency problems occur because the company's statements are reported in just one currency, its home currency.

1. Foreign Exchange Transactions

The method of accounting for foreign transactions and foreign-held assets can have a significant impact on the financial performance reported for a company. Unfortunately, accountants have devised no simple set of ways for dealing with these situations; thus the analyst must be particularly alert to the accounting rules that are used by any company being analyzed. To gain a perspective on the ways different countries choose to deal with the problem of foreign exchange transactions is to take what is called a transaction perspective.

One-Transaction Perspective. Accountants using this approach assume that gains or losses from changes in exchange rates should not be separated from the actions that initiated them—for instance, making sales abroad. Let us demonstrate this with an example.

Assume that a U.S. company buys raw materials from a company in the United Kingdom for £375 when the dollar/pound exchange rate is

---

[24] An example of the problem is a credit sale. A change in exchange rates between the two countries will result in a loss or gain. The loss or gain will be for the seller if the product is priced in the buyer's home currency.

$1.60/£1.00. At that time, the company's financial statements would show $600 of inventory and $600 in accounts payable. If, on April 1, the exchange rate is $1.75/£1.00, the financial statements would show an additional $56.25 in inventory and $56.25 in accounts payable [(1.75$/£ × £375) – (1.60$/£ × £375)]. With no further exchange rate changes, when the company pays for the goods, accounts payable and cash will be reduced by $656.25. When the inventory is sold, the cost, including any costs attributable to exchange rate changes, is charged to cost of goods sold and is reflected on the income statement.[25]

This method has a significant drawback: exchange rate gains and losses are combined with the actual cost of the company's supplies. This factor limits the comparability of the information.[26] When using this method, the analyst is left with the question: Did skillful management of the company or did exchange rate fluctuations create the performance?

Two-Transaction Perspective. The two-transaction perspective is designed to provide information so the analyst can determine whether a company's performance was based on its managers' ability to manage or from gains or losses in exchange rates. The two-transaction perspective separates the value of the event (in our example, the purchase of materials) from any subsequent exchange rate gains or losses by creating two new accounts. On the balance sheet the account is *loss/gain on foreign exchange*, and on the income statement the entry is *foreign exchange gains or losses*. To see how these statements would differ from those using the one-transaction perspective and from those of a company with no foreign purchases, see Exhibit 1A-9.[27]

2. Foreign Exchange Translation

When a company holds assets and liabilities in different countries there is another sort of reporting problem. It is not that we have to account for a transaction, but that the value of nondomestic assets and liabilities are changed by changes in exchange rates. These changes in values must be reflected on the balance sheet. Multinational companies, with divisions or subsidiaries in other countries, have long dealt with this problem. However, as more companies operate in more than one country, the problem becomes more urgent and widespread.

---

[25] Any exchange rate changes that occur before the accounts payable are paid are reported to cost of goods sold, even if the goods have already been used in the manufacture of the company's products and the products have been sold.

[26] This method is not used in the United States. It is used in other countries, for instance, in Brazil.

[27] The example transaction would be accounted for by showing 600 in inventory and 600 in accounts payable on January 1. On April 1, when the exchange rate changed, 56.25 would be added to accounts payable, and 56.25 to an account called "loss on foreign exchange." When the inventory is sold, on the balance sheet the inventory is reduced by 600 and loss on foreign exchange by 56.25; when the goods are paid for, accounts payable and cash are reduced by 656.25 and the income statement reflects a cost of goods sold of 600 and a foreign exchange loss of 56.25. All numbers are in units of currency.

Exhibit 1A-9

Effect of Different Accounting Methods for Foreign Exchange Transactions*

(in units of currency)	No Transactions	Foreign Exchange Method One- Transaction	Two- Transaction
Income Statement			
Revenue	1,000	1,000	1,000
Cost of goods sold	(600)	(660)	(600)
Selling, general, and administrative expenses	(100)	(100)	(100)
Operating profit	300	240	300
Depreciation	(50)	(50)	(50)
Research and development	(50)	(50)	(50)
Exchange rate gain (loss)	—	—	(56)
Earnings before interest and taxes	200	140	144
Interest	(50)	(50)	(50)
Earnings before taxes	150	90	94
Taxes	(60)	(36)	(38)
Net income	90	54	56
Balance Sheet			
Cash	50	14	14
Accounts receivable	250	250	250
Inventory	200	200	200
Property, plant, and equipment, net	400	400	400
Other assets	100	100	100
Total assets	1,000	964	964
Accounts payable	250	250	250
Long-term debt	400	400	400
Common equity	100	100	100
Retained earnings:			
Beginning of year	160	160	160
Net income	90	54	54
End of year	250	214	214
Total equity	350	314	314
Total liabilities and equity	1,000	964	964

* Figures reflect assumptions in this appendix. For simplicity, financial tax for reporting purposes (40 percent) equals the actual tax liability. Differences in taxes are accounted for by changes in cash.

Exhibit 1A-9

Effect of Different Accounting Methods
for Foreign Exchange Transactions *(continued)*

(in units of currency)		Foreign Exchange Method	
	No Transactions	**One- Transaction**	**Two- Transaction**
Ratios			
Return on sales	9.0%	5.4%	5.6%
Sales/Assets	100.0	103.7	103.7
Return on assets	9.0	5.6	5.8
Assets/Equity	285.7	307.0	307.0
Return on equity	25.7	17.2	17.8

The object of accounting is to develop financial statements that reflect the company's situation fairly and makes them understandable to and useful for investors, creditors, and managers. Since it would be impossible to understand statements where different currencies are just added together, the value of all foreign assets and liabilities are translated into the company's home currency. Whatever method of translation is used, the company must report both how it chose the exchange rate and how it accounted for exchange rate gains and losses.

There are three basic translation methods used for these translations: current/noncurrent, monetary/nonmonetary, and current.

1. **Current/noncurrent method.** In this method, assets and liabilities are grouped according to their maturity. Current assets and liabilities are translated at the date of the company's balance sheet; those that are noncurrent are translated at the rate in effect at the time of the transaction itself—for instance, when the liability was incurred or the asset purchased.
2. **Monetary/nonmonetary method.** Using this approach, assets are put into monetary or nonmonetary groups. **Monetary** or **financial assets and liabilities** are such things as cash receivables, payables, and long-term debt. In fact, you can think of them as any account that must be stated at current market value and must be translated at the exchange rate in effect at the date of the financial statement. **Nonmonetary assets** are translated at the rate in effect when the transaction first occurred, for instance, when a plant was purchased. A variation of this approach, called the **temporal method**, is used in the United States and other countries when accounting for the translation effects of foreign subsidiaries in high inflation countries.

3. Current method. This method is the easiest and most widely used method. All assets and liabilities are translated as of the date of the financial statements.[28]

Generally, all income statement accounts are translated at the average of the exchange rate prevailing over the period reported.[29] After the accounts are translated to reflect the effect of foreign exchange rates, a gain or loss is computed. There are two ways to account for foreign exchange translation gains or losses. Using the first method, a foreign exchange loss or gain would be shown as a separate income or expense item, thus affecting the income statement directly. The second method charges the gain or loss against the retained earnings account on the balance sheet. Exhibit 1A-10 shows the impact on a company of different methods of accounting for foreign exchange translations.

Translation gains and losses are not real losses as are transaction gains and losses. They are estimates of what the fair value would be if the asset was sold or a liability retired at the time the financial statements were prepared. The translated income statement shows an approximation of the revenues and expenses as if they had been incurred in the home currency. Although these figures are purely estimates, they do have a profound impact on financial statements and on measures of financial performance.

These are only some of the accounting principles that can profoundly impact both how information is reported, and how it is analyzed. These reporting differences also impact the way managers manage.

VII. Revenue Recognition

One issue that recently has been widely discussed in the press, the U.S. Congress, at the NYSE, and by numerous attorneys general is the issue of when to **recognize**, or record as a sale, revenue. Historically, financial reports have disclosed in the footnotes to the financial statements the revenue recognition policies. Unfortunately, these disclosures have been vague. Exacerbating the analysis difficulty caused by revenue recognition policies are increasing trends to bundle products, or products and services, to be delivered over time into one sales transaction, to develop creative financing arrangements to stimulate sales, and to lengthen the time for product returns in order to guarantee customer satisfaction. Trends such as these separate the origin of the sale from product delivery and from the collection of cash from the sale. As time between these events lengthens, more estimates are involved in revenue recognition. As a con-

---

[28] One curious problem that plagues historic, adjusted statements is whether they were adjusted for exchange rates of inflation. The problem is that the statement itself does not report the inflation index or exchange rate that was used. As a consequence, it is difficult to understand or reconstruct the statements later.

[29] The rationales are that revenue and expenses are received and paid fairly evenly over the year and that exchange rates change gradually. This assumption is often erroneous, however.

Exhibit 1A-10

Effects of Different Accounting Methods for Foreign Exchange Translations

Income Statement	U.S. Dollars	Income Statement Changes			Balance Sheet Changes		
		Current/ Noncurrent (yen)	Nonmonetary/ Monetary (yen)	Current Rate (yen)	Current/ Noncurrent (yen)	Nonmonetary/ Monetary (yen)	Current Rate (yen)
Revenue	$1,000	¥145,000	¥145,000	¥145,000	¥145,000	¥145,000	¥145,000
Cost of goods sold	(600)	(87,000)	(87,000)	(87,000)	(87,000)	(87,000)	(87,000)
Selling, general, and administrative expenses	(100)	(14,500)	(14,500)	(14,500)	(14,500)	(14,500)	(14,500)
Operating profit	300	43,500	43,500	43,500	43,500	43,500	43,500
Depreciation	(50)	(8,250)	(8,250)	(6,750)	(8,250)	(8,250)	(6,750)
Research and development	(50)	(7,250)	(7,250)	(7,250)	(7,250)	(7,250)	(7,250)
Exchange rate gain (loss)	—	(8,500)	(1,500)	(10,000)		0	—
Earnings before interest and taxes	200	19,500	26,500	19,500	28,000	28,000	29,500
Interest	(50)	(7,250)	(7,250)	(7,250)	(7,250)	(7,250)	(7,250)
Earnings before taxes	150	12,250	19,250	12,250	20,750	20,750	22,250
Taxes	(60)	(4,900)	(8,900)	(4,900)	(8,300)	(8,300)	(8,900)
Net income before inflation adj.	90	7,350	10,350	7,350	12,450	12,450	13,350
Inflation gains (losses)	—	—	—	—	—	—	—
Net income	$ 90	¥ 7,350	¥ 10,350	¥ 7,350	¥ 12,450	¥ 12,450	¥ 13,350

(continued)

Exhibit 1A-10

Effects of Different Accounting Methods for Foreign Exchange Translations (continued)

Balance Sheet	U.S. Dollars	Income Statement Changes			Balance Sheet Changes		
		Current/ Noncurrent (yen)	Nonmonetary/ Monetary (yen)	Current Rate (yen)	Current/ Noncurrent (yen)	Nonmonetary/ Monetary (yen)	Current Rate (yen)
Cash	$ 50	¥ 6,750	¥ 6,750	¥ 6,750	¥ 6,750	¥ 6,750	¥ 6,750
Accounts receivable	250	33,750	33,750	33,750	33,750	33,750	33,750
Inventory	200	27,000	33,000	27,000	27,000	33,000	27,000
Property, plant and equipment, net	400	66,000	66,000	54,000	66,000	66,000	54,000
Other assets	100	16,500	16,500	13,500	16,500	16,500	13,500
Total assets	$1,000	¥150,000	¥156,000	¥135,000	¥150,000	¥156,000	¥135,000
Accounts payable	$ 250	¥ 33,750	¥ 33,750	¥ 33,750	¥ 33,750	¥ 33,750	¥ 33,750
Long-term debt	400	66,000	66,000	54,000	66,000	66,000	54,000
Common equity	100	16,500	16,500	13,500	16,500	16,500	13,500
Retained earnings:							
Beginning of year	160	26,400	26,400	26,400	26,400	26,400	26,400
Net income	90	7,350	13,350	7,350	12,450	12,450	13,350
Other	0	—	—	—	(5,100)	900	(6,000)
Total equity	350	50,250	56,250	47,250	50,250	56,250	47,250
Total liabilities and equity	$1,000	¥150,000	¥156,000	¥135,000	¥150,000	¥156,000	¥135,000

Exhibit 1A-10

Effects of Different Accounting Methods for Foreign Exchange Translations *(continued)*

Ratios	U.S. Dollars	Income Statement Changes			Balance Sheet Changes		
		Current/ Noncurrent (yen)	Nonmonetary/ Monetary (yen)	Current Rate (yen)	Current/ Noncurrent (yen)	Nonmonetary/ Monetary (yen)	Current Rate (yen)
Return on sales	9.0%	5.1%	7.1%	5.1%	8.6%	8.6%	9.2%
Sales/Assets	100.0	96.7	92.9	107.4	96.7	92.9	107.4
Return on assets	9.0	4.9	6.6	5.4	8.3	8.0	9.9
Assets/Equity	285.7	298.5	277.3	285.7	298.5	277.3	285.7
Return on equity	25.7	14.6	18.4	15.6	24.8	22.1	28.3

sequence, inaccurate estimates can be made and outright manipulation of a company's earnings picture can increase. Because reported revenue impacts all income measures and most of the ratio analyses of operations, the area of revenue recognition is important to understand.

An example of one of these trends, product bundling, can be found in Xerox Corporation's financial statements.[30] Xerox sells a package of goods that includes hardware, services, and financing. Management must estimate the amount of the total revenue to allocate to each revenue stream: hardware, service contract, and financing. Xerox recognizes revenue associated with hardware sales immediately when the product is shipped. Revenue associated with service contracts and financing is recognized in future periods when the service contract is executed and the benefits of financing (i.e., interest income), are received. When Xerox Corporation experienced financial difficulties, management changed estimates and allocated more of the package revenue to hardware (revenue recognized immediately) and allocated less revenue to services contracts and financing activities. By changing estimates, more revenue was allocated to the current period, improving Xerox's reported earnings.[31]

Until footnote disclosure of revenue recognition practices becomes more transparent, users of financial data must be diligent in their understanding and analyses of a company's revenue recognition. Only if revenue recognition policies are understood can meaningful company assessments be made.

VIII. Conclusion

When a company operates in more than one country, whether it is selling or sourcing products or holding assets or liabilities, the analysis of financial statements becomes more complex. The ways a company can account for various income statement and balance sheet items is long, varies from country to country, and discretion exists within a country.

Exhibit 1A-11 provides a list of the various ways in which a company can account for each of the items discussed in this appendix. It is not an exhaustive list of differences in accounting principles throughout the world, but it does reflect the primary areas about which an analyst should be concerned when comparing the financial performance of companies from different countries. Exhibit 1A-12 provides a list of the ways in which various countries account for the major items discussed here. This list does not deal with every account or possibility, only with the most important and universal. Furthermore, due to changes in accounting rules, these rules should be verified before undertaking an analysis since the

---

[30] Xerox Annual Report to Stockholders, for the year ended December 31, 2001, pp. 19–21 of the footnotes.

[31] Management of other companies has chosen less forthright and sometimes fraudulent ways to recognize revenue. The accounting scandals of 2002 have prompted indictments, accounting reviews, and the requirement that CFOs must personally attest to the accuracy of their company's financial statements.

Exhibit 1A-11

Common Methods of Accounting around the World

Method	Balance Sheet Effect	Income Statement Effect
Inventory		
a. FIFO	Inventory value based on recent prices	Cost of goods sold based on obsolete prices of inventory units sold
b. LIFO	Inventory value based on obsolete prices	Cost of goods sold based on recent prices
c. Weighted average	Inventory value based on weighted-average prices for purchases during the current fiscal year	Cost of goods sold based on weighted-average costs for inventory units sold during the current fiscal year
d. Specific identification	Inventory value based on actual historical cost of each item purchased	Cost of goods sold based on actual historical cost of each inventory item sold
e. NIFO	Inventory value based on obsolete prices	Cost of goods sold based on current market prices of inventory units sold
f. Latest purchase price	Inventory value based on current market prices	Cost of goods sold based on obsolete prices for inventory units sold
e. Lower-of-cost-or-market	Inventory value based on lower-of-cost-or-market value	Cost of goods sold based on higher-of-cost-or-market value
Inflation		
a. Constant dollar, flow-through method	Various assets and liabilities revalued using a general price-level index	Inflation gains (losses) included in reported income
b. Constant dollar, balance sheet method	Various assets and liabilities revalued using a general price-level index; inflation gains (losses) recorded directly to the equity section of the balance sheet	Income statement does not reflect changes in profits caused by inflation
c. Specific cost, flow-through method	Various assets and liabilities revalued based on specific appraisals or specialized indices	Inflation gains (losses) included in reported income

(continued)

Exhibit 1A-11

Common Methods of Accounting around the World *(continued)*

Method	Balance Sheet Effect	Income Statement Effect
d. Specific cost, balance sheet method	Various assets and liabilities revalued based on specific appraisals or specialized indices; inflation gains (losses) recorded directly to the equity section of the balance sheet	Income statement does not reflect changes in profits caused by inflation
e. No adjustments	Balance sheet accounts do not reflect changes in value caused by inflation	Income statement does not reflect changes in profits caused by inflation

Foreign Exchange Transactions

a. One-transaction perspective	Receivables or payables are adjusted to reflect changes in the exchange rate prior to completion of the transaction	Gains (losses) from changes in exchange rates not separately recorded, but included with the other income statement accounts; the gain (loss) is only recorded if the transaction is completed
b. Two-transaction perspective	Receivables or payables adjusted to reflect changes in the exchange rate prior to completion of the transaction	Gains (losses) from changes in exchange rates reported as a separate item on the income statement, and reflect changes in the exchange rate prior to completion of the transaction

Foreign Exchange Translation

a. Current/ Noncurrent	Current assets and liabilities translated at the current exchange rate (balance sheet date); noncurrent assets, liabilities, and equity accounts translated at the rates in effect when each transaction occurred	Revenue and expenses translated using the average exchange rates for the period; depreciation expenses normally translated at the rate in effect when the asset was purchased; foreign exchange translation gains (losses) usually recorded in the current year in either a balance sheet reserve account or directly to the income statement

Exhibit 1A-11

Common Methods of Accounting around the World *(continued)*

Method	Balance Sheet Effect	Income Statement Effect
b. Monetary/ Nonmonetary	Monetary assets and liabilities translated at current rates; nonmonetary assets, liabilities, and equity accounts translated at historical rates	Same as current/noncurrent method
c. Current rate	All assets and liabilities translated at the current exchange rate; capital stock translated at the rate in effect when the stock was issued; ending retained earnings becomes the balancing item	Same as current/noncurrent method

rules can change. The intention in providing these exhibits is to highlight the basic differences between accounting methods, and to indicate how a company from that country would deal with these major items. Exhibit 1A-12 is a simple matrix and does not substitute for the more detailed analysis the professional analyst should undertake.

It should be clear by now that an analyst cannot simply compare companies operating from different countries. Differences in accounting alone can make the financial statements of two companies incomparable. The analyst must move beyond the simple comparisons to adjusting for the significant accounting differences. To do this there are three steps a good financial analyst will take:

1. Define the economic event that caused the accounting transaction.
2. Determine the accounting principle that governed the transaction.
3. Determine when the event will be or was reported on the financial statements.

As hard as it may be, whenever performance must be judged and the company operates outside the analyst's home-base economy or operates in several different countries, the analyst takes on the challenges of international accounting.

Exhibit 1A-12

Accounting Methods Available in Selected Countries[§§]

Country	Inventory	Inflation	Foreign-Exchange Translation	Foreign-Exchange Transaction
United States	a, b, c, d	e	c	b
United Kingdom	a, c, e	e	c	b
Germany	a, b, c, e	e	a, b, c*	b[†]
France	a, e	d, e	b, c	b[‡]
Spain	a, b, c, d	e	b, c	b
Japan	a, b, c, d, e	e	b[§]	b
Singapore	a, b, c, d	e	b, c	b
Canada	a, c, d, e	e	b, c	b"
Mexico	a, b, c	a, c	c**	b**
Brazil	a, b, c	a, d	b, c	a

[§§] Refer to Exhibit 1A-11.
* No specific requirements exist in German law or accounting principles as to which method must be used. The requirement is that whatever is chosen must be used consistently.
** There are no published accounting principles or regulations to account for the effects of foreign currency but companies generally follow U.S. accounting practices.
[†] No gains are recognized.
[‡] Losses may be deferred until the transaction is completed.
[§] Noncurrent monetary items are carried at historical rates.
" Unrealized gains (losses) on long-term monetary items are deferred until the transaction is completed.

Selected References

Afteman, Allan B. *International Accounting, Financial Reporting and Analysis.* Boston, MA: Warren, Gorham & Lamont, 1995.

Ball, Ray. "Making Accounting International: Why, How, and How Far Will It Go?" *Journal of Applied Corporate Finance*, Fall 1995, pp. 19–29.

Belkaoui, Ahmed. *Multinational Management Accounting.* New York: Quorum Books, 1991.

Carlsberg, Bryan. "FAS #52—Measuring the Performance of Foreign Operations," in *New Developments in International Finance*, Joel M. Stern and Donald Chew, Jr., eds. New York: Basil Blackwell, 1988, pp. 97–104.

Coopers & Lybrand (International). *International Accounting Summaries.* 2nd ed. New York: John Wiley & Sons.

Lessard, Donald, and David Sharp, "Measuring Performance of Operations Subject to Fluctuating Exchange Rates," in *New Developments in Inter-*

national Finance, Joel M. Stern and Donald Chew, Jr., eds. New York: Basil Blackwell, 1988, pp. 121–133.

Moffett, Michael. "Issues in Foreign Exchange Hedge Accounting," *Journal of Applied Corporate Finance*, Fall 1995, pp. 82–94.

Nobes, Christopher. *International Classification of Financial Reporting*. New York: St. Martin's Press, 1984.

Nobes, Christopher, Robert Parker, R. H. Parker eds. *Comparative International Accounting*. Upper Saddle River, NJ: Pearson Education, 2002.

Quick, Graham. *Global Reporting: A Guide*. London: Extel Financial Limited, 1989.

Saudagaran, Shahrokh M. *International Accounting*. Mason, OH: South-Western/Thomson Learning, 2003.

Shapiro, Alan C. *Multinational Financial Management*. 7th ed. New York: John Wiley & Sons, 2002, chaps. 8–11.

Stewart, Bennett. "A Proposal for Measuring International Performance," in *New Developments in International Finance*, Joel M. Stern and Donald Chew, Jr., eds. New York: Basil Blackwell, 1988, pp. 105–120.

Stickney, Clyde, and Roman L. Weil. *Financial Accounting*. 9th ed. Fort Worth, TX: The Dryden Press, 2000, chap. 4.

Helpful web sites among others:

For accounting terminology see http://www.nysscpa.org/prof_library/guide.htm.

For information on progress toward international accounting standards see http://www.pwcglobal.com.

For information on differences between local and international standards see http://www.ifad.net.

For information on the Sarbanes-Oxley Act see, among many other sites, http://www.aicpa.org/info/sarbanes_oxley_summary.htm.

Chapter Two

Forecasts are critical to evaluating future courses of action. To make useful forecasts, analysts must have the technical skill to forecast and the interpretive ability to understand the future. All forecasting depends upon the skill of the individual making the forecast, and skill comes from both knowledge and experience. A financial analyst must have skill in interpreting and understanding the company's past and current strategy and performance. The quality of an analyst's forecasts depends upon understanding the forces—technological, competitive and economic—that will affect the company in the future. The accuracy of any forecast depends on proper interpretation of historical data, and the identification and extrapolation of the forces that will impact the company's performance.

No one can really forecast the future. Yet every day we make decisions that require us to make forecasts: buy a stock, invest in Brazil, build a new plant, introduce and market a new product. All these decisions depend upon our interpretation of the future. To forecast the future, the analyst must make assumptions about what will happen. These assumptions are critical to creating forecasts and to understanding the scenarios behind the forecasts. The skilled analyst knows that these assumptions must be detailed and explicit. An inability to recognize the assumptions that have been made and failure to test them can result in tenuous or obscure forecasts, or forecasts that can be derailed by unforeseen changes in the company, industry, or economic conditions.

The forecasts discussed in this chapter are financial in nature. They represent the expected activity and condition of the company over time and at various points in the future, expressed in financial terms. These financial forecasts are the explicit details about what is expected from the way a company creates its products or services.

Financial analysts make a variety of forecasts. External analysts typically make forecasts to anticipate a company's performance. For example, a stock analyst may try to determine what returns might be expected from an equity investment in a company and whether its stock is attractive.[1] A lender will try to determine whether a company can generate sufficient cash to remain solvent and repay its obligations. Internal analysts, on the other hand, are often concerned with forecasting financial needs so managers can plan future operations and investments. This chapter's primary focus will be on the types of analyses used by internal corporate managers. These forecasts often rely on information unavailable to external analysts.

Financial analysts for a company turn forecasts for the company's future into two types of financial statements. For a view of the near future, a forecast known as the cash budget is most often used. When the forecasts are longer term, projected financial statements are developed.[2] Both will be discussed and some ways to test the assumptions used in creating the forecasts will be described.

I. Cash Budgets

A **cash budget** specifically focuses on the cash account of the company. It is a forecast of the cash receipts and cash disbursements the company will make. The objective of the forecast is to identify whether sufficient cash will be available to meet the financial needs or whether there is excess cash that can be invested. This cash-based approach differs significantly from the common method of accounting in corporations, the accrual method. **Accrual accounting** attempts to match the revenues earned with the expenses incurred during a specific period, without regard to actual cash receipts or disbursements. The cash budget looks only at when cash is received or spent.

A cash budget can be made for a whole company, a division, and/or a business unit, or even for an individual or family. To determine whether there is extra cash or a need for more cash, the analyst compares the expected cash receipts with the anticipated cash disbursements. The difference between cash receipts and disbursements reveals either an excess of cash or a need for additional cash for that particular period.

Whether a company has excess cash or a need for cash depends upon the timing of cash receipts and disbursements. If a company prices its products to break even, just cover costs, or to make a profit, and if the cash payments for its sales are received at the same time it makes payments for its production costs, it will not need additional cash. However, credit sales, seasonal demand, and other factors can combine to cause mismatches between disbursements and receipts. These mismatches re-

---

[1] Lately investors and analysts have even been forecasting whether a company's financial statements fairly reflect the actual activity of a company or industry.

[2] Some finance texts and finance professionals call forecasted financial statements pro forma. However the word *pro forma* means restated for different conditions. Here we are not restating statements but making forecasts.

sult in the need for cash or more cash than is needed to run the business.[3] Because of these timing differences, a cash budget is an essential planning tool for management.[4]

There are three steps in creating a cash budget:

1. *Choose an appropriate time period for the forecast.* For most companies a cash budget for monthly cash flows is normal. However, in industries with highly volatile cash flows or during times of high inflation or rapid economic or industry change, cash budgets may be for weekly or even daily cash flows. Not surprisingly, in some highly inflationary environments, companies have been known to prepare hourly cash budgets.[5]

2. *Choose a suitable length of time over which to forecast.* The forecast horizon depends on the firm's situation. If monthly cash budgets are suitable, a 12- or a 24-month forecast would be appropriate. Cash budgets based on shorter time periods are usually developed for correspondingly shorter forecast horizons.

3. *Determine what critical assumptions underlie the forecast.* Most forecasts begin with an assumption about the sales volume. The forecast for sales should be developed in light of the company's current market share, its product line, and its current and future competition. Once the sales forecast has been made, the analyst can use history, along with expected changes in the future, to determine what other assumptions underlie the forecasts. A good place to start is with an analysis of the company's past performance like that described in Chapter 1. For most cash budgets, asset, liability, and expense levels will be related to the forecasted level of sales. Thus, the expected relationships between sales and the assets and expenses are important and need to be stated explicitly.

The cash budget includes forecasts for cash and credit sales, and credit and inventory policies that result in a series of schedules to determine the cash receipts and disbursements for each period.

To demonstrate how to create a cash budget, let's develop one for Sport-Smart Fashions, Inc., a wholesale distributor of tennis and swimming clothing and accessories. Although Sport-Smart sustained some losses during its initial operations, management expects that continuing operations will be profitable. The company has been in existence for only

---

[3] The need for cash can create serious problems. For example, when a company does not have enough cash to meet its payroll, employees cannot cash their paychecks. This results in problems for the employees and a general decrease in confidence in the company. Extra cash does not cause the same problem. However, failing to invest the cash excess means a loss of income and less value for the shareholders.

[4] A cash budget requires considerable information, much of which is available only within the company. Hence, it is primarily a management tool, not a tool used by outside investors to assess the value of an investment. It also can be a critical family finance tool.

[5] Many corporate treasurers use daily intra-day forecasts so that they may borrow to meet needs or invest excess cash in very short-term instruments.

two years, and the owner has relied on a bank loan of $50,000 to offset the financial drain caused by the early losses. Although sales are expected to increase annually by 10 percent, the necessity of extending credit to customers for long time periods causes severe cash problems during the peak summer sales season. To determine the severity of the problem, monthly cash budgets, commencing on September 1, 2003 and extending through August 2004, are prepared.

The first assumption in creating a cash budget is the level of sales. Much of the activity of the company will depend upon the sales level. Sport-Smart management might have used information about customers—from its sales force, the industry, other companies, and trade organizations—to forecast sales growth of 10 percent. Starting with a forecast for sales growth of 10 percent, management makes the remaining assumptions. Management may use its experience or the experience of others in the industry to make the remaining forecasts. The assumptions made by Sport-Smart's management are listed in Exhibit 2-1. Based

Exhibit 2-1   Sport-Smart Fashions, Inc.

Cash Budget Assumptions

1. *Sales.* Sales, shown in Exhibit 2-2, are seasonal with the peak occurring during the summer months.
2. *Cash and credit sales.* Ten percent of the sales are for cash. Credit terms for Sport-Smart's customers are net 60 days, and customers meet the credit terms.
3. *Cost of goods sold.* Supplies are purchased the month prior to need. Cost of goods sold is 73 percent of sales.
4. *Accounts payable.* Suppliers require payment in 30 days.
5. *Selling, general, and administrative expenses.* Selling, general, and administrative expenses are 14 percent of sales. These expenses are paid in the month in which they are incurred.
6. *Fixed operating expenses.* Fixed operating expenses are $6,500 per month. This does not include $500 per month for depreciation.
7. *Lease and interest payments.* Lease and interest payments are $3,000 per month. This is a simplifying assumption since interest expense will depend upon the actual amount borrowed.
8. *Taxes.* The company has tax loss carryforwards, thus no tax payments need be made in 2003–2004. The fiscal year begins in September.
9. *New equipment.* New equipment will be purchased in March 2004 for $25,000, and must be paid for two months later.
10. *Credit line.* The bank will allow a credit line of no more than $50,000. This allows the company to borrow up to $50,000 as needed.
11. *August 31 balances.* Sport-Smart has a $9,000 cash balance at the end of August 2003. Its accounts payables are $70,100 and receivables are $246,100.
12. *Dividend payments.* No dividends will be paid.

on these assumptions, the expected sales volume, cash and credit sales, accounts receivable collections, and purchases of merchandise for each of the 12 months of the cash budget period are shown in Exhibit 2-2. In addition, since Sport-Smart sells primarily on credit, credit sales are included for July and August 2003. These are used to forecast the collections of credit sales for September and October 2003.

Exhibit 2-2 Sport-Smart Fashions, Inc.

2003–2004 Forecast for Sales, Purchases, and Collections

	Sales	Cash Sales	Credit Sales	Collections of Accounts Receivable	Purchases
2003 Actual					
July	$ 151.9	$ 15.2	$ 136.7	N.A.	N.A.
August	121.5	12.1	109.4	N.A.	$ 70.1
2003 Forecast					
September	$ 96.0	$ 9.6	$ 86.4	$ 136.7	$ 54.8
October	75.0	7.5	67.5	109.4	40.2
November	55.0	5.5	49.5	86.4	32.9
December	45.0	4.5	40.5	67.5	25.6
2004 Forecast					
January	$ 35.0	$ 3.5	$ 31.5	$ 49.5	$ 32.9
February	45.0	4.5	40.5	40.5	51.1
March	70.0	7.0	63.0	31.5	76.7
April	105.0	10.5	94.5	40.5	105.9
May	145.0	14.5	130.5	63.0	131.4
June	180.0	18.0	162.0	94.5	120.5
July	165.0	16.5	148.5	130.5	98.6
August	135.0	13.5	121.5	162.0	115.2
Total 9/1/03–8/31/04	$1,151.0	$115.1	$1,035.9	$1,012.0	$885.8

N.A. = Not applicable

As you look at the cash budget and the other forecasts that follow, note that in making forecasts the years increase going to the right. Historic financial statements most often show the most recent year to the left, as was shown in Chapter 1. Do not be confused. It is just one of the odd conventions to which you will become accustomed.

If Sport-Smart made all of its sales and purchases in cash, everything would be easy. However, it does not. Because of this we must estimate the impact on its cash position of delays in receiving payments from customers and making payments for what it owes. The following describes how to create the schedules, starting with the forecasts for September.

1. To determine the accounts receivable for September 30, add to the August 31 accounts receivable balance of $246,100 the credit sales for September. From the total subtract the accounts receivable collected: the credit sales from the two months ago. Do this for each month. The result is shown in Exhibit 2-3.
2. To determine the total receipts, add to the cash sales for September that month's collections on accounts receivable from the accounts receivable schedule in Exhibit 2-3. Do this for each month. The result is shown in the receipts' panel of Exhibit 2-5 (page 108). Sport-Smart has no receipts other than from its sales.
3. To determine the payments on accounts payable and the accounts payable balance, begin with the August 31 accounts payable balance of $70,100. Add to the balance the purchases for September (73 percent of October's sales), and subtract the payments on the accounts payable: the payments are the purchases from the prior month. Do this for each month. The complete schedule is shown in Exhibit 2-4.
4. The disbursements schedule, also shown in Exhibit 2-5, is the sum of the accounts payable payments from Exhibit 2-4, and the other disbursements listed in Exhibit 2-1.
5. The cash account is determined by adding to the August 31 cash balance the September receipts and deducting the September disbursements. The result of doing this for each month is shown in Exhibit 2-6 (page 109).

Using this cash budget, we can see that Sport-Smart would need $47,100 additional cash in June and a total of $53,200 in July. The need is relatively short term—it declines to $4,700 by the end of August. This short-term need for funds is typical of companies with seasonal sales, and most, Sport-Smart included, have significant cash balances to begin the next selling season.

This cash budget gives Sport-Smart management important information. The company has a credit limit of $50,000, but this is not enough to meet the needs in July. Management has two choices. It can change its marketing plan, thus reducing the need for sales-driven cash, or go to the bank and negotiate an increase in the credit line to accommodate the need. Since the forecast shows that the funds are needed because of the nature of the business, not because of poor planning or bad management, management should go to the bank well before the funds are needed and negotiate an increased credit line. By extending the cash budget for one month, management can show the bankers that Sport-Smart's cash need is a temporary supplement needed only to meet its seasonal requirements during the summer months. Graphically, Exhibit 2-7 (page 110) shows the cash balance and vividly demonstrates the impact on financing needs that can come solely from selling a product with seasonal demand.

Exhibit 2-3 Sport-Smart Fashions, Inc.

2003–2004 Accounts Receivable Schedule

(in thousands)	September	October	November	December	January	February	March	April	May	June	July	August
Beginning accts. receivable	$246.1	$195.8	$153.9	$117.0	$90.0	$72.0	$ 72.0	$103.5	$157.5	$225.0	$292.5	$310.5
Credit sales	86.4	67.5	49.5	40.5	31.5	40.5	63.0	94.5	130.5	162.0	148.5	121.5
Collection—accts. receivable	136.7	109.4	86.4	67.5	49.5	40.5	31.5	40.5	63.0	94.5	130.5	162.0
Ending accts. receivable	$195.8	$153.9	$117.0	$ 90.0	$72.0	$72.0	$103.5	$157.5	$225.0	$292.5	$310.5	$270.0

EXHIBIT 2-4 Sport-Smart Fashions, Inc.

2003–04 Accounts Payable Schedule

(in thousands)	September	October	November	December	January	February	March	April	May	June	July	August
Beginning accts. payable	$70.1	$54.8	$40.2	$32.9	$25.6	$32.9	$51.1	$ 76.7	$105.9	$131.4	$120.5	$ 98.6
Purchases	54.8	40.2	32.9	25.6	32.9	51.1	76.7	105.9	131.4	120.5	98.6	115.2
Payments	70.1	54.8	40.2	32.9	25.6	32.9	51.1	76.7	105.9	131.4	120.5	98.6
Ending accts. payable	$54.8	$40.2	$32.9	$25.6	$32.9	$51.1	$76.7	$105.9	$131.4	$120.5	$ 98.6	$115.2

Note: Shaded cells indicate beginning balances from the balance sheet.

Exhibit 2-5 Sport-Smart Fashions, Inc.

2003–2004 Monthly Cash Budget

(in thousands)	September	October	November	December	January	February	March	April	May	June	July	August
Receipts												
Cash sales	$ 9.6	$ 7.5	$5.55	$ 4.5	$ 3.5	$ 4.5	$ 7.0	$ 10.5	$ 14.5	$ 18.0	$ 16.5	$ 13.5
Collections on accts. receivable	136.7	109.4	86.4	67.5	49.5	40.5	31.5	40.5	63.0	94.5	130.5	162.0
Total receipts	$146.3	$116.9	$91.9	$72.0	$53.0	$45.0	$ 38.5	$ 51.0	$ 77.5	$112.5	$147.0	$175.5
Disbursements												
Accts. payable payments	$ 70.1	$ 54.8	$40.2	$32.9	$25.6	$32.9	$ 51.1	$ 76.7	$105.9	$131.4	$120.5	$ 98.6
Selling, general, & admin. expense	13.4	10.5	7.7	6.3	4.9	6.3	9.8	14.7	20.3	25.2	23.1	18.9
Operating expenses	6.5	6.5	6.5	6.5	6.5	6.5	6.5	6.5	6.5	6.5	6.5	6.5
Lease and interest expenses	3.0	3.0	3.0	3.0	3.0	3.0	3.0	3.0	3.0	3.0	3.0	3.0
New equipment payment									25.0			
Total disbursements	93.0	74.8	57.4	48.7	40.0	48.7	70.4	100.9	160.7	166.1	153.1	127.0
Receipts less disbursements	$ 53.3	$ 42.1	$34.5	$23.3	$13.0	$ (3.7)	$(31.9)	$(49.9)	$(83.2)	$ (53.6)	$ (6.1)	$ 48.5

Exhibit 2-6   Sport-Smart Fashions, Inc.

2003–2004 Cash Account Balance

(in thousands)	September	October	November	December	January	February	March	April	May	June	July	August
Beginning cash balance	$ 9.0	$ 62.3	$104.4	$138.9	$162.2	$175.2	$171.5	$139.6	$(89.7)	$ 6.5	$(47.1)	$(53.2)
Receipts less disbursements	53.3	42.1	34.5	23.3	13.0	(3.7)	(31.9)	(49.9)	(83.2)	(53.6)	(6.1)	48.5
Ending cash balance*	$62.3	$104.4	$138.9	$162.2	$175.2	$171.5	$139.6	$ 89.7	$ 6.5	$(47.1)	$(53.2)	$ (4.7)

Note: Shaded cells indicate beginning balances from the balance sheet.
* Negative cash balance indicates a need for financing.

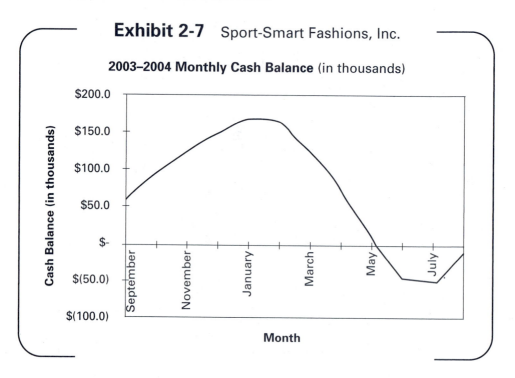

Exhibit 2-7 Sport-Smart Fashions, Inc.

2003–2004 Monthly Cash Balance (in thousands)

We have not mentioned the positive cash balances that Sport-Smart has for most of the year. What should Sport-Smart management do? Be pleased with the cushion, or plan for its use? The real question is, "Just how much reserve cash should Sport-Smart keep on hand?" The liquidity a company requires depends on its operating practices and the environment in which it operates. Companies operating in more volatile environments, with greater uncertainty about such things as sales, collections, and costs, need to maintain a higher cash balance than those operating in more stable economic conditions. Obviously, the more difficult it is to forecast future events, the greater the need to maintain a high cash reserve for unforeseen needs. Note that the cash reserve need not be maintained as an actual cash balance. Adequate liquidity protection can be established with a line of credit with a bank.[6] Other kinds of companies need actual cash. Companies with retail operations—for example, companies like Target, the department store we analyzed in Chapter 1—need cash for daily store transactions.

---

[6] A line of credit allows a company to borrow up to a preset limit at any time the credit line is in force. To provide such a credit line, the bank will charge a fee (interest) for what is borrowed, and a fee for keeping the credit facility available.

II. Projected Financial Statements

Cash budgets are used to track the ebb and flow of accounts, particularly the cash account. Management uses cash budgets the same way you track your own cash receipts and disbursements: to make certain that money is available when needed, and that excess cash is invested. The cash budget is a management tool, not a way to determine whether the company is profitable and healthy over the longer term. Most managers, stock analysts, and investors would rather see forecasted financial statements, the income statement and balance sheet, for that insight.

1. Developing Projections Directly

Forecasted financial statements, like normal financial statements, provide aggregate accrual information either over the forecast period for the income statement, or at a point in time for the balance sheet. You can also think of a projected financial statement as a summary of the information contained in the cash budget. Cash budgets provide the details, while financial statement forecasts provide information in the more familiar accrual-based accounting format.[7] Although financial statement forecasts can be prepared weekly or monthly, as was our cash budget, they are usually created for the same periods as those reported historically—quarterly or annually.

Like cash budgets, making a financial statement forecast requires defining one or more critical variables and the relationships of other variables to the critical variable(s). The relationships that underlie the forecast, and assumed by the analyst, should be explicit and written, just as they should with the cash budget.[8]

When you want to forecast how well a company will do in the future you can use a simple extension of ratio analysis on which to base the forecasts. The first step in this process is to determine the historical relationships among financial statement accounts for previous years, just as we did in Chapter 1 for Target. These relationships, expressed as ratios, are then adjusted to account for expected future events and trends. The second step is to forecast the various accounts on the basis of these adjusted ratios. As is the case with cash budgets, the first projection is for sales or revenues. In most cases, other accounts are then forecasted on the basis of their expected relationship with sales. Using Sport-Smart Fashions for our example, let's develop the forecasted financial statements.

Our first statement will be the income statement. All of what we need to create the forecast is found in Exhibits 2-1 and 2-2. The forecast,

---

[7] Projected income statements forecast earnings and expenses for the period; projected balance sheets forecast assets and liabilities at the conclusion of the period; projected cash flow statements forecast funds changes over the period.

[8] We will continue to argue for explicit, written, and detailed assumptions. These are easier to follow, interpret, change, and return to later.

along with notes about the sources of the data, is shown in Exhibit 2-8. The net income is expected to be $29,700.

Exhibit 2-8   Sport-Smart Fashions, Inc.

2003 Income Statement

(in thousands)

Sales	$1,151.0	Sum of September 2003–August 2004 sales, Exhibit 2-2.
Cost of goods sold	(840.2)	Assumption 3, Exhibit 2-1.
Gross income	310.8	Calculated.
Expenses:		
Selling, general, and administrative	(161.1)	Assumption 5, Exhibit 2-1.
Fixed operating	(78.0)	Assumption 6, Exhibit 2-1.
Depreciation	(6.0)	Assumption 6, Exhibit 2-1.
Lease and interest	(36.0)	Assumption 7, Exhibit 2-1.
Net income before taxes	29.7	Calculated.
Taxes	0	Assumption 8, Exhibit 2-1.
Net income	$ 29.7	Calculated.

The balance sheet for Sport-Smart is a bit more difficult to create than the income statement. One reason is that the forecasted balance sheet rarely balances. One of two things can happen. Either the assets will be larger than the liability and equity accounts, indicating a need for additional financing if the asset strategy is to be followed, or the liability and equity accounts will exceed the assets. An excess of liabilities and equity indicates that the company has additional sources of capital that may be used to increase assets or reduce liabilities and equity. One easy way to deal with this problem of balance in the forecasted balance sheet is to include a "net financing needed" account in the liabilities and equity portion of the projected balance sheet. This might be called a "plug" account because it is not a real account since it is used only to create the balance. If the amount in this account is positive, additional financing is needed. Because the account is part of the liabilities and equity portion of the balance sheet, if the amount is negative, the company has excess funds, and additional capital is available for investment. As you can see in the balance sheet in Exhibit 2-9, Sport-Smart needs at least $4.7 million at the end of August 2004.[9] This is the same figure calculated in the cash

---

[9] The statement is built using the assumptions from Exhibits 2-1 and 2-2 and the net income figure from Exhibit 2-8.

Exhibit 2-9 Sport-Smart Fashions, Inc.

Directly Forecasted Balance Sheets as of August 31

(in thousands)	Actual 2003	Forecasted 2004	
Assets			
Cash	$ 9.0	0	Assumption for simplicity.
Accounts receivable	246.1	$270.0	The sum of July and August 2004 credit sales from Exhibit 2-2.
Inventories	89.0	134.6	Inventory from fiscal year-end 2003 + purchases from July 2003–August 2004, less cost of goods sold.
Total current assets	344.1	404.6	
Net equipment	42.0	61.0	Equipment from year-end 2003 plus new equipment less depreciation (Exhibit 2-1 assumptions 6 and 9).
Total assets	$386.1	$465.6	
Liabilities and Equity			
Notes payable	$ 10.0	$ 10.0	No change.
Accounts payable	70.1	115.2	August 2003 purchases from Exhibit 2-2.
Total current liabilities	80.1	125.2	
Long-term debt	100.0	100.0	No change.
Equity	206.0	235.7	Equity from year-end 2003 plus net income from income statement in Exhibit 2-8.
Trial balance	$386.1	$460.9	
Net financing needed	0.0	$ (4.7)	Negative number here indicates that there is a cash need and the company must borrow at least this amount to support its assets at the end of August 2004.
Total liabilities and equity	$386.1	$465.6	

budget. Since the assumptions underlying both are the same, the amounts should be the same.[10]

It is essential to remember that the reliability of all forecasts depends on the assumptions. While these forecasts are simple, even they must be adapted for anticipated company and market conditions. More sophisticated forecasting approaches may be used if warranted.

2. Developing Financial Statement Forecasts from Cash Budgets

Cash budgets and financial statements are related. In fact, if you have a cash budget, you can derive the financial statement forecasts directly from it. To create the financial statements from a cash budget, you need two things: the balance sheet at the beginning of the forecast period and the cash budget. With these two statements, you can create an end-of-period income statement, balance sheet, and a sources and uses of funds or cash flow statement. Once again we will use Sport-Smart as an example to demonstrate this process.

To forecast the September 1, 2003 to August 31, 2004 income statement we use the assumptions from Exhibit 2-1. This is identical to the process we used in creating Exhibit 2-8 and the result is identical and will not be repeated here. For the balance sheet, the process is different.

We will use the balance sheet for August 31, 2003, the beginning of the forecast period, and information from the cash budget to create the projected balance sheet for August 31, 2004. The resulting balance sheet is shown in Exhibit 2-10.[11] This exhibit details the sources of the data and the changes that are expected to occur in the various accounts over the forecast period. Exhibit 2-11 (page 116), the sources and uses of funds, summarizes the changes over the forecast period.

These financial statement forecasts are the basis on which managers, shareholders, lenders, stock analysts, and portfolio managers make decisions and test possibilities. Thus, it is important to understand them and the assumptions behind them. The best way to be able to interpret forecasts made by others is to be skilled at making forecasts yourself.

Although projections do not provide the level of detail about the ebbs and flows in the cash account that is shown in the cash budget, they do show the cash balance at the end of the forecast period: they indicate the company's financing needs at the end of the period. For companies that do not experience a significant change in cash during a year, this approach to forecasting their cash requirements is usually adequate. Because cash budgets are more time-consuming to prepare, most managers elect to develop financial statement projections directly rather than on the basis of a cash budget.

---

[10] The cash budget and balance sheet give us the same forecast for what the company will need for August 2004. However, the balance sheet shows the financial condition on that date; the cash budget shows us the full year, month by month. If we had looked only at the balance sheet, we might miss the larger need in the months preceding August.
[11] The fact that the cash is negative indicates financing is needed.

Exhibit 2-10 Sport-Smart Fashions, Inc.

Balance Sheets from Cash Budget as of August 31

(in thousands)	Actual 2003		Forecasted 2004
Assets			
Cash	$ 9.0	From cash budget, Ex. 2-6.	$ (4.7)
Accounts receivable	246.1	From accounts receivable schedule, Ex. 2-3, 2003 balance plus purchases of $885.8, less cost of goods	270.0
Inventories	89.0	sold of $840.2.	134.6
Total current assets	344.1		399.9
		2003 inventory plus new equipment of $25, less	
Net equipment	42.0	depreciation of $6.	61.0
Total assets	$386.1		$460.9
Liabilities and Equity			
Notes payable	$ 10.0	No change.	$ 10.0
		From accounts payable	
Accounts payable	70.1	schedule, Ex. 2-4.	115.2
Total current liabilities	80.1		125.2
Long-term debt	100.0	No change.	100.0
		2003 balance plus net income of $29.7 from the income	
Equity	206.0	statement, Ex. 2-8.	235.7
Total liabilities and equity	$386.1		$460.9

III. Projecting Financial Statements in Highly Uncertain Conditions

A number of critical assumptions underlie the financial forecasts we made for Sport-Smart Fashions, Inc. Making assumptions is very difficult, even in circumstances that generate relative confidence. Analysts usually feel most confident when they make forecasts for companies that:

1. Are in a reasonably stable industry.
2. Have a strong position in their industry.
3. Are not making many changes to the:
   a. products they sell,
   b. methods used for production, and
   c. sources of financing.
4. Are in reasonably stable economic and political environments.

Exhibit 2-11   Sport-Smart Fashions, Inc.

Sources and Uses Statement September 2003 to August 2004
(in thousands)

Sources	
Decrease in cash	$13.7
Increase in accounts payable	45.1
Net profits	29.7
Total sources	$88.5
Uses	
Increase in accounts receivable	$23.9
Increase in inventories	45.6
Increase in net equipment	19.0
Total uses	$88.5

Sport-Smart operated in a relatively certain environment. However, many companies operate in situations that are challenging. While understanding the historical performance of companies that operate in highly volatile environments can be difficult, forecasting their future performance can seem impossible. As an example, let's use a company operating in a country where the economic environment has been quite volatile.

Terra Blanca SpA binds paper into notebooks for use by schools and businesses. The company has experienced difficulties since 2000. First, the country where it operates was on an economic roller coaster, with inflation reaching very high levels. Second, because of declines in individual and government incomes, sales of products had not met management's expectations. In addition, since some of the material Terra Blanca used to make its products came from outside the country, and those prices were not frozen by government mandate, costs have been difficult to control. The financial performance of the company for 2000–2002 is shown in Exhibit 2-12. As you can see, performance was erratic. This is most obvious when you look at the common-size statement (Panel B) and the growth rates in the various expense items (Panel C). You should note the strange profit figure in 2000. In that year the net financing income, income from financial transactions, dwarfed the sales.

Management, believing that planning was essential even though it had to be flexible, continued to make forecasts in spite of the volatility of the business and economy. However, management was confronted with a difficult problem: historical data was so erratic that it did not provide much information to use as a basis for estimating the future. What should they do?

After looking at the past, to understand how the economic environment had impacted Terra Blanca, the next thing management did was

Exhibit 2-12   Terra Blanca SpA

Historic Income Statement Data

(in thousands of currency units)	2000	2001	2002
Panel A:	Currency		
Sales	10,100	38,500	68,540
Cost of goods sold	(20,100)	(49,450)	(82,800)
Gross profit	(10,000)	(10,950)	(14,260)
Operating expenses	(6,500)	(38,450)	(48,840)
Operating profits	(16,500)	(49,400)	(63,100)
Net financing costs	73,010	77,900	66,400
Profit before taxes	56,510	28,500	3,300
Panel B:	Percentages		
Sales	100%	100%	100%
Cost of goods sold	−199	−128	−121
Gross profit	−99	−28	−21
Operating expenses	−64	−100	−71
Operating profits	−163	−128	−92
Net financing costs	723	202	97
Profit before taxes	560%	74%	5%
Panel C:	Growth Rates		
Sales		281%	78%
Cost of goods sold		146	67
Gross profit		10	30
Operating expenses		492	27
Operating profits		199	28
Net financing costs		7	−15
Profit before taxes		−50	−88

to assess the environment in which the company would be operating in the future. Recent events had led Terra Blanca management to believe that the economy was gradually coming under control and that a period of stability had been under way since late 2002. In this case management determined that the current situation was normal enough to use it as a basis for making forecasts. Explicit forecasts were made for inflation, as well as for the way in which Terra Blanca's business would react to the economic environment. Their analysts' forecasts are shown in Exhibit 2-13.

Exhibit 2-13 Terra Blanca SpA

2003–2007 Forecasted Financial Statements

(in thousands of units of currency)

	2003	2004	2005	2006	2007
Sales	99,109	130,625	149,174	176,324	208,415
Cost of goods sold	(67,394)	(73,150)	(82,046)	(88,162)	(104,207)
Gross profit	31,715	57,475	67,128	88,162	104,208
Operating expenses	(69,376)	(88,825)	(71,604)	(79,346)	(83,366)
Operating profits	(37,661)	(31,350)	(4,476)	8,816	20,842
Net financing costs	48,000	28,450	(22,100)	(16,000)	(12,000)
Profit before taxes	10,339	(2,900)	(26,576)	(7,184)	8,842

Assumptions:

	2003	2004	2005	2006	2007
Real annual sales growth rate	2.0%	5.0%	8.0%	12.0%	12.0%
Gross profit/sales	32.0	44.0	45.0	50.0	50.0
Operating expenses/sales	70.0	68.0	48.0	45.0	40.0
Inflation rate per month	3.0	2.0	0.5	0.5	0.5
Inflation rate per year	42.6	26.8	6.2	6.2	6.2
Taxes/profit before taxes	42.0	42.0	42.0	42.0	42.0
Nominal annual sales growth rate	44.6	31.8	14.2	18.2	18.2

Several things about the Terra Blanca financial statements, and those for companies in similar environments, are quite different from those shown for companies in more stable environments. First, for Terra Blanca, inflation had been high and had impacted revenues and costs unevenly. Second, operating profits in an uncertain and inflation-prone environment can be negative because of declines in demand brought on by decreases in real income, or because of price freezes instituted by the government in an attempt to reduce inflation rapidly. Third, inflationary environments provide profit-making opportunities for companies that have cash to invest: net financing costs turn into lending profits rather than interest expenses, and the profits from financial transactions can offset product/market losses.[12] When inflation reaches a lower level in 2005 Terra Blanca is expected to stop making financial gains and to borrow and incur financing costs. This situation is not unusual in inflationary environments.

---

[12] This is what happened to Terra Blanca: profits from financial transactions declined as did inflation. In 2005 you can see that Terra Blanca had to pay interest costs on debt that exceeded any financing income.

One solution to the complexity of making high inflation forecasts might be to make the forecasts in **real**, net of inflation, terms. The statements in Exhibits 2-12 and 2-13 are **nominal**, and include inflation's impacts. Creating real statements would be a good plan if, and only if, inflation impacted all the forecasted items identically. Unfortunately, this is rarely true. Costs can escalate faster than inflation, some costs may lag inflation, revenues may first go up with inflation and then stabilize, and the income from invested cash, the financial gains, might rise at quite a different rate. Since costs and revenues can be changed by inflation in different ways, real statements do not solve the problem of forecasting in an inflationary environment. Management must determine how inflation will impact their company and its financial forecasts, taking no shortcuts.

Terra Blanca provides a somewhat more complex forecasting problem than we had seen before. It is not harder than making forecasts for Sport-Smart; it is just more complex and requires market and economic intelligence.

IV. Analyzing Assumptions

Projections require assumptions. If the assumptions are not valid, then the subsequent forecasts are valueless. Whether an assumption is valid is recognizable only after the fact. Still, we want to be certain that our assumptions are realistic representations of a likely future. To test the reasonableness of an assumption several procedures have been used. These methods generally do one of two things: test for reality or demonstrate how the change in an assumption will impact a forecast. Rather than just describing the various ways you can gain perspective and confidence about assumptions, let's use an example.

Design Supplies, Inc. is a distributor of drafting and architectural supplies and software. The equity investment was provided by the owner/manager of the company, and a friend provided the remainder of the funding of $200,000 as a no-interest loan. The lender, a friend who considered herself more a silent partner than a lender, recently requested that she become involved in the operations of the company. However, she is willing to be paid off, or will remain silent as long as there are real prospects for having her entire loan repaid in the near future. The original agreement was that the owner/manager would fully repay the debt at the end of 2006. The owner/manager hopes that Design Supplies will provide sufficient funds to allow him to do so.

To determine whether adequate funds will be available for a buyout, the minority owner/manager has developed a five-year forecast. Exhibits 2-14 and 2-15 show the income statements and balance sheets for the previous three years and the projected statements for five more years. The assumptions used in developing the forecasts are shown at the bottom of the exhibits.

From the forecasts, it appears that the company will generate sufficient funds by 2006 to allow the manager/owner to fully pay off the debt. You will note, as should the owner, that while the total of these accounts is

Exhibit 2-14 Design Supplies, Inc.

Historic and Forecasted Income Statements

(in thousands)	Actual					Forecasted		
	2000	2001	2002	2003	2004	2005	2006	2007
Sales	$1,094	$1,360	$1,402	$1,612	$1,854	$2,132	$2,452	$2,820
Cost of goods sold	(792)	(980)	(984)	(1,128)	(1,298)	(1,492)	(1,716)	(1,974)
Gross profit	302	380	418	484	556	640	736	846
Operating expenses	(244)	(290)	(351)	(376)	(402)	(430)	(460)	(492)
Profit before taxes	58	90	67	108	154	210	276	354
Taxes	(15)	(30)	(14)	(36)	(51)	(70)	(92)	(118)
Net profit	$ 43	$ 60	$ 53	$ 72	$ 103	$ 140	$ 184	$ 236

Assumptions:
Sales will grow at 15 percent.
Gross profit will be 30 percent of sales.
Operating expenses will grow at 3 percent plus the expected 4 percent rate of inflation.
Taxes will be 33.3 percent of profit before taxes.

Exhibit 2-15 Design Supplies, Inc.

Historic and Forecasted Balance Sheets

(in thousands)	Actual					Forecasted		
	2000	2001	2002	2003	2004	2005	2006	2007
Assets								
Cash	$ 45.0	$ 54.0	$ 60.0	$ 64.2	$ 68.7	$ 73.5	$ 78.6	$ 84.2
Accounts receivable	118.0	168.0	165.0	177.4	204.0	234.5	269.7	310.2
Inventory	309.0	320.0	365.0	403.1	463.5	533.1	613.0	705.0
Other current assets	46.0	52.0	75.0	80.3	85.9	91.9	98.3	105.2
Total current assets	518.0	594.0	665.0	725.0	822.1	933.0	1,059.6	1,204.6
Fixed assets, net	13.0	19.0	14.0	14.0	14.0	14.0	14.0	14.0
Total assets	$531.0	$613.0	$679.0	$(739.0)	$(836.1)	$ 947.0	$1,073.6	$1,218.6
Liabilities and Equity								
Accounts payable	$ 41.0	$ 61.0	$ 73.0	$ 80.6	$ 92.7	$ 106.6	$ 122.6	$ 141.0
Other current liabilities	3.0	5.0	6.0	6.0	6.0	6.0	6.0	6.0
Total current liabilities	44.0	66.0	79.0	86.6	98.7	112.6	128.6	147.0
Long-term debt	200.0	200.0	200.0	200.0	200.0	200.0	200.0	200.0
Common stock	150.0	150.0	150.0	150.0	150.0	150.0	150.0	150.0
Retained earnings	137.0	197.0	250.0	322.0	425.0	565.0	749.0	985.0
Total equity	287.0	347.0	400.0	472.0	575.0	715.0	899.0	1,135.0
Trial balance	531.0	613.0	679.0	758.6	873.7	1,027.6	1,227.6	1,482.0
Net financing needed (excess funds)	—			(19.6)	(37.6)	(80.6)	(154.0)	(263.4)
Total liabilities and equity	$531.0	$613.0	$679.0	$ 739.0	$ 836.1	$ 947.0	$1,073.6	$1,218.6
Total excess funds plus cash	$ 45.0	$ 54.0	$ 60.0	$ 83.8	$ 106.3	$ 154.1	$ 232.6	$ 347.6

Assumptions

Receivables will be 11 percent of sales; inventory will be 25 percent of sales; cash and other current assets will increase at 3 percent plus the expected 4 percent inflation rate; accounts payable will be 5 percent of sales; other current liabilities will not change; new fixed asset investments will equal depreciation.

sufficient to pay off the partner, doing so would leave the company with a small amount of cash for operations. The owner will have to plan to have sufficient cash for operations when the loan is repaid.[13]

If you are the friendly lender, these forecasts look good—if you can wait until 2006. However, before accepting that the loan can be paid off five years from now, you would certainly want to understand the assumptions on which the forecasts are based. A reasonable way to look at the assumptions would be to compare Design Supplies' forecasts to its own recent performance.

1. Historical Comparisons

Just as ratios are used to examine the historical performance of a company, so to can they be used to test whether assumptions about future performance are reasonable. For Design Supplies, such a comparison is shown in Exhibit 2-16. There are several oddities that you might note: real and nominal sales growth is expected to be higher than the previous year, and operating expenses and inventory are expected to be lower. If you were the lender, would you feel confident in these forecasts?

Exhibit 2-16   Design Supplies, Inc.

Ratio Comparison of Actual Results and Forecast Assumptions

	Actual			Forecast
	2000	**2001**	**2002**	**2003–07**
Sales growth	N.A.	20%	11%	15%
Inflation	N.A.	6%	6%	4%
Real sales growth	N.A.	14%	5%	11%
Receivables/sales	11%	12%	12%	11%
Inventory/sales	28%	24%	26%	25%
Payables/sales	4%	5%	5%	5%
Gross margin	28%	28%	30%	30%
Operating expense growth	N.A.	19%	21%	7%

N.A. = Not Applicable

Let's look first at the sales growth. Is it too optimistic? As the lender you might note that the forecasted sales growth is above that obtained in 2002, but below what was experienced in 2001. Management may be as-

---

[13] Note that all we have planned for, thus far, was to pay off the lender's $200,000. What if the lender was expecting interest? If the lender was expecting only an annual rate of interest of 6 percent interest per year on her loan, the full value of the loan plus interest could not be repaid until 2007. If the interest rate were higher, it would take even longer.

suming a decline in inflation and an increase in the real rate of growth in the future. In addition to the important assumptions about inflation and real growth, management's forecast for operating expense decline is dramatic. This reduction in operating expenses coupled with lower inventories and receivables constitutes a forecast for a tightly controlled company that is growing. These forecasts may be overly optimistic.[14]

There are many other ways managers and analysts use to gain more confidence in their forecasts. Statistical tools such as regression analysis allow the analyst to project mathematical relationships based on several past periods of data. While this method provides the security of quantitative rigor, it may be false security if the analyst has good reason to expect future relationships between various accounts to differ from their historical patterns.

2. Sensitivity Analysis—One Scenario

One variable at a time. A valuable means of analyzing the assumptions is called **sensitivity analysis**. This process examines how the change in an assumption will change the forecasts. If changing a particular assumption has little impact on the forecasts, then the assumption is not considered critical. If changing one assumption causes a major change in the projected statements, then it is considered a critical variable that warrants further analysis and careful monitoring.

There were two assumptions, sales growth and the operating expenses/sales ratio, that were optimistic in the Design Supplies forecasts. But are they critical? If you were the lender, you would want to know what might happen to the loan repayment if sales were lower or the operating expenses were higher. To look at this we could make two new forecasts, one with lower sales and the other with higher operating expenses.

A simple change would be to forecast sales growth at the level achieved in 2002, 11 percent. With a sales growth rate of 11 percent there will be insufficient cash to repay the lender in 2006. We could expand this test of the sales growth rate by calculating the excess cash available at a variety of sales growth levels. This is done most easily in a computer spreadsheet. Even better than looking at a series of spreadsheets, we could graph the results. Such an analysis and the resulting graph for Design Supplies is shown in Exhibit 2-17. Here you can see that if sales growth is under 12 percent, the investor's $200,000 note cannot be paid off in 2006. Clearly, whether the lender can be fully repaid in 2006 depends upon Design Supplies' growth being better than that achieved in 2002.

Operating expenses were another of the critical assumptions, and it turns out that it is even more critical to our lender than sales growth. If the operating expenses grow at the rate of sales (not a really crazy assumption),

---

[14] One way to get some perspective would be to look at others in the industry. While we will not make the comparison here, recall that when comparing companies you must be certain that the companies to be compared are similar; that is, they should be in the same industry and have similar operating and marketing strategies. If such strictly comparable companies cannot be found for evaluation, then the analyst should adapt the comparison companies' ratios as needed.

Exhibit 2-17 Design Supplies, Inc.

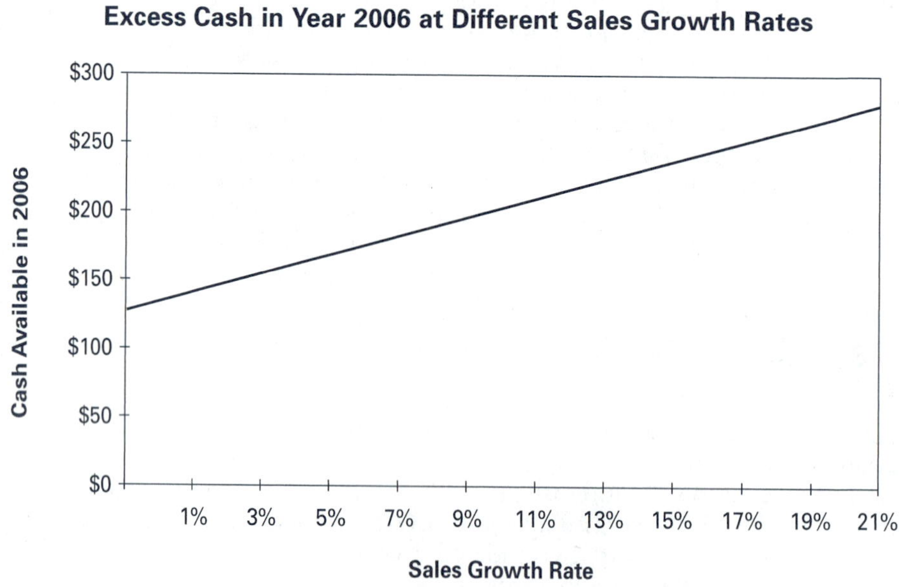
Excess Cash in Year 2006 at Different Sales Growth Rates
Cash Available in 2006
$300
$250
$200
$150
$100
$50
$0
1%
3%
5%
7%
9%
11%
13%
15%
17%
19%
21%
Sales Growth Rate

Design Supplies not only cannot pay off the lender, but also will need more funds. This is shown in Exhibit 2-18. This type of sensitivity-to-change analysis can be done on any of the other critical assumptions.

Although sensitivity analysis is a fairly simple concept it can give us important insight. As attractive as it is, however, it is rather time-consuming to execute properly. If the forecasts incorporate many assumptions, the analysis could take considerable time and effort. To ease this process, analysts attempt to simplify the assumptions and to estimate which factors will have a critical impact on the results. The sensitivity analysis is then confined to these factors.

As an alternative some analysts analyze only negative outcomes. Their reasoning is that while optimistic relationships may occur and create problems, those problems are easier to deal with than the problems pessimistic outcomes create. By focusing only on the downside risks, a range of potential negative results are forecast. In some cases, however, negative results arise from upside factors. For example, a large increase in sales may appear positive, but it could also result in an increased need for working capital, a need that should be foreseen and for which management needs to plan.

3. Sensitivity Analysis—Three Scenarios

The risk of looking only at the impact of one variable at a time is that simplifying some critical assumptions may be ignored. To concentrate on the key factors, analysts frequently design different **scenarios**, different sets

Exhibit 2-18   Design Supplies, Inc.

Total Excess Funds plus Cash, Operating Expenses Grow with Sales

(in thousands)	2003	2004	2005	2006	2007
Sales	$ 1,612	$ 1,854	$ 2,132	$ 2,452	$ 2,820
Cost of goods sold	(1,128)	(1,298)	(1,492)	(1,716)	(1,974)
Gross profit	484	556	640	736	846
Operating expenses	(404)	(464)	(534)	(614)	(706)
Profit before taxes	80	92	106	122	140
Taxes	(27)	(31)	(35)	(41)	(47)
Net profit	$ 53	$ 61	$ 71	$ 81	$ 93
Net financing needed (excess funds)*	(1)	23	49	78	112
Total excess funds plus cash*	$ 65	$ 46	$ 25	$ 0	$ (28)

*Cash and net financing needs come from balance sheets created as Exhibit 2-15 but not reproduced here.

of assumptions about the future. A widely used technique of scenario analysis combines three different sets of values for the crucial assumptions into three scenarios: most likely, optimistic, and pessimistic. The original forecast, or scenario, is usually the **most likely scenario**. Let's be clear, the optimistic and pessimistic forecasts are not the same as the absolute best and worst cases that can be imagined. We want to focus on scenarios with a real likelihood of happening, not those that are only remotely possible.

What might be these three probable scenarios for Design Supplies? The critical variables and the resulting excess cash available to repay the lender are shown in Exhibit 2-19. This exhibit contains three scenarios. You might disagree about which factors should be changed and by what degree. That is the prerogative of the analyst. What should be clear from this exhibit is the degree to which the outcome depends upon the assumptions, and that some assumptions are more critical than others.

Computer-based financial modeling systems have been developed that greatly increase the analyst's ability to undertake sensitivity analysis. The analyst can determine the most significant relationships and the effect that potential changes might have on performance. Not only can the modeling systems perform the calculations rapidly, they also facilitate the use of probability analysis.

4. Probability Analysis

Probability analysis is an extension of sensitivity analysis. There are three steps in doing probability analysis. First, forecast a range of possible out-

Exhibit 2-19   Design Supplies, Inc.

Three Scenario Forecasts

	Pessimistic	Most Likely	Optimistic
Sales growth	11%	15%	20%
Inflation	6%	4%	2%
Real sales growth	5%	11%	18%
Gross margin	27%	30%	32%
Operating expense growth	7%	7%	12%
Cash and other assets			
growth (real)	3%	3%	3%
Receivables/sales	12%	11%	11%
Inventory/sales	28%	25%	24%
Payables/sales	4%	5%	5%
Excess cash in 2007			
(financing needed)	$(45.44)	$347.3	$456.12

comes. Second, estimate the likelihood that each will occur. Third, combine the probabilities for each factor with the range of outcomes. As an example, we might take the three scenarios shown in Exhibit 2-19 and make estimates of the likelihood of each occurring. For example, management might expect the most likely scenario to have a 50 percent chance of occurring, while the other two have only a 25 percent probability. The weighted outcome is excess cash of $276.3. This is not the most likely outcome but the **expected value**—the probability-weighted average of the outcomes.[15]

More powerful than scenario-based probability is critical variable testing, in which the potential range and likelihood for each of the critical variables in the forecasts is estimated and tested. For example, the analyst might estimate that a 7 percent sales growth has a probability of 15 percent; a 10 percent sales growth, 70 percent; and a 15 percent sales growth, 15 percent; and so on for each item. By combining these probabilities with those estimated for other variables—such as cost of goods sold and rates of inflation—the analyst can calculate the overall probabilities of all possible outcomes. This series of calculations, called a **simulation**, provides more useful information than do projections relying on a single or point estimate for each variable. As you might guess, this is painstaking analysis, unless you have a computer with spreadsheet software. A simulation package makes this kind of analysis even easier. For the reader interested in doing such an analysis, suggested readings are listed at the end of the chapter.

---

[15] A more complete analysis is shown in Chapter 4.

V. Multi-Currency Financial Statements

The forecasts for Sport-Smart Fashions and Design Supplies were made in dollars, because the companies operated only in the United States. But what if a company made or sold products in more than one country or sourced materials outside its domestic environment, like Terra Blanca? How would the forecasts change? What would be different about a company that was owned by another company in another country? How would those forecasts change?

The first question concerns the proper currency in which to forecast, and the second is how to adapt the forecasts for multiple currencies. The answer to the first question is to forecast in the currency in which the cash will be spent and received. For Sport-Smart Fashions, that would be U.S. dollars, and for Terra Blanca, its home currency. Before we can answer to the second question we need to understand how exchange rates operate.

1. The Importance of Exchange Rates

The globalization of the economic world forces us to recognize that few companies operate in only one currency. A company may owe suppliers, sell products, or receive or pay dividends or interest to owners or lenders in other countries. This exposure to foreign currencies introduces a special problem when making forecasts—exchange rates. To make financial forecasts, analysts must forecast receipts and disbursements in whatever currency they occur. If the company is expected to change any of its receipts or disbursements into another currency, the analyst must forecast when the change will occur and the currency exchange rate that will be in effect at that time. Thus, to make cross-border forecasts, an analyst must have a basic understanding of foreign exchange markets, of how exchange rates affect their forecasts, and of what makes exchange rates change.[16] However, an analyst forecasting the financial performance of a company with currency exposure must understand the accounting issues as well as foreign exchange rates and how they change. So how are exchange rates determined and how do they change?

2. Exchange Rate Theories

An exchange rate is the rate at which one currency can be exchanged for another. This is the rate at which the demand for and supply of a particular currency are equal. There are two different theories about what governs exchange rates. One theory proposes that it is relative purchasing power between the two currencies, while the other hypothesizes that it is interest rates. The first theory, **purchasing power parity**, theorizes that exchange rates render currency denomination differences irrelevant—in a free-trade world, exchange rates make the cost of a good the same in

---

[16] In the Appendix to Chapter 1, we discussed how foreign exchange transactions and translations are handled by accountants. In this chapter our concern is transactional.

both countries. Theoretically, if a difference in the price of the same good offered in the two countries exists, someone will see the potential to profit.[17] They will take the opportunity to buy the good at the lower price and offer it to buyers in the country where it commands a higher price. This process is called **arbitrage**, and those acting on price differences are called **arbitrageurs**. Theoretically, exchange rates change only when there is a change in the rates of inflation in the two countries.

Purchasing power parity is simple, and it makes sense, except that it does not seem to work well in practice. The simplest version of this theory does not take into account differences in actual costs of buying, moving the product, and reselling it, or any barriers to arbitrage (e.g., tariffs) created by the two countries. Because purchasing power parity does not explain what actually occurs in the world very well, other theories have been developed. The major contender is interest rate parity.

Interest rate parity, or the **Fisher effect**, suggests that differences in *real* interest rates, and changes in those differences, are at the heart of exchange rates and their changes. In theory, exchange rates make the real returns in the two countries the same: if real rates are not the same, the potential exists to make a profit, and an arbitrageur will move in, take the profit, and drive the expected real rates of return together.[18] The mechanism that makes the rates the same is the exchange rate between the two countries. Arbitrageurs move out of the currency of the country with the lower real rate of return, buy the currency of the country offering the higher real rate of return, and thus create a demand for that currency. An increased demand for a currency puts pressure on the exchange rate, and it changes.

In reality, exchange rates are determined by a combination of such things as the differences in real interest rates, relative inflation, growth rates in available income, and perceptions about political and economic risk in the two countries.

Most exchange rates float; that is, they can change as conditions between two countries change. A **floating exchange rate** can depreciate or appreciate—go down or up—relative to another country's currency depending on supply and demand in the marketplace. Most industrialized nations have had floating exchange rates since the early 1970s.[19]

Some exchange rates are fixed. A **fixed exchange rate** is one where the rate of exchange is set relative to some other currency—often to the U.S. dollar. For example, Argentina and over 30 other countries have, or have had, a currency whose value was set relative to the U.S. dollar. A country's governing body, usually its central bank, can change fixed currency

---

[17] Of course, such costs as the cost of moving the product from country to country must be taken into account.

[18] Real rates are the rates after subtracting the rate of inflation.

[19] While this statement is true in theory, a country's central bank can intervene to maintain the relative exchange rates between two or more countries. This intervention is usually intended to smooth otherwise rapid exchange rate changes. Often, however, it creates overvalued currencies that rapidly revert to normal relationships once the intervention ceases.

relationships.[20] A decrease in the value of the currency relative to another is called a **devaluation** and an increase is called a **revaluation**.

Currencies are traded. Indeed, the foreign exchange market is the largest financial market in the world. A company or individual can trade one currency for another today (**spot market**) or for some time in the future (futures or forward market).

Exchange rates are generally quoted in the home currency relative to the currency of the other country. For example, on July 24, 2002, at 10:18 EDT, the spot rate for the Canadian dollar was U.S.$1.00: CDN1.5852. This means that it cost U.S.$0.6308 to buy CDN1.00. At the same time, the new European currency was trading at $1.00: EUR1.0063. To determine the exchange rate for the euro and the Canadian dollar, the exchange rates for those two currencies would be used. Exchange rates for major currencies are reported in the financial press daily and continuously on many financial web sites.

There are both **bid prices**, what a seller will pay for the currency, and **ask prices**, the price at which a seller will sell the currency, quoted for large currency transactions. Small transactions cost more than large transactions.

The futures or **forward markets** are markets in which transactions in the future can be settled today. For example, a company with a large payment to a supplier due 30 days from now could contract with a bank for the delivery of the needed currency at that time, for a price specified today. Bank **forward contracts** are arranged between the bank and its customer. The difference between the spot and the futures or forward rates depends on the volume of buyers and sellers of the particular currency for the date in the future and on the potential variability in the exchange rate. Forward contracts usually are for less than one year. The terms and conditions are arranged between the buyer of the contract and the seller.

The customer needing to make a payment or expecting to have an excess of a particular currency for a particular date in the future may also use the **futures markets**. The futures contract differs from a forward contract in that it is publicly traded and the contract is for a standardized quantity of the currency deliverable at a particular date. These contracts are similar to commodities' futures contracts and in the United States are traded on the Chicago Mercantile Exchange. On July 24, 2002, when the spot rate between the U.S. and Canadian dollars was US$1.00: CDN1.5852, the December futures' contract rate was U.S.$1.00: CDN1.5924.[21] This latter rate reflected a small expected change in U.S. to Canadian dollars over that time period. In contrast, the dollar:euro spot rate was $1.00:EUR1.0132. This implies an expected appreciation in the dollar relative to the euro.

Most currencies are quoted relative to every other currency. This is no longer true in the countries belonging to the European Monetary Union—all have and use a single currency, the euro. This has been a significant change in exchange rates and their trading.

---

[20] The central bank in the U.S. is the Federal Reserve Bank.

[21] Most of the currencies of major countries are freely convertible into currency of other major countries. This is not true for smaller countries with less stable currencies.

3. How Exchange Rates Affect Forecasts

When making a forecast for a company that has income or expenses from another country or countries, the analyst must make some assumptions about exchange rates at the time the cash will be transferred, not at the time the forecast is being made. For example, let's take the Sport-Smart Fashions, Inc. example and add some information about how and where the company does business. Sport-Smart uses fabric woven in another country to make some of its products. The assumption used to create the income statement shown in Exhibit 2-8 was that the cost of goods sold would be an unchanging 73 percent of sales. However, if 21.5 percent of the cost of sales is fabric purchased from the other country, and the exchange rate went from $1:1 to $1:0.67, there would be a significant increase in the cost of purchases. As a result of the cost increases, Sport-Smart's need for cash would be larger. The impact on the income statement of such a cost increase is shown in Exhibit 2-20. The changes in the cash balance are shown graphically in Exhibit 2-21.

Exhibit 2-20 Sport-Smart Fashions, Inc.

2003 Income Statement with Exchange Rate Change

(in thousands)

Sales	$1,151.0	**Current COGS**	
Cost of goods sold	(929.2)	78.5% COGS	$659.6
Gross profit	221.8	21.5% COGS	180.6
Expenses:		Current COGS	$840.2
Selling and administrative	(161.1)		
Fixed operating costs	(78.0)	**New COGS**	
Depreciation	(6.0)	U.S.	$659.6
Lease and interest expense	(36.0)	Non-U.S. ($180.6/0.67)	269.6
Taxes	0	New COGS	$929.2
Net profit	$ (59.3)		

Sport-Smart is a very simple example of what could occur if the exchange rate changes dramatically. Managers often insure against such potentially dramatic exchange rate changes by anticipating the need for funds and hedging that need with a forward or futures contract. **Hedging** is an activity where a future price is locked in today. There are a variety of ways to hedge, including the futures and forward markets as well as careful corporate financing and investment strategy. All hedging has a cost. The analyst would have to incorporate the hedging and its costs into the forecasts.

Many fabric imports come from one of the United States' trading partners, Mexico. Mexico is classified as a developing country, and many believe that exchange rates are more volatile in developing countries with floating

Exhibit 2-21   Sport-Smart Fashions, Inc.

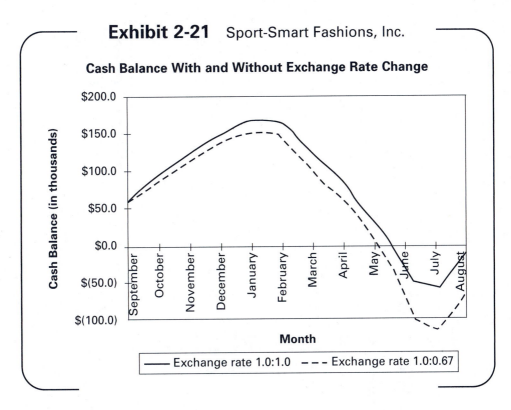

Cash Balance With and Without Exchange Rate Change

Month

— Exchange rate 1.0:1.0 – – – Exchange rate 1.0:0.67

exchange rates. A look at the U.S. dollar exchange rates with a number of U.S. major trading partners (Exhibit 2-22) shows that exchange rates can be volatile regardless of the level of the country's development.

For the analyst or manager, the more likely a relevant exchange rate will change, and the greater the impact that change can have on the financial viability of a company or strategy, the more effort the manager or analyst must make to understand the potential changes and to forecast them. Because this section is only a simple introduction to exchange rates and to what makes exchange rates change over time, the competent manager will need to know much more about exchange rates, the mechanisms governing them, and methods to hedge or take advantage of changes in them.[22]

Making forecasts in highly uncertain economic and political environments is difficult. The difficulty reinforces the need for a careful understanding of the company, its industry, and the economy in which it operates. In addition to the sensitivity to exchange rate changes, the impact

---

[22] Some companies choose to insulate themselves against changes in exchange rates through certain corporate strategies. One example is to match foreign sales revenues with costs denominated in the same currency. Alternatively, the manager might choose to hedge the currency risk with forward or futures contracts. Because speculating and hedging are sophisticated activities, references for further reading are provided at the end of this chapter. Hedging is also discussed further in Chapter 8.

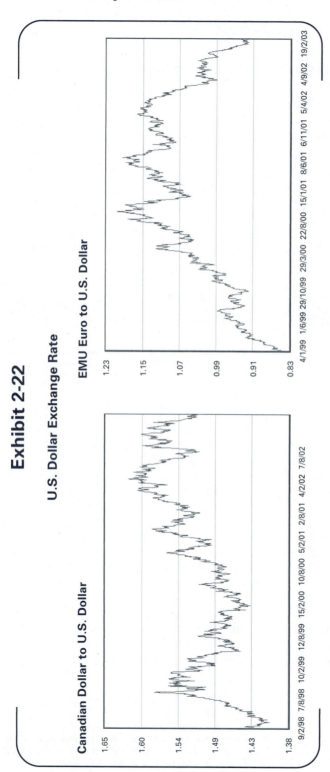

Exhibit 2-22

U.S. Dollar Exchange Rate

Source: http://www.ozforex.com.au/charts.asp.

(continued)

Exhibit 2-22

U.S. Dollar Exchange Rate *(continued)*

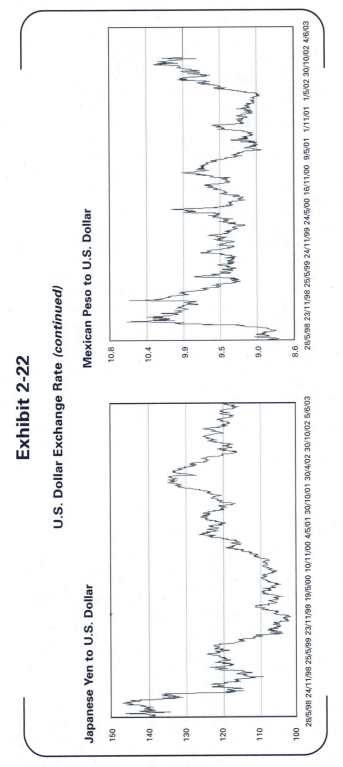

Source: http://www.ozforex.com.au/charts.asp.

of inflation must be understood as clearly as possible. In volatile environments, forecasts should be changed frequently as conditions change.

Note that forecasts are not irrelevant in rapidly changing environments; management just must make them more often than in stable environments. In fact, many managers contend that forecasts are more important in rapidly changing environments. Rather than despairing about forecast relevancy, we have other ways to approach uncertainty, whether that uncertainty is about the company's operations, its sales, or its environment. Sensitivity analysis, multi-scenario analysis, and simulation can help the manager deal with the dangers and opportunities and plan for them.

VI. Summary

Historical relationships can aid analysts in projecting the future performance of a company. History must be tempered, however, by the analyst's views of changes in the environment and in the company. Based on these assumptions, an analyst can estimate future cash needs using cash budgets and projected financial statements. The appropriate method depends on the needs of the company. Most often, companies use both.

Projections are only as useful as the validity or reasonableness of the underlying assumptions. An important part of any forecast is testing the assumptions through sensitivity analysis. In so doing, the analyst and manager become aware of the critical assumptions and are forewarned about areas needing additional analysis and special monitoring.

One other thing must be kept in mind by those creating and using forecasts: forecasts should be constantly updated as information and conditions change. The world is not as stable as we once thought it was, and basing the future of a company on a single set of assumptions that are not kept current or tested for veracity is worse than making no forecasts at all.

Selected References

For discussions of the impact of inflation on funds forecasting, see:
  Seed, Allen H., III. "Measuring Financial Performance in an Inflationary Environment." *Financial Executive*, January 1982, pp. 40–50.
  Vancil, Richard F. "Funds Flow Analysis During Inflation." *Financial Analysts Journal*, March–April 1976, pp. 43–56. .

For a discussion of simulation, see:
  Hertz, David B. "Risk-Analysis in Capital Investment." *Harvard Business Review*, September–October 1979, pp. 169–81.

For additional information on the differences between cash and accrual accounting, see:
  Kroll, Yoram. "On the Differences Between Accrual Accounting Figures and Cash Flows: The Case of Working Capital." *Financial Management*, Spring 1985, pp. 75–82.

For additional discussions of forecasting financial needs, see:

Brealey, Richard A., Stewart C. Myers, and Alan Marcus. *Principles of Corporate Finance.* 7th ed. New York: McGraw-Hill, 2002, chap. 29.

Brigham, Eugene F., Louis C. Gapenski, and Michael Ehrhardt. *Financial Management.* 9th ed. Fort Worth, Texas: The Dryden Press, 1999, chap. 14.

Ross, Stephen, Randolph Westerfield, and Jeffrey Jaffee. *Corporate Finance.* 6th ed. Boston, MA: McGraw-Hill Irwin, 2002, chap. 26.

For more information on foreign exchange exposure, management, and forecasts, see:

Abuaf, Niso. "The Nature and Management of Foreign Exchange Risk," in *New Developments in International Finance*, Joel Stern and Donald Chew, Jr., eds. New York: Basil Blackwell, 1988, pp. 29–43.

Brigham, Eugene F., Louis C. Gapenski, and Michael Ehrhardt. *Financial Management.* 9th ed. Fort Worth, Texas: The Dryden Press, 1999, chap. 27.

Cornell, Bradford. "Managing Foreign Exchange Risks," in *New Developments in International Finance*, Joel Stern and Donald Chew, Jr., eds. New York: Basil Blackwell, 1988, pp. 44–59.

Damodoran, Aswath. *Corporate Finance.* New York: John Wiley & Sons, 1997, chap. 26.

Heckmann, Christine. "Don't Blame Currency Values for Strategic Errors," in *New Developments in International Finance*, Joel Stern and Donald Chew, Jr., eds. New York: Basil Blackwell, 1988, pp. 29–43.

Pringle, John. "A Look At Indirect Foreign Currency Exposure." *Journal of Applied Corporate Finance*, Fall 1995, pp. 75–81.

Pringle, John, and Robert Connolly. "The Nature and Causes of Foreign Currency Exposure." *Journal of Applied Corporate Finance*, Fall 1995, pp. 61–74.

Solnik, Bruno. *International Investments.* 4th ed. Reading, MA: Addison-Wesley Longman, 1999, chap. 3.

For a discussion of taxes and corporate strategy, see:

Scholes, Myron, and Mark Wolfson. *Taxes and Business Strategy.* Upper Saddle River, NJ: Prentice Hall, 1992.

For the original interest rate parity discussion, see:

Fisher, Irving. *The Theory of Interest: As Determined by Impatience to Spend Income and Opportunity to Invest It.* New York: Augustus M. Kelley, 1965.

Study Questions

1. The chief financial officer of Liu Provenders (Liu) is meeting with two top analysts regarding working capital management. One analyst, Charles Fong, has suggested that a more lenient accounts receivable collection policy of 45 days would result in a sales growth of

20 percent, higher than previously forecasted for Liu. In addition, inventory turnover would increase to 600 percent and reduce bad debts to 2 percent. While management should expect operating expenses to increase 20 percent because of additional processing costs, Mr. Fong suggests that an increase in the minimum cash balance to 20 percent of gross sales would offset any liquidity problems.

Another analyst, Ginny Fisher, counters Mr. Fong's argument for an aggressive working capital policy. She cites, among other issues, the recession throughout the country, and notes that this strategy could help maintain operating expenses at current levels. She estimates that reducing the accounts receivable period to 30 days would stabilize the 5 percent bad debt level and still allow Liu to grow at 10 percent. Although she states that the inventory turnover could decrease to 300 percent, a minimum cash balance of 15 percent of gross sales appears possible. Operating expenses would not change. Liu has sufficient sources of short-term debt. The tax rate would remain at 40 percent, cost of goods sold at 40 percent of gross sales, and accounts payable at 114 days.

Of course, an argument ensues between the analysts. Mr. Fong contends that the rest of the world where Liu operates is not suffering from a recession. Rather, the unification of Europe and the growing purchasing power of the Chinese consumer have expanded potential and current markets. Mr. Fong argues that Liu should attack these markets without hesitation. The financial impact on Liu of these two strategies is not clear.

Compute an income statement, balance sheet, net working capital ratio, and current ratio under both Mr. Fong's and Ms. Fisher's alternatives. Compare the two alternatives.

From the financial forecasts you have created, decide which policy changes the chief financial officer should implement. The current financial statements are provided.

LIU PROVENDERS
Historic Financial Statements—Income Statement
(in thousands)

Sales	$8,600
Bad debt	(430)
Net sales	8,170
Cost of goods sold	(3,500)
Gross profit	4,670
Operating expense	(3,000)
Operating income	1,670
Taxes	(668)
Net profit	$1,002

LIU PROVENDERS
Historic Financial Statements—Income Statement
(in thousands)

Assets		Liabilities and Equity	
Cash	$1,200	Accounts payable	$1,400
Accounts receivable	850	Other short-term debt	1,500
Inventory	800	Total current liabilities	2,900
Total current assets	2,850	Long-term debt	550
Net property, plant,		Common stock	420
and equipment	4,000	Retained earnings	2,980
		Total equity	3,950
Total assets	$6,850	Total liabilities and equity	$6,850

2. Wendy Steele, financial manager of Agrilabs, SpA. was working on the company's financial forecast for the coming year. Agrilabs is located in Beaverton, Oregon, and produces specialized chemicals used in the deciduous (oranges, apples, pears, etc.) fruit industry. The company's financial statements are provided. Agrilabs had sales of $7.5 million in 2003. Ms. Steele is expecting sales to increase by 20 percent in 2004. Assuming that costs and expenses increase proportionally to sales, what would the income statements be in 2004? If sales grow 22 percent in 2005 and 2006, and 18 percent for each of the next two years, what would the Agrilabs financial statements be?

Agrilabs 2003 Financial Statements
(in thousands)

Income Statement	2003
Sales	$ 7,500
Cost of goods sold	(6,000)
Gross income	1,500
SG&A	(780)
Interest	(120)
Net income before taxes	780
Taxes (40%)	(203)
Net income	$ 305
Dividends	$ 153

Balance Sheet	2003
Cash	$ 300
Accounts receivable	657
Inventory	2,400
Net fixed assets	4,000
Total assets	$ 7,357
Accounts payable	$ 357
Accruals	100
Notes payable	250
Long-term debt	3,300
Common stock	2,500
Retained earnings	850
Total liabilities and equity	$ 7,357

3. 2002 annual reports have just come out for companies in your industry. As a new analyst for JM Motors you are assigned to study your toughest competitor, Wingate Motor Co., Ltd. Despite the slump in auto sales, Wingate was expecting further growth in revenues. Using the financial statements for 2002 and the following figures, forecast a Wingate balance sheet and income statement for 2003. In addition, to assist you in analyzing your competitor's strategic options, you should determine the change in net working capital and the current ratio for 2003. The exchange rate to the dollar for 2001 was ¥154:U.S.$1.00, but it strengthened to ¥140:U.S.$1.00 in 2002. Your assumptions are as follows:

   - U.S. sales are expected to grow by 25 percent in dollar terms over the next year.
   - Home country sales are expected to grow by only 5 percent in local currency terms. Cost of sales is 75 percent of total revenue.
   - Research and development spending will be maintained at its current amount.
   - Total operating expenses will grow 10 percent.
   - Sales should be collected within 45 days.
   - The company is pushing for a 60-day payables period.
   - Inventory turnover is 600 percent.
   - Management requires a minimum cash balance of 10 percent of sales. There will be no net changes in property, plant, and equipment. No dividends will be paid, and no long-term debt will be repaid. Funding will be in the form of short-term debt. The tax rate will remain at 40 percent.

Wingate
2002 Income Statement
(in billions)

Net sales	
Japan	¥ 1,300
United States	2,200
Total net sales	3,500
Cost of goods sold	(2,625)
Research and development	(200)
Gross profit	675
Operating expenses	(500)
Operating profit	175
Taxes	(70)
Net profit	¥ 105

Wingate
2002 Balance Sheet
(in billions)

Assets		Liabilities and Equity	
Cash	¥ 250	Accounts payable	¥ 400
Accounts receivable	400	Other short-term debt	350
Inventory	475	Total current liabilities	750
Total current assets	1,125	Long-term debt	1,050
Net property, plant,		Common stock	75
and equipment	1,500	Retained earnings	750
		Total equity	825
Total assets	¥2,625	Total liabilities and equity	¥2,625

4. After reviewing your analysis, JM Motors' management believes that you are slightly optimistic about your assumptions. Management expected Wingate's results to be less positive, and it suggests you look into the financial statements one more time with these revised assumptions:

   - Reduce the minimum cash balance to 7 percent of sales.
   - Decrease the payables period to 45 days.
   - Increase the collection period to 60 days.

   Is the current ratio in line with the industry average of 120 percent? What are the implications of these policy changes to you as a competitor?

5. Review how your analysis would change if the ¥:$ exchange rate dropped to an unprecedented rate of ¥85:$1.00. How would such an exchange rate impact your strategy if you were Wingate management? If you were JM Motors management?

6. Mary Turnbull, of Mary's Ski Chalet, is attempting to plan a monthly cash budget for the coming year but is having difficulty determining

her expected cash balance because of the seasonality of her sales. She has been able to accumulate the following data for 2004.

MARY'S SKI CHALET
Sales Forecasts and Balance Sheet Beginning Balances
(in thousands)

Projected Sales 2004				Beginning Balances 12/31/2003	
Jan.	$210	July	$ 30	Accounts receivable	$184
Feb.	175	Aug.	75	Accounts payable	173
Mar.	160	Sept.	90	Cash	65
Apr.	140	Oct.	125	Inventory	50
May	50	Nov.	165	Equity	471
June	30	Dec.	230	Plant, property, and equipment, net	345

- All collections and payments will be made on a 30-day basis.
- 25 percent of all sales will be paid for in cash.
- Cost of goods sold will be 75 percent of sales.
- Selling, general, and administrative expenses will be 19 percent of sales.
- Purchases will be 100 percent of cost of goods sold plus 8 percent of sales for a cushion against stock-outs (safety stock).
- Interest and lease expenses will be $24,000 for the year.
- Depreciation expense will be $12,000 for the year.
- Tax loss carryforwards will result in Mary's Ski Chalet paying no taxes in 2003.

Will Ms. Turnbull need additional financing to cover a monthly cash deficit?

7. Prepare a 2004 forecasted income statement and balance sheet for Ms. Turnbull using the information provided in Question 6.

8. Aries Corporation has entered a new market in early 2003 and has asked you to prepare a five-year projected balance sheet and income statement based on the following forecasts:

- Sales growth in 2003 will be the same as in 2002. In 2004, sales growth will dip to 10 percent, and then will increase 1 percent for each year thereafter.
- Negotiations with suppliers have reduced prices, resulting in an improvement in gross margin of 12 percentage points, if the payment period is decreased to 60 days. Purchases made at the higher rate and included in raw materials inventory will result in an average margin of only 10 percentage points in 2003.
- There will be no change in the percentage of sales historical relationships for operating expenses or cash balance.
- Legislation has been passed that will reduce the tax rate to 38 percent in 2005 from its current rate of 50.7 percent.

- Inventory turnover has been historically high. Management plans to increase the turnover in 2003 to 8 times and level it out in 2004 to 6 times.
- Management does not expect any change in days' sales outstanding.
- Property, plant, and equipment—net of acquisitions, disposals, and depreciation (which is included in the cost of goods sold allocation)—will be $265,000, $291,000, $323,000, $403,000, and $513,000 for 2003 through 2007, respectively.
- Any additional financing required will be short-term (notes payable) financing.

To assist in your analysis, financial statements for 2001 and 2002 are as follows:

ARIES CORPORATION
Income Statements
(in thousands)

	2001	2002
Sales	$221	$266
Cost of goods sold	(145)	(166)
Gross profit	76	100
Operating expenses	(38)	(35)
Operating profit	38	65
Taxes	(19)	(33)
Net income	$ 19	$ 32

ARIES CORPORATION
Balance Sheets
(in thousands)

	2001	2002
Assets		
Cash	$ 22	$ 37
Accounts receivable	49	31
Inventory	47	45
Total current assets	118	113
Fixed assets	70	122
Total assets	$188	$235
Liabilities and Equity		
Notes payable	$ 0	$ 0
Accounts payable	19	34
Total current liabilities	19	34
Equity	169	201
Total liabilities and equity	$188	$235

Chapter Three

Managing Working Capital

Most financial managers spend a significant amount of their time dealing with immediate problems and opportunities. There is no doubt that the development of a comprehensive financial strategy in conjunction with a corporate business strategy is critical for the long-term growth of the company. However, the financial manager must ensure that the corporation can successfully cope with the present challenges and opportunities, otherwise a long-term plan has no value.

One of the major problems facing managers is the company's need for working capital. **Working capital** includes both the current assets of the corporation—inventories, accounts receivable, cash, and marketable securities—and the current liabilities—accounts, notes, and taxes payable. The resources provided by the current assets are directly involved in the company's production and sales. The current liabilities are the immediate obligations of the company. Successful management of corporate working capital accounts allows managers to move their company into a prosperous future. This chapter will discuss the various working capital accounts and how they can be successfully managed.

I. The Working Capital Cycle

The term **working capital cycle**, or **production-sales cycle**, refers to the ebb and flow of funds through the company in response to changes in the level of activity in manufacturing and sales. When the company decides to manufacture a product, funds are needed to purchase raw materials, pay for the production process, and maintain inventory. If the product is sold on credit, the company also must have funds to support the accounts receivable until customers ultimately pay the company for the purchased products.

The word *cycle* refers to the difference between the time payment is due for production expenses and the time the customer pays for the product.

If the company received payment for the product at the same time it was required to pay the expenses of producing the product, there would be no working capital cycle, nor would firms have difficulty managing working capital.

This timing difference can be illustrated with the simple graph shown in Exhibit 3-1. The raw materials are ordered on Day 0, and materials arrive and production begins. As production proceeds, workers are paid, and by Day 30, all the costs for labor and materials have been paid. The product is completed and is put into finished goods inventory on Day 60. An order is received from a customer on Day 60, and the product is sold. Payment is received from the customer on Day 90. That payment, presuming that the company has priced its product properly, covers all the costs of production plus a profit. From a cash flow standpoint, the company has made all of the cash payments for labor and raw material costs by Day 30, but it receives no cash from the customer until Day 90. Consequently, the company requires some type of financing for at least 90 days. In this example, the working capital cycle is a total of 90 days, or three months.

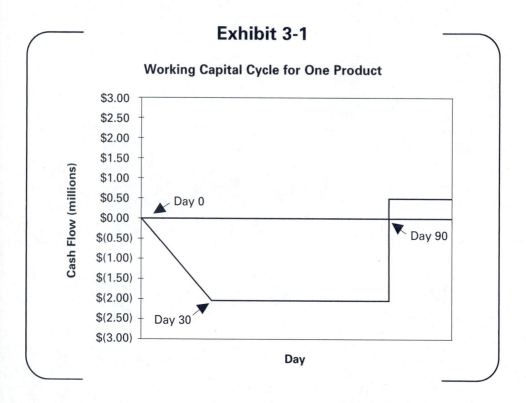

Exhibit 3-1

Working Capital Cycle for One Product

The working capital cycle length varies significantly among different kinds of companies and even among a company's different products. Two extreme examples of companies with different working capital cycles are distilled spirits producers and grocery retailers. The distilled spirits producer typically stores the product for several years to age; there are several years between the cash outflows for production and the receipt of cash from sales to customers. The grocery retailer usually has a rapid turnover of its perishable inventory and most sales are made for cash; the working capital cycle for the bulk of its inventory is short, and is measured in days or weeks.

Exhibit 3-1 shows the cycle for only one unit of a product. Most companies do not produce one unit of a product at a time. A grocery retailer is a good example of a company that has a variety of goods. Some have short cycles, like fresh produce; others have a much longer shelf life, like health and beauty products.[1] For companies like this, many products are produced and/or sold, and all are at various stages in the production-sales cycle at any given time. Thus, once a company is able to complete the start-up phase of operations successfully, it will be able to rely on a continuous flow of products through the cycle to provide funds for its needs. The company can use the cash from previous sales to pay for current production. When a company is in a stable environment with no inflation, sales growth, or changes in customer demand, these lags in the working capital cycle present little difficulty. However, it is rare to find such a situation. Thus, the cycle must be understood and managed.

1. The Impact of Inflation

In an inflationary environment, the cost of producing each unit increases over time. Thus, by the time the company has collected the cash from its previous sales, the production costs on subsequent units have increased due to inflation. Unless the company is able to price units with sufficient profit margins to cover expected inflation, it may not be able to meet subsequent production costs with revenues from prior production.

To illustrate this problem, let's look at a simple example of a production cycle in a steel manufacturing company. The company begins with a cash balance of $450, as shown in Exhibit 3-2. This cash balance is sufficient to cover the estimated costs of manufacturing 2 tons of steel at the current price of $225 per ton. However, an unexpected outburst of inflation of 1.5 percent per month (an annualized rate of 20 percent) occurs.[2] The company sells its first ton of steel on the 120th day for $301, but it does not collect payment until 60 days later. It does not charge interest on its accounts receivable. This entire cycle is shown in Exhibit 3-2.

Note that, in spite of the fact that management initially thought it could cover its needs with its cash balance, the company must borrow to finance the production of the second ton of steel as well as to carry the accounts receivable for the sale of the first ton. This is because the costs of production rose once the sale was made while the monetary value of

---

[1] Airplane manufacturers are at the opposite end of the rapid cycle/multiple product spectrum.

[2] The annualized rate of inflation is the compound rate at 1.5 percent per month, or an annual rate of 19.56 percent. A compound rate is not the simple sum of the monthly rates. To learn more about the compounding process, see Chapter 4.

Exhibit 3-2 Steel Manufacturer

Impact of Inflation on Cash Balance Over the Working Capital Cycle

Day	Activity	Cash Balance
0	Begin production of first ton.	$450
30	Complete one-third of first ton.	374
60	Complete two-thirds of first ton.	297
90	Complete production of first ton at total cost of 232.	218
90	Begin production of second ton.	218
120	Complete one-third of second ton.	138
120	Sell first ton at current price of 239.	138
150	Complete two-thirds of second ton.	57
180	Complete production of second ton at total cost of 243.	(25)
180	Receive payment for sale of first ton.	214

the accounts receivable did not. Management might choose to deal with this problem in a variety of ways, but identifying it is the first step.

This example is obviously highly simplified. Continual production and multiple products with varying working capital cycles and exposures to inflation complicate the analysis. Nevertheless, the conceptual framework for analyzing the increased working capital requirements caused by inflation is the same. The net effect of inflation is to increase the amount of working capital required by the company. Capital, you should note, is the critical item, not units of production.

2. The Impact of Sales Growth

The effect of sales growth on working capital needs is similar to that of inflation. In the case of sales growth, the problem is not caused by an increasing per-unit cost, but by an increasing number of units. Although the cost per unit may be stable, total costs increase because of the increased volume.

For example, a computer producer may have been very successful in developing a market for its products. Assume that the company can produce computers for a cost of $700 each. The company produces 500 computers and sells each for $800 during a particular month. The company extends credit for 30 days to buyers of the computers. During the ensuing month, the demand for computers is such that the company produces 600. At production costs of $700 each, the company incurs a total production cost of $420,000. However, the sales revenue collected from the previous month's sales will be only $400,000 (500 × $800). Thus, even if the company continues to charge $800 per unit, a price that allows a profit margin of 12.5 percent, the sales growth alone will result in a need for new working capital. A company in this situation will have insufficient cash inflow from collections each month to meet the expenses incurred for the production of new computers.

One way to see how the impact of sales growth on the working capital cycle is to calculate the net working capital/sales ratio. This ratio shows the dollars that need to be invested for each new dollar of sales. The higher the ratio, the more diligent management must be as the company grows. Growth demands increasing capital investment. As an example, in 2002 average net working capital/sales ratios for consumer staples' companies was $0.17/$1.00 of sales, while durable goods' manufacturers averaged about $0.48/$1.00.[3] The technology companies were much higher with average working capital to sales ratios of $1.47/$1.00. This is a very high burden when a company is growing.[4] Yet it was not the highest. Companies designated in the health sector had an average of $7.87 of working capital per dollar of sales. To give you some idea of the wide variation that can occur in one industry, on-line retailers averaged $0.72 per dollar of sales with some reaching over $10.00. As with technology companies with high working capital/sales ratios, our computer company did not misprice its products as you might have first thought; the company's prices allowed an adequate profit margin above the costs of production. The problem stemmed from the timing differences between the payment for production expenses and the receipt of payment from sales.

This example of the computer manufacturer illustrates the problem that growing a company faces—in order to grow, a company must finance

---

[3] These are averages for all the companies in a sector as defined by Morningstar in mid-2002. Other providers and other lists would have different results. In addition, there is a wide variation within a sector.
[4] For companies whose growth is declining, a high net working capital/sales ratio means the company will be awash in cash.

that growth. A lack of adequate funding will restrict the potential growth of the company. The maximum growth rate a company can fund with its existing financing policies is termed the sustainable growth rate, discussed in Chapter 1. Sustainable growth depends on the profitability of the company, the need for assets to support sales growth, the way the company is financed, and the company's dividend policy. In general, the more rapid the actual rate of growth, the greater the need for funds to support that growth. Conversely, if the rate of growth declines, the company will need less cash for its sales and cash will accumulate.[5]

3. The Impact of Variable Sales Demand

The other major factor that can cause working capital problems for a company's management is a changing level of sales. Changes in sales are of three types:

1. **Seasonal.** Peak demand occurs during particular periods of the year. Snow-skiing equipment is one example of a seasonal product with a peak before the winter skiing season.
2. **Cyclical.** Peak demand occurs during different phases of the business cycle; for example, the demand for building materials is cyclical.
3. **Secular.** Demand fluctuates over a long period of time. Revenues from gold are secular.

These are called cycles because they reoccur over time. Each of these cycles differs in duration but has a similar effect on the company's working capital: peaks typically coincide with the company's highest working capital needs. For simplicity's sake, we will focus on the seasonal cycle because it is of short duration and its impact on working capital needs is easy to trace. However, the only difference between the three cycles is their length and the point of highest and least impact on the working capital needs of the company.

In a seasonal industry, the company may not have sold the completed units before it must incur the costs of producing additional units. To illustrate the problem, we will use the example of the snow-skiing equipment manufacturer. This business is highly seasonal: peak consumer demand occurs during fall and winter. The producer's peak sales period occurs in late summer and early fall when retailers place their orders to have the equipment ready to sell during the peak snow-skiing months.[6] The peak sales period for the manufacturer is not, however, the peak production period. To produce skiing equipment as orders from retailers are received would be inefficient. The manufacturer would need large production capacity, which would be idle for most of the year, and new

---

[5] Using our sustainable growth formulas you can see that cash can accumulate, the company can buy more assets (for example another company or its own stock), pay down debt, pay a dividend, or pay a higher dividend. In the past, tobacco companies were those with slower or slowing growth in sales and thus with significant assets to put to work in some other way.

[6] Make sure you know in which hemisphere the company operates since the seasons are reversed in the southern hemisphere.

workers would have to be hired and trained for each production season.[7] During the peak production period the work force would be required to work overtime, and at the conclusion of the period workers would be laid off. In short, seasonal production typically is inefficient and expensive.

To avoid these problems, the ski-equipment manufacturer may produce skis year round. During the slack sales months, in the late winter and spring, production is continued but little equipment actually is sold to retailers. The manufactured equipment is stored, and the growing inventory is used to fill sales orders as they arrive in the late summer and early fall. As inventory builds up, the company still buys and pays for the raw materials and labor needed to produce the skiing equipment.

As retailers begin to place orders in the late summer, the manufacturer ships equipment from the warehoused inventory. During this period, the manufacturer starts to draw on the finished goods inventory if orders exceed the continuing production level. However, the manufacturer still has not received payment for any of the equipment it has shipped. The retailers buy from the manufacturer on credit, with perhaps 30 or 60 days in which to pay for the equipment.[8] During this period of high but decreasing inventories, continuing production, and increasing accounts receivable, most seasonal companies experience their greatest need for working capital.

As the ski-equipment producer's selling season progresses, additional orders will be received. As these orders are filled the large finished goods inventory is used more rapidly than it is being replenished from production. Accounts receivable increase from the credit sales, although the company does receive payment for shipments made in the late summer. By the end of the fall selling season, the company's inventory is depleted, and all of its receivables should have been collected. The company should have the cash ready to begin the next working capital cycle.[9]

No matter how a seasonal company chooses to produce its products, there are risks. The level production company chances the obsolescence of products or, in the case of the ski company, a poor snow year. The seasonal producer must rely on a ready source of labor to tide it over during peak demand periods. In certain industries and at certain times in the economic, weather, or fashion cycle, seasonal production can be very dangerous.

In any company the pattern of inflow and outflow of funds might exist for several seasonal peaks during a year, over a business cycle, or over a long-term secular trend. The working capital pattern in many businesses

---

[7] If the company can rehire the workers each season and thus avoid costly retraining, the workers must find off-season work.

[8] The industry custom for payment terms varies widely. In the agricultural industry where farmers order agricultural chemicals and seed at the season's beginning and earn revenues only when crops are sold after harvest, payment is usually due at harvest's end. The working capital cycle for companies supplying to farmers on these terms can be six months or longer.

[9] Looking back to Chapter 1, you can see how different the financial performance of a seasonal company might look at different points in its working capital cycle.

is determined by industry practice. When there is a choice (e.g., level versus seasonal production), the analytical techniques that will be discussed in Chapter 4 are useful in determining which approach is most economically attractive.

II. Cash Management

Because labor costs and material purchases must be paid for in cash, the critical resource in dealing with the working capital cycle is cash. Corporate managers need to ensure that sufficient cash is available to meet the obligations. This has led to the development of sophisticated, automated techniques to manage a company's cash. These techniques have three objectives: to accelerate the speed of cash receipts, decelerate the speed of cash disbursements, and maximize the return on investment of cash balances. In the 1970s and 1980s, high interest rates emphasized the importance of managing cash, while the development of computers allowed managers access to the information needed for close monitoring of cash balances.

1. Managing Receipts

The process of managing cash receipts involves collecting funds as quickly as possible and concentrating them in accounts so that the financial manager can control them.

Lockboxes. The use of lockboxes speeds the collecting, processing, depositing, and reporting of payments received through the mail. A lockbox is a special post office box to which the company's customers are instructed to mail payments. The box is checked several times daily by the processing operation, which is usually operated by a bank. On receipt the checks are immediately entered into the check-clearing process to be converted into funds for the company.

Electronic Funds Transfer. A faster method of collecting funds is to require that payment be made electronically rather than with a paper check. In this system, payment is made by transferring funds directly from the payer's bank account to the recipient's account. This makes the funds immediately available and also eliminates the cost of handling paper checks. For an individual, the debit card issued by a bank acts in the same way. Increasingly, banks, with their on-line services, offer to individual customers services that were once offered only to their corporate clients.

Preauthorized Checks. Preauthorized checks (PACs) are preprinted, unsigned checks. For fixed, repetitive payments, companies authorize their creditors to draw checks on their accounts. The creditor sends the PAC to the bank, which then deposits the funds into the creditor's account. This also may be done electronically.

Preauthorized Payments. Increasingly, companies are offering their customers an Internet solution to payment and a rapid way for companies to receive their payments.[10] A payer authorizes the recipient from whom they have obtained goods or services to charge their credit card or authorize the direct withdrawal from their account before the bill is presented. The payer can obtain a copy of the bill through their on-line account and any discrepancies are adjusted after the payment has been made.

On-Line Payments. Payments can be made by creating on-line checks through an intermediary like a bank. The payments are made electronically to well-known companies or through a bank-mailed check. Monthly bills can be preauthorized for payment.

Deposit Concentration. Because it is difficult to control funds in many different banks, most receipt management systems provide for transferring funds electronically into one or more large accounts. Central accounts can be more closely managed.

Note that all these systems can be used within a country and between parties in two or more different countries. When a payment must cross borders, the primary criterion is that the currencies of the two countries involved be freely convertible; that is, the currencies can be readily exchanged for each other at a known exchange rate. If the currencies are not freely convertible, the problem is somewhat more complex. International banks have specific expertise in dealing with payments across borders.

2. Managing Disbursements

The goal in managing disbursements is to delay payments so that the company can use funds as long as possible.

Managed Balance Account. A managed balance account is a special checking account that has a zero balance. As checks are presented to this account, a negative balance is created. Funds are then automatically transferred from a master account to bring the account back to zero or another predetermined balance. In this way, all funds are centralized and no idle balances remain in the disbursing account.

Controlled Disbursement System. The purpose of this system is to maximize the time it takes for checks to clear a company's account. By making payments through geographically remote banks, the clearing time, also called **float**, is increased. The purpose is to postpone the date when the company must provide funds to cover checks and to either allow funds to remain in interest-earning assets or reduce the need to borrow.

3. Investing Cash Balances

By carefully managing cash accounts, a financial manager can minimize the cash the corporation must maintain. This increases the amount of funds available to invest or reduces the need to raise additional capital. By

---

[10] Indeed, many companies are offering an economic incentive to switch.

maximizing the amount of funds available to invest in productive or working assets, the manager is operating efficiently.

Despite the efforts to control and predict disbursements, there may be unforeseen disbursements or slower than expected receipts. Therefore, companies typically maintain a positive cash balance for transaction liquidity or a line of credit on which they can readily draw. The most prudent approach is to have sufficient cash for foreseen needs, as well as a reserve. However, having idle cash is unproductive. Good managers maximize the return on these unused fund balances by investing them in the money market or by using a line of credit to cover any temporary imbalance.

The **money markets** match borrowers and lenders of short-term funds. Although technically money-market instruments can have a maturity of up to one year, most have shorter maturities, some overnight. Money-market instruments are considered to be "near cash" because the market is quite liquid (has many buyers and sellers) and the borrowers generally are institutions with high credit ratings.

Money-market instruments in the United States include

1. Treasury bills: short-term notes issued by the U.S. government with maturities of overnight to one year.
2. Treasury notes and bonds: U.S. Treasury debt that matures in less than a year but which originally had longer maturities.
3. Commercial paper: short-term notes issued by financial and nonfinancial corporations with a maturity of up to 270 days.
4. Certificates of deposit: short-term notes issued by banks for up to a year.
5. Eurodollar certificates of deposit: dollars deposited in a foreign bank.
6. Bankers' acceptances: an order to pay issued by an importer and guaranteed by a bank.

Although the returns from these short-term investments may be relatively low in comparison with longer-term, less liquid investments, the returns are superior to idle cash balances.

The short-term investment opportunities may be quite different in other countries. For example, in smaller economies, the shorter-term market may be arranged only through banks. Very short-term investments may exist exclusively through borrowing and lending between corporations. In countries where domestic currency values are volatile, there may be instruments issued by the government or banks that are denominated in a more stable currency, for example, U.S. dollars.

While the particular instruments available for short-term investments or to finance a company's short-term needs vary from country to country, one additional major, organized money market exists: the **Eurobond** or **Eurodollar market**. Eurobond borrowing can be in one of several widely tradable currencies. However, much of the borrowing and lending is done in U.S. dollars, even though the market is outside the United States. A company can borrow or lend in this market from overnight up to one year. One can also borrow and lend for more than one year, a subject we will discuss in Chapter 8. Because the lending is done in dollars, the interest rates paid for Eurodollar deposits and charged on loans are similar to those of similar transactions in the United States.

In order to invest in any of these short-term instruments, the financial manager must know how much cash is available to invest. Cash management systems are designed to provide daily, or even more frequent, information about the amount of funds that can be invested. In many cases, investments must be made for periods as short as overnight to maximize the return available from cash balances.[11]

In times of low interest rates and economic stability, cash by itself is not a productive asset. In such times, and in such countries, managers need to make sure that their companies have minimized the cash that is maintained in the company and that all available resources have been invested in assets being used to produce the company's products. The cash balance should be maintained at the level needed for the operations of the business alone.

Not all environments are stable or have low interest rates, however. In some circumstances, the most productive asset the company has is its cash. In situations where the company's management can lend at rates that generate higher returns than those that could be earned in the company's product market, management will want to adopt policies that maximize the cash at its command and invest it in the money market or the longer-term, capital markets.

Opportunities to invest cash in the capital and money markets became evident to many managers around the world in the 1980s. For many companies, the returns they made on their financial transactions exceeded those earned on selling their products. In some cases, financial profits compensated for product/market losses. Periods of above-normal inflation often provide such opportunities. Terra Blanca, the company we looked at in Chapter 2, is an example of such a company with inflation-driven financial gains.

III. Managing Other Working Capital Requirements

Just as a company's cash must be managed, so must other working capital investments. The general rule is to minimize working capital investments while still providing the resources required to produce quality products.

1. Accounts Receivable

To a large extent the competitive environment determines the size of a company's accounts receivable. The company often has little control over the magnitude of its credit sales; if competitors are selling goods on credit, the company may be forced to follow that practice to remain competitive. In that case, the only method of reducing accounts receivable is

---

[11] Some of these systems are quite complex. For those interested in such systems, see the references at the end of the chapter.

to ensure that credit collections are prompt. If goods or services are sold on 30-day terms, management should vigorously attempt to ensure that payment is received within the 30-day period. Any extension represents a non-interest-bearing loan by the producer to the customer. Some companies charge their customers overdue account penalties or interest to encourage timely payment or to compensate for inflation. Other companies offer an incentive, such as a discount, for early payment.

A method of monitoring accounts receivable based on the due date is called **accounts receivable aging**. In this process, receivables are categorized according to the number of days they are overdue. For example, they might be categorized as 30, 60, and 90 days overdue. Collection efforts can then focus on those accounts that are most overdue. The intent is to minimize the number of accounts that are not collected punctually. Because of the costs associated with the financing of a company's working capital needs, any unnecessary increases in accounts receivable caused by lax collection of overdue accounts must be recognized as an extraneous expense for the company.

In an environment in which a company can independently determine its accounts receivable policy, the critical factor is the relationship between sales and the credit policy. By reducing the financing offered to buyers, a company may be eliminating potential customers. Accounts receivable may be reduced, but only at the cost of reducing total revenues. In such an environment credit policy should be considered a marketing tool, and the cost of the resulting accounts receivable should be considered a cost of marketing the company's products.

On the other hand, extending more credit to customers may be used to reduce the amount of inventory the company must keep. With easier credit terms, buyers may purchase more goods, thereby assuming some of the costs of inventory maintenance from the manufacturer. However, while the company's inventory would decline, its accounts receivable would increase.[12]

An increased volume of credit sales has two other effects. First, it exposes the company to additional risk of uncollectable accounts. The potential cost of unpaid accounts (bad debts) must be weighed against the profits resulting from new sales generated by the easier credit terms.[13] Second, the company extending the credit must have adequate capital to finance its customers' purchases. As you already know, and we will discuss in later chapters, money has a cost. Whether the company borrows to extend credit, or diverts resources from other uses, there is a cost.

---

[12] This assumes that the company has a higher level of inventory than it wishes to maintain. However, if it does not, it may increase inventory turnover or force the company to increase its inventory.

[13] Many companies have a reserve account against bad debts—customers who do not pay their accounts. The reserve is a reduction of sales and the amount of the reserve is based on the company's history with its accounts. When the company enters new markets or extends its sales to new customers, the history is not available, and payment practices must be estimated.

2. Inventories

Like accounts receivable, inventory is directly related to sales volume.[14] While maintaining too much inventory is expensive, it will have no impact on sales volume. However, too little inventory may cause stock-outs, and may result in lost sales. Maintenance of an appropriate inventory level is so significant that sophisticated inventory models, including those based on neural networks and fuzzy logic, are used in inventory planning. The aim of these models is to determine the relationship between inventory levels and sales levels so that the company can have the optimum production and inventory levels.

During the 1980s, many managers reevaluated the size of the inventory their companies maintained. One reason for this reevaluation was high interest rates: the cost of financing additional current assets was high. A second reason for reevaluating inventory positions was the method introduced by Japanese companies called **just-in-time** inventory management. This method placed the burden for inventory maintenance on the suppliers and forced both buyers and sellers to institute new inventory management procedures. In effect, this inventory method minimized the inventory kept on hand: shipments of materials and/or goods arrived just as they were needed for production or sales. While this had the effect of reducing inventories, it did present the danger of **stock-outs**—not having enough inventory—particularly in cases where a supplier falters.[15]

Where inventory is kept, at the supplier or customer, depends upon the nature of the inventory and the balance of power between the supplier and customer. Both just-in-time inventory and more traditional systems, where inventory is stored at the customer, have their risks. Just-in-time systems place the responsibility for inventory storage, planning, and shipping on the supplier. This system places the risk of stock-outs on the customer, but obsolescence and warehousing costs and risks on the supplier. When inventory is kept at the customer, the risks are reversed. The choice of inventory system depends in part upon the kind of goods being sold, the geographic proximity of supplier and customer, the relative power of the supplier and customer, the concentration and strength of the suppliers, and the risks management is willing to take.

In sum, from the standpoint of reducing the need for working capital, the company should attempt to reduce its investment in accounts receivable and inventories. However, the company risks the loss of sales if these accounts are reduced inordinately. The managerial task is to ascertain the appropriate level for cash, accounts receivable, and inventory.

---

14 That is without a change in the system for managing inventory and/or inventory contents.

15 This problem was apparent as suppliers suffered disruptions due to the major earthquake in the port and production center of Kobe, Japan, in the spring of 1995. Computer chip scarcity was expected after the September 1999 earthquake in Taiwan, the biggest source of computer chips in the world. Serious disruptions were experienced in production throughout the United States after the attacks on September 11, 2001 shut down all air transport, and again in late 2002 with the West Coast dock workers' strike.

IV. Financing Working Capital

Having determined the minimum level of working capital needed to carry out the production and sales cycle, the manager must then select the most appropriate method of financing it. Not surprisingly, an important consideration is the cost of various sources of financing.

The most significant source of self-funding is a company's profits. If the competitive environment allows, the company may be able to price its products so that profits are sufficient to fund its working capital needs. For example, in an inflationary environment, the company might attempt to increase its prices in excess of the expected inflation rate in order to finance the working capital needs caused by inflating production costs. The company's ability to adjust its prices in this manner naturally depends on the competitive situation and the economic and political environment in which it operates, and good forecasts for inflation. In a restrained political environment, above-average price increases may create excessive scrutiny and the potential for price freezes or other industry controls by the government.[16] In a highly competitive environment, the company may not have much latitude in its pricing and will need to turn to other sources.

One of the most readily available external sources of funds is the company's suppliers, through the credit terms they allow. Unfortunately, there is a limit to supplier-supplied credit. The company's suppliers may refuse to ship materials needed for production, and such refusals might force the company to stop production. This is usually the last course of action a supplier will take, however, because it results in the loss of a customer.[17] For some companies, supplier credit is a major source of company financing. When a company sells its suppliers goods in a short period of time, but pays accounts payable over a longer time, supplier credit not only is a working capital source of financing, but also may provide considerable resources for other investments. This is the strategy followed by Amazon.com, and was the early distinguishing characteristic of Kmart.[18]

---

[16] Those reading this book who live and work exclusively in the United States may not recall any period of price freezes or price-induced government scrutiny, but both occurred in the 1970s—price freezes during the Nixon administration and price scrutiny of the oil industry during several periods of rapid price increases or lagging price decreases. Current discussions of the magnitude of prescription drug prices may result in price controls. For many readers who live in different economic and political environments, price scrutiny and price freezes are common, particularly in politically sensitive or highly visible companies or industries.

[17] In 2002, Kmart encountered suppliers that were reluctant to ship goods not paid for when received and in cash.

[18] For example, Amazon's customers pay when the order for books is placed. Thus Amazon has little or no accounts receivable. However, it takes Amazon almost two months to pay its suppliers for the books it sells. In its early history the accounts payable period was over three months.

More often, suppliers encourage prompt payment by providing an incentive. For example, the supplier may offer the customer a discount from the sales price if the payment is made within a specified time period. For example, suppliers may indicate payment terms of 2/10, net 30. This means that, if the purchaser pays within 10 days, a discount of 2 percent from the sales price is allowed, otherwise, the full sales price is due in 30 days. If the purchaser decides to wait 30 days to pay rather than paying in full within 10 days and taking the 2 percent discount, the cost of holding the funds for the additional 20 days is 43.5 percent on a compounded annualized basis.[19] Even if the purchaser decides to pay after 60 days rather than the 30 days specified by the terms of the sale, the effective cost is 15.5 percent for the 50 days. These figures suggest that, when a supplier offers a discount, stretching the payables period is an expensive source of funds unless payment is delayed for a long time.

In countries where tax authorities collect taxes as the profits are earned, another creditor or source of credit financing is the government. Note, however, that while some government taxing authorities may allow a temporary deferral of taxes, nonpayment of taxes is a punishable offense, thus limiting the usefulness of this source of funds. One view of this source of funds is the income taxes payable account on the balance sheet.[20]

A less expensive source of short-term financing is bank debt. A standard borrowing arrangement for creditworthy companies is a **line of credit** with a bank. This is an agreement that the bank will lend up to a specified amount during a specified period of time. The borrower can borrow, or draw down, against the credit line as the need arises. In situations where the borrower may not be considered a good credit risk, the bank may extend a **secured line of credit**. In this case, the bank has a claim on specific assets of the company—usually the accounts receivable and inventory—if the borrowed funds are not repaid as agreed.[21] A standard practice is for secured lines not to exceed some portion of the value of receivables and inventory.

Some companies have found it advantageous to sell their accounts receivable to a financial institution. This process is called **factoring**. The company receives immediate payment for the receivables and does not have to wait until accounts are collected to have funds available. The factoring company buys the receivables at a discount from their stated, or

---

[19] If the discount is not taken, and the bill is paid on the due date in 30 days, the customer has paid 2 percent for the use of the funds for 20 days—an annualized compound rate of 43.5 percent. Compounding is explained in Chapter 4. To make a simple estimate, divide 365 days by the period for which the discount is forgone (in this case, 20 days), then multiply this by the rate foregone (in this case, 2 percent). The result for our example is 36.5 percent. It is a crude estimate.

[20] Some companies in an extreme position or with little managerial knowledge even postpone or fail to pay payroll taxes. They should do so at their peril since the U.S. government is aggressive in prosecuting those that do.

[21] In some circumstances the inventory securing the credit is segregated and secured and only an officer of the bank can release it.

face, value, so the company incurs a cost in selling its receivables. The advantage of factoring is that it reduces the firm's need for working capital. In addition, for a somewhat higher discount, the receivables may be sold without recourse. This means that if an account is not collectible, the financial institution, rather than the company, absorbs the loss.[22]

Companies considered to be good credit risks have developed direct access to short-term financial markets without using commercial banks as intermediaries. These high-quality companies can issue short-term notes, called **commercial paper**, at interest rates that are usually below what the banks would have charged. Other companies, such as insurance companies, are large purchasers of commercial paper. Companies are using increasingly sophisticated and innovative methods of raising short-term funds. The objective is to obtain funds at the lowest cost.

Some companies have created their own finance companies to take advantage of their credit rating. These companies are usually those with customers who need to seek financing, for example, automobile buyers. General Motors' GMAC and General Electric's GE Capital are examples of lending institutions established by creditworthy companies.

Another method of financing for companies with accounts receivable is called **securitization**. Securitization has been used primarily by companies with financial assets, such as the financing subsidiaries of large corporations and financial institutions. In general, these companies bundle a number of receivables into a package that is then sold like a security in the capital markets, hence the name securitization. The first assets that were securitized in this way were mortgages. Other assets such as accounts receivable and even credit card receivables have also been securitized.

Our focus on financing for working capital needs has, in this chapter, been short-term sources. Short-term sources generally are considered appropriate because the need is short-lived. For this reason, a company's **net working capital** is defined as current assets minus current liabilities. While a current asset (that is, a particular credit sale or product in inventory) may be short-lived, the inventory or accounts receivable amounts on the balance sheet are not short-lived; they are a permanent part of the assets of the company. Thus, many believe that a more appropriate way of financing such working-capital investments is through a more permanent, long-term form of financing. This notion of using permanent financing for working capital is especially attractive when working capital increases are secular.

If a company chooses to use short-term, temporary financing for permanent or long-lived increases in working capital, there are risks to the strategy. The risk comes when a short-term source must be renewed. At that time the company is exposing itself to interest rate changes and the possibility that funds will not be available when needed. Financing with longer, more permanent sources of financing may be a more appropriate

---

[22] Factors frequently assume the credit-checking function for the company's new and existing customers to be certain that they are lending against a good asset.

strategy, even though it can be more costly. These sources will be discussed in Chapters 6 and 7.

V. Summary

Through the normal course of business operations, companies need current assets. These assets—inventories, accounts receivable, and cash—are required to allow the company to create and sell its products. However, because of the timing differences between the cash outflows for creating the products and the cash inflows from the sale of products, companies usually require some financing for these working capital needs.

Because of the magnitude of the amounts required for working capital, skillful managers of working capital can make a significant impact on a company's profitability. Such steps as shortening the working capital cycle or eliminating unneeded assets can reduce the need for cash. In assessing working capital needs, managers must balance reducing working capital and reducing sales and profits. Having achieved an appropriate working capital level, management's remaining responsibility is to finance working capital by taking cost and funds availability into consideration.

Selected References

For a discussion of cash management and cash management systems, see:

Baumol, W. S. "The Transactions Demand for Cash: An Inventory Theoretic Approach." *Quarterly Journal of Economics* 66, November 1952.

Brealey, Richard A., and Stewart C. Myers. *Principles of Corporate Finance*. 6th ed. New York: McGraw-Hill, 2002, chap. 31.

Brigham, Eugene F., Louis C. Gapenski, and Michael Ehrhardt. *Financial Management*. 9th ed. Fort Worth, Texas: The Dryden Press, 1999, chaps. 22 and 23.

Kamath, Ravindra R., Shahriar Khaksari, Heidi Hylton Meier, and John Winklepleck. "Management of Excess Cash: Practices and Developments." *Financial Management*, Autumn 1985, pp. 70–77.

Miller, M. H., and D. Orr. "A Model of the Demand for Money by Firms." *Quarterly Journal of Economics*, August 1966.

Mullins, David, and R. Hamonoff. "Applications of Inventory Management Models," in *Modern Developments in Financial Management*, S. C. Myers, ed. New York: Praeger, 1976.

Opler, Tim, Lee Pinkowitz, Rene Stulz, and Rohan Williamson. "The Determinants and Implication of Corporate Cash Holdings." *Journal of Financial Economics* 52, 1999.

Ross, Stephen A., Randolph W. Westerfield, and Jeffrey F. Jaffe. *Corporate Finance*. 6th ed. Homewood, Ill.: Richard D. Irwin, 2002, chap. 28.

For a discussion of accounts receivable management, see:

Brealey, Richard A., and Stewart C. Myers. *Principles of Corporate Finance.* 6th ed. New York: McGraw-Hill, 2002, chap. 32.

Brigham, Eugene F., Louis C. Gapenski, and Michael Ehrhardt. *Financial Management.* 9th ed. Fort Worth, Texas: The Dryden Press, 1999, chap. 23.

Gentry, James A., and Jesus M. DeLa Garza. "A Generalized Model for Monitoring Accounts Receivable." *Financial Management,* Winter 1985, pp. 28–38.

Halloran, John A., and Howard P. Lanser. "The Credit Policy Decision in an Inflationary Environment." *Financial Management,* Winter 1981, pp. 31–38.

Mian, Sherzad, and Clifford W. Smith, Jr. "Extending Trade Credit and Financing Receivables." *Journal of Applied Corporate Finance,* Spring 1994, pp. 75–84.

Ross, Stephen A., Randolph W. Westerfield, and Jeffrey F. Jaffe. *Corporate Finance.* 6th ed. Homewood, Ill.: Richard D. Irwin, 2002, chap. 29.

Scherr, F. C. "Optimal Trade Credit Limits." *Financial Management,* Spring 1996.

For information on inventory management, see:

Brigham, Eugene F., Louis C. Gapenski, and Michael Ehrhardt. *Financial Management.* 9th ed. Fort Worth, Texas: The Dryden Press, 1999, chap. 21.

Damodoran, Aswath. *Corporate Finance.* New York: John Wiley & Sons, 1997, chap. 14.

For more on financing working capital and securitization, see:

Ross, Stephen A., Randolph W. Westerfield, and Jeffrey F. Jaffe. *Corporate Finance.* 6th ed. Homewood, Ill.: Richard D. Irwin, 2002, chap. 29.

http://www.securitization.net/

For more on working capital management in an international company, see:

Shapiro, Alan C. *Multinational Financial Management.* 6th ed. New York: John Wiley & Sons, 1999, chaps. 12 and 13.

Study Questions

1. Chateau Royale International is anticipating explosive sales growth in 2004. As the company's account manager at Bank & Trust, you are concerned about the amount of short-term borrowing that will be required under current working capital policies. Forecast a balance sheet and income statement for 2004, as well as the change in net working capital and the current ratio, to assist management in understanding the effects of this increase in sales volume. Financial statements for 2003 follow.

CHATEAU ROYALE INTERNATIONAL
2003 Income Statement
(in billions of units of currency)

Sales	375,000
Cost of goods sold	(276,150)
Gross profit	98,850
Operating expenses	(75,000)
Depreciation	(5,100)
Operating profit	18,750
Taxes	(7,500)
Net profit	11,250

CHATEAU ROYALE INTERNATIONAL
2003 Balance Sheet
(in billions of units of currency)

Cash	75,000	Accounts payable	23,116
Accounts receivable	46,233	Short-term debt	51,867
Inventory	93,750		
Current assets	214,983	Current liabilities	74,983
		Long-term debt	125,000
		Common stock	100,000
Net property, plant,		Retained earnings	30,000
and equipment	115,000		
		Total liabilities and	
Total assets	329,983	owners' equity	329,983

Based on your knowledge of the company and the industry, you have made the following assumptions:

- Sales will increase 60 percent. Cost of goods sold will be 75 percent of sales. Operating expenses will grow 10 percent.
- Depreciation will be $8,000.
- For this analysis, common stock and long-term debt will remain constant from 2003 onwards.
- Receivables will be outstanding 45 days.
- Purchases equal the cost of goods sold. Payables payment period will be 30 days.
- Inventory turnover will be 3 times.
- Management requires a minimum cash balance of 20 percent of sales.
- There are no purchases or disposals of property, plant, or equipment.
- The tax rate will be 34 percent.
- No dividends will be issued in 2004.
- Additional funding will be in the form of short-term debt.
- Cash will be 20 percent of sales.

2. After reviewing your analysis, Chateau Royale management suggests the following working capital policy changes:

   - Reduce minimum cash balance to 15 percent of sales.
   - Increase payables payment period to 45 days.
   - Increase inventory turnover to 400 percent.

   Recompute the balance sheet and net working capital to reflect these changes. Is the current ratio in line with the industry average of 320 percent? What are the implications of these policy changes?

3. Cindy Brittain, chief financial officer of Kurz Corporation, located in Edmonton, Ontario, Canada, is meeting with her two top analysts regarding management of working capital. Tony Triano has suggested that a more lenient accounts receivable collection policy would result in higher sales. He has estimated that, by increasing the receivables collection period to 60 days, sales would be 50 percent higher than the original forecast, inventory/sales will increase to 700 percent, and bad debt will be only 2 percent of net sales. Furthermore, an increase in the minimum cash balance to 20 percent of net sales will offset any liquidity problems.

   Jim Dine, however, has advised against an aggressive working capital policy citing, among other issues, the expectation of slower economic growth. He has estimated that, by reducing the receivables collection period to 30 days, there will be no bad debt expense and sales growth will still be as originally forecast at 20 percent. Although inventory turnover will decrease to 500 percent, the minimum cash balance can be reduced to 15 percent.

   All additional financing will be in the form of short-term debt. The tax rate will remain at 35 percent, cost of goods sold at 75 percent of gross sales, accounts payable/COGS at 29.7 days, and operating expenses will be constant.

   a. Compute an income statement, balance sheet, net working capital, and current ratio under each alternative. To assist in your analysis, the financial statements, without the strategy change, are provided.
   b. Which policy changes should Ms. Brittain implement?

KURZ CORPORATION
Forecasted Income Statement
(in thousands of Canadian dollars)

Sales	CD$ 505,000
Bad debts	(5,000)
Net sales	500,000
Cost of goods sold	(375,000)
Gross profit	125,000
Operating expense	(90,900)
Operating profit	34,100
Taxes	(11,935)
Net profit	CD$ 22,165

KURZ CORPORATION
Balance Sheet
(in thousands of Canadian dollars)

Cash	CD$ 90,000	Accounts payable	CD$ 30,822
Accounts receivable	61,644	Short-term debt	86,322
Inventory	62,500	Current liabilities	117,144
Current assets	214,144	Long-term debt	110,000
Net property, plant,		Common stock	75,000
and equipment	130,000	Retained earnings	42,000
		Total liabilities and	
Total assets	CD$344,144	owners' equity	CD$344,144

4. Jose Dizon, a well-known Philippine architect, has completed the design for THE CRESCENT, to be constructed at the new financial center of the Philippines, the Ortigas Center. He has invited building contractors to bid for the work, and Pablo Lucas has won the bid for 45 million pesos (P). In the contract, Mr. Dizon agreed to pay Mr. Lucas P4.5 million at the beginning of construction, 20 percent of the total contract fee for every additional 25 percent of the job completed, and the final 10 percent 90 days after construction and a successful inspection is completed. Construction is expected to last one year, beginning January 2001. To start the project Mr. Lucas expects to have P1 million in cash on hand at the beginning of January 2004.

   Develop a monthly cash budget for 2004 for Mr. Lucas assuming:

   - Cement is now scarce because of a boom in the construction industry. As a result, it will have to be imported from Taiwan. Every other month, 33,750 bags will be needed at a cost of U.S.$3.60 per bag. A letter of credit will be used to finance the cement purchases from the Taiwanese supplier. The letter of credit will be opened with a bank one month prior to a shipment. The full value of the letter of credit must be deposited in the bank at the time the letter is obtained. The first shipment will arrive in February 2004, and the last in August 2004. The exchange rate in January 2004 is expected to be P28:U.S.$1, but it is expected to rise to P30:U.S.$1 as early as February.

- Granite tiles to be used for the building exterior must be imported from Italy. The order must be placed in May, and a letter of credit in U.S. dollars must be opened at that time. The total cost is expected to be P5 million.
- Beginning in March and ending in December 2004, 40 molded plastic window frames will be imported from Germany per month. Each window unit will cost $100. The supplier requires a letter of credit.
- Two elevators will be ordered from Korea's Goldstar in February, at a cost of U.S.$10,000 each. Goldstar requires a letter of credit in its favor when the order is placed.
- A generator will be ordered in January. Because the producer, Caterpillar Co., has a locally operated sales office, the payment can be made in local currency. Mr. Lucas expects the generator to be delivered in April and installed and paid for in May. The cost of the generator is P2 million.
- Bathroom fixtures will be imported from Italy. A total of 130 pieces are needed at an expected cost of U.S.$150 per piece. The fixtures will take two months to be delivered and are needed one month before the project is completed. A letter of credit will be used to facilitate this purchase.
- Employed on the job will be 200 people with an average monthly salary and benefits of P1,875.
- Overhead expenses are expected to be P10,000 per month.
- Mr. Lucas expects to complete the job in four equal portions in May, August, October, and December.
- No taxes will be paid until 2005.

Mr. Lucas has a revolving credit line with the United Coconut Planters' Bank. The bank has asked him to provide a forecast of the amount of funds he will need and the timing of those needs during THE CRESCENT project. As his financial analyst, you are expected to provide the detailed forecasts for Mr. Lucas to take to the bank.

Chapter Four

Valuation 1: Capital Budgeting

Forecasting the future is one of the most important and challenging tasks a manager faces. The task of making forecasts for the future and then turning them into financial forecasts forces the manager or analyst first to think in detail about what might happen, and second to turn the detailed and ambiguous forecasts into their explicit financial details. In Chapter 2 we discussed some simple methods of forecasting future financing needs. Most of the techniques used the history of the business to create forecasts for the future. These forecasts are useful for examining the financial effects of corporate strategy and policy. However, each forecast assumes that a specific strategy has been decided on and will be undertaken. What we did not discuss in Chapter 2 was how managers choose among different alternative investments and strategies. In this chapter, we will examine the process by which managers allocate capital among different courses of action. Because we are allocating a usually scarce resource, capital, this process of forecasting future performance and making investment decisions is called capital **budgeting**.

A **capital investment** involves an outlay of funds on which management expects a return. It is thought of as having potential benefits extending over a longer period of time, usually more than one year. Capital investments that come as a result of increases and decreases in current assets that can occur in businesses where sales are seasonal, cyclical, or growing are called **spontaneous capital investments**: they occur as the normal result of changing sales levels.[1] For example, a manufacturer making sales on credit will need funds for increasing inventories and accounts receivable during a cyclical upturn. Both the increases in accounts receivable and inventories are investments, even though they are spontaneous—the inevitable result of increasing sales. The return comes from the profit on the expected increased sales. Spontaneous investments often have short-term benefits and usually involve transient

---

[1] We discussed this in Chapter 3.

changes in working capital (for example, inventory or accounts receivable) rather than capital investments.

Spontaneous investments are only one type of capital investment. Investment of capital that comes as the result of a decision made by management is also called a capital investment. We might call these investments that occur as a consequence of management's actions **planned capital investments**. They include such things as permanent additions to working capital (such as an increase in accounts receivable as a result of a change in the company's credit policy); the purchase of land, buildings, or equipment to expand capacity; and the costs associated with an advertising campaign to expand sales or a research and development program to increase product offerings. Because capital investments are often irreversible, or the redeployment of assets comes only at considerable loss of time, money, and managerial effort, planned capital investments are evaluated more formally and intensely than are spontaneous investments.

In most firms, the capital budgeting process consists of five steps:

1. Generating and gathering investment ideas.
2. Analyzing the costs and benefits of proposed investments:
   a. Forecasting the costs and benefits for each investment.
   b. Evaluating the costs and benefits.
3. Ranking the relative attractiveness of each proposed investment and choosing among investment alternatives.
4. Implementing the investments chosen.
5. Evaluating the implemented investments.

These five steps are continuously repeated in any company. Because financial analysts are most involved in estimating and evaluating the costs and benefits and choosing among the alternative investments, we will concentrate on steps 2 and 3 in this chapter.

I. Cost-Benefit Analysis of Proposed Investments

The goal of investing is to create value for the owners of the firm. An investment creates value for its owners when the expected returns from the investment exceed its costs. In economic terms, we say that the **marginal** or **incremental benefits**—the benefits derived solely from the investment—must exceed the **marginal** or **incremental costs**. There are several hidden questions behind this concept. First we must ask incremental to what? The second question is how do we measure the costs and benefits?

In estimating the value of an investment, we care about only the costs and benefits that would not have occurred if the company had not undertaken this particular project. To estimate the investment's benefits and costs, the analyst forecasts the cash flows associated with the investment at the time they will be received or disbursed as measured by the receipt and disbursement of cash. Many companies use the accrual method of accounting: sales are recorded when an order is shipped, and obligations are recorded when incurred.[2] However, we want to know when cash is spent and received.

Accrual accounting can trick an investment analyst. We have already discussed the accrual accounting issues surrounding the purchase of a capital asset and its expensing over time as depreciation. Such timing issues complicate the analysis. There are more potential complications. For example, an investment may be charged with a portion of the ongoing expenses of the firm—the overhead.[3] This is an accounting allocation of costs, not a marginal or incremental cost associated with the investment itself. Thus, if this investment neither increases nor decreases overhead expenses, then overhead is not a cost or benefit for the purposes of the investment analysis. Only incremental, new expenses or benefits are relevant in the analysis of new investments. The real benefits and costs derived are the receipt or disbursement of cash that comes solely as a result of this investment, and it is cash that concerns the investment analyst. To identify and estimate the costs and benefits associated with any investment, the analyst will call on experts in marketing, engineering, accounting, operations, and the economy to provide needed forecasts.

1. Cash Benefits

Four sources of cash benefits or receipts may be derived from an investment:

1. Cost reductions when a more efficient process is substituted for one that is less efficient.
2. Cash received as a result of increased sales.
3. Cash received when replaced equipment is sold.
4. Cash received from the salvage value or sale of the plant or equipment at the end of its useful life.

To illustrate these benefits we will describe the analysis of a shipping company that is considering an investment in a sail-assisted tanker. Management is analyzing whether to replace one of its diesel-fueled, ocean-going tankers with a tanker that has auxiliary metal sails to take advantage of the wind. The firm might benefit from this investment in several ways.

1. The sail-assisted ship would use less fuel and thus be less expensive to operate than the diesel-powered vessel. This cost reduction would lower the operating costs for every year the ship would be in operation.
2. The new ship would have a larger cargo space, thus the tonnage carried by the ship would exceed that carried by the old tanker, resulting in increased yearly revenues.
3. In addition to the benefits from reduced operating expenses and increased sales, the company would sell the old diesel-powered ship for cash and gain favorable tax treatment as a result of the sale.

---

[2] We discussed this in Chapter 2.
[3] Overhead usually consists of charges for such things as cleaning and accounting services.

4. Finally, at the end of its useful life, the salvage value of the sail-assisted ship and any favorable tax effects would be benefits.

The sail-assisted tanker, like most investments, offers a variety of benefits at various times throughout its useful life. The analyst's task is to identify all the benefits (and costs) and their magnitude and timing.

2. Cash Payments

The cash payments are the costs associated with any investment. These fall into three categories:

1. The initial capital cost of the investment.
2. Added capital costs over the life of the investment, including capital improvements made to plant or equipment during the life of the project.
3. Operating costs.

Capital costs include the initial cash outlays associated with making the investment (e.g., buying equipment) as well as any subsequent major outlays of cash required to extend the life of the project or equipment. In our tanker example, capital costs include the costs of obtaining the new ship, the subsequent major engine replacements, and other major repairs needed to extend the life of the vessel. Operating costs are the recurring, annual cash outlays that are required once the investment becomes part of the company's operations. Finally, by purchasing the tanker, the company would have to cover such annual operating costs as wages, fuel, taxes, and maintenance that exceeded those that would have been spent on the old tanker.

Any cash already expended on the investment (for example, research to develop the new tanker's sails) is not a relevant cost in this investment analysis. Instead, such an expense is considered a **sunk cost** because it represents a past outlay of funds and has no bearing on the present decision. The manager's concern is not to recover sunk or irreversible costs but to create value from subsequent new investments. In other words, any investment being considered must have a positive marginal return.[4]

The company, as a result of making an investment, will also incur tax benefits and costs. Unfortunately, the exact effect tax laws will have over the life of a given project may not be known at the time an investment is made. If current tax laws are expected to continue in effect during the life of the project, the impact of taxes on the costs and benefits can be forecasted with relative ease. However, tax codes change, sometimes dramatically and quickly. For example, during the years 1981–1991 there were three major changes in the U.S. tax code that affected the tax treatment of capital investments. From 1981 to 1986, the Accelerated Cost Recovery System (ACRS) was in use. In 1986, a new tax code was enacted that lowered tax rates, removed the investment tax credit, and lengthened de-

---

[4] In fact this is true, in practice many managers ignore this and try to recreate and justify the past.

preciation schedules.[5] In 1991, the code was further adjusted and called the Modified Accelerated Cost Recovery System (MACRS).[6] In 2002 further changes were made. Clearly, the analyst must keep up with continuous changes in the tax code.[7]

The straight-line and double-declining-balance methods of depreciation were most used under the 1980 U.S. tax codes and are widely used in other countries.[8] With **straight-line depreciation**, the annual depreciation is calculated by simply dividing the investment cost by the allowed depreciable life. For example, if a company purchases a piece of equipment for $150,000 that has a depreciable life of five years, the annual depreciation expense is $30,000:

$$\text{Annual depreciation expense} = \frac{\text{Cost of asset}}{\text{Depreciable life}}$$

$$= \frac{\$150,000}{5 \text{ years}}$$

$$= \$30,000$$

Double-declining-balance depreciation allows a higher deduction from taxes in earlier years than does straight-line depreciation. This method is a little more difficult to calculate. To calculate double-declining-balance depreciation, we double the straight-line rate of depreciation and

---

[5] Under the tax law adopted in 1986, assets were assigned to different depreciable categories depending on their expected life. Personal property was divided into six different categories (expected lives of 3, 5, 7, 10, 15, and 20 years), and real property (real estate, not including land) was divided into two groups (expected lives of 27.5 and 31.5 years).

Capital costs in the 3-year to 10-year classes were depreciated using an accelerated type of depreciation called the double-declining-balance method, with a switch to the straight-line method permitted near the end of the life. The switch was allowed in order to optimize deductions. Costs in the 15- and 20-year categories were depreciated using a 150 percent declining-balance rate, switching later to the straight-line rate. Real estate, on the other hand, had to be depreciated using the straight-line method.

The rules were a little simpler in 1999. Buildings were depreciated for 39 years starting in the month in which they were put in service; property like computers and the bundled software could be written off on a 5-year schedule, with half the depreciation in the first and sixth years; and assets such as office furnishings were depreciated over 7 years. Unbundled software was considered to have a 3-year life. Costs associated with software developed by the company for its own use was expensed.

[6] The first year was considered a half year and depreciation was 20 percent, half that under ACRS. In the following five years, the rates were 32.00, 19.20, 11.52, 11.52, and 5.76, respectively.

[7] In addition to changes in the method of depreciation, the U.S. 1991 tax code stipulated a lower maximum tax rate for corporations of 34 percent (the ACRS marginal rate was 48 percent) and the 2002 change had the maximum of 35 percent, but only for corporations with $10 million or more in profits. For corporations with taxable incomes of more than $75,000 but less than $10 million, the rate was 34 percent; for those whose profits were less than $75,000 the rate was to 25 percent; and below $50,000 in profits the rate was 15 percent. Investment tax credits, amounting to 8 to 10 percent under ACRS, were abolished.

[8] Making life a little more interesting, these depreciation rules govern taxes paid by a company. The company in its report to its shareholders may choose a different method of depreciation than it used in calculating taxes.

multiply it by the undepreciated investment value. Note that the first year is considered a half year in this method.

For our example the straight-line rate of depreciation is 20 percent, based on a five-year life. Thus, the first year's depreciation using the double-declining-balance method would be twice 20 percent for a total of 40 percent. Remember, we take depreciation for only half of the first year.

$$\text{Double-declining-balance for the first year's depreciation} = \frac{[(0.20 \times 2) \times \$150,000]}{2}$$

$$= \$30,000$$

For the remaining years we take the undepreciated value ($150,000 – $30,000) times twice the straight-line rate. For the second year the following would be the result.

$$\text{Double-declining-balance depreciation for year 2} = (0.20 \times 2) \times \$120,000$$

$$= \$48,000$$

This depreciation expense is much higher than the amount that would be expensed during the second year using the straight-line method. **Accelerated depreciation** results in higher depreciation and lower taxes in the early years than does straight-line depreciation. Note that the total depreciation over the life of the investment is the same under both methods; only the timing of the depreciation expense differs. At some times, and in some countries, the double-declining-balance rate is simply double the straight-line depreciation, and the first year is considered a full year.

Exhibit 4-1 shows the differences in depreciation expense using three methods: straight-line depreciation; ACRS, the method under the tax code in force from 1981; and double-declining-balance and MACRS, the method under the 1999 U.S. tax code revision. By comparing the depreciation expense allowed under the two recent U.S. tax codes to straight-line depreciation, a method favored by many corporations for their public reporting, you can see how the depreciation method chosen can affect the company's reported profitability. Because depreciation expense is much larger in the early years under the double-declining-balance method, the company's taxes will be lower during those years and its cash flow larger. It is because of this that accelerated depreciation methods are believed to encourage investment in capital projects.

There is a dark side of accelerated methods: they decrease profits. Thus, most U.S. companies do not use accelerated methods of depreciation for their financial reports, in spite of the fact that accelerated methods are used to calculate tax payments. This difference in tax and reporting methods results in financial statements that do not accurately reflect the taxes that were paid in any given year. Over time, of course, the two are equal.

Because a tax code and its effect on a project's costs and benefits are sources of uncertainty, potential changes and their impact should be assessed. Some changes in a tax code can be anticipated; others cannot. In fact, the nature of the changes and their impact can be quite unexpected.

Exhibit 4-1

Depreciation Expense Using Three Methods of Depreciation

Year	Straight-Line	ACRS*	Double-Declining-Balance MACRS†	Traditional‡
1	$ 30,000	$ 22,500	$ 30,000	$ 30,000
2	30,000	33,000	48,000	48,000
3	30,000	31,500	28,800	28,800
4	30,000	31,500	17,280	17,280
5	30,000	31,500	17,280	12,960
6	0	0	8,640	12,960
Total	$150,000	$150,000	$150,000	$150,000

* Most machinery and equipment was depreciated over five years under U.S. ACRS rules. For those five years, depreciation was 15, 22, 21, 21, and 21 percent, respectively. An investment tax credit was allowed in the first year, generally amounting to 8 percent of the investment's cost, and the marginal tax rate was 48 percent.
† This is the 1999 tax code framework. The first year is considered to be one-half year, regardless of the actual length of time the asset is owned during the year. The depreciation rates for the six periods are 20.00, 32.00, 19.20, 11.52, 11.52, and 5.76 percent, respectively. Assets with different depreciable lives have different rates each year. The maximum tax rate was 35 percent. Current information on these is available from the IRS at http://www.irs.gov.
‡ This is simply double the straight-line depreciation rate with a switch to straight-line depreciation when it is advantageous. In this case the switch occurs in the fourth year. At the beginning of Year 5 there is a balance remaining of $25,920 to be depreciated equally over the remaining two years.

This uncertainty is only one of many that face the analyst in making forecasts. Later in the chapter we will describe methods for incorporating uncertainty into the analysis.

Before we conclude this section on costs and benefits, note that we have not dealt with one kind of costs and benefits—those associated with financing. It is important to determine both the value created from an investment and the value that comes from the way that investment is financed. In this chapter we discuss only the evaluation of an investment from the point of view of the owners of the corporation, without considering subcontracting any of the owners' financing responsibility. Therefore, no costs or benefits associated with financing the investment will be included in the analysis. The issue of financing, since it is a complex topic, is left to Chapters 7, 8, and 9. In Chapter 7 we will discuss how shareholders, or managers on their behalf, decide to subcontract some of the financing of the company to other capital providers, principally lenders. In Chapter 8 we discuss what tools can be used to determine the proportion of financing that should be subcontracted to lenders and whether value can be created or destroyed through judicious leverage. In Chapter 9 we show how financing costs (particularly interest payments and principal repayments) and financing benefits (primarily, new loan receipts) can be included in the analysis of an investment.

II. Evaluating Incremental Costs and Benefits

Once costs and benefits have been itemized, the analyst's major task is to determine the marginal or incremental effect the investment will have on the firm as a whole. To evaluate incremental costs and benefits, many analysts group investment proposals into categories that help them examine each proposal in terms of its relationship to the firm's business as a whole.

The most useful scheme is to group projects according to the degree of independence of their costs and benefits from the costs and benefits of the company and its other investments and projects. **Independent investments** are projects that can be accepted or rejected regardless of the action taken on any other investment, now or later. **Mutually exclusive investments** are projects that preclude one another: once one project is accepted, the others become unavailable or inappropriate. Mutually exclusive investments usually are designed to solve the same problem or to serve the same function. For example, managers often must choose among alternate means of adding plant capacity, or among advertising programs, or between two new product lines.

There is a second way to categorize independent and mutually exclusive investments: replacements and new products and processes. **Replacement investments** are investments made to modernize an existing process or to revitalize an old product line. Because estimating the net effect on the company of replacing a process or product can be especially difficult, analysts often place these investments in a separate category. They are, however, just an especially troublesome type of mutually exclusive or independent investment. To understand the process of evaluation, we will analyze two mutually exclusive investments, keeping in mind that independent investments would be evaluated using the same tools.

The management of Betty's Better Big Boys, one of the largest franchisers of fast foods in the West, is considering two investment proposals. Betty's Better Big Boys sells a variety of sandwiches, drinks, and other fast foods through its 500 restaurants. Management has capitalized on the public's health concerns by offering whole-grain sandwich buns, sandwich wraps, toppings such as tomatoes and sprouts, french fries with potato skins, fruit smoothies, and tofu shakes, as well as regular fare. Management is considering either of two investments—opening their restaurants for breakfast or adding salad, sushi, and pasta bars to their existing lunch and dinner menus. Because of the management effort needed to implement either project, management considers these investments mutually exclusive: it may choose one or the other, but not both.

1. Mutually Exclusive Investments: The Breakfast Proposal

Betty's Better Big Boys restaurants currently are open from 11 A.M. to 11 P.M. Because many of Betty's competitors have begun to serve breakfast, management is considering opening from 6:30 to 11:00 A.M. to serve breakfast. They believe Betty's Better Big Boys has an edge over its competition because it pioneered the healthy fast-food concept with its "healthy hamburger." Betty's would emphasize tasty and nutritious breakfast offerings as well as more traditional Southern breakfast items such as biscuits and gravy, sausage and ham biscuits, fried apples, and grits.

The same buildings and equipment would be used for serving breakfast, although the longer serving hours would increase overhead expenses. There would be added costs for ingredients, salaries of managers and employees, and advertising the new items and hours. Together, incremental overhead and operating expenses for all 500 restaurants are expected to total $14.25 million per year. In addition, since breakfast would be a new product, management is planning an extensive employee-training program. The program, to be completed before the company starts offering breakfast in July, would cost $1.75 million. New inventory would total $1,800 per restaurant, and all remaining inventory would be fully recovered at the end of the project in five years.[9] Management has forecast a $15 million increase in sales per year to be made from the breakfast service.

The first step in evaluating this proposal is to estimate the incremental costs and benefits the company will gain if the investment is made. These are detailed in Exhibit 4-2. Since management expects no inflation, costs and benefits are shown in real dollars.[10] Costs and benefits are forecast for five years because management believes that the equipment used in each restaurant will last only five years.

Exhibit 4-2 is a typical presentation of the analysis of a capital investment. The first part looks like an income statement forecast, but the second part, below the net profit entry, does not. Recall that this forecast is for *cash* costs and benefits. Then why is a noncash charge, such as depreciation, deducted in the top half of the exhibit and then added back in the second half as noncash charges? This is because depreciation reduces taxable income and thus taxes, and taxes are paid in cash.[11] By subtracting noncash charges in the income statement the tax payment can be accurately determined. In the second section of Exhibit 4-2 the noncash charges are added back, leaving only depreciation's impact on taxes.

You will also recall that, because we are assuming that only its owners finance the company, these cash flows belong to the shareholders.[12] Thus

---

[9] Little or no inventory would remain at the end of the project's life. All perishable and nonperishable goods would have been used and not replaced, thus reducing inventory to zero.

[10] Since there is no expected inflation, real and nominal dollars would be identical.

[11] Some analysts choose to put in an item called tax impact of depreciation, foregoing the deduction on the income statement and addition in the cash flow section of depreciation. They are equivalent methods. The explicitness of this approach avoids expository problems.

[12] Financial subcontracting occurs when shareholders' funds are supplemented from sources such as lenders.

Exhibit 4-2   Betty's Better Big Boys

Breakfast Proposal—Marginal Costs and Benefits

(thousands of real dollars)

	0	Period 1	2	3	4	5
Income Statement Changes						
Sales	0	$ 15,000	$ 15,000	$ 15,000	$ 15,000	$ 15,000
Operating expenses	0	(14,250)	(14,250)	(14,250)	(14,250)	(14,250)
Training costs	$(1,750)					
Depreciation	0	0	0	0	0	0
Profit before taxes	(1,750)	750	750	750	750	750
Taxes*	595	(255)	(255)	(255)	(255)	(255)
Net profit	$(1,155)	$ 495	$ 495	$ 495	$ 495	$ 495
Noncash Charges						
Depreciation		0	0	0	0	0
Capital Investments						
Property, plant, and equipment	0	0	0	0	0	0
Inventory	(900)	0	0	0	0	900
Residual net cash flow	$(2,055)	$ 495	$ 495	$ 495	$ 495	$ 1,395

* Positive taxes are a tax reduction in the rest of the company due to the training expenses in the year prior to start up. This benefit occurs only if the company has profits in other parts of its business.

there are no provisions for interest payments, principal payments, or new loans in the cash flows. Because these cash flows belong to the shareholders alone, and shareholders have the residual claim on the company's cash flows, we call them **residual cash flows**.[13]

The second set of adjustments shown to the net profit in Exhibit 4-2 are capital investments—cash payments for property, plant, and equipment or for investments in working capital. Property, plant, and various items of equipment are not expensed but are capitalized on the balance sheet. Since they are not expenses they do not affect taxes at the time they are purchased. Instead, plant and equipment are expensed over the period allowed by the tax code. This annual capital investment expense is

---

[13] We will show in Chapters 6 and 7 how financial subcontracting changes an analysis.

called depreciation. Property is put on the balance sheet at its purchase price and neither depreciated nor revalued.[14]

Working capital investments—increases in inventory, accounts receivable, or cash—are also included. These are considered to be investments just as real as investments in a piece of equipment, and thus are shown as cash investments when they are made. However, until the company, at its discretion, recovers these investments they remain a part of the firm's invested capital.[15] These assets may be recovered when a strategy is changed, a process reengineered, or when growth declines.

2. Mutually Exclusive Investments: Salad, Sushi, and Pasta Bar Proposal

As an alternative to adding breakfast, management at Betty's Better Big Boys is considering adding an all-you-can-eat salad, sushi, and pasta bar to the existing lunch and dinner menus starting in July. They have already spent $600,000 in developing the salad, sushi, and pasta bar concept in limited test marketing. To introduce the products into all of their restaurants, they estimate that personnel would have to be trained at a cost of $832 per restaurant and that display cases would have to be bought and installed at $2,800 per restaurant. Management expects that the display cases would be scrapped in five years and that the value of the scrap would be offset by disposal costs. Incremental (marginal) operating expenses include the cost of ingredients, additional refrigeration, and the salary of one additional employee per restaurant to stock the salad, sushi, and pasta bar. On the basis of test market results, the marketing department estimates sales of salad, sushi, and pasta at $15 million per year and operating expenses at $13.934 million. New inventories would be $1,800 per restaurant. The cash flows for this investment are shown in Exhibit 4-3.

The different effects these two proposals would have on Betty's Better Big Boys illustrate the usefulness of categorizing investments as independent or mutually exclusive. Management considers the two proposed investments to be mutually exclusive because they do not believe that they could adequately oversee both projects at the same time. The breakfast option would be independent of Betty's existing business because it would extend the existing product line. The salad, sushi, and pasta bar, however, would be a partial replacement since it would affect existing sales of sandwich meals at lunch and dinner. In fact, the marketing staff estimates that half of the salad, sushi, and pasta bar's sales would come from customers who would otherwise have purchased sandwiches and french fries. Thus, while total salad, sushi, and pasta sales would be $15 million, incremental sales would be only half of the total, or $7.5 million per year.

---

[14] Revaluation of assets is not allowed under the U.S. tax code except in the event that the company is acquired. However, asset revaluation is allowed and does occur in some high-inflation countries.

[15] Working capital investments, such as inventory and accounts receivable, are long-term assets, even though the constituents of the accounts change. This was described in Chapter 3.

Exhibit 4-3 Betty's Better Big Boys
Salad, Sushi, and Pasta Bar Proposal—Marginal Costs and Benefits

(thousands of real dollars)

	Period						
	0	1	2	3	4	5	6
Income Statement Changes							
Sales		$7,500	$7,500	$7,500	$7,500	$7,500	0
Operating expenses		(6,967)	(6,967)	(6,967)	(6,967)	(6,967)	0
Training costs	$ (416)						
Depreciation*		(280)	(448)	(269)	(161)	(161)	(81)
Profit before taxes	(416)	253	85	264	372	372	(81)
Taxes‡	141	(86)	(29)	(90)	(127)	(127)	28
Net profit	$ (275)	$ 167	$ 56	$ 174	$ 245	$ 245	$(53)
Noncash Charges							
Depreciation		280	448	269	161	161	81
Capital Investments							
Property, plant, and equipment	(1,400)						
New inventory	(900)					900	
Residual net cash flow	$(2,575)	$ 447	$ 504	$ 443	$ 406	$ 1,306	$ 28

*Depreciation based on the 1999 U.S. tax code rules. The five-year depreciation schedule has half the annual rate expensed in the first year with the last depreciation charge coming in the sixth year.

‡ Positive taxes that result from the expense of training are a tax reduction to the remainder of the company. This tax reduction is a benefit only if the company has profits from other businesses and these losses can offset the profits and lower the company's total taxes.

The salad, sushi, and pasta bar's status as a partial replacement would be responsible not only for lower net cash receipts but also for lower incremental overhead and operating expenses than the breakfast project. Unlike the breakfast option, it would add less to current overhead and operating expenses because it would be offered during existing hours and manned primarily by existing employees. If the analyst did not realize that the salad, sushi, and pasta bar option would be a replacement investment, he or she might erroneously include two inappropriate items. First, the analyst might include a portion of the costs of buildings and equipment as part of its incremental costs. These are not incremental since the company currently has the buildings and equipment and incurs the costs. A second error would be to include its total sales of $15 million as a benefit rather than the $7.5 million in incremental sales. The net cash flow for the salad, sushi, and pasta bar is the net incremental profit plus any non-cash charges that were deducted from profit before taxes for the purpose of calculating taxes, minus the new costs for the salad bar equipment and inventory.

Details of this evaluation of the net benefits of the project appear in Exhibit 4-3. Note that the $600,000 in expenses incurred in developing and test-marketing the salad, sushi, and pasta bar concept are not included. They are sunk costs: cash already spent and not relevant in making this decision.

Now that the incremental costs and benefits for the two projects have been estimated, Betty's management must decide whether to accept one of the plans or reject both projects and seek a different opportunity. To make these decisions, management needs a method for measuring the relative value of the two proposals. Without some measure of an investment's value, the choice becomes a question of preference and the power of persuasion.

III. Choosing Among Investments: Net Present Value and IRR

The relative attractiveness or value of investments may be determined and alternatives ranked in a number of different ways. Each of these methods has advantages and disadvantages.

The net present value is the most widely accepted and used method for gauging an investment's economic value to a company. This method is important because it recognizes that investors want to be rewarded for waiting for returns that are not immediate: it takes into account the time value of money. The **time value of money** is a rate of return that compensates investors for any temporary lack of liquidity by promising increased returns for more distant cash flows. It is not the only method used for evaluating and ranking investments; however, it is the most transparent and reliable method. Later in this chapter we will discuss other methods and compare them to the merits of our chosen standard—the net present value (NPV). However, first we must discuss how to take the timing of cash flows into account in our analysis—how to equate future and present cash flow values.

There is a straightforward way of determining the value of a cash flow in the future. It is called **future value**, which is the value of a sum of money today at a particular time in the future. To calculate the future value we need to know three things: the date in the future that is of interest to the investor, the investment rate for the time period, and the amount of money to be invested.[16]

Let's suppose that we have an investment of $6.27 million. We can invest the money, let's say in a money market account, at 5 percent per year. We want to know what we will have at the end of five years. To do this we could set up a table like that shown in Exhibit 4-4. Here we calculate the interest earned in a year by multiplying the beginning balance by the rate of 5 percent. As you can see, the first year we earn $313,500. Since we do not withdraw any of the money, the balance on which we can earn interest in the second year is the initial investment of $6.27 million plus the $313,500 in interest earned in the first year. The interest earned each year is added to the beginning investment the following year to determine the investment on which interest will be paid. Exhibit 4-4 shows that the value of $6.27 million invested at an annual rate of 5 percent at the beginning of the first year is worth a little over $8 million at the end of five years. This is the sum that the investor will have if all the annual earnings are reinvested at a compounding rate of 5 percent.[17] The $8 million is the future value of $6.27 million for five years at 5 percent. As you can see, this is a relatively simple calculation. Unfortunately, the task becomes more cumbersome when dealing with more complex situations.[18]

Exhibit 4-4

Future Value of an Investment at a 5 Percent Annual Rate of Return

	Year				
	1	2	3	4	5
Investment, beginning of year	$6,270,000	$6,583,500	$6,912,675	$7,258,309	$7,621,224
Interest (@ 5%)	313,500	329,175	345,634	362,915	381,061
Investment, end of year	$6,583,500	$6,912,675	$7,258,309	$7,621,224	$8,002,285

---

[16] We can think of this rate as the rate a bank might pay on a savings deposit, the yield on low risk bonds, or some other minimum return that an investor would certainly expect for illiquidity. We will discuss this rate in greater detail in Chapter 6.

[17] Compounding means we earn interest on previously accrued interest.

[18] For example, continuously compounding interest, multiple investments and/or withdrawals over time, and changing interest rates.

Fortunately, there is a much easier way to calculate the future value of a sum invested today. To use this shortcut we first need to create a factor that can be used as a beginning investment multiple. We then use the multiple with any initial investment. We call this factor the **future value factor**.

$$\text{Future value factor} = (1 + R)^n$$

Where:
   R = The rate of return
   n = The number of periods, usually years[19]

The process for creating this future value factor for an investment made for five years at a 5 percent compound rate of return is:[20]

$$\text{Future value factor} = (1.05)^5$$
$$= 1.276282$$

To calculate the future value of any investment, we multiply the cash flow investment by the factor as follows:

$$\text{Future value} = \text{Future value factor} \times \text{Cash flow}$$

Using this future value factor we can solve the problem in Exhibit 4-4.

$$\text{Future value} = \text{Future value factor} \times \text{Cash flow}$$
$$= 1.276282 \times \$6,270,000$$
$$= \$8,002,288$$

As you can see the answer varies only slightly due to rounding. However, using the future value factor was much easier.

We just calculated the future value of a single sum. To calculate the future value of a series of cash flows, we would compound each cash flow to the future value and sum these values. The future value of a dollar received in each of the next five years is shown in Exhibit 4-5. The sum is the future value of this annuity.

In Exhibit 4-5 the new investments are identical. A series of identical cash flows received over time is called an **annuity**. When we have an annuity, there is a shortcut to this tabular process for calculating the future value—we create a future value factor. To do this we simply sum the future value factors for each of the years the annuity will be earned.

$$\text{Future value of annuity} = \text{Sum of future value factors}_n$$

---

[19] Actually we can do this for periods of any length. We simply use the interest rate for a period of that length. For example, if we wanted to do the analysis over six-month periods, we would use the interest rate for six months.

[20] To calculate the future value factor without the exponential function, simply multiply $(1 + R)$ by itself n number of times. For five years at 5 percent the result would be:

$$\text{Future value factor} = [(1 + .05) \times (1 + .05) \times (1 + .05) \times (1 + .05) \times (1 + .05)]$$
$$= 1.276282$$

Exhibit 4-5

Future Value of an Annuity

	Year				
	1	**2**	**3**	**4**	**5**
Balance, beginning of year	0	$1.05	$2.15	$3.31	$4.53
New investment	$1.00	1.00	1.00	1.00	1.00
Total balance	1.00	2.05	3.15	4.31	5.53
Interest @ 5%	0.05	0.10	0.16	0.22	0.28
Ending balance	$1.05	$2.15	$3.31	$4.53	$5.81

For an annuity received for five years compounding at 5 percent, the future value annuity factor would be

$$\text{Future value of annuity factor} = (1 + .05)^1 + (1 + .05)^2 + (1 + .05)^3 + (1 + .05)^4 + (1.05)^5$$

$$= 1.05 + 1.10 + 1.158 + 1.216 + 1.276$$

$$= 5.8$$

Once again, we can multiply the annuity factor by the sum to be received in each year to get the future value of an annuity. For example, if you win a lottery of $1 million per year for five years, you will have $5.8 million ($1.0 million × 5.8) at the end of the fifth year. If you have a choice of taking the $1 million per year or a sum of $3.5 million today, what should you do? To answer this question we have to calculate the value in today's currency of the annual $1 million payments. We cannot do that yet.

To calculate the value today of a future sum we can use an adaptation of the compounding process. Today's worth or value is called **present value** or the **discounted present value**. The process of **discounting** is simply the inverse of compounding.

$$\text{Present value factor} = \frac{1.00}{(1 + R)^n}$$

The present value factor for a sum received five years from now at a rate of 5 percent would be:

$$\text{Present value factor} = \frac{1.00}{(1.05)^5}$$

$$= \frac{1.00}{1.276282}$$

$$= 0.783526$$

The 0.783526 means that a sum received in five years (using a 5 percent rate) is worth 78.35 percent of its future value today. To put it in dollar terms, $1.00 in five years is worth $0.78 today.[21] To calculate the present value of more than $1.00 received five years in the future just multiply the future value by the present value factor. For example, the present value of $8 million received in five years is $6.27 million ($8.0 million × 0.7835).

Now can we answer our question about the lottery payoff? Not quite. To determine whether we should take $1 million per year or $3.5 million today, we must calculate the present value an annuity. To answer the question you could create a table to calculate the present value of an annuity as shown in Exhibit 4-6.

Exhibit 4-6

Present Value of an Annuity

(in millions)

	Period Annuity Received				
	1	**2**	**3**	**4**	**5**
Cash flow from annuity	$1.00	$1.00	$1.00	$1.00	$1.00
Present value (@ 5%)	$0.952381	$0.907029	$0.863838	$0.822702	$0.783526
Total present value	$4.329476				

Note: Rounding of present or future value factors may cause small discrepancies in the results.

As an alternative to the tabular approach you can create and use a present value annuity factor as follows.[22]

$$\text{Present value annuity factor} = \frac{1.00}{(1 + R)^n}$$

$$= \frac{1.00}{1.05} + \frac{1.00}{1.10} + \frac{1.00}{1.158} + \frac{1.00}{1.216} + \frac{1.00}{1.276}$$

$$= 0.952381 + 0.907029 + 0.863838 + 0.822702 + 0.783526$$

$$= 4.329476$$

---

[21] Using the compounding approach, $0.783526 invested today is worth $1.00 in five years at a rate of 5 percent.
[22] You will note that the number of decimal places in the denominator will impact the result.

Using the present value annuity factor of 4.329476 we can determine the present value of the lottery's annuity payout of $1.0 million per year.

Present value of annuity = Present value annuity factor × Annual annuity

= 4.329476 × $1.0

= $4.33 million

The lottery choice is a lump sum of $3.5 million or an annuity of $1 million a year for five years. Since the present value of the annuity is $4.3 million and the lump sum is only $3.5 million, the annuity is the better choice.

Fortunately, one does not have to go through the laborious process of calculating compound and present value factors. Lists of factors are available on web sites. Moreover, computer spreadsheet models perform the calculations and all but the simplest modern calculators perform compounding and discounting functions quite painlessly, thus rendering the direct use of discount factors an unnecessary step. Now let's see how we can use the compounding and present value calculations to help us determine which investment Betty's Better Big Boys should make.

1. Net Present Value

The **present value** (PV) calculates today's lump sum value of all current and future benefits. The **net present value** (NPV) is the present value of the benefits less, or net of, the present value of the costs.[23] The NPV is calculated using a discount rate. The rate is used to adjust each year's returns according to the time between it and the present—the date the decision would be implemented, usually the time of the initial investment. The discount rate is better known as the investors' **required rate of return**.[24] A discount rate has a variety of names, including hurdle rate. The **hurdle rate** is used to signify that the project must exceed or "jump over" the hurdle. Net present value is calculated as follows:

$$NPV = \frac{NCF_0}{(1 + R)^0} + \frac{NCF_1}{(1 + R)^1} + \frac{NCF_2}{(1 + R)^2} + \cdots + \frac{NCF_n}{(1 + R)^n}$$

Where:

NCF = The net cash flow for the period (cash flow benefits minus cash flow costs)

R = Periodic discount rate

$0, 1, 2, \ldots, n$ = Periods from the date of original investment

Any initial investment is a cash flow in time zero (NCF_0).

---

[23] The net present value can also be described as the present value of the net worth an investment will contribute to a company by the end of its useful life. This is a particularly useful way to think about net present value if you are an owner or shareholder.

[24] Later in the chapter we will discuss how to adjust this rate for the risk inherent in an investment.

While we have described the discounting and compounding processes in terms of annual rates of return and years, any period can be used. For instance, shorter periods are useful when cash flows vary over the year. This can be especially true in development projects and in inflationary environments. The analyst using different periods must, however, make sure that the rate of return, the discount rate, is appropriate for the length of the periods being used in the cash flows. For instance, if the analyst were evaluating the project over quarters, the rate of return would be a quarterly rate of return. In our example, the annual 5 percent rate of return would be equivalent to a 1.23 percent quarterly rate.[25] This latter rate would be used to discount or compound quarterly cash flows.

For Betty's Better Big Boys, the net present value of the breakfast option using 5 percent as an annual discount rate is calculated as follows:

$$NPV = \frac{-\$2,055,000}{(1 + .05)^0} + \frac{\$495,000}{(1 + .05)^1} + \frac{\$495,000}{(1 + .05)^2} + \frac{\$495,000}{(1 + .05)^3} +$$

$$\frac{\$495,000}{(1 + .05)^4} + \frac{\$1,395,000}{(1 + .05)^5}$$

$$= \$793,265$$

The initial investment of $2.055 million is considered a negative cash flow in period zero and thus is undiscounted.

The NPV of $793,265 is the present value of the breakfast project to Betty's. You also can think of it as the present value of the net worth the project will add to Betty's balance sheet at the end of five years, if all goes as forecasted by management. The NPV of the salad, sushi, and pasta bar project is $68,734 at a 5 percent discount rate. As you can see, the breakfast project is economically superior by $724,532 in present value terms.

The NPV approach offers a logical method of evaluating investments. The process is quite simple when a calculator with a net present value function or a computer spreadsheet is used. The method takes into account the timing of cash flows by placing a higher value on those received immediately than on those to be received in the future. Once the timing of cash flows has been taken into account, acceptable investments are those with net present values *equal to or greater than zero.*

Some people require that the NPV be greater than zero. However, if we have used a discount rate that includes the time value of money and compensates the investor for the risk being taken, the investor is already adequately compensated for both illiquidity and risk. In finance lingo, shareholders' value is neither being created nor destroyed. A NPV greater than zero would signify that value is being created and shareholders are getting a return greater than they require. Creating value is difficult, but

---

[25] This rate takes compounding into account. The simple rate, 1.25 percent, is less accurate.

it is the job of management.[26] Even though we and shareholders may wish for more, maintaining value is the acceptable objective.

2. Profitability or Present Value Index

Some managers prefer to use the profitability or present value index (PVI) rather than net present value. The PVI is simply an adaptation of the benefit/cost ratio. A ratio of 1 or more shows that the present value of the benefits equal or exceed the present value of the costs:

$$\text{Present value index} = \frac{\text{Present value of net benefits}}{\text{Present value of investment costs}}$$

Calculating the present value index (PVI) is simple and straightforward. Using the breakfast project and a 5 percent discount rate, the index is calculated as follows:

$$PVI = \left[\frac{\$495,000}{(1 + .05)^1} + \frac{\$495,000}{(1 + .05)^2} + \frac{\$495,000}{(1 + .05)^3} + \frac{\$495,000}{(1 + .05)^4} + \frac{\$1,395,000}{(1 + .05)^5} \right] / \$2,055,000$$

$$= \frac{\$2,848,265}{\$2,055,000}$$

$$= 1.39$$

The present value index is 1.39, meaning that the benefits are 139 percent of the costs. For the salad, sushi, and pasta bar project, the PVI is 1.027. Both projects have a PVI greater than our minimum of 1.0.

Internal Rate of Return A second discounted cash flow technique is the internal rate of return (IRR). The IRR is the average rate of return that will be earned over the life of the project. To calculate the IRR the same formula for calculating net present value is used; however, we set the net present value equal to zero and solve for R, the discount rate.

Solving for R is somewhat more difficult than solving for the NPV, and the method is not as reliable.[27] To solve for R we must use a trial-and-error method. To begin the process we choose an arbitrary discount rate, say 5 percent, and calculate the NPV for an investment. If the resulting NPV is positive, a higher discount rate is next selected and the NPV is re-calculated. We continue choosing discount rates until we find the discount rate that yields an NPV of zero. Alternatively we can use a calculator or spreadsheet with an IRR function. For the Betty's Better Big

---

[26] You may remember that we used the market price/book value to show how satisfied shareholders are with the performance of a company. We could now say that if the market price/book value is greater than 1.0, shareholders believe that the company and its management have created value.

[27] One might ask, then why show it? The reason it is included is that many companies and managers choose to use the IRR rather than the NPV; they are more comfortable with a rate than a currency value. If you work at such a company, you can understand the method and test for its frailties using the NPV.

Boys' breakfast project, the IRR is obviously larger than 5 percent since, at that rate, the NPV is $793,265.[28]

It is easy to get lost in this trial-and-error analysis. We could keep track of the NPVs in a table. However, this is where a graph is much better, as you can see looking at Exhibit 4-7. This graph, also called a **net present value profile**, shows the results of this trial-and-error approach for both of Betty's investment alternatives. As you can see, the IRR for the breakfast project is 15.9 percent. For the salad, sushi, and pasta bar project the IRR is 5.8 percent. At all discount rates, the breakfast project is superior. The graph makes this clear.

Exhibit 4-7

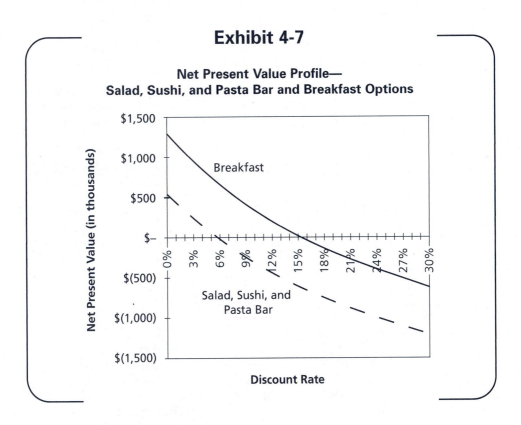

Net Present Value Profile— Salad, Sushi, and Pasta Bar and Breakfast Options

While management would certainly prefer the breakfast option if choosing between the two, how do they know if either is acceptable using the IRR? Will the investment maintain or create value for shareholders? An acceptable IRR for a project is a return that equals or exceeds the investors' required rate of return. Here we have used 5 percent as the required return for these investments. Thus, both projects would be

---

[28] Note that at a discount rate of zero the net present value is the simple sum of the undiscounted cash flows.

acceptable, but the breakfast option is best. A different required rate of return may be used, and we will discuss rate development and choices later in this chapter and Chapter 6.

Investors are accustomed to using rates of return in analyzing potential investments. This is the attraction of IRR. However, while the IRR method is purported to be equivalent to the net present value method, there are some situations in which it does not provide a clear picture of the investment. For instance, some cash flow patterns can produce more than one IRR. This can occur when:

- Investments are of different sizes.
- The timing of the cash flows is different for each project under consideration.
- Negative and positive net cash flows alternate over the life of the project.

When one or more of these is true, the internal rate of return can give results that are misleading and/or difficult to interpret. The analysis of the sail-assisted tanker project presented earlier in the chapter is just such a situation.

In evaluating the sail-assisted tanker project, we noted there would be significant investments at several points over the useful life of the tanker: positive and negative cash flows alternate over the life of the project. At the beginning of the project the tanker will be purchased. Later, extensive engine overhauls will be needed. Thus its net cash flows will be negative in the first year and when the vessel is overhauled in the future. During the intervening years, cash flows will be positive as the company operates the tanker. As a result of having alternating negative and positive net cash flows, several different discount rates exist that make the NPV equal zero. Exhibit 4-8 shows the net present value profile for the sail-assisted tanker project. There are IRRs of both 8.1 and 21.0 percent: the NPV is zero at both discount rates. Does this mean that for companies using discount rates below 8.1 and above 21 percent, the project is acceptable? Yes, it does. Furthermore, if the required rate of return is between 8.1 and 21 percent, the investment should be rejected.

Unfortunately, most computer models and calculators are designed to solve for only one IRR. Thus the analyst may erroneously believe he or she has the complete information necessary to analyze and make a decision about the investment. Because of this and other issues with the IRR, it is helpful to use the net present value profiles. These graphs provide more complete data, and let management avoid making decisions on the IRR alone.

The net present value will tell management or the investor if the investment will maintain or create value at the required rate of return. Thus it provides an unambiguous choice, while the IRR may not. For these and other reasons, the net present value technique is the preferred approach. For those who find rates more comfortable, a net present value profile provides adequate information on which to make a decision.

Exhibit 4-8

Net Present Value Profile—Sail-Assisted Tanker

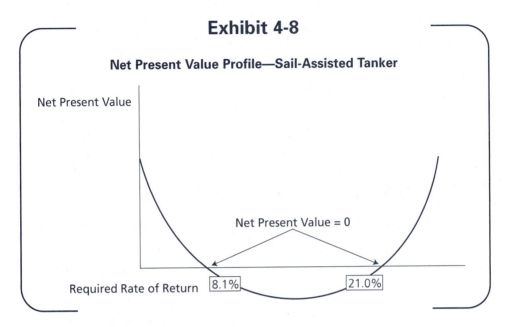

IV. Choosing Among Investments: Simple Valuation Methods

Net present value and IRR by no means are the only two ways that people use to evaluate and rank investments. Most other methods are simple, and have their use in a first glance analysis. However, for understanding the economic benefit of an investment to a company and its shareholders, NPV is preferred.

1. Benefit/Cost Ratio

The easiest way to compare two investments is to compare their benefit/cost ratios. If the benefits of an investment exceed the costs—if the benefit/cost ratio is greater than 1.0—the project is deemed acceptable. In fact, this should be the baseline minimum for any investment: if the undiscounted benefits do not exceed the undiscounted costs, the NPV will not be positive.[29] Keep in mind, however, that the benefit/cost ratio at best is a blunt tool for determining the attractiveness of a project and is a poor measure of relative attractiveness.

For Betty's Better Big Boys' proposed investment in breakfast, the benefit/cost ratio is calculated as follows. This analysis uses the cash flow figures in Exhibit 4-2.

---

[29] This may not be true in the rare case where the benefits of the project are front-loaded and the investment comes late in the project's life. This is not a normal investment.

$$\text{Benefit/cost ratio} = \frac{\text{Benefits}}{\text{Investments}}$$

$$= \frac{\$495 + \$495 + \$495 + \$495 + \$1,395}{\$2,055}$$

$$= \frac{\$3,375}{\$2,055}$$

$$= 1.64$$

A comparable analysis of figures in Exhibit 4-3 yields a ratio of 1.22 ($3,134/$2,575) for the salad, sushi, and pasta bar alternative.

2. Average Payback Period

Average payback period or average payback is similar to the benefit/cost ratio. Quite simply, average payback is used to measure the number of years before the annual benefits of the project are equal to its initial cost. For the breakfast proposal, the average payback period is calculated as follows:

$$\text{Average payback} = \frac{\text{Investment}}{\text{Average yearly benefit}}$$

$$= \frac{\$2,055}{\$675}$$

$$= 3.04 \text{ years}$$

A similar analysis of the salad, sushi, and pasta bar proposal yields an average payback of 4.15 years, using five years to average the yearly benefits.[30]

The average payback period is fraught with problems. First, it does not take into account the fact that the cash flows occur at different times over a five-year period, and we know that the timing of the cash flows is important. Let's look at an example to demonstrate how important timing can be. If we had two projects, one paying all the benefits in the first year, the other paying all the benefits in the final year, both would have identical average payback periods. Obviously they are not identical and management would prefer the investment with the earlier benefits, a fact that this measure disregards.

3. Payback Period

The payback period is similar to the average payback period calculation, except that the actual yearly benefits, rather than the average benefits, are used to calculate the payback period. This method is widely used. Exhibit 4-9 shows the payback calculation for the breakfast option: the payback equals 4.05 years. For the salad, sushi, and pasta bar, the payback is 4.6 years.

---

[30] In this exhibit we use five years of benefits since the depreciation shield that occurs in the sixth year is a convention under IRS depreciation rules. The sixth year has no other benefits from the project.

Exhibit 4-9 Betty's Better Big Boys

Payback Calculation for Breakfast Options

(in thousands)

Period	Investment	Cash Flow	Remaining Investment
0	$2,055		$ 2,055
1		$ 495	1,560
2		495	1,065
3		495	570
4		495	75
5		$1,395	$(1,320)

Total payback is
4 + ($75/$1,395)
= 4.05 years

Whether a payback of 4.05 years is adequate for the breakfast option is a decision for Betty's management. To use the measure, management typically sets a limit on the length of the payback period it will accept and reject those investments with longer paybacks. To choose among several projects with acceptable payback periods, management selects the project with the fastest payback period.

Payback period can be a useful quick approximation of a project's relative attractiveness. The best use is to determine whether a firm can recover an investment's costs in time to make another planned investment. This is particularly useful when there are rapid changes in products, technology, or the political and economic environment. The problem with the payback method is that it ignores all benefits that are received after the payback date, thus arbitrarily excluding potentially attractive investments with longer lives. It also ignores the time value of money.

Let's look at an example to illustrate this problem. Vast Resources, Inc. (VR) has two projects in which it can invest the $1.5 million it has available. VR management uses a payback criterion of three years and will not accept a project that fails to meet this standard.

Exhibit 4-10 presents data for VR's two projects. On the basis of this data management has chosen to invest in Project A and reject Project B. Do you agree with this choice? Under most circumstances, Project B would be the preferred investment. The situation where Project A is preferred is when VR needs the $1.5 million by the second year for another investment or to pay an obligation. Project B eventually provides a much larger cash flow and should be the most attractive project to management.

The VR example points out obvious problems that can occur when using payback. Similar problems exist when using benefit/cost analysis

Exhibit 4-10   Vast Resources, Inc.

Alternative Investments

(in millions)

	Project A	Project B
Cost	$1.50	$1.50
Residual cash flows:		
Year 1	$1.60	0
2	0	0
3	0	0
4	0	0
5	0	$8.00
Payback	0.94 years	4.19 years
Benefit/cost ratio	107%	533%
Net present value (@ 5%)	$0.02	$4.77

and average payback. None of these methods take the timing of cash flows into account. The benefit/cost ratio treats cash received at all points in time as equal. This presumption does not reflect the reality of investor preferences. While the payback method attempts to take investors' preferences for early cash flows into account, it fails to take into consideration cash flows beyond the payback period. We know later cash flows are not irrelevant to investors, particularly if they are large. Thus, none of these methods that evaluate investments solely on the size or speed of their returns adequately incorporate the investor's time value of money—the return the investor would expect to earn on a riskless investment.

4. Present Value Payback

In an attempt to meld present value techniques and payback, analysts have developed this simplistic adaptation of the payback called the present value payback. To calculate a present value payback, discount each residual net cash flow to its equivalent present value. These discounted present values are summed until the total equals the amount of the original investment. Exhibit 4-11 provides the data needed to calculate the discounted payback for the breakfast project. Using 5 percent as the discount rate, the discounted payback value of this project is 4.27 years. The salad, sushi, and pasta bar project's discounted payback is 4.95 years.

While including the time value of money, the discounted payback still ignores cash flows beyond the payback period. This is a particularly critical fault when projects with large future returns, such as new products, are being considered. It is neither necessary nor appropriate to discriminate arbitrarily against projects with returns in the more distant future.

Exhibit 4-11

Breakfast Proposal—Present Value Payback

(in thousands)

Year	Residual Net Cash Flow	Present Value Cash Flow		Remaining Investment
0	$(2,055)	$(2,055)/(1.05)^0 =	$(2,055.00)	$2,055.00
1	495	495/(1.05)^1 =	471.43	1,583.57
2	495	495/(1.05)^2 =	448.98	1,134.59
3	495	495/(1.05)^3 =	427.60	706.99
4	495	495/(1.05)^4 =	407.23	299.76
5	1,395	1,395/(1.05)^5 =	1,093.02	

Present value payback = 4.27 years. The 0.27 is calculated as follows:

$$\frac{\$299.76}{\$1,093.02} = 0.27$$

Better methods should, and do, exist to take into account those critical future cash flows.

Net present value and internal rate of return are two frequently used discounting techniques that take all cash flows into consideration. Either method provides a better measure of value than do the simpler ranking methods.

So far, we have assumed that if an investment creates value it should be accepted—the company can and should invest in all attractive projects. In a company with more projects than resources, projects must be ranked from highest to lowest in value, with management choosing the investments with the highest relative values. Since Betty's management had decided that it could accept only one of the two business expansion alternatives, the projects needed to be compared and ranked. The rankings using all our methods are shown in Exhibit 4-12.

No matter which valuation method we use the breakfast option is superior. If there were a disagreement, we would use the net present value as the preferred method: it provides a ranking that is consistent with the goal of value creation. For Betty's Better Big Boys, does this mean that the breakfast proposal is the one management should choose? Maybe, but the breakfast proposal is riskier: customers may not come to breakfast. The salad, sushi, and pasta bar seems less risky because it merely supplements the present sale of sandwiches, a product line and meal in which the restaurants are firmly established. So should management choose the investment that creates less value because it is less risky? Since risk is obviously an issue we must include it in our analysis.

Exhibit 4-12

Value of Breakfast versus Salad, Sushi, and Pasta Bar Options

(dollars in thousands)

Method	Breakfast	Salad, Sushi, and Pasta Bar	Decision Rule

Net present value
   at discount rate of 5%
                      10%
	$793.27
	$380.27
		$68.73
		$(315.24)
			NPV ≥ 0

Present value index at discount rate of 5%	1.39 or 139%	1.03 or 103%	PVI ≥ 1.0
Internal rate of return	15.9%	5.8%	IRR ≥ hurdle rate
Benefit/cost ratio (times)	1.64	1.22	B/C ≥ 1.0
Average payback period	3.04 years	4.15 years	Average payback ≥ management minimum
Payback period	4.05 years	4.60 years	Payback period ≥ management minimum
Present value payback	4.27 years	4.95 years	PV payback ≥ management minimum

V. Assessing and Incorporating Risk

1. Defining Risk

To assess risk we first must define risk. For capital investments the risk is that our residual cash flow forecasts might be wrong—that we might have a higher or lower than expected return.[31] We know that investors, in addition to preferring large and rapid returns, also prefer certain returns. They do not like to take risk unless rewarded to do so. To induce the typical risk-averse investor to invest in risky projects, that investor must anticipate higher returns. The higher the risk, the larger the return premium that is required to compensate for that risk.

Of all the problems facing the investment analyst, risk is the most troublesome. In spite of the fact that many have sought the best definition and way to analyze risk, so far there is no ideal method for incorporating risk into the formal assessment of an investment's value. There are some ways that investors and managers include risk, and while none is flawless, we will discuss several and describe both how they are used and the prob-

---

[31] There are a number of sources of risk in any kind of strategy or investment, but all result in either wrong or highly variable forecasts. We will discuss what can be done about both kinds of risk—errors and variability—later in this chapter.

lems with each. To be clear, understanding, analyzing, and intelligently incorporating risk into our analysis is critical to valuation.

In analyzing most corporate investments, management assumes that it does not change the company's risk. Explicitly, management assumes that the risk of the investment is identical to that of the company as a whole: the cash flows for the project are as predictable as those from the firm's current business. Once that assumption is made, management can use the company's average required return as a discount rate for any new investment prospect, even though this is rarely the situation. In this chapter we will assume that we know the company's discount rate—investors' required return on equity. In Chapters 6 and 7 we will discuss how this return, often called the cost of capital, is estimated.

2. Changing the Discount Rate

The simplest way to incorporate risk into investment analysis is in the discount rate. To do this we can use the company's required return on equity to discount an investment's cash flows, especially if the rate is provided. This required return on equity is what the shareholders require for the risk as the company currently exists. However, if the risk of a particular investment clearly is higher or lower than the company's average risk, we would expect that the shareholders would reassess their required ROE for the company plus the new investment. To adjust for the risk differences, management typically increases or decreases the corporate required return on equity. Because we are using the required return on equity to evaluate new investments, it is no longer called the corporate required rate of return or required return on equity, it is called a hurdle rate. As the hurdle rate increases—that is, as investors require greater returns to compensate for greater risks—the net present value of an investment diminishes. You can see the dramatic impact of increasing hurdle rates if you look at the net present value profile in Exhibit 4-7. When the discount rate is 5 percent, the breakfast and salad, sushi, and pasta bar options provide net present values of $793,260 and $68,730, respectively. However, if a 10 percent discount rate is used, the net present values diminish dramatically to $380,269 and a loss of $315,243.[32] In this case, no matter what rate is used, the breakfast proposal is better for Betty's shareholders.

These calculations assume that the risks of Betty's two projects are equal. On the contrary, management believes that opening for breakfast is more risky than adding salad, sushi, and pasta bars: new employees must be hired, a new advertising campaign must be undertaken, new food items will be offered, and a large unrecoverable investment in training is required. The fact is that management is concerned that the forecasts of potential sales and costs of the breakfast option could be wrong. Salad, sushi, and pasta bars, on the other hand, add little to the risk of the firm:

---

[32] A 5 percent rate is typical of a risk-free rate of return. The 10 percent rate is more like a corporate required return on equity. The rates do change, however, with changes in the economy.

the initial investment is small and a portion of it is recoverable; training costs are low; few additional employees must be hired; and if customers don't choose a salad, sushi, or pasta, they are likely to choose items from the old menu. As a result of this analysis, management might conclude that the two projects have different levels of risk, and be concerned about how to include the differences in the comparison.

So far neither academics nor business practitioners have answered this question very well, although many techniques are currently being used. One approach is to present the problem of risk directly to the managers. There are two ways to do this. First, the managers can adjust the company's required rate of return on equity for the risk they perceive in the investment, and use that adjusted rate to calculate the NPV. The method or methods they use to make the adjustment to the required return on equity need not be explicit.

The second way managers can incorporate risk into their analysis is by using the firm's required rate of return on equity as a discount rate. The managers can judge for themselves whether the resulting net present value compensates for the risk of the project. For example, the net present value of the breakfast option at a discount rate of 10 percent is greater by $695,510 than that of the salad, sushi, and pasta bar alternative. Now the managers must ask themselves whether this amount is adequate to compensate for the differences in risk between the two investments. It is up to them to decide.

These two management-adjustment methods can also be called "interrogate the manager" approaches. However, the methods are not scientific or even obvious, so managers often preferred a more structured approach.

3. Risk Categories by Investment Type

Another approach to risk adjustment is to modify the discount rate according to the apparent risk of the investment. For example, new products may be considered to have greater risks than the risk of the firm as a whole. Consequently, management will set a higher hurdle rate for new products than the firm's marginal required return on equity. Many firms use a scheme, such as the one shown in Exhibit 4-13, to categorize investments.

Managers who use a scheme like this believe that investments in cost reductions are less risky than their firm's average risk and that new products are more risky. Using this notion, Betty's management might discount the salad, sushi, and pasta bars' cash flows at a rate of 5 percent, but since breakfast is a new product and is considered by management to be riskier its cash flows might be discounted at an even higher rate, for instance, 10 percent. Doing this, the NPV for the breakfast proposal is $380,269. This still exceeds by $311,539 the NPV for the less risky salad bar. Thus, the breakfast proposal would be selected.

While some variety of this risk-adjustment scheme is often used, it has two flaws. First, it leads to predictable results: discounted at higher rates the new products are less attractive, whereas cost-reduction projects are

Exhibit 4-13

Risk Categories for Investment Analysis

Investment Category	Risk Level	Hurdle Rate
Cost reduction	Less than firm's average risk	Lower than firm's required rate of return
Plant expansion	Average risk	Marginal average required rate of return
New products	Higher than average risk	Higher rate than required rate of return

usually acceptable.[33] This may or may not be appropriate for the specific firm or investment. Second, it is difficult to determine the appropriate changes to make to the discount rate: should the differences between "risky" and "less risky" projects be 5 or 10 percent, or more or less? These two problems make finding a better method for dealing with risk very important.

4. Risk Adjustment by Division or Product Line

In many of the methods of risk adjustment we have used, management uses as its rate the company's required return on equity. However, this rate is an average of all the risks in the company, and thus may not reflect the risk of a particular division or product line. Managers of companies with a number of divisions or lines of business often adapt the overall company-required return on equity for the specific risks of a division or product line.[34] Because the required rate of return for a division is not available, a number of methods are used to estimate the appropriate discount rate. Most often the rate is calculated by using information about a number of publicly traded proxy firms—firms with similar characteristics. These proxy methods, while imprecise, are better than using a single rate for businesses and investments that have different levels of risk.[35]

5. Danger of Raising Discount Rates: New Products and New Processes

Companies face real risks when introducing new products or processes. When new products are introduced to customers, management does not

---

[33] In fact, if management wants to encourage the "riskier" projects, such as new products, to build the company's future, this scheme effectively cuts off those opportunistic growth projects, or forces managers who champion them to adapt the numbers to get them accepted.

[34] This divisional or line-of-business required rate of return may be further adapted for the risk inherent in the individual investment being considered.

[35] Estimating required returns for divisions and projects will be discussed in Chapter 6.

know if the customers will accept the product or, if they do, how enthusiastically. Such things as test markets, focus groups, product sampling, and advertising are designed to increase the trial rate of customers, and thus the size of the market for the product. But will those strategies work? Will the consumers buy the product? How many? Will the competition emulate the product, or even introduce a more attractive alternative? These are real risks that face management when introducing a new product. Because of this, management often raises the discount rate for new products. The same occurs for new technologies where management is not certain of the technology or its impact on the workforce or process.

Should management raise the discount rate for these high-risk investments? Maybe it should, but maybe not. The question management must ask itself is, Will the risk persist over the life of the investment, or is it a short-term phenomena? Will we know with much greater certainty what the cash flows for this investment will be after the initial shakeout period?

Often the high levels of uncertainty last only a short period of time: the product is introduced and either the customers buy it or not; the new process is put in place and it either works as expected or not. Once the initial period of uncertainty is over, management knows much better what to expect. This does not mean that the returns will be good—they could be bad. Good or bad once the trial period is over, management has much greater certainty about the outcome, and thus risk is reduced.

Is raising a discount rate, a rate that impacts the cash flows over the whole life of the project, the best way to deal with this temporary risk? No. The discount rate should reflect the risk over the life of the project, not just the short term. It should reflect the risks that come from changes in the basic assumptions about the economy. There are better ways to deal with these company-specific, shorter term, shakeout period risks. Scenario analysis is one approach and contingent claims another. Both of these will be discussed in the following sections.

6. Cash Flow Manipulation to Incorporate Risk

Instead of changing the discount rate, some managers and analysts manipulate the cash flows to account for risk. The most simplistic method of revising the cash flows for risk is commonly called "conservative" forecasting. To do this, Betty's management might decide to use a conservative forecast for breakfast sales, lower than their best estimate, and a conservative forecast for costs, higher than their best estimate. This is not an unusual approach. However, a conservative forecast is one that typically overestimates costs and underestimates revenues, even if in management's best judgment that is not what is likely to happen. The conservative forecast does not reflect a set of likely circumstances, and it often has little likelihood of actually occurring. Thus, rather than being conservative, such a forecast is wrong. "Conservative" estimates paint an inaccurate picture of the real potential of the project. While such conservatism is broadly practiced, the good analyst will seek the most accurate forecasts and analyze risk using a different method.

There are two other ways to include management's uncertainty into our analysis. Both of these methods are based on forecasting multiple scenarios—several probable outcomes for costs and benefits for the investment. Each scenario should be based on a realistic forecast of what might happen to the investment under different economic, competitive, or technological futures.

7. Multi-Scenario Analysis

In the simple use of multiple scenario analysis, an analyst forecasts just three alternative outcomes for an investment—optimistic, pessimistic, and most likely—for each of the costs and benefits.[36] The forecasts made for the breakfast project (shown in Exhibit 4-2) were management's most likely estimates. However, management was uncertain about what would occur if it opened Betty's restaurants for breakfast. If sales from the new breakfast menu exceeded the most likely estimate of $15 million, the operating costs as a percentage of sales might be expected to be slightly lower since some costs (for instance, maintenance) would not increase with sales. Likewise, if sales were lower than expected, operating costs would not decrease as fast as sales and the net profit might be lower. Exhibit 4-14 provides management's optimistic, most likely, and pessimistic

Exhibit 4-14   Betty's Better Big Boys

Breakfast Proposal—Annual Residual Cash Flows

(in thousands of real dollars)

	Pessimistic	Most Likely	Optimistic
Incremental sales	$ 3,300	$ 15,000	$ 26,000
Operating expenses*	(3,168)	(14,250)	(24,440)
Depreciation	0	0	0
Pretax profit	132	750	1,560
Taxes (34%)	(45)	(255)	(530)
Profit after taxes	87	495	1,030
Noncash charges	0	0	0
Residual net cash flow†	$ 87	$ 495	$ 1,030
Net present value (@ 5%)	$ (973)	$ 793	$ 3,110

*Operating expenses are projected by management to decline as sales increase. Management expects them to be 96, 95, and 94 percent of sales, respectively.
† This assumes that each year's cash flows follow the pattern shown in Exhibit 4-2.

---

[36] This is a different use of the three-scenario forecast that we first used in Chapter 2.

scenarios for the breakfast proposal's cash flows. The net present value for each scenario is given at the bottom of the exhibit. Obviously, the investment cost of $2.055 million remains the same regardless of the success of the project.[37]

If the pessimistic scenario materializes, the company will experience a loss from offering breakfast. The net present value of the breakfast project is negative: the costs exceed the benefits. Using a higher discount rate reduces the net present value further. However, if customers find the new breakfast menu appealing the project could be quite a boon to Betty's and its shareholders: the net present value would be very attractive. What should management do given these three different potential outcomes?

To decide whether to proceed with the breakfast proposal, management must decide on the likelihood of the pessimistic scenario occurring and whether the most likely and optimistic scenarios are attractive enough, that is it will create enough value, to offset this danger.

Those who use this three-scenario analysis approach implicitly assume that each scenario is equally likely and use the information to decide whether the company, the management, and the shareholders could tolerate the pessimistic scenario if it were to occur, or if the upside, the optimistic scenario, is sufficiently attractive to offset the potential pessimistic outcome.

When creating the scenarios, management does not need to believe that each of the outcomes is equally likely to occur. Using the breakfast proposal as an example, management might think it most likely, based on the experience of other fast-food restaurants in introducing a breakfast menu, that the breakfast proposal will have sales of $15 million as predicted in Exhibit 4-2. While $15 million is a good estimate of the expected sales, there is a reasonable chance that the innovative menu Betty's management is planning will be very successful. Thus the three outcomes would not be equally likely. In addition, management may estimate more than three possible scenarios. In Exhibit 4-15 you see that management has estimated five alternative outcomes for the breakfast proposal. In addition, the likelihood of each is estimated.

Once the estimates are made, management weights the net present value for each scenario by the probability that it will occur. The result is the probability-weighted net present value, the **expected value**.[38] Exhibit 4-15 provides the result of such an analysis. While the net present value of $957,000 is not one that management explicitly forecasted, it represents an average expected for the project.[39]

---

[37] A reminder: these scenarios should not be based on the worst (or best) outcomes possible for every cost and benefit. Such a forecast is usually possible but quite improbable. Possible but not probable forecasts give management very little information on which to base decisions. Therefore, in making these forecasts the analyst must take care that all three sets of forecasts are probable, not just possible.

[38] To calculate the expected value you multiply each outcome by its probability and sum the products.

[39] Management also could compute a standard deviation to obtain a measure of risk.

Exhibit 4-15

Probabilistic Analysis—Breakfast Proposal

(in thousands of real dollars)

Scenario	Probability	Net Present Value	Weighted Value
1	15%	$ (977)	$(147)
2	20	(102)	(20)
3	30	793	238
4	20	2,100	420
5	15	3,105	466
Expected value =			**$ 957**

This is a rather simple analysis. Management may have an investment with numerous costs and benefits for which it could assess probabilities. In these cases, computer-assisted analysis, especially simulation, provides a good means for analyzing the complex data and estimating the expected.[40]

One word of caution in the use of multiple scenario, expected value analysis: the method depends upon the company engaging in a number of projects at the same time, or over time. If only one project is undertaken, only one outcome can occur—no other project exists with which to average the results. In order for the expected value to represent the company's average net present value, the company must analyze and make a number of investments: it must have a portfolio of investments.[41] In a portfolio the company earns the weighted average of the returns from all its investments. This is particularly true if the investments are not all concentrated in one product, process, market, and/or technology.[42]

Simulation analysis is used by an increasing number of companies. Managers find that the discipline of deciding what might occur for each of the various costs and benefits keeps their assumptions reasonable and makes the analysis even more useful. Although this technique is time-consuming, the increasing use of computers has made multiple scenario simulation and analysis more accessible and useful.

Probabilistic analysis can yield rich information for a knowledgeable user, but it holds dangers for the naive. For managers, analysts, and in-

---

[40] One way to measure the potential variation of the net present value is the standard deviation.

[41] For a single investment there is just one outcome. In this case, expected value is useless. For a group of projects with different outcomes, the company receives the average.

[42] This is the basis of portfolio theory, the basics of which were discussed in the context of a securities portfolio. The theory and mathematics are rich, and sources for greater understanding of these portfolio concepts are listed at the end of the chapter.

vestors, much of the value of forecasting and multiple scenario analysis comes from the insight gained during the modeling process.

8. Upside Risk Analysis—Contingent Claims Analysis

All the forms of risk analysis that we have described in this chapter treat risk as a negative attribute: as risk increases so must the investors' required rate of return; decreases in risk reduce the required return. Virtually all investments have upsides and downsides. Virtually none are immune to changes in customers' requirements, competitive pressures, and economic change. All these investments have the possibility that their cash flows, and thus their value, could be higher or lower. Not all investments have the same sort of upside and downside possibilities, however. In some cases, management can avoid some or most of the downside—the negative cash flows—by purchasing insurance, arranging a partnership with another company, or halting a losing project. Eliminating the downside typically has a cost, however, and managers will want to be certain that the cost is appropriate.

The usual approaches to risk analysis require that roughly equivalent upside and downside cash flow potentials exist. In statistics we would call this a normal distribution. How does a manager or analyst evaluate an investment where the potential losses have been reduced or eliminated? Analysts have adapted option-pricing techniques to value the investment with a non-normal distribution. The methods developed for valuing options in the securities markets have real potential for analyzing certain kinds of capital investments. Those investments are called contingent claims or investments with embedded options. A **contingent claim**, or **option**, is the right to buy or further invest later in a set of assets at a particular price, or the right to abandon the investment at a point in the future at a known cost.

In the capital markets, standardized contingent claims, called calls and puts, are available and traded. A traded **call option** gives the option holder the right to buy a stock or index at a particular price up until some specified date in the future. A **put option** allows the holder to sell a stock or index at a preset price up to a date in the future. Using the option is called **exercising** the option. There are some calls and puts that are only exercisable at a particular time. These are called **European options**. Those that can be exercised for a period of time are called **American options**.

What is the advantage to having a contingent claim, or option, rather than making the investment in the first place? First, the cost for this contingent claim is much smaller than the cost of making the full investment. Second, the investor can choose to exercise the claim on the investment or not: if the investor chooses not to exercise the claim, the only cost is the initial cost of the option. Thus, for a small price, the investor has the right, but not the obligation, to make the investment.

To demonstrate this, let's use an example. Consider the following: Strike-It-Rich Oil Co. has just heard that the government is going to sell drilling rights in a remote jungle area in the interior of the country. From satellite maps, the area appears to have the necessary conditions for oil, so Strike-It-Rich management is interested. If it buys the right to drill in the area, management can decide later, or after more exploration, whether to make the investment in complete exploration and development of oil wells. The cost of the right to drill is small, the cost of developing wells is large, but Strike-It-Rich does not have to drill.

The typical discounted cash flow analysis that we have used in this chapter would discount all the costs associated with this investment and all the benefits that might accrue. Those costs would include exploration, drilling, and transporting the oil, as well as the benefit of the proceeds from the sale of the oil. Yet, at this point, management is not even sure that it is going to drill. With an option, Strike-It-Rich management can stop investing at any point and walk away from the project. The option places a management-controlled limit on the losses, and it is up to management's discretion whether to invest. Discounted cash flow has a hard time dealing with this sort of dynamic, if/then sort of possibility that is coupled with an investment. This is dynamic decision making, and it is not incorporated into a traditional discounted cash flow analysis.

Discounted cash flow analysis is static. It presumes that management cannot make changes once the investment is made. Contingent claims or options analysis is dynamic. Management can make changes to the investment once it is made. Thus contingent claims analysis is more realistic. One of the critical differences between the two forms of analysis is that a static technique like NPV does not adequately consider the risk of projects that have **embedded options**—options to be taken later at the discretion of management. When the investor has an option, high potential variability is attractive: it increases the possibility of reaping the rewards from the investment, without having locked in the potential downside. NPV analysis treats variability as risk, assigns it a cost, and discounts the higher risk (more variable) cash flows at higher rates than the rate at which it discounts more certain cash flows. The result is that NPV analysis often unduly penalizes the value of investments that have contingent claims embedded in them. In a dynamic world, they should not be penalized but sought.

Option-pricing techniques are one form of capital investment analysis that allow us to value dynamic projects where decisions about what will happen can be made later. Since these techniques are rather new in their application to capital investment analysis, a detailed description of how they are implemented is not included in this chapter but is in Appendix 4A to this chapter. Whether you have a fleeting or in-depth knowledge of this type of analysis, the forward-thinking analyst should know that discounted cash flow analysis deals with both limited-loss and later investment-in-growth projects very poorly, and that option-pricing methods lend themselves well to analyzing such problems. Thus, analysts and managers who are faced with analyzing investments that have such characteristics should read further.

None of the widely available risk-adjustment methods is completely satisfactory. Therefore, while new methods for incorporating risk into capital investment decision making are being developed or learned, some managers assign different hurdle rates to divisions or strategic business units that are exposed to different levels of risk. Other managers attempt to quantify risk differences for each individual investment. Still others use statistical techniques, such as probabilistic simulation analysis, to estimate directly the riskiness of investments. Still others try to incorporate and value options. To date, risk is the most difficult problem in assessing value.

VI. Other Considerations in Creating Value

Not all investments are as complex or as risky as our Betty's Better Big Boys examples. Some are simple replacements of old, antiquated, or technologically inferior equipment. Analysis of one of these replacement investments will allow us to examine the impact of such things as different methods of depreciation and taxes on an investment's cash flows and its value.

1. The Impact of Taxes and Depreciation on Value

Depreciation and taxes can have a major impact on the value of an investment. While most managers and investors would tell you not to invest when the only real value comes from avoiding taxes, let's turn to Betty's Better Big Boys to look at the impact of taxes.

Management is considering a replacement investment—microwave ovens. Currently, each of Betty's restaurants uses conventional electric ovens to heat foods. Such ovens are large, take an average of 10 minutes to heat the food and, because they warm up slowly, must be kept hot whether they are being used or not.

Microwave ovens have been proposed to replace these ovens. They are small, cook much more rapidly and, because the method of heating and cooking is totally different, need only be turned on when actually in use. Thus, the primary savings would be in the expense for electricity.

Management has made the following estimates of the costs and benefits associated with each new oven.

1. Microwave ovens can be purchased, fully installed, for $630 by July.
2. The old ovens can be sold to a used-equipment dealer for their book value of $25 each. Thus the sale is not taxable.
3. While annual usage and costs of electricity vary from restaurant to restaurant, the average cost per year per oven has been $300. The new ovens would use about one-third the electricity, for a cost of $100 per oven per year.
4. The new ovens are expected to be fully useful for five years. After that time, the ovens will be obsolete or in need of substantial repair. Management believes the ovens would have no salvage value at the end of the fifth year. Management would depreciate the new ovens over six years, according to the 1999 tax code.

This is a straightforward problem. As you can see in Exhibit 4-16, reduced costs are treated the same as increased income. The NPV (at a 10

Exhibit 4-16 Betty's Better Big Boys

Microwave Oven Investment Analysis—Per Oven

(in thousands)				Period			
	0	1	2	3	4	5	6
Income Statement Changes:							
Revenues		0	0	0	0	0	0
Electricity:							
Old oven		$(300.0)	$(300.0)	$(300.0)	$(300.0)	$(300.0)	0
New oven		(100.0)	(100.0)	(100.0)	(100.0)	(100.0)	0
Electricity cost decrease		200.0	200.0	200.0	200.0	200.0	0
Depreciation:							
Old depreciation		0	0	0	0	0	0
New depreciation		(121.0)	(193.6)	(116.2)	(69.7)	(69.7)	$(34.8)
Depreciation increase		(121.0)	(193.6)	(116.2)	(69.7)	(69.7)	(34.8)
Change in pretax profits		79.0	6.4	83.8	130.3	130.3	(34.8)
Taxes (@ 34%)*		(26.9)	(2.2)	(28.5)	(44.3)	(44.3)	11.8
Profit after taxes		52.1	4.2	55.3	86.0	86.0	(23.0)
Noncash Charges:							
Net depreciation		121.0	193.6	116.2	69.7	69.7	34.8
Asset Changes:							
Property, plant, and equipment:							
Microwave oven	$(605.0)						
Old oven salvage value	25.0						
Net cash flow	$(580.0)	$ 173.1	$ 197.8	$ 171.5	$ 155.7	$ 155.7	$ 11.8
Net present value at 10% =	$79.44						
Internal rate of return =	15.3%						

*Negative taxes are a tax credit against earnings in other portions of the company's business.

percent discount rate) is $79.44 per oven and the IRR is 15.3 percent. This appears to be a reasonable investment opportunity.[43]

However, there are changes within management's discretion that can increase the value of the investment. As an example, under certain tax codes management could have elected to use a different method of depreciation. Exhibit 4-17 shows the impact of using other depreciation methods on the value of the microwave oven investment. The double-declining-balance method yields the largest increase in the project's value.

At first glance, this may seem like numerical black magic, but it is a real change in the value of the investment to the company. While the same total depreciation is taken over the life of the investment regardless of the depreciation method, the amount taken in each year is different. It is the timing of the taxes that is different. Since the discounting process deems earlier cash flows to be more valuable than those received later, and since accelerated depreciation methods result in larger, earlier cash flows, the method of depreciation chosen by management can create value. As shown in Exhibit 4-17, the present values under each tax code are different. Accelerated depreciation methods result in higher values, and the double-declining-balance method has the highest net present value.

This analysis of the differences in the way the tax law treats depreciation illustrates the impact external factors can have on the operations and decisions of the company. With the tax shield having a significant impact on the attractiveness of a project, the analyst should always be informed of not only current tax regulations but pending legislation as well. Keeping abreast of the economic, social, and political environment is essential for the analyst in order to analyze managerial decisions properly.

2. Including Investment-Size Considerations

We have looked at three investments Betty's Better Big Boys' could choose—the breakfast service; the salad, sushi, and pasta bar; and an investment in microwave ovens. Each alternative has a different net present value. While the breakfast option appears to be the best choice, we have failed to take note of the fact that each investment requires different amounts of capital. If we simply compare the net present values of the three alternatives, we have ignored the magnitude of invested capital—more capital should provide a higher net present value. As an example, all 500 microwave ovens require a net investment of only $302,500 while the breakfast proposal requires $2.055 million, a difference of $1.7525 million. That means that if management chose the microwave investment it would have $1.75 million still available for another investment. What would management do with the added $1.75 million? To compare the investments fairly, we must compare the investments of the same size. To do otherwise is to compare different corporate strategies for using $2.055 million.

---

[43] An analysis for ovens for all 500 restaurants would yield the same IRR of 15.3 percent, but an NPV of $39,720 (500 × $79.44).

Exhibit 4-17

Yearly Depreciation Charge—Different Depreciation Methods for the Microwave Oven Investment (in thousands)

	0	1	2	3	4	5	6
Cash Flows							
Straight line*	$605.0	$121.0	$121.0	$121.0	$121.0	$121.0	
Double-declining balance†	605.0	242.0	145.2	87.1	65.3	65.3	
Sum-of-years' digits‡	605.0	201.7	161.3	121.0	80.7	40.3	
U.S. ACRS§	605.0	90.8	133.1	127.1	127.1	127.1	
MACRS/1999 U.S. tax code§§	605.0	121.0	193.6	116.2	69.7	69.7	$34.8
Net Present Value (@ 10%)							
Straight line	$76.3						
Double-declining balance	$87.2						
Sum-of-years' digits	$86.2						
U.S. ACRS	$74.6						
MACRS/1999 U.S. tax code	$79.4						
Internal Rate of Return							
Straight line	15.0%						
Double-declining balance	16.1%						
Sum-of-years' digits	16.0%						
U.S. ACRS	14.9%						
MACRS/1999 U.S. tax code	15.3%						

*The depreciation rate is calculated by dividing 100 percent by the number of years. In this case, the depreciation rate is $100/5 = 20$ percent per year. To determine yearly depreciation, multiply the purchase price, minus the salvage value, by the depreciation rate.

† Double the straight-line depreciation rate is multiplied by the fully depreciated value of the asset. A switch to straight-line depreciation occurs when it is larger.

‡ To calculate the sum-of-the years' digits factor:

a) Sum the numbers of the years, in this case $5 + 4 + 3 + 2 + 1 = 15$.

b) For each year, divide the number of remaining years by the summed years. In this case, the depreciation factor for the first year is $5/15$ or 0.33.

c) Multiply the depreciable value by this factor.

§ Five-year U.S. ACRS rates are 15 percent the first year, 22 percent the second year, and 21 percent the remaining three years.

§§ MACRS depreciates at the following rates: 20, 32, 19.2, 11.52, 11.52, and 5.76 percent, for years one through six, respectively.

Must management know the intended use for the extra capital in order to compare the projects? No, management can examine the value the added investment would create for the owners and decide if the return is sufficient. To do this we must follow a two-step process. First, management must forecast the cash flows for the two alternatives and, second, calculate the differences in the initial costs and the annual residual cash flows between the two investments. Exhibit 4-18 shows the results of this analysis of differences between the breakfast and microwave oven options for Betty's Better Big Boys. By looking at the last column in the exhibit, you can see that the breakfast option would require an additional investment of $1.75 million beyond that required for installing microwave ovens in all the restaurants. But what does Betty's and its shareholders get for its investment?

To determine the benefit, we can discount the differences between the two sets of cash flows. The discounted value of the differential benefits, also shown in column 3, is $340,545. The incremental investment the breakfast option requires makes a significant contribution to the shareholders' value. This is the incremental present value from investing $1.75 million more in the breakfast proposal than what is invested in the microwave ovens. Of course, Betty's management will want to compare this with the present values that could be earned on other ways to invest $1.75 million. Whatever use management might have for the $1.75 million, the exhibit clearly shows that the return would have to be more than 16.0 percent (the incremental IRR) to render any other use equal to the

Exhibit 4-18 Betty's Better Big Boys

Residual Net Cash Flows—Two Alternatives

(in thousands)

	(1) Breakfast Option	(2) 500 Microwave Ovens	(1) – (2) Breakfast – Microwave Oven Difference
Net investment	$(2,055,000)	$(290,000)	$(1,765,000)
Annual net cash flows			
0	(2,055,000)	(290,000)	$(1,765,000)
1	495,000	86,570	408,430
2	495,000	98,912	396,088
3	495,000	85,747	409,253
4	495,000	77,848	417,152
5	1,395,000	77,848	1,317,152
6	0	5,924	(5,924)
NPV (at 10%)	$380,269	$39,723	$340,545
IRR	15.9%	15.3%	16.0%

return from the breakfast investment. Management would likely conclude that the incremental return on the added investment in the breakfast option is attractive.[44]

3. Incorporating Timing Differences into Investment Analysis

In the last section we laid out a method for making two investments of different sizes comparable. Comparability on every dimension is important for making realistic, economically appropriate capital budgeting choices. While there are many other differences that can make investments noncomparable, another frequent and important one is a difference in lives. When two investments will exist for different lengths of time, they are not comparable.

When investments have different lives, we need a way to make them comparable. To do this we make them have the same life. This may sound a bit odd so let's use an example to show what we would do. We have a choice of two machines that will serve the same purpose. One machine costs $800 and will result in a net cash flow of $300 per year for six years. The second machine costs only $400, and it, too, will produce a cash flow of $300 per year for three years. Which is the best? From the data in Exhibit 4-19, it appears as if the more expensive machine is the clear winner. However, the two have different lives: one produces cash flows for six years, the other for only three years.

Exhibit 4-19

Net Present Value of Two Alternative Machines—Unequal Lives

Panel A: More Expensive Machine

| | | | | Year | | | |
	0	1	2	3	4	5	6
Net cash flow		$300	$300	$300	$300	$300	$300
Purchase of equipment	$(800)						
Net present value (@ 10%)	$506.58						

Panel B: Less Expensive Machine

| | | | Year | |
	0	1	2	3
Net cash flow		$300	$300	$300
Purchase of equipment	$(400)			
Net present value (@ 10%)	$346.06			

---

[44] If Betty's Better Big Boys had a number of investments of different sizes, the comparisons made in Exhibit 4-18 would have to be repeated for each pair of investments.

The problem with this analysis is that we are comparing two different strategies: a machine lasting six years with one lasting three. We want to compare equivalent strategies for machine use. To do this we can compare the more expensive six-year machine with two machines with three-year lives. This is done in Exhibit 4-20. To create this exhibit we simply assumed that the company bought two less expensive machines: one at time zero and the other at the end of the third year.

Exhibit 4-20

Net Present Value of Two Alternative Machines—Equal Lives

Panel A: More Expensive Machine

	0	1	2	Year 3	4	5	6
Net cash flow		$300	$300	$300	$300	$300	$300
Purchase of equipment	$(800)						
Net present value	$506.58						

Panel B: Two Sequential Less Expensive Machines

	0	1	2	Year 3	4	5	6
Net cash flow		$300	$300	$300	$300	$300	$300
Purchase of equipment	$(400)			$(400)			
Net cash flow	$(400)	$300	$300	$(100)	$300	$300	$300
Net present value	$606.05						

As you can see from Exhibit 4-20, two machines are better than one; they have a higher net present value.[45] Clearly, the wrong decision would have been made had the lives of the project not been taken into account.[46]

4. Incorporating Expected Inflation

Inflation can have a neutral, positive, or negative effect on the value of an investment, depending on whether managers can pass on their costs in the form of prompt or leading price increases. If cost increases can be passed on immediately and fully, the relative value of the project will re-

---

[45] We have used real, not nominal, numbers so the two machines are the same price.

[46] In reality, the two sequential machines are even more valuable. Management could, at its discretion, choose a different machine or abandon the project altogether at the end of the third year, with no consequences. The flexibility has a value. In Appendix A we discuss this.

main the same regardless of the level of inflation. If there is a lag between the company's costs increase and when it can raise prices, however, inflation can have a negative effect on the value of a project. Of course, if management can raise prices in advance of, or more than, inflation or has cash that it can invest, the company can prosper from inflation.[47]

Inflation can have yet other effects. Revenues themselves may rise or fall depending on the rate of inflation. For instance, if more people eat breakfast at fast-food restaurants than at traditional restaurants when inflation and prices rise, Betty's Better Big Boys may find that its revenues rise in both real terms (more customers are eating breakfast) and in nominal terms (prices rise to account for the increased costs of producing the same number of breakfasts).

The effects of these increases should be well understood by management. Up to now, all the cash flows forecasted for Betty's investments were in real terms—they did not include inflation. Exhibit 4-21 provides a forecast for the salad, sushi, and pasta bar proposal that management is considering, with 10 percent inflation. In this example there is no real increase in revenues and unit sales remain the same; the only increases arise from the expected inflation. Cash flow inflation alone increases the net present value (at a discount rate of 10 percent) from a negative $315,240 to a positive $452,408

Before you conclude that inflation has increased the value of this project, remember that we discounted these cash flows at 10 percent, the same rate we used on the cash flows before we introduced inflation. Investors do not ignore inflation. If the required return for this project was 10 percent before inflation, investors certainly will expect a higher return once they expect inflation. Using a more appropriate discount rate of 20 percent (10 percent for the required return and 10 percent for inflation) results in an NPV loss of $331,315.[48] Obviously, inflation's effect on value in this case is negative, not positive.

You might have noted that depreciation in Exhibit 4-21 did not change from that in Exhibit 4-3. This is because in many countries depreciation schedules for capitalized property are calculated on the basis of **historical cost**, the cost when it was purchased. Companies are not allowed to revalue assets to incorporate inflation-driven changes. As a result of this situation, as the rate of inflation increases, depreciation does not change, and neither do the taxes that are deferred by the depreciation tax shield. Thus, in an inflationary environment, the investment in a capitalized asset is less valuable. Appendix 4B describes this inflation drag, which is one of the insidious costs of inflation. In some countries, particularly those with high rates of inflation that have persisted for some time, companies are allowed to increase the book value of fixed assets to keep pace with inflation. As the book value rises, the depreciation

---

[47] Terra Blanca, an example used in Chapter 2, showed such inflation-related gains.
[48] We will discuss the impact of inflation on discount rates in Chapter 6. In this case, adding the two rates together slightly undercounts the combination of the two rates. More appropriately it would be 21 percent (1.1 × 1.1).

Exhibit 4-21 Betty's Better Big Boys

Salad, Sushi, and Pasta Bar Proposal—Marginal Costs and Benefits with Annual Inflation of 10%

(thousands of dollars)	0	1	2	3	4	5	6
Income Statement Changes							
Sales		$ 8,250	$ 9,075	$ 9,983	$ 10,981	$ 12,079	
Operating expenses		(7,664)	(8,430)	(9,273)	(10,200)	(11,220)	—
Training costs	$ (416)	0					
Depreciation		(280)	(448)	(269)	(161)	(161)	$(81)
Profit before taxes	(416)	306	197	441	620	698	(81)
Taxes	141	(104)	(67)	(150)	(211)	(237)	28
Net profit	(275)	202	130	291	409	461	(53)
Noncash Charges							
Depreciation		280	448	269	161	161	81
Capital Investments							
Property, plant, and equipment	(1,400)						
New inventory	(900)	0	0	0	0	1,449	0
Residual net cash flow	$(2,575)	$ 482	$ 578	$ 560	$ 570	$ 2,071	$ 28

Net present value @ 5%	$1,004.14
Net present value @ 10%	$452.41
Net present value @ 20%	$(331.32)

Note: If we had not grown the inventory with inflation, the NPVs would have been lower.

increases as well, keeping pace with inflation.[49] For companies operating in these environments, profits actually increase at a rate comparable to that of inflation.

VII. Summary

Good investments are critical to the future of a company. The analyst's job is to gather and analyze the relevant information and present it in a way that allows managers to make informed decisions. Analysts have four major problems in assessing potential investments:

1. Determining the appropriate cash costs and benefits. That process, as we have suggested, can be difficult, particularly when evaluating replacement investments or when operating in an inflationary environment.
2. Evaluating the relative attractiveness of the investment's net marginal benefits. We suggest that the NPV method is the most appropriate technique to use in measuring this value.[50]
3. Incorporating risk into the evaluation of any investment. If all of the investments are of a risk similar to that of the firm, it is appropriate to adjust for risk by using the firm's marginal required return as a hurdle rate. If the investment is more or less risky than the firm, the analyst may leave it to the managers to decide subjectively whether the return is adequate to compensate for the risk. Other managers find the information from multiple scenario or simulation analysis to be useful in making their decisions, while still others prefer to adjust the required return to compensate for risk. Understanding and incorporating risk into an analysis is one of the most difficult things that faces investors, and ignoring it is not a sensible approach.
4. Determining whether the investment meets the analytical criteria of the NPV analysis. If the investment is deterministic, it is. If the investment has contingencies, the analyst must consider them using a form of contingent claims analysis.

After reading this chapter you should have no doubt that analyzing the investments a company makes is challenging and critical.

Selected References

For comprehensive reviews of the capital budgeting process, see:
   Bierman, Harold, and Seymour Smidt. *Capital Budgeting Decision.* 8th ed. Englewood Cliffs, NJ: Prentice Hall, 1992.

---

[49] It depends upon the index used to calculate the inflation adjustment. The adjustment usually is statutory.
[50] Augmented by contingent claims analysis when appropriate.

Brealey, Richard A., and Stewart C. Myers. *Capital Investment and Valuation*. New York: McGraw-Hill, 2002.

Levy, Haim, and Marshall Sarnot. *Capital Investment and Financial Decisions*. Englewood Cliffs, NJ: Prentice Hall International, 1990.

Peterson, Pam, and Frank Fabozzi. *Capital Budgeting: Theory and Practice*. Hoboken, NJ: John Wiley and Sons, 2002.

Shapiro, Alan. "Corporate Strategy and the Capital Budgeting Decision." *Midland Corporate Finance Journal*, Spring 1985, pp. 22–36.

For an analysis of the capital budgeting and planning process in one firm, see:

Bower, Joseph. *Managing the Resource Allocation Process: A Study of Corporate Planning and Investments*. Homewood, IL: Richard D. Irwin, 1970.

For descriptions of various approaches to risk analysis, see:

Bodie, Zvi, and Robert Merton. *Finance*. Upper Saddle River, NJ: Prentice Hall, 2000, chap. 10.

Bower, Richard S., and J. M. Jenks. "Divisional Screening Rates." *Financial Management*, Autumn 1975, pp. 42–49.

Damodoran, Aswath. *Corporate Finance*. New York: John Wiley & Sons, 2001, chaps. 10 and 11.

Hertz, David B. "Risk Analysis in Capital Investment." *Harvard Business Review*, September–October 1979, pp. 169–81.

Weston, J. Fred. "Investment Decisions Using the Capital Asset Pricing Model." *Financial Management*, Spring 1973, pp. 25–33.

For information on the effects of inflation on capital budgeting analysis, see:

Bodie, Zvi, and Robert Merton. *Finance*. Upper Saddle River, NJ: Prentice Hall, 2000, chap. 4.

Rappaport, Alfred, and Robert A. Taggart, Jr. "Evaluation of Capital Expenditure Proposals Under Inflation." *Financial Management*, Spring 1982, pp. 5–13.

For more on international capital budgeting, see:

Shapiro, Alan C. *Multinational Financial Management*. 6th ed. New York: John Wiley & Sons, 1999, chap. 21.

Shapiro, Alan C. "International Capital Budgeting." in *New Developments in International Finance*, Joel Stern and Donald Chew, eds. New York: Basil Blackwell, 1988, pp. 165–180.

For information on capital budgeting in general, see:

Aggarwal, Raj. *Capital Budgeting Under Uncertainty*. Englewood Cliffs, NJ: Prentice Hall, 1993.

Brealey, Richard A., and Stewart C. Myers. *Principles of Corporate Finance*. 7th ed. New York: McGraw-Hill, 2002, chaps. 5, 6, and 9.

Brigham, Eugene F., Louis C. Gapenski, and Michael Ehrhardt. *Financial Management*. 9th ed. Fort Worth, TX: The Dryden Press, 1999, chaps. 11 and 12.

Damodoran, Aswath. *Corporate Finance*. New York: John Wiley & Sons, 2001, chaps. 7–11.

Ross, Stephen A., Randolph W. Westerfield, and Jeffrey F. Jaffe. *Corporate Finance*. 6th ed. Homewood, IL: Richard D. Irwin, 2002, chaps. 3, 4, 6, 7, and 8.

For information on discounting, see:

Bodie, Zvi, and Robert Merton. *Finance*. Upper Saddle River, NJ: Prentice Hall, 2000, chap. 4.

Brealey, Richard A., and Stewart C. Myers. *Principles of Corporate Finance*. 7th ed. New York: McGraw-Hill, 2002, chaps. 2 and 3.

Brigham, Eugene F., Louis C. Gapenski, and Michael Ehrhardt. *Financial Management*. 9th ed. Fort Worth, TX: The Dryden Press, 1999, chap. 7.

Study Questions

1. In December 2002, Metalwerks' management was considering the development of a new assembly line. The necessary machinery was estimated to cost 1.4 million deutsche marks. The tax code would allow the equipment to be depreciated in 20 years, its useful life, using the double-declining-balance method of depreciation with a switch to straight-line depreciation when advantageous. Management estimated that the costs associated with owning and running the machinery (gas, electricity, and minor repairs) would be constant over time and total DM260,000 over its 20-year estimated life. Twenty people would be required to work the assembly line. These would be new employees, each earning an average of DM24,000 a year in salary and benefits. Sales from the new assembly line were estimated to total DM1.625 million a year, with raw materials representing 37 percent of that amount. No other costs specific to the project were anticipated. Metalwerks had a 34 percent tax rate and a required payback period of four years on all new projects. Should the company develop the assembly line? What is the project's benefit/cost ratio?

2. BELLA LUNA was considering an investment that would cost €200,000 initially. The new equipment was estimated to have a useful life of five years but would require an additional investment of €60,000 in the third year for specialized equipment. The initial investment would be depreciated under the tax code for five years. The second investment would meet the guidelines for the three-year class. Sales specific to the project are forecasted at €120,000 in year one, increasing 15 percent per year for five years. Necessary raw materials, labor, etc., are estimated at 39 percent of sales.

    The tax code allows the following depreciation schedules.

Year	5-Year Schedule	3-Year Schedule
1	15%	26%
2	22	32
3	21	42
4	21	
5	21	

   a. Compute the project's net present value using a 10 percent discount rate and a 45 percent tax rate. Recalculate the NPV using a 34 percent tax rate.

   b. What is the major factor creating the project's net present value?

3. Cloud Frame Company operates in an environment where capital is scarce. Management is trying to decide between the following two capital projects. Evaluate each of the projects on the basis of their payback period, benefit/cost ratio, and net present value. Which project would you recommend Cloud Frame Company undertake? Why?

Project 1: Expand existing production by acquiring new machinery costing Libra 800,000 and having a productive life of ten years:

- Incremental sales = Libra 500,000 a year
- Cost of goods sold = 49 percent of sales
- Advertising = Libra 50,000 a year
- Depreciation computed using double-declining-balance for ten years.

Project 2: Expand product line by undertaking a project estimated to cost Libra 600,000 for production facilities, depreciable using double-declining-balance for its ten-year life, and Libra 200,000 for production training for employees. Cloud Frame management has already funded Libra 100,000 worth of market research, which documented the product's sales potential. Cloud Frame management hopes to recoup this outlay through further sales.

- Sales in year 1 are estimated to be Libra 350,000, increasing 10 percent a year in years 2–4, 15 percent a year in years 5–7, and 10 percent a year in years 8–10
- Cost of goods sold is projected at 50 percent of sales
- Advertising is to be 25 percent of sales for first three years and to level off at Libra 100,000 thereafter

Cloud Frame has a 34 percent tax rate and uses a 10 percent discount rate to evaluate all projects.

4. Based on financial forecasts from the sales department, Barry Nilson, the director of sales and marketing for New Age, Inc., recommended that his company accept a proposal from the Department of Defense. The proposal was for the delivery of specialized biological hazard

suits to be used by the Army for its decontamination unit soldiers operating in overseas campaigns. The contract was for 100 suits per year for each of the next 5 years at a fixed price of $30,000 per suit. The Department of Defense was obliged to buy all 100 suits produced each year, and New Age, Inc. was obliged to accept the payment of $30,000 per suit. New Age had never been confronted with a fixed-price, long-term contract before and management wanted to analyze the figures before accepting the contract. New Age's top management asked Nel Diamond, their new hire, to analyze the figures from the sales department staff and determine whether the company should accept the contract. Ms. Diamond wanted the analysis to be perfect so the decision would be economically sound, and her job secure.

The following were the important facts Ms. Diamond had gathered to analyze the forecasts.

- The plant in which the specialized suits would be made is currently under-utilized and there are no contracts in sight for the use of the facility.
- The plant is fully depreciated. The original purchase price of the land was $10,000.
- The plant sits on the edge of a new summer home development just outside of Asheville, North Carolina, a very desirable summer vacation area. If the land were sold, it is expected that New Age could realize about $600,000. Local real estate brokers estimated that land prices would continue to be quite stable, thus the price is a good estimate of the land's value now and in five years.
- Renovating the plant for the production of the suits would cost $500,000. There is not expected to be a salvage value. Depreciation for renovations would be done over five years using the following MACRS schedule.

Five-year MACRS Schedule

Year	Rate
1	20.00%
2	32.00%
3	19.20%
4	11.52%
5	11.52%
6	5.76%

- New machinery would cost $1 million. This too would be depreciated over five years using the MACRS percentages shown above.
- Inventory would be needed to begin the project. In addition, there would be accounts receivable—the Department of Defense

is not a particularly prompt payer. The result would be a net working capital of 10 percent of sales.

- There was no expectation that any further sales of this product would be made to this customer or any other customer after the five-year contract expired. At that time, the equipment would be sold (with little hope of a salvage value) or left idle. The plant would also be left idle.

New Age, Inc. Sales Department Forecasts— Biological Hazard Suits

	1	2	3	4	5
Price per unit	$ 30,000	$ 30,000	$ 30,000	$ 30,000	$ 30,000
Sales in units	100	100	100	100	100
Revenue	3,000,000	3,000,000	3,000,000	3,000,000	3,000,000
COGS	(2,100,000)	(2,184,000)	(2,271,000)	(2,362,000)	(2,457,000)
Gross income	900,000	816,000	729,000	638,000	543,000
Depreciation	(250,000)	(250,000)	(250,000)	(250,000)	(250,000)
EBIT	650,000	566,000	479,000	388,000	293,000
Taxes (34%)	(221,000)	(192,400)	(162,860)	(131,920)	(99,620)
Net income	$ 429,000	$ 373,560	$ 316,140	$ 256,080	$ 193,380

a. Evaluate the sales department's forecasts, and fix any problems that are apparent. Describe any changes you made and why you made them.

b. Evaluate the economic benefits of accepting the contract, making sure to use the appropriate measures, including the NPV. A discount rate of 10 percent should be used in this analysis.

c. Decide whether New Age, Inc.'s management should accept the contract. State your conclusions and reasons for them.

Appendix Four A

In Chapter 4 we discussed ways to evaluate capital investment opportunities with emphasis on the preferred method—the net present value. In NPV analysis we forecast our best estimate of the future cash flows from the investment and discount them at a rate that reflects the risk of the investment. We define risk as the possibility that our cash flows could be wrong, and vary the discount rate according to the risk. Discounted cash flow analysis has one big flaw: it assumes that once management makes an investment nothing can be changed. It's a kind of "what will be, will be" analysis, and it is not a good reflection of what can really happen.

With many investments, management later alters the investment. This can happen when management evaluates the investment results and decides that the prospects are good enough to expand the investment. When an investment's results do not meet expectations, management may decide to "cut their losses" and abandon or scale back the investment. If the investment results exceed expectations, management may choose to invest more or expand. As you can see, management can influence the final outcome from an investment after the initial investment is made. Traditional NPV analysis does not account for changes management makes to alter the investment's prospects, but it should.

Net present value analysis is a good method for analyzing investment opportunities when no changes can be made once the investment is made. NPV evaluates a **static decision**—a decision where the outcome cannot be altered. If, however, a manager has future discretion to alter the investment, it is a **dynamic decision**. Dynamic decisions are not appropriately analyzed using net present value.

Options for later action are all around us. Every time we use the conditional phrase "if . . . then," we are talking about a **contingency**, an optional choice, an action we can take if something else happens. For

---

[1] This appendix benefited greatly from the fine work of Asst. Professor Diane Lander, University of Southern Maine, Gorham, Maine.

managers making investments, a number of options for future action exist:

1. **Investment option.** Option to acquire or use something that currently has little or no value, but could if conditions change.
2. **Growth** or **production option.** Option to increase the investment or commitment to an investment or strategy, if it is attractive to do so. These options usually offer the opportunity to grow.
3. **Abandonment** or **bailout option.** Option to abandon a project or strategy in the future if it is not proceeding as desired.

An investment project can have both static and dynamic features. Some things about an investment may be unchanging and unchangeable once the investment is made. Other features are optional. In some cases these options are a natural part of the investment; in other situations management designs future choices into the investment. Because the option or options often are bundled together with an investment project, these options generally are called **embedded options**.[2] An example will make this clear.

The RAPTOR Group needs a new plant to build its products. The primary reason that it needs to expand is to manufacture a new product developed by the Mesozo Division. The new technology product is the brainchild of their hot new designer, but it is so revolutionary the marketing staff is not sure just how many the company will sell. Management has secured a limited-production contract from a long-time customer. The amount the customer purchases will not grow over time. This customer's contract gives RAPTOR management time to fully develop the product, establish its production, and engage new customers. If the market is as large as the Mesozo Division head has forecasted, the company will need a large plant with special equipment to produce the product, called the X Design. If, however, most customers decide not to adopt the new product, the company's sales after three years will not grow.

Management has been presented with two possible ways to satisfy X Design's production needs: build a small plant that can be expanded in three years or build a large plant now. The combination of the smaller plant and the later expansion would cost more than the large plant, but the smaller plant would allow management to test the market's acceptance of the new product before expanding the plant. If the market for X Design does not develop, management would continue to produce for their one customer, but sales would not grow and management would not expand the small plant. If management chooses the larger plant and the market does not develop, the company would have a large, expensive, partially used plant that would be hard to use for any other purpose.

The option in this investment is embedded in the investment in the smaller plant—to expand later. There is no option embedded in the larger plant investment. At first glance, management believes that the more flex-

---

[2] In this appendix, we limit ourselves to real options such as options to invest, disinvest, or grow. The company also can use options in its financing activities.

ible two-stage construction is better. However, before making a decision about which to choose, management needs to value the two alternatives.

In this appendix we will show how net present value analysis is not up to the task of valuing the small plant with later expansion.[3] Through an example we will show why using the net present value to compare the two alternatives is not appropriate. While we will present an explicit approach to valuing this real option, first we must set the groundwork and look at options where they are valued most frequently, in the capital markets.

I. Financial Options

While options exist all around us, the formal valuation of options has been highly developed in the capital markets where standard option contracts are used. Because of the magnitude of the markets for financial options, standard approaches have been developed to deal with them. These methods also can be used for the real options that accompany capital budgeting decisions.[4]

There are options on a variety of financial instruments that are designed to suit the insurer or the owner. There are two basic kinds of **financial options**: calls and puts. **Call options** give the owner the right, but not the obligation, to buy a specific asset (the **underlying** asset) at a specific price (the **strike** or **exercise price**) at, on, or before a specific time (the **maturity** or **exercise date**). **Put options** allow the owner to sell a specific asset, at a specific price, on or before a specific time. In essence, a put option is the reverse of a call option. Options that can be exercised from the date of purchase to expiration are called **American options**. Options that can be exercised only on a specific date are called **European options**. Embedded options can be either American or European.

In the capital markets both put and call options are publicly traded. However, not all financial securities have puts or calls or both. Options that are freely traded are listed on an organized exchange, such as the Chicago Board Options Exchange (CBOE).

Financial options allow the investor to take later action. For instance, a call option on a specific common stock allows an investor to acquire a particular number of shares of the stock at a later date at a specified price. Exhibit 4A-1 shows the call prices listed for International Business Machine shares on August 16, 2002. Options expire on the third Friday of the month. The last date on which the call can be used, the third Friday

---

[3] We will not discuss the use of financial options to craft the risk characteristics of financial investments and strategies here. This use of financial options, also called financial engineering, is discussed in Chapter 7.

[4] In this appendix we will use the most general of the option-valuation methods, the binomial model. Other models, most notably the Black-Scholes option-pricing model, provide us a standard way to value traded options. However, they do not allow us to examine real options as carefully or to consider changes as dynamically as does the binomial option-pricing approach.

Exhibit 4A-1 IBM

Options on Stock—August 16, 2002, Stock Price of $79.35

(all prices in dollars)

Strike Price	Expiration	Call	Put
70	Aug	9.50	0.05
	Sept	10.40	0.80
	Oct	11.20	1.70
75	Aug	4.50	0.05
	Sept	6.10	1.70
	Oct	7.40	2.90
80	Aug	0.05	0.55
	Sept	2.95	3.40
	Oct	4.40	4.90
85	Sept	1.05	6.40
90	Oct	1.05	12.20

of the month it expires, is listed in the second column. As you can see there are a variety of options with different expiration dates. The first column is the strike or exercise price, the price for which the stock can be acquired. You will note that for the IBM options the exercise prices are near the stock price of $79.35. The calls at the various strike prices allow the owner of the call to purchase shares at that price on or before the expiration date. The calls are sold or **written** by an owner of IBM shares.[5] The owner of the call does not have to buy the shares now. The owner can wait, conserving his or her capital, in the hope that the actual share price will rise and a profit will be earned from exercising the call.[6] As the stock price rises the value of the call depends upon the difference between the stock price and the stock price at which the option can be exercised.[7] Notice that IBM call prices at exercise prices below $75 are rather high. These are called in-the-money options: the exercise price is below the current stock price.

Put options allow the owner to sell shares at the strike price on or before the put expiration date. Put options become more valuable as the

---

[5] Owners of stock write calls for two reasons. First, they presume the stock will move in the opposite direction from the call price, thus rendering the call useless and leaving them with the premium paid for the call. Second, the stock owner may find the call price high enough to be attractive if it is reached and the call exercised.

[6] The owner of the call does not actually have to buy the stock to make money. Since the option price reflects the rise in prices, the option can be sold to realize the gain. Furthermore, if the option has not expired, it is more profitable to sell the option than to exercise it.

[7] If the stock price is below the exercise price, the value of the call option is zero, even though the price is not. The price reflects investor expectations.

strike price rises above the actual price.[8] Put option prices are in the last column of Exhibit 4A-1. To understand the true value of options, let's look at what can happen to the value of a put and call option at the moment of expiration.

The value of a stock is reflected in its current market price. Whatever the price may be today, that price could be much higher or lower at the time the option expires. This is because many things can happen to the company, its competitors, and the economy between the time the option is bought and the time it expires. The longer the length of time between the purchase of the option and its maturity or exercise date, the more that can happen to the company, its competitors, and the economy, and thus to its stock price. As a result, the longer the period of time the option has until expiration, the more valuable it is.

The value of an option is the difference between the exercise price of the option and the market price of the stock.[9] The call-option holder gains from share price increases; the put-option holder, from price decreases. Reflecting on the nature of call and put options, we can see that an option's price depends upon five things:

1. *The price of the underlying asset.* If the price rises, the value of a call (put) option rises (falls). If the price declines, the value of a call (put) option falls (rises). Theoretically, the lowest value of the option is zero. However, if the option has time remaining before it expires, it will only approach but not reach zero.
2. *The exercise price.* If we hold the price of the asset constant, the higher (lower) the exercise price, the lower (higher) will be the value of the call (put).
3. *The time until the option expires.* The longer the remaining life of the option, the greater is its price. As we said before, the longer the time to expiration, the greater chance that things can happen, and there is, therefore, a greater possibility that the option will have value.[10]
4. *The variability of the returns of the underlying investment.* The more variable the price of the underlying asset, the greater the possibility that the price will change and that the option can be profitably exercised.
5. *The current market interest rate.* The higher the rate, the more valuable the option. This is because by owning the option rather than the underlying investment we have avoided investing the full value of the underlying investment. Since the option has a lower price and the underlying investment a much larger price, we defer making the investment and can invest the difference in something else. Thus the

---

[8] The owner of the put could buy shares at a price below the stock price and then force the seller of the put to buy them at the higher strike price.

[9] The call option is worth nothing when it is at maturity and the stock price is lower than the exercise price.

[10] For European options all the actions are the same, except the time to expiration. With these options, this impact has outcomes that cannot be easily classified as positive or negative.

higher the interest rate, the more we earn on this investment. This is the reverse of net present value analysis where the higher the discount rate, the less valuable the investment. Exhibit 4A-2 summarizes how the critical variables impact the prices of put and call options.

Exhibit 4A-2

American Call Price Changes from Changes in Critical Variables

Increase in Critical Variables	Option Price Impact	
	Call	Put
Stock price	Positive	Negative
Exercise price	Negative	Positive
Volatility of stock price	Positive	Positive
Time to expiration	Positive	Positive
Risk-free rate	Positive	Negative

There are five things that we know about the price of an option on a stock.

1. The option price is never greater than the stock price.
2. The option price cannot drop below zero.
3. The option price is never below the value that could be earned if the option were exercised immediately.
4. The option price, less the present value of the price paid for the option, will approach the stock price when there is a large stock price increase.[11]
5. Because an option has a small price relative to the stock, the option's price volatility is higher than the underlying stock's price volatility. The higher the price of the stock and the option, the lower the option's volatility. The lower the price of the stock and option, the higher the volatility. Thus the risk of an option is always higher than that of the stock, but it changes and the change depends upon the relationship between the stock price and the exercise price.

These factors are used in different ways in options and net present value analysis, thus they have a very different impact on the value of a capital investment. The major differences are shown in Exhibit 4A-3.

Financial options often come in bundles. There may be several puts and/or calls contained in one instrument. These combinations of options

---

[11] This is different for European options.

Exhibit 4A-3

Impacts on Option and Net Present Values
from Changes in Critical Variables[12]

Variable	Option Value	Net Present Value
Risk-free rate rises	Increases value*	Decreases value
Variability of outcomes increases	Increases value	Decreases value
Life of investment lengthens	Increases value*	Decreases value

* For a put the impact may be different.

are usually called synthetic securities. We will discuss these briefly in Chapter 8.

Options on such things as common stocks are called **financial options**; options embedded in corporate investment decisions are called **real options**. In this chapter we take what we know about financial market options and apply it to corporate investment options.

II. Real Options

Real options allow managers to increase their potential returns while limiting their potential losses. In the past, many managers, not having the proper tools to value real options, called these strategic or intangible investments. They intuitively knew that these real options had a value, but net present value analysis did not allow a value to be placed on them. Thus managers would argue on strategic grounds in support of an investment that had a negative net present value. Purists would say that anything could be valued using net present value techniques. Realists knew that net present value analysis did not provide a complete valuation. To see what the valuation differences might be between net present value and an option valuation method let us return to the plant expansion example. RAPTOR can build a new plant now for $10 million. The analysis of this alternative is shown in Exhibit 4A-4. Note, in this analysis, management has to make an assumption about sales from the third year onwards. It assumed that sales would grow at 5 percent from year 3 onwards.

The net present value of investing in the larger plant today is almost $12.5 million. The net present value of building a smaller plant now for $8 million and waiting to build the remainder (at a cost of $5 million in

---

[12] There are some exceptions to this simplistic scheme, but in general the impact shown in this chart is accurate.

Exhibit 4A-4   RAPTOR

NPV of Large Plant Expansion with 5 Percent Terminal Growth

	0	1	2	3
Sales		$ 7,962,400	$ 9,395,632	$11,086,846
Variable costs		(3,821,952)	(4,509,903)	(5,321,686)
Depreciation		(1,000)	(1,000)	(1,000)
Fixed costs		(5,000)	(5,000)	(5,000)
EBIT		4,134,448	4,879,729	5,759,160
Taxes @ 40 percent		(1,653,779)	(1,951,891)	(2,303,664)
Operating profit		2,480,669	2,927,838	3,455,496
Depreciation		1,000	1,000	1,000
Operating cash flow		2,481,669	2,928,838	3,456,496
Change in plant	$(10,000,000)			
Terminal value*				26,588,430
Net cash flow	$(10,000,000)	$ 2,481,669	$ 2,928,838	$30,044,926
Net present value @ 18%	$ 12,492,825			

Assumptions:
Operating characteristics:
Year 1:

Sales volume (units)	592,000
Sales price per unit	$13.45
Variable cost per unit	48.00%
Fixed costs	$5,000
Depreciation	$1,000
Sales growth rate	
(years 1–3)	18.00%
Required rate of return	18.00%
Risk-free rate of return	7.00%
Terminal value	
growth rate	5.00%
Marginal tax rate	40.00%
Initial cost	$10,000,000

* Terminal value calculated using the perpetuity for a growing cash flow. Thus the terminal value is $26,588,430 in year 3 [$3,456,496/(0.18 − 0.05)].

three years) is close to $11.5 million, as shown in Exhibit 4A-5. Since the large plant investment has the larger NPV, RAPTOR management would choose to build the larger plant now rather than the two-phase building plan.

In spite of the higher net present value from building the larger plant today, there is a value to being able to wait before deciding to build the rest of the plant. The value comes from being able to expand *if and only*

Exhibit 4A-5

NPV of Expansion in Year 3 with 5 Percent Terminal Growth

	0	1	2	3
Sales		$ 7,962,400	$ 9,395,632	$11,086,846
Variable costs		(3,821,952)	(4,509,903)	(5,321,686)
Depreciation		(800)	(800)	(1,300)
Fixed costs		(5,000)	(5,000)	(5,000)
EBIT		4,134,648	4,879,929	5,758,860
Taxes @40%		(1,653,859)	(1,951,972)	(2,303,544)
Operating profit		2,480,789	2,927,957	3,455,316
Depreciation		800	800	1,300
Operating cash flow		2,481,589	2,928,757	3,456,616
Change in plant	(8,000,000)			(5,000,000)
Terminal value*				26,589,354
Net cash flow	$ (8,000,000)	$ 2,481,589	$ 2,928,757	$25,045,970
Net present value @ 18%	$11,450,180			

*Terminal value is calculated using the perpetuity for a growing cash flow. Thus the terminal value is $3,456,616/(0.18 − 0.05)] or $26,589,353.
Note: Depreciation in year 3 reflects the depreciation from the initial plant plus depreciation for the expansion.

if the market materializes. Since management is not sure that the market will materialize, this option is interesting and potentially valuable.

Note that our analysis in Exhibit 4A-5 assumes that sales will grow and that management will expand the plant regardless of whether the new market develops. But management does not know whether the market will grow after the third year, and it would not expand the small plant if it did not. The question management must ask itself is, "What is it worth to be able to wait until there is more information about the market before deciding to build the second phase of the plant?" To understand the value of this flexibility to expand later if the market develops, management should look at what will happen if the added capacity is not needed.

We know that sales will be the same for the first three years, regardless of management's plant choice. However, if the product does not meet expectations, no new customers will buy from RAPTOR and sales will not grow after the third year. If management builds the large plant, it will have more capacity than it needs. If it builds the small plant, it will not expand. Exhibit 4A-6 shows the analysis of the wait-and-see strategy if terminal sales growth is zero and management decides not to expand the plant. As you can see, the net present value is almost $10 million.

Exhibit 4A-6

Cash Flows and NPV of Wait-and-See Strategy: No Growth or Plant Expansion Beyond Year 3

	0	1	2	3
Sales		$ 7,962,400	$ 9,395,632	$11,086,846
Variable costs		(3,821,952)	(4,509,903)	(5,321,686)
Depreciation		(800)	(800)	(800)
Fixed costs		(5,000)	(5,000)	(5,000)
EBIT		4,134,648	4,879,929	5,759,360
Taxes		(1,653,859)	(1,951,972)	(2,303,744)
Operating profit		2,480,789	2,927,957	3,455,616
Depreciation		800	800	800
Operating cash flow		2,481,589	2,928,757	3,456,416
New plant	$ (8,000,000)			
Terminal value*				19,202,311
Net cash flow	(8,000,000)	$ 2,481,589	$ 2,928,757	$22,658,727
Net present value	$ 9,997,230			

*Terminal value is calculated as a perpetuity with no growth and a discount rate of 18 percent.

Management is not certain what the market demand will be. Depending upon the growth, the cash flows from the third year onwards could be much higher or lower than our expected value of 5 percent. This growth rate impacts the terminal value, and thus the NPV. Exhibit 4A-7 summarizes the present and terminal values with different assumptions about terminal growth.

If the growth is zero, management does not have to build the added plant. However, if the growth is 8 percent, the added terminal value from being able to build the plant is $15.4 million. Since the plant costs $5 million management would build the plant. If the growth were only 2 percent, management would gain only $2.4 million, and the added terminal value would not cover the cost of building the plant.[13]

The only trouble with this analysis is that at the time the investment is made, management does not know what sales growth will be after the third year. How can it decide about the plant when it just does not know what will happen? In the past when managers believed that the option to build later had a value they could either assert that the option had a value, construct NPV numbers to fit their beliefs, or use their persuasive abilities. Now they can put a value on the option using option-pricing techniques.

---

[13] By the way, the difference between the zero-growth scenario and the expected value of 5 percent growth is $7,385,504. The expected value is the mean of the outcomes, or in terms we used in Chapter 4, it is the most likely outcome. This is a probability-weighted outcome, not an explicit scenario.

Exhibit 4A-7

Present and Terminal Values of Wait-and-See Strategy: Different Rates of Growth with No New Plant in Year 3

Terminal Rate of Growth	Present Value	Terminal Value
0%	$ 9,997,230	$19,202,311
1%	10,684,708	20,331,859
2%	11,458,120	21,602,600
5%	14,492,276	26,587,815
8%	19,346,926	34,564,160

We already know most of what we need to know to value this option.

- The value of the ability to grow at 2 percent after year 3 is $2,400,289: the difference between the terminal values at zero and 5 percent. At 8 percent the value difference is $15,361,849.
- The annual discount rate is 18 percent per year, or 64.3032 percent for the three-year period.[14]
- The present value of the difference between the terminal values at 2 (the lowest expansion growth rate) and 5 (the average expansion growth rate) percent growth is $4,985,215.
- The risk free rate is 7 percent per year, or 22.5043 for the three-year period.

What we need to know now is the chance that the growth will be 8 or 2 percent: the conditions under which management would consider expanding the plant in the third year. What we do know is that the probability-weighted upside change in terminal value plus the probability-weighted downside change in terminal value must be equal to $4,495,046, the differences in present value at zero and 5 percent. From this we can determine the probabilities. Exhibit 4A-8 shows the calculations.

Now we can calculate the value of the option. Exhibit 4A-9 shows the binomial option-pricing framework that we use for this problem. Notice several things about this exhibit. First, we describe the outcomes in terms of what management might do. If the downside occurs, management could spend $5 million to get $2.4 million, but it does not make economic sense to do so. Thus they would forgo the $2.4 million benefit and the $5 million cost, and get nothing more than originally expected: the terminal value without any growth. We can show that this branch is not sensible by putting a cross on the line leading from the present value to the outcome. If the upside occurs, management is faced

---

[14] Actually, we are treating the three years as if it is one three-year period. Thus the discount rate is 64.3032 percent $(1.18)^3$.

Exhibit 4A-8

Expected Value of Terminal Values

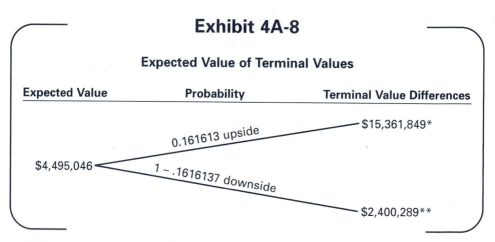

Expected Value	Probability	Terminal Value Differences
$4,495,046	0.161613 upside	$15,361,849*
	1 − .1616137 downside	$2,400,289**

*Difference between terminal values at 0 and 8 percent growth.
**Difference between terminal values at 0 and 2 percent growth.
Note: Discount probability-weighted terminal value at the risk-free rate for one three-year period.

with the same possibilities, do nothing and get no added terminal value, or get $15.4 million at a cost of $5 million. The present value is the value of the probability-weighted present value of each of the logical outcomes. Since the downside branch is cut off, the value of the downside is zero. Thus, the present value of the upside terminal value simply is the value of the option to wait-and-see before building the plant expansion.[15] The option is worth $1,366,980.

Exhibit 4A-9

Option Value Using Binomial Option Pricing

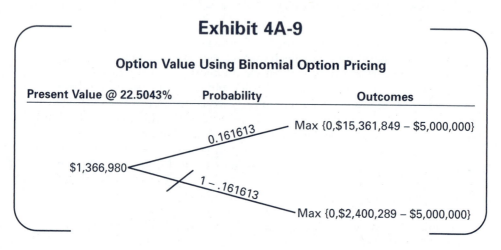

Present Value @ 22.5043%	Probability	Outcomes
$1,366,980	0.161613	Max {0,$15,361,849 − $5,000,000}
	1 − .161613	Max {0,$2,400,289 − $5,000,000}

---

[15] Notice we are using the risk-free rate of return for discounting. Again, we are assuming this is a one three-year period. We use the risk-free rate for discounting because option valuation depends upon a concept called the riskless hedge. This assumption rests on the notion that the investor preserving capital by taking the option would invest it to earn a return at a risk-free rate of return. For more about this see the references at the end of the chapter.

Management now has the information it needs to make an informed decision. What should it do? If the value of the small plant plus the option is greater than building the large plant today, management should invest in the small plant. The value of the first phase of the small plant with no growth after the third year plus the option is $11,364,210 as shown in Exhibit 4A-10. The value of the large plant, shown in Exhibit 4A-4 is $12,492,825. Management should, in economic terms, have a preference for building the large plant, in spite of its inclination to hedge their bet with the two-stage plant.

Exhibit 4A-10

Present Value of Large Plant and Small Plant Plus Option[16]

	Net Present Value
Asset in Place—Small Plant	$ 9,997,230
Option	1,366,980
Total NPV Small Plant	$11,364,210
Large Plant	$12,492,825

III. Conclusion

This is the briefest of introductions to the basics of embedded or real options. As you can see, this is a powerful, realistic analysis that is and should be gaining widespread acceptance. The mathematics of the methodology, particularly some of the shortcut methods like the widely used Black-Scholes option-pricing model, can be daunting. However, using the binomial method can be relatively straightforward. It portrays decisions as they are likely to be taken by management, and incorporates into the valuation of an investment the likely courses of action management may take.

More and more corporate managers are recognizing that net present value analysis depends upon static, unchanging, outcomes—outcomes that are unlikely even at the outset of an investment. Managers already knew that many investments held options to abandon, expand, or grow, and those that did not could be adapted to do so. What they did not have was a method for analyzing the options. Analyzing and valuing embedded options is a skill analysts must gain. Creating the options and understanding their value is the job of good managers.

---

[16] Note: Using the Black-Scholes method, a widely used formulaic method, results in a similar outcome.

Selected References

On options in general, see:

Brealey, Richard A., and Stewart C. Myers. *Principles of Corporate Finance.* 6th ed. New York: McGraw-Hill, 2002, chap. 20.

Brigham, Eugene F., Louis C. Gapenski, and Michael Ehrhardt. *Financial Management.* 9th ed. Fort Worth, TX: The Dryden Press, 1999, chap. 24.

Bodie, Zvi, and Robert Merton. *Finance.* Upper Saddle River, NJ: Prentice Hall, 2000, chap. 15.

Cox, John, and Mark Rubinstein. *Options Markets.* Englewood Cliffs, NJ: Prentice-Hall, 1985.

Damodoran, Aswath. *Corporate Finance.* New York: John Wiley & Sons, 1997, chap. 27.

Ross, Stephen A., Randolph W. Westerfield, and Jeffrey F. Jaffee. *Corporate Finance.* 6th ed. Homewood, IL: Richard D. Irwin, 2002, chap. 23.

Stoll, Hans, and Robert Whaley. *Futures and Options.* Cincinnati, OH: South-Western Publishing, 1993.

Thomsell, Michael. *Getting Started in Options.* 3rd ed. New York: John Wiley & Sons, 1997.

On real options, see:

Amran, Martha, and Nalin Kulantilaka. *Real Options: Managing Strategic Investment in an Uncertain World.* Cambridge, MA: Harvard Business School Publishing, 1998.

Brealey, Richard A., and Stewart C. Myers. *Principles of Corporate Finance.* 6th ed. New York: McGraw-Hill, 2002, chap. 21.

Brennan, Michael, and Lenos Trigeorgious, eds. *Project Flexibility, Agency and Product Market Competition: New Developments in the Theory and Application of Real Options Analysis.* Oxford University Press, 1999.

Brigham, Eugene F., Louis C. Gapenski, and Michael Ehrhardt. *Financial Management.* 9th ed. Fort Worth, TX: The Dryden Press, 1999, chap. 13.

Bodie, Zvi, and Robert Merton. *Finance.* Upper Saddle River, NJ: Prentice Hall, 2000, chap. 15.

Damodoran, Aswath. *Corporate Finance.* New York: John Wiley & Sons, 1997, chap. 27.

Dixit, Avinash K., and Robert S. Pindyck. "The Options Approach to Capital Investment," *Harvard Business Review,* May–June 1995.

Leuhrman, Timothy A. "Capital Projects as Real Options: An Introduction," *Harvard Business School Case Series,* 1994.

Ross, Stephen A., Randolph W. Westerfield, and Jeffrey F. Jaffe. *Corporate Finance.* 6th ed. Homewood, IL: Richard D. Irwin, 2002, chap. 7.

Trigeorgious, Lenos. *Real Options: Managerial Flexibility and Strategic Resource Allocation.* Cambridge, MA: MIT Press, 1996.

Appendix Four B

Tax codes in highly inflationary environments often have a feature that an analyst must incorporate into an investment analysis: companies are allowed to revalue their assets to compensate for the erosive effects of inflation. For many analysts, especially stock analysts dealing with companies in many different countries, this asset revaluation presents a special challenge. To fully understand financial statements, the analyst must know the accounting rules that impact statements in the inflationary environment and must be able to adapt the statements to compare companies from different countries. This is the reason that the EBITDA ratio, described in Chapter 1, is considered so useful in cross-border analysis.

Let's use an example to make clear why asset revaluation occurs and how the revalued asset depreciation expense will be quite different from that based on the asset's historic cost. Exhibit 4B-1 shows the depreciation that a company can expense in a country with 35 percent inflation, a rate reached by many countries each year. Since this exhibit would be very large if all the data were included, we show only 3 of the 10 years.

Exhibit 4B-1 Panel A shows the impact on a company's financial statements when the asset is not revalued: the depreciation is based on historical cost. From this exhibit you can see that the tax shield stays the same each year—it does not rise to offset the changes in the value of the currency over time. By the tenth year, the depreciation shield is virtually meaningless. Panel B shows the results when the asset is revalued: its value is restated to reflect inflation. As you can see, the asset value and depreciation grow with inflation. Perhaps the most important item, the cumulative cash flow, is higher when assets are revalued to keep pace with inflation. The differences in profits and cash flows under the two scenarios are shown most clearly in the graph in Exhibit 4B-2.

For the analyst, this creates a real problem. Let's suppose that Panel A and B represented two companies in countries where inflation was identical but asset revaluation was allowed only for the Panel B country. The

Exhibit 4B-1

Inflationary Impact on Financial Performance: Depreciation With and Without Asset Revaluation—Inflation 35 Percent per Year

(in units of currency)

Panel A
Asset Value Based on Historical Cost

	Year 1	Year 5	Year 10
Net asset value (beginning of year)	500,000	300,000	50,000
Depreciation	(50,000)	(50,000)	(50,000)
Asset value (end of year)	450,000	250,000	—
EBITDA	100,000	332,151	1,489,375)
Depreciation	(50,000)	(50,000)	(50,000)
EBIT	50,000	282,151	1,439,375
Taxes (40%)	(20,000)	(112,860)	(575,750)
Profit after taxes	30,000	169,290	863,625
Cumulative profit after taxes	30,000	286,913	1,495,569
Cumulative taxes	20,000	298,175	1,983,606
Cash flow*	80,000	219,290	913,625
Cumulative cash flow	80,000	697,263	3,475,410

Panel B
Asset Value Based on Inflated Asset Value

	Year 1	Year 5	Year 10
Net asset value (beginning of year)	500,000	1,220,703	3,725,290
Depreciation	(50,000)	(122,070)	(372,529)
Inflated asset value (end of year)	675,000	1,647,949	5,029,142
Asset value less depreciation (end of year)	625,000	1,525,879	4,656,613
EBITDA	100,000	332,151	1,489,375
Depreciation	(50,000)	(122,070)	(372,529)
EBIT	50,000	210,081	1,116,846
Taxes (40%)	(20,000)	(84,032)	(446,738)
Profit after taxes	30,000	126,049	670,108
Cumulative profit after taxes	30,000	215,077	1,153,238
Cumulative taxes	20,000	234,035	1,518,548
Cash flow*	80,000	248,119	1,042,637
Cumulative cash flow	80,000	761,404	3,940,468

* Cash flow is the profit after taxes plus depreciation.

Exhibit 4B-2

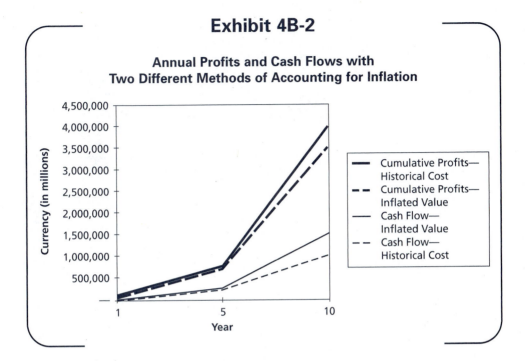

Annual Profits and Cash Flows with Two Different Methods of Accounting for Inflation

sales of the two companies would be identical, the EBITDA the same, but the ROS ratios would be different. Thus you can see why EBITDA has become an attractive ratio. As much as an analyst would like this measure to solve the comparisons, EBITDA ignores the impact of on depreciation and the resulting taxes and cash flow. EBIT and ROS comparisons are flawed, but in different ways.

What should be clear from this very brief example is that an analyst or manager working in or analyzing a company from an environment with high inflation must be aware of what the accounting rule can do to the company and its asset-investment plans.

Chapter Five

Valuation 2: Company Valuation, Acquisitions, Divestitures, and Mergers

Valuing a company is important when evaluating the:

1. Company's common stock as a potential investment.
2. Price to be paid for acquiring another company or business.
3. Price to be asked for a company or division that is for sale.

There are some differences between the valuation methods analysts use in the three situations. For the most part, however, the differences lie in the perspective being taken, the depth of the information available, and the amount of control those doing the valuation may have over the future of the business being valued. For those valuing the shares of a company as an investor, publicly available data must be used.[1] However, when a company is merging, acquiring another, or selling itself, more detailed information about one or both of the companies usually is available.[2] Since this book is about corporate financial analysis, in this chapter we will concentrate on the valuation of a business that may be sold to or acquired by another company, not the valuation of shares by investors in the capital markets.

I. Reasons for Acquisition and Merger

There are many reasons to acquire a company. Managers engaged in merger activity report they have used mergers to:

1. Lower financing costs.
2. Diversify the company and thus reduce its risk.
3. Increase the earnings per share of the acquiring firm.

---

[1] Stock analysts, money managers, and individual investors are typical of those who value the shares.
[2] This may not be the case in an unfriendly tender offer.

4. Use excess funds.
5. Provide needed funds.
6. Purchase an undervalued company and its assets.
7. Take advantage of economies of scale or size.
8. Enter a business or market.
9. Gain market share or presence.

While the reasons for making an acquisition or merger vary, all the reasons can be reduced to one: to create value for the acquiring company's shareholders. This creation of value comes only as the result of synergy between the merging firms.[3] **Synergy** comes from combining unused capacity in one company with a need for that capacity in another. While value for an acquiring firm's shareholders can be the result of paying less for the targeted company than it is worth, real synergy comes from combining or better using such things as plant capacity, sales forces, distribution systems, equity or debt-market access, brand presence, or management talent. Synergy can also come from the willingness of one company's owners to take risk, combined with another's too-conservative approach. Acting on potential synergies can result in the creation of value, the goal of shareholders.

Creating value was discussed in relation to capital investment decisions in Chapter 4. Creating value is the goal whether it is the sale or purchase of a business or an investment in plant or marketing strategy. Although a business is usually larger than the typical capital investment, the acquired firm, division, or line of business must still generate an adequate return for the risk being taken by the acquiring company's shareholders. Thus the tools used in Chapter 4 apply here. An acquisition is just like any other corporate investment. If capital budgeting and acquisition analysis are the same, why do we devote another chapter to its discussion? There are five reasons.

1. Since acquisitions usually require large investments, companies frequently have a separate staff of acquisition analysts and their analysis must be understood.
2. The acquisition decision is an excellent example of the way a manager can create or destroy value for a company's owners.
3. Since the costs and benefits are unusually influenced by tax and accounting issues, the real benefits of an acquisition can be difficult to identify and awkward to evaluate.
4. Companies often rely on outside advisers, such as consultants, investment bankers, or business brokers, to identify, analyze, and value potential acquisitions or divestitures. These outside advisors and their analysts may use special language to describe their analysis and special tools to value a business. Managers who are acquiring or di-

---

[3] We do not mean that shareholders' interests should beggar the customers, employees, or any other stakeholder. The goal is not to maximize shareholder value at the expense of others, but to create value. Value creation is returning more than the shareholder requires for the risk being taken, not the most.

vesting a business should be aware of the basic valuation concepts and how experts use, interpret, and augment them.

5. Merger analysts often borrow the analytical tools of stock analysts, using them instead of or as a supplement to traditional valuation (capital investment) techniques and criteria. The stock analyst's approach is used because many acquisitions are made by purchasing the stock of the acquired firm with cash or securities of the acquiring firm. Because stock often is used or exchanged in the transaction, stock analysis techniques appear appropriate. However, they must be augmented by capital investment analysis.

Analyzing a corporate strategy—whether the investment is in property, plant, or equipment; a line of business; or a whole company—requires valuation tools. The only real differences between capital budgeting and corporate valuation lie in the scope and availability of the data needed to create estimated cash flows and discount rates. Because acquisitions and divestitures are large, are strategically important, and seem to require special analytical approaches, we consider their analysis as a separate topic in valuation.[4]

The capital investment framework presented in Chapter 4 can be used to determine whether a potential acquisition will create value for the acquiring firm's owners. In this chapter, we will describe how to use present value analysis of cash flows as a method for valuing and pricing a business. We will then discuss some of the other valuation techniques currently used by analysts. Note that while an acquisition is our primary focus, a divestiture is the same transaction seen through the seller's eyes, and the approach to the analysis is the same.

Acquisitions are done to create value. There are two ways in which value can be created in making an investment. First, value can be created by finding unusual benefits that accrue from the investment itself. Second, value can come from the way the investment is financed. Because these sources of value are quite distinct, the analysis of these sources should also be distinct. In Chapter 4 we discussed the methods for valuing an investment, but we did not consider whether special forms of financing might enhance or detract from this value. In this chapter we will follow the same process, saving the discussion of how a company should finance itself to Chapters 7 and 8 and how that financing might affect the value of capital investments, including mergers, for Chapter 9. In the appendix to that chapter we will discuss leveraged mergers, also called leveraged buyouts.

Before we begin to look at how capital budgeting tools are adapted to value businesses, a word of warning: the combination of poor analysis, misuse of tools, and overenthusiasm among buyers can create a dangerous situation. Buyers can let their enthusiasm for a merger cloud the analysis of the potential costs and benefits of the merger. When enthusiasm overwhelms judgment, management can overvalue the benefits and misjudge

---

[4] In the past, the words *merger* and *acquisition* were used to denote different forms of corporate combinations. In general, the word *merger* now is used to designate the physical combining of companies after acquisition is complete.

the costs. In this chapter you will see that when management pays too much for an acquisition, the acquiring company's shareholders' value is reduced. Shareholders recognize that enthusiasm often impacts their value in an acquisition. That is why in the United States the stock price of an acquirer is often negatively affected by the announcement of a pending merger, whereas the shareholders of the company being acquired often find positive and significant returns from their shares.[5]

Now, armed with our knowledge about basic valuation techniques gained in Chapter 4, we are ready to value lines of business, divisions, or whole companies.

II. Valuing Cash Flows

There are two steps in valuing the target company—the company to be acquired or divested:

1. Identify the value of the target company (NPV_T).
2. Identify the value of the synergies that may result as the acquired firm's business is joined with that of the acquirer (NPV_S).

The marginal value of the acquisition depends both on the value of the company to be acquired and on the value of the synergies, the value that comes only as a result of the combination:[6]

$$\text{Acquisition value} = NPV_T + NPV_S$$

What follows is an example to demonstrate the analysis of an acquisition using these two steps. We will first value an acquisition that has no synergies.

1. The Value of an Acquisition Without Synergies

The management of NUVUE Co., a manufacturer of knit goods such as sweat pants, has identified another company that is potentially an interesting acquisition, Delphi Company. Delphi Co. is a printer, binder, and distributor of books for little-known religious organizations whose beliefs are based on early Greek mythology. Since the demand for Delphi's books has been level for years and is not expected to rise, the current cash flow for Delphi is expected to continue without change into the foresee-

---

[5] A major consulting firm, McKinsey and Company, verified this stock market impact in a study it conducted of 200 acquisitions made by the largest U.S. public corporations in the late 1970s and early 1980s. McKinsey found that 70 percent of the acquirers failed to earn the required return on their investments. Few, it found, added value for the acquiring company's shareholders. In fact, many mergers during the period studied provided returns below those of very low-risk U.S. Treasury securities. This result is disheartening, but it continues to exist today. Because of findings like these, it is critical that the analyst evaluating the purchase of another business do so with great care, and for management to temper its enthusiasm with solid analysis.

[6] The concept of marginal value was discussed in Chapter 4.

able future. Management expects Delphi Company's 2004 sales to be $10.3 million, cost of goods sold and operating expenses to total 92 percent of sales, depreciation to be $50,000, equipment purchases to be $50,000, and taxes to be 34 percent of income before taxes. Net income is expected to total $510,840. Income and costs are not expected to grow, and there is a widely held view among economists that there will be no inflation. Using these assumptions, management has produced the forecasted earnings and residual cash flow forecast shown in Exhibit 5-1.[7]

Exhibit 5-1 Delphi Co.

2004 Income and Residual Cash Flow Forecast

(in thousands)

	2004
Sales	$10,300.00
Operating expenses	(9,476.00)
Depreciation	(50.00)
Earnings before taxes	774.00
Taxes (@ 34%)	(263.16)
Income after taxes	510.84
Depreciation	50.00
New equipment purchase	(50.00)
Annual residual cash flow	510.84
Terminal value	0
Residual cash flow	$ 510.84

You will note that while some acquisition and stock analysts discount earnings rather than cash flows, we do not do so here: earnings reflect the impact of accounting rules on the timing of expense and revenue recognition, but do not necessarily show when cash inflows or outflows occur. Cash flows adjust the earnings for noncash expenses and for capitalized items and represent the actual cash the company receives or disburses. If the tax authorities allowed companies to recognize revenues when customers paid for their orders and costs when the company paid for its purchases, earnings and cash flows would be identical. Since few, if any, tax authorities allow companies to do this, cash flow best recognizes when cash is received and paid by the company.

---

[7] Residual cash flow is the cash flow that is available after the company has paid all its suppliers. For this example we are assuming that the whole company is financed by its shareholders, thus there are no interest payments. Chapter 9 will discuss how to include financing into these decisions.

The earnings of a company should not be discounted to estimate the value of a business, only the cash flows.[8] Earnings are useful for perspective and communication, however. After we do our valuation of Delphi's cash flows, we will show you how to use the earnings to gain valuable insights.

Now let's return to the valuation. First, note that in Exhibit 5-1 we have only one year of cash flows. Is that all that NUVUE will get from Delphi? No. We need to forecast all the cash flows NUVUE expects to get from Delphi in the future. Usually that would mean we need years and years of forecasts. However, since Delphi's cash flows are expected to be the same for every year in the future, we can use a shortcut—the perpetuity method of valuation.

To use the **perpetuity** or **perpetual** method of valuation, divide the annual cash flow by the discount rate less the long-term growth rate.[9]

$$NPV_T = \frac{NCF_T \times (1 + g)}{R_{eT} - g}$$

Where:

R_{eT} = Investors' required return on equity for the target company

NCF_T = Yearly residual net cash flow for the target company

NPV_T = Net present value of equity cash flows for the target company

g = Long-term growth rate in cash flows

Since Delphi management expects no cash flow growth—the residual cash flow will remain the same every year—we can use the perpetuity method of valuation. Management estimates that the investors require a return of 13.8 percent.[10]

$$NPV_D = \frac{NCF_D}{R_{eD} - g}$$
$$= \frac{\$510,840}{0.138 - 0.0}$$
$$= \$3,701,739$$

The present value of Deplhi's future cash flows is $3.7 million. This method gives us a valuation that is identical to one calculated if we discounted the annual cash flows of $510,840 far into the future—but it is much easier and quicker.[11] However, the perpetuity method comes with a warning: *use it only when unchanging cash flows will last a very long time* or when *the rate of growth in the future is low and unchanging*. In a situ-

---

[8] In some circumstances, and for some companies, earnings and cash flows are identical. This can occur with slow-growing, mature companies.
[9] We will discuss this method in great depth later in this chapter.
[10] Chapter 6 will discuss how to calculate a discount rate. In this chapter we use the management-determined rate.
[11] If you are not certain that the two methods are equivalent, try it yourself.

ation where the cash flows do not follow this pattern, the perpetuity method of valuation cannot be used.[12] One must forecast the cash flows far into the future, and then discount them.

Now that we have valued a nongrowing Delphi, the decision about its acquisition by NUVUE depends upon the price that NUVUE management will pay. If NUVUE management pays a fair price for Delphi there will be no expected benefit or loss to the owners of either firm. That price is $3.7 million. Delphi's shareholders get what their company is worth and NUVUE's shareholders pay what it is worth. A price of $3.7 million is one that neither creates nor destroys value—one that exactly equals the present value of the benefits from Delphi. If Delphi is purchased for $3.7 million neither set of shareholders are better off than they were before the acquisition. A simple formula can be used to show the important relationship between price and value:

$$NRC_T = Price_T - NPV_T$$

Where:

NRC_T = Net real cost to the acquirer for the target company
$Price_T$ = Purchase price of the target company
NPV_T = Present value of the target company, with no synergistic benefits

At a price of $3.7 million for Delphi, the value created for NUVUE's owners will be zero.

$$NRC_N = \$3.7 - \$3.7$$
$$= \$0$$

If NUVUE management pays more than $3.7 million, NUVUE's owners would expect to lose value.[13] As you can see below, if the price paid were $4.0 million, then the expected cost, or loss in present value, to NUVUE shareholders would be $300,000.

$$NRC_N = \$4.0 - \$3.7$$
$$= \$0.3 \text{ million, or } \$300,000$$

NUVUE's shareholders' cost is a gain to the shareholders of Delphi as shown in Exhibit 5-2. The lines cross where the price is equal to the value, $3.7 million. Obviously, it is both the value of the acquisition and price paid for it that are important.

2. The Benefits from an Acquisition With Synergies

Our calculations thus far have assumed that the acquisition offers no synergies between NUVUE and Delphi. What if the combined companies were expected to have synergies: cash flows in excess of those the

---

[12] Actually there are adaptations of the perpetuity to value companies with various stages of growth. Most were developed to ease the tedium of analysis before there was widespread use of calculators and computer spreadsheets.
[13] Of course, Delphi's shareholders gain from NUVUE's shareholders' loss.

Exhibit 5-2

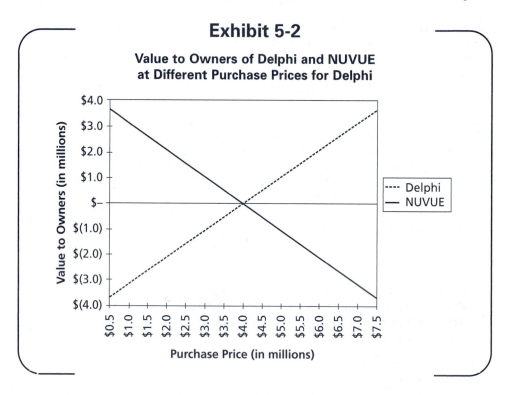

**Value to Owners of Delphi and NUVUE
at Different Purchase Prices for Delphi**

companies would have had without each other? This increase in cash flows might come from a variety of different sources. In this example, if Delphi were operating at full capacity with a large backlog of orders for its products and NUVUE had an empty manufacturing facility that could be used with no change to produce products for Delphi's customers, the combination of NUVUE's unused capacity and Delphi's need for capacity would produce new benefits from the synergies. The benefits from synergies clearly have value, but their cash flows can be hard to estimate. The benefits from synergies can be estimated directly or indirectly.

Direct Forecasts of the Benefits from Synergies. To use the direct method to estimate synergies, management forecasts the cash flows that result from the synergies and discounts them. To do this for the unused plant capacity example, NUVUE management would estimate the increase in Delphi's sales from producing more tracts, the marginal costs incurred in using NUVUE's plant to produce them, and any other new (marginal) costs associated with producing, selling, and delivering the additional pamphlets. In the case of the Delphi acquisition, NUVUE management estimated that:

- Revenues from the sales of the new booklets would be $350,000 per year.
- New expenses, expenses not already being incurred by either company, would be $85,000. This would include the taxes on the incremental income.

- There would be no need for new equipment since Delphi had equipment that was not being used, and since Delphi had the skilled workers to install it there would be no installation expenses.
- All the booklets printed would be sold. There would be no further growth.
- The booklet sales were more certain than Delphi's regular business, thus management estimated investors' required return for these cash flows of 13 percent. This was lower than the discount rate used to value the company as a whole.
- The perpetuity method of valuation could be used since the benefits from the synergies would last for a very long time.

Given these estimations, the present value of the benefits from the synergies with no growth is just over $2 million.

$$NPV_S = Cash\ flows_s/(R_{es} - g)$$
$$= (Benefits_s - Costs_s)/(R_{es} - g)$$
$$= \frac{\$350,000 - \$85,000}{0.13 - 0.0}$$
$$= \$2,038,462$$

The value of the benefits from the synergies is $2.0 million. This $2.0 million would be added to NUVUE's estimate of Delphi's value without synergies for a total value of Delphi plus the synergies of $5.7 million ($3.7 million + $2.0 million). By taking the benefits from the synergies into account, NUVUE management could offer up to $5.7 million for Delphi without losing value for its shareholders. However, if NUVUE management did offer $5.7 million for Delphi, the full value of the synergies would go to Delphi's shareholders. At a price of $4.7 million the buyer and seller share the benefits from the synergies equally, and at a price of $3.7 million Delphi's owners are not paid for their contribution to the synergistic benefits. Price and value are both critical to value creation.

This direct valuation of the benefits from synergies focuses management on forecasting what can be achieved. For those who find estimating the value of synergies difficult, there is the indirect method.

Indirect Method of Forecasting the Benefits from Synergies.   Indirect valuation of the benefits from synergies is a three-step process:

1. Estimate the present values of NUVUE and Delphi operating alone.
2. Estimate the value of the combined firms after the merger.
3. Subtract the two.

The difference between the two cash flow forecasts is the benefits from synergies.[14] For our example the result of each step is shown in Exhibit

---

[14] Many companies forecast the with-benefits-from-synergies cash flows. However, these cash flows are often the only ones valued and the acquiring company pays for the full value of the synergies while the acquired company's shareholders gain the full value of the synergies. Clearly, when the synergies are positive, forecasting and valuing these cash flows can lead to overpayment by the acquirer.

5-3. As you can see the synergies are worth $2.038 million, the same amount we just calculated directly. Of course, whether the Delphi shareholders, or those from NUVUE, will actually receive the value of the benefits from synergy depends upon the purchase price.

Exhibit 5-3

Net Present Value of Combined Firms with Benefits from Synergies

	NUVUE	Delphi Co.	Combined Companies
Residual net cash flow per year	$600,000	$510,840	$1.376 million
Investors' required return	12.0%	13.8%	12.8143%
Net present value	$5.00 million	$3.70 million	$10.738 million

*If the investors' required rate of return were rounded, the NPV would be an approximation.

The analysis of the NUVUE–Delphi merger and its synergies was deceptively straightforward. Projecting the costs and benefits of the synergies of the combined companies is often subject to even greater forecasting error than is forecasting the cash flows for the original entities. Our example has the potential for several forecast errors. For example, the benefits that management believes Delphi would receive from using NUVUE's excess capacity to print Delphi tracts depend upon such factors as the availability of local labor, the suitability of the space, and the actual conversion costs to the plant. The actual benefits that NUVUE receives may be quite different from what management had originally forecast.

As uncertain as the NUVUE forecasts may be, most acquisitions valuations provide far greater forecasting ambiguity than does our example, and most managers hot on the trail of an acquisition underestimate the costs of merging the companies. Simply put, the acquirer often pays too much.

Risk and Synergies.   Thus far most of the discussion has been about cash flow forecasting. However, risk and the impact of an acquisition on risk also must be estimated. This can be very difficult. In the NUVUE–Delphi example, the analyst's life was made simple by assuming that the business risk of the new firm was the weighted average of the two companies' risks prior to acquisition plus the risk associated with the synergistic benefits. This simplifying assumption rarely holds true in practice. For example, joining a cyclical to a countercyclical firm can greatly reduce the risk of the combined firm, all other factors being equal. However, joining two firms with the same cycle would not have the risk-reducing effect.[15]

---

[15] In Chapter 6 we discuss the portfolio effect.

3. The Value of Redundant Assets

In the example of Delphi, NUVUE management valued Delphi's cash flows to determine the company's value. In creating the cash flows, management assumed that Delphi used all its assets to produce the cash flows, and all its assets were dedicated to the publishing business. What if Delphi had assets it did not use in the publishing business, the business that NUVUE wanted to own? Since these assets are not needed to produce the publishing-related cash flows, we must consider how these should be included in the valuation. Does the discounted cash flow fully value these assets?

Redundant assets, assets not needed to support the business, should be valued independently of the business-related cash flows. To value these assets, segment any cash flows associated with the redundant assets and remove them from the business-related cash flows. The redundant assets and/or their cash flows are valued independently. The value of the company is the sum of the values of the business and the redundant assets. An example will demonstrate how to deal with these assets.

Suppose Delphi has a piece of property purchased years ago that it has never used. On this property Delphi pays property taxes but earns no income. While the property is reported on the balance sheet at its original cost, and the property taxes are expensed on the income statement, Delphi management knows that it will never use the property. Unless the property cannot be sold, NUVUE management can value the property at the price for which it could be sold.[16] In net present value terms, the company is worth the net present value of the tax-adjusted cash flows plus the sale value of the property.[17]

To include redundant assets in a valuation, you must be certain that the:

- Asset is truly redundant.
- Asset can be valued and the value realized.
- Cash inflows or outflows associated with the asset are removed from business-related cash flows.
- Value of the asset is added to the net present value of the ongoing business.

There are a wide variety of redundant assets. Such things as excessively large cash accounts and real property are the most obvious.[18] To value the redundant asset, any of the tools discussed in the chapter may be appropriate depending upon the nature of the asset.

---

[16] Remember to eliminate the property's tax payments from forecasted business cash flows for Delphi.

[17] Because of the elimination of property taxes, the income would rise, but so would the company's income tax.

[18] Excess cash typically is invested in marketable securities. The cash is valuable, and its total value can be added to the net present value if, and only if, any of the interest earned on the marketable securities is deducted from the cash flows before the net present value is calculated.

4. The Marginal Benefit of a Growing Acquisition

Both analyses of Delphi assumed that the company was anticipating no growth in its future cash flows. However, forecasts by industry experts suggest that growth in splinter religions is expected to increase from 2003 for the next five years. Management believes that this means that Delphi will experience sales growth: growth in sales could be as high as 10 percent for the next five years, before it drops to zero. The current equipment would not be adequate to sustain this growth, and added investments would be necessary. This growth, and the investment needed to sustain it, will change the value of Delphi. To value this, management must estimate the cash flows that might result from the change, and deal with the following questions.

1. What is the value of Delphi with growth?
2. What should be the least NUVUE should pay to acquire Delphi?
3. What should be the most NUVUE should pay to acquire Delphi?

The analysis shown in Exhibit 5-4 was prepared by management, based on the assumption that Delphi sales and operating expenses would grow at a rate of 10 percent from 2004 to 2008, and would not grow thereafter. The value of a growing Delphi is $4.7 million, $1.0 million more than the value calculated without growth.[19] The value would be even greater if management could grow without investing in the new assets to support that growth.

To value Delphi, we forecast the cash flows for six years. During the first five years revenues are growing at 10 percent. Once Delphi's growth stops at the end of the fifth year, we can use the perpetuity method to value the cash flows for the ensuing years. To do this we first normalize the 2008 cash flows to represent the cash flows that would occur in the zero growth years. These cash flows show no changes in working capital, and all new investments in property, plant, and equipment equal depreciation for the year. The perpetuity method is used to value the cash flows from 2008 onwards.

The calculation for the perpetuity value for 2008 and onward is shown at the bottom of Exhibit 5-4. This value is also called the terminal value. This value, $6.091 million, is added to the cash flow of $535.0 thousand forecasted to be received in 2008. The sum of these two cash flows, $6.63 million, is discounted back to its present value, the value at the beginning of 2004, to determine the present value of the growing Delphi Co.

5. Terminal Value

Terminal value is a curious concept. In general, **terminal value** means the value of an investment at the time the investment is liquidated or terminated. In valuing a business, however, the terminal value usually represents the present value of an investment's cash flows from that point

---

[19] The analysis shown is the same sort used in Chapter 4 to value capital investments.

Exhibit 5-4 Delphi Co.

Income and Residual Cash Flow with Growth

(in thousands)	2004	2005	2006	2007	2008	Normalized 2008
Sales	$ 11,330.0	$ 12,463.0	$ 13,709.3	$ 15,080.2	$ 16,588.3	$ 16,588.3
Operating expenses	(10,423.6)	(11,466.0)	(12,612.6)	(13,873.8)	(15,261.2)	(15,261.2)
Gross income	906.4	997.0	1,096.7	1,206.4	1,327.1	1,327.1
Depreciation:						
Original	(50.0)	(50.0)	(50.0)	(50.0)	(50.0)	(50.0)
Growth-induced	(0.5)	(1.1)	(1.7)	(2.3)	(3.1)	(3.4)
Income before taxes	855.9	945.9	1,045.0	1,154.1	1,274.0	1,273.7
Taxes	(291.0)	(321.6)	(355.3)	(392.4)	(433.2)	(433.1)
Income after taxes	564.9	624.3	689.7	761.7	840.8	840.6
Depreciation:						
Original	50.0	50.0	50.0	50.0	50.0	50.0
Growth-induced	0.5	1.1	1.7	2.3	3.1	3.1
Change in property, plant, and equipment:						
Original	(50.0)	(50.0)	(50.0)	(50.0)	(50.0)	(50.0)
Growth-induced	(5.0)	(5.5)	(6.1)	(6.7)	(7.3)	(3.1)
Working capital change	(206.0)	(226.6)	(249.3)	(274.2)	(301.6)	0
Annual cash flow	354.4	393.3	436.0	483.1	535.0	840.6
Terminal value*					6,091.3	6,091.3
Residual cash flow	$ 354.4	$ 393.3	$ 436.0	$ 483.1	$ 6,626.3	
Net present value @ 13.8% = $4,671.						

Assumptions:
Growth of 10 percent until 2008; depreciation is 10 years straight line; working capital is 20 percent of the change in sales

*Terminal value is the perpetuity value of the annual residual normalized cash flow in 2007 at a discount rate of 13.8% [$840.6/(0.138 − 0.0)].
The growth is zero from 2008 onwards.

onwards. That point should be when the cash flows are not expected to change in the future. At that point the perpetuity method can be used to calculate the NPV of the future cash flows.[20] The perpetuity method of valuation is easy, so we must ask when can an analyst use this shortcut? The answer to that question is when the cash flows are not expected to change. Let's use an example to show how the calculation is done.

Suppose you were making an investment in a company that was expected to return $100 forever, and the required return for its level of risk was 10 percent. What would it be worth, what price would be fair for this investment? Using the perpetuity approach, without growth, your answer would be:

$$\text{Present value perpetuity} = \frac{\text{Annual cash flow}}{\text{Investors' required rate of return}}$$

$$= \frac{\$100}{0.10}$$

$$= \$1,000$$

The perpetuity also can be used when the cash flows are expected to grow at a constant, low rate for a very long time.[21] By constant rate, we mean a rate that does not change. Since the rate of growth will not change for a very long time it implies that the rate must be relatively low. Let's use an example of valuing a slow-growing cash flow before we turn to Delphi's terminal value.

Suppose someone told you that you could have an investment that, while otherwise identical to the first investment, would provide $100 plus 3 percent every year. What would this investment be worth?

$$\frac{\text{Constant growth}}{\text{present value}} = \frac{\text{Annual cash flow} \times (1 + \text{Growth in cash flows})}{\text{Investors' required rate of return} - \text{Growth in cash flows}}$$

$$= \frac{\$100 \times (1 + 0.03)}{0.10 - 0.03}$$

$$= \$1,471.43$$

Obviously growth increases the present value of the cash flows. Since a low constant rate of growth is what characterizes Delphi Co.'s future, we were able to use the **constant-growth perpetuity** to value the cash flows after 2008 as shown in Exhibit 5-4.[22]

The question of when an analyst can use one of the perpetuity shortcuts is widely debated. Analysts often use this shortcut to value cash flows

---

[20] This is called the present value of an annuity in Chapter 4.

[21] At a high rate of growth into perpetuity, the company would eventually be unrealistically enormous. Thus when high growth is expected for some time, the cash flows must be forecasted annually until the abnormal growth is exhausted.

[22] This is also called the Gordon Model when used with dividends. It is named after Myron Gordon, who devised it.

long before the cash flows are either steady or growing at a slow but steady rate. This is generally because the analyst's fear of forecasting overcomes their common sense: they just do not know what the cash flows are likely to be, so why not use a shortcut? Fear, however, is not a good reason to use a shortcut, especially when it can lead to significant errors in value.[23] One general rule about when a shortcut can be used can be developed from the concept of sustainable growth rate described in Chapter 1: when the expected growth rate of the company into the future is equal or very close to its long-term sustainable rate of growth, the analyst can feel more confident in the use of a perpetuity shortcut.

A bit later in this chapter we will discuss other methods of valuation, for example, the use of price/earnings ratios in valuation.[24] As you read that section, keep in mind that market price/earnings multiples are frequently used as a way to estimate a terminal value. You will see the benefits and the dangers: it is easy to use but it buries all assumptions into one simple and simplistic number.

6. Inflation and Growth

Inflation is a factor that can profoundly affect the value of a company, and it is an important one. Inflation affects both the cash flows and the discount rate—sometimes in unexpected ways. In the appendix to Chapter 1, we discussed the impact of inflation on depreciation. When the tax code requires that assets be depreciated at their historical cost, depreciation does not keep up with inflation: depreciation is calculated based on a currency value that has changed. In Chapter 2 we looked at an example of the problems that one can encounter in making forecasts in a highly inflationary environment. Clearly, inflation affects cash flows and discount rates, and both impact value.

Exhibit 5-5 shows cash flow forecasts for Delphi with 10 percent inflation from 2003 to 2007. Compare the depreciation shown in Exhibit 5-5 with the depreciation with real growth of 10 percent (Exhibit 5-4). You can see that the depreciation is lower and the taxes higher under inflation.[25] This is the so-called depreciation penalty of inflation we discussed earlier.

Inflation has another impact on the value of a company. It increases the investors' required rate of return.[26] A higher discount rate reduces the value of any given set of cash flows, as you can see by looking at the net

---

[23] The more important reason not to use this shortcut inappropriately is because the information and insight gained from doing the detailed analysis is glossed over, buried, and provides neither insight nor information.

[24] There are other methods of valuation that can be used, but they are dependant upon the condition and strategy of the company at the point the terminal value is estimated. For example, if the company expects to dissolve and distribute its assets to the owners, liquidation value might be appropriate.

[25] We have assumed that Delphi operates in a country where the tax code does not allow for the revaluation of assets due to inflation. This revaluation of assets due to inflation is described in the appendices to Chapters 1 and 4.

[26] This is because investors do not want to lose money in real terms, as you will learn in Chapter 6.

Exhibit 5-5   Delphi Co.

Cash Flows with No Real Growth and 10% Inflation for Five Years and No Inflation or Growth Thereafter

(in thousands)	2004	2005	2006	2007	2008	Normalized 2008
Sales	$ 11,330.0	$ 12,463.0	$ 13,709.3	$ 15,080.2	$ 16,588.3	$ 16,588.3
Operating expenses	(10,423.6)	(11,466.0)	(12,612.6)	(13,873.8)	(15,261.2)	(15,261.2)
Gross income	906.4	997.0	1,096.7	1,206.4	1,327.1	1,327.1
Depreciation:						
Original	(50.0)	(50.0)	(50.0)	(50.0)	(50.0)	(50.0)
Growth-induced	—	—	—	—	—	—
Income before taxes	856.4	947.0	1,046.7	1,156.4	1,277.1	1,277.1
Taxes	(291.2)	(322.0)	(355.9)	(393.2)	(434.2)	(434.2)
Income after taxes	565.2	625.0	690.8	763.2	842.9	842.9
Depreciation:						
Original	50.0	50.0	50.0	50.0	50.0	50.0
Growth-induced	—	—	—	—	—	—
Change in property, plant, and equipment:						
Original	(50.0)	(50.0)	(50.0)	(50.0)	(50.0)	(50.0)
Growth-induced	—	—	—	—	—	—
Working capital change	(206.0)	(226.6)	(249.3)	(274.2)	(301.6)	—
Annual cash flow	359.2	398.4	441.5	489.0	541.3	842.9
Terminal value					6,108.0	6,108.0*
Residual cash flow	$ 359.2	$ 398.4	$ 441.5	$ 489.0	$ 6,649.3	

Net present value at 13.8% = $4,698
Net present value at 23.8%** = $3,277

*The terminal value is $6,108 ($842.9/(0.138 − 0.0)), since there is no inflation from 2008 onwards, and Delphi is not expected to grow.
** A discount rate of 23.8 percent includes 10 percent for inflation.

present values shown in Exhibits 5-4 and 5-5. The higher discount rate better reflects the rate that investors would require in a world with 10 percent inflation. The twin impacts of inflation on cash flows and on the investors' required rate of return point out a critical element in valuation—the forecasts for the discount rate and the cash flows must both rest on the same assumptions for the future.

Thus far we have not discussed how the acquisition of Delphi would be financed by NUVUE. We will postpone that discussion until Chapters 8 and 9, and confine ourselves to the valuation of a company for the shareholders' perspective alone. Financing of an acquisition is a critical decision. However, we need to discuss financing in more detail before we can discuss the acquisition financing decision and its implications for value.

III. Valuation Using Market Multiples

Some analysts discount earnings rather than cash flows. We have not done that so far. There is one major reason: earnings do not reflect the real earning power of the company. Earnings reflect the impact of accounting rules on the timing of expenses and revenues. In some circumstances a company's earnings and cash flows are the same. This can occur with slow-growing, mature companies. Since this is rare, the analyst is safe when using cash flows, and not earnings. Thus an easy, reliable rule is that under no circumstance should the earnings (or EBITDA) of a company be discounted to estimate the value of a business, only the cash flows. Earnings are useful for perspective and communication, however.

1. Earnings Multiples

Most of us would like an easier way to estimate the value of a company since making assumptions and cash flows is laborious. To avoid elaborate projections of cash flows, risks, and required rates of return, some analysts use the relationship of a firm's projected earnings to its stock price to value a company. From this ratio the analyst estimates the price per share for the business to be acquired as follows:

$$\text{Price per share} = \text{EPS} \times \text{P/E}$$

Where:
    EPS = Earnings per share
    P/E = The firm's estimated price/earnings ratio after acquisition

A company with publicly traded stock already has a P/E. This P/E reflects the relationship between the company's earnings per share and the share's current market price—the market's assessment of the company's value. So how can you use the P/E multiple to value a company when the P/E itself is created from the market's assessment of a company's value? There are a variety of companies for which there is no P/E or where the current P/E cannot be used. These are companies:

1. With no publicly traded stock.

2. Where the expectations for the future are quite different from the current circumstances:
   a. An acquisition or merger is expected to create synergies.
   b. The acquisition is expected to change the structure of the company.
3. The company is over- or undervalued in the stock market.

For the company with no publicly traded stock, analysts either use the discounted cash flow or create an estimated P/E for valuation. Let's use our example to show how to use an estimated P/E.

Suppose that NUVUE's management expects Delphi's earnings over the next 12 months to be $510,840.[27] With 100,000 shares of stock outstanding, expected earnings per share would be $5.11. But Delphi is not publicly traded and has neither a market price nor a P/E ratio to use as a starting point for the valuation. To overcome this lack of information NUVUE management must estimate the appropriate P/E to use in the valuation. To do this management will turn to other sources of information about the appropriate P/E to use as a proxy for Delphi's unobservable P/E. As a proxy management might use the average P/E for a group of similar, but publicly traded firms, or the P/E for the most similar company it can find. Note that by using a proxy P/E you are assuming that companies in the same industry or with similar characteristics are equally risky and that the market will pay a standard multiple of earnings for stocks of equivalent risk. This is a big assumption, but one that is critical to remember.

Proxies are tricky and should be used with care. The price/earnings multiples of comparable stocks in the same industry can be very different, as are the P/Es for Delphi's industry that are shown in Exhibit 5-6. These are P/Es from the most recent four years.

Exhibit 5-6

Selected Publishing Companies' Average Annual P/E Multiples: 2000–2003

	2000	2001	2002	2003
Banly	6	7	15	10
Brown Inc.	8	4	NA	5
C.C.&H.	8	6	12	18
Delfin	6	7	15	18
Grants Industries	19	28	40	37
Hightower	24	21	55	69
John Howard	11	12	15	18
McDougal	8	6	11	9
Average	11.3	11.4	23.3	23.0

---

[27] As shown in Exhibit 5-1.

If management chooses to use the industry average of the most recent P/Es, the estimated price per Delphi share would be:

$$\text{Price per share} = \text{EPS} \times \text{P/E}$$
$$= \$5.11 \times 23.0$$
$$= \$117.53$$

At a price per share of $117.53, the total value for the company would be $11.8 million ($117.53 × 100,000 shares). This price is higher than any of the present values we calculated for Delphi using the cash flow method.

The fact that we found Delphi's value using the cash flow and earnings multiple methods quite different is not unusual. There can be any number of reasons why this can happen. The most important reason for valuation differences is that the proxy companies and the company being valued are different. The differences can be in size, markets, customers, strategies, and/or products. In the case of Delphi, it is not publicly traded, it sells different products and to different customers, it has had virtually no growth in the recent past, and it is smaller than the other book publishers.

In addition to the fact that the universe of competitors is not reflective of the character of Delphi, several of the proxy companies have P/Es that are much higher than that which Delphi might command if it were publicly traded.[28] To rectify the differences, the analyst may choose to exclude one or more of the companies on the list to create a group that is more comparable to Delphi. In this situation the analyst might choose to remove those with the highest P/Es—Hightower and Grants. The average P/E would be 13.0. Using this P/E, the estimated value of Delphi would be $6.6 million (13.0 × $5.11 × 100,000 shares). This is closer to our NPV valuation.

When none of the comparison companies closely resemble the company being valued, the analyst must seek other companies for comparison or adapt the proxy P/E average. For instance, the analyst might choose to use the company's most similar competitor, or the P/E implied from the purchase prices of recent acquisitions of similar companies. For example, on our proxy list the only company that is both small and publishes religious material is McDougal. The P/E McDougal commands is lower than the industry average. Using McDougal's P/E of 9 as a proxy for Delphi, the value of Delphi would be $45.99 per share, and the total value of the company would be $4.6 million. This is close to our NPV valuation.

The price/earnings method of valuation requires an estimate that is difficult to make no matter how we might choose to find a proxy P/E. There are other reasons why using the P/E is tricky. First, to use it we must assume that recent earnings represent the real earning power of the

---

[28] As an analyst if you knew more about why Grants' and Hightower's P/Es were so high, or why Brown's P/E was so low, you might choose to exclude them from the sample. Indeed, in 2003, Hightower's P/E had risen so much it required more investigation.

firm. In the recent past we have been faced with evidence that the reported earnings of U.S. corporations have become less and less representative of companies' economic earnings. Changes in accounting methods for such items as retiree health benefits, revenue recognition, and option valuation have made the reported earnings of U.S. corporations resemble only vaguely the firms' real earning power. This, in addition to some corporate reporting choices and even managements' fraudulent actions, make reported earnings difficult to use without significant evaluation and revision. As for the veracity of earnings of companies in other countries, they vary greatly.

Second, the P/E method assumes that the price/earnings ratio is a reliable indicator of value. While the current P/E of a publicly traded firm reflects its shareholders' present estimates of its future as an independent company, it is just the relationship between the market price of the company's stock and its earnings.[29] It does not reflect the potential synergies that might result from a merger.[30] To estimate the value of synergies using the earnings-valuation approach, the analyst must forecast both the new earnings after the merger and the P/E multiple as if the merger and its benefits were known to investors. The current P/E reflects prospects without a merger, and a P/E reflecting the potential for a merger is different and very difficult to estimate. If the acquisition is expected to create value, the analyst is justified in using a higher estimate; just how high is the question. The problem is that no simple method exists for making this estimate.[31]

There are still other assumptions behind the earnings-valuation method: that the earnings stream will remain constant over time, and that short-term earnings and market prices are good indicators of value. These are dangerous assumptions. The NPV method, on the other hand, assumes that any acquisition with a positive marginal value will increase the value of the acquiring company and that the increased value will eventually be reflected in the market price of its stock. The logic behind the NPV method is clear and powerful.

While we dismiss the P/E multiple method as the sole approach to valuing an acquisition, it can be very useful in putting the present value analysis into a capital market perspective. For instance, we can compare the P/E that is implied by a present value analysis to a P/E estimated

---

[29] Actually, stock analysts may choose to use the current 12 months, the trailing 12 months, the last fiscal or calendar year, or an estimate of the future earnings in calculating the P/E. When using published P/E ratios the analyst must know what data was used to calculate the ratio.

[30] In addition, P/Es of growing companies depend heavily upon future expectations. The P/E can be temporarily, and perhaps unrealistically, high. This was certainly true with Internet stocks during the stock market bubble. In addition, healthy cyclical companies typically have high P/Es when they are at their cyclical lows for earnings, and low P/Es when their earnings are at their best.

[31] In an earlier section about terminal values, we noted that P/E ratios can be used to estimate terminal values. In the discussion of P/Es and their use in valuation, it should be clear that forecasting a P/E in the future is virtually impossible and holds no details about the assumptions being made by the analyst.

using the earnings analysis. Exhibit 5-7 summarizes information from Exhibits 5-1 and 5-4.

Exhibit 5-7   Delphi Co.

Valuation Information

Cash flow per year	$510,840
Earnings per year	$510,840
Discount rate	13.8%
Net present value with 10 percent growth for five years	$4.7 million
Number of shares	100,000

The **implied price/earnings ratio** is equal to the present value divided by the earnings.[32] It also can be calculated on a per share basis.

$$\text{Implied P/E} = \frac{\text{PV}}{\text{Earnings}}$$

$$= \frac{\$4,670,850}{\$510,840}$$

$$= 9.1 \text{ times}$$

The implied P/E is lower than the average ratio for all but one of the companies in Exhibit 5-6. Why is the implied P/E only 9.1? Should we use a higher P/E? There are several possible reasons for the difference between the implied P/E for Delphi and others in the publishing business:

1. The predicted cash flows and their underlying growth rates may be less than what the market is forecasting.
2. The predicted risk incorporated in the required rate of return may be higher than the market's prediction.
3. There may be an error in the inflation forecasts.
4. The P/E of Delphi could be lower than that of the industry because of its size, markets, products, or prospects.

A good analyst will return to the analysis to determine which cause is likely, and adjust the analysis or conclusions where needed. As for Delphi, the implied P/E is lower because the expected rate of growth is lower than that expected for others in the industry over the long run. This is due to Delphi's concentration in the religious materials publishing business. Thus the lower P/E seems justified.

---

[32] Since the denominators of the PV and earnings are both the same number of shares, the analysis can be done on the totals.

There are serious problems with using the P/E for valuing a whole company, but what about using it for estimating the terminal value? In the analysis of Delphi's value once growth had slowed, we used the perpetuity valuation method. Some analysts choose to use a multiple of the terminal year's earnings to calculate the terminal value. This approach has the same problems as using a P/E to value the whole company, and one more: we have to forecast what the company or industry P/E will be at some point in the future. This adds a degree of fragility to the forecast.

2. Other Multiples for Valuation

Price/earnings ratios depend both upon the company's earnings, its earning prospects, and the capital markets' general level of optimism. Over time the average P/Es for the market change. At times of robust economic prospects or market enthusiasm P/E ratios, as well as other multiples like the market/book value and price/cash flow or sales, may be quite high. This indicates that investors feel confident and are willing to take risk. Such was the case in 1999 to 2001, particularly among many companies with Internet-related businesses. Exhibit 5-8 shows this quite dramatically, particularly when you look at the differences between the Panel A and Panel B data.

Exhibit 5-8

Standard and Poor's 500 Market Multiples[33]

Panel A: 1999

| Multiples | S&P 500 | | | Technology Stocks |
	1999	5-Year Average	Difference	
Price/earnings	32.6	23.7	9.0	166.1
Market/book value	6.1	2.9	3.2	61.3
Price/sales	2.9	2.1	0.8	64.9
Price/cash flow	20.7	16.2	4.5	132.1

Panel B: 2001

| Multiples | S&P 500 | | | Technology Stocks |
	2001	5-Year Average	Difference	
Price/earnings	30.5	36.7	−6.2	51.6
Market/book value	4.9	4.8	0.1	3.1
Price/sales	2.4	3.1	−0.7	4.3
Price/cash flow	16.2	16.3	−0.1	28.4

---

[33] In this exhibit we show the data in multiples, not in percentages. You may choose to use either multiples or percentages. We use both in this book.

The very high or low multiples can be a very short-lived phenomenon. To forecast them would have been difficult. In fact, if you had been in the middle of 1999, would you have forecast that multiples would be lower, the same, or higher in five years? Could you have forecast the magnitude of the changes, and how these changes would impact various industries? Such forecasts are virtually impossible. Yet from the middle of 1999 to 2003 change did come, and it was dramatic.[34]

Managers, corporate and investment analysts, and investment managers often use multiples in their valuations. The multiples often are used as a shorthand by those who fully know industries and companies, or for cross-border (EBITDA) comparisons. There are industry-specific multiples that have been developed to represent value—for instance, multiples of revenue per subscriber line for cable companies or same-store sales for growing retailers. For companies with no earnings—for instance, Internet or biotechnology companies—some analysts use multiples of revenues.

While it is simple to use P/Es and other price multiples, using them avoids the detail and explicitness of cash flow forecasts. Multiples can be useful in describing valuations and in communicating. However, using them to shortcut a full discounted cash flow valuation results in a loss of critical information that is needed for good decisions and a complete valuation. This is a particularly important loss when the investment is significant and/or large, as are most mergers, acquisitions, and divestitures. No manager can afford to lose information, know less than possible, or lack information about how the forecasts and valuation might be impacted by changes in the company, the industry, and/or the economy. Cash flow forecasting forces us to look at the details. Big investments deserve this careful attention.

IV. Other Valuation Techniques

Acquisition analysts use several other valuation techniques. Each is used to value the company or to estimate a terminal value. However, these methods are best used as supplements to the present value analysis, not as substitutes for it.

1. Book Value

The book value is the value of the equity on a company's balance sheet—its common stock and retained earnings. To use the book value method to value a company or terminal value, the analyst multiplies the book value of the company by a market/book value ratio.

$$\text{Company value} = \text{BV} \times \text{MV/BV}$$

Where:

BV = Book value of equity of a company
MV/BV = Stock market price/book value of a company

---

[34] At one point the average P/E for on-line retailers was over 100.

The ratio might come from any one of the sources we discussed in the previous section on P/E multiples. Recent ones are listed in Exhibit 5-8.

Using market/book value multiples as a valuation technique is quite basic and lacks any but the most simplistic reasons for its use. In addition to the problem with using any multiple, book value has its own peculiar problem—it is a poor estimate of economic value. There are several reasons for this. Book value:

1. Depends on the accounting practices of a firm. It is usually only an approximation of the real economic value of the firm.
2. Ignores intangible assets. Intangibles—copyrights, trademarks, patents, franchise licenses, and contracts—protect a company's right to market its goods and services and thus have value. If the book value of the assets is less than the present value of the cash flows of the firm, intangible assets can account for the discrepancy.
3. Ignores liabilities not reflected on the balance sheet. These liabilities may be such things as lawsuits pending against the company, or employee retirement benefits or off-balance-sheet financing not reported on the balance sheet.
4. Ignores the price appreciation of real assets. Since assets are valued on the balance sheet at their depreciated costs, some assets may be valued far below even their liquidation value. Assets such as land and mineral reserves are prone to valuation discrepancies.

Owners of privately or closely held firms often believe that book value is the least they should receive when selling the company.[35] When this is true, book value often provides a floor below which a successful price offer is unlikely to go. It is not necessarily a reasonable estimate of the floor value since the book value can overstate the value of the company.[36] Since it is thought to provide a floor for valuation, you should be aware of it in contemplating the price at which a merger offer might succeed.

2. Liquidation Value

Liquidation value is the cash value the acquirer would receive if the assets of the acquired firm were sold.[37] It may also be used to aid in determining the fair value of over- or undervalued assets. Analysts sometimes use liquidation value as a floor price for an acquisition. If liquidation value exceeds the present value, the company is worth more if its assets are sold. Liquidation value can also be used as a terminal value in valuing a company when its products or services have a definite life. This valua-

---

[35] This can be true for more widely held companies, too.
[36] Overstating occurs when management has invested, at book value, and still holds assets that are obsolete, worthless, or worth less than what was paid for them.
[37] This can also be used by stock analysts considering the potential for an acquisition and the value of the deal if pieces of the acquired company are sold. This kind of analysis might be called "the-parts-are-greater-than-the-whole" analysis.

tion method might be useful, for instance, in valuing the patent protection on prescription drugs.[38]

3. Replacement Cost

Replacement cost is a measure of the cost of replacing the assets of the potential acquisition. While some analysts use it to set a ceiling price on the acquisition, replacement cost estimates can be difficult to make. In spite of this, there are times when this method of analysis has been of special interest. When the cost of acquiring assets by buying a whole company is less than buying the assets themselves, replacement cost is a valuable approach. This has happened at various times with such things as oil reserves, brand franchises, mineral rights, and manufacturing facilities.

4. Market Value

The market value of the firm's stock is often a good starting point in estimating an acquisition's price. If the stock is publicly traded its market value is simply the market price per share times the number of shares. The reason market value is only a starting point should be clear from the present value analysis we performed for Delphi and NUVUE. If the acquisition is expected to increase value for the shareholders of one or both firms, this increase in value is unlikely to be reflected in the public price of the common stock of either firm.[39] Thus, if there are synergies and value will be created from those synergies, the current market prices underestimate the present value of the merged firms. Still, the market price of the stock is a benchmark from which the analyst can begin.[40]

Under certain circumstances, all these values should be the same. Liquidation value should reflect what a buyer is willing to pay for the earning power of the firm's assets. Thus, a liquidation value should be close to the value estimated using present value analysis. Likewise, if book value truly reflects the company's economic value (the earning power of the assets), it, too, estimates a value that is the same or similar to other valuations.[41] Only because of estimation errors and accounting conventions, coupled with inflation's impact, will the values be different.

---

[38] This and other methods are used to value companies in a sum-of-the-parts valuation. Such a valuation is performed when the acquirer expects or is expected to sell off assets, divisions, or lines of business.

[39] Of course, the expectation of increased value may be reflected in the price once the merger becomes public knowledge. In addition, if a company is buying controlling interest in a company, there may be a control premium.

[40] For an investment manager, companies with a stock price that is less than the intrinsic value are undervalued: they are the stocks to buy. Managers who seek undervalued securities are called value managers. They seek stocks where the intrinsic/market value is greater than 1.0, and as high as possible. They also look for a catalyst: some event or action that will allow the market price to reach the intrinsic value.

[41] When the earning power of the asset is greater than the book value, management has created value.

5. Dividend Discount Valuation

Dividend discount models are among the earliest versions of discounted cash flow models in finance. They are commonly used by investment analysts and managers. Closely akin to discounted cash flow and earnings models, they concentrate only on what the investor actually receives in cash payments and when the cash is received.

$$\text{Present value dividends} = \sum \frac{\text{DPS}}{(1 + R_e)^n}$$

Where:

Σ = Sum

DPS = Future dividends per share

R_e = Required return on equity

n = The period, usually a year

The perpetuity version of the dividend discount model is as follows:

$$\text{Present value dividends} = \frac{\text{DPS}(1 + g)}{R_e - g}$$

In this case the g in the formula is the expected growth rate in the cash to be received—the future dividends—not the growth in earnings or cash flows.

Once again we will use an example to show how this model is used to determine the intrinsic value of the equity of a company. Let's estimate the equity value for a company that pays dividends and is well-known in the United States and around the world: Kellogg's, a producer of ready-to-eat cereals including Corn Flakes, Frosted Flakes, Nutri-Grain, and Fruit Loops as well as other convenient breakfast and snack foods, such as Pop Tarts, Eggo Waffles, Nutri-Grain Bars, and Rice Krispies Treats. Kellogg's acquired Keebler Foods, a snack food, cracker, and cookie producer, in 2001. The company has paid dividends for years. For the year ending December 2002 the dividend was $1.01, an 87 percent payout of net income. Dividend growth has been regular—over the prior five years the dividends have been $0.87, $0.92, $0.96, $0.99, and $1.01, a growth rate of 3.2 percent per year.[42]

Since the dividend is steadily growing, the perpetuity model can be used for valuation. Remember, we are forecasting the dividend one year beyond the date of the stock price, January 2003. The required return that we will use for the discount rate is 6.4 percent. This is a rate we estimated to reflect the very low risk of Kellogg's business and the fact that key investment rates were very low in January 2003.[43]

---

[42] Just because dividends have grown at 3.2 percent over the five years does not mean they will grow by that amount in the following years. In fact, another analysis might have the increase slowing. However, Kellogg's dividends have grown every year and the 3.2 percent growth rate is one reasonable estimate.

[43] The 6.4 percent required return is quite low by historic standards.

$$Value = \frac{DPS(1 + g)}{K_e - g}$$

$$= \frac{\$1.01(1 + .032)}{0.064 - 0.032}$$

$$= \frac{\$1.042}{0.032}$$

$$= \$32.56$$

The stock price in January 2003 was just over $33 but had been fluctuating, as had been the market. In spite of the late summer 2002 gyrations of the market, the low-risk nature of Kellogg's had kept the fluctuations relatively low. With an estimated price of $32.56 and an actual market price per share of between $33 and $34, our model did a good job of valuing Kellogg's.[44] This may not be the case with other companies where dividends are not paid, the dividend payment is not steady, or the company or investors' sentiments are undergoing change.

6. Relationship among Earnings, Cash Flow, and Dividend Discount Models of Valuation

We now have three valuation models. Each model discounts a different thing, cash flows, earnings, or dividends. Which model is correct? Are these models related? Will the dividend and cash flow discount models find the same value for a company and/or its stock? The answer is all the models are correct, but they will give identical answers if and only if you are discounting information about the same company at the same point in time using the same assumptions.

Look at the chart in Exhibit 5-9. This shows one company's cash flows, earnings, and dividends at the three stages of its life cycle.

> **Stage 1—Fledgling.** As a company first begins its life its cash flows are negative as are its earnings: the company is making investments into such things as product development, brand franchise, equipment, and inventory. At this stage the company cannot and does not pay a dividend.
>
> **Stage 2—Growing.** As the company produces its products, markets them, and gains success, its cash flows and earnings go from negative to positive, and are growing. As we saw in Chapter 1, such growth still requires investments, and paying a dividend, at least as the company grows rather rapidly, is not feasible.
>
> **Stage 3—Mature.** Finally, the company is mature. In sustainable growth terms, the rate of growth and the sustainable rate of growth are close and the company is able to pay dividends.

---

[44] We earlier discussed how stock prices keep changing as there is news about the company, the economy, and investors' sentiments. This was particularly true in the summer and fall of 2002.

Exhibit 5-9

Life Cycle of a Company's Earnings, Cash Flows, and Dividends

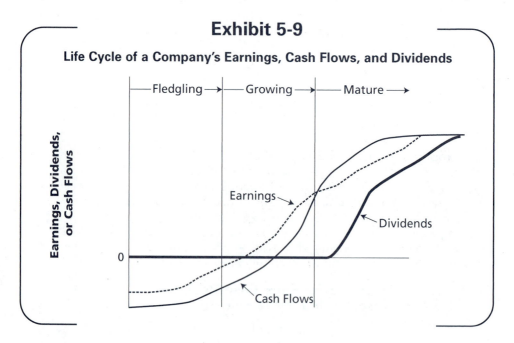

Over the company's life the cash flows and dividends are different and grow at different rates: early cash flow growth is positive and high, while dividend growth is zero. Later dividend growth is high and cash flow growth is low. Finally, the rates of growth of cash flows and dividends are quite similar. Thus you must consider the life cycle of a company in your valuation: so long as the data used reflects the position of the company in its life cycle, the dividend and cash flow discount models will result in the same valuations. So should you use earnings, dividends, or cash flows in your valuation?

The dividend discount model requires that you describe the dividend policy of the company; the cash flow model does not.[45] The earnings model relies on tax-code adjusted data; the cash flow model does not. The cash flow model requires that the company invest all retained funds, the funds that we discount, at the required rate of return for later payment to shareholders in the form of dividends.[46] All three models require assumptions about what the company will do. The cash flow model does not require assumptions about when and how much the company will pay in dividends. It deals with companies that pay no dividends as well as those that are constantly growing or changing dividends: it does not care if and when dividends are paid. The cash flow model is explicit about the

---

[45] Remember that we earlier discussed the earnings model and the way earnings can be managed. Both the cash flow and dividend models discount cash either in the form of dividends or cash flow, the dividends plus cash retained on the shareholders' behalf. The earnings model does not.

[46] This assumption of neutral (NPV = 0) investment, the investment of retained earnings at the investors' required rate of return, is crucial to this model.

corporate actions that create the cash flows. For those reasons, and others, the cash flow model is superior to others.[47]

7. Cross-Border Acquisitions

The increase in cross-border and non-U.S. merger activity in the latter half of the 1990s was extraordinary. In its increase it has posed for the analyst all the problems that we discussed in other chapters and then some. The problems that must be addressed in these mergers are:

- *In what currency should the company be valued?* In Chapter 2 we discussed forecasting in multiple currencies. The same rules apply to the analysis of a merger, with one special consideration. When using the dividend discount model an analyst must forecast when the dividend will be paid, and what the relevant exchange rate will be at the time of transfer.
- *Do local customs dictate the use of special analysis?* In some countries special analytical customs exist. For instance, in countries with a large number of closely held companies, a measure like book value may be an important consideration.
- *Are the financial statements reliable indicators of the company's past performance?* There are two primary considerations in dealing with this problem: do the accounting rules allow for transparency, and has the economy been sufficiently stable that the information has meaning?[48] If the accounting masks what has actually occurred or the economy has had a recent outburst of inflation, the historic information may be relatively meaningless.
- *Is there capital market information on which to rest forecasts or obtain proxies?* In many countries the capital markets are either very small or represent a narrow spectrum of the companies operating in the country.[49] When valuing an acquisition in such an economy, proxies and information from other countries may be adapted to help with the valuation.
- *Is the company considered a part of its domestic industry or a part of the global industry?* Companies operating as a part of the global industry, for instance, telecommunications companies, may be valued on the basis of their expanded industry rather than as purely domestic companies. Larger companies in a global industry tend to be valued higher than smaller, domestic-industry players.[50]

These are a few of the considerations in valuing a merger candidate from another country. The issues are the same, though somewhat more complicated, when dealing with companies with a multi-country structure.

---

[47] Many analysts, especially stock analysts, use a discounted cash flow to verify valuations based on P/E, MV/BV, EBITDA, or other multiples.

[48] We used to believe U.S. accounting was transparent. We know that U.S. financial statements must be scrutinized with care.

[49] For instance, a large number of the companies in Canada are natural-resource based.

[50] Actually, analysts and investors are just becoming better able to deal with valuing companies and industries with global franchises.

V. Mergers Waves and Troughs

Interestingly enough, merger activity is not constant—it has peaks and troughs. For example, as globalization of business became paramount, acquisitions of non-U.S. by U.S. companies rose, peaking in 1999 in both value and numbers as you can see in Exhibit 5-10. During this period Canada was the primary destination of U.S. acquirers, with the United Kingdom, Mexico, and Germany following.

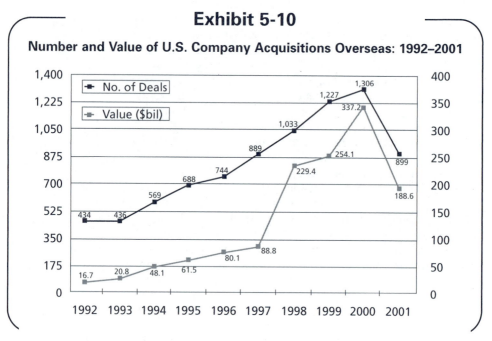

Exhibit 5-10

Number and Value of U.S. Company Acquisitions Overseas: 1992–2001

Source: "2002 M&A Profile," *Mergers and Acquisitions*, February 2002, p. 32.

At the same time as U.S. companies were making acquisitions abroad, non-U.S. companies were acquiring companies in the United States. Exhibit 5-11 shows that this activity rose through 2000, only falling prey to economic forces starting in 2001. In Europe, with its restructuring toward monetary union and economic integration, activity grew rapidly, particularly toward the end of the decade. While the number of deals increased, the size of the mergers increased even more rapidly. This data is depicted in Exhibit 5-12. You will note that the size of the mergers both in Europe and outside the United States increased. This merger boom was termed a "juggernaut" by *Mergers and Acquisition*, the bi-monthly reporting of mergers and acquisitions. In 1998 the total value of deals was over $1 trillion. By 2001, the decline in global economic activity had also profoundly impacted both the number and size of mergers in Europe by European companies as well as around the world. This continued into 2003.

Exhibit 5-11

Number and Value of Acquisitions of
U.S. Companies by Non-U.S. Companies: 1992–2001

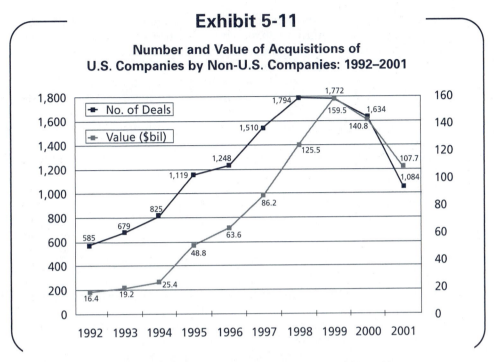

Source: "2002 M&A Profile," *Mergers and Acquisitions*, February 2002, p. 32.

Exhibit 5-12

Cross-Border Merger Activity in Europe

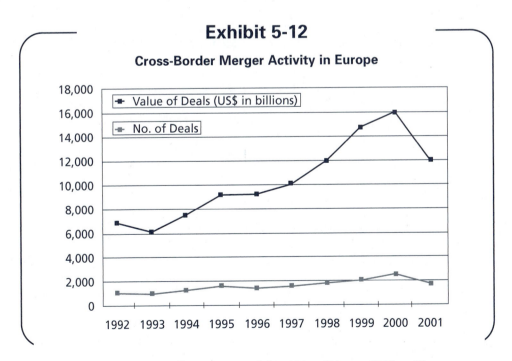

Data source: "2002 M&A Profile," *Mergers and Acquisitions*, February 2002, p. 34.

By early 2003 two things were clear. First, the number of strategic mergers, mergers to expand or enhance business, had declined dramatically. The very large increase in intra-European mergers, including mergers involving Eastern European companies that characterized the late 1990s, had stopped. Companies that facilitated mergers, in particular, investment bankers that had begun expanding their Japanese operations in advance of what they believed would be a serious period of restructuring and mergers in Japan, were in serious trouble, with many downsizing or eliminating their operations. Merger activity around the world, and those who assisted in creating the merger expansion in the late 1990s, had seen serious declines in their business. These declines continued into 2003.

Globalization contributed to merger activity prior to 2002. However, another event was believed to have contributed to the merger activity before 2002. Until mid-2001 U.S. companies could choose either the pooling or purchase method to account for a merger.[51] In **pooling** the acquired company and acquirer combine their assets and earnings. This method does not seriously impact earnings, and thus, it was believed, the merger would not impact stock price.[52] These mergers were paid for in stock, thus the shareholders of the acquired company received a tax-free transaction.

The **purchase** method of accounting for a merger already was used in the rest of the world by the time it was adopted as the sole method in the United States. In the purchase method one party to the merger must be identified as the purchaser. Anything that the purchaser pays for the acquired company above its net asset value is called goodwill, and it is placed on the purchaser's balance sheet and written off over time.[53] This reduces future earnings, the event the pooling method was trying to avoid. Goodwill being written off is not a tax-deductible expense in most countries, but it can be taken as a tax deduction in the United States.[54]

As a consequence of these waves of merger activity, it is important for analysts and managers to understand why companies combine, why they do not, and how to properly value potential activity. Lest we forget, the stratospheric prices paid for some companies at the end of the twentieth

---

[51] Some attributed the increase in U.S. mergers before 2001 to the impending demise of the purchase method of merger accounting in the United States in 2001. Some believed that some of the 2001–2002 declines in stock prices were impacted by goodwill being written off by companies that retrospectively overpaid for their acquisitions.

[52] Most believe that investors are aware of and take into account any impact a merger will have on a company's earnings. Thus the impact of the change from pooling to purchase was overstated since investors see through a mere accounting event to the real economic impact of the event. What we discovered in 2002 is that investors must have data on which to form an opinion. That lack of useful data led off a discussion of accounting transparency.

[53] Goodwill is typically written off over 15 years in a way similar to depreciation.

[54] A quarterly impairment test is done by the acquiring company. If the value of the acquisition has fallen below the goodwill account, it must be written down. Thus the future write-off of goodwill for accounting and taxes is impacted. This has particularly affected companies that acquired high-priced "dot com" companies during the stock market bubble. The goodwill accounts have been severely impaired and have had to be written down, sometimes virtually wiping out the goodwill account.

century will not guide us when we reach another peak of activity in an industry, country, or globally.

VI. Summary

There is only one purpose in making an acquisition. That purpose is to create value for the owners. Value can be created by increasing returns or reducing risk. In general, an increase in value comes from excess capacity or assets being matched with a need for that resource—a matching that cannot occur unless the two firms merge. The analyst's task is to estimate the effect of a merger on a firm's return and risk characteristics. Since projected earnings are, at best, only a vague indication of real earning power of the company, the analyst should project cash flows with and without the benefits of the synergies from the merger, and discount them to determine the acquisition's value. It is up to management to determine, in light of this valuation, the price that can and should be paid for the acquisition. Other valuation techniques, such as earnings analysis, should be used merely to corroborate the discounted cash flow analysis.

Selected References

For methods of analyzing a merger, see:

Brealey, Richard A., and Stewart C. Myers. *Principles of Corporate Finance.* 7th ed. New York: McGraw-Hill, 2002, chap. 34.

Brealey, Richard A., and Stewart C. Myers. "A Framework for Evaluating Mergers." In *Modern Developments in Financial Management.* New York: Frederick A. Praeger, 1976.

Copeland, Tom, John Wiley, Tim Koller, and Jack Murrin. *Valuation: Measuring and Managing the Value of Companies.* 3rd ed. New York: John Wiley & Sons, Incorporated, 2000.

Myers, Stewart C. "The Evaluation of an Acquisition Target." *Midland Corporate Finance Journal,* Winter 1983, pp. 39–46.

Ross, Stephen A., Randolph W. Westerfield, and Jeffrey F. Jaffe. *Corporate Finance.* 6th ed. Homewood, IL: Richard D. Irwin, 2002, chap. 30.

Shrives, Ronald E., and Mary M. Pashley. "Evidence on Association between Mergers and Capital Structure." *Financial Management,* Autumn 1984, pp. 39–48.

Weston, J. Fred, Brian A. Johnson, Kwang S. Chung, and Juan A. Siu. *Takeovers, Restructuring, and Corporate Governance.* Upper Saddle River, NJ: Prentice Hall Professional, August 2000.

For more on shareholder value creation, see:

Finegan, Patrick T. "Maximizing Shareholder Value at the Private Company." *The Journal of Applied Corporate Finance,* Spring 1991, pp. 30–45.

Mergers & Acquisitions, various issues.

Rappaport, Alfred. *Creating Shareholder Value*. New York: Free Press, 1986.

Shleifer, Andrei, and Robert W. Vishny. "The Takeover Wave of the 1980s." *Journal of Applied Corporate Finance*, Fall 1991, pp. 49–56.

For more on estimating divisional required returns, see:

Fuller, Russell, and H. Kerr. "Estimating the Divisional Cost of Capital: An Analysis of the Pure Play Technique." *Journal of Finance*, December 1981, pp. 997–1009.

Gup, Benton E., and Samuel W. Norwood, III. "Divisional Cost of Capital: A Practical Approach." *Financial Management*, Spring 1982, pp. 20–24.

Harrington, Diana R. "Stock Prices, Beta, and Strategic Planning." *Harvard Business Review*, May/June 1985, pp. 157–164.

Harris, Robert S., Thomas J. O'Brien, and Doug Wakeman. "Divisional Cost-of-Capital Estimation for Multi-Industry Firms." *Financial Management*, Summer 1989, pp. 74–84.

For studies on the relative values of mergers, see:

Cusatis, Patrick, James Miles, and J. Randall Wooridge. "Some New Evidence That Spinoffs Create Value." *Journal of Applied Corporate Finance*, Summer 1994, pp. 100–107.

Mueller, D. C. "The Effects of Conglomerate Mergers: A Survey of the Empirical Evidence." *Journal of Banking and Finance*, December 1977, pp. 315–348.

Rappaport, Alfred. "What We Know and Don't Know About Mergers." *Midland Corporate Finance Journal*, Winter 1983, pp. 63–67.

Rumelt, Richard. *Strategy, Structure and Economic Performance*. Boston: Harvard Business School Press, 1986.

Study Questions

1. Magnus Corporation and Carr Company both operate in the same industry, and although neither is experiencing any rapid growth, both provide a steady stream of earnings. Magnus's management is optimistic about the acquisition of Carr because it has excess plant capacity that Magnus hopes to use. Carr Company has 50,000 shares of common stock outstanding, which are selling at $6.00 per share. Other data are shown in the following tables.

	Magnus Corporation	Carr Company	Combined Entity
Profit after taxes	$48,000	$30,000	$92,000
Residual net cash flow/year	$60,000	$40,000	$120,000
Required return on equity	12.50%	11.25%	12.00%

CARR COMPANY
Balance Sheet

Assets		Liabilities and Owners' Equity	
Current assets	$273,000	Current liabilities	$134,500
Net PP&E	215,000	Long-term liabilities	111,000
Other	55,000	Owners' equity	297,500
		Total liabilities and	
Total assets	$543,000	owners' equity	$543,000

- Compute the maximum price the management (for the shareholders) of Magnus Corporation should be willing to pay to acquire Carr Company, and the minimum price Carr's management should accept.
- What is the value of the synergies, and which shareholders should receive this value?

2. Smythe Instrument Company wishes to acquire Robinson Research Lab through a merger. Both companies are Canadian and operate exclusively in Ontario Province. Smythe Instrument expects to gain operating efficiencies from the merger through distribution economies, advertising, manufacturing, and purchasing.

   The required rates of return for Smythe and Robinson are 16.2 percent and 14.5 percent, respectively. These rates include the market's consensus for long-term inflation of 4 percent. Neither company has any long-term debt outstanding. The effective required rate of return after the merger is estimated to be 15.5 percent. The projected real growth rate for each of the firms is 4 percent per year, and management expects that growth rate to continue when the two companies are merged. All revenues and costs are expected to keep pace with inflation of 4 percent annually. The current net cash flow per year is Canadian $6.45 million for Smythe and Canadian $2.20 million for Robinson. Based on management's analysis of the synergies for the combined company, the combined net cash flow would have been Canadian $10.92 million if the two had been combined for the past year.

   Calculate the price Smythe Instrument should offer to acquire Robinson Research and the price above which Robinson should accept the merger offer.

3. Action Corporation makes cardboard boxes for a wide range of clients. It is located in Lima, Ohio. The industry is experiencing a severe slowdown in terms of sales. Several substitute products are threatening to win over Action's major clients. In spite of the fact that entry into the industry is relatively cheap, fixed costs account for a large percentage of the total expenses. Thus volume is important, and there is pressure on margins.

In late 2003, Action was approached by a large packaging company that wanted to add a cardboard box manufacturer to its portfolio of companies. Mr. Santiago, CFO at Action, was concerned about the price he should expect for this acquisition and wondered how best to maximize the return to Action's owners.

Action was rated by Moody's rating service as a moderate risk. Mr. Santiago believed that Action's owners would demand at least an 11.2 percent return on their investment. Sales in 2003 were $250 million and were expected to grow at 5 percent annually until 2010, and 3 percent thereafter; cost of sales is 75 percent of sales; and selling, general, and administrative expenses are 10 percent of sales. Taxes are 34 percent. Depreciation is $7 million per year and not expected to change, and PP&E and working capital investments total $7 million per year. The company has no debt. In the past, Action paid dividends of 10 percent of net income, and the return on the investment was about 3.4 percent. At what price should Mr. Santiago sell to provide the Action owners a fair return?

4. Mr. Santiago assumed the company that was interested in acquiring Action was a U.S. company. Thus your cash flows and valuation are in U.S. dollars. How would Mr. Santiago change the analysis if he discovered the potential acquirer was Mexican? Be explicit about what would change in each step of the valuation process.

Chapter Six

Valuation is one of the most important topics in finance. Whether valuing an investment in a new product, process or technology, a company, or its stock, valuation requires that the analyst know about the investment, its prospects, and how changes in competition, technology, and the economy will affect its value. The analyst also must know how to go about assigning a value to the future.

In Chapters 4 and 5 we looked at valuation. In Chapter 4 we looked at capital budgeting, and how managers decide whether to make investments. In Chapter 5 we valued a company. For the most part we used the residual cash flow method of valuation in our analyses: we valued the owners' cash flows. We discussed the cash flows and how to calculate and evaluate them but we did not discuss where the discount rate came from or how to estimate it. The rate was given.[1]

In this chapter we discuss how to estimate discount rate. Please note that we have not yet discussed how a company or investment is financed, nor will we in this chapter. We save that important discussion for Chapters 7 and 8. We continue to assume that the cash flows belong only to the shareholders, and that the discount rate is the rate they require from their investment: the required return on equity.[2] The required return on equity is forward looking. It is an estimate of how investors think about an investment, how they process the information about it and determine what a fair return might be for the risk of the investment. Getting into somebody else's mind, especially when that mind is the collective mind of those in the capital markets, is a real challenge. In this chapter, we discuss how that challenge might be met, and how a discount rate that reflects the investors' required rate of return might be estimated.

---

[1] We did discuss risk-adjusting rates in Chapter 4 and 5, but not where to get the rate to be adjusted.

[2] Investors call this required return the required return on equity; however, from the company's point of view, it is a cost, and thus is called the cost of equity. It is forward looking and is not the historic return on equity.

I. What Is a Shareholders' Required Return?

Investors expect to earn a return on the funds they invest—a return that compensates them for both the time that the funds are made available to the company and the risk that the expected return will not be earned. Returns from common stock come from the dividends the common shareholders receive over the life of their investment and from any gains that may realized when they sell the stock.[3]

How do we know what equity investors expect to earn on their investment in a company? How would we estimate the returns shareholders require? We might start by thinking about how we would do this if there were only one or a small group of shareholders to whom we could talk. Let's ask that shareholder(s) some questions. First we would ask, "What return do you expect this company to earn on your behalf?" If the shareholder replied, "Fifteen percent would satisfy me; with that return I would not want to buy a larger share of the firm, nor would I want to sell the ownership position I already have," we would know that the shareholder's required return was 15 percent. That seems simple enough until you consider the number of shareholders in most companies. Most companies whose stock is bought and sold in the public markets do not have such limited ownership, and it is impossible to know how their shareholders would answer the question.[4] As a result, we must find a way to estimate the return on equity required by a large number of dispersed shareholders.

There are two categories of methods used to estimate the required return on equity. The first category places a value on the cash the company generates for its shareholders. Essentially this is a fundamental, company-specific, cash-flow based approach. The second category includes all capital market–based estimates. Capital market methods categorize all securities into risk classes and then use the classifications to estimate the owners' required return on equity. To understand how these models work, a basic introduction to the equity markets is useful.

II. Capital Market Basics

The markets for long-term funds for corporations are called **capital markets**. Capital markets differ from the money markets discussed in Chapter 3: **money markets** trade short-term investments with maturities of less than one year; **capital market investments** are longer-term invest-

---

[3] Those gains come when the investor sells the investment to someone with different expectations about the future dividends of the company. The return is called a return on equity since it is an investment in the equity of a company.

[4] Even if we could ask all the shareholders what they need to earn, we could not do so simultaneously. We would need to do this because things change over time and the answer taken at different times would not be based on the outlook for the same company, industry, and/or economic circumstances.

ments with maturities exceeding one year. In addition to providing debt funds with a stated **maturity**, the date when the instrument must be fully repaid, capital markets trade equities that have no stated maturity.[5]

Equity capital markets exist on two levels: primary markets and secondary markets. **Primary market** transactions occur when companies issue equity to investors. Typically, these securities are sold through investment bankers who, through their relationships with investment brokers, act as agents for the companies selling the instruments. The proceeds from the sales of financial instruments, minus the investment bankers' commissions, are paid to the issuing companies.[6] The primary markets are the major source of new equity capital for companies. New equity issued by companies that have never raised equity in the public markets is called **initial public offerings**, or **IPOs**.

After the securities have been sold in an IPO, the purchaser of the securities may then trade them in the **secondary markets**.[7] Financial instruments may be sold individually or bundled together and then traded between individuals or institutions that have no relationship with the original issuing company. Although the company does not gain any direct benefit from this trading, it is not indifferent to activities in the secondary markets. The prices of its securities may change as a result of changing prospects for the company, its industry, and the economy. The prices for secondary market trading of securities are reported in such U.S. publications as *The Wall Street Journal, Barron's,* and *Investors' Business Daily.* In the United Kingdom, publications such as *The Financial Times* carry daily prices, as do the major financial or daily newspapers in the United States and other countries. In addition, there are numerous web sites where current or slightly delayed prices are available.[8]

In recent years, derivative instruments, such as options and futures contracts, have been widely traded in mature capital markets and in some emerging markets.[9] These instruments, which are designed to provide a means of protecting investors against price movements in the capital markets, are all secondary market instruments. They are not a source of capital for corporations.[10] Company treasurers and investment bankers have

---

[5] We discuss the debt markets more extensively in Chapters 7 and 8.

[6] The sale can be "best efforts," where the sales proceeds are delivered to the company, or on a contractual basis where the proceeds are guaranteed. The cost of the transaction depends upon the risk being taken by the intermediary.

[7] Major shareholders and management owning shares may offer them to the market as a secondary offering.

[8] See the references at the end of the chapter.

[9] Derivative instruments are those based on another instrument. For instance, a call option on a common stock gives the owner of the option the right to buy a particular number of shares of a stock at a particular price within a given time period. Put options are the right to sell a number of shares during a particular time period for a given price. Futures are the right to buy or sell a commodity for a given price on a given day. These two option types plus futures are the basic forms of derivatives. More exotic securities can be fashioned from bundles of these derivatives.

[10] For corporations, options and futures primarily are used for hedging risk and, sometimes, speculating.

gained a real appreciation for the attractiveness of the features of some of these new instruments and have incorporated some of their characteristics into new forms of corporate securities.[11] For those working in corporate treasury offices or in investment banks, or considering investing in synthetic or exotic securities, a careful review of the features of each security is critical.[12]

Trading in capital market instruments can take place in organized market exchanges or **over the counter (OTC)**. Organized stock exchanges, such as the New York Stock Exchange (NYSE) and the American Stock Exchange (AMEX) in the United States, as well as stock exchanges around the world, allow trading only in listed securities. To achieve listed status a company must meet the specific qualifications of the exchange, including such things as the size of the company, the total market value of the publicly traded shares, the share price, and the amount of trading in the company's securities. Trading on these exchanges can be done only by members of the exchange. Members are typically brokerage companies that buy and sell securities for their customers. Increasingly, large blocks of securities can be and are traded between buyer and seller using an electronic trading system.[13] Comparable, but not identical, arrangements exist in other countries.

Unlike the organized exchanges that have a specific location where trading takes place, the **over-the-counter market** consists of numerous traders located throughout a country and even internationally. These traders do what is called *making a market*. That means that they buy, sell, and keep an inventory in one or more securities. Brokerage firms are market makers.[14] In the United States a computerized network called NAS-DAQ, sponsored by the National Association of Securities Dealers and the American Stock Exchange, ties market makers as well as buyers and sellers of non-exchange-traded securities together. Many more securities are traded OTC than on the organized exchanges. Because listed companies tend to be larger, the average trading volume for the securities listed

---

[11] These are used to enhance the value of the basic instrument, such as a bond or preferred stock.

[12] Synthetic securities are those that mimic the characteristics of some other instrument or security. Exotic securities, which have a variety of features, are generally the special creation of a particular investment bank for one issuer or a group of issuers, and normally are in vogue for a short period of time.

[13] Some exchanges themselves are electronic (for instance, the Singapore exchange), and in some areas (for instance, Europe and increasingly in the United States) the electronic trading systems compete for trades with organized exchanges. These electronic trading networks are increasingly important.

[14] In the past, stocks were traded in fractions such as $30\frac{1}{2}$ or $30\frac{1}{32}$. Trading is now done in decimals, for instance, $30.50 or $30.03125. For smaller stocks you will find two prices listed: **the bid**, the price for which the stock will be bought; and **the ask**, the price for which it will be sold by the market maker. Market makers are the investment organizations that hold inventories, or **make a market**, in a particular, usually small company, stock. Investors must buy or sell through the market maker at the bid or ask prices. The difference between the bid and ask prices is called **the spread** and is the market makers' profit. Since decimalization the spreads have dramatically declined, as have the market makers' profits and their incentive to make a market.

on the exchanges is much greater than that for the vast majority of OTC trades. In 2003, exceptions to this existed among the large technology and biotech companies. These companies, such as Dell, Microsoft, and Genzyme, are large, but choose to continue to be traded on the NAS-DAQ national market. Exhibit 6-1 shows the changes in trading volume from 1996 to 2002. Prior to the mid-1990s, the NYSE trading dwarfed that of the NASDAQ. In terms of dollar volume, the two had reached parity in 1999 as shown in Exhibit 6-2. The NASDAQ dollar volume fell well below that of the NYSE when the Internet bubble subsided.

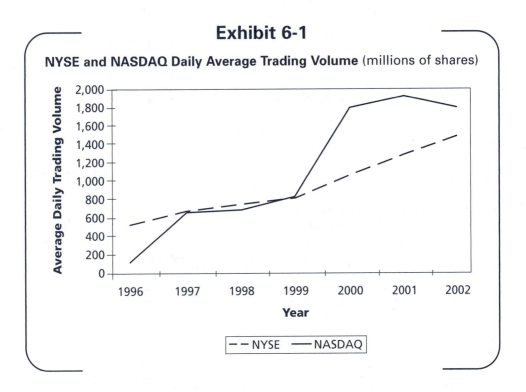

Exhibit 6-1

NYSE and NASDAQ Daily Average Trading Volume (millions of shares)

In the past few years a number of new trading systems have evolved that allow those who have a large quantity of one security, a **block**, to trade directly with a buyer or buyers; for individual investors to trade at costs close to those of large, institutional investors; and to trade outside the usual trading hours. In addition, the Internet has provided increasingly sophisticated data and tools to make and manage investments.[15] All this has expanded the interest in investing and trading, in particular to individuals.[16] This is all secondary market activity.

---

[15] See the references at the end of the chapter.
[16] Some call this the democratization of the capital markets. Individuals, who lost considerable money in the stock market "bubble," call it a disaster.

Exhibit 6-2

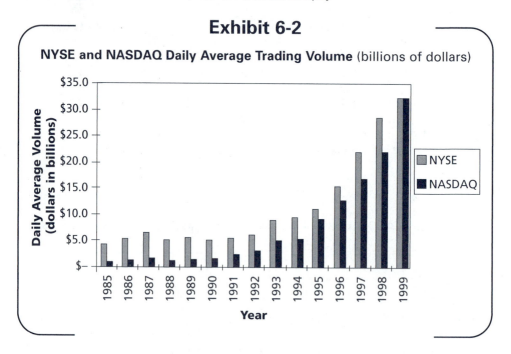

NYSE and NASDAQ Daily Average Trading Volume (billions of dollars)

While most countries have equity markets, the level of individual equity ownership varies substantially. For instance, in the United Kingdom most securities are owned by institutions. In Germany, banks own many of the securities. In Japan, cross-ownership, where shares of two or more companies are owned by each other, is common. Institutional investors such as mutual funds, insurance companies, and pension funds are the largest investors in the equity markets worldwide. While many of these relationships have been stable for a long period of time, there significant changes have and are occurring. Companies are listing their shares in more than one country and issuing bonds in more than one currency, government-run pension funds are becoming private and are being invested in the capital markets, and the volatility of markets has increased substantially.[17] In particular, the intra-day trading volatility in the United States and other markets has become dramatically higher than at any other time recorded.

Equity is the fundamental core of capital for a company. Many investors buy common stock in the expectation that the company will grow and prosper and, therefore, the stock price will increase. These increases in price come when investors revise their expectations for the company: investors increase or decrease their estimates of the company's dividend payments in the future. A change in the market price of the stock is

---

[17] Yet another set of events is influencing where shares trade: the accounting and fraud scandals that first became apparent in 2002. As a consequence of the problems of World-Com, Enron, Adelphia, and others, new requirements for companies have come from the stock exchanges and the SEC. Because of the new rules, several non-U.S. companies have decided not to list shares on U.S. exchanges.

termed a **capital appreciation** if the change is positive and a **capital loss** if it is negative. **Realized capital gains or losses** are those that come from selling shares. **Unrealized capital gains or losses** come without a sale and may subsequently disappear. In addition to owning the residual or the income of the company after all other providers are paid, common shareholders, unlike owners of preferred shares, elect the board of directors and vote on policy changes.[18]

Determinants of changes in stock prices are not easy to isolate. Factors that affect the general economy, such as changes in interest rates and the rate of economic growth, affect stock prices. In addition, the market price of a company's shares can be affected by a revised industry outlook as well as by changes in prospects for the specific company.

Dividends are the only source of income from equity investments. If expectations change regarding future dividends, and the stock price changes, the equity holder can sell some stock and capture these revised dividend forecasts.[19] The relative importance of the dividend or capital gain depends on how long the investor has held the shares. However, since future return is uncertain at the time the equity is purchased, investors must determine the return they require and decide if the current market price is fair, that is, if the cash flows that are expected to be generated from their investment will provide the return they require and want.

Having said all this, how can we use this information to ferret out the shareholders' required rate of return? To get into the shareholders' collective heads, we will take the information they give us, the stock price, and use a model of how investors make decisions. One set of models is based on the cash flow models we used for capital budgeting and valuation in Chapters 4 and 5. However, when we used these models in the earlier chapters we solved for the net present value. Now we will be looking for the required return on equity. Since we are looking at a company from the market's point of view, we will call the net present value the company's **intrinsic market value**.

$$\text{Intrinsic market value} = \sum \frac{RCF_n}{(1 + R_e)^n}$$

Where:

Σ = Sum over n time periods
RCF = Residual or shareholders' cash flow
R_e = Required return on equity
N = Time period

Now let's make one more change. Instead of solving for the intrinsic market value, let's solve for the shareholders' required return on equity

---

[18] A word of caution—some companies have more than one class of common shares. These classes are normally labeled alphabetically and often have different voting rights. This is particularly true in companies that were previously family owned and where the family maintains a higher proportion of the voting rights. Share classes can also exist to represent claims on different portions of the company's assets.

[19] A company may liquidate some or all of itself by paying an unusual dividend, selling to another buyer, or returning the equity investors' capital.

(R_e). Remembering your algebra, you know that we can have only one unknown in a formula. Since we have forecast the residual cash flows (RCF), to solve for R_e we must know the intrinsic market value, the net present value. By making one assumption about the capital markets, we can substitute the price of the company's stock in the market for the intrinsic market value in the formula. The assumption that we must make is that capital markets are efficient.

In an **efficient market** all available information is known and knowable to market participants and is reflected in the current market price of a security, for example, a company's stock.[20] That means that the intrinsic market price (the net present value) for a company should be the same as its stock market price. While a market price may change, and frequently does so, and often quite dramatically, in an efficient market the price changes only when the market participants gain new information about the company, the markets, or the economy, or change their attitude about the company.[21] Inefficient markets are markets in which no one can forecast changes in stock prices, at least not at a cost that allows them to make money repeatedly.

Research has shown that the capital markets are relatively efficient, especially the major markets, even though some studies conclude that the market may have some inefficiencies that an astute investor can exploit.[22] By assuming that equity markets are relatively efficient, we can use a company's current stock price as the value investors have placed on the company's future cash flows—their intrinsic value. Now we have two of the formula's unknowns, and that is all we need to solve for the required rate of return. Let's look in depth at how to use the cash flow valuation models.

III. Cash Flow Valuation Models

In previous chapters we discussed a variety of discounted cash flow models using cash flows, earnings, or dividends as our cash flows. Up to this point we said that the residual cash flows are the best cash flows to discount to determine the value of an investment, whether it is a company's internal investment or an investment in an acquisition. In the equity markets, however, the custom has been to look only at the cash the shareholders receive—the dividends. Since we are trying to emulate how investors think, and dividends are the equity market custom, that is the model with which we will start.

---

[20] In theory there are different degrees of efficiency from the weak form, where the current price cannot be used to forecast the future price, to the strong form, the version we are using here.

[21] This change can come from information about the company, the industry, the economy, or a change in investors' appetite for risk.

[22] The question of whether stock price changes can be forecasted is controversial. Most researchers conclude, however, that the markets are relatively efficient. In the late 1990s, the study of behavioral finance shed light on why some of the seeming inefficiencies are really the result of investors acting like humans with all of their greed, fear, and herd instincts.

1. The Dividend-Discount Model

The dividend-discount model is:

$$\text{Market price}[23] = \sum \frac{\text{Dividends}_n}{(1 + R_e)^n}$$

To use this model to value a company we must forecast the dividends forever, or at least for a very long time, and discount them at the shareholders' required return on equity. An example will serve to demonstrate how to estimate the required return on equity using the dividend-discount model.

The 3M Company, once known as the Minnesota Mining and Manufacturing Company, makes a variety of products. Its original strength was in coating and bonding for abrasives. Now it is widely known for its integrated approach to research, manufacturing, and marketing in six major business groups: health care, electro and communications, consumer and office, industrial and graphic, and safety and transportation. Best known among its products are Scotch tape and other tape products, Scotchgard fabric protector, and Post-It notes. Sales in the United States are 45 percent of 3M's total worldwide revenues. For the first nine months of 2002, 3M's revenues were $12.19 billion, and net income ($1.46 billion) increased by 39 percent. Exhibit 6-3 shows 3M's historic performance.

As you can see from the financial statements, 3M has had steady performance over the five-year period, in spite of the economic slowdown in 2001–2003 that hurt 2001 sales, income, and cash flow. The reaction of the shareholders to this otherwise steady and profitable performance is shown by the market price/book value and P/E ratios. The stock performance, shown in Exhibit 6-4, also shows the positive reaction of the capital markets to 3M's performance, especially when it is compared to the more recent performance of the overall market represented by the Standard & Poor's 500 index.[24] By early 2003, 3M's stock price was just under $127 per share; the total equity value was about $49.4 billion with just over 390 million shares outstanding.

Now that we become acquainted with 3M, let's turn to estimating the required return on equity for their shareholders using the dividend-discount model. As you can see in Exhibit 6-3, the dividends have grown every year for the last five years. However, the last few years have been difficult for many companies. In the face of a global economic recession, revenues, earnings, and cash flows have been battered. 3M Company showed some of these effects in 2001, and will do so when it reports financial results for 2002.[25] Since we have a somewhat unusual period, let's look at the returns over longer periods of time.

Exhibit 6-5 (page 282) shows 3M's earnings, dividends, and cash flows per share. At the bottom of the chart, you can see their growth rates over

---

[23] Depending upon how you are using the model, this can be called the net present value, intrinsic market value, or market price. All are the present value of the cash flows.

[24] This shows the link between performance and stock price. For some companies the link is not as obvious. That is because the future performance is expected to be dramatically different from the present performance. For 3M, it is reasonable to expect that the recent performance is a precursor to the future.

Exhibit 6-3　3M Company

Historic Performance—1997 to 2001

(in millions, except per share)

Basic Data	2001	2000	1999	1998	1997
Sales	$16,079	$16,724	$15,659	$15,021	$15,070
Net income	1,430	1,782	1,763	1,175	2,121
Depreciation	1,089	1,025	900	866	870
Cash flow	2,519	2,807	2,663	2,041	2,991
Earnings per share	3.63	4.69	4.39	3.01	5.14
Dividends per share	$2.40	$2.32	$2.24	$2.20	$2.12
Key Ratios					
Return on sales	8.9%	10.7%	11.3%	7.8%	14.1%
Sales/Assets (times)	1.1x	1.2x	1.1x	1.1x	1.1x
Return on assets	9.8%	12.8%	12.4%	8.6%	15.5%
Assets/Equity (times)	2.4x	2.2x	2.2x	2.4x	2.2x
Return on equity	23.5%	28.1%	27.2%	20.7%	34.1%
Dividend payout ratio	67.0%	52.1%	51.6%	76.4%	41.9%
Earnings retention ratio	33.0%	47.9%	48.4%	23.6%	58.1%
Self sustainable growth	7.7%	13.5%	13.2%	4.9%	19.8%
Market price/Book value (times)	7.6x	7.3x	6.2x	4.8x	5.6x
Price/Earnings (times)	29.7x	21.7x	19.9x	27.5x	18.3x

ten-, five-, and one-year periods. The rates vary depending upon the economic environment: dividend increases have varied from a high of $0.20 to a low of $0.04.

Forecasting growth rates can be a challenge. In more mature companies estimates for future growth can be found in sources such as *Value Line* and *S&P Industry Reports*, as well as numerous web sites.

In 2002, 3M's shareholders received dividends of $2.48 per share, an increase of 3.3 percent or 8 cents, from the year before.[26] However, in 2002 the economy was weak and dividend growth was lower than it had been for the previous five and ten years. With an expectation that long-term economic conditions will stabilize, and 3M will likewise recover, 3M is likely to return to its historic growth rates.[27] Since we expect future growth to be low and steady, we can use the perpetuity method of the dividend-discount model to estimate 3M's shareholders' required return on equity.[28] We also will use the growth rate in dividends for the last five years. While we would ordinarily focus on the most recent date, eco-

---

[25] Data for a year is typically reported several months after the end of the fiscal year.

[26] Dividends are made public before the annual financial statements.

[27] It is here where analysts can differ in their forecasts. However, 3M has had a rather stable dividend growth except in the recent economic recession. Thus, 4.5 percent growth in dividends is a reasonable estimate for future dividend growth.

Exhibit 6-4 3M Company

Stock Price and Standard & Poor's 500 1997–Early 2003

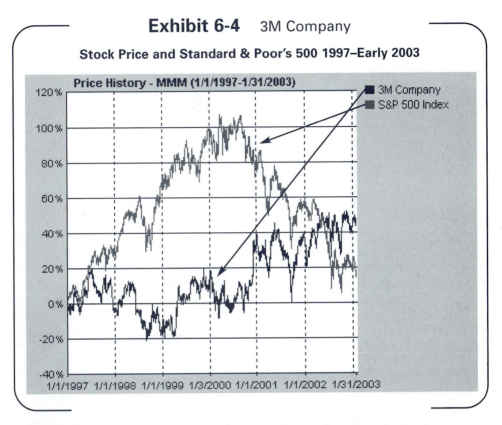

Source: MSN Money http://moneycentral.msn.com/investor/home.asp.

nomic conditions for 2001 were difficult and thus influenced that year's dividend growth rate. Note, since it is the dividend-discount model, it is proper to use the dividend growth rate (g).

$$\text{Market price} = \frac{\text{Dividend} \times (1 + g)}{R_e - g}$$

$$\$126.44 = \frac{\$2.48 \times (1 + 0.045)}{(R_e - 0.045)}$$

Rearranged:

$$R_e = \frac{\text{Dividend}}{\text{Market price}} + g$$

$$= \frac{\$2.59}{\$126.44} + 0.045$$

$$= 0.0655 \text{ or } 6.55\%$$

---

[28] In all these models, as the market price and/or company's prospects changes, these numbers will change.

Exhibit 6-5   3M Company

Earnings, Cash Flows, and Dividends: 1991–2001

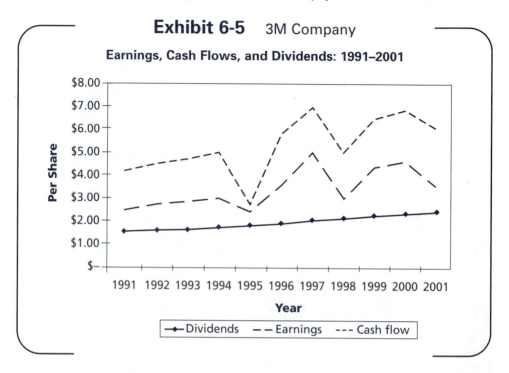

At the time 3M stock was trading at $126.44 per share, and the U.S. Treasury 30-year bond rate was 4.97 percent, 1.58 percent less than our estimated return required by 3M shareholders. Given 3M is a high-quality company with stable earnings, cash flows, and dividends, in normal times, it seems reasonable the shareholders would require a rate somewhat higher than the safe U.S. Treasury bonds. However, since this is an estimate we should corroborate it. Before we do that let us discuss the long version of the dividend-discount model.

The dividend-discount model is in widespread use. But this widely used model has its limitations. The constant growth or perpetuity version of the dividend-discount model cannot be used when:

1. A company pays no dividends. When this situation exists, the company's revenues, earnings, cash flows, and eventual dividend policy must be forecasted in order to estimate future dividends and thus the required return on equity. When a company does not pay dividends, the perpetuity dividend-discount model cannot be used.[29]

2. When either the expected rate of growth is higher than the discount rate or the rate of growth is not constant. Either of these situations

---

[29] Many people contend that some companies will never pay a dividend. This means that they will never provide any return to their investors. Logically, such a company can have no value. What we know is that as companies mature, and their need for funds declines, dividend payments become more likely. As an example of this mature move to dividend payments, in early 2003 Microsoft, long a dividend hold out, announced that its cash flow was higher than its needs and it would begin to pay its shareholders dividends.

signals that the company is entering an abnormal growth phase. Thus explicit, annual forecasts must be made for dividends, and the long version of the dividend-discount model must be used.[30]

Even if a company does not currently pay a dividend, one thing is clear—it would be impossible for the dividend growth rate to exceed that of the cash flows over a very long time. Eventually the dividends would greatly exceed the cash flows—a situation that cannot exist. For some companies the disparity between the cash flow and dividend growth rates is wide and the perpetuity versions of the valuation models cannot be used. To deal with abnormal growth, either positive or negative, year-by-year forecasts must be made. These forecasts are then compared to the current market price to estimate shareholders' required return on equity, the R_e.

To demonstrate this process let's create a fictitious future for 3M. We will assume that we hear that 3M is introducing a blockbuster line of new products. The new line will increase growth and interrupt the level, low-growth forecast we previously made for dividends. At the same time that we hear about the new products, we read that economists are forecasting a strong global economic recovery that, even without the new products, is expected to spur 3M's return to its normal growth rates. Using the information about 3M's prospects for future sales of the new products and the impact of the economic recovery, we might devise a scenario for the future such as the following:

1. For years 1–5, growth will come from cost cutting and higher-than-usual sales arising from the introduction of the new line of products and the strong economic recovery.
2. For years 6–10, growth will be lower than in the first five years but still higher than the company can sustain for a long period of time. During this period 3M continues to expand its new products with a series of line extensions. The strong economic recovery slows. At this point, it is likely that dividend growth will increase as the company's growth in sales declines and its need for funds for growth decreases.[31]
3. For years 11–15, sales, earnings, and cash flow growth slows further. Dividend growth reflects a continuing decline in the company's need for additional capital for growth. By the end of the 15 years, the dividend, earnings, and cash flow growth will be virtually identical.

The actual historic growth rates for 3M are shown in Panel A of Exhibit 6-6. The growth rates that would result from our fictitious forecast are shown in Panel B. The forecast of earnings, dividends, cash flows, and revenues, based on these growth rates, is shown Exhibit 6-7.[32] Stock analysts in investment management companies frequently do this type of forecasting.

---

[30] This long version of the dividend-discount model sums the forecasted dividends and discounts them at the required return on equity. The dividend forecasts are explicit for each year.
[31] This follows the company life cycle description we used in Chapter 5.
[32] As with any set of forecasts, different analysts will make different forecasts. These forecasts are consistent with the history of 3M and a forecast for successful new product introductions and economic recovery.

Exhibit 6-6   3M Company

Historic and Forecasted Growth Rates in Sales, Earnings, Cash Flows, and Dividends

Panel A: Historic Growth Rates

	10 Years	5 Years	1 Year
Dividends	4.4%	4.50%	3.3%
Earnings	3.3%	−0.10%	−20.0%
Cash flow	3.4%	1.20%	−1.3%

Panel B: Forecasted Growth Rates—Fictitious Scenario

Period (years)	Sales	Earnings	Cash Flow	Dividends
1–5	14.0%	10.0%	9.5%	4.0%
6–10	7.0	5.0	4.5	4.0
11–15	3.5	2.5	2.5	4.0
16 onward	2.5	2.5	2.5	3.0

Exhibit 6-7   3M Company

Summarized Forecasted Financial Performance Fictitious Scenario*

(dollars in millions except per share)

	Actual			Forecasts			
	2000	2001	2002 est.	2003	2008	2012	2018
Revenues	$16,724	$16,079	$16,337	$18,624	$33,657	$44,118	$53,708
Net income	1,782	1,430	1,879	2,067	3,177	3,862	4,478
Cash flow	2,807	2,663	2,870	3,143	4,947	5,145	5,967
Dividends/ Share	2.32	2.24	2.48	2.58	3.14	3.67	4.64

* Note that this exhibit has data only for the years when the growth rate forecasts change.

Using the data from Exhibit 6-7, and the long version of the dividend-discount model, we estimate a required return on equity of 7.5 percent for our fictitious 3M future.[33] This is higher than our earlier estimate, and

---

[33] To estimate the owners' required return, we forecast dividends from 2018 at 2.2 percent over a very long time (more than 50 years). The R_e was calculated using the internal rate of return method described in Chapter 4.

should be, since we are using different dividend growth rate forecasts than those we used in the perpetuity version of the dividend-discount model. The assumptions for 3M used in this long version of the dividend-discount model are fictional forecasts and do not reflect the assumptions we used in the perpetuity version. If the assumptions behind the two versions of the dividend-discount model are not identical, neither will be the results.[34] If they are identical, so will be the results.

Because 3M is expected to have a stable, low-growth future, we can use the perpetuity version of the dividend-discount model. Our perpetuity estimate for 3M's required return on equity was 6.55 percent, but we said that we should corroborate it. A fictitious forecast will not corroborate the perpetuity forecast. For that we have to turn to other methods.

2. Discounted Cash Flow Models

Up to now we have based our forecasts on dividends. This is reasonable since 3M has had rather predictable dividend payments. Even in times of economic contraction, the dividends have grown rather steadily, as you can see in Exhibit 6-8.[35] However, dividend payout policy and dividend payments are decisions made by a company's board of directors. The dividends may or may not follow the pattern of earnings and cash flows. As such, the forecasts for dividend policy, especially for companies without dividends, are difficult at best. Because cash flows reflect the earning power of the company and its ability to pay dividends now and in the future, the cash flows typically provide a better forecast for our required return on equity estimations. Thus we can use the discounted cash flow model we discussed and used in Chapter 5 to provide corroboration. The formula is:

$$\text{Net present value} = \sum \frac{RCF_n}{(1 + R_e)^n}$$

This, too, has a shortcut—the perpetuity version of the formula. It can be used when a company's residual cash flow is growing at a low, constant rate (g) for a long time period.

$$\text{Net present value} = \frac{RCF \times (1 + g)}{R_e - g}$$

For 3M, we can use a cash flow perpetuity model if we assume that its cash flows will grow in the future at a low steady rate. From our previous analysis it seems likely that 3M can grow at the rate it has achieved over the past five years, 1.2 percent.[36] For the net present value we substitute

---

[34] Suppose 3M management determined that it needed to slow the dividend growth for the first five years. The required return on equity would then drop. Any other changes in the growth rate for short periods of time mean that we must use the longer form of the dividend-discount model; the perpetuity version will not do. However, since 3M is mature, the short cut perpetuity dividend-discount model is appropriate.

[35] The recession that began in 2000 has had profoundly impacted all companies and 3M was no exception.

[36] Once again this is a judgment call. You may choose to support and use a different rate.

Exhibit 6-8 3M Company

Historic Earnings, Cash Flows, and Dividends per Share

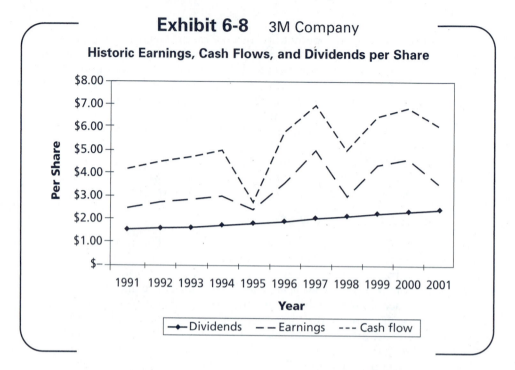

the market price of $126.44, and for the cash flow growth rate we will use the five-year average from Panel A of Exhibit 6-6 and the cash flow per share of $6.46 (390.1 million shares) from Exhibit 6-3.

$$\text{Net present value (Market price)} = \frac{RCF}{R_e - g}$$

$$\text{Market price} = \frac{RCF \times (1 + g)}{R_e - g}$$

$$\$126.44 = \frac{\$6.46 \times (1 + .012)}{(R_e - 0.012)}$$

Rearranged:

$$R_e = \frac{\$6.54}{\$126.44} + 0.012$$

$$= 0.0637 \text{ or } 6.37\%$$

The 6.37 percent we estimated using cash flows is close to our dividend-discount model estimate of 6.56 percent.[37]

As with the dividend-discount model, if we expect changes in the company before it reaches its slow-growing, mature phase, then we must

---

[37] Don't expect that the results will be identical unless you are working with a fictitious problem instead of a real situation.

use the long form of the residual cash flow model. The data used for this model would be like that shown in Exhibits 6-6 and 6-7, and the model is that shown below. We will not produce the results.

$$\frac{\text{Net present value}}{\text{(Market price)}} = \frac{RCF_1}{(1 + R_e)^1} + \frac{RCF_2}{(1 + R_e)^2} + \frac{RCF_3}{(1 + R_e)^3} + \frac{RCF_n/(R_e - g)}{(1 + R_e)^n}$$

One issue that faces us in using the long versions of the models is the length of time for the forecast. A company's life, and thus its cash flows, earnings, and dividends, will exist far into the future. Earlier in this chapter when we estimated the required return on equity using the long version of the dividend-discount model, we forecast that the fictional 3M would pay dividends for more than 50 years. However, an analyst would rarely forecast for that long. They might truncate their forecasts at fifteen years as we did with our fictitious forecasts for 3M. However, we could not stop there since we believed that 3M would still exist in 2018 and would continue to pay dividends for years into the future. To incorporate that future into our analysis we assumed that from year 16 onwards dividends would grow slowly. To value this low-growth dividend from 2018 onwards, we used a perpetuity.[38] To estimate the required return on equity we used the forecasts for the first fifteen years plus the perpetuity to compare to 3M's current market price of $126.44. The internal rate of return from these infinite forecasts was 10.55 percent. This is the estimate of the shareholders' required rate of return on equity for our fictitious forecasts for 3M.[39]

Using a perpetuity at some point in the future is only one of the ways common stock analysts estimate the terminal value. Another, more common, approach is to forecast the market price at some time in the future by multiplying the forecasted earnings in that year by an estimated price/earnings ratio. This is the value estimated in the terminal year.[40] To do this for 3M, we would estimate the 2018 earnings per share, $11.48 in our fictitious scenario, and the appropriate P/E.[41] As simple as this seems, forecasting a P/E ratio in practice, especially one years from now, is at best very difficult and at worst, impossible. The P/E forecast is much more tenuous than forecasting the cash flows, dividends, or earnings themselves. Far better is the perpetuity value of the residual cash flows the company will generate from the terminal, or low-growth, year onwards. This is the method described in Chapters 4 and 5.

---

[38] This also can be thought of as the market price for the stock at that point in the future.

[39] To estimate the owners' required return, we used the internal rate of return method and a terminal growth rate from the forecasts.

[40] This terminal value is added to the forecasts before that point just as it was in the 3M example.

[41] The P/E for 3M has ranged from 18.3 to 29.7 over the past five years. If we used those numbers, the terminal value estimate would go from $341 to $210. That does not include forecasting what will happen to the company, investors' enthusiasm for it, the economy, and the stock markets by 2018.

3. Implicit Required Return on Equity

In addition to the cash flow and dividend-discount models, analysts use numerous abbreviated approaches to estimate shareholders' required return. Many of these approaches rely on earnings, or the relationship between earnings and the market price. These are some of the same models described in Chapter 5. The most widespread method is called the **implicit required return on equity** or **implicit cost of equity**. For 3M at the beginning of 2003, the implicit required return on equity is:

$$R_e = 1/(\text{Market price/Earnings per share})$$

or

$$R_e = \text{Earnings per share/Market price}$$
$$= \frac{\$4.82}{\$126.44}$$
$$= 0.038 \text{ or } 3.8\%$$

The implicit required return on equity is well below the shareholders' required return we estimated thus far. The discrepancy arises because the model has no provision for any future growth. You might note that this model is similar to the others, only the company does not grow, that is, it either (1) pays out all earnings to its shareholders or (2) does not create value for its shareholders with any funds that it retains. In other words, the equation assumes that the net present value of a company's investments is zero.

Only for the most mature companies in stable and highly competitive industries would the implicit required return on equity be anything more than a rough approximation of the shareholders' required return on equity. For companies in declining industries, investors may believe that today's earnings and dividends are higher than they will be in the future. For new companies in growing markets, present earnings and dividends are less than investors expect to gain in the future. When a portion of the company's earnings will be reinvested in the firm, and these investments will create value for the owners, a simple approach to determining the required return on equity that fails to account for growth is useless.[42]

IV. Capital Market Estimations—Risk Premium Models

The cash flow and dividend-discount models use forecasted corporate data and the current stock price to estimate the shareholders' required return on equity. As you have seen, these forecasts can be difficult to make. An analyst may, however, use a different approach—one that estimates the required return according to the risk of the security in comparison to others available in the capital markets.

---

[42] This also holds for companies with negative growth.

The capital markets are the great arbitrageur of risk and return. Investors, both large and small, and security traders monitor the market constantly looking for profit-making opportunities. In doing so, these market participants constantly compare the returns they are getting with the risk they are taking. We can use this same process of arraying securities by their relative levels of risk on the understanding that riskier securities must promise higher levels of return to be attractive. This approach, called **capital market estimation** or risk-premium, assumes that investors require additional return to compensate them for added risk. This additional return is known as the **risk premium**. The concept can be expressed mathematically as:

$$R_e = R_f + R_p$$

Where:
R_e = Investors' required return on equity
R_f = Return required from a hypothetical risk-free security
R_p = Risk premium for the particular asset

There are several different ways to use this simple concept to estimate the cost of equity. We will discuss two methods: the stock-bond yield spread method and the capital asset pricing model.[43]

1. The Stock-Bond Yield Spread

This simple model estimates the cost of equity by means of two key variables: (1) the firm's marginal pretax cost of debt and (2) the historical difference between the firm's costs of debt and equity. Expressed mathematically,

$$R_e = R_d + (\overset{\circ}{R}_e - \overset{\circ}{R}_d)$$

Where:
R_e = Required return on equity
R_d = Required return (pretax) on debt, for instance, the yield to maturity on the firm's bonds
$\circ$ = Indicates historical data

We will demonstrate how it is used by calculating 3M's shareholders' required return on equity. If 3M's historical equity/debt cost difference (the spread) has been 2 percent and the company's marginal required return on debt is 6.3 percent, we can calculate 3M's shareholders' required return on equity.[44]

---

[43] There is another risk premium model called arbitrage pricing theory. This model relies on more factors as a source of return on a security, while the capital asset pricing model uses only "the market." This is a very interesting model, but much more difficult to use in practice. Thus, we will not feature it here. The references at the end of this chapter will help you find information on this model if you are interested.

[44] In early 2003, the cost of debt on very high-quality credits such as 3M was low, ranging from 5.47 to 6.4 percent for the highest quality corporate debt.

$$R_e = R_d + (\overset{\circ}{R}_e - \overset{\circ}{R}_d)$$
$$= 6.3\% + 2.0\%$$
$$= 8.3\%$$

This percentage is a bit above the cost of equity we calculated with the cash flow discount model. These two methods usually do not yield the same results. With marginal rates on corporate debt at record lows, the results are rather close. Often they are not, and the difference may be because the spread between the yields of stocks and bonds is not always constant. Panel A of Exhibit 6-9 shows annual returns on the Standard & Poor's (S&P) 500 Index and a high-grade corporate bond index. Panel B of this exhibit shows that the differences between Standard and Poor's stock returns and those on corporate bond returns are not as constant as the stock-bond yield spread method implies. Thus the stock-bond yield spread provides a quick estimate, but it should not be used unless its results are verified by another method.

2. The Capital Asset Pricing Model

A simple adaptation makes the simple risk premium model more universal. To do this we add a term denoting the difference between the average risk of all assets in the market and the risk of a particular asset, in this case a common stock. The new equation would be as follows:

$$R_{ej} = R_f + X_j(R_m - R_f)$$

Where:
- j = Term to denote a particular asset
- X = Measure of the risk for an asset
- R_m = Return required on an asset of average risk
- R_f = Return required on a hypothetical risk-free asset
- R_e = Return required on equity

This formula could also be called the **relative risk premium model**, because it contains a factor, X, to indicate the relative risk of the particular asset. Notice that in this formula, only X_j changes, and all other factors remain constant from asset to asset. Exhibit 6-10 depicts this relationship, and it is similar to the value creation framework used in previous chapters. Since investors require a return for illiquidity the line starts at R_f, the return required from a risk-free security.[45] The solid line represents the return required at each level of risk. This risk/return concept seems quite realistic: investors do expect greater rewards for taking greater risks, and the expected return for the common stock of any company is relative to its risk. However, in order to use this method, we must define and measure risk.

---

[45] The investor is illiquid since the invested capital is not available for their use. When investors cannot access their capital, they require a return.

Exhibit 6-9

Realized Returns on Common Stock and Corporate Bonds (1926–2002)

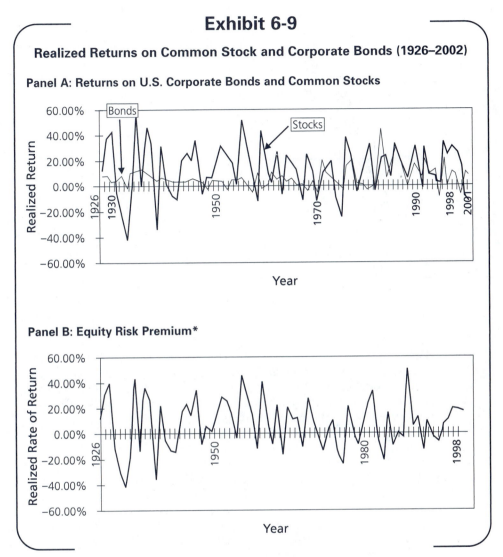

Panel A: Returns on U.S. Corporate Bonds and Common Stocks

Panel B: Equity Risk Premium*

* Realized stock returns minus corporate bond returns.[46]
Source: Data from Ibbotson Assoc. Yearbook, *Stocks, Bonds, Bills, and Inflation*, 2002.

[46] We plotted the difference between the realized return for the large company stocks (S&P 500) and corporate bonds. We could also have chosen to take the differences between the stocks and long-term U.S. government bonds. The means and standard deviations of the two series are similar. The plots of the two are almost identical.

	Mean Realized Return	Standard Deviation
Stock—Corporate bonds	6.58%	21.16%
Stock—Government bonds	6.98%	20.87%

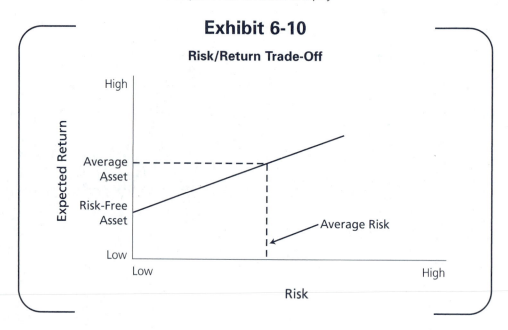

Exhibit 6-10

Risk/Return Trade-Off

The capital asset pricing model (CAPM) is an adaptation of this basic relative risk premium approach. It is an attempt to make the relative risk premium model usable. In the CAPM, risk is defined as the covariance of a stock's returns with those of an asset of average risk. This definition is a bit different from the usual definition of risk as total variability, most often measured as variance and/or standard deviation. Covariance rests on a simple idea—it is not the total variability of the returns of each security that are important to the investor, but how each security's return variability contributes to the variability of the investor's total portfolio.[47] We could, for instance, place a security with cyclical returns (such as an automobile company's common stock) with a security whose returns are countercyclical (such as an automobile replacement parts manufacturer's common stock). Both of these stocks have risky returns. The returns from the two stocks over time are shown in Exhibit 6-11. Note, when the auto manufacturer is doing well, the replacement parts manufacturer is experiencing a slump, and the stock returns reflect the business performance. The reverse is also true—replacement parts sell well when people defer new car purchases. As you can see, returns from the portfolio containing both stocks would be quite stable, that is, they would not be very risky according to the CAPM's definition of risk even though the returns from each are quite risky. You should note our optimism about these stocks

---

[47] This is called portfolio risk, and comes from portfolio theory. Portfolio theory rests on the assumption that investors care about the risk of their portfolio, not the individual risks of the assets contained in the portfolio.

Exhibit 6-11

Portfolio Returns in a Portfolio with Two Assets

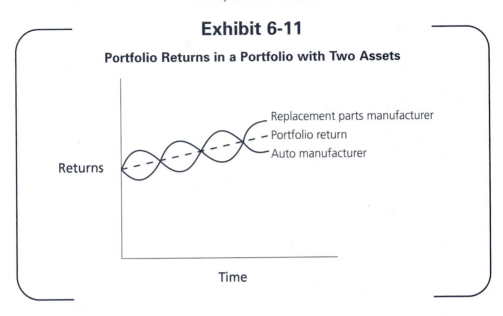

since we show the returns for both companies growing, not diminishing, over time.

The only difference between the relative risk premium formula and the CAPM is how the latter defines risk. Risk is relative to the market for all assets. It is the covariability of the asset's returns, here a stock, with those of the overall asset market. The relative risk premium model does not define risk but the CAPM does. The CAPM equation is:

$$R_{ej} = R_f + \beta_j (R_m - R_f)$$

In this equation β_j stands for **beta**, a measure of the covariance between the total returns (dividends plus capital gains) of the asset market and those of company j's stock. All the other equation notation has been used before.[48]

To estimate 3M's shareholders' required return on equity using the CAPM, we must have estimates for the risk-free rate of return, the expected return on the average asset, and the covariability—the beta—of the returns on 3M's stock with those on the average asset.[49] To use the CAPM, therefore, we need forecasts for the returns from R_f, R_m, and an estimate of the asset's expected β.

---

[48] Covariance $(j_1, j_2) = 1/n \times \Sigma(j_{1i} - j_{1 \text{ average}}) \times (j_{2i} - j_{2 \text{ average}})$, where j_1 and j_2 are the annual rates of return from each of two investments (j_1, j_2) over time, n is the total number of returns (i), and $j_{1 \text{ average}}$ and $j_{2 \text{ average}}$ are the averages of the returns for j_1 and j_2.

[49] Considerable controversy surrounds the theory and use of the CAPM. The reader should become familiar with the problems before becoming a frequent user. Since these problems are lengthy and complex, they are beyond the scope of this book.

The Risk-Free Rate of Return. R_f stands for the risk-free rate of return. In theory, the returns from this asset should entail no risk, none at all, not even the risk of a loss of purchasing power from the impact of inflation on prices. It is difficult to find a truly risk-free rate or even conjure one up. Thus most analysts choose a proxy. As we examine all the possible proxies, we must deal with the fact that all of them include a return to compensate the investor for expected inflation.[50] For investors in U.S. securities, the proxy probably would be a U.S. Treasury instrument with a maturity that matches the life of the asset being evaluated.[51] Because equity securities have long lives, a longer term U.S. Treasury bond is a good choice. Even though the longest lived bond seems an appropriate choice, since the typical U.S. Treasury **yield curve**—the yields for many maturities—is upward sloping, in actuality the normal curve is rather flat from 10 years onward. Thus many analysts choose a U.S. Treasury bond with a 7- to 10-year maturity as an appropriate proxy for the CAPM. Recent yield curves are shown in Exhibit 6-12.

There are a number of problems that the analyst faces in choosing and using U.S. Treasury securities as a proxy for the risk-free rate. First, rates change, and sometimes rather rapidly. You can see the kind of change that took place from September 1998 to two and three years later in Exhibit 6-12. A second problem is that rates and/or the yield curve can be unusual. For example, rates might reflect high short-term inflation forecasts or unusual demand or supply imbalances. The yield curve configurations in Exhibit 6-12 are rather unusual. Exhibit 6-13 (page 296) shows a more normal, upward-sloping yield curve.

A U.S. Treasury bond is priced by the capital markets so that the rate will compensate the investor for the time value of money and the real rate of return, generally thought to be about 2.5 percent. In addition, its price includes a return to compensate for domestic inflation that investors anticipate during the life of the bond. This is true for assets in other countries as well—they must return enough to compensate for the expected domestic inflation in those countries. Thus when estimating the return required for an investment in non-U.S. assets, a more appropriate risk-free proxy must be chosen than a U.S. Treasury security.[52]

Choosing the wrong proxy can make quite a difference. Exhibit 6-14 (page 296) shows yield curves for Japan, the United Kingdom, and

---

[50] Even very short-term government returns include investors' estimates for the life of the investment.

[51] There are those who argue that we should use the shortest term Treasury bill here since it includes the least risk. However, in this chapter we bundle the capital markets' estimate of the return required for the lowest risk instruments we can find in the United States, Treasury instruments, with the market's estimate for inflation over the life of the investment will be outstanding. Only for investments lasting 30 days or less should a 30-day Treasury bill rate be used as the risk-free rate.

[52] Some analysts use the U.S. Treasury rate and adjust it for the inflation difference between the United States and the home country of the asset. This differential inflation method rests on the exchange rate theory discussed in Chapter 2.

Exhibit 6-12

U.S. Treasury Security Yield Curves— September 1998, October 2002, and January 2003

Panel A: The Yield Curves

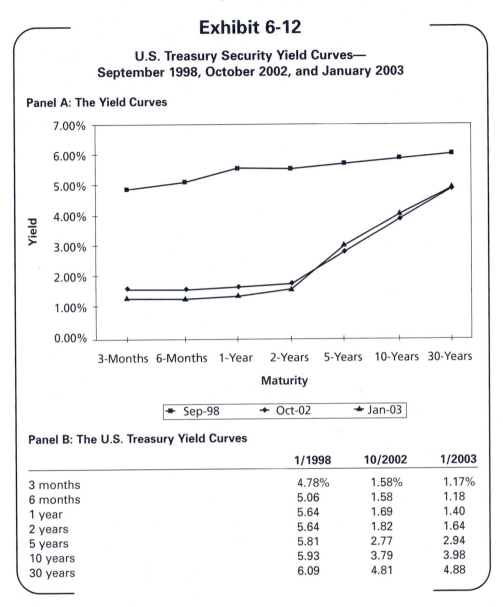

Panel B: The U.S. Treasury Yield Curves

	1/1998	10/2002	1/2003
3 months	4.78%	1.58%	1.17%
6 months	5.06	1.58	1.18
1 year	5.64	1.69	1.40
2 years	5.64	1.82	1.64
5 years	5.81	2.77	2.94
10 years	5.93	3.79	3.98
30 years	6.09	4.81	4.88

Source: Bloomberg LP.

Canada. Here you can see why there is real concern about the level of Japanese interest rates—all except the longest term rates are less than one percent.[53] This indicates there is not a high cost of money in real terms, and there is little, if any, inflation expected over the next 30 years.

---

[53] At various times, the Japanese rates have been praised and derided for their impact on Japanese company investment policies and practices.

Exhibit 6-13

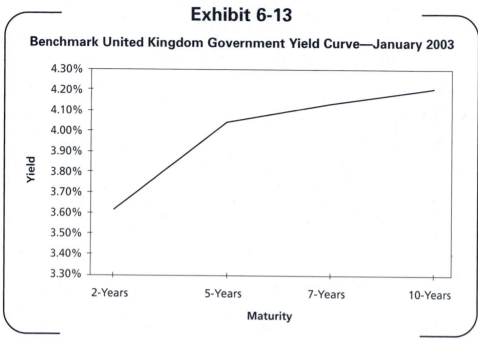

Benchmark United Kingdom Government Yield Curve—January 2003

Source: Bloomberg LP.

Exhibit 6-14

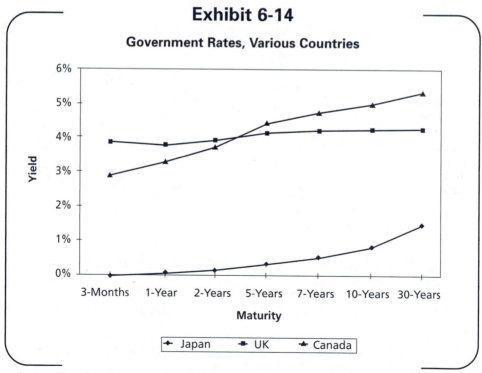

Government Rates, Various Countries

Source: Bloomberg LP.

After all this discussion of yield curves and inflation, what proxy should be used for 3M?[54] A reasonable risk-free rate would be that for the 10-year U.S. bond, a rate of 3.98 percent.[55]

The Market Rate of Return. The risk-free rate is difficult to estimate and the market return estimation is no easier. Before you stop here and decide all this is just too difficult, remember that we have the same problem whenever we make a forecast. Instead of avoidance, practice and knowledge bring skill and confidence.

The R_m in the CAPM is the expected return on an asset of average risk. Analysts have used two ways to determine the average expected return on the market average. One is a variation of the risk premium approach: the long-term historical return on the risk-free asset is subtracted from the historical return on a proxy for all assets.[56] In the United States, analysts have often used data like that shown in Exhibit 6-15 to estimate the premium. At year-end 2001, the geometric 75-year return on the U.S. large capitalization stocks was 10.7 percent and the premium of U.S. equities above U.S. Treasury bonds was 5.4 percent.[57]

Instead of using the data from 1926 to 2001, you might choose to customize your forecast by choosing the period in the past that is most like what you expect for the future. For instance, if you believe that the next 20 years will be like the 17 years ending in 1999, we will have a market boom. Over the boom years of 1983 to 1999, the large capitalization stocks returned 18.4 percent and its premium over long-term U.S. Treasury bonds was 10.6 percent. If you expect the two years from 2000–2001 to be our future, the results are quite different. The two-year returns showed a loss of 10.5 percent for stocks and a return of 12.2 percent for U.S. Treasury bonds. The data from 2000 and 2001 influence

---

[54] There is a problem using a single proxy for a company that does business in several countries. Actually, we should use a rate that reflects the minimum rate of return plus the appropriate inflation rate. Fortunately, in this case worldwide rates are very low and rather similar. Thus we are spared dealing with the practicalities of deriving either a worldwide market rate of return or a weighted average of the rates where the company operates.

[55] In 1999, the U.S. Treasury began reducing its debt at the longest maturities. This, plus the fact that the typical yield curve flattens at about 10 years, would ordinarily suggest that the 10-year yield is a good choice. However, the yield curve in early 2003 was unusual. Short-term rates were at a 45-year low, U.S. business was in recession, potential war was imminent, and the U.S. government was amassing a deficit at a high rate. This suggests that the 30-year rate, including a longer-term outlook for inflation, may be a better choice. Thus we have chosen to use the 30-year rate. As you can see, judgment is the critical issue in all these choices.

[56] Equities are used as a proxy for the average risk asset because, if you consider all possible investments that an investor can make, equities are rather average in risk.

[57] There is considerable controversy over what is the right period of history to use as a proxy for the future. Some argue that a period longer than 40 years should be used and, because the data are easily available, they use data from 1926 to the present. Some choose to exclude the period from 1926–1950. They do so because of the market turmoil that occurred from 1929–1935 and the fact that rates were set by the government during World War II. Still others choose a period of history as much as possible like the future they foresee. To complicate matters, there is considerable discussion about whether the arithmetic or geometric averages should be used. Finally, some argue that realized returns, however long term, are not a good proxy for expectations.

Exhibit 6-15

Basic Series: Summary Statistics of Annual Returns (1926–2001)*

Series	Geometric Mean	Arithmetic Mean	Standard Deviation	Distribution
Large Company Stocks	10.7%	12.7%	20.2%	
Small Company Stocks**	12.5	17.3	33.2	
Long-Term Corporate Bonds	5.8	6.1	8.6	
Long-Term Government	5.3	5.7	9.4	
Intermediate-Term Government	5.3	5.5	5.7	
U.S. Treasury Bills	3.8	3.9	3.2	
Inflation	3.1	3.1	4.4	

-90%   0%   90%

* This data begins in 1926 and has not been calculated to extend further into the past.
Source: *Stocks, Bonds, Bills and Inflation® 2003 Yearbook*, © 2003 Ibbotson Associates, Inc. Based on copyrighted works by Ibbotson and Sinquefield. All rights reserved. Used with permission.
** The 1933 Small Company Stocks Total Return was 142.9 percent.

the long-term geometric averages—the average from 1926 to 2002 was 14.9 percent for stocks, a premium of 2.7 percent over the bond return of 12.2 percent.[58] The data you choose to use as a basis of your forecast of the future is very important. The data is available to make your own calculations. For our analysis of the 3M shareholders' required return, we will use the 75-year average premium of 5.4 percent.

Analysts also use an estimate of the expected market premium. This estimate may come from information derived from security analysts working in money management companies whose job it is to make forecasts for individual stocks. Putting all their forecasts together produces a consensus estimate of the expected U.S. stock market return.[59]

The Risk—Beta. The beta is a measure of the asset's or stock's risk relative to that of the overall market. This risk comes from sensitivity to changes in things that impact the market returns, such as changes in interest rates and GDP growth rates. However, our most direct approach is to go first to history to develop our beta forecast.

---

[58] Adding the stock return data from 2002 makes the return for stocks lower and the spread smaller.
[59] The analyst forecasts and the historic returns can be quite different. For instance, in late 1991 when historic data would have shown a long-term average market return of 12.1, one group of analysts forecasted a long-term rate of return for U.S. equities of 14 percent.

To use history, the typical method for estimating a beta is to use a version of the simple linear regression. Below you see a dressed-up version of the formula for a straight line, y = a + bx, to create the security characteristic line and the beta estimate. We will use this formula and the monthly total rates of return for the stock and for an index like the S&P 500:[60]

$$R_j - R_f = a_j + \beta_j(R_m - R_f) + e_j$$

Where:

a = Intercept of the linear regression
β = Slope of the line
e = Errors that occur because the fit of the line to the data is not perfect
j = Designated stock or portfolio

The regression for the 3M stock and S&P 500 index returns is shown in Exhibit 6-16. Each dot shown on the graph represents the returns for 3M and the Standard & Poor's 500 for one period, here a month.[61] The line is one that minimizes the absolute distance of the dots from the line and is called the **security characteristic line**. Each stock will have a somewhat different security characteristic line. The beta, the slope of the line, from this regression is 0.521, the coefficient of the x shown in Exhibit 6-16.[62] We will use this beta in our estimate of the 3M shareholders' required return on equity.

Several companies calculate and publish betas for a number of publicly traded U.S. common equities. Standard & Poor's *Industry Survey* and Value Line's *Investment Reports* are two sources that are widely available.[63] In addition, many money management companies estimate and sell proprietary versions.

As any financial analyst knows, using history as a predictor for the future is dangerous. The danger is no less here. An historical beta is only a guideline for what the beta might be in the future. In fact, it is the analyst's role to make the forecast using whatever data is available tempered by analysis and judgment. This is particularly true when a company has

---

[60] We are using the S&P 500 as a proxy for the market. This is a long-standing custom, even though the S&P 500 hardly is the whole market for assets. Using monthly returns for 60 months is customary, though not necessarily the best way to approach the beta forecast. Sixty months was chosen to balance the need for sufficient data to perform the analysis, and a desire not to include data from a different economic and business climate.

[61] For those of you with such an interest, the regression statistics are:

$$Y = 0.0067 + 0.5121x$$

The R^2, which measures the relationship between the two sets of data, is 0.1351. The highest R^2 is 1.0, and the average for stocks is about 0.30. For those of you seeing this for the first time, the mystery of regression can be deciphered in many of the readings listed at the end of this chapter.

[62] Beta represents a company's systematic risk—the risk relative to the market—not risk specific to the company. Specific risks are called unsystematic risks.

[63] Betas are available from sources such as those listed at the end of the chapter.

Exhibit 6-16   3M and Standard & Poor's 500

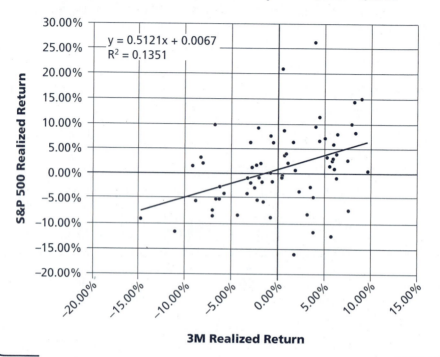

Security Characteristic Line: Monthly Data 2/1997–1/2003

y = 0.5121x + 0.0067
$R^2 = 0.1351$

(y-axis) S&P 500 Realized Return

(x-axis) 3M Realized Return

Data from MSN.com.

made an acquisition, divested part of its business, or is expected to change in the future.

3. Using the CAPM

To demonstrate how an analyst might use the model, we will use 3.98 percent as the current yield on a 30-year U.S. Treasury bond for R_f, and 5.4 percent for the historical return premium of equities over long-term U.S. government bonds for $R_m - R_f$. For the systematic risk of 3M's returns, the beta, we will use 0.51, the estimate from Exhibit 6-16. Using these estimates, we can calculate 3M's shareholders' required return on equity as follows:

$$R_{ej} = R_f + \beta_j (R_m - R_f)$$
$$R_{3M} = 3.98\% + (0.51 \times 5.4\%)$$
$$= 6.73\%$$

The CAPM provides a result that is a bit higher than the dividend-discount and cash flow discount models we used earlier. Since these are all estimates, our results are very close.[64] For the most part, the various models will give consistent, though not identical, answers when the company is relatively mature and the inputs are reasonably forecastable. Whenever you estimate a required return on equity you would be wise to use several approaches to corroborate any cost of equity estimate.

V. Other Concerns in Determining Required Return on Equity

1. New Equity Issues

When a firm issues new equity, it incurs some additional expenses. The firm issuing new equity must register the issue with a regulatory body such as the U.S. Securities and Exchange Commission (SEC), and the firm must rely on the advice of lawyers, accountants, and underwriters to design, plan, register, and sell the new security. In addition to registering the stock, the underwriter usually buys the issue from the firm, thus guaranteeing its sale. The underwriter then resells the stock to the public—for a fee.[65] The average cost of these services can range from 4 to 15 percent of the equity issue, depending on the size of the company, the amount of stock to be issued, and the underwriter's confidence that the firm's stock will sell quickly. As a consequence of these costs, newly issued equity has a higher required return than does seasoned stock—stock that has already been issued.

We can demonstrate how to calculate the required return on newly issued equity. To do so we will use the perpetuity version of the dividend-discount model (the long version makes it harder to see the impact of new issue costs). If we were a small regional company with a current stock price of $20.00, paying an annual dividend of $0.80 per share and anticipating a growth of 4 percent per year, our required return on equity would be 8.2 percent:

$$R_{ej} = \frac{D_1(1.0 + g)}{MP_o} + g$$

$$= \frac{\$0.80(1.0 + 0.04)}{20.00} + 0.04$$

$$= 0.042 + 0.04$$

$$= 0.082 \text{ or } 8.2\%$$

---

[64] We might have any one of a number of inconsistencies in the models. For example, our historical beta might be an over- or underestimate of the future beta, or the dividend or cash flow growth rates might be too low. Whenever there are discrepancies between the estimates, particularly if they are large, the analyst should examine the assumptions. Here they are quite close.

[65] For a smaller fee, the underwriter may make a "best efforts" to sell the stocks or bonds. In a "best efforts" sale, the underwriter does not guarantee the sale of the securities.

However, if the cost of issuing new stock, U, were 8 percent, the return we would have to earn on this newly issued capital would be:

$$R_{ej} = \frac{D_1(1.0 + g)}{MP_o(1 - U)} + g$$

$$= \frac{\$0.80(1.0 + 0.04)}{\$20.00(1.0 - 0.08)} + 0.04$$

$$= \frac{\$0.832}{\$18.40} + 0.04$$

$$= 0.045 + 0.04$$

$$= 0.085 \text{ or } 8.5\%$$

Obviously, the cost to the company is higher since their proceeds are lower. Shareholders still expect a return of 8.2 percent on their $20 investment.

2. Cost of Retained Earnings

Each year a company can generate net income after taxes and dividends. This is the earnings retained on behalf of the shareholders for that year, and it is added to the retained earnings balance in the equity section of the company's balance sheet. Managers may use the new retained earnings funds to increase the firm's assets (a change in the assets) or to reduce its debt (a change in the liabilities), or the funds may be held temporarily in cash or marketable securities (an asset change). Some managers consider retained earnings to be free funds, but that is certainly not true from the shareholders' point of view. If managers had returned the funds to the shareholders, the shareholders could have invested the funds. Thus, retained earnings must generate a fair return.

In exchange for this **opportunity cost**, shareholders expect retained earnings to create value for them. So the return required on retained earnings is the same as the return that the manager must earn on equity investments.

3. Preferred Stock

Preferred stock presents special analytical problems because preferred stock is a cross between debt and equity. Like debt, preferred stock offers a fixed payment—fixed dividends. In bankruptcy, preferred shareholders take precedence over common shareholders. However, if preferred dividends are not paid the firm cannot be forced into bankruptcy as it may be if it fails to pay the interest on its debt. For investors, owning preferred equity is somewhat less risky than holding common stock but more risky than being a lender. Preferred stock is also unlike debt in that the firm does not repay the investment.

Keeping these things in mind, we can calculate the return required by preferred stockholders as follows:

$$R_p = \frac{PD}{PP_o}$$

Where:
  PD = Preferred dividend[66]
  PP_O = Preferred stock price
  R_p = Return required on preferred stock

This analysis of the required return by preferred shareholders is applicable only to preferred stock, not stock that is convertible into any other security. Convertible preferred stock, typically convertible into common stock, is a security that has some of the characteristics of debt and some of equity's characteristics. Therefore, a convertible security is more complex to analyze than ordinary preferred stock. Knowledge of option theory and practice is necessary. A simple introduction to options is included in Chapter 4 and extended in Appendix 4A.

VI. Required Return on Equity for Private, Non-U.S., or Companies Experiencing Change

The analysis we have performed thus far was for 3M, a U.S. company that is traded on the NYSE, the largest stock exchange in the world. Considerable data are available for such companies, and there are stock analysts whose job it is to know as much about public companies as possible. Much of the writing about how to use the methods was based on the U.S. market and meant for students and practitioners in the United States. The models are equally applicable to any company, however, whether it is public or private; operates in the United States, another developed, or a developing country; or is stable or undergoing considerable change. The adaptations are simple, but require much experience and rely on the analyst's skill:

1. *Beta.* Instead of relying on history, you must use judgment about what the beta will be: you must understand that the magnitude of the beta depends on the company's sensitivity to changes in factors that, to a greater or lesser degree, negatively or positively affect the returns from all assets worldwide.[67] Examples of such factors are inflation, worldwide industrial production growth, GDP changes, and investors' propensity to take risk. Companies that are highly sensitive to changes in these factors will have a higher than average beta.

---

[66] There is no tax adjustment because preferred dividends are not a tax-deductible expense for companies in the Unites States and other parts of the world. The tax deductibility is dependent upon the tax laws in the particular country where the company operates.

[67] Actually, all betas are the analysts' forecast for the future sensitivity of the company's returns to changes in those of the market. In turning to history to help us forecast, often we think that is the only approach to estimating a beta. It is not.

Those that are insulated from the impact of changes in these factors will have higher than average betas. Since beta is an index, the average beta is 1.0, and most betas are from 0.5 to 1.8.

2. *Market and risk-free rates of return.* For companies outside the United States, market returns and risk-free rates must be changed from the U.S.-only rates. The nominal risk-free rate for companies operating in other countries must include the forecast for that country's inflation. The market return, the return on average assets, also must be adapted for that economy. More and more we are developing a global CAPM—one that is usable for all assets, and adapted for differences in inflation and sensitivity of the domestic economy to global changes.[68] It is with non-U.S. and private companies, as well as companies undergoing significant changes, that the analyst has the biggest challenge.

To estimate the required return on equity for all companies requires ingenuity and judgment. For private and non-U.S. companies, the ingenuity and judgment may be more than most analysts are used to exercising. However, with experience an analyst will gain skill in dealing with more varied situations where information is not available, and where an analyst's judgment is critical.

VII. Summary

In this chapter we looked at what returns shareholders expect to earn on their investments. We call this return the required return on equity or the company's cost of equity. The models used to estimate what investors require are attempts to replicate the methods investors themselves are using to price an equity security. These models can be used with publicly traded companies for which there are considerable data, or they can be applied, using proxies or analogy, to companies that are privately held or are in small or developing markets.

Each of the required return on equity models we have described and used has analyst judgment as its major ingredient. If the results are approximately the same from these models, the analyst can have more confidence in their estimate. However, if each method results in a very different required return on equity, the analyst must think carefully about the source of the variations. The analyst's choice of data from model to model may be inconsistent; the forecasts may be optimistic or pessimistic; or the shareholders' concept of future returns may be quite different from that of the analyst. To be secure in a forecast the analyst should use

---

[68] You might think of the local market return as a combination of the return expected on the average global asset, adapted for the sensitivity of the local market to changes in the global economy. Thus countries that are relatively insulated from changes in such things as inflation and those that have diverse economies might be less sensitive than the average, while countries that are profoundly impacted by global changes, for example, raw material/commodity exporters, might be more sensitive.

more than one model and corroborate the forecasts, remembering that the purpose of all forecasts and calculations is to capture the shareholder's expectations of future returns, not the analyst's or management's hopes and beliefs.

The required return on equity is the rate that is used to discount the residual cash flows—that is, the cash flows to equity shareholders, the owners of the company. In many companies, however, the shareholders have chosen to share their financing obligation with others, especially with those investing in debt instruments. What happens to the company's required return when the shareholders share their rights and obligations with lenders is the subject of Chapters 7 and 8.

Selected References

For information on equity markets, see:
Ball, Ray. "The Theory of Stock Market Efficiency: Accomplishments and Limitations Values." *Journal of Applied Corporate Finance*, Spring 1995, pp. 4–17.
Bodie, Zvi, Alex Kane, and Alan Marcus. *Investments*. 4th ed. Homewood, IL: McGraw-Hill, 2001.
Clark, J. F., and Roger G. Ibbotson. *Investments: A Global Perspective*. Upper Saddle River, NJ: Prentice Hall Professional Technical Reference, 2001.
Malkiel, Bernard. *A Random Walk Down Wall Street*. New York: W. W. Norton & Co., 2002.
Reilly, Frank K., and Edgar Norton. *Investments*. 6th ed. Cincinnati, OH: South-Western College Publishing, 2002.
Shiller, Robert J. *Irrational Exuberance*. New York: Broadway Books, 2001.
Teweles, Richard, and Edward Bradley. *The Stock Market*. 7th ed. New York: John Wiley & Sons, 1998.
Thaler, Richard H. *Advances in Behavioral Finance*. New York: Russell Sage Foundation, 2001.

For information about equity valuation methods, see:
Bodie, Zvi, Alex Kane, and Alan Marcus. *Investments*. 5th ed. Boston, MA: Richard D. Irwin, 2001, chaps. 18 and 19.
Bodie, Zvi, and Robert Merton. *Finance*. Upper Saddle River, NJ: Prentice Hall, 2000, chap. 9.
Brealey, Richard A., and Stewart C. Myers. *Principles of Corporate Finance*. 7th ed. New York: McGraw-Hill, 2002, chap. 4.
Brigham, Eugene F., Louis C. Gapenski, and Michael Ehrhardt. *Financial Management*. 9th ed. Fort Worth, TX: The Dryden Press, 1999, chap. 9.
Ross, Stephen A., Jeffrey F. Jaffe, and Randolph W. Westerfield. *Corporate Finance*. 6th ed. Homewood, IL: Richard D. Irwin, 2001, chap. 5.

Woolridge, J. Randall. "Do Stock Prices Reflect Fundamental Values?" *Journal of Applied Corporate Finance*, Spring 1995, pp. 64–69, 102.

For more on warrants and convertible securities, see:
Brigham, Eugene F., Louis C. Gapenski, and Michael Ehrhardt. *Financial Management.* 9th ed. Fort Worth, TX: The Dryden Press, 1999, chap. 2.

For general information about the stock market, see:
Fogler, H. Russell, Frank Fabozzi, and Diana Harrington. *Analyzing the Stock Market.* 2nd ed. Chicago, IL: Probus Publishing, 1988.
Levy, Haim. *Introduction to Investments.* Cincinnati, OH: South-Western College Publishing, 1996.
Sharpe, William F., Gordon J. Alexander, and Jeffery V. Bailey. *Fundamentals of Investments.* 6th ed. Englewood Cliffs, NJ: Prentice Hall, 2001.
Teweles, Richard, and Edward Bradley. *The Stock Market.* New York: John Wiley & Sons, 1998.

For those with a further interest in the capital asset pricing model and discounted cash flow methods of equity valuation, see:
Harrington, Diana R. *Modern Portfolio Theory, The Capital Asset Pricing Model and Arbitrage Pricing Theory: A Users Guide.* 2nd ed. Englewood Cliffs, NJ: Prentice Hall, 1987.
Kothari, S. P., and Jay Shanken. "In Defense of Beta." *Journal of Applied Corporate Finance*, Spring 1995, pp. 53–58.

For historical data from the stock and bond markets and information about comparable firms, see:
Arnold Bernhard & Co., Inc. *Value Line Investment Survey.*
Dun & Bradstreet, *Key Business Ratios.*
Ibbotson Associates. *Stocks, Bonds, Bills and Inflation, 2002 Yearbook.*
Robert Morris Associates, *Annual Statement Studies.*

For information on estimating the risk premium, see:
Harrington, Diana R. *Modern Portfolio Theory, The Capital Asset Pricing Model and Arbitrage Pricing Theory: A Users Guide.* 2nd ed. Englewood Cliffs, NJ: Prentice Hall, 1987.
Sharpe, William, and Katrina Sherrerd. *Quantifying the Market Risk Premium Phenomenon for Investment Decision Making.* Charlottesville, VA: Institute of Chartered Financial Analysts, 1989.

For the basics on arbitrage pricing theory, see:
Bodie, Zvi, Alex Kane, and Alan Marcus. *Investments.* 4th ed. Boston, MA: Richard D. Irwin, 1999, chap. 11.
Bodie, Zvi, and Robert Merton. *Finance.* Upper Saddle River, NJ: Prentice Hall, 2000, chap. 13.
Brigham, Eugene F., Louis C. Gapenski, and Michael Ehrhardt. *Financial Management.* 9th ed. Fort Worth, TX: The Dryden Press, 1999, chap. 6.

Damodoran, Aswath. *Corporate Finance*. New York: John Wiley & Sons, 1997, chap. 6.

Haugen, Robert A. *Modern Investment Theory*. Upper Saddle River, NJ: Pearson Education Communications, 2000.

Web sites of note:
Historic interest rates, the St. Louis Federal Reserve Bank at http://www.stls.frb.org
International interest rates, the Federal Reserve Bank at http://www.federalreserve.gov
Current interest rates and other market data, http://www.bloomberg.com
LIBOR rates can be found at http://www.kuhlmann.com, a site operated by Kuhlmann Commercial Capital.

The following web sites are of interest to investors with price charts and fundamental information:
http://www.bigcharts.com
http://www.bloomberg.com
http://www.hoovers.com
http://www.moneycentral.msn.com
http://www.sec.gov
http://www.thomsoninvest.net
http://finance.yahoo.com

Study Questions

1. Bakelite Company is a commercial bakery specializing in biscuit making that is located in rural Ohio. Recent substantial declines in grain prices have resulted in significant raw material savings. Since prices do not need to be cut, because Bakelite is already at the low-priced end of the market, cash reserves have built up well beyond historical levels. This wealth of cash spurs management, with the support of the board, to consider some capital investments they have long deferred. The various division heads have been asked to propose capital investments to Carl Borg, vice president of finance. Mr. Borg has the job of evaluating the projects and making recommendations to the board. Because it has been years since Bakelite made any significant investments, Mr. Borg is concerned about choosing the right ones. To get some advice about making these decisions, he calls an old college friend, Jane Wilson, now a finance professor at a nearby university. Professor Wilson says that, since Mr. Borg already has cash flow forecasts from the divisions, the only thing left to be done is to discount the flows at the appropriate discount rate.

   Bakelite is too small a company to be followed by investment services like *Value Line*. However, a regional investment banker has just published a brief report on the company. It includes the following information: Bakelite's beta is 0.66 and the analyst's estimate for Bakelite's nominal long-term growth in dividends is 2.9 percent, a figure with which management agrees. The company recently paid a $2.86 dividend, and its current market price in the over-the-counter market is $45. At present, U.S. Treasury 10-year bonds are yielding 6.7 percent and 90-day Treasury bills are yielding 4.9 percent. Historically, the stock market has yielded about 6.5 percent above Treasury bills and 4 percent above longer term Treasury bonds. Bakelite's taxes are 34 percent. Its balance sheet is shown below.

Bakelite Corporation
(in millions)

Assets		Liabilities and Owners' Equity	
Cash	$0.2	Accounts payable	$1.4
Marketable securities	2.3	Taxes payable	0.3
Accounts receivable	1.1	Total current liabilities	1.7
Total current assets	3.6	Common stock	1.2
Net property, plant,		Retained earnings	1.9
and equipment	1.2	Total equity	3.1
Total assets	$4.8	Total liabilities and equity	$4.8

What is Bakelite's owners' required return on equity, using the:
a. dividend-discount model, where $g = (1 - \text{Payout})(\text{Return on equity})$?
b. capital asset pricing model?

2. Kelly Services is one of the largest U.S. providers of temporary personnel for large companies. The temporary help business has been suffering from contract-building practices and the U.S. recession. In spite of this, the company's growth has been a relatively steady 4.2 percent. With U.S. Treasury 10-year bonds yielding 6.3 percent and 90-day Treasury bills yielding 3.8 percent (on average 8.9 percent below the U.S. stock market), what is Kelly's cost of equity? The company paid a $2.80 dividend this year, its stock price is $36.00, and *Value Line* reports a beta of 0.95.

3. The Grupo Mercado Tropical management is considering purchasing Hannaford Bros., a chain of U.S. grocers located primarily in the northeastern United States. The "Grupo," a Mexican company, currently owns chains of stores in Central America, Mexico, and several of the Caribbean islands. For some time it has been considering opening markets in the increasingly Hispanic northeastern United States. Purchasing Hannaford might be a good way to gain a foothold in this market, without having to start from scratch. Already

many small bodegas are operating in many of Hannaford's areas, and local grocery chains, including Hannaford, are carrying increasing amounts of fresh and dry goods catering to this rapidly growing market. Grupo Mercado Tropical management has asked you to use the information below to determine what required return on equity should be used by management in valuing Hannaford's cash flows.

Mexican Treasury bonds	22.5%
Mexican inflation	17.0
U.S. 20-year Treasury bonds	6.0
U.S. inflation	1.8
72-year U.S. stock market premium over Treasury bonds	7.5
Beta:	
Grupo Mercado Tropical	1.84
Hannaford	1.02

Grupo Mercado Tropical growth rates:

Revenues	18%
Net Income	21
Cash flows	23
Dividends	None

4. In Chapter 4, Problem 4, Barry Nilson of New Age, Inc., received financial forecasts from the sales department for a Department of Defense proposal for the delivery of specialized biological hazard suits to be used by the Army for its decontamination unit soldiers operating in overseas campaigns. In that problem, Mr. Nilson asked you, Nel Diamond, to determine whether the company should accept the proposal by

   - Evaluating the sales department forecasts, and fixing any problems that are apparent in the forecasts. Describe any changes you made and why you made them.
   - Evaluating the economic benefits of accepting the contract, making sure to use the appropriate measures, including the NPV.
   - Deciding whether New Age, Inc., management should accept the contract.

   You were told to use a discount rate of 10 percent in your analysis.
   Now Mr. Nilson has forwarded to you the following data from the New Age, Inc., treasury department.

Capital Market Information—December 2002

Beta

Department of Defense	0.10
New Age, Inc.	0.80
Other similar manufacturers	0.93

U.S. Treasury rates

Bills (less than 1 year to maturity)	4.1%
Notes (5 years to maturity)	5.8%
Bonds (20 years to maturity)	6.1%
Expected Premium on Average Asset	6.4%

a. Use the data to determine the appropriate discount rate to use for this proposal, making clear what method(s) and data you used and why you chose them.

b. Determine the value of the contract using your new discount rate and whether you should recommend that New Age accept the contract.

Appendix Six A

Dividends, Dividend Policy, and the Value of the Company

In Chapters 5 and 6 we used several methods to value a company and to estimate its required return on equity. The dividend-discount model was one of the methods we used, although not enthusiastically. The reason is that this long-used method is plagued with the problems caused by the relationship between dividends to earnings and cash flows—or better yet, the lack of a relationship between them. For example, many companies have positive earnings and cash flows, yet pay no dividends. Others have no earnings or earnings losses, and still pay dividends.[1] At best, these situations make the dividend-discount model challenging to use.[2] In this appendix we discuss dividends, and how and why they are paid. This discussion of a company's dividend policy and strategy will shed some light on the reasons for dissatisfaction with the dividend-discount model and elucidate the way in which dividend policy is decided and implemented by a company.

I. How Companies Pay Dividends

Dividends are the distribution of corporate earnings to company shareholders. They frequently are distributed quarterly. Companies are not required to pay dividends, indeed, for some companies it is not desirable to do so. For example, companies that are in a rapid growth phase typically have investors who would rather have their residual earnings reinvested in the company's future growth. This is particularly true because dividends in the United States are taxable twice—first to the corporation and

---

[1] Typically this is a short-term phenomenon for a company that has paid regular dividends for a long period of time.
[2] Other challenges come when valuing companies that pay no dividends or that pay dividends in excess of their earnings.

second to the investor.[3] In many countries dividends are not taxed at the corporate level.[4]

Each year the magnitude and timing of the dividends are determined and declared by a company's board of directors. The date on which the board decides to issue dividends is called the **dividend declaration date**. Once declared, the dividends will be distributed to shareholders owning shares as of a particular date in the near future, the **date of record**.[5] Shares purchased after this date are sold without the dividend, or are sold **ex dividend**. For ex dividend shares, the selling shareholder receives the dividends but the buyer does not.

Normally, at the time dividends are declared the stock price drops by the amount of the dividends per share.[6] For example, if shares of a company are selling for $30 and a $1 dividend is declared, the shares should sell for $29. The shareholder has lost $1 because of the share price decline but has gained $1 from the coming dividend payment—the total per-share value of the owners' holdings, prior to personal tax payments, is still $30.[7] The date the dividend is actually paid is called the **payment date**. All this dividend activity takes place over a relatively short period of time.

II. Why Companies Pay Dividends

When a company's board of directors considers whether to pay a dividend and how big that dividend should be, they are really asking themselves, do shareholders want dividends or would they rather have us invest the money back into the company? Investors prefer that the company retain and invest the capital if the company can create value for the shareholders. If the company has no opportunities superior to those of the investor, the excess earnings should be paid to the shareholders. We can call this the **excess capital** explanation for paying dividends. This also fits with the Dupont analysis in Chapter 1. There we saw that when the growth of the company is less than its sustainable growth, and it has no value-creating investment opportunities, it can raise its dividend.

As clear as this objective may seem, there are some issues that make the decision a bit more messy. It may help if we start by thinking about what would make the decision irrelevant—what would make the investor

---

[3] This means that a corporation pays dividends out of after-tax earnings. The investor pays personal income taxes on them. In 2003 there is a proposal in the United States to end this double taxation of dividends. Whether it will be enacted by the U.S. Congress and signed by the President, and what the exact form of the legislation will be, are unknown.

[4] In Chapter 7 you will see the relevance of taxation of interest and/or dividends on the capital structure of the company.

[5] There are some issues regarding investors who purchase right before the declaration date, but whose trade is not yet reported to the company. Typically shareholders have the right to the dividends if they purchased the shares three days before the declaration date.

[6] This is true in the logical world, of course. There has been considerable research into whether personal taxes impact the drop.

[7] While this is true in theory, in practice stock prices can drop less than the dividend.

neutral on whether the company pays dividends. This brings us to the first of the theories about why companies choose to pay dividends—the dividend irrelevance theory. While the evidence in the capital markets tells us that dividends are not irrelevant, the dividend irrelevance theory helps us understand how companies' boards evaluate whether to pay dividends and what their dividend policy should be. This can lead us to understand the potential value of and cost of paying dividends. It is these values and costs that corporate boards must weigh in making their dividend policy decisions.

The **dividend irrelevance theory** says that it does not matter whether a company pays dividends since the value of the company will not be impacted by dividend payments. This theory rests on four illuminating assumptions:

1. The company's investment plan is set and will not be changed by paying dividends.
2. There are no taxes impacting dividend payments or costs to distributing dividends.
3. All market participants have the same outlook for the future, in particular for the company's future dividends and earnings, and no single investor can dictate the price of a company's shares.[8]

Since nothing about the company's future will be changed by paying dividends, paying them is irrelevant to the shareholders—the company's value stays the same. This is because, given the assumptions, the value of the company is derived only from its expected return and risk, not from whether it pays dividends. Paying dividends, in light of these assumptions, does not change that value. Dividend payments change only the timing of the shareholders' returns. As interesting as this theory may be, companies do pay dividends. We need to know how those decisions are made.

Obviously the dividend irrelevance assumptions are unrealistic. However, examining them can lead to more useful insights about dividends, and assist in the development of theories that are more practical. Two of the assumptions are obviously not realistic. We know that investors and companies do pay taxes, and that corporate investment opportunities and budgets can change.[9]

1. Dividend payments do not impact the investment plan and today's dividend is equal to a future dividend.

Implicit behind these assumptions is that shareholders do not care whether they receive dividends or not—the company's future will be the same and so will be what they receive. But what if investors believe

---

[8] Together the first two conditions constitute what is called by economists a perfect market.

[9] A couple of other things play into this discussion. First, it is assumed that investors who don't want the dividends can buy more shares with the unwanted dividends, at no cost. Second, it is assumed that investors who want more dividends can sell shares, again with no cost.

dividends today are more certain than future earnings and dividends? If this is the case, and it seems logical, shareholders would rather have the certain cash flow now, the dividends today, rather than a promise—even if the promise is for a larger dividend later. This theory has been labeled, quite descriptively, the **bird-in-the-hand** proposition.

We can think of the bird-in-the-hand mentality of investors in the context of the perpetuity version of the dividend-discount model. The bird-in-the-hand theory is roughly equivalent to investors saying that the g in the perpetuity dividend-discount model is more risky than the present dividend, D.

$$\text{Dividend-Discount Model of Corporate Value} = \frac{D}{(1 + R_e)} + g$$

Where:
    D = Next period dividends
    R_e = Shareholders' required return on equity
    g = Growth in dividends in the future

If investors prefer dividends today to future growth, the obvious conclusion is that companies should pay dividends today. Those who are skeptical of this notion ask if shareholders receive dividends, what do they do with them? Those who dismiss this theory say that investors will take their dividends and invest them in the stock of the same or a similar company. The result is that the risk of the shareholders' cash flows in the future does not change whether the company keeps the residual income or disperses it to shareholders.

The self-made risk argument is not the only one that makes many skeptical about the bird-in-the-hand theory. First, not all companies pay dividends and the theory does not take taxes and transaction costs into account.

Let's look at dividend payments by U.S.-based corporations. The simple chart in Exhibit 6A-1 gives some insight into what companies pay dividends and how high those dividends are. As you can see, utilities have very high payout ratios while software producers pay out a very small proportion of their earnings—not all companies act as if the investor wants immediate dividends. The second thing that the theory ignores is taxes and transaction costs.

2. Taxes do not impact dividend payments.

We know that taxes do make a difference in investors' returns and their perceptions of returns. There are three reasons why this is so:

1. Dividends are taxed twice—once at the corporate level and again at the shareholders' level.
2. Tax rates on dividends and capital gains can be different.[10]
3. Capital gains taxes are paid when stock is sold. Thus its timing is under the control of the investor. Dividends are declared by the

---

[10] This depends upon the tax code. A tax code can change over time.

Exhibit 6A-1 Different Industry Groups

Dividend Payout Ratios and Dividend Yields, 2002

	Software	Hardware	Utilities	S&P 500
Dividend yield	0.0%	0.2%	5.1%	1.4%
Dividend payout ratio	2.2%	13.8%	90.0%	44.6%

company's board of directors and shareholders have little control over the size and timing of the payments and their tax consequences.

4. There is no capital gains tax if the investor leaves shares to others in his or her estate.

Thinking about how taxes impact dividends can lead us to some useful ideas about investors' preferences. The **clientele effect** suggests that different kinds of investors have different preferences for dividends.

1. *High dividends.* Since a corporation pay no taxes on dividends it receives from investments, it would prefer high dividend payments from its investments.
2. *Medium to low dividends.* Individuals in low tax brackets prefer low to medium dividend payouts.
3. *Low to no dividends.* Individuals in high tax brackets prefer no or very low dividends.

The tax circumstances of different investor, or client, types would attract them to companies with different dividend payment levels. Thus, companies should pay dividends to attract a particular constituency. That constituency, or clientele, should be the one that best supports the company and its future funding needs. Changing dividend policies would force a change in clientele. In practice, a change in dividend levels normally changes the interested investment group and this impacts the share price as the transition occurs. These share price impacts are negative and sometimes large and sustained. The Potlatch dividend cut is one example from many. On August 13, 2001, *CFO Magazine* reported the following:

> Potlatch Corp. late Friday announced it has slashed its quarterly dividend by 66% to 15 cents a share from 43.5 cents due to poor markets and an uncertain economy.
>
> A Potlatch spokesman said the company found its dividend had "actually been rather high," compared with competitors. Potlatch's yield—the dividend divided by the share price—had been about 5% before the cut. After Friday's reduction, the yield would be about 1.7%, assuming the stock doesn't dip on news of the cut, the spokesman noted. At 4 p.m. EDT on the New York Stock Exchange, shares of Potlatch were up 54 cents, or 1.6%, at $34.09.

The company has about 28.3 million shares outstanding, and its stock was bumped last month from Standard & Poor's S&P 500 Index.[11]

The reason for the dividend cut was clearly spelled out, and management hoped that the dividend cut would not impact the share price. As you can see in Exhibit 6A-2, its hopes were dashed as the stock price dropped from just over $34 to under $27 as investors reconsidered their ownership of Potlatch. The dividend reduction conveyed news about future dividends and the company and its future, albeit news that was negative.

Exhibit 6A-2   Potlatch

Stock Price, June–November 2002

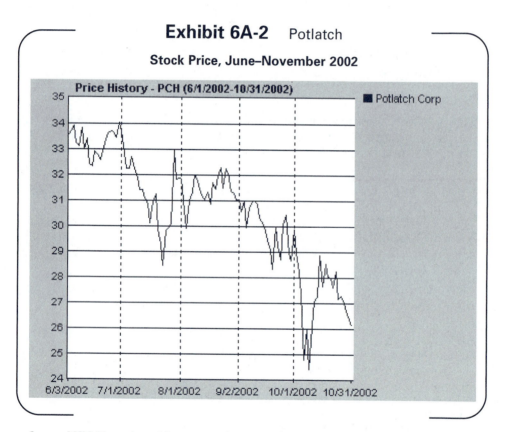

Source: MSN Money http://moneycentral.msn.com/investor/home.asp.

3. Dividend payments do not impact investors' outlook for the future.

Dividends can be a signal to investors. Underlying **signaling theory** is the notion that managers know more about the company and its future

---

[11] *Dow Jones Business News,* August 13, 2001, from http://www.cfo.com.

than do investors.[12] By deciding to pay a dividend the company management and the board of directors are confident that the dividend can be paid in the future, and the shareholders can trust that the future is bright. By cutting dividends the company's board of directors and management are clearly stating that the current dividend policy cannot be sustained in the future.

Dividend signals are positive when the company institutes a dividend or when it increases the rate at which it will pay dividends in the future. Deciding to cut a dividend is interpreted as a signal of potential problems, and negatively impacts share prices as shown with the Potlatch example. When dividends are cut, they should be accompanied by robust communication with shareholders to soften the negative news. While Potlatch management did issue press releases describing the reasons for the cut, it appeared to reinforce previous bad news. In Exhibit 6A-3 you can see that the share price had dropped by $10 over the year prior to the dividend announcement. It took almost six months for the stock price to recover from the dividend cut announcement. The dividend cut signaled management and the board's agreement that the company had financial difficulties.

4. Pay it if you have it.

We have looked at various theories for companies to pay or not to pay dividends that range from differential taxes, excess cash, bird-in-the-hand, signaling, and the clientele effect. From each of these theories a company's board can devise a dividend policy and strategy. However, the theories do not seem to fit every company. We need yet another reason—one that takes the view of the shareholders.

Shareholders want management to act in their best interests. But how can shareholders keep management aligned with their objective? They could do this by reducing excess capital that management might choose to use unwisely. By paying dividends, management is implicitly obliged to pay dividends in the future.[13] Dividend payments reduce financial slack and give management less discretion to make decisions about spending the excess capital. We might call this the **if-you-got-it-you-better-pay-it theory**—a company with excess capital, capital beyond its legitimate investment needs, should return that capital to its shareholders. We can put it in a slightly more cynical way—if management has excess capital, it might get into trouble. Paying dividends forces fiscal discipline on the company and its management.[14] In the next chapter we discuss **agency theory**, the arrangement of formal and informal contracts among the

---

12 We could also say there is asymmetric information—management knows more than the shareholders.

13 Remember, dividend cuts can be disastrous to the company's share price.

14 There are numerous examples of companies that have used excess capital to make investments in new processes or acquisitions that were not in the shareholders' long-term best interests. One you might examine is the history of Philip Morris and its acquisition and dividend policies.

Exhibit 6A-3 Potlatch

Stock Price, January 2000–2003

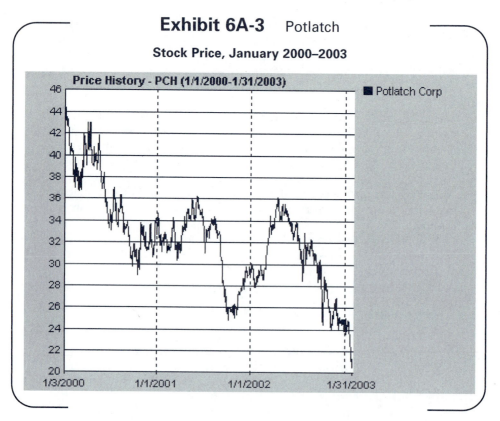

Source: MSN Money http://moneycentral.msn.com/investor/home.asp.

major agents in a company. The shareholders and management are two such agents, and they must find ways to align their interests. Dividend payments are one way to shackle management to investors' interests.

5. Everybody is doing it.

There is one more impetus behind dividend policies: industry practice. It is difficult for a company to fall outside the industry practice. It brings attention to the company that may not be wanted. Such differences can hamper a company's capital market access. The classic example is the electric utility industry. Of the 72 electric utilities listed on the New York Stock Exchange only 11 fail to pay dividends, and most of those are in serious economic circumstances. The average dividend payout in 2002 was over 70 percent, and some companies were paying out over 200 percent of their earnings.[15] This sort of payment is done to maintain the shareholder base and usually is a short-term phenomenon. In another ex-

---

[15] Using the Chapter 1 Dupont relationships, this means that the company had to sell assets, borrow, or issue new stock to pay dividends in excess of earnings.

ample, significant pressure has been brought by large investors on more mature technology companies to pay dividends. Some of these companies have significant excess cash flows, but pay no dividends. The poster child for this dividend payment campaign in 2002 was Microsoft.

So, what have we learned? Shareholders may or may not want dividends. Their desire for dividends may be because of taxes, management mistrust, or to access management information about the future. It appears that the higher taxes on dividends are not enough to repress investors' desire for them—at least some investors prefer dividends for their monetary value. Others want them to exert control over management's spending. As for companies, it is the obligation of the company, its board of directors, and management to act in the best interests of shareholders, while taking into account the company's future viability. With these conflicting views, there is no clear answer to what the appropriate policy should be. However, companies do pay dividends and each must have a policy with regard to dividend payments.

III. Developing the Dividend Policy

As we saw in Exhibit 6A-1, dividend practices vary widely from industry to industry. However, a few basic questions will guide a company's board in establishing a dividend policy that is positive for the shareholders and realistic for the company. They must take into account the following questions when developing the company's dividend policy.

1. *Shareholder preference.* What dividend policy do our investors prefer? Would they rather have dividends today or growth—capital gains— in the future?
2. *Corporate investment outlook.* What investments is the company expected to make in the future? Is the company mature or is it early in its growth phase?
3. *Capital structure and financial slack.* What is the current capital structure of the company? Could it be changed? Is capital easily available and reasonable? Could the company raise capital to pay dividends in a bad year?
4. *Company change.* Is there some reason that we want to change our dividend policy?

1. Shareholder Preference

We already discussed the various reasons that investors prefer or do not prefer dividends: taxes and certainty. The board should take into account the preferences of the current shareholders. The shareholders' preference is often reflected in the dividend policy of the company, the policy that attracted the current investors.

As management and the board of directors consider the future policy, they should keep in mind that change can cause disruptions as shareholders who preferred the old policy sell their shares and other shareholders are attracted to the new policy.

2. Corporate Investment Outlook

Early stage companies that have low or no earnings and negative cash flows are not in the position to pay dividends. All their available capital is being invested in projects designed to create the company's future. Companies that are mature often have a much lower need for new investments. These are the companies with excess cash flow that can be paid to shareholders in dividends or can be delivered in share repurchases.[16] The choice of whether the dividend is in cash or discretionary through a stock repurchase depends upon the shareholders' preference and tax situation.

3. Capital Structure and Financial Slack

The amount of flexibility needed for the future can limit the company's dividend-paying ability. While we will discuss the capital structure issues in Chapter 7, at this point it is sufficient to know that companies with little flexibility in their capital structures and a demanding schedule of corporate investments rely heavily on the company's own earnings. Little is available for shareholder dividend payments.

4. Company Change

Companies mature, enter a new business, or become financially troubled. These are times when companies change their dividend policies.

- As a company matures its need for investment capital declines. At this point, many companies choose to institute a dividend or to increase the dividend.
- A company that enters a new business, technology, or market may make a case to its investors for curtailing the dividend or limiting its normal growth.
- A company in financial difficulty may be forced to limit or suspend its dividend. Companies in businesses or economic circumstances that have limited their long-term ability to pay dividends take this difficult step. It is rarely a reaction to one or two years of poor financial performance.

IV. Dividend Practice

Once the board and management have assessed the situation, what are their choices for a dividend policy? The company can pay out the earnings that are not needed for investments each year, it can smooth the annual payout with attention to the long-term availability of earnings, or it can pay a set amount.

1. **Residual dividend policy.** The annual dividends that are declared are the result of an analysis of the company's needs and its capital

---

[16] We will discuss share repurchases at the end of this appendix.

sources for the year. The dividends are paid only if there are sufficient earnings after all its needs are met. Under this policy dividends
can vary substantially from year to year. This makes the growth in
dividends very difficult to predict, and shareholders are not fond of
this sort of uncertainty.

2. **Long-term dividend policy.** The management and the board determine a reasonable long-term strategy given the company's potential investments and capital resources. This long-term policy is an
adaptation of the residual dividend policy, but the company's capital
needs and sources are planned over a longer period of time. This
policy ensures that the dividends are not volatile from year to year—
it is a more certain dividend stream to shareholders. Companies
using this approach typically raise dividends only when they can be
sustained.

3. **Smoothed dividends.** This is a variation of the residual dividend
policy approach, with the annual dividends smoothed to take out
some of the annual variability. This method provides some policy
guidance to shareholders, reducing the uncertainty of the dividends
for the shareholders somewhat, but allowing the company flexibility.
Looking at the relationship of 3M's dividends and earnings discussed
in Chapter 6, it appears that this is the policy of 3M. Its earnings varied over time but its dividends followed a slow growth trajectory.

4. **Special dividend for windfall earnings.** Unusual earnings wind-
falls typically are dealt with by paying a special, one-time dividend,
or by repurchasing shares. This windfall dividend strategy is designed to signal that the event is unusual and will not change the
basic dividend payment policy of the company in the future. Thus
the investors' expectations are not raised, but the money is distributed. A company that has practiced this windfall dividend strategy is
National Presto Industries from 1983 to 1999, shown in Panel A,
Exhibit 6A-4. In 1992 a windfall dividend was paid followed by a
year with no dividends. In Panel B you can see that National
Presto's dividends followed a level dividends approach for the last
few years, even paying out over 200 percent of earnings in 2001 in
order to maintain the $2.00 dividend.[17]

V. Dividends Companies Pay

Over time dividend-paying patterns have changed. The dividend payout
ratio of the S&P 500 is shown in Panel A of Exhibit 6A-5. As dividend
payouts have declined, so too have the dividend yields shown in Panel B.
In spite of the recent declines in the stock market from the internet bubble of the late twentieth century, the dividend yields remain at historic
lows.

---

[17] Recollect the Dupont Model from Chapter 1. In order to pay out at this rate, National
Presto had to reduce assets or increase debt or equity.

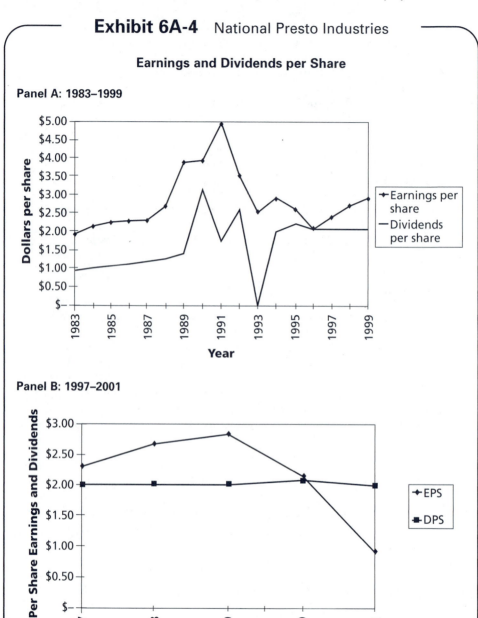

Exhibit 6A-4   National Presto Industries

Earnings and Dividends per Share

Panel A: 1983–1999

Panel B: 1997–2001

Exhibit 6A-5 Standard & Poor's 500

Dividend History

Panel A: Dividend Payout Ratio, 1925–2000

S&P Dividend Payout Ratio
S&P dividend as percentage of EPS

1970–2000 Average 45%

UBS Warburg

Panel B: Dividend Yields, 1946–2001

S&P 500 Dividend Yield

Morgan Stanley

Source: Edward Mathias, "Economics & Investment Environment." Washington, D.C.: The Carlyle Group, August 2001 and January 2002.

VI. Alternate Ways to Pay Dividends

Companies may pay out earnings as dividends, or they may use the cash to repurchase shares in the open markets. A corporation's board may choose to distribute their earnings in noncash transactions. Most typically these distributions take the form of an action related to the company's stock such as a stock repurchase, stock split, or stock dividend. These have a direct economic benefit for shareholders only if the dividend levels per share remain the same.

1. Stock Repurchase

In a stock repurchase the company takes the cash it might otherwise pay shareholders and repurchases some of its stock.[18] Shareholders who need cash can sell some of their shares and pay any capital gains taxes. Those who do not want cash can ignore the share repurchase. As shares are repurchased, the number of outstanding shares decreases. As a result, the earnings and cash flow per share increase for the remaining shareholders. Since the business and financial risk of the company do not change with the repurchase, the discount rate for the cash flows (or price earnings ratio for the earnings) does not change, and the value of the company remains the same. Since the number of shares decreases, the value per share increases as does the earnings and cash flow per share. Thus the shareholders who choose to hold their shares gain from the repurchase as do those whose shares are repurchased. In a perfect world without taxes and transactions costs, the gains for both sets of shareholders should be the same.[19]

2. Stock Split or Reverse Split

In a **stock split** the company increases or decreases the number of shares outstanding. In a split the shareholder receives two or more shares for every share owned. Typically stock splits are done to reduce the price per share for which the company trades.[20] A split should have no impact on the value of the shareholder's position—the price per share will drop but the number of shares owned increases. A 2 for 1 stock split of a $50 share would result in the shareholder owning two $25 shares. There are two reasons for a stock split. The first is to make high-priced shares more attractive to the investing public. The second is to attract a larger number of potential buyers. A stock split is declared by the board and ratified by the shareholders for shareholders of record on a particular date. The split is made on a subsequent date.

---

[18] A company can use other sources of cash, for instance, asset sales or new debt, to repurchase shares.

[19] Stock repurchases often are viewed as positive signals by the market. The repurchase can be viewed as a strategy to increase the share price to the level deemed appropriate by management and the board of directors and/or a signal that management believes that the company needs less cash and financial flexibility.

[20] The number of shares received in the split reflects management's and the board's view of the appropriate resulting price.

A **reverse split** decreases the number of outstanding shares. Thus a 5 for 1 reverse split of a $2 stock should result in the shareholder's number of shares being reduced by 80 percent. However, the price per new share should rise to $10. With a stock split or reverse split, there is no economic consequence absent a change in dividends.[21]

3. Stock Dividends

A stock dividend is the delivery of additional shares to holders of record. Typically the dividend is small, for instance, 5 percent. This increases the shareholders' number of shares, but not the proportion of the company that they own—the company has not changed, only the number of shares. Stock dividends can be misunderstood, but have no real economic consequences.

VII. Conclusion

In many ways a company's dividend policy is part of the financing question—if it pays out dividends the company has less self-generated funds on which to grow. What we do know about dividend policy is that it should be set so that:

1. A company does not have to forgo value-creating investments.
2. Personal taxes do not offset the value of the dividend to most investors.
3. Special dividends and/or stock repurchases are used for windfall or surplus cash.
4. Repurchases are considered as a cash alternative when the company's shareholders pay taxes.

In the next chapter we discuss capital structure—how a company finances itself.

Selected References

For more on basic dividend theory, see:

Bernstein, Peter L. "Dividends: The Puzzle." *Journal of Applied Corporate Finance*, Spring 1996.

Gordon, Myron. "Optimal Investment and Financing Policy." *Journal of Finance*, May 1963, pp. 264–272.

Lintner, John. "Dividends, Earnings, Leverage, Stock Prices, and the Supply of Capital to Corporations." *Review of Economic and Statistics*, August 1962, pp. 242–269.

---

[21] The only economic consequence is if the number of potential investors is increased. This can change the stock's clientele and its recognition, resulting in a transitory price change.

Miller, Merton H., and Franco Modigliani. "Dividend Policy, Growth, and the Valuation of Shares." *Journal of Business*, October 1961, pp. 411–433.

For more on agency costs and corporate cash flow, see:
Jensen, Michael. "Agency Costs of Free Cash Flows, Corporate Finance and Takeovers." *American Economic Review*, May 1986.

For more on taxes, dividends, and investor preferences, see:
Elton, Ned, and Martin Gruber. "Marginal Shareholder Tax Rates and the Clientele Effect." *Review of Economic and Statistics*, February 1970.
Litzenberger, Robert, and Krishna Ramaswamy. "The Effects of Dividends on Common Stock Prices: Tax Effects of Information Effect." *Journal of Financial Economics*, May 1982.
Miller, Merton, and Myron Scholes. "Dividends and Taxes." *Journal of Financial Economics*, December 1978.
Shefrin, H., and M. Statman. "Explaining Investor Preference for Cash Dividends." *Journal of Financial Economics*, June 1984.

For more on current dividend practice and dividend and stock behavior, see:
Fama, Eugene F., and Kenneth R. French. "Disappearing Dividends: Changing Firm Characteristics Or Lower Propensity To Pay?" *Journal of Applied Corporate Finance*, Spring 2001.
Frank, M., and R. Jagannathan. "Why Do Stock Prices Drop by Less than the Value of the Dividend? Evidence from a Country without Taxes." *Journal of Financial Economics*, February 1998.
Rozeff, Michael. "How Companies Set Their Dividend Payout Ratios," in *The Revolution in Corporate Finance*, Joel Stern and Donald Chew, eds. New York: Basel Blackwell, 1986.
Soter, Dennis, Eugene Brigham, and Paul Evanson. "The Dividend Cut Heard Round The World. The Case Of FPL." *Journal of Applied Corporate Finance*, Spring 1996.

For more on stock repurchase, see:
Gup, Benton E., and Doowoo Nam. "Stock Buybacks, Corporate Performance, And EVA." *Journal of Applied Corporate Finance*, Spring 2001.
Grullon, Gustavo, and David Ikenberry. "What Do We Know About Stock Repurchases?" *Journal of Applied Corporate Finance*, Spring 2000.

For basic overviews on dividend theory and practice, see:
Brealey, Richard A., and Stewart C. Myers. *Principles of Corporate Finance*. 7th ed. New York: McGraw-Hill, 2002, chap. 16.
Brigham, Eugene F., Louis C. Gapenski, and Michael Ehrhardt. *Financial Management*. 9th ed. Fort Worth, TX: The Dryden Press, 1999, chap. 17.
Ross, Stephen A., Randolph W. Westerfield, and Jeffrey F. Jaffe. *Corporate Finance*. 6th ed. Homewood, IL: Richard D. Irwin, 2002, chap. 18.

Chapter Seven

Financial Leverage and Shareholder Value

In Chapter 6 we learned how to estimate the fair return that should be expected for an equity investment. We found that all investors require a return for:

1. *Illiquidity*: The time that their money is invested.
2. *Inflation*: The losses caused by changes in the purchasing power of money.
3. *Risk*: The chance that the returns from an investment may be higher or lower than was expected.

We used the following formula to determine this required return:

Required return = Risk-free rate + Inflation premium + Risk premium

In this formula we used the rate from a U.S. Treasury security as a proxy for the risk-free rate of return. For U.S. investors it combines the return required for the time value of money and for expected inflation.[1] As for risk, we know that investors expect more return for increased risk. To determine what they expect, we asked capital market experts what they believed was a fair return for risk—their market price of risk. Up to this point we have assumed that all our investments are financed only by the owners of the company, but this is rarely true. Many owners, or the managers on their behalf, subcontract some of their financing obligations to others, particularly to those who prefer investments that have a predetermined repayment schedule and pay rent for the use of the money. These financing subcontractors are called **lenders**, the investment is called **principal**, and the annual rent is called **interest**.

How do shareholders, or managers on their behalf, decide whether they want to subcontract the financing of their company? The answer is shareholders should subcontract to lenders when doing so increases the shareholders' value. If, however, it makes no difference at all to the value

---

[1] Similar proxies could be chosen in other countries.

of the shareholders' position, then the shareholders will be indifferent as to the source of the company's capital—the company can subcontract or not. Thus the crucial question is, can subcontracting some of the financing obligations to lenders create value for the shareholders?

Let us begin to answer that question with what we know. First, we know that shareholders want managers to create value for them. Second, we know that to create value, managers must make decisions that will increase the present value of the company either by reducing risk, increasing cash flow, or both. Keeping the shareholders' value-increasing objective in mind, let us see if financing the corporation with some mixture of debt and equity can actually make the company worth more than financing it with equity alone.

I. The Value of Financial Leverage

A company has two kinds of leverage—operating and financial. **Operating leverage** is the degree to which the company utilizes its assets to produce revenues. We measure operating leverage with the sales/asset ratio. **Financial leverage** is the degree to which the company uses debt financing to enhance shareholders' returns. The assets/equity ratio measures financial leverage.[2] The amount of debt and equity used by the company determines its **capital structure**.

With the objective of determining whether a particular capital structure can enhance shareholders' value, let's look at an example. Greenway Corporation currently has no debt. It is located in a country where interest is not tax-deductible, unlike the United States and many other countries. Greenway's cash flows are shown in Exhibit 7-1. In addition, we have calculated the value of the cash flows using methods from previous chapters using the following information.

- Debt costs 10 percent.
- Required return on equity is 15 percent with no leverage and 15.6 percent with 10 percent debt/total capital.
- New debt retires a portion of the outstanding equity. It is not new money adding to the assets of the company.
- Total market value of the company is calculated using cash flow perpetuity.

$$\text{Value of company} = \frac{\text{Residual cash flows}}{\text{Required return} - \text{Growth in cash flows}}$$

- As leverage increases, shareholders require an increasing return to compensate for their subordinate position in the capital structure.[3]

---

[2] There are many ways to measure leverage. The ratio depends upon who is assessing the role of debt in the firm. For example, shareholders would use assets/equity; lenders would use debt/total capital, debt/assets, or debt/equity. We discussed leverage ratios in Chapter 1.

[3] In bankruptcy or liquidation, shareholders' claims on the assets of the company follow those of the creditors and lenders.

Exhibit 7-1   Greenway Corporation

Earnings, Cash Flow, and Value: No Tax Deduction for Interest Expense

(in millions, except per-share data)

	100% Equity Financed	90% Equity/ 10% Debt
Cash Flows		
Profit before taxes	$15.00	$15.00
Taxes	(5.00)	(5.00)
Profit after taxes	$10.00	$10.00
Depreciation	5.00	5.00
New plant and equipment	(5.00)	(5.00)
Added working capital	0.00	0.00
Cash flow to all capital providers	$10.00	$10.00
Residual cash flow*	$10.00	$ 9.40
Number of shares outstanding	10	9
Residual cash flow per share	$ 1.00	$ 1.04
Required Return on		
Company	15.0%	15.0%
Debt	0	10.0%
Equity	15.0%	15.6%
*Market Value***		
Debt	0	$ 6.67
Equity	$66.67	$60.00
Company	$66.67	$66.67
Equity value per share	**$ 6.67**	**$ 6.67**

*Residual cash flow is cash flow after interest expense of 10 percent has been deducted—$0.67 with 10 percent debt in the capital structure.
**Market value is cash flow/required return.

- Interest is not tax-deductible. Thus it is not an expense before taxes.
- The resulting profits and cash flows belong to all capital providers.

Now we can determine whether shareholders gain value from leverage. If they do, the value of their shares should increase as debt/total capital increases. In this example, it does not. As you can see by the bold numbers near the bottom of Exhibit 7-1, the share price is the same with or without debt—the value of the shares is $6.67 whether the company borrows to buy back shares or not.

Investors require higher returns as they take a subordinate position in the capital structure.[4] Exhibit 7-2 illustrates why the shareholders' return

---

[4] In the event of financial distress or bankruptcy, all other capital providers have claim on assets before shareholders.

Exhibit 7-2 Greenway Corporation

**Forecasted Earnings and Cash Flows: Three Outcomes
With and Without Leverage: Interest Not Tax-Deductible**

(dollars in millions)

	Bad Times	Most Likely	Good Times
Profit before taxes	$ 5.0	$15.0	$25.0
Taxes	(1.7)	(5.0)	(8.5)
Profit after taxes	3.3	10.0	16.5
Depreciation	5.0	5.0	5.0
New plant and equipment	(5.0)	(5.0)	(5.0)
Added working capital	0.0	0.0	0.0
Cash flow	$ 3.3	$10.0	$16.5
Without Financial Leverage			
Net income and cash flow to:			
All capital providers	$3.30	$10.00	$16.50
Shareholders	$3.30	$10.00	$16.50
Book value of equity	$66.67	$66.67	$66.67
Return on debt	10.00%	10.00%	10.00%
Return on equity	**4.95%**	**15.00%**	**24.75%**
With 10% Debt/Total Capital			
Net income and cash flow to:			
All capital providers	$3.30	$10.00	$16.50
Shareholders	$2.60	$9.30	$15.80
Book value of equity	$60.00	$60.00	$60.00
Return on equity	**4.33%**	**15.50%**	**26.33%**

requirements increase with increased leverage. The exhibit shows the shareholders' returns, the ROE, as the company's earnings change from those originally forecasted in Exhibit 7-1 to those earned under better and worse business circumstances. Without leverage, the maximum return is 24.8 percent in good times, but it increases to 26.3 percent when 10 percent of the company's capital comes from lenders. Increase the leverage even more than the 10 percent, and the ROE is higher. In bad times, of course, leverage increases the downside for the shareholders. It is this range of outcomes that become wider with leverage, and which cannot be known beforehand, that shareholders recognize as risk. For the increased risk from leverage, shareholders expect a higher return—in this case the required return increases from 15 to 15.6 percent.[5]

---

[5] Later we will discuss how to estimate the increase in required return with increased leverage.

As leverage increases, the required return for the whole company does not change. The 15 percent return is the return required by all capital providers for the risk of the company. This is because the company's risks and cash flows do not change with leverage, only the risks and cash flows for each capital provider change. The process for calculating the average capital cost for the company with no tax impact on interest, usually called the weighted-average cost of capital (WACC), is as follows:

$$\text{WACC} = [R_d \times (D/V)] + [R_e \times (E/V)]$$

Where:
R_d = required return on debt
R_e = required return on equity
D = debt capital
E = equity capital
V = total capital

For Greenway, the tax-free WACC would be

$$\text{WACC} = [R_d \times (D/V)] + [R_e \times (E/V)]$$
$$= [0.10 \times 0.10] + [0.156 \times 0.90]$$
$$= 0.15 \text{ or } 15\%$$

Leverage does not change the average cost of capital for the company, and it does not change the company's value. What it does change is the relative positions of the capital providers—at low levels of debt, lenders charge less than equity providers because of their contractual position.[6] As debt increases, the return required by each increases, as seen in Exhibit 7-3.[7]

There are exceptions to the rule that leverage does not affect shareholders' value. Exceptions occur when the way a company is financed changes its risk, its cash flows, or both. The question is, what could change the company's cash flows and/or its risk?

One thing that can change cash flows is taxes, or rather the tax deductibility of any financing expense. In many countries, for example, the United States, interest is a tax-deductible expense—interest payments lower the taxes a company pays, increase the company's cash flows, but do not change risk. The following formula is the weighted average cost of capital in a world where interest is tax-deductible.

---

[6] The payment schedule interest and maturity is contractual. Shareholders earn only the residual income—the income left after all providers, including lenders, are paid.

[7] Chapter 9 discusses free cash flow valuation, a shortcut method of valuation that depends on a company's capital structure remaining constant. The method uses a weighted-average cost of capital to discount the cash flows to all capital providers. It is a quick alternative to forecasts that include the financing of cash flows in determining the value of an investment. It is useful only under certain restrictive conditions.

Exhibit 7-3   Greenway Corporation

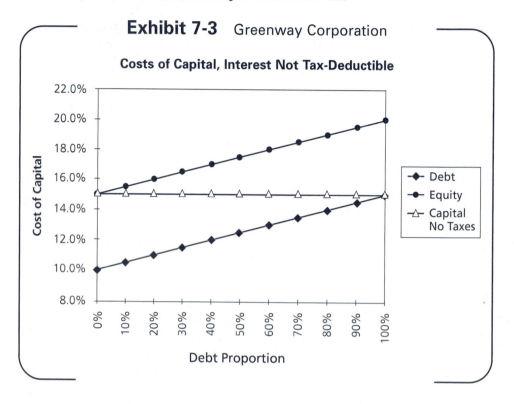

Costs of Capital, Interest Not Tax-Deductible

$$\text{WACC} = [R_d \times (1 - t)] \times (D/V)] + [R_e \times (E/V)]$$

Where:

R_d = required return on debt
R_e = required return on equity
D = debt capital
E = equity capital
V = total capital
t = tax rate

Exhibit 7-4 shows the impact of interest deductibility on Greenway's cost of capital and the shareholders' value per share. The value per share is higher with leverage and it is entirely due to the tax-deductible interest.

The shareholders' value does increase when interest is tax-deductible —the cash flows increased. Exhibit 7-5 shows graphically the effect of taxes on the cost of capital—when interest is tax-deductible the average cost of the company's capital decreases and the value of the company increases. This is in spite of the fact that debt and equity costs increase as lenders provide a larger proportion of a company's capital. Why then, in a world where there are taxes, don't companies finance themselves with more debt? In fact, why don't shareholders force companies to finance themselves with almost 100 percent debt?

There is no definitive answer to why there seems to be a limit to a company's financial leverage. There are several theories. One of the most

Exhibit 7-4 Greenway Corporation

**Impact of Tax-Deductible Interest on
Shareholder Value: 10 Percent Debt/Total Capital**

(dollars in millions, except per share value)

	Interest Not Tax-Deductible	Interest Tax-Deductible
Profit before interest and taxes	$15.0	$15.0
Interest	0.0	(0.7)
Profit before taxes	15.0	14.3
Taxes (34%)	(5.0)	(4.9)
Profit after taxes	10.0	9.4
Depreciation	5.0	5.0
New equipment	(5.0)	(5.0)
Added working capital	0.0	0.0
Cash flow to all capital providers	$10.0	$9.4
Residual cash flow (after interest of $0.67)	$9.3	$9.4
Cost of equity	15.6%	15.6%
Cost of debt	10.0%	10.0%
Weighted-average capital cost	15.0%	14.7%
Equity market value of company	$59.62	$60.26
Debt value	—	$6.67
Corporate value	$66.67	$67.31
Number of shares	9	9
Equity value per share	**$6.62**	**$6.70**

interesting theories is the notion of financial distress. A company that is **financially embarrassed** is unable to pay the interest on its debt. **Financial distress** occurs when a company cannot pay the interest or principal on its debt. A company that fails to pay its lenders can be forced into bankruptcy: the contract with the lender is broken and the lender, because it has a contract, can require debt repayment. When the company cannot meet the required payment, it may have to resort to bankruptcy or reorganization.[8] Shareholders have no such contract, and thus cannot force the company into bankruptcy or reorganization. Obviously, shareholders are not happy when a company is financially distressed, but they have no contract, only expectations. When shareholders' expectations are not met, they can sell their shares, or they can use their voting rights to change the board of directors.

---

[8] In reorganization creditors may have to negotiate their bills and capital providers may have to renegotiate their positions. The shareholders have little power in such a situation and often lose their equity. In that case the bondholders may have to accept an equity position.

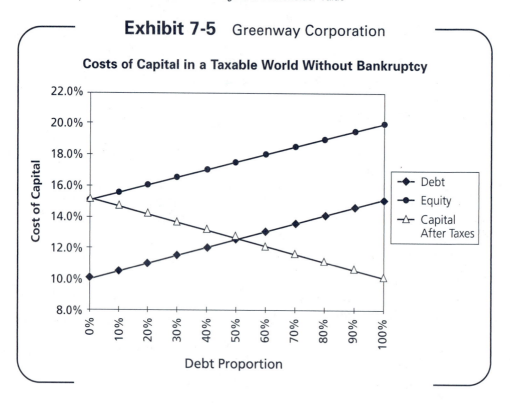

Exhibit 7-5 Greenway Corporation

Costs of Capital in a Taxable World Without Bankruptcy

In the case of a company with modest amounts of debt, most lenders do not worry about the possibility of bankruptcy. As the amount of debt increases, however, bankruptcy becomes more probable, and lenders begin to incorporate the expected costs of possible bankruptcy into their required return. Thus, at the point when lenders begin to be concerned about bankruptcy, they appear to have added an extra charge to the cost of debt—a charge for possible bankruptcy. Exhibit 7-5 showed what happens to a company's cost of capital when lenders and shareholders are not concerned about bankruptcy. With bankruptcy, the costs of debt and equity jump at the point of lender concern, and the cost of capital starts to rise. Exhibit 7-6 shows the sort of rise that can occur. Finally, Exhibit 7-7 compares Greenway's cost of capital under the various conditions.

We have suggested that the lender's required return—the interest on the debt—increases when the probability of bankruptcy becomes real. This is only one theory that may explain a jump in the cost of capital as leverage increases. Many theories have been used to explain this phenomenon. Two of the prominent ones are agency and pecking order theories.

Agency Theory. The corporation is a group people with different roles—lenders, managers, and employees. Agents are those who work on behalf of the shareholders but are not owners of the company, such as managers and lenders. Those who work for lenders, and who are acting in their personal best interests, may become wary of lending to a company long

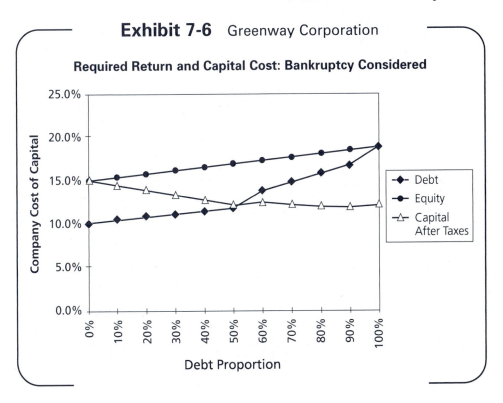

Exhibit 7-6 Greenway Corporation

Required Return and Capital Cost: Bankruptcy Considered

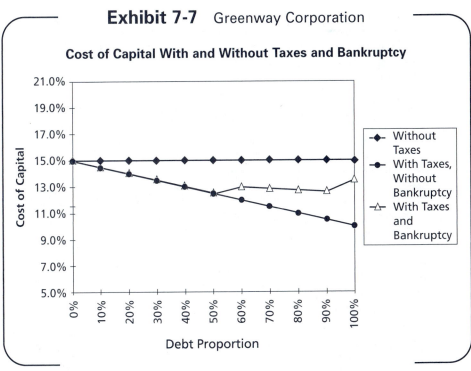

Exhibit 7-7 Greenway Corporation

Cost of Capital With and Without Taxes and Bankruptcy

before their employer would—the impact of a loss on the lending agent is considerable, while the impact on the lending institution may be negligible.

Agents are bound together by informal and formal agreements that allow them to seek the success of the company. However, their personal goals may be at odds with each other and with the company's owners, its shareholders. For example, shareholders prefer that a company have considerable debt—their potential loss is their investment, but the upside is considerable. Lenders, on the other hand, stand to gain nothing if the firm does better than expected—the interest and principal is set in their contract. Managers are caught between the two competing goals. This tension is thought to limit the amount of debt held by companies. Various strategies have been used by companies and their boards to align the interests of the various agents with the shareholders and thus reduce the potential agency costs—costs such as under leveraging.

Pecking Order Theory. This theory rests on the assumption that companies have a preference for particular kinds of financing. There are two key ideas that are behind this theory. First, managers do not want all the information they know about the company and its business to be broadly known.[9] Second, managers' allegiance is to current shareholders—they will forgo value-creating opportunities if it involves issuing new equity. The result is that managers prefer internally generated funds to all other sources of capital. If additional capital is needed, the preference first is debt, and then convertible securities, preferred stock, and common stock, in that order.

Whatever the reasons or theory, there does appear to be some limit on the debt financing of a company. As a company reaches that limit, its weighted-average cost of capital begins to increase and its value starts to decrease. Companies seek to know where this limit is reached, and where the company has the lowest capital cost. The capital structure at this point is called the **optimal capital structure**. It is optimal because the value of the company is highest when the company is at its optimal capital structure. Beyond this point the company's cost of capital increases and the value of the company and the shareholders' value both decrease.

The manager must consider all the risks and returns in determining the appropriate mix of debt and equity. In some ways, this task is a marketing problem: the manager has several different products (the company's financial securities) and several different markets (potential investors in the company). The financial manager must match securities with investors in a way that creates the greatest value for the company. He or she does so by analyzing the potential effects of various financing alternatives on the total market value of the company. To understand the decisions that face managers as they consider the appropriate capital structure for their company, a basic understanding of debt and debt markets is important.

---

[9] This is called having asymmetric information.

II. What Do Subcontractors Want?

Most companies are financed with a combination of equity and debt. Debt is different from equity in that it is contractual, typically specifying the amount to be borrowed, the interest charged for the money, and the time at which the money will be returned. The debt contract may also have some **covenants**, which are provisions that restrict the company's activities (e.g., allow no further increase in debt) or require that certain standards be met (e.g., a particular current ratio). Lenders' claims appear before the shareholders' residual claim both on the balance sheet and in law.

In addition to the public markets for debt, which are similar to those for equity described in Chapter 6, capital can be raised through **private placements**.[10] Public issues are regulated by the Securities and Exchange Commission (SEC) in the United States and by similar commissions in other countries. They require the issuing company to disclose specific information about the company's business activities, the financial instrument being issued, and the intended use of the proceeds. Such disclosure provides the public with information that facilitates subsequent trading in the secondary market. Private placements are direct placements of the securities with investors such as large insurance companies. They are not registered and generally are not traded in the secondary market. However, because the issuer can negotiate directly with the investor, private placements allow more complicated and specialized financial arrangements between borrower and lender than are possible in the public capital markets. In general, it is debt, and debt with some equity characteristics that are placed privately.

Private institutional investors such as mutual funds, insurance companies, and pension funds are the largest investors in the capital markets. Although precise data are difficult to obtain, estimates suggest that well over half of publicly traded securities in the United States are owned by these institutions. Individual shareholders account for the remainder. In other countries, the level of institutional ownership is quite different, and can be much higher.

While the two primary types of securities used by companies to raise long-term capital are debt and equity, some instruments combine the two types through convertible provisions. **Convertible instruments** typically allow the investor to convert debt or preferred stock into equity, usually common stock, at a specified price and usually during a particular period of time. This is done to make the security more attractive to the investor at times when investors may prefer non-equity investments. In addition,

---

[10] The market for certain bonds can be much less liquid than markets for equity issues. This even can be true for bonds of large companies. This is because a company may have many different debt instruments (bonds), each with a different set of characteristics, and because one or a few large investors own large quantities of a particular debt instrument, making trading infrequent.

there are investors that have a preference for convertible securities because of their tax or other circumstances.

1. Debt Markets

Long-term debt instruments are frequently called **bonds** or **debentures**.[11] A bond is a contractual debt obligation to repay a stated amount on a specified date, termed the **maturity**, and to make periodic interest, or **coupon**, payments. The stated amount is called the **principal** or **par value**. The par value is typically a standard amount in each country. For instance, in the United States the usual par value is $1,000. Specific features of the bonds issued are described in a contract called an **indenture agreement**. The stated interest or coupon payments are determined by a specified interest rate or coupon rate at the time the bond is issued. If the contractually obligated payments are not made, the bond is in default and the bondholders may have to call on, or take, some or all of the assets of the company as compensation.

For most bonds, the coupon rate is fixed for the life of the bond. Because of large fluctuations in interest rates in recent years, some bonds have been issued with variable, or floating, interest rates. For **variable-rate bonds**, the interest rate is restated at specified intervals based on a particular market index of interest rates—for example, LIBOR (the London Interbank Offer Rate) or the prime rate, the rate charged the best customers of a bank. These bonds are also called **floating-rate bonds** or **floaters**.

For fixed-coupon bonds, changes in interest rates subsequent to the date of issue affect the bond price in the secondary market but do not affect the cost to the company. If general market interest rates go up (or down), the price of the bond will go down (or up) in order to continue to provide a fair rate of return in the subsequent interest rate environment. These adjustments occur so that the bond's **yield to maturity**, the return from interest plus principal repayments, will approximate the current market rate of interest for bonds of similar maturity, quality, and special features.

The price that an investor is willing to pay for a bond is a function of the par value of the bond, the coupon rate, the maturity, and prevailing interest rates. The following formula for determining the proper secondary price of a bond is similar to the present value calculations discussed in Chapters 4 and 5.

$$P = \frac{CP_1}{(1 + R)^1} + \frac{CP_2}{(1 + R)^2} + \cdots + \frac{CP_m}{(1 + R)^m} + \frac{PAR}{(1 + R)^m}$$

Where:

P = market price of the bond
CP = periodic coupon payment (interest payment)
R = current market interest rate
PAR = par value of the bond
m = maturity period of the bond

---

[11] Bonds are often backed by security—some asset of the company; debentures are not.

Let's use an example and calculate the price of a bond when interest rates change. In the past a company had issued $2 million in bonds at 12.0 percent coupon. If the rate of interest on bonds of a similar maturity and quality rose from 12.0 to 15.7 percent, the market price of the bonds with two years remaining until maturity would drop from $2 million to $1.88 million. This new price would yield the market rate of 15.7 percent to new purchasers:

$$P = \frac{\$240,000}{(1 + 0.157)^1} + \frac{\$240,000}{(1 + 0.157)^2} + \frac{\$2,000,000}{(1 + 0.157)^2}$$

$$P = \$1,880,762$$

Conversely, if market rates dropped to, say, 10 percent, the bond price would increase to $2,069,421.

$$P = \frac{\$240,000}{(1 + 0.10)^1} + \frac{\$240,000}{(1 + 0.10)^2} + \frac{\$2,000,000}{(1 + 0.10)^2}$$

$$P = \$2,069,421$$

Prices (present values) of bonds with longer maturities are more affected by interest rate changes than are values of bonds with short maturities.[12]

We can use the same formula to determine the bond's yield to maturity if the price is known. The method for determining the yield to maturity is like that used in Chapter 4 for calculating the internal rate of return. A calculator with basic financial functions is all you need.

For conventional bonds, the amount the company borrows is the same as the principal or par value of the bond, net of issue costs of course. This statement is not true for **zero-coupon bonds**. These bonds require no periodic coupon payments. Instead, the par value of the bond to be paid at maturity is much larger than the amount originally borrowed, the price when the bond was issued and bought by the investor. Essentially, interest is accrued during the bond's life and paid at the time the principal is repaid at the bond's maturity. Determining the return on these bonds is a simplification of the yield-to-maturity calculation, because there are no coupon payments. The following simplified formula would be used:

$$\text{Price} = \frac{\text{PAR}}{(1 + i)^m}$$

Where:
  i = yield to maturity
  m = years to maturity

Using this formula, if a firm issues a zero-coupon bond today at a price of $275 per bond returning $1,000 in 10 years, the effective yield, or yield to maturity, would be 13.78 percent ($275 = [1,000/(1 + i)^{10}]$).

---

[12] For those of you with an interest in bonds and bond price changes, the primary measure of the bond's price sensitivity to interest rate changes is duration. See the references at the end of this chapter for further reading.

In the 1980s, we saw the explosion of a relatively new version of debt, junk bonds. There had always been a market for bonds of companies that had fallen into disfavor after their debt was issued, and whose debt-quality ratings had declined. These bonds, sometimes called fallen angels, were traded at discounts to their original issuing price.[13] **Junk debt**, however, was debt of companies that were not highly rated or of companies that were issuing unusually high levels of debt for their size or risk. The debt carried very high interest rates and was issued at a discount to its par value. Today it is called, more formally, **original issue discount (OID) debt**.

Not all bonds require the issuer to retire the entire principal amount at the specified maturity date of the bond. Many bonds require the company to make periodic principal reductions, into what is called a **sinking fund**. The purpose of these sinking funds is to reduce the risk that the borrower will not be able to repay the principal. While the amount going into the sinking fund may be placed in a trust account to be held until the maturity date, this practice is not typical today. It is more likely that when the sinking fund payments are due, the company will retire a portion of the issued bonds, even though they have not reached maturity. The way in which bonds are chosen to be purchased or retired before maturity is specified at the time the bonds are first issued by the company and noted in the **indenture agreement**, the debt contract. For publicly traded bonds, commonly the company will simply purchase some of the existing bonds in the market, thus reducing the total amount of bonds outstanding. In addition to the actual retirement of debt by the sinking fund payments, the company may set aside funds equal to the sinking fund payment to be used for retirement at maturity.[14]

In addition to reducing the amount of bonds outstanding to meet sinking fund requirements, companies may choose to retire the bonds before the specified maturity. This process is termed **refunding** or **calling** the bonds. Companies are especially interested in refunding when interest rates fall. The existing bonds can be called and refinanced with lower cost debt. To protect against this possibility many bonds have **call protection**—the bonds cannot be called and retired for a specified period of time, or may be called only if a stated premium is paid to the bondholders. Call provisions are specified in the indenture agreement.

As a further protection for bondholders, the bond contract, the indenture, may limit the company in other ways. Frequently the company will be required to maintain certain levels of assets, to limit its total amount of debt, or to not issue any debt without the permission of the lender. Often these restrictions, or **covenants**, are specified in the form of ratios—the kind we discussed in Chapter 1. If any of the bond covenants are violated, the bond is deemed to be in technical default and is immediately due for payment. It is up to the bondholder whether the

---

[13] This discount existed with no marketwide change in interest rates.
[14] Often these funds are U.S Treasury securities with a maturity or duration that meets the obligation. The company has no access to these funds except to repay the principal.

company will be forced to pay off the debt or whether the covenant will be waived or rewritten.

The general risk to the borrower is reflected in the **bond rating**. Bond ratings are important because bonds with higher potential for default (lower ratings) must have a higher coupon (that is, pay a higher interest rate) to compensate investors for the increased risk. Several organizations publish bond ratings; Moody's and Standard & Poor's (S&P) are the two most widely known in the United States. Based on these independent organizations' assessments of the general credit risk of the borrower, bonds are assigned a rating, with Aaa (Moody's) or AAA (S&P) indicating the most creditworthy bonds—those with the lowest risk of default. The ratings decrease through Aa/AA, and so on, to high-risk bonds rated Caa/CCC or below. A bond's rating may be changed because of changes in the issuer's situation.[15]

A company may have several kinds of debt at the same time. The debt may have been issued to different lenders, at different times, and under different market conditions. The indenture agreement stipulates the differences: the amount of debt, the coupon rate of interest, payment terms, specific assets on which the lenders may call in event of default, the priority in which the lenders' claims will be settled, and criteria the company must meet in order to have the debt without covenant revision. Debt that holds claim to specific assets in event of default, particularly land or buildings, is usually called **mortgage debt**. Debt that, by contract, allows other debt precedence in event of default is called **subordinated debt**. Different issues of debt are listed separately on a company's balance sheet. The balance sheet and the accompanying notes describe the major differences in each debt instrument. Bond guides such as S&P and Moody's in the United States provide more detail for the potential investor or company analyst.

2. Cost of Debt

Most companies use debt to finance a portion of their assets. The proportion of debt used by U.S. firms has changed dramatically over rather short periods of time, as shown in Exhibit 7-8. In the 1990s, equity had regained favor with investors, as shown in Exhibit 7-9. In the early part of the twenty-first century, debt, with its historically low rates, has been much more attractive to companies. Changes in the securities that are issued is due more to capital market interest rather than what companies want to issue although low interest rates and stock prices can spur an interest in debt.

Not only does the debt proportion of new financing change, so do interest rates. At a high in the early 1980s, they have, until the past year, declined. Exhibit 7-10 shows the market rates of interest during the last 18 years on publicly traded debt of varying qualities. Note that the interest rate on the best quality corporate debt is higher than that on

---

[15] Only the best quality bonds are considered investment grade. Many institutional investment portfolios may invest only in investment grade bonds.

Exhibit 7-8

New Bond and Equity Issues: 1969–2001

(all nonfinancial business corporations)

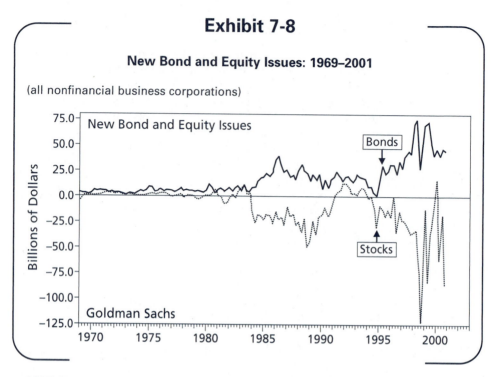

SOURCE: Mathias, Edward J., *Economic and Investment Environment*, August 2001, Washington, D.C.: The Carlyle Group.

government debt of the same maturity, and that the lower the corporate debt is rated, the higher the interest rate—the lender's required return.

Just as the reliability of the borrower affects the interest rate, so does the length of time the borrower wishes to use the principal. Exhibit 7-11 shows the market rate of interest on debt of the same quality but different maturities at several points in time. Each of the lines is a **yield curve.** An upward slope is normal because lenders who provide capital for longer times require, quite logically, more return. At some points in time, this upward-sloping yield curve does not exist. This has been particularly true in periods of high inflation. For instance, during the 1970s, the relationship between the market rate of interest and debt of different maturities was sometimes perverse. Exhibit 7-11 shows two typical yield curves and two inverse yield curves (March 1, 1981, and December 1, 1981). The rapidity of the change, coupled with the change from a normal to an inverse yield curve, has not been repeated since that time.

In addition to interest payments, a number of special features may be required by the lender. For example, specific assets may be pledged to support the loan, the lender may require seniority over others' claims in the case of bankruptcy, or the loan may be convertible into common or preferred stock under certain conditions. Each feature offers the lender different levels of protection from risk and thus carries a somewhat different cost, which is reflected in the interest rate.

Exhibit 7-9

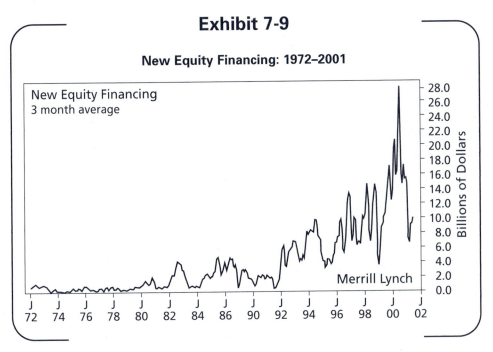

New Equity Financing: 1972–2001

SOURCE: Mathias, Edward J., *Economic and Investment Environment*, August 2001, Washington, D.C.: The Carlyle Group.

Exhibit 7-10

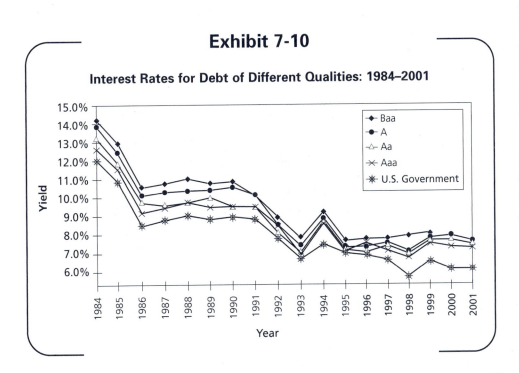

Interest Rates for Debt of Different Qualities: 1984–2001

Exhibit 7-11

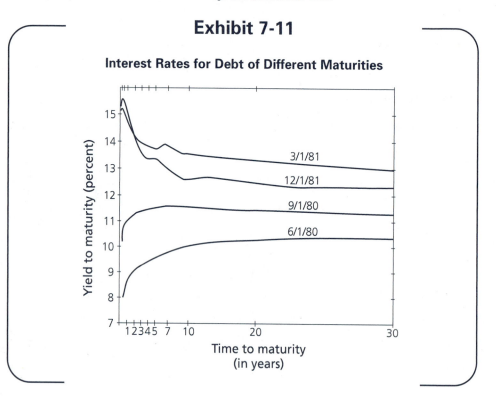

Interest Rates for Debt of Different Maturities

Earlier we showed that the lenders' required return on debt was the ratio of the interest rate to the principal amount of the debt.

$$R_d = \frac{\text{Interest payment}}{\text{Debt principal}}$$

However, the company's interest expense is tax-deductible, making the company's cost of debt K_d:

$$K_d = \frac{\text{Interest payment (1 - Tax rate)}}{\text{Debt principal}}$$

Let's use an example to show the difference in the calculations. If a company wanted to borrow $2 million, and the lender expected interest payments of $163,000 per year, the investor's required return would be 8.15 percent ($163,000/$2,000,000). However, taking into account the tax deductibility of debt, if the tax rate is 34 percent, the company's cost of debt would be:

$$K_d = \frac{\text{Interest payment (1 - Tax rate)}}{\text{Debt principal}}$$

$$= \frac{\$163,000 \ (1 - 0.34)}{\$2,000,000}$$

$$= \frac{\$107,580}{2,000,000}$$

$$= 0.0538 \text{ or } 5.38\%$$

This formula applies whether the company issues bonds at par or at a discount. If the company issues zero-coupon bonds, however, there are no interest payments during the life of the bond, and the investor's return comes from the difference between the price paid and the principal returned at maturity. Following our example, if the company's lenders' required yield to maturity was 8.5 percent on zero-coupon bonds, and it wanted to borrow $2.0 million for 10 years, the principal returned at the maturity of the bonds would be $4.5 million, not $2.0 million.[16]

III. The Impact of Leverage on Shareholders' Required Return

In the Greenway example we said that the required return on equity increases as a company increases its leverage. In theory this is true, since we assume that the financing costs have no relationship, or correlation, to the returns of the company.[17] Using the CAPM, and assuming that the beta increases as does financial leverage in a linear fashion, the following formula demonstrates the impact of leverage on beta.

$$\text{Beta levered} = \text{Unlevered beta} \times [1 + ((1 - \text{Tax rate}) \times \text{Debt/Equity})]$$

With an unlevered, equity, beta of 1.0, debt to total capital ratio of 50 percent, (debt/equity ratio of 100 percent), and a tax rate of 34 percent, the following shows the levered beta. You can see from the analysis how the degree of financial leverage increases or decreases the levered beta (β_L).

$$\beta_L = 1.0 \times [1 + ((1 - 0.34) \times 1.0)]$$
$$= 1.66$$

One caveat. This assumes that the relationship between interest and earnings does not exist. However, companies may organize their capital structures to mitigate their earnings variability. For example, a company with earnings from oil may choose debt with a floating interest rate. Typically, as oil prices increase, so do interest rates. This would yield a constant spread, or difference, between the earnings and interest charges. The lesson to learn is know your company.[18]

---

[16] To determine the $4.5 million principal to be repaid, compound $2.0 million by 8.5 percent for 10 years.

[17] We also could say that there is no correlation between the earnings of the company and the costs of debt.

[18] In addition, in looking at proxy betas, Russ Fuller and Kerr Halbert in "Cost of Capital: An Analysis of the Pure Play Technique," *Journal of Finance*, December 1981, found that when trying to find proxies, the betas were more reliable if they were not adjusted for differences in leverage between the proxy and the company.

IV. Conclusion

What should be clear from this chapter is that financial leverage can be important in creating value for shareholders. However, the sources of value must be identified and understood. It is not enough to believe that debt is a good source of financing, but we must measure its impact on the value of a company.

In addition to determining the optimal capital structure—the debt/total capital ratio that most enhances the value of the company—management's job is to choose financing over time. This financing depends upon the condition of the company and capital markets. The process for making financing decisions is discussed in Chapter 8.

Selected References

For the origination of the debt irrelevance theory, see:

Miller, Merton. "Debt and Taxes." *Journal of Finance* 32, May 1977, pp. 261–276.

Modigliani, Franco, and Merton Miller. "Corporate Income Taxes and the Cost of Capital: A Correction." *American Economic Review* 53, June 1963, pp. 433–443.

For more on agency theory, see:

Jensen, Michael, and W. Meckling. "The Theory of the Firm: Managerial Behavior, Agency Costs and Ownership." *Journal of Financial Economics* 3, 1976.

For more on capital structure and its value, see:

Altman, E. "A Further Investigation of the Bankruptcy Cost Question." *Journal of Finance* 39, September 1984, pp. 1067–1089.

Barclay, Michael J., and Clifford W. Smith, Jr. "The Capital Structure Puzzle: Another Look At The Evidence." *Journal of Applied Corporate Finance*, Spring 1999.

Bierman, Harold. *Capital Structure Decision.* New York: Kluwer Academic Publishers, 2002.

Brealey, Richard A. "The Capital Structure Puzzle." *Journal of Finance*, July 1984.

Brealey, Richard A., and Stewart C. Myers. *Principles of Corporate Finance.* 7th ed. New York: McGraw-Hill, 2002, chaps. 17 and 18.

Brigham, Eugene F., and Michael C. Ehrhardt. *Financial Management.* 10th ed. Cincinnati, OH: South-Western College Publishing, 2001, chaps. 12 and 13.

DeAngelo, H., and Ronald Masulis. "Optimal Capital Structure Under Corporate and Personal Taxation." *Journal of Financial Economics*, March 1980, pp. 5–29.

Graham, John. "Estimating The Tax Benefits Of Debt." *Journal of Applied Corporate Finance,* Spring 2000.

Jensen, Michael. "Agency Costs of Free Cash Flow, Corporate Finance and Takeovers." *American Economic Review* 26, May 1986, p. 323.

Miller, Merton H. "Leverage." *Journal of Applied Corporate Finance,* Summer 1991, pp. 6–12.

Miller, Merton H. "The Modigliani-Miller Propositions after Thirty Years." *Journal of Applied Corporate Finance,* Spring 1989, pp. 6–18.

Myers, Stewart. "Still Searching for the Optimal Capital Structure." *Journal of Applied Corporate Finance,* Spring 1993, pp. 4–14.

Patrick, Steven C. "Three Pieces to the Capital Structure Puzzle: The Cases of Alco Standard, Comdisco, and Revco." *Journal of Applied Corporate Finance,* Winter 1995, pp. 53–61.

Ross, Stephen A., Jeffrey F. Jaffe, and Randolph W. Westerfield. *Corporate Finance.* 6th ed. New York: McGraw-Hill, 2001, chaps. 15–16.

Shapiro, Alan C. "Guidelines for Long-Term Corporate Financing Strategy." *Midland Corporate Finance Journal,* Winter 1986, pp. 6–19.

Warner, J. B. "Bankruptcy Costs: Some Evidence." *Journal of Finance* 26, September 1984, pp. 1067–1089.

For more on international capital structure issues, see:

Jacque, Laurent, and Gabriel Hawawini. "Myths and Realities of the Global Capital Markets." *Journal of Applied Corporate Finance,* Fall 1995, pp. 81–94.

Shapiro, Alan C. *Multinational Financial Management.* Upper Saddle River, NJ: Prentice Hall, 1996, chap. 17.

For information about financial distress and bankruptcy, see:

Brigham, Eugene F., and Michael C. Ehrhardt. *Financial Management.* 10th ed. Cincinnati, OH: South-Western College Publishing, 2001, chap. 25.

Ross, Stephen A., Jeffrey F. Jaffe, and Randolph W. Westerfield. *Corporate Finance.* 6th ed. New York: McGraw-Hill, 2001, chap. 31.

For information on duration and debt markets and valuation, see:

Fabozzi, Frank J., *Bond Markets: Analysis and Strategies.* Pearson Education. 1999.

Fabozzi, Frank J., *Duration, Convexity, and Other Bond Risk Measures.* New York: McGraw-Hill Professional. 1999.

Zipf, Robert. *How the Bond Market Works.* Upper Saddle River, NJ: Prentice Hall Professional, 2002. http://invest-faq.com/articles/bonds-duration.html.

Study Questions

1. Meg Malvern is thinking about changes to her portfolio. She has done very well over the past few years with her low-risk, bonds only,

investment strategy. One bond concerns her. She has $100,000 invested in a very high-quality, zero-coupon bond. The bond is a 10-year bond. Its value at maturity is $232,428. Currently it has five years until maturity and is trading for $152,500 in the capital markets. Should she sell the bond? What would be her return if she sold it now? If she keeps it? Under what circumstances should she sell it (keep it)?

2. MAH Assoc. is considering a stock repurchase to support its stock price. The uncertainty in the economic, political, and global situation has driven the stock price down. However, the news from the company is all good—it is having the best year it has ever had. In order to have the capital markets recognize its performance, management has been advised by their investment banker to repurchase stock. Since the interest rates on debt are at 40-year lows, and MAH Assoc. currently has no debt, the CEO is considering the recommendation. As the CFO of the company, you have been asked to estimate the increase in stock price that would come solely from issuing debt to replace equity.

   MAH's earnings after depreciation, but before taxes and interest, will be $250 million this year. Since it has no debt it pays no interest. Its depreciation will be $75 million, and it expects to replace $75 million in equipment this year. It has estimated that its current required return on equity is 9.2 percent, and it has 110 million shares outstanding. It will replace 22 percent of its equity with debt. Debt will cost 8 percent. Taxes are 34 percent and MAH management expects the company to grow at a 3 percent rate into the future. The beta without leverage is 1.075. The U.S. Treasury bond is yielding 4.9 percent, and typically common stock trades about 4 percent above U.S. Treasury bonds in this sort of market environment.

   a. What is the company's value with its all-equity capital structure?
   b. What are the shareholders' earnings and cash flow per share?
   c. What is the required return for the company?
   d. What is your estimate of the stock's value per share?
   e. Repeat a–d assuming that the company repurchases 22 percent of its equity by issuing debt with an interest rate of 8 percent.

3. Melissa Hackett had worried about her cash flow figures for the analysis of the investment for Bigg Corp. What she had not thought about was the tax rate—she had used the statutory rate of 40 percent for all her calculations. When she presented her analysis to Mr. Bigg he had said, "I just got back from the Young Presidents' Organization meeting in Acapulco. Before we went paragliding one day, a speaker talked about tax rates and how they might change. I had never thought about it. With this new administration, tax rates for corporations could decline. However, many of my crowd thought the rising deficit would make rates rise." With that he asked Ms. Hackett to come back to him in the morning and brief him on:

- The impact of tax rate increases and decreases on Bigg Company's cost of capital.
- Whether a tax decrease (increase) would be better for Bigg's WACC, and its value?
- A plan for how to incorporate uncertain tax rates into the WACC.

Chapter Eight

Practical Aspects of Financing a Company

Up to Chapter 7 we avoided the capital structure issues by analyzing and making decisions in a company financed only by its owners. As the basis for decision making we said that management's objective was to create value for the shareholders. This objective remains the same as management considers how to finance its company. This objective translates into a straightforward task for management making decisions about financing—choose a capital structure that minimizes the company's cost of capital thus maximizing the value of the company.

As you read Chapter 7 you found that the capital structure analysis rests on complex theory.[1] Theory sheds light on the decisions that face management. However, it does not describe a straightforward decision-making process for management to follow in making its decision.[2] On the way to choosing the cost-minimizing, value-maximizing capital structure, two decisions face management. First, management must choose an appropriate long-term capital structure, and, second, it must choose the appropriate financing vehicles to support that structure over time. The first task is a policy decision; the second task depends upon the conditions in the capital markets and with the company at the time financing is sought. Both the long-term capital structure and the financing vehicles, if chosen wisely, will create and may maximize the value of the company.

In spite of the lack of a theoretical roadmap, some practical steps are useful in guiding management in choosing the appropriate capital structure and financing vehicles for its company. In this chapter we lay out such an approach, called RICHS. In general, RICHS is used to decide whether to issue debt or equity when the company is seeking new capital. It takes

---

[1] In this chapter we are faced with the same dilemma we had in the dividend appendix to Chapter 6—theory only helps us understand the complexity of the decision. Just as with dividends, boards of directors and management need practical steps to guide their decision.

[2] For example, the decision-making process described in Chapter 4 for making investment decisions using net present value was unambiguous and logical.

into account the impact of financing on the company and its stakeholders—shareholders, lenders, and management. Before we move to the RICHS framework, however, we need some basic information about equity and debt from the point of view of the company considering using it as part of its financing.

I. Basics for Companies Financing with Equity

All companies have owners. Most companies begin as small businesses financed primarily by their owners. As a company grows it needs more capital. It becomes important to increase its equity capital—first from friends and employees, and then from outside investors. For rapidly growing and innovative companies, private investors, individuals, investment pools, and venture capitalists are early outside investors. When a company establishes itself, and has a record of positive growth and performance, it may decide to seek public investment from the capital markets. We call this first access to the equity capital markets **going public**.

Public markets provide access to equity capital for a company, but at a cost.[3] The cost is that the company must:

1. Report its performance on a quarterly and annual basis to its owners and to the Securities and Exchange Commission. This information becomes part of the public record and is readily available to any interested party, including competitors.
2. Contend with pressure and scrutiny regarding its performance from regulators and investors.
3. Disclose information about its markets, products, performance, management, and officers.
4. Contend with low trading volume and potential under- or overvaluation if it is a small company.
5. Face potential takeovers by outside investors or other companies.

Stock is issued with a **par value**, a value stated on the stock certificate of ownership. This usually is a small amount. For example, you can see in Exhibit 8-1 the par value of Kellogg, the company we evaluated in Chapter 6, is $0.25. The par value of the **outstanding**, available, stock is reported as *Common stock* on the balance sheet. This item also lists the number of shares the board of directors has created, or **authorized**, and the number that have been **issued**, or sold, to shareholders.[4]

The par value is not the price for which the stock was sold when it was issued. The price for which it was sold is the value per share given the market and economic conditions on the day the stock was first sold. The difference between the par value and the value for which the stock was sold to the public is reported on the balance sheet as *Capital in excess of par value*. *Retained earnings*, the other equity account, is the sum of all

---

[3] Having stock that trades publicly places a value on the company that is otherwise uncertain.
[4] The number of shares can only be increased by the board of directors with shareholder agreement.

Exhibit 8-1   Kellogg Company and Subsidiaries

Consolidated Balance Sheets: 2001 and 2000

(millions, except share data)

At December 31,	2001	2000
Current assets		
Cash and cash equivalents	$ 231.8	$ 204.4
Accounts receivable, net	762.3	685.3
Inventories	574.5	443.8
Other current assets	333.4	283.6
Total current assets	$ 1,902.0	$1,617.1
Property, net	2,952.8	2,526.9
Other assets	5,513.8	742.0
Total assets	$10,368.6	$4,886.0
Current liabilities		
Current maturities of long-term debt	$ 82.3	$ 901.1
Notes payable	513.3	485.2
Accounts payable	577.5	388.2
Other current liabilities	1,034.5	707.8
Total current liabilities	$ 2,207.6	$2,482.3
Long-term debt	5,619.0	709.2
Other liabilities	1,670.5	797.0
Shareholders' equity		
Common stock, $.25 par value, 1,000,000,000 share authorized; Issued: 415,451,198 shares in 2001 and 415,451,198 in 2000	103.8	103.8
Capital in excess of par value	91.5	102.0
Retained earnings	1,564.7	1,501.0
Treasury stock at cost: 8,840,028 shares in 2001 and 9,812,543 shares in 2000	(337.1)	(374.0)
Accumulated other comprehensive income	(551.4)	(435.3)
Total shareholders' equity	$ 871.5	$ 897.5
Total liabilities and shareholders' equity	$10,368.6	$4,886.0

Source: Kellogg 2001 Annual Report.

the past earnings that were not paid out in dividends to the shareholders. Kellogg also reports the stock that it holds, but that is not held by investors, as *Treasury stock at cost.*

When a company issues stock, it will use an expert to help manage the process. That expert, an **investment banker**, will advise the company's management on the regulations governing stock issuance; help prepare the appropriate legal and selling documents; help price the stock; organize a selling group, a selling **syndicate**; and may underwrite the issue.[5] **Underwriting** means that the investment banker, or a group of underwriters called the **underwriting syndicate**, buys the entire stock issue from the company. If the stock cannot be sold at the stated price, the stock price must be discounted by the underwriter and the underwriter suffers the loss, not the issuing company.[6] Before the stock is issued, the company provides potential investors with information about the company—its history, its management and directors, and the intended use of the proceeds from the stock sale—in a document called the **prospectus**. In spite of the fact that the prospectus has been distributed and potential investors alerted that the stock is for sale, the price is not set until the night before the stock actually is issued. This is to eliminate as much as possible the potential impact of market and company changes on the share price.[7]

Most small and/or young companies list their stock in the over-the-counter market. Larger, more mature companies may decide to list on an organized exchange such as the New York Stock Exchange. Organized exchanges have requirements regarding minimum number of shares, stock price, and rules regarding required disclosure.[8]

A company that already has stock traded in the public markets, but wishes to issue more, has several alternatives. It may make a public offering, issue **rights**—an option to buy—to existing shareholders, or it may make a public offering allowing current shareholders the right to buy shares to maintain their current ownership percentage.[9] It may also make a **private placement**—placing the newly issued stock with one or several investors. These investors normally are institutions such as insurance companies or private equity investment groups. Private placements are used more often with bonds.

Once stock is issued it is traded in the capital markets. The company does not receive any direct benefit from changes in the stock price once the stock has been issued. Indeed, regardless of when a company's stock was issued, the characteristics of all the shares are identical.[10] This is not

---

[5] As you might imagine, the stock price is set the night before the stock is to be sold. This is done to minimize the impact of company, economic, and market changes on the share price.

[6] The alternative to an underwritten issue is a best efforts offering. The company bears the risk since the investment banking syndicate sells the stock for what the market will bear. If the stock does not sell out at the offering price, the price must be reduced and the company bears the loss. This method of issuance is less expensive but more risky for the company. Normally it is used only by well-known, widely traded companies. It would not be done when the company first goes public.

[7] A prospectus that does not include the price is called a **red herring** and has red printing on the margin of the front page. A prospectus that includes the price simply is called the prospectus. Except for the price, the two are identical.

[8] In addition, since the accounting scandals of 2002, the NYSE has instituted other requirements.

[9] These are called pre-emptive rights.

[10] Stock can be issued a number of times. All shares of stock that have the same characteristics are identical once they are traded in the stock market. However, a company may issue several kinds of shares with different voting rights or backed by different parts of the company. These are different stocks and are usually designated as A or B shares.

true for bonds. Bonds are a contractual arrangement between lender and borrower. Each time a group of bonds is issued, called an **issue**, the contract terms are peculiar to the issue and may be different from any other bonds the company or any company has outstanding. While the debt markets dwarf the equity markets, common stock is the backbone of the financing of U.S. corporations.

II. Basics for Companies Financing with Debt

Bonds are financial instruments used to finance a company.[11] In contrast to equity they are a contract between the lender (the investor) and the borrower (the company). In general the contract (also called the **indenture agreement**) will spell out:

1. The type of bond.[12]
2. Its cost.
3. The interest rate and the timing of interest payments.
4. The bond's maturity.
   a. When the bond will be repaid.
   b. Whether and how a bond can be called before maturity.
5. The covenants—certain activities that must or must not be undertaken by the company while the debt is outstanding.

We began our discussion of bonds in Chapter 7; there is a bit more information needed to determine when and whether to issue various kinds of debt.

1. Bond Type

There are three types of bonds: notes, debentures, and bonds. A **debenture** is debt that is not secured by specific property, a **note** is unsecured debt with less than ten years to maturity, and a **bond** is debt secured by property.[13] We use the word *bond* to refer to all kinds of long-term debt even though we should be more precise.

2. Cost

A corporate bond is denominated in units of $1,000.[14] This is also called the **principal**, or **par value**, and is the amount to be returned to the investor upon the bond's maturity. Most bonds are issued at their par

---

[11] We discussed bonds in Chapter 7 to define their cost. Here we are concerned with the details of issuance and ownership.

[12] The quality of the bond is evaluated by an independent bond rating agency such as Moody's or Standard & Poor's.

[13] A mortgage is a property-guaranteed version of a bond.

[14] Peculiarly, we quote this as 100, or 100 percent of par. If the bond sells later for less, say $900, we would quote it as 90.

value.[15] **Original issue discount bonds**, bonds sold for less than their par value, or **zero coupon bonds**, bonds that do not pay interest, are issued below par value. After the original sale of the bonds by the company the bond price may drop because of changes in the prevailing market rate of interest or company conditions. The par value does not change.[16]

3. Interest Rate

The interest rate and its payment dates are listed in the indenture agreement. A debt instrument may have a fixed or adjustable interest rate. Debt with an adjustable, or **floating**, interest rate is called a **floater**. The indenture agreement will specify how and when the rate can change. Most floating rate debt is tied to a base rate such as LIBOR, the London Interbank Offer Rate; the prime rate, the rate banks lend to their best customers; or a U.S. Treasury bill or bond rate. Many floaters have maximum and minimum rates and rate changes. The indenture also will detail the frequency of the rate change.

4. Maturity

The **maturity**, the date the par value of the bond must be repaid to the investor by the borrower, the company, is noted in the indenture agreement. Some bonds have **sinking fund** provisions—a way to retire the bond issue over time rather than all at one time. A traditional sinking fund requires that the company actually buy, or **redeem**, a stated percentage of the bonds each year. The company can **call**, or require to be redeemed, particular bonds, usually by serial number, or the necessary bonds may be purchased by the company in the capital markets.[17] In some cases the company can place the sinking fund monies with a trustee who invests them, usually in U.S. Treasury securities, until the full issue of the bonds is redeemed at maturity. The sinking fund is not available to the company. Sinking fund details are listed in the indenture agreement.

5. Covenants

The indenture agreement may require that the company meet certain conditions. These conditions may limit the company's new debt, its dividend payments, or oblige the company to meet certain financial targets. If the conditions are not met, the debt may be called by the lender. When the covenants are not met the lender can call the debt (force it to be repaid). At that point the lender and borrower either renegotiate the agreement or the company is forced to repay the debt in full. Renegotiation is more typical with lenders who are banks or when the whole issue was sold to one investor.

---

[15] We use the word *issue* to represent a single sale of stock or a sale of bonds under one indenture agreement.

[16] We can use the tools from Chapter 4 to value the bond when the interest rate has risen or fallen in the capital markets.

[17] Each bond has a unique number.

To encourage lenders or reduce interest costs, borrowers can **sweeten the deal** by adding extra benefits. The benefit might be the right to convert the debt into common stock at some time in the future, called **convertible debt**, or it might be the addition of **warrants** to the bond—the bondholder's right to buy stock in the future.[18] Bonds that are convertible or have warrants sell at lower interest rates than do straight debt for the same company.

There are many kinds of debt traded in the capital markets. Some issues trade frequently, others do not trade at all. Some debt is privately placed, arranged between a borrower and lender, and never trades in the open market. A company may have more than one issue of debt **outstanding** (not yet repaid). The characteristics of the issue reflect the capital market preferences and market and company conditions at the time the debt was issued.[19] The footnotes to the company's financial statements describe the various debt issues the company has outstanding. Exhibit 8-2 shows part of the footnote for 2002 for Kellogg's outstanding long-term debt. Details regarding each issue further support the footnote.

Exhibit 8-2   Kellogg Company and Subsidiaries

Financial Footnote Detailing Debt

Long-term debt at year-end consisted primarily of fixed rate issuances of U.S. and Euro Dollar Notes, as follows: (millions)

	2001	2000
(a) 4.875% U.S. Dollar Notes due 2005	$ 200.0	$ 200.0
(b) 6.625% Euro Dollar Notes due 2004	500.0	500.0
(c) 6.125% Euro Dollar Notes due 2001	—	500.0
(d) 5.75% U.S. Dollar Notes due 2001	—	400.0
(e) 5.5% U.S. Dollar Notes due 2003	998.4	—
(e) 6.0% U.S. Dollar Notes due 2006	994.5	—
(e) 6.6% U.S. Dollar Notes due 2011	1,491.8	—
(e) 7.45% U.S. Dollar Debentures due 2031	1,085.3	—
(f) 4.49% U.S. Dollar Notes due 2006	375.0	—
Other	56.3	10.3
	5,701.3	1,610.3
Less current maturities	(82.3)	(901.1)
Balance, December 31	$5,619.0	$ 709.2

Source: Kellogg 2001 10-K filing with the SEC.

---

[18] At conversion the bond is traded for the stated number of shares—no money changes hands. Warrants, however, are the right to buy. The lender keeps the bond and can buy the designated number of shares.

[19] It can also reflect the relative strength of the borrower's and lender's positions.

In addition to the financial statement information about the debt, various outside analytical services provide information about the characteristics of each debt issue for potential investors in the capital markets.

The magnitude of bonds issued and traded in the United States and worldwide dwarfs the stock markets. As shown in Exhibit 8-3, the bond market is dominated by U.S. Treasury and agency debt, as well as debt issued by municipalities. Global markets also trade sovereign, or country, debt. In spite of the magnitude of government-issued debt, debt is a major source of capital for companies.

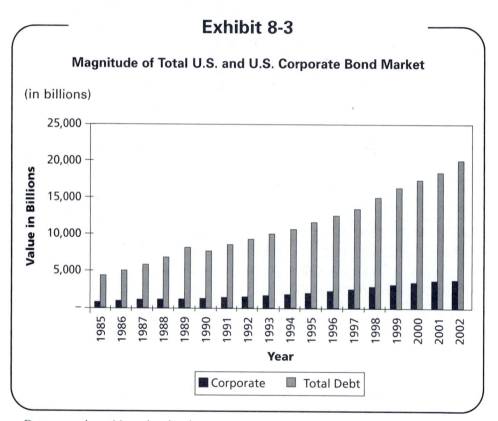

Exhibit 8-3

Magnitude of Total U.S. and U.S. Corporate Bond Market

Data source: http://www.bondmarkets.com.

III. RICHS Analysis

The capital markets are complex and ever-changing. Deciding to add debt to a company's all-equity capital structure adds risk and potential return to its owners' position. How do a company's owners, or the managers on the owners' behalf, decide whether to subcontract some of their financing responsibilities? A convenient framework for analyzing the many different, and sometimes conflicting, forces that affect the capital structure decision is provided by the RICHS process. This acronym is used to represent five major factors that should be considered:

R — Risk
I — Income
C — Control
H — Hedging
S — Speculating

These factors are not listed in order of priority or importance; for each firm, and in different economic environments, the relative importance of the factors will differ. However, the manager should ensure that all factors have been considered before proceeding with establishing or changing the company's financial strategy.

The process of making the decision about a company's capital structure is not a strictly mechanical process in which computational abilities can be substituted for analytical skill and judgment. In every case management must interpret the results of the analysis. For this reason, the RICHS analytical process can best be explained through a specific example—management's decision about whether to finance Greenway Corporation's expansion in production capacity through a public equity offering or a privately placed debt issue.[20]

Greenway is the leading producer and marketer of sand trap graders for golf courses. The company was a market leader in both the manufacture and sale of graders until the rising value of the dollar made it economically attractive for Greenway to sell its production plants and produce the needed parts in a joint venture with a French firm. Up to 2003, parts for the graders were manufactured in Europe and assembled and sold in the United States by Greenway. Recently the value of the dollar has declined relative to the euro and it has become economically attractive to manufacture as well as assemble the grader parts in the United States. Greenway has decided to buy a parts manufacturing plant. A plant that is readily adaptable is available. Exhibit 8-4 shows Greenway's 2004 financial statements with and without the new plant.

As you can see in Exhibit 8-4 after 2004 earnings retained, Greenway will need a total of $6.7 million to fund its new plant, working capital, and the dividends it plans to pay.[21] While management is expecting reduced costs from on-shore manufacturing, those will not be reflected in the financial statements in 2004. Greenway management plans to pay a dividend of $1.50 per share each year—a total of $1.39 million each year if it finances with debt.[22]

---

[20] We have chosen these alternatives to make the example as simple as possible. We will discuss the issues of publicly placed debt where appropriate.

[21] This is smaller than the $6.4 million for the plant and working capital because of differences in depreciation and taxes that result from making the new investment.

[22] Remembering financial statement forecasting, dividend payments do not reduce earnings except those reported to retained earnings. For example, the 2003 year-end equity balance of $28.28 million, plus 2004 earnings of $2.55 million less the $1.39 million in dividends with debt financing, yields a 2004 equity balance of $29.44.

Exhibit 8-4   Greenway Corporation

2004 Financial Statements: No Additional Financing

(dollars in millions)

	Without Plant	**With Plant**
Income Statement		
Sales	$ 36.00	$ 36.00
Manufacturing expenses	(29.70)	(29.70)
Depreciation*	(1.74)	(2.19)
Earnings before interest & taxes	4.56	4.11
Interest	(0.70)	(0.70)
Earnings before taxes	3.86	3.41
Taxes (@34%)	(1.31)	(1.16)
Net earnings	$ 2.55	$ 2.25
Balance Sheet		
Assets		
Total current assets	$ 31.01	$ 32.91
Net property, plant, and equipment	14.26	18.76
Total assets	$ 45.27	$ 51.67
Liabilities and Equity		
Total current liabilities	$ 8.63	$ 8.63
Long-term debt	7.20	7.20
Equity	29.44	29.14
Subtotal	45.27	44.97
Net financing needed*	0	6.70
Total assets and liabilities	$ 45.27	$ 51.67

* New assets are depreciated for 10 years on a straight-line basis for purposes of this example.

Greenway currently has 19.7 percent of its $36.6 million of long-term capital (debt plus equity) in the form of 25-year debt issued in 1998. The coupon, or interest rate, on that debt is 9.74 percent. It has no principal repayments due until 2009. At that point it must be fully amortized over 15 years. Any new debt would be subordinated to the old debt—that is, it would not have as strong a contract for its lenders. Greenway's investment banker believes that it would have to offer a coupon of 12 percent on 20-year bonds to attract buyers. Greenway would pay interest only until 2009, when it would begin paying principal payments sufficient to fully amortize the debt on maturity. There would be no measurable costs in placing the debt.

Greenway's investment banker has estimated that the company could issue, and the investment banker underwrite, up to 300,000 shares of stock. While the final price would, of course, depend upon market conditions the day the stock was issued, it was estimated that the company would realize $26 per share, after all issuance costs. Since markets had been quite stable for some time it appeared that $26 was a good estimate of what Greenway could realize from a sale of shares.[23]

To decide whether to issue equity or debt to obtain the $6.7 million needed, management will want to look at all the important factors to determine which financing method will have the biggest impact on the value of the company. To begin, let's look at the first RICHS factor, risk, if it uses debt financing.

1. Risk

In Chapter 7 we saw that how a company finances itself does not impact its risk. While the risk of the company does not change, how those risks are shared between the lenders and shareholders does change.[24] From the company's point of view, however, some financing arrangements may strain the company's ability to pay—the affordability of the debt.

Affordability—Interest Payments. To ensure that the company can meet its debt obligations, management should determine how much cash is available to **service the debt**—to meet interest and principal payments. The cash that will be available for debt service sets an upper limit on the amount a company should borrow. Companies that take on obligations in excess of their ability to service them readily court disaster.

The first step in assessing how much debt a company can bear is to use the coverage ratios from Chapter 1. We will determine both the interest coverage and, since Greenway intends to maintain its dividend, the fixed charge coverage ratios. We will look at these ratios with and without the new debt financing. Because Greenway does not have to repay principal until 2009, let us look first at the interest coverage ratio without the new plant.

$$\text{Interest coverage ratio} = \frac{\text{Earnings before interest and taxes}}{\text{Interest}}$$

$$= \frac{\$4.56}{\$0.7}$$

$$= 6.51 \text{ times, or 651 percent.}$$

This means that without new debt, EBIT covers Greenway's 2004 interest payments 6.5 times—a generous coverage ratio. With the new plant, and its associated increased depreciation, the coverage ratio drops to 5.87 times. However, as you can see in Exhibit 8-5, if it finances the $6.7 million with debt, the coverage ratio drops to 2.7 times. This is much lower, but still above the minimum of 1.0 times we discussed in Chapter 1.

Since Greenway has committed itself to pay dividends of $1.50 per share, we must take that into account. In Chapter 1 we discussed incor-

---

[23] This is net of fees.
[24] It may, however, reach the point where the probability of bankruptcy increases and investors radically change their required return.

Exhibit 8-5   Greenway Corporation

**Interest and Fixed Charge Coverage Ratios:
With and Without New Financing**

(in thousands except per share)

	Without Plant	With Plant — Debt Financed	With Plant — Equity Financed
Income Statement			
Sales	$36.00	$36.00	$36.00
Manufacturing expenses	(29.70)	(29.70)	(29.70)
Depreciation	(1.74)	(2.19)	(2.19)
Earnings before interest & taxes	4.56	4.11	4.11
Interest	(0.70)	(1.50)	(0.70)
Earnings before taxes	3.86	2.61	3.41
Taxes (@ 34%)	(1.31)	(0.89)	(1.16)
Net earnings	$ 2.55	$ 1.72	$ 2.25
Interest coverage ratio (times)	6.51	2.74	5.87
Fixed charge coverage ratio calculations:			
Number of shares (in thousands)			
Old	0.926376	0.926376	0.926376
New	0	0	0.261538
Total shares outstanding	0.92638	0.92638	1.18791
Dividends per share	$1.50	$1.50	$1.50
Total dividends	$1.3896	$1.3896	$1.7819
Total dividends before taxes	$2.1054	$2.1054	$2.6998
Total fixed charges before taxes	$2.805	$3.605	$3.400
Fixed charge coverage ratio (times)	1.62	1.14	1.21
Earnings per share	$2.75	$1.86	$1.89

porating other fixed charges into the interest coverage ratio. We called that ratio the fixed charge coverage ratio. Financing itself with debt, the ratio for Greenway would be:

$$\text{Fixed charge coverage ratio} = \frac{\text{Earnings before interest and taxes}}{\text{Interest} + \text{Dividends before taxes}^{[25]}}$$

$$= \frac{\$4.11 \text{ million}}{\$1.50 + (\$1.39/0.66)}$$

$$= 1.14 \text{ times, or } 114 \text{ percent.}$$

[25] Dividends are $1.50 per share after taxes. The total after-tax dividends must be converted to a pretax number since it is this that is compared to EBIT.

Incorporating dividends into the coverage ratio shows there is little margin for error. In fact, if the EBIT were to drop by only 12.3 percent, it would cover the fixed charges 1.0 times. If Greenway has stable EBIT, the risk of not covering interest and dividends is low. However, if its earnings are expected to be unstable, the dividends could be jeopardized.

In looking at coverage ratios, both the magnitude and variability of future cash flows are important. Companies with steady, predictable cash flows can bear more debt than companies with more volatile cash flows. Because periods of cash flow shortage can impair the company's ability to service its debt, a manager will want to be sure to forecast financial performance for the company in lean times—times of cash flow shortages.

The most common source of risk, and thus unstable earnings and cash flows, is the impact of business cycles. Cyclical expansions and contractions strain a firm's ability to service product demand, maintain proper inventories, and control its resources adequately. These strains are most vividly seen in their effects on earnings and cash flow. As economic conditions deteriorate, companies are pressed to find adequate cash to meet their obligations.

In addition to the problems caused by business cycles, companies face other types of risks. In some industries strikes occur with almost the same regularity as business cycles. These disruptions cause problems not only for the companies experiencing strikes but also for their suppliers and customers. Other unforeseeable problems such as periodic market gluts and shortages of basic raw materials can affect particular industries or companies. In each of these situations, a company's ability to marshal its cash resources is critical to its ability to service debt. There may be actions management can take to free up cash during difficult periods. For example, during a recession a company might postpone capital investments, or if a cash shortfall is caused by rapid growth, management might decide to tighten credit terms and thus decrease accounts receivable.

Greenway may be able to generate additional cash internally through astute management of inventories, accounts payable, accounts receivable, and capital expenditures. Thus, cash could increase during periods of declining sales and decline during periods of increasing sales. This strategy is, in fact, what most companies have discovered. The critical factor in the management of a company is to identify the economic situation and respond quickly to minimize any adverse impact it may have on the cash position of the company.

The factors that might lead to cash shortages are different for each business. For some companies an unusual demand for its products, with the resulting need for cash to finance growth, might be the time when more cash, and thus greater debt financing, is needed. For other companies an economic recession with a decline in sales might cause cash problems. Whatever is the case for the particular company, the managers should examine the cash flows under the maximum likely cash shortfall in order to determine the business's ability to meet debt payments and remain solvent. Exhibit 8-6 shows what would happen if Greenway's revenues varied by $10 million. These calculations provide only an approximation of the cash available to service obligations during an adverse cycle.

Exhibit 8-6   Greenway Corporation

2004 Interest Coverage Ratios and Earnings per Share: Alternative Financing Schemes

(in thousands except per share)

	LOW EBIT		EXPECTED EBIT		OPTIMISTIC EBIT	
	Debt	**Equity**	**Debt**	**Equity**	**Debt**	**Equity**
Revenue	$26.00	$26.00	$36.00	$36.00	$46.00	$46.00
EBIT	$ 2.36	$ 2.36	$ 4.11	$ 4.11	$ 5.36	$ 5.36
Net income	0.56	1.10	1.72	2.25	2.87	3.41
Old interest	0.70	0.70	0.70	0.70	0.70	0.70
New interest	0.80	0	0.80	0	0.80	0
Total interest	$ 1.50	$ 0.70	$ 1.50	$ 0.70	$ 1.50	$ 0.70
Interest coverage ratio	1.57	3.37	2.74	5.87	3.57	7.66
Dividends	1.39	1.78	1.39	1.78	1.39	1.78
EBIT/contractual payments	0.65	0.69	1.14	1.21	1.49	1.58
Earnings per share	$ 0.60	$ 0.93	$ 1.86	$ 1.89	$ 3.10	$ 2.87

As you can see, the interest coverage ratio is over 1.00 in every scenario. However, if Greenway finances with equity and revenues drop by $10 million, the EBIT of $2.36 million will not cover both dividends and interest. Indeed, it covers interest payments only 1.57 times when the company uses debt to finance the new plant.

Greenway's earnings and revenues have been very stable in the past. Management has been able to secure equipment orders far in advance of delivery and has not been badly hurt in previous recessions. Thus the coverage ratios should hearten lenders, if not shareholders. However, regardless of the financing method chosen, Greenway will be somewhat more risky in 2004 than it has been without the new plant. Common stock financing provides better interest coverage in 2004.

Based on our analysis, management, lenders, and shareholders should conclude that if the forecasted earnings materialize, the company can cover its interest obligations and dividend payments. In later years, because management expects revenue and thus EBIT to grow, coverage ratios will improve. In 2004, EBIT covers interest more than two times. Is this enough of a cushion to comfort lenders? That depends on how volatile Greenway's earnings might be. Lenders to companies with very volatile earnings will want a larger cushion than lenders to companies whose earnings are quite stable.

After evaluating the impact of all the cash-freeing alternatives, management can determine how much cash will be available to pay the company's debt obligations. The amount of debt this cash can service (cover interest and principal payments) should establish a company's debt limit or debt capacity.

Companies may decide to borrow less than their capacity. The actual debt level that management decides to attain is termed the **debt policy**. While **debt capacity** is limited by the ability of the company to service the debt, the debt policy is determined by management's judgment of the markets' reactions. The objective of debt policy is to create company value by minimizing its cost of capital.

Affordability—Principal Repayments. Thus far we have evaluated Greenway's ability to pay interest and dividends in 2004. The company has a comfortable margin regardless of how it finances its needs, *without* considering principal payments. In 2009 Greenway is obliged to begin to repay the principal on both its old debt and any new debt it may choose to acquire. Interest payments will remain the same. Debt principal must be fully repaid by 2024 through 15 equal annual installments.[26] Exhibit 8-7 shows Greenway's debt service ratio for 2009 if it built the new plant and financed it with debt. As you can see, the EBIT is adequate to cover Greenway's fixed obligations in 2009 (interest, dividends, and principal payments).[27] If management and the board were willing to forgo dividends in 2009 the total fixed charge coverage would be over 2 times.

Lenders are concerned not only with interest payments; they want to be certain the principal they have lent can be repaid. Since a lender's business is to make money by lending money, the lender does not want the money returned because that means the loss of interest income or creates the need to find another customer. What a lender wants is to be sure the money can be repaid. When firms are **financially embarrassed**, they cannot pay the interest on their debt; when they are **financially distressed**, they cannot repay the principal. To determine whether they could lose their principal, lenders often use ratios that measure the relative proportion of the company's capital they have provided. The ratio of debt to total capital is a good measure of the exposure of a lender's principal to loss.

Greenway currently has 19.7 percent of its capital in the form of debt. Exhibit 8-8 shows what will happen when Greenway adds $6.7 million in either debt or equity. Greenway's ratio of debt to total capital increases to 32.7 percent if it uses debt. The ratio drops to 16.8 percent if equity is raised. Increased leverage does increase the lender's risk, but does it raise it beyond a level that is acceptable?

To determine the impact of leverage and whether it is acceptable, analysts often examine the practice of others in the same industry. Exhibit 8-9 (page 368) provides information on others in Greenway's industry. Producers of lawn and garden equipment obtain about one-third of their capital from lenders—just about what Greenway will have if it raises $6.7 million in debt. Its interest coverage ratio would be similar to others in that

---

[26] As does the old debt.

[27] Since revenues and earnings are expected to grow by 5 percent from 2005 onward, the debt service ratios will improve each year.

Exhibit 8-7   Greenway Corporation

Income Statements and Coverage Ratios 2004–2009: Debt Financing

(dollars in millions)

	2004	2005	2006	2007	2008	2009
Sales	$ 36.00	$ 38.52	$ 41.22	$ 44.10	$ 47.19	$ 50.49
Manufacturing expenses	(29.70)	(31.78)	(34.01)	(36.38)	(38.93)	(41.65)
Depreciation	(2.19)	(2.29)	(2.39)	(2.49)	(2.59)	(2.69)
Earnings before interest & taxes	4.11	4.45	4.82	5.23	5.67	6.15
Interest	(1.50)	(1.50)	(1.50)	(1.50)	(1.50)	(1.50)
Earnings before taxes	2.61	2.95	3.32	3.73	4.17	4.65
Taxes (@ 34%)	(0.89)	(1.00)	(1.13)	(1.27)	(1.42)	(1.58)
Net earnings	$ 1.72	$ 1.95	$ 2.19	$ 2.46	$ 2.75	$ 3.07
Interest coverage ratio	2.73	2.97	3.21	3.49	3.78	4.10
Total dividends	$ 1.39	$ 1.39	$ 1.39	$ 1.39	$ 1.39	$ 1.39
Dividends before taxes	$ 2.11	$ 2.11	$ 2.11	$ 2.11	$ 2.11	$ 2.11
Fixed charge coverage ratio	1.14	1.23	1.33	1.45	1.57	1.70
Principal payment, old debt						$ 0.81
Principal payment, new debt						0.48
Total principal payments						$ 1.29
Principal before taxes						$ 1.95
Total fixed charges and principal						$ 5.56
Debt service ratio, times						1.10

industry. Based on these comparisons, if Greenway raises debt, it would still be following a conservative financing plan. However, Greenway does not really fall into the lawn and garden equipment industry. A better comparison is with producers of golf course equipment. In this case, Greenway would be following a more aggressive strategy.

Based on these comparisons, management must ask itself, "Why do golf course equipment producers have less debt and higher coverage ratios than lawn and garden equipment makers?" The likely answer is that they are more affected by economic cycles than producers of lawn and garden equipment, and lenders have decided that they require more protection in that industry. Lenders obtain protection by lending less to producers of golf equipment, leaving them a greater margin for error.

Exhibit 8-8 Greenway Corporation

2004 Measures of Leverage

Panel A: Balance Sheets—Debt or Equity Financed

	No Plant	New Plant Financed with	
		Debt	Equity
Balance Sheet			
Assets			
Total current assets	$31.01	$32.91	$32.91
Net property, plant, and equipment	14.26	18.31	18.31
Total assets	$45.27	$51.22	$51.22
Liabilities and Equity			
Total current liabilities	$8.63	$8.63	$8.63
Long-term debt	7.20	13.90	7.20
Equity	29.44	28.59	35.55
Subtotal	45.27	51.12	51.38
Net financing needed*	0.00	(0.10)	(0.16)
Total liabilities and equity	$45.27	$51.22	$51.22

Panel B: Leverage Ratios

	No Financing	Debt Financed	Equity Financed
Debt/Total capital	19.7%	32.7%	16.8%
Debt/Equity	24.5%	48.6%	20.1%
Assets/Equity	153.8%	179.1%	144.1%

* Rounding errors lead to financing needed figure.

While Greenway may well be stronger and more able to handle higher levels of debt than others in its industry, following a different financing plan is likely to cause lenders to scrutinize Greenway, its strategy, and its management very carefully. Because of this, management must be certain that debt financing will be better than equity financing for Mr. Greenway and the rest of the shareholders. How about the shareholders? Which would they prefer? Which alternative will create more value for the owners?

2. Income

One of the obvious impacts of debt financing on shareholder value is its effect on their income—the "I" in RICHS. Since new funds often are invested in productive assets, shareholders should expect new benefits—

Exhibit 8-9

Industry Comparisons

	Debt/Total Capital	Interest Coverage (times)
Lawn and garden equipment producers		
Ride Rite Enterprises	33.1%	3.10
TopFlight Irrigators	34.3%	2.54
General Crop Harvester, Inc.	46.0%	3.05
Greenway Corporation:		
Debt financed	32.7%	2.74
Equity financed	16.8%	5.87
Golf course equipment producers		
Fairway Products, Inc.	11.2%	14.30
Green's Keepers Corporation	18.1%	23.01
Sam Speed, Inc.	15.3%	18.36
Greenway Corporation:		
Debt financed	32.7%	2.74
Equity financed	16.8%	5.87

benefits from investment that accrue to the shareholders.[28] Thus, management must analyze the financing from the shareholders' point of view. Such an analysis is consistent with management's objective: to create value for the shareholders.

In determining the impact the financing decision will have on the income of shareholders, management must consider both the **explicit cost** (the impact on the earnings and cash flow per share) and the **implicit cost** (the impact on the market price of the stock).

Explicit Cost. To determine explicit cost Greenway managers must estimate the effect that each financing alternative would have on the company's EPS. This analysis is similar to the coverage analysis that was undertaken to estimate the impact on lenders of increased financing, but done from the investors' point of view. In Exhibit 8-6 you can see the earnings per share that result from the two different financing plans.[29] Equity financing lowers the EPS in all but one scenario—the optimistic one. The lower EPS results from the increase in the number of shares outstanding when equity is used for financing. These newly issued shares **dilute**, or reduce, each shareholder's ownership position and his or her

---

[28] These returns come to shareholders because the debtholders' claim, although senior, is fixed. Thus the residual benefits belong to the common shareholders.

[29] You may have noted that we are doing our analysis on a per-share basis. This is because different numbers of shares will be outstanding depending on whether management chooses debt or equity financing.

earnings for each share. Each owner now holds a smaller piece of the company and its earnings.

A reduction in earnings per share is a common occurrence as additional common stock dilutes the benefits of stock ownership. Still, the higher the EBIT, the more attractive debt will look to the shareholders, because once the interest is covered the remaining earnings, the residual, go to the shareholders alone. Only in the optimistic scenario is the EPS with debt financing greater than that with equity financing.

Up to this point we have looked at the EPS at one level of EBIT. We know that the EBIT could vary, and vary dramatically. One way to examine the impact of financing on shareholders' EPS is to create an EBIT/EPS chart. By charting the EPS for various levels of EBIT for each of the sources of financing, we can see which is better for shareholders, and under what conditions. To create such a chart we can use the data from Exhibit 8-6. Each line shows the earnings per share for a financing alternative under different EBIT levels. Since the relationships are linear, only two points are necessary to plot each of the lines. The resulting graph is shown in Exhibit 8-10.

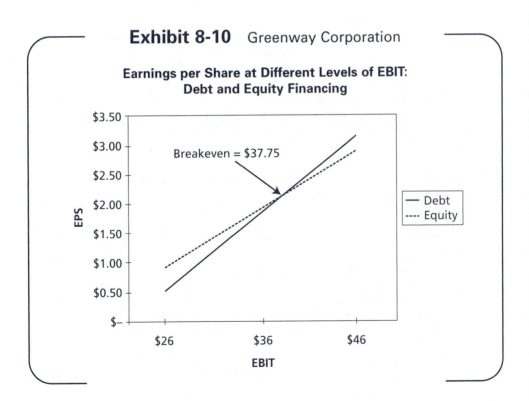

Exhibit 8-10 Greenway Corporation

Earnings per Share at Different Levels of EBIT: Debt and Equity Financing

The **breakeven point**, the point where shareholders would be indifferent between debt and equity financing, can be deduced from the chart or more precisely calculated using the following formula:

$$\frac{(EBIT - I_n - I_o)(1 - t) - P}{CS_d} = \frac{(EBIT - I_n - I_o)(1 - t) - P}{CS_e}$$

Where:

$EBIT$ = Breakeven EBIT level

I_o = Interest payments on old debt

I_n = Interest payments on new debt

t = Tax rate

P = Preferred dividends applicable to the alternative under consideration

CS_d = Number of common shares outstanding with the debt alternative

CS_e = Number of common shares outstanding with the equity alternative

The breakeven formula can be solved for the EBIT level as follows:

$$EBIT = \frac{(CS_d \times I_o) - (CS_e \times I_o) - (CS_e \times I_n)}{CS_d - CS_e} + \frac{P}{(1 - t)}$$

For Greenway's two methods of financing the breakeven EBIT is $37.5 million. Since Greenway management is predicting $36 million in EBIT for 2004, the debt alternative will not dominate equity until the EBIT exceeds $37.5 million, which occurs in 2005. The driver to the breakeven analysis is the fixed cost of debt. Thus there is some risk to choosing debt immediately—Greenway has never surpassed the breakeven EBIT levels above which debt is preferable. However, the company has steadily grown with few surprises, and management is confident that EBIT will surpass $37.5 million from 2005 onwards. Still, there is some danger the EBIT may not reach break even. It is up to management to determine the magnitude of that risk.

The EPS/EBIT chart in Exhibit 8-10 demonstrates the impact of financial leverage on shareholders' EPS, and by inference the company's value. As you can see, the slope of the debt financing line is greater than the slope of the equity financing line. In fact, the bigger the difference in the slopes of the two lines, the faster the rate of change and the greater the impact of leverage on earnings and cash flow.[30] This increased rate of change is the primary advantage of using leverage in financing a company.

Although our focus has been on the benefits to shareholders of leverage at higher levels of EBIT, below the EBIT breakeven point leverage

---

[30] There is one more thing to notice about this analysis before we use it to help Greenway management make its decision—we focused on earnings, not cash flow per share. The same sort of graphic and breakeven analysis can be done with cash flow per share. We should look at the cash flows since they are the basis for valuation, and we will do so later in the chapter. In this case, however, the earnings and cash flow for Greenway are the same—depreciation offsets new investments from 2004 onwards—and the analysis would look and be the same.

works against shareholders. When the EBIT falls below break even the impact of the leverage is reversed and shareholders suffer.[31]

Implicit Cost. We have seen that income to shareholders increases with debt. We also concluded that lenders should not see an increased risk to their position since the coverage ratios are adequate.[32] The question remains, however, will Greenway's shareholders perceive greater risk with either financing scheme?

Leverage certainly affects the shareholders' position—their risk. Greenway will have higher fixed costs, and while its EBIT will not be any more sensitive to changes in economic conditions after financing costs than before, earnings and cash flows will be more sensitive. These changes affect the safety of the shareholders' returns and thus their risk.

In Exhibit 8-10 we saw that the value of the equity rose and fell as leverage increased. Because the shareholders' risk increases with added leverage, so should the shareholders' required return. Using the two models from Chapter 6, the capital asset pricing model (CAPM) and the dividend-discount model, let us look at the effect of leverage on Greenway of the shareholders' required return. Let's begin with the CAPM.

Think for a moment about how changes in leverage would affect the factors used in the capital asset pricing model. No change in a company's financial leverage will impact the risk-free rate of return or the average market premium—they are the basic required rates of return for all investments. Only one factor in the CAPM is company specific—the beta.[33] If Greenway takes on fixed-rate debt, the beta will increase. That is because the after-tax earnings of the company will become more volatile. The increased volatility comes from deducting a fixed charge, interest, from the potentially volatile EBIT.[34] Currently, Greenway's beta is 1.3. Using a theory about how leverage impacts beta as we discussed in Chapter 7, we can estimate a beta at any other capital structure. The theoretical relationship is:

$$\beta \text{ of Leveraged firm} = \beta \text{ of Unleveraged firm} \times \{1 + [\text{Debt/Equity} \times (1 - \text{Tax rate})]\}$$

Exhibit 8-11 shows the results of using this formula. Greenway's required return on equity is shown in the last column. In calculating the required return, we have assumed that the yield on a 10-year U.S. Treasury security is 4.9 percent, the market premium is 6 percent, the tax rate is 34 percent, and that the formula above represents the relationship between capital structure and beta for the company. As you can see, as

---

[31] The same analysis can be used to study the effect of financing alternatives on dividends per share at different EBIT levels when the payout ratio is kept constant.

[32] That risk is the increased probability of bankruptcy.

[33] The nominal risk-free rate of return and market premium are common CAPM factors for all risky assets.

[34] That is if the company uses fixed rate debt. If the debt has a floating rate, the risk impact will depend upon how changes in interest rates and company EBIT are related.

Exhibit 8-11   Greenway Corporation

Beta at Different Capital Structures

Debt/Equity	Beta	CAPM Required ROE
0.0%	1.12	11.6%
21.0%	1.28	12.6%
24.5%	1.30	.12.7%
48.6%	1.48	13.8%
60.0%	1.56	14.3%

financial leverage (debt/equity) increases so does the shareholders' required return.

We also can think of what happens to shareholders' risk in the framework of the dividend-discount model:

$$\text{Shareholders' required return} = \frac{\text{Dividends}}{\text{Market price}} + \text{Growth}$$

Because of the increase in leverage, Greenway will have to pay more interest. This fixed cost can affect the company's ability to pay or increase its dividends in the future. As a result, investors' estimates of dividend certainty could change. Currently, Greenway pays $1.50 per share in dividends. Greenway is mature and has had few uses for its profitability inside the company. The Greenway family has expressed a need for the money. Before the financing the earnings growth rate was expected to be 6.8 percent, and the required return 12.6 percent. After financing, the growth rate will increase to 7.9 percent with debt financing. Given this increase in expected growth, shareholders might expect that management will increase dividends, perhaps at the earnings and cash flow growth rate of 7.9 percent. Using this information, if Greenway finances with debt, the dividend-discount model cost of equity would be:

$$\text{Shareholders' required return} = \frac{\text{Dividends}}{\text{Market price}} + \text{Growth}$$

$$= \frac{\$1.50}{\$25.50} + 0.079$$

$$= 0.059 + 0.079$$

$$= 0.138 \text{ or } 13.8\%$$

This is the same as the cost of equity we calculated using the CAPM.

Value. We know that the required return for shareholders increases with increases in financial leverage. But do the changes impact the value of the company—the value of interest to shareholders? What is the value of the company to its shareholders if the $6.8 million is debt- or equity-financed?

To determine the answer we will use a discounted cash flow analysis. We will do this on a per-share basis since the two different financing methods result in different numbers of shares outstanding. Exhibit 8-12 shows the cash flow per share under the different financing scenarios. First we forecast the 2004–2008 cash flows. Second, we normalize Greenway's 2008 cash flows to calculate the terminal value.[35] The result of the analysis is shown in Exhibit 8-12.

Exhibit 8-12   Greenway Corporation

Equity Value per Share: Two Different Financing Plans[36]

	Equity Financing	Debt Financing
Equity required return	12.6%	13.8%
Cash flow growth rate	6.8%	7.9%
2008 residual cash flow per share	$2.56	$2.72
Value per share	$27.79	$30.54

Debt financing increases shareholders' value almost $3 per share. As for risk, a debt-to-total-capital ratio of 32.7 percent should not be considered too extreme by lenders. In addition, the price/earnings ratio, often a measure of the relative value of a company, should increase under debt financing as shown in Exhibit 8-13.

Exhibit 8-13   Greenway Corporation

Impact of Financing on Price/Earnings Ratio: 2004

	New Plant	
	Equity Financing	Debt Financing
Earnings per share	$1.89	$1.85
Market price per share	$28.79	$30.54
Implied price/earnings ratio	15.2	16.5

---

[35] EBIT in 2004 is expected to be $4.11 million. With no new additions to working capital, and all capital investments offset by depreciation, the net income and cash flow both would be $1.72 million.

[36] In Appendix 8A we discuss the valuation of leveraged cash flows using two methods. Here we present the valuation results only.

3. Control

Up to now our evidence suggests that Greenway should use debt to finance its capital needs. However, there are other issues of concern. For Greenway's shareholders a major issue would be control.

There are two ways in which financing can impact the owners' control of the company. First, new shares dilute the earnings, cash flow, and voting rights of existing shareholders. Second, if the company has not had debt financing, introducing lenders creates a relationship that has not existed. Debt covenants, as we have seen, can exert control, or at the minimum restrain management decision making and increase reporting. Thus, management is not as free to take action, particularly action without lender knowledge.

Equity Financing. In addition to diluting cash flow and earnings per share, issuing equity involves a potential loss of ownership control—the "C" in RICHS: a new issue of new common stock can expand the existing ownership and dilute voting control of the current owners of the company. Whether this dilution is important depends on the distribution of ownership of the company. For companies with a significant proportion of ownership in the hands of an individual or a small group of shareholders, and where the existing owners wish to maintain a dominant voting position without buying the new stock, then an equity issue may not be appropriate. Typically, the dilution issue is critical at three levels of ownership: when the ownership block will be reduced below 100, below 50, and below 25 percent.

The problem of introducing outside owners for the first time (reducing ownership below 100 percent) is usually more of a psychological problem. If the original owners can still maintain an ownership position greater than 50 percent they are in a position to continue to control the affairs of the company—they can elect the board of directors. The primary change will be that outside owners now have an interest in the operations of the company and may create additional accounting, reporting, and legal requirements.

In spite of the desire to own the company, there may be compelling reasons for obtaining outside equity, not the least of which is the need to develop a market for the equity to provide for liquidity in the owners' holdings. This is particularly true for owners who are aging and whose family members are not interested in an active role in the company. Another factor that may force a company to admit outside owners is rapid growth accompanied by capital needs that exceed the company's debt capacity or the owner's ability to provide new equity. For these or other reasons, the owner or ownership block may believe that selling equity to outsiders is necessary.

Once outside owners are involved, the original owners can maintain operating control only so long as they own at least 50 percent of the voting common stock. Thus, the 50 percent hurdle is a very difficult one for many owners to pass. Usually the need for outside equity must be severe before the controlling owners will relinquish their 50 percent position.

For publicly held companies with a widely distributed ownership position, effective control can usually be maintained with an ownership block of 20 to 25 percent. Through solicitation of proxy votes, an insider group with a significant minority position usually can dominate managerial decisions and control the operations of the company.[37] Because dilution of this block through the issuance of additional shares could eliminate effective control, dilution below this level is another critical point in evaluating equity control.[38]

Other than at these critical points, the dilution of control is not usually a significant concern when issuing equity. Obviously, for the company with a widely dispersed ownership and no significant ownership blocks, the control issue is moot.

Debt Financing. Although the control issue is more easily assessed when financing with equity, debt financing may also create some control issues. Lenders frequently impose restrictions on company operations in the form of debt covenants. These covenants may specify certain actions the company may or may not undertake, or may limit other actions. For example, loan covenants may require the company to maintain specific levels of working capital, to limit additional borrowings, or to limit the amount of dividends. The purpose of the covenants is to protect the lender's investment, but their effect may be to restrict the ability of owners or managers to operate the company as they believe necessary.

Jim Greenway and the Greenway family own 30 percent of the stock of Greenway Corporation. Since the rest of the shares are held by a large number of unrelated people, the Greenway family effectively controls the company. However, they certainly will be concerned about what happens to their control if equity is issued.

Greenway has 926,376 shares outstanding. If the company were to finance its needs with equity, 230,769 new shares would be sold. Jim Greenway and his family would then own:

$$\text{New proportion} = \frac{\text{Old proportion} \times \text{Old shares}}{\text{Total old and new shares}}$$

$$= \frac{0.30 \times 926,376}{1,157,145}$$

$$= 0.240 \text{ or } 24.0\%$$

If even one person were to buy all the new shares, he or she would control only 20 percent of the company. Thus the family would not lose effective control if the new equity were issued, although they are close. Even so, the issue of control, when coupled with the fact that debt fi-

---

[37] Proxy votes are the right to vote shares on behalf of the shares' owners.
[38] Companies can use equity dilution as a means of thwarting unwanted takeover bids. Through issuing new stock, the company dilutes the ownership an unfriendly suitor may have gained, thereby making the takeover more difficult. Poison pill covenants, where new stock is automatically issued upon an unfriendly takeover attempt, are often designed to create this situation.

nancing will increase the value of the company, should lead management to choose debt to finance the company and shareholders to prefer it.

4. Hedging/Speculating

Hedging, using special techniques to minimize financing risk, and **speculating**, financing in an attempt to create financial gain, are the final factors in the RICHS analysis. Most of us think of them as actions taken in the commodities or securities markets. While these generalizations are true, they require special action by companies when financing.

Hedging is a mechanism investors use to insulate themselves from a change in price. One way to hedge is in the futures markets. A **futures contract** is a contract to deliver a particular quantity of a commodity (including Treasury bills, bonds, and stock market indices) at a particular time at a given price. A producer or owner of the commodity can lock in the price at which it will be sold, hedging against a change in price, by selling a futures contract that is large enough to cover the commodity that will be delivered in the future. Regardless of what happens to the price between the time the future is sold and the date the commodity is to be delivered, the hedger has a guaranteed price—he or she has "hedged the risk." On the other side is the buyer of the contract, someone who wants to lock in the delivered price of the commodity in the future. A classic example might be a bakery. The company uses flour, eggs, sugar, and natural gas to produce its products. It cannot change the prices of its products easily and quickly to reflect changes in raw materials prices. If the bakery buys contracts from the producers of eggs, sugar, flour, and natural gas to sell their products at a fixed price to the bakery at a future date, the bakery can, with comfort, know what raw material prices will be in the future and how to price the bakery products. If prices on the raw materials decline, the bakery will have lost potential profit, but prices will still cover costs.

The same futures contract can be used to speculate. For example, a speculator, believing a commodity price will decline in the future, can sell a futures contract (without owning the commodity) and, if the price declines, cover the obligation to deliver with another, less expensive, futures contract later. The speculator gains the difference between the price at which the first contract was sold and the price for which the covering contract was bought. When the reverse happens the speculator loses.

Investors who are satisfied with the current price can hedge by locking in the price and eliminating price volatility. Investors willing to bet on the upward or downward direction of prices can speculate. Corporate managers do the same thing every time they make a financing decision. Implicitly or explicitly, they bet on the direction of interest rates and stock market levels, and they either hedge or speculate. In the past, managers have used a simple rule: match the maturity of the need (e.g., new plant to be used for a long time) with that of the financing instrument (e.g., long-term debt or equity). Using this matching principle, financing decisions were made by default. In fact, the "match financing and asset life" rule created a natural hedge.[39] While the rule is reasonable in environments where interest rates and the stock market are relatively stable, management must make a decision whether to speculate or hedge when markets are not stable. Decisions by default can be costly.

For managers planning new financing there are three outlooks for the future. If they are considering equity, the stock market can go up, down, or sideways (change little). For those planning a debt issue, interest rates can rise, fall, or remain roughly the same. When deciding what and when to issue equity or debt, management must make explicit forecasts for the future. Each forecast implies a different strategy and potential outcome.

Issue Debt:

1. *Interest rates are expected to remain the same.* Unless management is expecting the quality of the company to rise or deteriorate, debt is issued by the company without hedging.
2. *Interest rates are expected to rise.* In this case, the company issues debt, perhaps more than enough for its immediate needs.[40]
3. *Interest rates are expected to fall.* When management forecasts a decline in interest rates it has several alternatives:
   a. It can use short-term debt to finance its long-term needs, replacing the short-term with long-term debt when interest rates decline. The risk is that long-term rates don't decline.
   b. It can use floating rate debt, anticipating that the rate will decline when the rate is reset. The risk is that rates rise.
   c. It can use interest rate futures to hedge some of the risk.[41]
4. *Market conditions or company conditions or preferences change after debt is issued.* Once debt has been issued by the company it can find the debt structure less than optimal. For example, a company may have fixed rate debt and, in retrospect, prefer floating rate debt. Such a situation can occur when a company enters a new business with revenues that are highly related to changes in interest rates. Floating rate debt could provide a natural hedge, yet its debt is fixed rate. What can it do?
   a. Retire the debt. It can completely buy back the debt issue financing it with new, floating rate debt. An alternative is to **defease** the debt, which is to remove it from the company's balance sheet without retiring it. To do this the company sets aside sufficient monies in a trust fund to fully pay the interest and principal payments to the bondholders. The debt is no longer reported on the

---

[39] A natural hedge is one where the company hedges risk in its business with a business action. An example is a company with sales in another country hedging income variability by building a plant in the same country. That way the costs of production match local sales in local currency. The other choice is to take foreign exchange risk by producing in one country and selling in the other. A financial solution to the natural hedge uses foreign exchange hedges. These are shorter term in nature than is the natural hedge.

[40] The additional debt issued would constitute a speculation on future rates.

[41] This is a sophisticated analysis including how many futures to buy and how to adjust for the shorter term nature of the futures. See the references at the end of the chapter.

company's financial statements. This is a popular strategy when interest rates fall and bond prices are lower than their book value.

b. Execute a swap. If the rate is attractive, although the fixed interest payments are unattractive, the company could execute a **swap** with another company. In this case the company swaps its fixed rate obligation with another company that has, but does not want, floating rate debt. The debt does not change hands, only the interest payment obligation. Currency obligations also can be changed through the use of swaps.

Issue Equity:

1. *Equity prices are low and expected to rise.* Managers deciding to finance with equity face a dilemma: should they issue stock at the going price, or wait until the market rises and fewer shares need to be issued to raise the same money? Typically, managers are tempted to delay issuing new equity as long as possible because they believe that, in a growing company, earnings will steadily increase, and the stock price will follow. In that case, a stock issue should be delayed to take advantage of the impact of increased profitability on the stock price. However, there are times when financing cannot be delayed.

An alternative when a company wants to issue equity, but its stock price is low, is **convertible debt**.[42] This is debt that can be converted at a specified time into the equity of the company. No money changes hands on conversion; the bondholder surrenders the bond and receives shares, the company changes the debt with equity at no cost. The conversion can be required by the company or can be at the discretion of the convertible bondholder.[43]

Convertible bonds, given they have equity possibilities, are usually issued at a lower interest rate than straight debt. If the equity does not rise to the conversion price, the company has straight debt, but at a lower rate than it otherwise would have had. Unfortunately, convertible bond buyers in the future can take an unconverted issue as a signal of potential danger to new convertible issues.[44]

There is another way to piggyback equity on debt. That is to issue debt with warrants.[45] **Warrants** are the right to buy equity in the future. The bondholder who exercises these warrants pays for the shares at a prearranged price and continues to hold the bonds. Each bond has a specified number of warrants, which are like call options with longer lives.

---

[42] For more on preferred stock, convertible preferred stock, convertible debt, and warrants, see the appendix to this chapter.

[43] Often convertible bonds are callable by the issuer. The owner has a short period either to convert the bond or take the call price in cash. The bond value is the floor value of the security to the investor. These bonds usually are unsecured and subordinated to other debt.

[44] Convertibles typically are issued by companies that have lower bond ratings, are smaller, and are faster growing.

[45] For more on warrants, see the appendix to this chapter.

2. *Equity prices are high and are expected to fall.* This situation is a moral conundrum: should management, expecting prices to fall, issue new shares? Is this destroying value for the shareholders for whom they are obliged to create value?
3. *Equity prices are expected to remain flat.* Here the issue confronting management is the better financing vehicle relative to market prospects and the company's optimal capital structure.

In addition to considering the direction of the market and interest rates, management must consider (1) the use of long-term versus short-term financing, (2) the sequencing of financing methods over time when the company needs money frequently or continuously, and (3) how to deal with multiple-currency financing. With the increased integration of the global capital markets, other questions arise:

1. Should nondomestic currency obligations be matched with debt borrowed in the same currency?
2. Should the manager take advantage of perceived opportunities for reduced-rate financing?
3. Should the manager take advantage of profit-making (arbitrage) opportunities that appear to present themselves to the financing corporation?[46]

Whenever a financing decision is made, these questions must be addressed. Forecasting interest rates and market prices is difficult, and the consequences of incorrect forecasts are especially severe in planning capital structure. If forced to raise capital in unfavorable markets, a company will bear the impact of that decision for several years. We have recently seen how rapidly interest rates can change in and outside the United States. Rate changes in the last 20 years have been especially severe and rapid. For most growing companies, the problem is not whether to issue debt or equity, but when to do so. Growth brings with it a continuous need for funds, and most companies find that they are unable to finance growth solely through internal sources. Recognizing that the use of external capital is inevitable, companies should seek the most opportune time to enter the markets.

The implicit and explicit speculating and hedging activities involved in financing corporations today are increasingly complex.[47] A wise manager will call on experts inside the company and at its investment bank to explore hedging and speculating in:

1. The general level of interest rates.
2. The level of the stock market.

---

[46] Some of these arbitrage issues arose in corporate malfeasance cases such as Enron.
[47] We also know from a number of examples that some managers who believed they were hedging were in fact speculating, or did not understand the limits of their hedging activities. Major U.S. banks and others have been involved in both unexpected activities and in lawsuits that have resulted from these activities. The references listed at the end of the chapter provide further reading into some of these situations.

3. The company's stock price.
4. The quality rating of the company's debt.
5. Multiple capital markets.

These are just a few of the difficult issues that concern present-day managers. These issues are complex, increasing, and continuously changing. Because of these uncertainties, the financing decision lends itself to the sort of multiple-scenario analysis we discussed in Chapter 4. Let's use Greenway's decision to demonstrate the process.

Suppose the treasurer of Greenway decided to issue debt to obtain the $6.8 million the company needs, but she believed that rates would decline in the future. The treasurer would consider three probable scenarios:

1. Interest rates do not decline and the money must be renegotiated later at the same rate.
2. Interest rates decline and the money is borrowed later at the lower rate.
3. Interest rates rise and the money is borrowed later at a higher rate.

Using the framework described earlier, the manager would find that each of the three scenarios would result in a different debt cost and different values for Greenway's shareholders. Greenway's treasurer must balance the value gained if rates decline against the value lost if rates rise. In addition, the probability that each scenario will occur must be considered. This analysis can become complex and sophisticated.

5. Greenway's Financing Decision

Now back to Greenway. On the basis of Risk, Income, Control, Hedging, and Speculating, what should Greenway management choose to finance the company's needs? Since good managers' objective is to create value—they add to their shareholders' RICHS—Greenway management should borrow: value will be created for its shareholders without subjecting them to undue risks.

IV. Leasing

Greenway management considered one other way to finance a part of the company's needs: it could lease new equipment for the fabrication operation in the new plant. It may seem peculiar to be discussing leasing in a chapter on financing, but leasing is a form of financing. There are some who believe that the decision management should make is whether to lease or to buy equipment. That is not the decision facing management. Management must determine whether, once it has decided to get the equipment, it should use equity or debt financing to purchase the equipment or to lease it.

In outfitting the new plant, the equipment would cost Greenway $446,975. Management could borrow this amount at 12 percent. However, the equipment manufacturer's representative has suggested that the company might want to lease it for $76,000 a year for 10 years. To analyze the decision we will use net present value analysis.[48] The discount rate for our analysis will be 7.92 percent (12 percent after taxes). If leasing provides a higher net present value than borrowing and buying the equipment, management should lease it. However, if borrowing yields a superior net present value, debt is the way it should be financed.

Exhibit 8-14 illustrates an analysis of the alternative financing schemes. By purchasing the equipment and borrowing the money, Greenway gets tax shields from deductions for both depreciation and interest. By leasing the equipment, Greenway benefits from the fact that lease payments are tax-deductible expenses. The total after-tax cost of the lease over its life is less than that from borrowing. However, these payments are level, and the costs from borrowing and owning the equipment are not: they start lower and rise. Thus, borrowing and buying the equipment is superior to leasing since the present value of the costs is lower. In fact, the present value of the lease payments is $2,538 higher.

V. Leverage in Valuing Acquisitions

We began this long chapter by discussing whether leverage can create value for shareholders and, if so, where that value comes from. It is clear that unused debt capacity reduces shareholder value. Companies that do not fully use their debt capacity are less risky for their shareholders, but they fail to take advantage of the tax advantages of debt and thus provide the owners lower returns. These companies also are prey for acquirers willing to take more risk and use unused debt capacity.

In Chapter 5 we discussed the valuation of acquisitions and divestitures. What we did not discuss was the value of debt capacity in making an acquisition. Leveraged buyouts are examples of acquisitions in which value is created when the acquirer permanently or temporarily increases the leverage of the target. Since this is an ancillary topic, but one that deserves special attention, Chapter 9 discusses the evaluation of leverage corporate acquisitions and other valuations.

VI. Summary

This chapter introduced you to the markets for debt and methods for determining whether using debt capital can create value for the firm's shareholders. We determined that to create value, a company's owners (or managers on their behalf) must find debt financing that increases the company's after-tax cash flows per share or reduces the company's risk. We identified one potential source of value—the tax deductibility of interest payments. With the tax advantages of debt comes increased risk to the shareholders, however. We asked, therefore, given these opposing

---

[48] There is considerable disagreement about the best way to analyze the lease-borrow decision. See the references at the end of the chapter for further reading.

Exhibit 8-14

Analysis of Borrow and Buy versus Lease Equipment

| | Borrow and Buy | | | | Borrow and Buy | Lease | |
Year	Loan Payment (1)	Interest (2)	Depreciation (3)	Tax Shield (4) [(2) + (3)] × .34	After-Tax Cash Cost (1) − (4)	Payment (5)	Lease After-Tax Cash Cost (5) × 0.66*
1	$79,107	$53,637	89,395	$48,631	$30,476	$76,000	$50,160
2	79,107	50,581	71,516	41,513	37,594	76,000	50,160
3	79,107	47,157	57,213	35,486	43,621	76,000	50,160
4	79,107	43,323	45,770	30,292	48,815	76,000	50,160
5	79,107	39,029	36,616	25,719	53,388	76,000	50,160
6	79,107	34,220	29,293	21,594	57,513	76,000	50,160
7	79,107	28,834	29,293	19,763	59,344	76,000	50,160
8	79,107	22,801	29,293	17,712	61,395	76,000	50,160
9	79,107	16,044	29,293	15,415	63,692	76,000	50,160
10	79,107	8,477	29,293	12,842	66,265	76,000	50,160
Total					$522,103		$501,600
Net present value (@ 7.92%)					$335,258		$337,796

*Double-declining balance depreciation.

forces, how should management determine the best financing mix for their firm?

To investigate the decisions that had to be confronted by managers, we used the RICHS analysis, looking specifically at the risk, income, and control aspects of the financing decision, and whether management, given the financing alternatives, should hedge or speculate. To see how the RICHS analysis works in practice, we examined the decision facing Greenway management. We then used net present value to determine the best choice. However, Greenway's decision was a simple one, and each decision about financing is different. The current and future capital market conditions, coupled with the company's size, condition, and its current and future needs, require analysis, insight, and judgment. The tools discussed in this chapter help the manager confront the decisions.

Selected References

For more on the characteristics of debt and debt markets, see:

Alexander, Gordon, William F. Sharpe, and Jeffery V. Bailey. *Fundamentals of Investments*. Upper Saddle River, NJ: Pearson Education, 2000.

Brealey, Richard A., and Stewart C. Myers. *Principles of Corporate Finance*. 7th ed. New York: McGraw-Hill, 2002, chaps. 23 and 24.

Brigham, Eugene F., and Michael C. Ehrhardt. *Financial Management*. 10th ed. Cincinnati, OH: South-Western College Publishing, 2001, chaps. 15 and 16.

Bodie, Zvi, Alex Kane, and Alan Marcus. *Investments*. 3rd ed. New York: McGraw-Hill, 2001, chaps. 2, 3, and 4.

Fabozzi, Frank J. *Handbook of Fixed Income Securities*. 6th ed. New York: McGraw-Hill, 2001.

Haugen, Robert A. *Modern Investment Theory*. 5th ed. Upper Saddle River, NJ: Pearson Education, 2000, chaps. 2, 12–14.

Madura, Jeff. *International Financial Management*. 7th ed. Cincinnati, OH: South-Western College Publishing, 2002, chap. 18.

Ross, Stephen A., Jeffrey F. Jaffe, and Randolph W. Westerfield. *Corporate Finance*. 6th ed. New York: McGraw-Hill, 2001, chaps. 19 and 20.

For more on equity markets and company financing, see:

Brealey, Richard A., and Stewart C. Myers. *Principles of Corporate Finance*. 7th ed. New York: McGraw-Hill, 2002, chap. 15.

Ibbotson, Roger, J. L. Sindelar, and J. R. Ritter. "The Market's Problems with Pricing of Initial Public Offerings." *Journal of Applied Corporate Finance*, Spring 1994.

Ross, Stephen A., Jeffrey F. Jaffe, and Randolph W. Westerfield. *Corporate Finance*. 6th ed. New York: McGraw-Hill, 2001, chap. 19.

For more on hedging financial risk, see:

Brealey, Richard A., and Stewart C. Myers. *Principles of Corporate Finance*. 7th ed. New York: McGraw-Hill, 2002, chap. 25.

Ross, Stephen A., Jeffrey F. Jaffe, and Randolph W. Westerfield. *Corporate Finance*. 6th ed. New York: McGraw-Hill, 2001, chap. 25.

For more on finance theory and financial practice, see:

Carow, Kenneth A. "A Survey of U.S. Corporate Financing Innovations: 1970–1997." *Journal of Applied Corporate Finance*, Spring 1999.

Myers, Stewart C. "Finance Theory and Finance Strategy." *Midland Corporate Finance Journal*, Spring 1987, pp. 6–13.

Wruck, Karen Hopper. "Financial Policy as a Catalyst for Organizational Change: Sealed Air Corporation's Leveraged Special Dividend." *Journal of Applied Corporate Finance*, Winter 1995, pp. 20–37.

For more on financing corporate growth, see:

Amram, Martha. *Value Sweep: Mapping Corporate Growth Opportunities*. Boston, MA: Harvard Business School Publishing, 2002.

Cornell, Bradford, and Alan C. Shapiro. "Financing Corporate Growth." *Journal of Applied Corporate Finance*, Summer 1988, pp. 6–22.

For information about the effects of different financing instruments on capital costs, see:

Smith, Clifford W. "Raising Capital: Theory and Evidence." *Midland Corporate Finance Journal*, Spring 1986, pp. 6–22.

Stanhouse, Bryan, and Duane Stock. "How Changes In Bond Call Features Affect Coupon Rates." *Journal of Applied Corporate Finance*, Spring 1999.

For more on capital structure and its value, see:

Barclay, Michael, and Clifford W. Smith, Jr. "The Capital Structure Puzzle: Another Look At The Evidence." *Journal of Applied Corporate Finance*, Spring 1999.

Brealey, Richard A., and Stewart C. Myers. *Principles of Corporate Finance*. 7th ed. New York: McGraw-Hill, 2002, chaps. 17 and 18.

Damodaran, Aswath. "Financing Innovations and Capital Structure Choices." *Journal of Applied Corporate Finance*, Spring 1999.

Miller, Merton H. "Leverage." *Journal of Applied Corporate Finance*, Summer 1991, pp. 6–12.

Ross, Stephen A., Jeffrey F. Jaffe, and Randolph W. Westerfield. *Corporate Finance*. 6th ed. New York: McGraw-Hill, 2001, chaps. 15 and 16.

Shapiro, Alan C. "Guidelines for Long-Term Corporate Financing Strategy." *Midland Corporate Finance Journal*, Winter 1986, pp. 6–19.

For more on financing strategy, see:

Barclay, Michael J., Clifford W. Smith, and Ross L. Watts. "The Determinants of Corporate Leverage and Dividend Policies." *Journal of Applied Corporate Finance*, Winter 1995.

Booth, Laurence. "Estimating The Equity Risk Premium And Equity Costs: New Ways Of Looking At Old Data." *Journal of Applied Corporate Finance*, Spring 1999.

Brealey, Richard A., and Stewart C. Myers. *Principles of Corporate Finance.* 7th ed. New York: McGraw-Hill, 2002, chaps. 17 and 18.

Carow, Kenneth, Gayle Erwin, and John McConnell, "A Survey Of U.S. Corporate Financing Innovations: 1970–1997." *Journal of Applied Corporate Finance*, Spring 1999.

Damodaran Aswath. "Financing Innovations and Capital Structure Choices." *Journal of Applied Corporate Finance*, Spring 1999.

Pettit, Justin. "Corporate Capital Costs: A Practitioner's Guide." *Journal of Applied Corporate Finance*, Spring 1999.

Ross, Stephen A., Jeffrey F. Jaffe, and Randolph W. Westerfield. *Corporate Finance.* 6th ed. New York: McGraw-Hill, 2001, chaps. 15 and 16.

For more on leasing, see:

Bayless, Mark E., and J. David Diltz. "An Empirical Study of the Debt Displacement Effects of Leasing." *Financial Management*, Winter 1986, pp. 53–60.

Brealey, Richard A., and Stewart C. Myers. *Principles of Corporate Finance.* 7th ed. New York: McGraw-Hill, 2002, chap. 26.

Brigham, Eugene F., and Michael C. Ehrhardt. *Financial Management.* 10th ed. Cincinnati, OH: South-Western College Publishing, 2001, chap. 25.

Ross, Stephen A., Jeffrey F. Jaffe, and Randolph W. Westerfield. *Corporate Finance.* 6th ed. New York: McGraw-Hill, 2001, chap. 21.

Schall, L. "The Evaluation of Lease Finance Options." *Midland Corporate Finance Journal*, Spring 1985, pp. 48–65.

For more on finance theory and financial practice, see:

Myers, Stewart C. "Finance Theory and Finance Strategy." *Midland Corporate Finance Journal*, Spring 1987, pp. 6–13.

Wruck, Karen Hopper. "Financial Policy as a Catalyst for Organizational Change: Sealed Air Corporation's Leveraged Special Dividend." *Journal of Applied Corporate Finance*, Winter 1995, pp. 20–37.

For data on the web, see:

Bond markets: http://www.bondmarkets.com and http://www.bloomberg.com, among others.

Equity markets: http://www.moneycentral.msn.com, http://www.bigstocks.com, http://www.bloomberg.com, and http://www.hoovers.com, among others.

For links to many other sites, see http://www.wallstreetview.com.

Study Questions

1. Management at Zumar, Inc., a chain of gourmet food stores located primarily in New York, was planning to expand its main store in Manhattan. By expanding, Zumar management could add an imported

beer and wine section. Management believed this $15 million addition would increase sales by 20 percent, to $120 million, in the next year, 2004. The new EBIT sales would be the same as Zumar had on its current product lines, 13 percent, and once the new beer and wine lines were established, management expected overall growth to go back to its traditional 2 percent. Taxes were expected to be 34 percent. Zumar currently had $40 million in 7 percent coupon long-term debt. While principal payments on this debt were $2.8 million per year, management expected to keep debt at this level and thus borrowed whenever principal payments were due. In addition to the debt, Zumar had 2 million shares of stock outstanding, with a par value of $2. The current balance sheet for the company follows.

Zumar, Inc.
2003 Balance Sheet
(in millions)

Assets

Cash	$ 54
Long-term assets	80
Total assets	$134

Liabilities and Equity

Current liabilities	$ 40
Long-term debt	40
Common stock ($2 par)	4
Retained earnings	50
Total debt and equity	94
Total liabilities and equity	$134

To finance the $15 million needed for expansion, management had two alternatives:

a. Borrow $15 million of ten-year, 10 percent coupon debt with annual principal payments beginning after five years.
b. Issue equity of 750,000 common shares, netting $20 per share after issue costs.

Prepare an EPS-EBIT table and chart using the existing and proposed levels of EBIT. What is the breakeven EBIT? How do you interpret these data?

2. Zumar management currently had a policy of increasing dividends about 5 percent per year. In 2003 the dividend per share was $0.75. Analyze and compare the present dividend coverage with that likely under both debt and equity financing schemes at the projected level of sales.

3. Which of the two financing schemes is expected to create more value for Zumar's shareholders, assuming:

   a. There will be no changes in net working capital, and corporate expenditures will be equal to depreciation? (These aspects are typical of a low-growth company.)
   b. The required return on equity is 16.9 percent if the expansion is financed with debt, and 15.4 percent if the expansion is financed by equity?

4. In December 2002, Babson Air's management team met in the Center for Executive Education at Babson College. The goal for the meeting was to discuss whether Babson Air should purchase five short-haul aircraft for $25 million to continue the expansion of their mail delivery service. Conservative management estimates were that the annual EBIT from the five aircraft would be $4 million per year once they were put in service. The aircraft had a life of 20 years and were expected to be used and useful for all 20 years. They would be placed into service almost as soon as they were received. The aircraft were available and would be delivered once the order was placed and the planes were paid for.

   While there was general enthusiasm for the purchase of the aircraft, the real question facing management was how to finance the purchase. At present the company had $20 million in cash and marketable securities, but only $10 million could be used to purchase the aircraft. The remaining $10 million was needed for normal business operations and for a reserve against emergencies. The current financial statements and market information are shown below.

Babson Air Financial Statements
(in millions)

Balance Sheet

Assets

Cash & marketable securities	$ 20
Other current assets	20
Net fixed assets	250
Total assets	$290

Liabilities and Equity

Notes payable	$ 50
Other current liabilities	20
Long-term debt (10% rate due in 2020)	100
Shareholders' equity (10 million shares outstanding)	120
Total liabilities and equity	$290

Income Statement

Gross profit	$ 58
Depreciation	(20)
EBIT	38
Interest	(10)
EBT	28
Taxes (35%)	(10)
Net profit	$ 18
Dividends	$ 6.5

Capital Market Information—December 2002

Beta

Aircraft manufacturers	1.88
Air freight companies	1.65
Babson Air	1.50

U.S. Treasury rates

Bills (less than 1 year to maturity)	4.1%
Notes (5 years to maturity)	5.8%
Bonds (20 years to maturity)	6.1%
Expected premium on average asset	6.4%

Since only $10 million of the cash and marketable securities could be used to purchase the aircraft, the company would have to finance the additional $15 million. The choices were to sell $15 million in common stock at $10 per share or borrow the $15 million at 5 percent per year for 20 years. Management was divided on what to do:

- The CFO argued for issuing common stock: even though the company was in the most stable segment of the industry, the company was subject to profit swings. "Only two years ago our revenues dropped so low that we had an interest coverage ratio of 1.0. That meant that we had to really dig to pay the dividend, and we dare not cut that. Borrowing will increase risk." At present the market value of the debt is $180 since rates have fallen to 5 percent from the 10 percent rate when the $100 million of debt was issued. The debt/total capital ratio, in market value terms, is 60 percent.
- The COO countered with a question about how investors would react. He asked, "Won't investors jump to the conclusion that the stock is fully or overvalued if we issue stock in this environment?" He continued, "Even if we explain why we are issuing the stock and the benefits we will get from the new planes, I'm afraid the stock price will decline, and it has already declined by nearly a fifth in the last year." He suggested that issuing stock might need to be accompanied by an increase in the dividend payment

to get people to purchase the stock without a significant decline in price.

- The CEO didn't agree. She said, "I understand your arguments, but don't agree. Why should we sell more equity when our stock price has fallen recently? Even if we sell equity I think it would be stupid to pay out a higher dividend at the same time we issue stock: that is like taking the shareholders' money just to return it to them. And what about dilution? Given the book value of the shares, we would be selling stock at a discount to book value.

  As for debt, I don't believe it increases risk. We aren't about to go bankrupt, so borrowing doesn't increase risk at all. Besides, the debt ratio should be calculated on the book value of the debt since the market value is a moving target."

Still, the decision had to be made if the company was to increase its fleet. You have been asked to help management determine the best alternative for financing the new aircraft. To do this you must answer the following questions:

a. Should Babson Air use debt or equity to finance the new aircraft if revenues and operating costs are expected to remain the same (the EBIT will not change)? What evidence and/or analysis did you use to come to this conclusion?

b. Should Babson Air use debt or equity to finance the new aircraft if revenues and costs drop to the level of two years ago? What evidence and/or analysis did you use to come to this conclusion? Please show your calculations, and you're your results graphically.

c. What is the company's cost of capital before financing?

d. What would be the costs of capital under each alternative assuming that the required return on equity does not change?

e. What would be the debt/total capital ratios if Babson financed with debt? With equity?

f. Draft a brief memo to the CEO, COO, and CFO stating your recommendation and the reasons for it. Please address in the memo whose arguments regarding debt or equity are right or wrong and why.

5. Tyson's Autos was a simple business. It sold cars for cash. It bought the cars it sold at the beginning of each quarter and paid the importer for the cars at the end of the quarter. The revenues from the sales of the cars paid for the cars it imported for sale and for running the business. Needless to say, Mad Mike Tyson, the owner, made a good living from the business.

   In the fourth quarter of 2000, 250 cars were sold. The selling price averaged $20,000 per car, and the average cost was $18,000. Early 2001 was a different economic environment: car sales slumped, and the U.S. dollar fell, thus increasing the cost of the imported cars Tyson's sold. Mad Mike reacted aggressively by increasing his well-known, but zany, advertising; keeping the price to the customer unchanged; and offering six months of free credit. Mad Mike, along with his loyal employees, managed to reduce costs. By eliminating capital expenditures cash needs were further reduced. Although sales fell during the quarter, the company still was profitable. Mad Mike was proud that the company had weathered another economic story.

Mid-2001 saw a rebirth in consumer confidence borne of lower interest rates and massive home refinancing. Consumers had cash to invest and it was a new car they sought. As new customers came into Mad Mikes they continued to expect the six months of free credit. By the fourth quarter of 2001, sales had recovered. By the end of the first quarter of 2002, sales had increased to a new high for Tyson's: 275 cars. Mad Mike was delighted: sales were at an all-time high, profits were up from the dismal third quarter of 2001, and his equity had grown from $1 million to over $2 million. The accompanying exhibit shows these results.

Mad Mike Tyson's Autos Financial Statements

	2000	2001				2002
	Quarter 4	1	2	3	4	1
Number sold	250	200	200	225	250	275
Price/unit	$20	$20	$20	$20	$20	$20
Cost/unit	18	18	18	18	18	18

Income Statements ($ in thousands)

	2000 Quarter 4	2001 1	2001 2	2001 3	2001 4	2002 1
Revenues	$ 5,000	$ 4,000	$ 4,000	$ 4,500	$ 5,000	$ 5,500
Cost of goods sold	(4,500)	(3,600)	(3,600)	(4,050)	(4,500)	(4,950)
Other costs	(200)	(150)	(150)	(150)	(150)	(150)
Depreciation	(80)	(80)	(80)	(80)	(80)	(80)
EBIT	220	170	170	220	270	320
Net interest	(4)	—	(76)	(153)	(161)	(178)
EBT	216	170	94	67	109	142
Taxes (35%)	(76)	(60)	(33)	(23)	(38)	(50)
Profit after taxes	$ 140	$ 110	$ 61	$ 44	$ 71	$ 92

Balance Sheets

	End Q3 2000	End Q1 2002
Cash	$ 10	$ 10
Accounts receivable	—	10,500
Inventory	4,500	5,400
Total current assets	4,510	15,910
Net fixed assets	1,760	1,280
Total assets	$6,270	$17,190
Notes payable, bank	$ 230	$ 9,731
Accounts payable	4,500	5,400
Total current liabilities	4,730	15,131
Shareholders' equity	1,540	2,059
Total liabilities & equity	$6,270	$17,190

Mad Mike knew how to sell cars and spend money, but he left the financial aspects of the business to his nephew, who he had put through college. What disturbed Mad Mike now was the mounting level of debt the company owed the bank. Before Mad Mike could call his nephew to find out why the debt had reached the current levels, he received a call from the bank. The lending officer, an old friend from the Culpepper Country Club, said that the bank would not extend any more credit to Tyson's; moreover, the bank's lending committee was questioning the bank's current level of exposure and were considering reducing the amount it had lent to Tyson's. Mad Mike's old friend asked him to explain why the company needed such a large loan and when it would be repaid so he could calm the lending committee's fears.

As Mad Mike hung up the phone he wondered how a successful year could result in such a call from the bank. He was sure that when the bank's lending committee saw the forecasts for the rest of 2002 (he was certain that sales would rise steadily to 325 cars by the fourth quarter), the lending committee would understand that the profits were abundant and the bank's loans were secure. He placed a call to his nephew.

If you were Mad Mike's nephew, how would you answer the following questions (making sure you support your conclusion with evidence)?

a.   Can Tyson's afford the loans they currently have?
b.   Can the company pay off the loan if the bank calls some or all of it? Show your work.
c.   Is the company in trouble?
d.   Should the bank lower its exposure/call the loan? Why?
e.   What happened to create the situation?
f.   If you were the nephew would you get your resume ready?

6. Sam's Equestrian Centers, once a one-barn operation, had expanded nationwide. Its early capital came from the owner, later supplemented by a few investors, followed by a public offering of its shares. Sam's had a unique organization—its centers attracted both amateur and highly skilled riders who competed at international levels. As such, Sam, now the CEO, and her board were considering raising new capital for international expansion. Their investment banker had told them that preferred stock was a better alternative than debt. Debt would cost 7.7 percent, and the preferred stock would be priced to have a dividend of 4.9 percent. The issue would be $100 million. Issue costs were expected to be about average, 4 percent if it issued preferred shares. Debt issue costs were negligible. Sam's has an ROE of 18 percent and its tax rate is 34 percent.

    a.   What is the cost of the preferred stock to the company after issue costs?

    b.   How does the cost of preferred stock compare to the cost of debt?

    c.   How might the signaling effect play into this decision?

    d.   What should Sam choose to do?

Appendix Eight A

Hybrid Securities

In addition to straight debt and equity, there are an increasing number of financing vehicles that combine features of both. While we mentioned convertibles and warrants in Chapter 8, primarily we discussed how to determine whether to issue equity or debt to finance the company. By their nature, hybrid securities include considerable uncertainty about their value and cost. In this appendix we discuss three hybrid vehicles and their characteristics. You will see that they can be very attractive financing vehicles, particularly when a company has a series of financing needs. The oldest and simplest of these hybrid securities is preferred stock.

I. Preferred Stock

Preferred stock is nonvoting stock with a set dividend and no maturity. The dividend is paid at the discretion of the board of directors. While the dividend can be unpaid for one or more periods, to protect preferred shareholders most preferred stock is **cumulative preferred**. This means that all unpaid preferred stock dividends in arrears must be paid before any common stock dividends can be declared and paid. The investors' required return on preferred stock would be:

$$\text{Required return on preferred stock} = \frac{\text{Preferred dividend}}{\text{Preferred stock price}}$$

If the preferred stock has a dividend of $4.00 and a price of $50, the required return would be:[1]

$$\text{Required return on preferred stock} = \frac{\$4.00}{\$50.00}$$

$$= 0.08 \text{ or } 8 \text{ percent}$$

---

[1] To price a preferred stock, we would need information about the dividend to be paid and an estimate of the return required by investors for investments with this level of risk.

Note that since the preferred stock has no maturity and the dividend does not change, there is no growth term in the formula.[2] In addition, since preferred dividends are not tax deductible to the company, the required return to the investor is identical to the company's cost.

Since preferred stock has a set dividend, it is like bonds. Since the preferred shareholders have no vote, it is like bonds. However, since the payment of preferred dividends is at the discretion of the board of directors, and the dividend is not tax deductible to the company, it is like common equity. This is why preferred stock is considered a hybrid financing vehicle. A company can have several versions of preferred stock that it has issued over time. Each may have different dividend arrangements.

Preferred stock seems to go in and out of favor in the capital markets. One thing that enhances its attractiveness is the possibility of converting it to common stock at some point in the future. With convertible preferred stock the investor receives a preset dividend until the time he or she decides to convert it into common stock. After that time, the investor is a common shareholder.

II. Convertible Securities

Convertible securities give the investor an instrument with both fixed return and common equity potential. Debt or preferred stock may be issued with conversion features. Because of the potential convertibility, the instruments typically have a rate lower than those without a conversion feature.[3]

Every convertible security has a **conversion ratio**, the number of shares the preferred shareholder or bondholder will receive if and when the instrument is converted into common stock. Given the price the investor paid for the preferred stock or bond, we can determine the **conversion price**, the effective price paid for each share of common stock.[4]

At the time the convertible securities are issued, the implicit conversion price is set above the prevailing equity price per share. That premium depends upon the company and the market's appetite for convertible securities, but typically it is under 30 percent. The conversion ratio and price are related in the following way:

$$\text{Conversion ratio} = \frac{\text{Par value of convertible security}}{\text{Conversion price}}$$

---

[2] Actually, there could be a provision for a change in dividends over time.
[3] Interest rate on debt and dividend on preferred stock.
[4] Normally the conversion ratio does not change over the life of the convertible security, although it could, particularly if new stock is issued, diluting the ownership percentages. In addition, the issue usually has call features for the issuer and call protection for the investor.

If the par value of the security is $50 and 5 shares are to be received at conversion, the implicit conversion price would be $10 per equity share.

Convertible securities join two distinct types of investments together. The first portion sets the minimum return and, since it provides a set return, might be characterized as a bond. The other portion, the convertibility, provides the upside potential. Since the investor has the right, but is not required to convert, this upside potential is an option on the company's equity.[5]

1. Bond Portion of the Convertible

The value of the bond sets a floor to the value of the convertible security. Determining the value of debt is rather straightforward—we need the interest rate, par value, price, and maturity of the debt.[6] Such a floor value also exists for convertible preferred stock—the preferred dividend sets the minimum return the security holder will receive, regardless of the potential for conversion.

2. Option on Equity Portion of the Convertible

Since the convertible bond or convertible preferred stockholder can choose to convert his or her security into common equity, each of these securities can be thought of as having an option on the company's stock. The security itself details the conversion ratio and how and when the investor may convert to common stock. It will also spell out the conditions under which the company may call the security, or force conversion. To value a convertible bond we add the value of the bond (or preferred stock) to the value of the options.[7]

Value of convertible bond = Value of bond at current market rates + Value of conversion options [8]

Nel Reyes is considering buying a Spurious Corp. convertible bond. The current yield in the capital markets for bonds of Spurious' quality and maturity is 10 percent. As you can see in Exhibit 8A-1, a bond with a 10 percent coupon would sell for $1,000. The Spurious Corp. convertible has a coupon of 8 percent. With a coupon of $80 per year the Spurious convertible bond sells for $924.18. The difference between the two bonds is $75.82. This is the value of being able to convert the bond into common shares. Because the convertible bond can be converted into 10 shares of stock in the fifth year, each option is worth $7.58.

---

[5] Actually, these instruments frequently contain call provisions—the company can require conversion. However, the investor can always sell the instrument before the call.

[6] To determine the after-tax cost to the company of the bond portion of the convertible, we also would need to know the company's tax rate.

[7] We can value a convertible preferred stock using this same approach.

[8] We discussed options in the appendix to Chapter 4. Return to that appendix for valuing options.

Exhibit 8A-1

Value of Straight Bond and Convertible Bond

Assumptions:

Market Rate = 10%
Bond's par value = $1,000
Maturity in years = 5

Straight Bond at 10 Percent Coupon

	Year				
	1	2	3	4	5
Interest payment	$100	$100	$100	$100	$ 100
Bond repayment					1,000
Cash flow per year	$100	$100	$100	$100	$1,100

Bond value* = $1,000

Convertible Bond at 8 Percent Coupon

	Year				
	1	2	3	4	5
Interest payment	$80	$80	$80	$80	$ 80
Bond repayment					1,000
Cash flow per year	$80	$80	$80	$80	$1,080

Bond value* = $924.18

* Present value of interest payments for 5 years and the principal repayment in the fifth year. The discount rate is 10 percent—the current interest rate on bonds of this quality.

We know the convertible bond is underpriced relative to a normal bond. But is it fairly priced? To determine this we must value the option.[9] To value the option we need to know:

Criteria for Valuing an Option	Spurious Corp. Convertible Bond
The current stock price	$30.00
The exercise price (the conversion value)	$39.00
The time the conversion option is exercisable	5 years
The variance of the stock	30%
The risk-free rate of interest	4.7%

[9] Most analysts use a version of the Black-Scholes option pricing methodology widely used to value financial options. For more on option valuation and references, see the appendix to Chapter 4.

Using the Black-Scholes option pricing model and the data for Spurious Corporation's convertible bond, we calculate that the each option is worth $7.58 per bond for a total for the 10 options of $75.82. Thus the value of the bond is:

$$\text{Value of convertible} = \text{Value of bond at current market rates} + \text{Value of conversion options}$$
$$= \$924.18 + \$75.82$$
$$= \$1,000$$

The convertible bond is fairly priced.[10] However, if the option value were higher (lower) than $7.58, the bond would be underpriced (overpriced).

Convertible securities are attractive to investors so long as the price is fair in the current market conditions. A convertible security provides downside protection and upside potential for investors.[11] For a company, there are advantages and disadvantages to issuing convertible securities.

- *A convertible allows a company to pre-sell stock at a price higher than current market conditions would otherwise allow.*
    - If the company's stock price does not rise as management expects, the convertible can be **hung**—it does not rise to its conversion price. As a result, investors who hold securities that yield below-market returns are disappointed, and this disappointment can taint future convertible financing.
    - The company, on the other hand, had expected the hybrid security to be converted. When it is not, the company unexpectedly is stuck with debt or preferred stock that will not convert.
- *A convertible allows the company to obtain below-market-rate financing.*
    - The lower rate is attractive to the company until conversion. At that point, the low-priced financing disappears, replaced with equity.
    - For investors, the low-priced investment is attractive only if conversion is economically attractive.

Convertible securities have advantages and disadvantages for companies and investors.

III. Warrants

A convertible preferred stock or convertible bond allows investors to convert their security into common equity at some future time. Once the security is converted it no longer exists. The investor does not pay for the stock and the company receives no cash at the time of the conversion, and the company no longer reports the security as convertible preferred or

---

[10] So you might value these options we used an Internet-based Black-Scholes option pricing model. See the references at the end of the appendix.
[11] The downside for the investor is that the conversion price may never be reached, rendering the option of conversion worthless.

debt on its financial statements. Instead, the investment now is reported as part of the common stock account.

Alternatively, a company wanting to add an equity sweetener can issue a bond with warrants. Warrants give the bondholder the right, but not the obligation, to buy stock in a particular company, at a stated price and time. Warrants are very similar to call options on a company's common stock, although most have longer lives.

Call options are sold by individuals in the financial markets and have no direct impact on the company. Warrants are issued by companies, and when the warrant is exercised the company must issue new shares and the investor exercising the warrant must pay the company for the shares. The bonds are not retired.

The exercise price typically is set between 20 and 30 percent of the stock price when the bond was first sold. Most warrants can be detached from the bond and sold separately.[12] Since warrants can trade, and their price will reflect the current stock price plus its potential, investors will not exercise the warrants unless one of the following exists:

- The warrants are near their date of expiration and the stock price is above the exercise price.
- The dividends on the stock exceed the interest paid on the bond.
- The warrant's exercise price increases, or **steps up**, over time. When the exercise price is about to increase, and the stock price is above the exercise price, the investor will exercise the warrant.

For a growing company, warrants are a way to pre-sell equity.[13] When the warrant is exercised, the investor buys the common shares at the warrant's stated price. The investor still owns the underlying instrument, the bond, and buys the stock. The warrants allow the company to issue debt at below-market rates. Investors gain the potential upside of the stock and the limited downside of the bond. Similar to a convertible bond, the value of the bond with warrants is:

Value of bond plus warrants = Value of bond at current market rates + Value of warrants[14]

We would value them in a way similar to that we used with convertible securities.

Conclusion

There are other hybrid instruments that have and could be designed. Most are combinations of bonds, stock, and options. It is up to the com-

---

[12] There are warrants that do expire. They are called evergreen warrants.

[13] There are reporting consequences of having unexercised warrants. Fully diluted EPS show the EPS if warrants were exercised.

[14] While the binomial option pricing method may be used to value warrants, typically the Black-Scholes model is used. Many financial calculators are programmed with this option valuation method.

pany to issue securities that are attractive to investors and useful in financing the company and supporting its target capital structure. Management, as they consider financing vehicles, must be mindful of how they impact the company and its value to the owners.

Selected References

For information on convertible bonds and/or warrants, see:

Brealey, Richard A., and Stewart C. Myers. *Principles of Corporate Finance.* 7th ed. New York: McGraw-Hill, 2002, chap. 22.

Brigham, Eugene F., and Michael C. Ehrhardt. *Financial Management.* 10th ed. Cincinnati, OH: South-Western College Publishing, 2001, chap. 20.

Ganshaw, Trevor, and Derek Dillon. "Convertible Securities: A Toolbox Of Flexible Financial Instruments For Corporate Issuers." *Journal of Corporate Finance*, Spring 2000.

Mayers, David. "Convertible Bonds: Matching Financial and Real Options." *Journal of Applied Corporate Finance*, Spring 2000.

Ross, Stephen A., Jeffrey F. Jaffe, and Randolph W. Westerfield. *Corporate Finance.* 6th ed. New York: McGraw-Hill, 2001, chap. 24.

For information on Black-Scholes option pricing, see:

Black, Fischer, and Myron Scholes. "The Pricing of Options and Corporate Liabilities." *Journal of Political Economy*, May–June 1973.

Brigham, Eugene F., and Michael C. Ehrhardt. *Financial Management.* 10th ed. Cincinnati, OH: South-Western College Publishing, 2001, chap. 24.

Ross, Stephen A., Jeffrey F. Jaffe, and Randolph W. Westerfield. *Corporate Finance.* 6th ed. New York: McGraw-Hill, 2001, chap. 22.

Hull, John. *Options, Futures, and Other Derivatives.* 5th ed. Upper Saddle River, NJ: Prentice Hall, 2002.

Marlow, Jerry. *Option Pricing: Black-Scholes Made Easy.* New York: John Wiley & Sons, Incorporated, 2001.

For websites for pricing and understanding Black-Scholes option pricing, among others, see:

http://www.freeoptionpricing.com/
http://www.finance.wat.ch/cbt/Options
http://www.snowgold.com/financial/calc1.html

Chapter Nine

Valuation in a World of Financial Leverage

Throughout this book our perspective has been that of the company's owners.[1] Even when we were discussing how to finance a company we took the owners' point of view—we treated the introduction of debt into a company's capital structure as owners subcontracting their financing obligation. We discussed investment and financing decisions in different chapters, never explicitly discussing how to incorporate investment and financing decisions into one analytical framework.

Keeping our discussion of investment and financing decisions separate served to clarify the issues; rarely do and never should companies make such decisions independently. How a company finances itself enhances or limits its ability to make investments; the character of its investments provides the base on which capital providers judge their opportunity and safety. Since these decisions are separate only in the abstract, we need a method that merges the analysis of the value of an investment with the impact the financing of the investment has on value. There are three valuation methods that merge financing and investment decisions:

1. *Residual cash flow valuation*, in which the cash flows from the investment and financing decisions are merged. The result is a combined valuation.
2. *Adjusted present value*, in which the financing and investment cash flows are valued separately before the two valuations are merged.
3. *Free cash flow valuation*, which is a shortcut method to merge the investment and financing decisions. This method can be used in limited circumstances.

All of these methods are useful in different circumstances. In this chapter we will discuss each of the methods and when they can and should be used.

---

[1] Or management working on behalf of the owners.

I. Residual Cash Flow Valuation

Repeatedly we have taken the shareholders' perspective when valuing capital investments, acquisitions, and financing schemes. We used residual cash flows, cash flows to the shareholders alone, as the basis for our valuations. We discounted them at the owners' required return on equity to determine their value to the owners. We first discussed this approach in Chapter 4 when we discussed capital budgeting. We valued only the cash flows associated with the investment itself, not its financing. We did not worry about how the investment was financed. To incorporate financing into our analysis, we combine the costs of debt financing with the investment's cash flows. To do this, we:

- Forecast the cash flows from the investment, taking into account the income statement and balance sheet impacts.
- Subtract interest payments as a cash expense on the income statement.
- Add the new debt principal to the cash flows at the time it is received and subtract it when it is repaid. These cash flows, along with any asset investment and noncash (depreciation) charges, are added to or subtracted from the net income to create the forecasted of the cash flows.

To demonstrate this analysis let us lay out a set of investment and financing cash flows. For our example we will value a financially leveraged company, Tai Chin, Inc. The financing and investment cash flows needed to do the valuation are shown in Exhibit 9-1.[2] To create this exhibit, we used the following assumptions:

- Tai Chin's sales and costs, including depreciation, are expected to grow at 6 percent for five years after which they level off—the residual cash flow growth rate will be 3 percent. Sales for the next year, 2004, are expected to be $10,000.
- The company currently has $7.1 million in debt. It's current debt/total capital ratio is 61.5 percent. Tai Chin operates in a stable market where debt levels often exceed 70 percent. Management expects to continue providing 61.5 percent of the company's capital from owners in the form of equity. This means that the capital structure will not change, even though new debt will be added to maintain debt at 61.5 percent of total capital.[3]
- Required return on equity is 20 percent. The marginal cost of debt is 13.9 percent.
- Depreciation and capital expenditures will be $1,200 in 2004 and grow with sales.

---

[2] For our example we will value the entire company. This analysis also can be done for a division or investment project.

[3] As the company is profitable and adds to its retained earnings, new debt will be added to maintain the debt/total capital ratio.

In the residual cash flow valuation all the costs and benefits are included—all providers are paid, and all debt payments, including interest and principal, are made. As a result of this the residual net cash flows belong to the shareholders alone.

Once we have forecasted the residual cash flows we discount them by the required return of equity, in this case 20 percent. To calculate the terminal value, the value of Tai Chin from 2008 onwards, we discount the cash flows from 2009—cash flows based on the long-term growth rate of 3 percent. We add that terminal value to the 2008 cash flow. The result is a residual cash flow value—the present value of the shareholder's equity—of $9.574 million.

This process is straightforward. It includes in the cash flows the inflows and outflows to all suppliers except the shareholders—it is a complete assessment of the shareholders' cash flows from Tai Chin. Using the required return on equity to discount the cash flows yields the value of the company to the shareholders. The company, given our assumptions, is worth $9.574 million.

Residual cash flow analysis is clear, detailed, and disliked by some critics. Their main objection is that this method mixes the investment and financing decisions into one analysis. Indeed, it does and that is the objective. However, the critics would suggest that by mixing the cash flows, we do not know the source of the value—or the investment, the financing, or both.

To calm the concerns of the critics, we can use another technique. This method, adjusted present value, separates the investment from the financing cash flows. This approach is especially useful in highlighting the sources of value in such things as leveraged acquisitions or leveraged buyouts, acquisitions made using unusually high levels of financial leverage.

II. Adjusted Present Value

Leveraged acquisitions, or **leveraged buyouts**, are acquisitions in which the form of the financing has the potential of significantly affecting the value of the company being bought. These highly leveraged acquisitions might be made by a management group buying its publicly held company or by an individual or company with the objective of holding, dismantling, or selling all or part of the company acquired.

In general, those making these acquisitions use substantial amounts of debt to acquire a company. The expectation is that the debt will be repaid from the acquired company's future cash flows or from the proceeds of selling assets owned by the acquired company.[4]

In the 1980s leveraged takeovers became well-known and important transactions. In the earliest part of the highly leveraged takeover binge in

---

[4] In the analysis of Tai Chin, the debt/total capital ratio was within industry norms and management intended for it to remain at that level.

Exhibit 9-1 Tai Chin, Inc.

Residual Cash Flow Forecast and Valuation

(in thousands of dollars)

Assumptions

Sales growth	6.0%	Debt	$7,100	Debt/Total capital 61.5%
Terminal sales growth	3.0%	Required ROE	20.0%	Sales 2003 $9,434
Operating expenses	64.2%	Marginal cost of debt	13.9%	Tax rate 34.0%

Income Statement Changes	2004	2005	2006	2007	2008	Normalized 2009
Sales	$10,000	$10,600	$11,236	$11,910	$12,625	$13,004
Operating expenses	(6,420)	(6,805)	(7,214)	(7,646)	(8,105)	(8,348)
Gross profit	3,580	3,795	4,022	4,264	4,520	4,655
Depreciation	(1,200)	(1,272)	(1,348)	(1,429)	(1,515)	(1,560)
Profit before interest and taxes	2,380	2,523	2,674	2,835	3,005	3,095
Interest	(1,146)	(1,306)	(1,465)	(1,625)	(1,785)	(1,938)
Profit before taxes	1,234	1,217	1,209	1,210	1,220	1,157
Taxes	(420)	(414)	(411)	(411)	(415)	(393)
Profit after taxes	$ 814	$ 803	$ 798	$ 799	$ 805	$ 764
Noncash Charges						
Depreciation	1,200	1,272	1,348	1,429	1,515	1,560
Balance Sheet Changes						
Capital expenditures	(1,200)	(1,272)	(1,348)	(1,429)	(1,515)	(1,560)
Debt principal	1,038	1,022	1,015	1,016	1,024	972
Annual residual cash flows	1,853	1,825	1,813	1,815	1,829	$ 1,736
Terminal value					10,210*	
Residual cash flows			$ 1,813	$ 1,815	$12,039	
Net present value	$ 9,574					

* Terminal value is $10,210 [$1,736 ÷ (0.20 − 0.03)].

the United States in the 1980s, attractive candidates had several or all of the following characteristics:[5]

1. Stable, predictable cash flows.
2. Little, if any, debt.
3. Assets that could be stripped from the company and sold.
4. Good quality management.

These characteristics gave those who took over companies using significant financial leverage a way to reduce that leverage quickly. As many of the prime candidates for highly leveraged transactions disappeared, many companies were acquired that met few or none of these characteristics. Many of these companies were the ones that, in the 1990s, had considerable difficulty repaying the debt that had been used to acquire them.

It is important for the manager to understand highly leveraged transactions for three reasons.

1. These transactions created some of the problems that were evident in the early 1990s in the United States.
2. *Highly leveraged* is a matter of semantics and its meaning varies by country, industry, and over time within a country or industry. The good manager needs to understand the difference between high and excessive leverage and will not underutilize leverage in the future in an overreaction to the difficulties faced by some companies acquired during periods of market excess.[6]
3. The analysis of these transactions is somewhat different from the basic cash flow analysis discussed in the preceding chapters. While residual cash flow analysis can be used, adjusted present value is a particularly useful valuation approach.

Adjusted present value analysis can be used when the analyst wants to be explicit about forecasting and independently valuing the operating and financing cash flows. To demonstrate this method we will return to an example that was used in Chapter 5, the acquisition of Tract Co. by Lifelike Cabinet. We will evaluate the transaction using very high levels of financial leverage to acquire Tract.

You may recall that Lifelike Cabinet Co. management agreed to pay the full value for Tract Co., $3.7 million. Once they agreed, management approached lenders about financing the acquisition. A group of lenders agreed to provide $2.4 million in debt, 65 percent of the price of the acquisition, if the debt would be fully repaid by 2009. The question that must be answered is, will the value of the acquisition change if significant amounts of debt are used in its acquisition?

---

[5] These characteristics describe any investment made using high levels of financial leverage.
[6] Some of the difficulties can be traced to overleveraging companies that were not good candidates for high leverage. Other difficulties can be traced to the fact that the euphoric 1980s had not prepared many managers for the unexpectedly deep and protracted recession that followed.

We will use a two-step process, separating the residual cash flows from the cash flows associated with the financial leverage, for this valuation. This method is called adjusted present value because it adjusts the residual cash flow value of the investment by the positive or negative debt-derived value.

1. Residual Value

Forecast and value the residual cash flows. These cash flows are shown in Exhibit 9-2.[7] To value the cash flows, we use the required return on equity as the discount rate—these cash flows belong to the shareholders alone. The value of Tract *without financing* is $3.7 million, the same value we calculated in Chapter 5.

Exhibit 9-2 Tract Co.

Residual Cash Flows and Value

(in thousands)

	2004	2005	2006	2007	2008
Sales	$10,300.00	$10,300.00	$10,300.00	$10,300.00	$10,300.00
Operating expenses	(9,476.00)	(9,476.00)	(9,476.00)	(9,476.00)	(9,476.00)
Depreciation	(50.00)	(50.00)	(50.00)	(50.00)	(50.00)
Income before taxes	774.00	774.00	774.00	774.00	774.00
Taxes	(263.16)	(263.16)	(263.16)	(263.16)	(263.16)
Income after taxes	510.84	510.84	510.84	510.84	510.84
Depreciation	50.00	50.00	50.00	50.00	50.00
Change in PPE	(50.00)	(50.00)	(50.00)	(50.00)	(50.00)
Annual residual cash flow	510.84	510.84	510.84	510.84	510.84
Terminal value*	—	—	—	—	3,701.74
Residual cash flow	$ 510.84	$ 510.84	$ 510.84	$ 510.84	$ 4,212.58

Net present value @ 13.8 percent = $3,701.74

*No growth from 2008 onwards. For discount rate calculations, see Chapter 5.

---

[7] These are the cash flow forecasts from Exhibit 5-1 in Chapter 5. We repeat them here so you may follow the valuation process. Actually, in Chapter 5 we showed only one year of cash flows and used the perpetuity method of valuation. Here we extend the analysis to five years to match the debt financing's life. You will note that Tract's cash flows are the same for each year, except for those related to the financing.

2. Value of Financing

To value the financing, we first forecast the debt-related cash flows. The interest rate on the debt will be high because the acquisition of Tract will be financed with significant levels of debt. At an interest rate of 11 percent, and five annual equal payments to amortize the debt, the repayment schedule is as shown in Exhibit 9-3.[8]

Exhibit 9-3 Tract Co.

Acquisition Debt Repayment Schedule

(in thousands) Debt Payment Schedule	2004	2005	2006	2007	2008
Debt—beginning of year	$2,400.0	$2,014.6	$1,586.8	$1,112.0	$585.0
Payments	649.4	649.4	649.4	649.4	649.4
Interest	264.0	221.6	174.6	122.4	64.4
Principal	385.4	427.8	474.8	527.0	585.0
Debt—end of year	$2,014.6	$1,586.8	$1,112.0	$ 585.0	$ 0.0

Debt has both cash costs and benefits in the acquisition of Tract. The costs are the interest payments and principal repayments that must be made for five years. The interest payments are an expense that reduces the taxes that Tract would otherwise pay. The tax shield forecasts are shown in Exhibit 9-4.

Exhibit 9-4

Tax Shield from Debt

(in thousands)	2004	2005	2006	2007	2008
Interest	$264.0	$221.6	$74.6	$122.3	$64.4
Tax shield (taxes @ 34%)	$89.8	$75.3	$59.3	$41.6	$21.9
Present value of tax shield (@ 11%) = $225.775					

To value the tax shields we will discount. The discount rate used for the tax shields should reflect their risk. Since lenders require an 11 percent return, the discount rate should be 11 percent.

---

[8] Note that after the five years the company has returned to a normal capital structure.

3. Value of the Acquisition of Tract Co.

Tract's adjusted present value is the combination of Tract's residual value and the value of its financing—the debt-derived tax shields.

Adjusted present value = Present value of residual cash flows + Present value of financing

Adjusted present value of Tract = $3.701 million + $0.226 million
= $3.927

The residual value of Tract is $3.701 million without financing. The financing cash flows add $225,775 to the value of the acquisition. This added value comes from the debt tax shields alone. It should be clear that the value that comes from the financing should not be ignored. The total value of the financed acquisition is almost $4 million.

We have valued the cash flows associated with the tax shields from financial leverage. There are many other financing benefits that can be analyzed using adjusted present value—the value of below-market-rate debt, or special financing advantages from government authorities. All of these can increase the value of the acquisition.

Our adjusted present value analysis was straightforward and, perhaps, a bit too simple. For example, in our valuation we used required return on equity of 13.8 percent as we had done in Chapter 5. However, we know that the shareholders are going to worry about the amount of leverage that is used in making this acquisition and this will impact their required returns. In the early years of the acquisition's life, leverage is 65 percent of the financing—shareholders' required return will be higher. As leverage declines, the required return will return to that for an all-equity-financed investment. Using the beta releveraging formula from Chapter 7, the required return in the first year of the Tract valuation would be over 23 percent. It would decline in subsequent years until it reaches 13.8 percent in 2009.[9] Exhibit 9-5 shows the present value using the risk-adjusted required returns on equity. Note, to value the cash flows with varying required ROEs, we discounted each cash flow and summed the values. In large transactions every detail should be carefully calculated and assessed.[10]

Residual cash flow and adjusted present value analysis requires considerable data, much of which is hard to forecast. However, both methods present the most accurate reflection of the potential value of the company to its shareholders. They are detailed, explicit, and can be difficult to produce. Surely there must be a shortcut. There is, and it is one that works

---

[9] This is the required ROE used in Chapter 5.

[10] In this example we used very high leverage. However, it is not excessive if the company can service its debt (pay the interest and principal payments). Using the cash flow forecasts and doing some simple interest coverage ratios, we can determine that Tract is able to cover its interest payments, and appears to have considerable flexibility in case of an economic or business downturn. The cash flows from Tract alone cannot cover the principal payments. This may be an issue for Lifelike management. In essence, the limits on leverage depend on the supply of willing lenders and the buyer's appetite for risk.

Exhibit 9-5 Tract Co.

Net Present Value—Residual Cash Flows at Varying Required ROEs

(dollars in thousands)

	Period (n)				
	1	2	3	4	5
Residual cash flow (from Exh. 9-3)	$511	$511	$511	$511	$4,213
Discount rate (required return on equity)*	23.0%	20.7%	18.4%	16.1%	13.8%
Present value of annual cash flow**	$415	$351	$308	$281	$2,207

Net present value, varying required ROE = $3,563
Net present value @ 13.8 percent = $3,702
Difference from valuation using single required ROE = $(140)

* Calculated using the formula for a levered beta from Chapter 7.
** Each cash flow is discounted to its present value using cash flow $\div (1 + \text{required ROE})^n$.

for companies in Tai Chin's circumstances. It is called the free cash flow valuation, or the WACC valuation.

III. Free Cash Flow Valuation—The Cash Flows

The free cash flow valuation is simple, combines the costs of capital and the cash flows in a straightforward way, and is useful if, and only if:

- The company's capital structure is unchanging.[11]
- Its required returns on debt and equity are expected to stay the same over time.
- The tax rate will not change.

Since the Tract Co. leveraged buyout's capital structure changes as it repays the debt, we cannot use the free cash flow method to value Tract.[12] We can use it to value Tai Chin—the company plans to keep its capital structure constant. To use the free cash flow shortcut we include the cost of the debt into the discount rate, and assume that when debt must be repaid it is replaced with an equal amount of debt at the same cost.

---

[11] This means that the *proportions* of debt and equity as a percentage of total capital are unchanging. Some call the total capital *value*. The meaning is identical.
[12] In fact we could use it to value Tract, but the process is far more laborious than using the adjusted present value of residual cash flow analysis. Thus, in these circumstances, it is not a shortcut.

The debt-free cash flows are called **free cash flows**, or **cash flows to all capital providers**. Exhibit 9-6 shows the free cash flows for Tai Chin. The difference between the free cash flows (Exhibit 9-6) and the residual cash flows (Exhibit 9-1) is in the treatment of debt-related cash flows—the interest and principal. In the residual cash flow analysis the interest expense and principal payments are included in the cash flows. In the free cash flows all the capital costs are incorporated into the discount rate. The discount rate is the **weighted average cost of capital**—the average of the lenders' and shareholders' after-tax required returns.

To value Tai Chin using the free cash flow method we discount the free cash flows, Exhibit 9-6, by Tai Chin's WACC of 13.32 percent.[13] The value of Tai Chin to all its capital providers is $16.68 million. This is $7.106 million higher than the value we calculated using the residual cash flows and the cost of equity. How can Tai Chin be worth $16.68 million and $7.1 million at the same time? Does the change in method actually change the value of Tai Chin?

The method does not change the value of Tai Chin. The free cash flow valuation values the total company to its lenders *and* shareholders. The residual cash flow value belongs to the equity shareholders alone. Thus to determine the shareholders' value when using the free cash flow method, we must deduct the debt. The free cash flow value is $16.68 million. After deducting the value of the debt, $7.1 million, the shareholders' position is worth $9.58 million. Except for rounding errors, this is identical to the residual cash flow valuation.[14]

Because many people believe using the free cash flow valuation frees them from having to determine the explicit debt service schedule associated with any investment, they choose to use it exclusively. However, the free cash flow discount rate, the WACC, includes an *implicit* forecast of the capital structure and capital costs. Thus it is an acceptable shortcut when the company's capital structure, its costs of debt and equity, and its tax rate are not expected to change. Only when these circumstances are in place can we use this method. Otherwise, we believe that the explicit forecasts of the residual cash flow valuation or adjusted present value methods are superior to the error-prone shortcut.

IV. Free Cash Flow Valuation— The Weighted Average Cost of Capital

Since the free cash flow method includes all capital costs into a single discount rate, let us look in greater depth at the calculations and the assumptions behind it.[15] To calculate the weighted average cost of capital

---

[13] We will discuss how the WACC was calculated later in the chapter.

[14] Since both forecasts were based on the same assumptions, the result should be the same. The only difference in these two methods is how the costs of debt are incorporated into the analysis.

[15] We have discussed WACC briefly before, but it is important to look in greater depth as we consider the free cash flow method of valuation.

Exhibit 9-6 Tai Chin, Inc.

Free Cash Flow Forecast and Valuation

(in thousands of dollars)

Assumptions

Sales growth	6.0%	Debt	$7,100	Debt/Total capital	61.5%
Terminal sales growth	3.0%	Required ROE	20.0%	Sales 2003	$9,434
Operating expenses	64.2%	Marginal cost of debt	13.9%	WACC	13.32%

Income Statement Changes	2004	2005	2006	2007	2008	Normalized 2009
Sales	$10,000	$10,600	$11,236	$11,910	$12,625	$13,004
Operating expenses	(6,420)	(6,805)	(7,214)	(7,646)	(8,105)	(8,349)
Gross profit	3,580	3,795	4,022	4,264	4,520	4,655
Depreciation	(1,200)	(1,272)	(1,348)	(1,429)	(1,515)	(1,560)
Profit before interest and taxes	2,380	2,523	2,674	2,835	3,005	3,095
Profit before taxes	2,380	2,523	2,674	2,835	3,005	3,095
Taxes	(809)	(858)	(909)	(964)	(1,022)	(1,052)
Profit after taxes	$ 1,571	$ 1,665	$ 1,765	$ 1,871	$ 1,983	$ 2,043
Noncash Changes						
Depreciation	1,200	1,272	1,348	1,429	1,515	1,560
Balance Sheet Changes						
Capital expenditures	(1,200)	(1,272)	(1,348)	(1,429)	(1,515)	(1,560)
Annual residual cash flows	1,571	1,665	1,765	1,871	1,983	$ 2,043
Terminal value					19,789*	
Residual cash flows	$ 1,571	$ 1,665	$ 1,765	$ 1,871	$21,772	
Net present value to all capital providers	$16,680					
Value of debt	$ 7,100					
Residual value	$ 9,580					

* Terminal value is $19,789 [$2,043 ÷ (0.1332 − 0.03)].

we multiply the after-tax costs of debt and equity by their respective portions in the company's expected capital structure.

$$R_{WACC} = [(R_d \times (1 - \text{Tax rate})) \times D/V] + [R_e \times E/V]$$

Where:

R_{WACC} = Weighted average cost of capital (WACC)
  D = Amount of debt expected in the firm's capital structure
  E = Amount of equity expected in the firm's capital structure
  V = D + E, the value of the firm's capital
  R_d = Marginal required return on debt
  R_e = Marginal required return on equity

Let's demonstrate how we calculated the WACC of 13.32 percent for Tai Chin.

Lenders making new loans to Tai Chin say that they would require a return of 11.4 percent. Tai Chin analysts have determined that the equity holders require a return of 20 percent for their investment in the company.[16] Management's target debt/value ratio is 56 percent debt.[17] Management does not expect the company's current tax rate of 40 percent to change in the future. Using these assumptions, Tai Chin's weighted average cost of capital is 11.67 percent:

$$R_{WACC} = [(0.139 \times (1 - 0.34)) \times 0.615] + [0.20 \times 0.385]$$
$$= 0.1332 \text{ or } 13.32\%$$

To estimate the WACC we used four things—the marginal:

1. Required return on debt,
2. Required return on equity,
3. Tax rate, and
4. Proportions of debt and equity in the capital structure.

Marginal is the critical word in this analysis. We cannot use past costs—we are using the returns currently required by lenders and shareholders. Let us look at each one of these forecasts in turn.

1. Required Return On Debt

As the discount rate in the free cash flow valuation we use the company's WACC. It is the future we are considering and everything—the free cash flows and required rates of return—must be those that are expected to occur in the future. This means that any rates we use, including the required return on debt, must take into account the potential risk of the investment and expected market conditions. Thus we do not use the price the company has paid for debt borrowed in the past, the **embedded cost**, but the **marginal cost** of debt, the cost if the company borrowed today.[18]

---

[16] Using the methods described in Chapter 6.
[17] Debt/value and debt/total capital are synonymous.
[18] Analysts mistakenly take the interest payments from the income statement and divide that number by the total debt principal from the balance sheet. This is the cost of debt borrowed in the past under different conditions. It is not appropriate to use this figure to evaluate future opportunities.

How do we find the marginal cost of debt for a company? If the company is in the process of borrowing, the marginal cost of debt is obvious—it is the rate at which lenders say they will lend. If the company is not borrowing, then we have to estimate what debt would cost if it were borrowing. One estimate of this cost would be the yield-to-maturity on the company's outstanding debt.[19]

When debt is first issued its coupon (the interest rate on its face value) is appropriate for the market conditions: if the rate for new Aaa corporate bonds is 10 percent, an Aaa rated company's debt would cost 10 percent. However, as market conditions change investors change their required return for Aaa debt and the price of the bond will change to reflect this new reality. Thus if Aaa bond rates have risen (fallen), the bond's price will decline (rise) in order to keep the yield competitive. The change in market-wide rates is reflected in the bond's yield on its new price. This new rate is called the **yield-to-maturity**.[20]

Many companies issue debt and debt of different kinds, over time. Some debt may have been placed with banks or insurance companies, and other debt may have been sold in the capital markets. Each debt issue has different features. The differences in such things as maturity, coupon, relative priority, and security will result in different interest rates.[21] The embedded or historic cost of debt is the after-tax weighted average of the costs of all the company's debt reported on the financial statements. The marginal cost of debt is the interest rate at which new debt of various kinds can be obtained or, as a proxy, the cost at which the company's previously issued debt trades in the current market environment.

Most analysts exclude short-term (current) debt from the WACC calculation because it will be repaid within one year. However, analysts have reconsidered the exclusion of short-term debt when a company:

- Uses it as a stop-gap financing source while it waits for long-term rates to drop.
- Uses it as long-term financing.[22]
- Has lenders who prefer it in order to monitor the borrower or to frequently revise rates.

The best rule for an analyst to follow in dealing with short-term debt is to ignore it if it is used to finance temporary needs (such as seasonal inventory buildup) but include it if the short-term funds represent permanent financing for the firm's assets.

---

[19] This is the debt that was issued in the past but has not yet been repaid.

[20] If there is no publicly traded debt the analyst might use the yield-to-maturity on the debt of a comparable company or companies as a proxy. The yield-to-maturity is the rate of return that equates interest and principal payments to the current market price of the debt.

[21] By security we mean the assets backing the debt or the debt's subordination to other debt the company has issued.

[22] In this case the company intends to replace, or **roll over**, the short-term debt whenever it comes due. This is done more often using commercial paper, a kind of private placement. Accountants in these cases can choose to treat the short-term debt as a form of long-term capital.

Many companies do not have traded debt. When that is the case, we can use an analogy process. To do this we determine the bond rating the company might command if it had publicly traded debt and then find companies that have publicly traded debt of the same quality.[23] We then can use the rates on those securities as our proxy.

2. Tax Rate

The tax rate is important in determining the company's after-tax cost of debt.[24] Since this is a forward-looking analysis we are interested only in the marginal tax rate, not the company's historic rate.[25] For a cursory analysis, typically we use the statutory rate, the rate required by law. However, that rate can change and any expected changes should be incorporated into the analysis. For a large investment or acquisition the actual expected tax consequences should be built into the analysis. If you are using free cash flow valuation, the WACC would change whenever the tax rate changes.[26]

3. Required Return on Equity

In Chapter 6 we discussed at length methods for estimating required return on equity, the company's cost of equity. For Tai Chin we used the CAPM to calculate the marginal required return on equity of 20 percent. In situations where the capital structure changes over time we must recalculate the required ROE for each change in financial leverage.[27]

4. The Capital Structure

Finally, we need to estimate the proportions of debt and equity that will be used to finance the company.[28] While doing this appears to be simple it is, like most of the analyst's jobs, not completely straightforward. We have four choices of capital structure to use in the WACC:

1. *Book value capital structure.* This is the proportion of debt and equity to total capital reported on the financial statements. This is the cumulative impact of all of the company's past financings.

---

[23] These rates are available in the financial press and from many Web sites.

[24] You should note that in the residual cash flows, interest is a tax-deductible expense. In the free cash flows the interest expense and its impact on taxes is taken into account in the discount rate.

[25] One of the facts to keep in mind is that the financial statements provided to shareholders are not those submitted to the Internal Revenue Service. Thus using the historic relationship between the earnings before taxes and taxes does not necessarily reflect the underlying relationship, nor is it forward looking.

[26] In fact, the WACC method can be used with changing capital structure, tax rates, or capital costs. However, the tediousness of adjusting the WACC each year for the changes suggests that either the residual cash flow valuation or the adjusted present value would be more appropriate.

[27] You saw this change in required return on equity for changing leverage for Tract Co. in Exhibit 9-5.

[28] In the WACC we assume that any debt repayments would be offset by new debt, keeping the debt/total capital ratio the same.

2. *Market value capital structure.* This capital structure represents the weights of debt and equity at their capital market values. This represents the value of past financings in light of the current market and company conditions.
3. *Target capital structure.* This capital structure represents management's financing policy over the long term.
4. *Investor anticipated capital structure.* This is the percentages of debt and equity investors *believe* will be used to finance the company in the future.[29] The investors determine their required returns, in part, based on the relative position of capital providers in the future.

Book Value Capital Structure. To calculate this capital structure we use the company's most recent financial statements. Exhibit 9-7 shows the book value capital structure of a hypothetical company. The values of debt and equity reflect the values at the time they were initially issued—this capital structure does not reflect current market or company conditions. As easy as it is to calculate, it is not the basis on which lenders and shareholders determine their required returns.

Market Value Capital Structure. Just as rates change in the marketplace, so do the values of the securities. The value of debt, for instance, declines as rates rise and the market value of stock rises as the company and/or the economy prospers.[30] Because this is so, the book value of the debt and equity may not reflect their market values. Exhibit 9-7 compares the book and market value capital structures for a hypothetical company. The data used to calculate the market values of the debt and equity is shown at the bottom of the exhibit.

The market value of the equity is the current market price per share times the number of shares. It is reported by this company as common stock, at par, and retained earnings. For debt the price at current market yields provides the market value for each issue of debt.[31] The total debt is the sum of the market values of the various issues. The combined market value of the debt and equity are the total market value of the company's capital.

Target Capital Structure. This is the capital structure management plans to maintain or achieve over time. Some managements describe their intentions in the company's annual report to shareholders or detail their expectations to market analysts. Unless they do so, the target is not observable.

---

[29] It is this expected structure on which lenders and shareholders determine their required rates of return.

[30] Given no change in market-wide required returns, the risk-free and market rates of return in the CAPM.

[31] Many companies' bonds are publicly traded and their market values are available. However, for those that are not, we can use present value techniques to determine their market values. The market value of the bond is the present interest payments per year over the remaining life plus the present value of the book value of the bond at the end of its life. The discount rate is the current market rate of interest on bonds with these characteristics.

Exhibit 9-7   Hypothetical Company

Book and Market Value Capital Structures

	Book Value		Market Value	
	Dollars	Percentages	Dollars	Percentages
Current liabilities	$100		$100	
Long-term debt:				
Mortgage debt @ 9.8%,				
due 2009	100	18.18%	100	11.71%
Debentures @ 14%				
due in 2025	100	18.18%	128	14.99%
Subordinated debtures				
@ 17% due in 2020	100	18.18%	136	15.93%
Common stock (par of $1.00,				
30,000 shares outstanding)	30	5.46%	30	3.51%
Retained earnings	220	40.00%	460	53.86%
Total equity	250	45.46%	490	57.37%
Total long-term debt				
and equity	550	100.00%	854	100.00%
Total liabilities and equity	$650		$954	

Information for Market Values

Current rates on:	
Mortgage debt	9.80%
Debentures	10.70%
Subordinated debentures	12.00%
Market price per share	$16.33

Management's target capital structure reflects its estimate of the company's optimal capital structure—the capital structure that results in the company's lowest cost of capital and allows it to fund all value-creating investments. However, most managements keep the company's leverage within a certain range for a variety of other reasons.[32]

Investor Anticipated Capital Structure. This is the capital structure on which lenders and shareholders price their positions. While this anticipated capital structure is the appropriate one to use in the WACC, it is impossible to observe. Thus most analysts revert to an observable capital structure—the book value, market value, or target. The capital structure most often used as a proxy for that anticipated by the investors is the market value.

---

[32] For example, to reduce the lender's influence on the company or to match industry practice.

The analyst must try to estimate what investors expect from owning a share of the company, what lenders will require, and how the company is expected to raise its capital. While we have discussed approaches that will help the analyst make these estimates, each must be used thoughtfully. Furthermore, as conditions in the world and domestic economies change, the capital markets react, and investors' expectations change—sometimes quite rapidly. While these changes occur, the company itself may change—new projects may be announced, and old projects succeed or fail. Once again, investors' and lenders expectations will change, and so will their required returns. The analyst must not only estimate these elusive figures, but must do so at the same time that figures are changing. Skill and judgment take the financial analyst's job beyond the mechanical and the routine, making it a continual challenge.

We have been very clear that the free cash flow method of valuation assumes that the debt proportion of capital must stay the same and that the tax rate and the costs of debt and equity are constant. If any of these three are expected to change, we have said the residual cash flow or adjusted present value methods are preferable. That is not quite true. One can adapt the WACC for the free cash flow valuation for changes in capital structure as well as expected debt and equity costs and tax changes. To do this the changes must be forecast before recalculating each year's WACC. This is a laborious process and is based on the very data used to create the residual cash flow analysis and the adjusted present value. The shortcut has no advantage.

In spite of our reservations, there is a logical and defensible use of the free cash flow valuation—to value small investments that are frequently made by a company. These investments are too small to deserve the time and effort needed to make explicit forecasts of financing arrangements. While using the free cash flow valuation eases the pain of valuing the myriad of small investments companies make, the result of using this shortcut is to discount some investments at a rate that is too low and others at a rate that is too high.[33] In an effort to deal with the problem, and still use the free cash flow valuation, managers have adapted discount rates for risk, grouping investments into so-called risk classes. We showed such a risk class scheme in Chapter 4. In spite of its ease, one would do better to avoid such arbitrary WACCs except when valuing the many small investments a company considers.

V. Summary

When making investments or valuing a company, the analyst should use an explicit and detailed method of analysis. The residual cash flow valuation is such a method. It details the investment and financing cash inflows and values them for the shareholders. For the analyst who prefers to

---

[33] The WACC we use is the weighted average costs of capital for the company, not for the particular investment.

separate the financing and investment valuations, the adjusted present value method is appropriate. Either method is explicit and detailed.

The free cash flow method is neither as detailed nor as flexible. It is, however, a useful shortcut when the company's capital structure, financing costs, and tax rate are unchanging into the future. It is an especially useful approach when valuing the frequent and small investments made by a company.

Regardless of the method chosen by the analyst, it requires considerable skill in forecasting the future.

Selected References

For more on estimating and using the weighted average cost of capital, see references in Chapter 7 and:

Brealey, Richard A., and Stewart C. Myers. *Principles of Corporate Finance.* 7th ed. New York: McGraw-Hill, 2002, chaps. 18 and 19.

Ehrhardt, Michael C. *The Search for Value: Measuring the Company's Cost of Capital.* Boston, MA: Harvard Business School Press, 1994.

For more on the weighted average cost of capital in an international context, see:

Cooper, Ian, and Evi Kaplanis. "Home Bias in Equity Portfolios and the Cost of Capital For Multinational Firms." *Journal of Applied Corporate Finance*, Fall 1995, pp. 95–102.

Stulz, Rene. "Globalization of Capital Markets and the Cost of Capital: The Case of Nestle." *Journal of Applied Corporate Finance*, Fall 1995, pp. 30–38.

For a good explanation of adjusted present value, see:

Brealey, Richard A., and Stewart C. Myers. *Principles of Corporate Finance.* 7th ed. New York: McGraw-Hill, 2002, chap. 19.

Ross, Stephen A., Jeffrey F. Jaffe, and Randolph W. Westerfield. *Corporate Finance.* 6th ed. New York: McGraw-Hill, 2001, chap. 17.

For the interaction between investment and financing decisions, see:

Brealey, Richard A., and Stewart C. Myers. *Principles of Corporate Finance.* 7th ed. New York: McGraw-Hill, 2002, chap. 19.

Ross, Stephen A., Jeffrey F. Jaffe, and Randolph W. Westerfield. *Corporate Finance.* 6th ed. New York: McGraw-Hill, 2001, chap. 17.

For information on leveraged buyouts, see:

Brealey, Richard A., and Stewart C. Myers. *Principles of Corporate Finance.* 7th ed. New York: McGraw-Hill, 2002, chap. 19.

Brigham, Eugene F., and Michael C. Ehrhardt. *Financial Management.* 10th ed. Cincinnati, OH: South-Western College Publishing, 2001, chap. 24.

Clark, John J., John T. Gerlach, and Gerard Olson. *Restructuring Corporate America*. Fort Worth, TX: Dryden, 1996.

Donaldson, Gordon. "Corporate Restructuring in the 1980s—and Its Import for the 1990s." *Journal of Applied Corporate Finance*, Winter 1994, pp. 55–69.

Ferenbach, C. "Leveraged Buyouts: A New Capital Market Evolution." *Midland Corporate Finance Journal*, Winter 1983, pp. 56–62.

Fridson, Martin S. "What Went Wrong with the Highly Leveraged Deals?" *Journal of Applied Corporate Finance*, Fall 1991, pp. 57–67.

Rock, Milton, and Robert H. Rock. *Corporate Restructuring*. New York: McGraw-Hill, 1990.

Ross, Stephen A., Jeffrey F. Jaffe, and Randolph W. Westerfield. *Corporate Finance*. 6th ed. New York: McGraw-Hill, 2001, chaps. 16 and 33.

Study Questions

1. Rapid Rebound Sports Drink Company, located in eastern Massachusetts, produces sports drinks for the high school and college athlete. Mayana recently took over as CEO of the company. As an internationally known sportswoman she had helped develop and then endorse Rapid Rebound's products. While they were not as well known as sports drinks developed in Florida, Rapid Rebound's formulas were equal to or better than other drinks, and priced competitively.

   Mayana was known for her athletic skill, but she also is a canny and experienced businessperson. Her skills became obvious when she took over Rapid Rebound. She was ready to expand the business substantially. To start she began by looking at Rapid Rebound's financial statements with an eye toward making new investments in production and marketing of its flagship brands. Once she understood the financial statements, she asked her CFO to estimate the required return that Rapid Rebound should use in evaluating its investments. She said, "Return is not one of the criteria in evaluating investments, it is the only criteria. Once we have good cash flow estimates, it all comes to returns."

   Rapid Rebound's bonds had been issued years ago at a coupon of 17.5 percent. They had been rated B at the time they were issued. Mayana told her CFO, Jen Rockwell, that since Rapid Rebound was still a small company, if it issued debt today the rating would be B. At present, two insurance companies held all the bonds, so they did not trade. The current yield on newly issued B-rated bonds is 10.5 percent.

   Rapid Rebound is too small a company to be followed by investment services such as *Value Line*. It pays a $1.17 dividend on each of its 240,000 shares, and its current market price in the over-the-counter market is $14.95. However, Rapid Rebound's investment banker has just published a brief report on the company. It includes a beta of 1.32. Mayana and Jen Rockwell believed that Rapid Rebound could grow at about 5 percent for the next 10 years. At present, U.S. Treasury 10-year bonds are yielding 4.9 percent, and 90-day Treasury bills yield 3.65 percent. Historically, the stock market has yielded about 8 percent above Treasury bills and 6 percent above longer-term bonds. Rapid Rebound's balance sheet is as follows:

Rapid Rebound, Inc. Balance Sheet 2004
(in millions)

Assets		Liabilities and Equity	
Cash	$0.2	Accounts payable	$0.8
Marketable securities	2.3	Taxes payable	0.3
Accounts receivable	1.1	Total current liabilities	1.1
Total current assets	3.6	Long-term debt (due in 2020)	1.3
Net property, plant,		Common stock	0.5
and equipment	1.2	Retained earnings	1.9
		Total equity	2.4
Total assets	$4.8	Total liabilities and equity	$4.8

a. Mayana believes that Rapid Rebound's current capital structure represents the mix the company will continue to use. Its taxes are 34 percent. What is Rapid Rebound's weighted average cost of capital?

b. If Rapid Rebound were to have a target capital structure equal to its market value capital structure and a tax rate of 34 percent, what would be Rapid Rebound's weighted average cost of capital?

c. Mayana and her staff believe that if a new tax bill before the U.S. Congress is passed, tax rates will drop to 22 percent in 2005. How would that affect your answers to a and b?

2. There has been a raging argument among the new financial analysts at Rapid Rebound. Each of them are new to the company and recent graduates of prominent business schools. The crux of the problem derived from the fact that each of their alma maters were proponents of different methods of analyzing new investments.

- Jen Rockwell graduated from a prestigious school in her home state of Virginia. She argues that adjusted present value is the only way to value an investment. In her words, "All other methods are obsolete and wrong."

- Renata Bonner, a recent graduate of a Boston business school, just laughed. "All my professors agreed that APV is just a weird and hard way to do a valuation. WACC and free cash flow have been around forever and are widely used. Why argue with what works?"

- Melissa Hackett laughed at them both. A Chicago native, she had not ventured far for her education. In trying to calm the fierce rhetoric she said, "Let's just use residual cash flow analysis. You can do anything with it, and since the shareholders are our customers, let's value their interests."

Mayana presented them with three investments that top management was considering. The company had sufficient resources to do all the projects if they met her criteria.

A. Investment #1: The company had a series of small investments to make over the next six months. Most were small investments in upgrading the bottling plant. Mayana asked the analysts to determine the value of the current upgrade proposal.

The production line had inferior capping equipment. As a consequence one worker had to stand by the capping machine to fix and restart it when the process broke down, which it did several times a day. The worker had asked to retire, but was the only person in the plant who knew how to manage the cranky capping machine. The machine could be replaced for a total of $525,000, would last 10 years and be depreciated using straight-line depreciation for 10 years. The worker's annual salary is $25,000, and since added products could be produced because the capping process would not break down, $35,000 in added gross income is expected. There is no growth expected in the future.
- What method should be used in valuing the capping equipment investment?
- What is the value of the investment with the current tax rate? With the 22 percent tax rate?
- Should Rapid Rebound buy the capping machine?

B. The second investment being considered by Rapid Rebound is the purchase of Very Berry Drink Co. of Cape Cod in Massachusetts. The company had struggled when consumers turned away from their main ingredient during a pesticide scare. The company had state-of-the-art production facilities located in Chelmsford, MA. The bottling plant could serve an area of growing demand for Rapid Rebound's products.

Martin Cranford was willing to sell Very Berry Drink Co. for $1.2 million, with full payment coming at the end of the first year. Mayana and her staff projected that EBIT from the acquisition would be $145,000 in the first year, growing by 5 percent for eight years. Thereafter management expected the growth rate to be 2 percent.

Rapid Rebound knew that analysts had estimated the beta for Very Berry at 1.0, lower than the 1.2 for Rapid Rebound. The current long-term U.S. Treasury rate was 6 percent as was the risk premium. The tax rate is 34 percent.
- What method should be used to value the acquisition of Very Berry Drink Co.?
- What is its value?

C. A lender was willing to lend 90 percent of the purchase price at 14 percent so long as the debt was paid off in eight years.
   - How should you include this in your valuation?
   - How does the financing impact the value of Very Berry?

3. Select Company is in the process of developing a discount rate to evaluate capital projects that have been proposed for the following year. The company, with net income of $504,000 in 2003, has been growing steadily, with both sales and earnings increasing at about 5.7 percent per year. The firm's return on equity has also been fairly constant at about 7.5 percent per year. Without any change in the company's strategy, these trends are expected to continue into the future. At the end of 2003, the Select Company bonds had a Baa rating. Debt on the balance sheet had been issued at an average rate of 10 percent. Long-term Baa-rated bonds are currently being sold at 9.96 percent. Select's stock is selling for $6.90, 300,000 shares are outstanding, and the company consistently pays out 24 percent of earnings in dividends. Because of its growth and steady performance, Select's beta is estimated at 0.85.

Select Company's actual 2003 and projected 2004 equities and liabilities follow.

	2003	2004
Current liabilities	$1,227.7	$1,421.5
Long-term debt	2,261.5	2,487.7
Common stock par value	1,500.0	1,500.0
Retained earnings	2,700.0	3,120.0
Long-term debt and equity	6,461.5	7,107.7

Based on the data, compute the company's marginal weighted average cost of capital, using:
   a. The dividend discount model, where $g = (1 - \text{Payout})(\text{ROE})$.
   b. The capital asset pricing model (six-month Treasury bills are selling for approximately 5.57 percent; U.S. Treasury 7-year bonds are selling for 6.54 percent; the expected market return over 7-year Treasury bonds is 12.5 percent).

Appendix

Solutions to Study Questions

CHAPTER 1

1. To calculate the ratios, use the formulas in the chapter and the data provided in the problem.

   Step 1. To determine the sustainable growth rate, both the return on equity and the earnings retained must be computed. The return on equity for 2000 is net income divided by total equity ($26.5/$178.8 = 0.148, or 14.8 percent).

   Step 2. To determine the earnings retained, subtract the dividends from net income. The percentage is calculated by dividing the result by net income. Make sure that the amounts are all totals for the company or per-share amounts.

   The following table provides the results of these calculations for 1998–2002. As you can see, the company's sustainable growth rate has declined over the 5-year period.

EASY CHAIR CO.
Financial Data

(in millions, except per share)

	2002	2001	2000	1999	1998
Sales	$592.3	$553.2	$486.8	$420.0	$341.7
Net income	28.3	27.5	26.5	24.7	23.0
Dividends per share	$0.50	$0.50	$0.40	$0.40	$0.40
Number of shares	17.9	17.9	18.3	18.4	18.3
Total assets	$361.9	$349.0	$336.6	$269.9	$233.0
Total equity	$214.6	$194.3	$178.8	$165.3	$147.0

Financial Ratios

	2002	2001	2000	1999	1998
Return on sales	4.8%	5.9%	5.4%	5.0%	5.0%
Sales/assets (times)	1.64	1.59	1.45	1.56	1.47
Return on assets	7.8%	7.9%	7.9%	9.2%	9.9%
Assets/equity (times)	1.69	1.80	1.88	1.63	1.59
Return on equity	13.2%	14.2%	14.8%	14.9%	15.6%
Earnings per share	$1.58	$1.34	$1.45	$1.54	$1.54
Dividend payout ratio	31.6%	32.5%	27.6%	29.8%	31.8%
Retention rate	68.4%	67.5%	72.4%	70.2%	68.2%
Sustainable growth rate	9.0%	9.5%	10.7%	10.5%	10.7%
Net income growth	7.07%	13.64%	15.90%	22.91%	

Step 3. To compare EASY to the industry, the simplest approach is to subtract the company's ratios from those of the industry. The result is shown in the table that follows.

EASY CHAIR CO.
Difference Between Home Furnishings Industry and EASY

	2002	2001	2000	1999
Return on equity	−1.9%	−1.3%	−0.5%	−0.8%
Retention ratio	−2.6%	−3.5%	1.4%	−1.8%
Sustainable growth rate	−1.7%	−1.5%	−0.2%	−0.8%

EASY's return on equity and sustainable growth rate have been below the industry average. In 2002, the difference widened. These figures should concern management.

2. Because there have been changes in the EASY Chair Co. ratios over the past five years, the next thing the analyst should examine is the income statement. To do this, first do a percentage of sales analysis by dividing each income statement item by sales and then calculate the change in each item from year to year. The results of these two analyses are shown in the following tables.

EASY CHAIR CO.
Income Statement—Percentage of Sales

(in millions)

	2002	2001	2000	1999
Net sales	100.0%	100.0%	100.0%	100.0%
Cost of sales	–72.6%	–72.0%	–72.3%	–69.0%
Gross profit	27.4%	28.0%	27.7%	31.0%
Selling, general, and administrative expenses	–18.9%	–19.3%	–18.7%	–20.5%
Income from operations	8.5%	8.7%	9.0%	10.5%
Interest expense	–1.2%	–1.4%	–0.8%	–0.5%
Other income	0.5%	0.5%	0.6%	0.5%
Income before taxes	7.8%	7.8%	8.8%	10.5%
Taxes	–3.0%	–2.7%	–3.3%	–4.5%
Net income	4.8%	5.1%	5.5%	6.0%

EASY CHAIR CO.
Income Statement—Percentage Changes

(in millions)

	2002	2001	2000
Net sales	7.1%	13.6%	16.0%
Cost of sales	8.0%	13.1%	21.4%
Gross profit	4.5%	14.8%	3.8%
Selling, general, and administrative expenses	4.7%	17.6%	5.8%
Income from operations	4.2%	9.1%	0.0%
Interest expense	–12.5%	100.0%	100.0%
Other income	0.0%	0.0%	50.0%
Income before taxes	7.0%	0.0%	–2.3%
Taxes	20.0%	–6.3%	–15.8%
Net income	0.0%	3.7%	8.0%

As you can see from these analyses, EASY's revenues have slowed their growth and, in two of the three years, the cost of goods has grown faster than the sales. This leaves gross profit margin varying considerably. In addition, EASY management does not seem to have firm control of the selling, general, and administrative costs when sales increases are large. These changes should focus management of EASY Chair Co. on cost control and achieving stability in the relationships, particularly in the face of erratic sales growth.

3. To forecast financial statements for EASY Chair Co. based on Ms. Hampton's target ratios, the following process is used.
   - To calculate dividends of $0.78 per share, multiply the market price of $15.00 by the dividend yield of 5.2 percent.
   - Since the dividend payout ratio is 45 percent, divide it into the dividend to calculate the net income of $1.73 per share, or a total net income of $31,200.
   - With net income of 5.1 percent of sales, return on assets (net income/ assets) of 9.4 percent, and a return on equity of 13.7 percent, the equity, sales, and assets amounts can be determined by dividing the net income by the relevant ratio.
   - Once the sales are determined, accounts receivable and accounts payable can be calculated. To do so, divide the sales of $611,765 by 360 and multiply by the days in accounts receivable or by the payables payment period.
   - Inventory is calculated by dividing cost of sales by the inventory turnover of 733 percent.
   - Debt is 27.3 percent of equity.
   - Current liabilities are total assets minus debt and equity.
   - Current assets are 573.2 percent of current liabilities.
   - Cash is current assets minus inventory and accounts receivable.
   - Other current liabilities are current liabilities minus accounts payable.
   - Interest is operating profit less taxes.

The statements that result from this analysis follow.

EASY CHAIR CO.
Financial Statements
(in millions)

Income Statement	Revised
Sales	$ 611,765
Cost of sales	(442,918)
Gross profit	168,847
Selling, general, and administrative expense	(115,623)
Operating profit	53,224
Interest	(5,951)
Earnings before taxes	47,273
Taxes	(16,073)
Net income	$ 31,200

Balance Sheet

Cash	$ 15,988
Accounts receivable	155,036
Inventory	60,425
Total current assets	231,449
Net property, plant, and equipment	100,465
Total assets	$ 331,914
Accounts payable	$ 25,240
Other current liabilities	16,765
Total current liabilities	42,005
Long-term debt	62,172
Total liabilities	104,177
Owners' equity	227,737
Total liabilities and owners' equity	$ 331,914
Dividends per share	$0.78

4. To determine Peterson's position relative to the industry, estimate the ratios using the formulas described in the chapter. The result is shown below.

PETERSON'S CHEMICALS
Financial Ratios Relative To Industry

	Industry	Peterson's 2001	2002
Current ratio	150.0%	163.7%	112.9%
Acid-test ratio	90.0%	108.0%	72.8%
Receivables collection period	65 days	111.2 days	106.7 days
Payables payment period	60 days	139.8 days	154.4 days
Debt/equity	110.0%	75.0%	78.8%
Return on assets	7.0%	−9.5%	−14.3%
Return on equity	19.0%	−28.8%	−77.0%

From the analysis of the ratios, Peterson's is apparently not in a favorable position relative to its industry on any dimension except its debt ratios—current, acid-test, and debt/equity.

5. To revise the statements, recalculate the sales, cost of goods sold, accounts payable and receivable, and debt as described in the problem. The only challenge is the debt. To estimate the debt, determine the 2001 equity account (the 2000 equity account balance added to the revised 2001 earnings). From this, deduct the new equity balance, accounts payable, and other liabilities from the total assets for 2001. The difference between the two is the debt.

The revised 2001 statements are as follows.

PETERSON'S CHEMICALS
Revised Financial Statements
(in millions)

Income Statement	Original	Revised
Sales	$ 1,478	$ 1,434
Cost of goods sold	(1,182)	(1,076)
Gross profit	296	358
Selling and administrative expenses	(443)	(443)
Operating profit	(147)	(85)
Interest expense	(27)	(27)
Net income	$ (174)	$ (112)

Balance Sheet	Original	Revised		Original	Revised
Cash and equiv.	$ 120	$ 120	Accounts payable	$ 500	$ 202
Accounts receivable	432	306	Other current	309	309
Inventory	324	324	Total current liabilities	809	511
Other current	37	37	Long term debt	178	288
Total current assets	913	787	Total liabilities	987	799
Plant, property,			Owners' equity	226	288
and equipment	300	300	Total liabilities and		
Total assets	$1,213	$1,087	owners' equity	$1,213	$1,087

The ratios, calculated in the usual way, follow:

PETERSON'S CHEMICALS
Financial Ratios Relative To Industry

Ratios	Industry	2001	2002	Revised
Current ratio	150%	164%	113%	154%
Acid-test ratio	90%	108%	73%	91%
Receivables collection period (days)	65 days	111	107	78
Payables payment period (days)	60 days	140	154	69
Debt/equity	110%	75%	79%	100%
Return on assets	7	-10	-14	-10
Return on equity	19%	-29%	-77%	-39%

If Peterson's management had implemented the changes in 2001, Peterson's ratios would have been significantly improved, but the company still would have lost money.

CHAPTER 2

1. To create pro forma financial statements for Liu Provenders (statements that are adapted for changes in assumptions), a number of steps are needed:

Step 1. To create the changes that Mr. Fong suggests are possible:
a. Multiply the current sales by 1.2 to obtain Mr. Fong's estimate of sales.
b. Multiply sales per day by 45 [($10,320/360) × 45] to calculate accounts receivable.
c. Divide Mr. Fong's estimate of inventory turnover (600 percent) into sales.
d. Multiply the revised sales by 2 percent for the bad debt expense, 0.2 × $1,320.
e. All else remains the same.

Step 2. To create the changes Ms. Fisher suggests:
a. Multiply current sales by 10 percent.
b. Multiply revised sales by 5 percent to calculate bad debt expense.
c. Maintain operating expenses at $3,000.
d. Multiply revised sales by 15 percent to estimate cash.
e. Take 30 days of average sales for accounts receivable.
f. For inventory, use 1/3 of cost of sales.

The current and revised financial statements are as follows:

LIU PROVENDERS
Current and Revised Financial Statements and Ratios
(dollars in millions)

Income Statements	Historic	Fong	Fisher
Sales	$ 8,600.0	$10,320.0	$ 9,460.0
Bad debt	(430.0)	(206.4)	(473.0)
Net sales	8,170.0	10,113.6	8,987.0
Cost of goods sold	(3,500.0)	(4,128.0)	(3,784.0)
Gross profit	4,670.0	5,985.6	5,203.0
Operating expense	(3,000.0)	(3,600.0)	(3,000.0)
Operating income	1,670.0	2,385.6	2,203.0
Taxes	(668.0)	(954.2)	(881.2)
Net income	$ 1,002.0	$ 1,431.4	$ 1,321.8

Balance Sheets	Historic	Fong	Fisher
Assets			
Cash	$ 1,200.0	$ 2,064.0	$ 1,419.0
Accounts receivable	850.0	1,272.3	777.5
Inventory	800.0	688.0	1,261.3
Total current assets	2,850.0	4,024.3	3,457.8
Net property, plant, and equipment	4,000.0	4,000.0	4,000.0
Total assets	$ 6,850.0	$ 8,024.3	$ 7,457.8
Liabilities and Equity			
Accounts payable	$ 1,400.0	$ 1,289.3	$ 1,181.9
Short-term debt	1,500.0	1,500.0	1,500.0
Total current liabilities	2,900.0	2,789.3	2,681.9
Long-term debt	550.0	550.0	550.0
Common stock	420.0	420.0	420.0
Retained earnings	2,980.0	4,411.4	4,301.9
Total equity	3,400.0	4,831.4	4,721.9
Subtotal	6,850.0	8,170.7	7,953.8
New financing needed	0.0	(146.4)	(495.9)
Total liabilities and equity	$ 6,850.0	$ 8,024.6	$ 7,457.9
Net short-term debt	$ 1,500.0	$ 1,353.6	$ 1,004.1
Ratios			
Net working capital	$ (50.0)	$ 1,381.4	$ 1,271.8
Current ratio	98%	152%	158%

Step 3. After reviewing the financial statements you created, you can see that either of the analysts' plans results in greater profits for the company than does the current approach. Under both plans, the current ratio is improved from its marginal position and net working capital is positive, and no new capital is needed. In spite of the positive results, however, the forecasts raise questions:

a. Mr. Fong's plan of relaxing credit policy would actually result in a 20 percent increase in sales. This increase is substantial, and it would not be accompanied by significantly increased bad debts.

b. Ms. Fisher's concerns regarding Mr. Fong's forecasts seem warranted. Her forecasts contain increased bad debts and a smaller increase in sales because of the recession. She also includes an increase in inventories to service the new sales. However, she does not increase the company's liquid cash reserves as did Mr. Fong.

The question of which plan to follow depends largely on your view of the impact of the widespread recession on the company's markets. At the time, a recession appeared to be affecting Asian and European countries. However, the time might have been right for the company to lure new customers to its products with increased credit availability.

2. To create the 2004 financial forecast for Agrilabs, simply forecast the sales increase of 20 percent, and all other items are proportional to sales. To determine the proportions, you must create common-sized financial statements for 2003. The following years are identical except for the sales growth rates. The resulting financial statements follow.

AGRILABS SPA FINANCIAL STATEMENTS

(in thousands)

Income Statements	2003	Percent of Sales	2004	2005	2006	2007	2008
Sales	$ 7,500	100.0%	$ 9,000	$10,980	$ 13,396	$ 15,807	$18,652
Cost of goods sold	(6,000)	–80.0%	(7,200)	(8,784)	(10,717)	(12,646)	(14,922)
Gross income	1,500	20.0%	1,800	2,196	2,679	3,161	3,730
SG&A	(780)	–10.4%	(936)	(1,142)	(1,393)	(1,644)	(1,940)
Interest	(213)	–2.8%	(213)	(213)	(213)	(213)	(213)
Net income before taxes	507	6.8%	651	841	1,073	1,304	1,577
Taxes (40%)	(203)	–40.0%	(260)	(336)	(429)	(522)	(631)
Net income	$ 304	4.1%	$ 391	$ 505	$ 644	$ 782	$ 946
Dividends	$ 153		$ 153	$ 153	$ 153	$ 153	$ 153
To retained earnings	$ 151		$ 238	$ 352	$ 491	$ 630	$ 794

(continued)

Balance Sheets	2003	Percent of Sales	2004	2005	2006	2007	2008
Assets							
Cash	$ 300	4.0%	$ 362	$ 442	$ 539	$ 636	$ 750
Accounts receivable	657	8.8%	788	962	1,173	1,385	1,634
Inventory	2,500	33.6%	3,000	3,660	4,465	5,269	6,217
Total current assets	3,457	46.4%	4,150	5,064	6,177	7,290	8,601
Net fixed assets	4,000	53.6%	4,800	4,680	4,560	4,440	4,320
Total assets	$ 7,457	100.0%	$ 8,950	$ 9,744	$ 10,737	$ 11,730	$ 12,921
Liabilities and Owners' Equity							
Accounts payable	$ 357	4.8%	$ 428	$ 523	$ 638	$ 752	$ 888
Accruals	100	1.3%	100	100	100	100	100
Notes payable	250	3.4%	250	250	250	250	250
Total current liabilities	707	9.5%	778	873	988	1,102	1,238
Long-term debt	3,300	44.3%	3,300	3,300	3,300	3,300	3,300
Common stock	2,500	33.5%	2,500	2,500	2,500	2,500	2,500
Retained earnings	850	11.4%	1,088	1,440	1,931	2,561	3,355
Total liabilities and equity	7,357	98.7%	7,666	8,113	8,719	9,463	10,393
Trial balance	7,357	98.7%	1,284	1,631	2,018	2,267	2,528
Net financing needed	0						
Total liabilities and equity	$ 7,357	98.7%	$ 8,950	$ 9,744	$ 10,737	$ 11,730	$ 12,921

3. To create the financial statements for Wingate Motors, follow these steps.

Step 1. Sales. Increase the 2002 U.S. sales by 25 percent and the sales in Japan by 5 percent. To do this for Japan, multiply the 2002 sales by 1 plus the rate of growth, 5 percent. However, because the U.S. sales reported in 2002 are in yen:

a. translate the 2002 U.S. sales into dollars by dividing by the exchange rate of ¥154:$1.00
b. multiply the U.S. dollar sales by 1 plus the rate of growth (25 percent) to determine the estimated 2003 sales in the United States in dollars
c. convert the 2003 sales in the United States in dollars to yen by multiplying the U.S. sales in dollars by the estimated yen/dollar exchange rate of ¥140:$1.00.

The total sales figure for Wingate in 2003 is the sum of the yen-translated U.S. sales and the sales in Japan.

Step 2. Cost of Sales. Cost of sales is expected to be 75 percent of total U.S. and Japanese sales, in yen terms. Operating costs grow at a simple rate of 10 percent, and research stays at ¥200.

Using this information, the following income statement is created.

WINGATE MOTOR CO. LTD.
Actual 2002 and Forecast 2003 Income Statements

(in billions of yen)

	2002	2003
Net sales		
Japan	¥ 1,300	¥ 1,365.0
United States	2,200	2,500.0
Total sales	3,500	3,865.0
Cost of goods sold	(2,625)	(2,898.8)
Research and development	(200)	(200.0)
Gross profit	675	766.2
Operating expenses	(500)	(550.0)
Operating profit	175	216.2
Taxes	(70)	(86.5)
Net profit	¥ 105	¥ 129.7

Step 3. Balance Sheet. To estimate the balance sheet, the following steps must be taken:

a. Calculate the average daily sales:

$$\text{Average daily sales} = \text{Total sales}/360$$
$$= ¥3,865/365$$
$$= ¥10.59 \text{ million}$$

b. Multiply the average daily sales by the collection period of 45 days to obtain the value of the accounts receivable.
c. Inventory is 1/6 of cost of sales.
d. Cash is 10 percent of sales.
e. Payables are 60 days × (Cost of sales/365).
f. Retained earnings are the sum of the 2002 retained earnings and the 2003 profit after taxes.
g. The short-term debt is the "plug" or balancing figure for the balance sheet. The total liabilities and equity, with no change in short-term debt, are ¥2,831.2 million, and the assets are ¥2,846.1 million. Thus, the new short-term debt will be ¥14.9 million.

The balance sheet is as follows.

WINGATE MOTOR CO. LTD.
Actual 2002 and Forecasted 2003 Balance Sheets

(in billions of yen)

	2002	2003
Assets		
Cash	¥ 250.0	¥ 386.5
Accounts receivable	400.0	476.5
Inventory	475.0	483.1
Total current assets	1,125.0	1,346.1
Net property, plant, and equipment	1,500.0	1,500.0
Total assets	¥ 2,625.0	¥ 2,846.1
Liabilities and Equity		
Accounts payable	¥ 400.0	¥ 476.5
Other short-term debt	350.0	350.0
Total current liabilities	750.0	826.5
Long-term debt	1,050.0	1,050.0
Common stock	75.0	75.0
Retained earnings	750.0	879.8
Total equity	825.0	954.8
Subtotal	2,625.0	2,831.3
New short-term financing	—	14.9
Total liabilities and equity	¥ 2,625.0	¥ 2,846.1

Step 4. Net Working Capital. To determine the change in net working capital, first subtract the current liabilities from the current assets in 2002 and 2003. The change of ¥145 billion is divided by the 2002 net working capital of ¥375 to determine the change of 38.7 percent.

Step 5. *Current Ratio and Working Capital.*

Current ratio = Current assets/Current liabilities

For 2002, the current ratio is:

Current ratio = ¥1,125/¥750

= 1.50 or 150 percent

The current ratios and net working capital changes are as follows:

WINGATE MOTOR CO. LTD.
Current Ratios and Changes in Working Capital

(currency in billions of yen)

Working Capital	2002	2003
Net working capital	375	520
Change in net working capital	N.Ap.	39%
Current ratio	150%	163%

To revise your forecasts, use the assumptions detailed in the problem and follow the steps described in the solution to Study Question 1. The balance sheet is as follows.

WINGATE MOTOR CO. LTD.
Actual 2002 and Revised 2003 Forecasted Financial Statements

(currency in billions of yen)

	2002	2003
Assets		
Cash	¥ 250.0	¥ 270.6
Accounts receivable	400.0	635.3
Inventory	475.0	483.1
Total current assets	1,125.0	1,389.0
Net property, plant, and equipment	1,500.0	1,500.0
Total assets	¥ 2,625.0	¥ 2,889.0
Liabilities and Equity		
Accounts payable	¥ 400.0	¥ 357.4
Other short-term debt	350.0	350.0
Total current liabilities	750.0	707.4
Long-term debt	1,050.0	1,050.0
Common stock	75.0	75.0
Retained earnings	750.0	879.8
Total equity	825.0	954.8
Subtotal	2,625.0	2,712.2
New short-term financing	—	176.9
Total liabilities and equity	¥ 2,625.0	¥ 2,889.0

The current ratios and net working capital changes are as follows.

WINGATE MOTOR CO. LTD.
Current Ratios and Changes in Working Capital

(currency in billions of yen)

Net working capital	¥375.0	¥681.6
Change in net working capital	N.Ap.	82%
Current ratio	150%	196%

Note: N. Ap. represents data not applicable.

As you can see from your analysis, the changes that occur if Wingate extends its collection period (relaxes its credit terms) and pays its suppliers more quickly include a greater need for financing. This need results from the increase in accounts receivable. While the changes in accounts receivable and payables ought to have a net negative impact on the working capital and current ratio, they do not in this case: The decrease in cash and increase in financing from short-term sources offset the increase.

Thus the impact on Wingate Motor Co. of these changes appears to be neutral. If Wingate management decided not to reduce its cash position, and if it financed the changes from long-term sources of capital, the change would not be neutral.

This analysis reveals Wingate's financial strength. Its current ratio exceeds the average for the industry. If payables lengthened and receivables were to be collected more slowly in economic downturns, Wingate could easily endure the changes. This should concern Wingate's competitors.

4.

WINGATE
2002 Balance Sheet

(in billions)

Assets				Change
Cash	¥	250	¥	245
Accounts receivable		400		575
Inventory		475		475
Total current assets		1,125		1,295
Net property, plant, and equipment		1,500		1,500
Total assets		¥2,625		¥2,795

Liabilities and Equity				Change
Accounts payable	¥	400	¥	324
Other short-term debt		350		350
Total current liabilities		750		674
Long-term debt		1,050		1,050
Common stock		75		75
Retained earnings		750		750
Total equity		825		825
Total liabilities and equity		¥2,625		¥2,549

The Liabilities and Equity account is less than the assets with these changes. The company would need to find new financing or modify one of the changes.

5. With a change in the dollar:yen exchange rate, the following statements would result.

WINGATE MOTOR CO. LTD.
Actual 2002 and Revised 2003 Financial
Statement Forecasts—¥85:$1.00

(currency in billions of yen)

Income Statements	2002	2003
Net sales		
Japan	¥ 1,300.0	¥ 1,365.0
United States	2,200.0	1,517.9
Total sales	3,500.0	2,882.9
Cost of goods sold	(2,625.0)	(2,162.1)
Research and development	(200.0)	(200.0)
Gross profit	675.0	520.8
Operating expenses	(500.0)	(550.0)
Operating profit	175.0	(29.2)
Taxes	(70.0)	11.7
Net profit	¥ 105.0	¥ (17.5)

Balance Sheets	2002	2003
Assets		
Cash	¥ 250.0	¥ 201.8
Accounts receivable	400.0	355.4
Inventory	475.0	360.4
Total current assets	1,125.0	917.6
Net property, plant, and equipment	1,500.0	1,500.0
Total assets	¥ 2,625.0	¥ 2,417.6
Liabilities and Equity		
Accounts payable	¥ 400.0	¥ 266.6
Other short-term debt	350.0	350.0
Total current liabilities	750.0	616.6
Long-term debt	1,050.0	1,050.0
Common stock	75.0	75.0
Retained earnings	750.0	732.4
Total equity	825.0	807.4
Subtotal	2,625.0	2,474.0
New short-term financing	0	(56.4)
Total liabilities and equity	¥ 2,625.0	¥ 2,417.6

Working Capital		
Net working capital	¥375	¥301
Change in net working capital	N.Ap.	–20%
Current ratio	150%	149%

The drop in the yen relative to the dollar would negatively impact the condition of Wingate.

6. To forecast a monthly cash budget for Mary's Ski Chalet for 2004, first create 12 columns headed by the months of the year beginning with January. Then determine the cash receipts and disbursements.

Step 1. Cash receipts are determined as follows:
a. Cash is received from cash sales and collections from accounts receivable. Credit sales—75 percent of sales—are collected 30 days after the sale is made. Sales forecasts and beginning accounts receivable are provided in the problem.
b. Cash collections are the total of cash sales—25 percent of sales—plus the collections from accounts receivable.

Step 2. Disbursements are determined as follows:
a. Purchases are cost of goods sold (75 percent of sales) plus 6 percent of sales (a total of 81 percent of sales), and are paid for 30 days after the goods are ordered. The accounts payable account at the end of the month is the beginning accounts payable less the accounts payable payments plus the purchases.
b. The disbursements are the payments of accounts payable plus the selling, general, and administrative expenses of 19 percent of sales and lease and interest expenses of $2,000 per month ($24,000 for the year).

Step 3. Net receipts are the receipts less the disbursements.

Step 4. The cash balance is the beginning cash account plus the net receipts.

The forecasts for Mary's Ski Chalet are shown in the following table. As you can see, although Mary's Ski Chalet will have negative receipts for most months until August, the beginning cash balance of $65 plus the receipts in January will provide sufficient cash to operate through the difficult spring and summer months.

MARY'S SKI CHALET
2004 Cash Receipts and Accounts Receivable Account

(in thousands)	Jan.	Feb.	March	April	May	June	July	Aug.	Sept.	Oct.	Nov.	Dec.
Sales	$210.0	$175.0	$160.0	$140.0	$ 50.0	$30.0	$30.0	$75.0	$90.0	$125.0	$165.0	$230.0
Cost of goods sold	$157.5	$131.3	$120.0	$105.0	$ 37.5	$22.5	$22.5	$56.3	$67.5	$ 93.8	$123.8	$172.5
Accounts Receivable Schedule												
Beginning accounts receivable	$184.0	$157.5	$131.3	$120.0	$105.0	$37.5	$22.5	$22.5	$56.3	$ 67.5	$ 93.8	$123.8
Credit sales	157.5	131.3	120.0	105.0	37.5	22.5	22.5	56.3	67.5	93.8	123.8	172.5
Collections on accounts receivable	184.0	157.5	131.3	120.0	105.0	37.5	22.5	22.5	56.3	67.5	93.8	123.8
Ending accounts receivable	$157.5	$131.3	$120.0	$105.0	$ 37.5	$22.5	$22.5	$56.3	$67.5	$ 93.8	$123.8	$172.5
Receipts												
Cash sales	$ 52.5	$ 43.8	$ 40.0	$ 35.0	$ 12.5	$ 7.5	$ 7.5	$18.8	$22.5	$ 31.3	$ 41.3	$ 57.5
Collections on accounts receivable	184.0	157.5	131.3	120.0	105.0	37.5	22.5	22.5	56.3	67.5	93.8	123.8
Total receipts	$236.5	$201.3	$171.3	$155.0	$117.5	$45.0	$30.0	$41.3	$78.8	$ 98.8	$135.1	$181.3
Accounts Payable Schedule												
Beginning accounts payable	$173.0	$170.1	$141.8	$129.6	$113.4	$40.5	$24.3	$24.3	$60.8	$ 72.9	$101.3	$133.7
Purchases	170.1	141.8	129.6	113.4	40.5	24.3	24.3	60.8	72.9	101.3	133.7	186.3
Payments on accounts payable	173.0	170.1	141.8	129.6	113.4	40.5	24.3	24.3	60.8	72.9	101.3	133.7
Ending accounts payable	$170.1	$141.8	$129.6	$113.4	$ 40.5	$24.3	$24.3	$60.8	$72.9	$101.3	$133.7	$186.3

(continued)

	Jan.	Feb.	March	April	May	June	July	Aug.	Sept.	Oct.	Nov.	Dec.
Disbursements												
Payments on accounts payable	$173.0	$170.1	$141.8	$129.6	$113.4	$40.5	$24.3	$24.3	$60.8	$ 72.9	$101.3	$133.7
Selling, general, and administrative expense	39.9	33.3	30.4	26.6	9.5	5.7	5.7	14.3	17.1	23.8	31.4	43.7
Lease and interest expenses	2.0	2.0	2.0	2.0	2.0	2.0	2.0	2.0	2.0	2.0	2.0	2.0
Total disbursements	$214.9	$205.4	$174.2	$158.2	$124.9	$48.2	$32.0	$40.6	$79.9	$ 98.7	$134.7	$179.4
Cash Account												
Beginning cash	$ 65.0	$ 86.6	$ 82.5	$ 79.6	$ 76.4	$69.0	$65.8	$63.8	$64.5	$ 63.4	$ 63.5	$ 63.9
Receipts less disbursements	21.6	(4.1)	(2.9)	(3.2)	(7.4)	(3.2)	(2.0)	0.7	(1.1)	0.1	0.4	1.9
Ending cash	$ 86.6	$ 82.5	$ 79.6	$ 76.4	$ 69.0	$65.8	$63.8	$64.5	$63.4	$ 63.5	$ 63.9	$ 65.8

Once the cash balance has been determined, it is straightforward to create the income statement and balance sheet.

7. Following are the steps to create the 2004 financial statements.

Step 1. Income Statement.
a. The sales are the sum of the monthly sales for the year.
b. Cost of goods sold is 81 percent of sales.
c. Selling, general, and administrative expenses are 19 percent of the total sales.
d. Interest and lease expenses are $24,000.
e. Depreciation is $12,000.
The income statement for 2004 follows.

MARY'S SKI CHALET
2004 Income Statement

(in thousands)

Sales	$ 1,480.0
Cost of goods sold	(1,110.0)
Gross income	370.0
Selling and general expenses	(281.2)
Depreciation	(12.0)
Lease and interest expenses	(24.0)
Net income	$ 52.8

Step 2. Balance Sheet.
a. The cash, accounts receivable, and accounts payable accounts are those for the ending balances from the cash budget.
b. Inventory is the beginning inventory account given in the problem, plus the purchases, less cost of goods sold.
c. To calculate property, plant, and equipment, subtract depreciation of $12,000 from year-end 2003 property, plant, and equipment (beginning of 2003).
d. Equity is the beginning equity plus the net income for the year.
The balance sheets for 2003 and 2004 follow.

MARY'S SKI CHALET
Actual 2003 and Forecast 2004
Balance Sheets
(in thousands)

	2003	2004
Assets		
Cash	$ 65.0	$ 65.8
Accounts receivable	184.0	172.5
Inventory	50.0	138.8
Current assets	299.0	377.1
Net property, plant, and equipment	345.0	333.0
Total assets	$644.0	$710.1
Liabilities and Equity		
Accounts payable	$173.0	$186.3
Current liabilities	173.0	186.3
Equity	471.0	523.8
Total liabilities and equity	$644.0	$710.1

8. To make forecasts for Aries Corporation you must use the information in the problem and information from the 2001 and 2002 actual financial statements. The first step is to do a percentage of sales analysis of the 2001 and 2002 financial statements. This analysis is shown in the "Actual" columns on the left of the statements that follow. Once the analysis is done, the forecasts can be made. These forecasts are made like those in preceding problems.

ARIES CORPORATION
Actual and Projected Financial Statements

Income Statements	HISTORIC				FORECAST				
	2001	Percentage	2002	Percentage	2003	2004	2005	2006	2007
Sales	$ 221.0	100.0%	$ 266.0	100.0%	$ 320.2	$ 352.2	$ 390.9	$ 437.8	$ 494.8
Cost of goods sold	(145.0)	−65.6	(166.0)	−62.4	(167.8)	(177.5)	(197.0)	(220.7)	(249.4)
Gross profit	76.0	34.4	100.0	37.6	152.4	174.7	193.9	217.1	245.4
Operating expense	(38.0)	−17.2	(35.0)	−13.2	(42.1)	(46.3)	(51.4)	(57.6)	(65.1)
Operating income	38.0	17.2	65.0	24.4	110.3	128.4	142.5	159.5	180.3
Taxes (percent of operating income)	(19.0)	−8.6	(33.0)	−12.4	(56.0)	(65.1)	(54.1)	(60.6)	(68.5)
Net income	$ 19.0	8.6%	$ 32.0	−12.0%	$ 54.3	$ 63.3	$ 88.4	$ 98.9	$ 111.8
Sales growth			20.4%		20.4%	10.0%	11.0%	12.0%	13.0%

(continued)

Balance Sheets	HISTORIC				FORECAST				
	2001	Percentage	2002	Percentage	2003	2004	2005	2006	2007
Assets									
Cash	$ 22.0		$ 37.0		$ 44.5	$ 49.0	$ 54.4	$ 60.9	$ 68.8
Accounts receivable	49.0		31.0		37.3	41.0	45.6	51.0	57.7
Inventory	47.0		45.0		21.0	25.4	32.8	36.8	41.6
Total current assets	118.0		113.0		102.8	115.4	132.8	148.7	168.1
Net property, plant, and equipment	70.0		122.0		265.0	291.0	323.0	403.0	513.0
Total assets	$ 188.0		$ 235.0		$ 367.8	$ 406.4	$ 455.8	$ 551.7	$ 681.1
Liabilities and Equity									
Accounts payable	$ 19.0		$ 34.0		$ 27.6	$ 29.2	$ 32.4	$ 36.3	$ 41.0
Total current liabilities	19.0		34.0		27.6	29.2	32.4	36.3	41.0
Equity	169.0		201.0		255.3	318.5	406.8	505.7	617.4
Subtotal	188.0		235.0		282.9	347.7	439.2	542.0	658.4
New notes payable	—		—		84.9	58.8	16.6	9.7	22.6
Total liabilities and equity	$ 188.0		$ 235.0		$ 367.8	$ 406.5	$ 455.8	$ 551.7	$ 681.0

CHAPTER 3

1. Forecasting the 2004 financial statements for Chateau Royale requires several steps:

Step 1. Income Statement.
a. Sales for 2004 are 160 percent of 2003 sales.
b. Cost of goods sold is 75 percent of 2004 sales.
c. Operating expenses are 110 percent of 2003 operating expenses.
d. Depreciation is $8,000.
e. Operating income is sales minus cost of goods sold, operating expenses, and depreciation.
f. Taxes are 34 percent of operating income.
g. Net income after taxes is operating income minus taxes.
The resulting income statements follow.

CHATEAU ROYALE INTERNATIONAL
2003–2004 Income Statements

(in millions)

	2003	Forecast 2004
Sales	$ 375,000	$ 600,000
Cost of goods sold	(276,150)	(450,000)
Gross profit	98,850	150,000
Operating expenses	(75,000)	(82,500)
Depreciation	(5,100)	(8,000)
Operating profit	18,750	59,500
Taxes	(7,500)	(20,230)
Net profit	$ 11,250	$ 39,270

Step 2. Balance Sheet.
a. Long-term debt and common stock remain unchanged from 2003.
b. Property, plant, and equipment assets are the 2003 account less the 2004 depreciation of $8,000.
c. Retained earnings are the prior year's retained earnings plus net profit from 2004.
d. Accounts receivable are 45/365 times 2004 sales, and inventory is one-third of cost of goods sold.
e. Accounts payable are 30/365 times 2004 cost of goods sold. We use cost of goods sold since no information about purchases is given.
f. Cash is 20 percent of 2004 sales.
g. Since we do not know what Chateau Royale management expects to do with short-term debt, we enter a zero.

h. Forecasted assets will not balance with liabilities and equity. The best way to balance the assets and liabilities is to put in a balancing account called net financing needed.

The balance sheets for Chateau Royale follow.

CHATEAU ROYALE INTERNATIONAL
2003–2004 Balance Sheets

(in millions)

	2003	Forecast 2004
Assets		
Cash	$ 75,000	$ 120,000
Accounts receivable	46,233	73,973
Inventory	93,750	150,000
Current assets	214,983	343,973
Net property, plant, and equipment	115,000	107,000
Total assets	$ 329,983	$ 450,973
Liabilities and Equity		
Accounts payable	$ 23,116	$ 36,986
Short-term debt	51,867	0
Current liabilities	74,983	36,986
Long-term debt	125,000	125,000
Common stock	100,000	100,000
Retained earnings	30,000	69,270
Subtotal	329,983	331,256
Net financing needed (excess cash)	0	119,717
Total liabilities and owners' equity	$ 329,983	$ 450,973

Step 3. The net working capital is current assets minus current liabilities. To calculate the current ratio divide the two accounts. The net working capital and current ratios for 2003 and 2004 follow.

CHATEAU ROYALE INTERNATIONAL
Working Capital Ratios

Ratios	2003	Forecast 2004
Current ratio	287%	930%
Net working capital change	N.A.	$166,986

2. Only these assumptions for Chateau Royale International change for 2004:
   a. Cash/sales ratio is reduced to 15 percent.
   b. Days of cost of goods sold in payables is increased to 45 days.
   c. Inventory turnover is increased to 400 percent.
   The following statements reflect these changes.

CHATEAU ROYALE INTERNATIONAL
2003–2004 Revised Financial Statements

(in millions)

Income Statements	2003	Revised 2004
Sales	$ 375,000	$ 600,000
Cost of goods sold	(276,150)	(450,000)
Gross profit	98,850	150,000
Operating expenses	(75,000)	(82,500)
Depreciation	(5,100)	(8,000)
Operating profit	18,750	59,500
Taxes	(7,500)	(20,230)
Net profit	$ 11,250	$ 39,270

Balance Sheets (as of December 31)	2003	Revised 2004
Assets		
Cash	$ 75,000	$ 90,000
Accounts receivable	46,233	73,973
Inventory	93,750	112,500
Current assets	214,983	276,473
Net property, plant, and equipment	115,000	107,000
Total assets	$ 329,983	$ 383,473
Liabilities and Equity		
Accounts payable	$ 23,116	$ 55,479
Short-term debt	51,867	0
Current liabilities	74,983	55,479
Long-term debt	125,000	125,000
Common stock	100,000	100,000
Retained earnings	30,000	69,270
Subtotal	329,983	349,749
New financing needed (excess cash)	—	33,724
Total liabilities and owners' equity	$ 329,983	$ 383,473

Ratios	2003	Revised 2004
Current ratio	287%	498%
Net working capital change		$80,993

As a result of the lower cash balance and quicker inventory turnover, the current ratio is above the industry average of 320 percent. Chateau Royale management must take into consideration that the increase in the payables period may result in higher supplier costs, such as interest on unpaid balances, or may result in increased prices. Management should also consider whether lower cash and inventory balances could result in insufficient inventory to service customers or insufficient cash to transact business.

3. The process used in forecasting the statement revisions according to Mr. Dine and Mr. Triano is similar to the process used in solving Study Questions 1 and 2. The assumptions are those provided in the problem and are used to create the following financial statements.

KURZ CORP.
Financial Statement Forecasts

(Canadian dollars in thousands)

Income Statements	Original	Triano	Dine
Sales	CD$ 505,000	CD$ 757,500	CD$ 505,000
Bad debt	(5,000)	(15,150)	0
Net sales	500,000	742,350	505,000
Cost of goods sold	(375,000)	(568,125)	(378,750)
Gross profit	125,000	174,225	126,250
Operating expenses	(90,900)	(90,900)	(90,900)
Operating profit	34,100	83,325	35,350
Taxes	(11,935)	(29,164)	(12,373)
Net profit	CD$ 22,165	CD$ 54,161	CD$ 22,977

Balance Sheets	Original	Triano	Dine
Assets			
Cash	CD$ 90,000	CD$ 148,470	CD$ 75,750
Accounts receivable	61,644	124,521	41,507
Inventory	62,500	108,214	101,000
Current assets	214,144	381,205	218,257
Net property, plant, and equipment	130,000	130,000	130,000
Total assets	CD$ 344,144	CD$ 511,205	CD$ 348,257
Liabilities and Equity			
Accounts payable	CD$ 30,822	CD$ 46,280	CD$ 30,853
Short-term debt	86,322	—	0
Current liabilities	117,144	46,280	30,853
Long-term debt	110,000	110,000	110,000
Common stock	75,000	75,000	75,000
Retained earnings	42,000	73,996	42,812
Subtotal	344,144	305,276	258,665
New financing needed (excess cash)	0	205,929	89,592
Total liabilities and owners' equity	CD$ 344,144	CD$ 511,205	CD$ 348,257

Ratios	Original	Triano	Dine
Current assets	CD$ 214,144	CD$ 381,205	CD$ 218,257
Current liabilities	117,144	46,280	30,853
Net working capital	CD$ 97,000	CD$ 334,925	CD$ 187,404
Current ratio	183%	824%	707%

Based on these statements, Ms. Brittain should implement Mr. Triano's plan. Despite the higher cost, this plan results in higher net profits and higher asset growth. However, this policy also results in having to borrow more short-term money and thus increases the risk of financial distress if sales decline substantially.

4. The steps followed in making the forecast for THE CRESCENT are similar to those followed in the previous problems. The only special considerations that this problem presents are as follows:

   a. Some of the payments are made in Philippine pesos and some in dollars.

   b. The dollar/Philippine peso exchange rate is expected to change as early as February, and that exchange rate change must be built into the forecasts.

   c. Some of the goods ordered require a funded letter of credit before delivery. Thus, some of the expenses are incurred well before the goods arrive. For instance, the letter of credit for the cement purchases must be opened one month prior to delivery. Thus, the first payment for cement is for the letter of credit in January.

   The full forecasts are in the following table. These forecasts show that Mr. Dizon will need to have a credit line with United Coconut, and will be rapidly paid down as revenues are received. Mr. Lucas should ask United Coconut Planters' Bank for a revolving line of credit of at least P10,732,000. This is the total needed by July, before the expenses begin to decline and the revenues begin to offset the costs of building materials for THE CRESCENT. Mr. Dizon will not need the credit line after September 2004.

THE CRESCENT
Monthly Cash Flow Forecasts, 2004

(currency in millions of Philippine pesos)

Receipts	Jan.	Feb.	March	April	May	June	July	Aug.	Sept.	Oct.	Nov.	Dec.	Jan.	Feb.	March
Cash receipts	4,500				9,000			9,000		9,000		9,000			4,500
Cash disbursements															
Cement	3,402		3,645		3,645		3,645								
Granite tiles					5,000										
Window frames			120	120	120	120	120	120	120	120	120	120			
Elevators		600													
Generator					2,000										
Bathroom fixtures									585						
Salaries and benefits	375	375	375	375	375	375	375	375	375	375	375	375			
Overhead	10	10	10	10	10	10	10	10	10	10	10	10			
Total disbursements	3,787	985	4,150	505	11,150	505	4,150	505	1,090	505	505	505			
Cash Balance															
Beginning cash	1,000	1,713	728	(3,422)	(3,927)	(6,077)	(6,582)	(10,732)	(2,237)	(3,327)	5,168	4,663	13,158	13,158	13,158
Receipts less disbursements	713	(985)	(4,150)	(505)	(2,150)	(505)	(4,150)	8,495	(1,090)	8,495	(505)	8,495	—	—	4,500
Cumulative net cash flow	1,713	728	(3,422)	(3,927)	(6,077)	(6,582)	(10,732)	(2,237)	(3,327)	5,168	4,663	13,158	13,158	13,158	17,658

CHAPTER 4

1. *Step 1.* The first thing the analyst must do to determine whether Metalwerks' management should develop a new assembly line is to forecast the residual cash flows for the project. These cash flows are straightforward. If the pattern in the chapter is followed, only two tricky things must be considered—depreciation and calculating the payback period.

   a. To calculate the double-declining-balance depreciation, take the balance left to be depreciated and calculate double the straight-line depreciation. For instance, in the first year, the machinery is valued at DM1,400,000. Straight-line depreciation would be DM1,400,000 divided by 20, the number of years remaining in the equipment life. The double-declining-balance depreciation is twice the DM70,000 of straight-line depreciation, or DM140,000. The table calculating the depreciation follows the residual cash-flow forecast.

   b. The depreciation for any year is either the double-declining-balance amount or the straight-line value if the latter is larger. Straight-line depreciation is larger in the 12th year. The depreciation for years 11-20 is the straight-line value that depreciates the equipment in the remaining 8 years, or DM 48,815 per year.

   Step 2. To determine the payback, subtract the annual residual cash flow from the initial cost of DM 1,400,000. In the fourth year, the remainder to be covered is DM 338,500, while the residual cash flow is DM 530,750, which means that the equipment will be fully covered by the residual cash flow in an additional 0.64 years (DM 338,500/ DM 530,750). Because the payback is less than the four years the management requires, the project should be accepted. However, to analyze this project fully, management should estimate the net present value using an appropriate discount rate.

   The full forecasts and calculations for payback and depreciation are shown in the following table.

METALWERKS
Analysis of New Assembly Line—Residual Cash Flows (in thousands of DM)

PERIOD	0	1	2	3	4	5	6	7	8	9
Income Statement Changes										
Sales		1,625	1,625	1,625	1,625	1,625	1,625	1,625	1,625	1,625
Cost of goods sold		(601)	(601)	(601)	(601)	(601)	(601)	(601)	(601)	(601)
Gross Income		1,024	1,024	1,024	1,024	1,024	1,024	1,024	1,024	1,024
Repairs and utilities		(13)	(13)	(13)	(13)	(13)	(13)	(13)	(13)	(13)
Salaries and benefits		(480)	(480)	(480)	(480)	(480)	(480)	(480)	(480)	(480)
Depreciation		(140)	(126)	(113)	(102)	(92)	(83)	(74)	(67)	(60)
Income before taxes		391	405	418	429	439	448	457	464	471
Taxes		(133)	(138)	(142)	(146)	(149)	(152)	(155)	(158)	(160)
Net income		258	267	276	283	290	296	302	306	311
Noncash Charges										
Depreciation		140	126	113	102	92	83	74	67	60
Balance Sheet Changes										
New equipment	(1,400)									
Net residual cash flow	(1,400)	398	393	389	385	382	379	376	373	371
Payback										
Unrecovered investment value	1,400	1,002	609	(220)	(165)					
Partial year calculation			57.1%							
Payback (years)	2.57									
Benefit/cost ratio	4.76									
Depreciation Schedule										
Value not yet depreciated	1,400	1,260	1,134	1,021	919	827	744	670	603	
Straight-line rate	5%									
Depreciation		140	126	113	102	92	83	74	67	60
Straight-line for remaining life		70	66	63	60	57	55	53	52	50
Depreciation		140	126	113	102	92	83	74	67	60

(continued)

METALWERKS (continued)

PERIOD	10	11	12	13	14	15	16	17	18	19	20
Income Statement Changes											
Sales	1,625	1,625	1,625	1,625	1,625	1,625	1,625	1,625	1,625	1,625	1,625
Cost of goods sold	(601)	(601)	(601)	(601)	(601)	(601)	(601)	(601)	(601)	(601)	(601)
Gross income	1,024	1,024	1,024	1,024	1,024	1,024	1,024	1,024	1,024	1,024	1,024
Repairs and utilities	(13)	(13)	(13)	(13)	(13)	(13)	(13)	(13)	(13)	(13)	(13)
Salaries and benefits	(480)	(480)	(480)	(480)	(480)	(480)	(480)	(480)	(480)	(480)	(480)
Depreciation	(54)	(49)	(49)	(49)	(49)	(49)	(49)	(49)	(49)	(49)	(48)
Income before taxes	477	482	482	482	482	482	482	482	482	482	483
Taxes	(162)	(164)	(164)	(164)	(164)	(164)	(164)	(164)	(164)	(164)	(164)
Net income	315	318	318	318	318	318	506	318	318	318	319
Noncash Charges											
Depreciation	54	49	49	49	49	49	49	49	49	49	48
Balance Sheet Changes											
New equipment											
Net residual cash flow	369	367	367	367	367	367	367	367	367	367	367
Payback											
Unrecovered investment value											
Partial year calculation											
Payback (years)											
Benefit/cost ratio											
Depreciation Schedule											
Value not yet depreciated	542	488	439	391	342	293	244	195	146	97	48
Straight-line rate											
Depreciation	54	49	44	39	34	29	24	20	15	10	24
Straight-line for remaining life	49	49	49	49	49	49	49	49	49	49	49
Depreciation	54	49	49	49	49	49	49	49	49	49	24

Metalwerks' new assembly line investment meets management's criteria for payback. The benefit/cost ratio is 4.76 indicating that there are $4.76 benefits to every $1 of cost. However, neither of these criteria should be used without calculating the NPV. In this case there is no discount rate. Because the IRR is 27.3 percent, management should accept the investment: this is a rather high return, and thus is likely to be greater than the company's discount rate.

2. The difficulty in making these forecasts is dealing with the depreciation associated with the two investments. The cash flows show that depreciation is important in this case since the largest portion of the net present value is directly related to the high depreciation allowances.

Given the magnitude of the net present value, management of BELLA LUNA should pursue this investment. The forecasted residual cash flows are as follows.

BELLA LUNA
Residual Cash Flow Analysis—45 Percent Tax Rate

(in thousands of euros) PERIOD	0	1	2	3	4	5
Income Statement Changes						
Sales		€120.0	€138.0	€158.7	€182.5	€209.9
Operating expenses		(46.8)	(53.8)	(61.9)	(71.2)	(81.9)
Depreciation—initial investment		(30.0)	(44.0)	(42.0)	(42.0)	(42.0)
Depreciation—additional investment		0	0	(15.6)	(19.2)	(25.2)
Profit before taxes		43.2	40.2	39.2	50.1	60.8
Taxes (@ 34%)		(19.4)	(32.0)	(34.4)	(41.2)	(48.5)
Net profit		23.8	8.2	4.8	8.9	12.3
Noncash Charges						
Depreciation		30.0	44.0	57.6	61.2	67.2
Capital Investments						
Property, plant, and equipment	€(200.0)		(60.0)			
Residual net cash flow	€(200.0)	€ 53.8	€ −7.8	€ 62.4	€ 70.1	€ 79.5
Net present value (@ 10%)	€ (13.4)					

The NPV is negative with a 45 percent tax rate. However, when the tax rate drops to 34 percent, the NPV is €55.7. The tax rate makes an important difference in the value of this project.

3. In general, the solution to this problem follows that of the previous problems in this chapter. Project 1 is the most straightforward of the two. The cash flows are forecasted on the basis of data in the problem and are shown in the following project evaluation. The depreciation schedule requires that the larger of the double-declining-balance or straight-line methods be used on the undepreciated balance. The schedule to calculate the depreciation follows the residual cash flow forecasts.

Three things may be a problem in making the forecasts: Market research expenses have already been spent and, thus, are irrelevant to this project's value; production training is an expense at the beginning of the project life; and tax credit of $68,000 is expected to offset income received by Cloud Frame from other parts of its business. For the tax credit, if Cloud Frame had no other business, the tax credit could be carried forward; if no income were ever earned, the tax credit would be useless.

The net present value, benefit/cost ratio, and payback are calculated as demonstrated in the chapter. For Project 2, the same pattern is followed. However, there are two tricky cash flows—the production training and the market research. The production training is a tax-deductible expense that results in a tax credit in time zero; the market research is a sunk cost and thus not a part of the analysis.

CLOUD FRAME COMPANY
Analysis of Two Projects

(libras in thousands)

Project 1	0	1	2	3	4	5	6	7	8	9	10
Income Statement Changes											
Sales		500.0	500.0	500.0	500.0	500.0	500.0	500.0	500.0	500.0	500.0
Cost of goods sold		(245.0)	(245.0)	(245.0)	(245.0)	(245.0)	(245.0)	(245.0)	(245.0)	(245.0)	(245.0)
Gross income		255.0	255.0	255.0	255.0	255.0	255.0	255.0	255.0	255.0	255.0
Advertising		(50.0)	(50.0)	(50.0)	(50.0)	(50.0)	(50.0)	(50.0)	(50.0)	(50.0)	(50.0)
Depreciation		(160.0)	(128.0)	(102.4)	(81.9)	(65.5)	(52.4)	(52.4)	(52.4)	(52.4)	(52.4)
Income before taxes		45.0	77.0	102.6	123.1	139.5	152.6	152.6	152.6	152.6	152.6
Taxes		(15.0)	(26.0)	(35.0)	(42.0)	(47.0)	(52.0)	(52.0)	(52.0)	(52.0)	(52.0)
Net income		30.0	51.0	67.6	81.1	92.5	100.6	100.6	100.6	100.6	100.6
Noncash Charges											
Depreciation		160.0	128.0	102.4	81.9	65.5	52.4	52.4	52.4	52.4	52.4
Balance Sheet Changes											
New equipment	(800.0)										
Net residual cash flow	(800.0)	190.0	179.0	170.0	163.0	158.0	153.0	153.0	153.0	153.0	153.0
Payback											
Unrecovered investment value		610.0	431.2	261.1	97.9	(59.7)					
Partial year calculation						62.1%					
Payback (years)		4.62									
Benefit/cost ratio											
Benefit/cost ratio (times)		2.01									
Net present value (libras)		217.7									
Depreciation Schedule											
Value yet undepreciated		800	640	512	410	328	262	210	157	105	52
Double-declining balance		160	128	102	82	66	52	42	34	27	21
Straight-line for remaining life		80	71	64	59	55	52	52	52	52	52
Depreciation to be taken		160	128	102	82	66	52	52	52	52	52

Project 2

	0	1	2	3	4	5	6	7	8	9	10
Income Statement Changes											
Sales		350	385	424	466	536	616	708	779	857	943
Cost of goods sold		(175)	(193)	(212)	(233)	(268)	(308)	(354)	(390)	(429)	(472)
Gross income		175	192	212	233	268	308	354	389	428	471
Advertising		(88)	(96)	(106)	(100)	(100)	(100)	(100)	(100)	(100)	(100)
Production training	(200)										
Depreciation		(120)	(192)	(115)	(69)	(69)	(35)	—	—	—	—
Income before taxes	(200)	(33)	(96)	(9)	64	99	173	254	289	328	371
Taxes	68	11	33	3	(22)	(34)	(59)	(86)	(98)	(112)	(126)
Net income	(132)	(22)	(63)	(6)	42	65	114	168	191	216	245
Noncash Charges											
Depreciation		120	192	115	69	69	35				
Balance Sheet Changes											
New equipment	(600)										
Net residual cash flow	(732)	99	130	111	103	115	117	122	134	147	162
Payback											
Unrecovered investment		633	534	404	293	190	75	(42)			
Partial year calculation							0.6				
Payback (years)	5.6										
Benefit/cost ratio (times)	1.7										
Net present value											
(libras @ 10%)	6.55										

Based on the three measures of attractiveness, Project 1 is dominant, and management should choose to expand the existing production facilities.

3. The object of this exercise is to adjust the New Age Sales Department's forecasts so they may be used in making an investment decision. This includes using MACRS depreciation rather than straight-line depreciation, and calculating the net residual cash flow. The following shows the adjustments to the forecasts.

NEW AGE CASH FLOW FORECASTS

	1	2	3	4	5	6
Price per unit	$30,000	$30,000	$30,000	$30,000	$30,000	
Sales in meters	100	100	100	100	100	
Revenue	$ 3,000,000	$ 3,000,000	$ 3,000,000	$ 3,000,000	$ 3,000,000	
COGS	(2,100,000)	(2,184,000)	(2,271,000)	(2,362,000)	(2,457,000)	
Gross income	900,000	816,000	729,000	638,000	543,000	
Depreciation	(300,000)	(480,000)	(288,000)	(172,800)	(172,800)	$(86,400)
EBIT	600,000	336,000	441,000	465,200	370,200	(86,400)
Taxes (.34%)	(204,000)	(114,240)	(149,940)	(158,168)	(125,868)	29,376
Net Income	396,000	221,760	291,060	307,032	244,332	(57,024)
Depreciation	300,000	480,000	288,000	172,800	172,800	86,400
Refurbishing plant	$ (500,000)					
Machinery	(1,000,000)					
Working capital change	(300,000)				300,000	
Cash flow	$ 396,000	$ 701,760	$ 579,060	$ 479,832	$ 717,132	$ 29,376
NPV (@ 10%)	$ 664,620					

The NPV of the investments required to accept the Department of Defense contract is $664,620. However, this must be compared to what New Age could gain on the sale of the property. Sold now, the property would yield $600,000. The contract is preferable.

The analysis of the property could be included in the cash flows, treating the value of the land as a foregone cash flow in period zero and an inflow in period 5. In this case, the contract would still be accepted.

CHAPTER 5

1. The maximum price that Magnus' management should be willing to pay to acquire Carr is the value of Carr plus the value of the synergies that result from the merger. To determine this total, first determine the value of Magnus, of Carr, and of the combined companies. Because the problem states that there will be no growth, the value of each of the entities can be estimated using the shortcut perpetuity:

Value = Residual net cash flow/(Required return on equity – Growth in residual cash flow)

Step 1. Use the formula to calculate the value of Magnus, $355,556 ($40,000/(0.1125 – 0.0).

Step 2. The value per share is $7.11, the value of Magnus divided by the number of shares ($355,556/50,000).

Step 3. The value of Carr and the combined companies are calculated in the same way.

Step 4. The value of the synergies is $164,444, the value of the combined companies less the values of Carr and Magnus.

Step 5. The maximum price that Magnus' management should offer for Carr Co. is the value of the synergies, $164,444, plus the value of Carr, $355,556. This is a total of $520,000, or $10.40 per share price.

These values are shown in the following table.

	Magnus Corp.	Carr Co.	Combined Companies
Profit after taxes	$48,000	$30,000	$92,000
Residual net cash flow/year	60,000	40,000	120,000
Required return on equity	12.50%	11.25%	12.00%
Value	$480,000	$355,556	$1,000,000
Number of shares	N.Ap.	50,000	N.Ap.
Value per share	N.Ap.	$7.11	N.Ap.
Equity book value	N.Ap.	595,000	N.Ap.
Book value per share	N.Ap.	$11.90	N.Ap.

Step 6. The minimum price that Carr should accept from Magnus' management for the sale of Carr is the value of Carr in the market-place, in other words, its share price. Carr management should target a price equal to the value of Carr, however, because this value is higher than the current stock price. The current stock market equity value is $300,000 ($6.00/share with 50,000 shares). The value from the per-petuity shortcut valuation is $355,556, $7.11 per share—or $1.11 per share higher. Book value, often considered the floor value, is lower than the current market valuation and thus should play no role in de-termining the minimum acceptable price. While the minimum price is the current stock market value, Carr management should price the sale at the value of the company and bargain for Carr's shareholders to gain some of the $164,444 in synergies. Thus, the final price of this acquisition should be above $355,556 and below $520,000—be-tween $7.11 per share and $10.40 per share.

2. To estimate the price Smyth should offer for Robinson Research, the first step is to estimate the value of each of the entities—Smyth, Robinson, and the combined companies. The simple approach is to use the shortcut perpetuity method of valuation, as we did in Study Question 1. The only problem in dealing with this analysis is the net residual cash flow/year for the combined companies. That cash flow is management's estimate of the cash flow that would have been earned had they been merged. The residual cash flow is $10.92. Since the estimate is for the prior year, the CD$10.12 is grown at 8 percent, the real rate of growth plus the estimate for inflation.

   Using this data, the following table shows the values of each of the three companies.

SMYTH ACQUISITION OF ROBINSON LABS

(in millions of Canadian dollars)

	Smyth Instrument Co.	Robinson Research Lab	Combined Companies
Net residual cash flow/year	CD$6.45	CD$2.20	CD$10.93
Expected real growth in residual cash flow	4.0%	4.0%	4.0%
Expected nominal growth in residual cash flow	8.0%	8.0%	8.0%
Required return on equity (nominal)	16.2%	14.5%	15.5%
Value of company	CD$78.66	CD$33.85	CD$145.73

Once the value of each of the companies has been found, use the following formula to estimate the maximum price that Smyth could pay and still maintain value for its shareholders:

$$\begin{array}{c}\text{Maximum value of} \\ \text{merger to Smyth}\end{array} = \begin{array}{c}\text{Value of} \\ \text{combined companies}\end{array} - \begin{array}{c}\text{Value of} \\ \text{Smyth}\end{array}$$

$$= \text{CD\$145.73} - \text{CD\$78.66}$$

$$= \text{CD\$67.07}$$

Robinson Research Lab management should accept a price no lower than its current value of CD\$33.85 million. Any price above that will result in value being created for the Robinson shareholders. The difference between the combined values of Smyth and Robinson operating separately of CD\$112.51 (CD\$78.66 + CD\$33.85), and the value of the combined companies of CD\$145.73 is CD\$33.22. This is the value of the synergies. Smyth management can pay up to the value of Robinson plus the value of the synergies before it risks losing value for its shareholders.

3. To determine the value of Action and the price for which the company should be sold, first forecast the 2004 residual net cash flow:
   1. Forecast the 2004 sales at a growth of 5 percent from 2003 sales of \$250 million. Sales from 2003 to 2010 grow at 5 percent per year; sales thereafter grow at 3 percent.
   2. Cost of sales and selling, general, and administrative expenses are 75 and 10 percent of sales, respectively, and are deducted from sales.
   3. Depreciation of \$7 million is deducted from sales.
   4. To calculate the profit before taxes, deduct all expenses except taxes from the sales. Taxes are 34 percent of the profit before taxes.
   5. Once net income has been estimated, add back the noncash expense (depreciation) and deduct the \$7 million spent on additions to working capital and property, plant, and equipment.
   6. Because the rate of growth slows after 2003, the perpetuity shortcut can be used to estimate the value of Action from then on. But since the cash flows in this level growth world will be different from those when the company was growing more rapidly, first estimate the 2004 residual cash flow (a "steady-state" cash flow) and then estimate the terminal value from then on.
   7. The terminal value is the 2010 cash flow, divided by the required return on equity of 11.2 percent, less the permanent growth rate of 8.2 percent. The resulting terminal value is \$381.7 [\$31.3/(0.112 − 0.03)].

The forecasted residual cash flows are as follows.

ACTION CORPORATION
Residual Cash Flows 2003–2011

(in millions)

Income Statement Changes	2003	2004	2005	2006	2007	2008	2009	2010	2011
Sales growth	N.Ap.	5%	5%	5%	5%	5%	5%	5%	3%
Sales	$ 250.0	$ 262.5	$ 275.6	$ 289.4	$ 303.9	$ 319.1	$ 335.0	$ 351.9	$ 362.5
Cost of sales	(187.5)	(196.9)	(206.7)	(217.1)	(227.9)	(239.3)	(251.3)	(263.8)	(271.9)
Gross profit	62.5	65.6	68.9	72.3	76.0	79.8	83.7	88.1	90.6
Selling, general, and admin.	(25.0)	(26.3)	(27.6)	(28.9)	(30.4)	(31.9)	(33.5)	(35.2)	(36.2)
Depreciation	(7.0)	(7.0)	(7.0)	(7.0)	(7.0)	(7.0)	(7.0)	(7.0)	(7.0)
Profit before taxes	30.5	32.3	34.3	36.4	38.6	40.9	43.2	45.9	47.4
Taxes	(10.4)	(11.0)	(11.7)	(12.4)	(13.1)	(13.9)	(14.7)	(15.6)	(16.1)
Profit after taxes	$ 20.1	$ 21.3	$ 22.6	$ 24.0	$ 25.5	$ 27.0	$ 28.5	$ 30.3	$ 31.3
Noncash Charges									
Depreciation	7.0	7.0	7.0	7.0	7.0	7.0	7.0	7.0	7.0
Balance Sheet Changes									
PP&E and working capital changes	(7.0)	(7.0)	(7.0)	(7.0)	(7.0)	(7.0)	(7.0)	(7.0)	(7.0)
Annual residual cash flow	20.1	21.3	22.6	24.0	25.5	27.0	28.5	30.3	31.3
Terminal value	0	0	0	0	0	0	0	0	380.5
Net residual cash flow	$ 20.1	$ 21.3	$ 22.6	$ 24.0	$ 25.5	$ 27.0	$ 28.5	$ 30.3	$ 411.8

Present value (@ 11.2%) = $ 281.6

4. Nothing would change about the forecasts. The value of the company is as a company located in the United States and valued in its home currency. However, if the buyer were Mexican, it might want to know the total value in pesos of the purchase price. The purchase price would still be in dollars.

CHAPTER 6

1. The following data are provided in the case:

Dividend	$2.86
Market price	$45.00
Beta	0.66
Long-term growth	2.9%
10-year Treasury-bond yield	6.8
90-day Treasury-bill yield	4.9
Market risk premium above:	
Treasury bonds	4.0
Treasury bills	6.5%

To determine the cost of equity, two methods can be used.

Method 1. **Dividend-Discount Model.**

Required return on equity = [Dividend(1 + g)/Market price] + Dividend growth

The dividend yield, the dividend divided by the market price, is 6.5 percent [$2.86 × (1.029)/$45.00]. To the dividend yield, add management's estimated growth rate of 2.9 percent, for a total required return on equity of 9.4 percent.

Method 2. **Capital Asset Pricing Model.**

Required return on equity = Risk-free rate + Beta × (Market risk premium)

Using the 10-year Treasury bond rate as the nominal risk-free rate of 6.8 percent and the matching market risk premium of 4.0 percent yields a required return on equity of 9.44 percent [6.8 percent + 0.66 × (4.0 percent)]. This required return on equity is virtually identical to that estimated by the dividend-discount model. Because equity is a long-term instrument, the short-term Treasury bill rate and its matching premium are not appropriate to use.

2. Using the following data and the pattern used in the answer to Study Question 1, the dividend-discount model required return on equity for Kelly Services is 12.3 percent [($2.80 (1 + .042)/$36.00) + 4.2 percent]. Make sure that you calculate the next year's dividend, rather than using the past year's dividend of $2.80.

Growth rate	4.2%
U.S. Treasury bill yield	3.8
U.S. Treasury bond yield	6.3%
Beta	0.95
Dividend	$2.80
Market price	$36.00
Market return above Treasury bill	8.9%

To use the capital asset pricing model, the market expected return first must be estimated. The problem says that the market's return is expected to be 8.9 percent above the yield on U.S. Treasury bills. Thus, the market return is estimated at 12.7 percent. Using this, the U.S. Treasury bond return of 6.3 percent as the risk-free rate of return, and a beta of 0.95, the required return on equity is 12.38 percent [6.3 percent + 0.95 × (12.7 percent − 6.3 percent)]. Note, adding the U.S. Treasury bill rate to the premium to create a market estimate does not mean that the Treasury bill rate is being used as the risk-free rate of return.

3. Quite simply, the required return on equity should be that of Hannaford since it is Hannaford's cash flows that Grupo Mercado Tropical management would be buying. That required return on equity would use the U.S. longer term Treasury rate of 6 percent, the U.S. stock market premium of 7.5 percent, and the Hannaford beta of 1.02 for a required return on equity of 13.65 percent.

4. To determine the rate to use in discounting the New Age, Inc. cash flows for the DOD proposal, one must consider the risk of the project. There are two things that must be considered. First, for five years the price quantity for the product is contractually guaranteed by the DOD. This guarantee makes the cash revenues certain, and this argues for a very low required return, perhaps the return on five-year U.S. Treasury note of 5.8 percent. In addition to the fact that it is nominally risk free, the note matches the life of the project—it includes a fair return for risk (none), and a return to compensate for expected inflation.

   While there is not risk in the revenue stream, there is some operating risk. The cost of raw materials could rise, the production process could incur problems or added costs, and inflation in wages and raw materials could outpace the implicit forecast contained in the U.S. Treasury note rate. Since there is some risk, the required return would be higher. Depending upon how you view the various risks, the required return would be some average of the 5-year U.S. Treasury note of 5.8 percent, and the New Age, Inc. shareholders' required return of 10.9 percent (beta of 0.80, premium of 6.4 percent, and a nominal risk-free rate of 5.8 percent). The results for a various percentages of the U.S. Treasury note rate are shown as follows. As you can see, only with the highest percentages of the shareholders' required ROE is the rate equal to or above that used in the analysis in Problem 4, Chapter 4. Thus, the DOD proposal should be accepted.

Percentage Risk-Free Rate	Weighted Average Required Return
10.0%	10.4%
20.0%	9.9%
30.0%	9.4%
40.0%	8.9%
50.0%	8.4%

CHAPTER 7

1. If Ms. Malvern holds the bond for the full 10 years, she will earn 8.8 percent per return on her money. Using the IRR to compare the price today, $152,500, with the value at maturity, $232,428, you can see that the rate of return is 8.8 percent. By comparing the sales price today of $152,500 with her initial cost, the return is 8.8 percent as well—the return of 8.8 percent on the price of the bonds today suggests that interest rates have not changed since she bought the bond. Thus, she could, in all likelihood, reinvest her money at 8.8 percent. However, to sell the bond and purchase a new bond would incur transaction costs. Thus, given the current conditions, she should hold her bond to maturity.

2. The MAH potential restructuring follows the example in the chapter. The result is as follows.
   - First calculate the EPS, cash flow per share, the WACC, and corporate value with no change in the capital structure. The value of the company is the residual cash flow divided by the required return on equity less the growth rate ($165 million/(0.092 − 0.03) = $2,661 million.
   - Next do the same for the company with leverage. To do this you must estimate the WACC.
     - Calculate the beta with leverage. The unlevered beta is 1.075. Multiply this unlevered beta times [1 + (1 − tax rate) × Debt/Equity]. The levered beta is 1.275. The required return on equity is 10 percent.
     - Calculate the WACC. The analysis is shown as follows.

WACC Calculation	100% Equity Financed	78% Equity – 22% Debt
Required return on debt		
Required return on debt	0	8.0%
After-tax cost of debt	0	5.3%
Required return on equity data		
Unlevered beta	1.075	1.075
Tax rate	34.0%	34.0%
Debt/Equity	0	28.2%
Debt/Capital	0	22.0%
Levered beta	1.075	1.275
Required return on equity (CAPM)		
Risk-free rate of return	4.9%	4.9%
Risk premium	4.0%	4.0%
Required return on equity	4.9%	10.0%
WACC	9.20%	8.96%

The earnings, cash flow, company, and equity value with and without leverage are shown below.

	100% Equity Financed	78% Equity – 22% Debt
Income Statement and Cash Flows		
Profit before interest and taxes	$ 250.00	$ 250.00
Interest	0	(46.84)
Profit before taxes	250.00	203.16
Taxes	(85.00)	(69.07)
Profit after taxes	165.00	134.09
Depreciation	75.00	75.00
New plant and equipment	(75.00)	(75.00)
Added working capital	0.00	0.00
Residual cash flow	$ 165.00	$ 134.09
Number of shares outstanding	110	85.8
Earnings per share	$ 1.50	$ 1.56
Residual cash flow per share	$ 1.50	$ 1.56
Required return on		
Company	9.20%	9.20%
Debt	0	8.00%
Equity	9.20%	10.00%
WACC	9.20%	8.96%
Market value		
Debt	0	$ 585.48
Equity	$2,661.29	$2,249.08
Company	$2,661.29	$2,834.56
Equity value per share	$ 24.19	$ 26.21

The share price of MAH rises because of the interest tax shield. If the share repurchase brings attention to the company and that what potential investors see is positive, the share price could rise even further. The cost of the signaling is the new scrutiny that lenders bring to the company.

3. Melissa Hackett has an interesting set of questions to answer. Tax rates impact value, but sometimes in unexpected ways.
   - Cash flows are reduced by higher tax rates, but the after-tax cost of debt decreases.
   - Cash flows are increased by lower tax rates, but the after-tax cost of debt increases.
   - The effects of the impact on cash flows and cost of debt are not offsetting.
   - To incorporate uncertain tax rates into an investment's analysis, Ms. Hackett must build an analytical model where the tax rates can be analyzed using scenario analysis. While this is possible with WACC, it is more difficult than using required ROE and the discount rate and incorporating the cash flows from debt into the cash flows. This analytical structure is further discussed in Chapter 9.

CHAPTER 8

1. In order to determine the EPS-EBIT breakeven table:

   Step 1. Calculate the earnings per share at two different levels of earnings before interest and taxes. The most logical choices for the two EBIT levels are based on Zumar's current revenues and the revenues when the store is expanded, $100 million and $120 million, respectively.

   Step 2. Calculate the profit after taxes. To do this, you must account for $2.8 million in interest expense on existing debt ($40 million at 7 percent), and the costs of new financing. The cost of debt financing is 10 percent, and the cost of equity financing is dilution, or the increase in the number of shares from 2.0 million to 2.75 million. The following table provides the EBIT and EPS under the two financing schemes for two levels of revenue.

ZUMAR, INC.
Earnings with Existing and Expected Revenues

(in millions, except per share)

	Debt Financing		Equity Financing	
	Old Revenues	New Revenues	Old Revenues	New Revenues
Revenues	$100.0	$120.0	$100.0	$120.0
Earnings before interest and taxes	13.0	15.6	13.0	15.6
Interest:				
Old	(2.8)	(2.8)	(2.8)	(2.8)
New	(1.5)	(1.5)	0.0	0.0
Profit before taxes	8.7	11.3	10.2	12.8
Taxes	(3.0)	(3.8)	(3.5)	(4.4)
Profit after taxes	$ 5.7	$ 7.5	$ 6.7	$ 8.4
Number of shares	2.00	2.00	2.75	2.75
Earnings per share	$2.85	$3.75	$2.44	$3.06

Step 3. To determine the equivalency point, the following data are used:

Debt (millions):
    Old $40.0
    New $15.0
Interest rate:
    Old   7.0%
    New   10.0%
Number of shares (millions):
    Debt financing   2.00
    Equity financing   2.75

The formula for the breakeven EBIT or equivalency point (with no preferred dividends) is:

$$\text{Breakeven EBIT} = \frac{(2.0 \times \$2.8) - (2.75 \times \$2.8) - (2.75 \times \$1.5)}{2.0 - 2.75} \times \frac{P}{(1-t)}$$

$$= \$8.3$$

Graphically, the result is as shown on the following page.

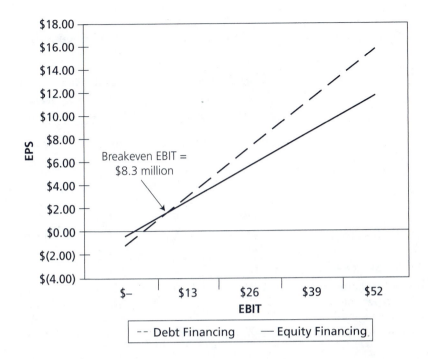

If Zumar expects to earn more than $8.3 million in earnings before interest and taxes, the debt is the better financing alternative because it results in a higher EPS for the shareholders.

2. To determine the dividend coverage, the dividends per share is divided into the earnings per share for each alternative method of financing, as follows.

ZUMAR, INC.
2003 Dividend Coverage with Existing and Expected Revenues

(in millions)

	Debt Financing		Equity Financing	
	Old Revenues	New Revenues	Old Revenues	New Revenues
Revenues	$100.0	$120.0	$100.0	$120.0
Earnings before interest and taxes	13.0	15.6	13.0	15.6
Interest:				
Old	(2.8)	(2.8)	(2.8)	(2.8)
New	(1.5)	(1.5)	0.0	0.0
Profit before taxes	8.7	11.3	10.2	12.8
Taxes	(3.0)	(3.8)	(3.5)	(4.4)
Profit after taxes	$ 5.7	$ 7.5	$ 6.7	$ 8.4
Number of shares	2.00	2.00	2.75	2.75
Earnings per share	$2.85	$3.75	$2.44	$3.06
Dividends per share	$0.75	$0.75	$0.75	$0.75
Dividend coverage (times)	3.80	5.00	3.25	4.06

Regardless of the financing method Zumar management chooses, it has sufficient earnings to cover its dividend payments generously.

3. To determine the value of Zumar for its shareholders under the two financing alternatives, we use the dividend-discount model and this data:

Dividends	$0.75
Dividend growth	5.00%
Required return on equity:	
Debt alternative	15.40%
Equity alternative	16.90%

The per-share value of the company under the two financing alternatives is:

$$\text{Debt alternative value per share} = \frac{\text{Dividends}}{\text{Required return on equity with debt financing} - \text{Dividend growth}}$$

$$= \frac{\$0.75}{0.154 - 0.05}$$

$$= \$7.21$$

$$\text{Equity financing value} \atop \text{per share} = \frac{\text{Dividends}}{\text{Required return on equity} \atop \text{with equity financing} - \text{Dividend growth}}$$

$$= \frac{\$0.75}{0.169 - 0.05}$$

$$= \$6.30$$

The value per share of Zumar with debt financing is higher than with equity. Thus Zumar management should finance the expansion with debt.

4. a. In determining which of the two financing alternatives is best for Babson Air, management must first look at the earnings per share and interest coverage ratios under the two financing alternatives. The analysis for the debt and equity financing is shown as follows. The EBITs were chosen as $38 million plus or minus $20 million.

Babson Air Debt and Equity Financing Alternatives

Debt Financing	EBIT		
Earnings before interest and taxes	$ 18.0	$ 38.0	$ 58.0
Interest:			
Old	(10.0)	(10.0)	(10.0)
New	(0.8)	(0.8)	(0.8)
Earnings	7.2	27.2	47.2
Taxes (35%)	(2.5)	(9.5)	(16.5)
Profit after taxes	$ 4.7	$ 17.7	$ 30.7
Number of shares	10	10	10
Earnings per share	$0.47	$1.77	$3.07
Interest coverage ratio	1.7	3.5	5.4

Equity Financing			
EBIT	$ 18.0	$ 38.0	$ 58.0
Interest:			
Old	(1.0)	(1.0)	(1.0)
New	—	—	—
Earnings	17.0	37.0	57.0
Taxes (35%)	(6.0)	(13.0)	(20.0)
Profit after taxes	11	24	37
Number of shares	11.5	11.5	11.5
Earnings per share	$0.96	$2.09	$3.22
Interest coverage ratio	18.0	38.0	58.0

The EBIT-EPS breakeven is $75.5 million, and the EBIT-EPS breakeven chart follows.

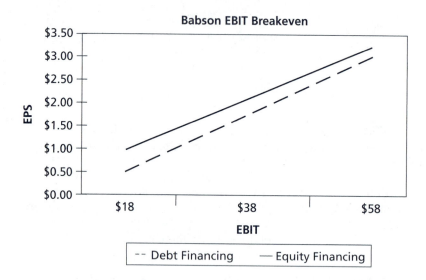

Unless management is expecting a major increase in EBIT beyond that forecast for the company with the new aircraft, equity is the superior alternative.

b. If the EBIT drops to a level where the coverage ratio is 1.0 with debt financing (an EBIT level of $11), equity still is the superior method of financing. In fact, given the slopes of the lines, it is more attractive.

c. To determine the WACC for the aircraft, the following information is used.
    a. Tax rate = 35%.
    b. Marginal cost of debt = 5%.
    c. Company beta = 1.50.
    d. Nominal risk-free rate of return = 5.8% (matches the life of the investment).
    e. Expected return on average asset = 6.1%.
    f. The appropriate capital structure is open to some discussion.
        • The CEO asserts the book value capital structure should be used. The current book value is 45 percent debt/total capital. This results in a WACC of 9.68 percent.
        • The CFO has stated that market value capital structure of 60 percent debt/total capital should be used. The resulting WACC would be 7.93 percent.

Actually, neither should be used. The target structure provides the appropriate weights. Thus, the argument is about which best represents the target structure.

d. After financing, the capital structure will change. Thus, the capital structures must be determined before the WACC can be calculated.

e. The capital structure after financing in book value and market value terms is shown below:

Debt/Total Capital	Debt Financing	Equity Financing
Book value	52.3%	61.4%
Market value	65.0%	45.0%

Given these weights, the WACCs would be:

WACC After Financing Capital Structure	Debt Financing	Equity Financing
Book value	8.8%	7.8%
Market value	7.3%	9.7%

f. Given the arguments, perhaps a hybrid security might be interesting to Babson Air. In that way, the company could finance with less expensive debt, and, anticipating a stock price increase, see a conversion of the debt after a reasonable time. However, the arguments for equity financing all run to equity.

5. Mad Mike is not suffering from capital structure problems, but from growth. Had Mad Mike thought about the impact of the financing scheme when sales recovered, he might have planned for the financing needs rather than having to react to the banker's call.

6. For Sam's Equestrian Centers, the cost of preferred is 5.1 percent after deducting issue costs.

$$Preferred\ Cost = (0.049 \times \$100)/(\$100 \times (1 - 0.04))$$
$$= \$4.9/\$96$$
$$= 0.051\ or\ 5.1\%$$

The cost of debt after taxes is:

$$After\text{-}tax\ cost\ of\ debt = Required\ return\ on\ debt \times (1 - tax\ rate)$$
$$= 0.078 \times 0.66$$
$$= 0.51\ or\ 5.1\%$$

The costs of the preferred and debt to the company are the same. Sam's does have some discretion about paying the preferred dividend on time, although it probably would have to pay it before any dividends could be paid on common stock. The debt is a bit more restrictive—lenders require more information and supervision. This oversight may not be attractive to Sam's.

As far as signaling, the preferred stock and debt would be attractive to different constituencies. Thus, Sam's should take into account what they are planning for the future, and what groups they would like to use for future capital.

CHAPTER 9

1. The following data are provided in the problem:

Dividend	$1.17
Market price	$14.95
Beta	1.32
Long-term growth	5.00%
Treasury bond yield	4.90
Treasury bill yield	3.65
Market risk premium above:	
Treasury bonds	6.00
Treasury bills	8.00
Tax rate	34.00

To calculate the WACC, the following steps must be performed.

a. *Step 1.* **The Cost of Equity.** To determine the cost of equity for Rapid Rebound, several methods can be used:

Method 1. Dividend-Discount Model.

Required return on equity = (Dividend/Market price) + Dividend growth

$$= (\$1.17/\$14.95) + 0.05$$

$$= 0.128 \text{ or } 12.8\%$$

Method 2. Capital Asset Pricing Model.

Required return on equity = Risk-free rate + Beta × (Risk premium)

Using the 10-year Treasury bond rate of 4.9 percent as the nominal risk-free rate, the matching market risk premium of 6.0 percent, and a beta of 1.32, results in a required return on equity of 12.8 percent [4.9% + (1.32 × 6.0%)]. This is a required return on equity that is the same as that estimated by the dividend-discount model. Since equities are a long-term instrument, the short-term Treasury bill rate and its matching premium are not appropriate to use.

Step 2. **Cost of Debt.** The next step is to determine the cost of debt for Rapid Rebound. The marginal cost of debt is best estimated from the current yield-to-maturity on newly issued B-rated bonds of 10.5 percent. The coupon of 17.5 percent on the company's bonds reflects its cost of borrowing in an economic environment when rates were higher. The cost of debt to the company is partially offset by the tax deductibility of the interest expense on the debt. With a tax rate of 34 percent, the after-tax cost of debt is 6.93 percent [10.5% × (1 − 0.34)].

Step 3. **Capital Structure.**
Embedded. The final step is to determine the capital structure that is anticipated. Since Mayana believes the current structure represents the future capital structure, we use the balance sheet information to calculate the proportions. The embedded debt/total capital ratio is currently 35 percent:

1) Since debt is $1.3 and equity is $2.4, total capital is

$$\text{Total capital} = \text{Debt} + \text{Equity}$$
$$= \$1.3 + \$2.4$$
$$= \$3.7$$

2) As a proportion of the capital structure:

$$\text{Debt/Total capital} = \$1.3 \div \$3.7$$
$$= 0.35 \text{ or } 35\%$$

$$\text{Equity/Total capital} = \$2.4 \div \$3.7$$
$$= 0.65 \text{ or } 65\%$$

Step 4. **WACC.** Weighting the debt cost and required return on equity by their proportions, the weighted average cost of Bakelite's capital is 10.75 percent.

Source	Cost	Proportion	Weighting
Debt	6.93%	35%	2.43%
Equity	12.80%	65%	8.32
Weighted average cost of capital			10.75%

b. Capital Structure—Market Value. The market value weightings are:
  • Equity. Market value of equity is 240,000 shares times the market price per share of $14.95—a total of $3.588 million.
  • Debt. The market value of debt is $1.991 million:
    • $1.3 million discounted at the market interest rate of 10.5 percent until maturity (16 years) is $263,116.
    • The present value of 16 annual interest payments (17.5 percent times $1.3 million) at a discount rate of 10.5 percent is $1.728 million.
  • Capital structure. Total debt and equity at market value is $5.579 million. The debt is 36 percent of capital. The proportions are virtually identical to the book value proportions.

c. If the tax rate changes, the after-tax cost of debt will increase to 8.2 percent. In book value terms the WACC would be 11.2 percent. Since the book and market value capital structures are nearly identical, the costs of capital would be roughly the same. Rapid Rebound would have to use the new WACC starting in the year the tax rate was reduced to 22 percent.

2. A. Capping Machine. The following is the analysis of the capping machine with a tax rate of 34 percent. Note we used the free cash flow method since this is a small investment that will not change the capital structure of the company. For the WACC, we used Rapid Rebound's overall WACC. The analysis was done as a perpetuity since no growth is expected in the future.

Rapid Rebound Capping Machine
With 34 Percent Tax Rate

	Year 0	Annual Cash Flows
Added gross income		$ 35,000
Salary		25,000
Depreciation		(52,500)
Earnings before taxes		7,500
Taxes		(2,550)
Net income		4,950
Depreciation		52,500
Capping machine	$(525,000)	
Cash flow	$(525,000)	$ 57,450
WACC	10.75%	
Perpetual growth rate	0.00%	
Perpetuity value	$534,419	
Net present value	$9,419	

With a change in the tax rate to 22 percent, both the cash flows and the WACC would change making the project undesirable shown as follows. Thus the capping machine should be bought if the tax rate expected remains unchanged.

Rapid Rebound Capping Machine
With 22 Percent Tax Rate

Added gross income		$ 35,000
Salary		25,000
Depreciation		(52,500)
Earnings before taxes		7,500
Taxes		(1,650)
Net income		5,850
Depreciation		52,500
Capping machine	$(525,000)	
Cash flow	$(525,000)	$ 58,350
WACC	11.20%	
Perpetual growth rate	0.00%	
Perpetuity value	$520,982	
Net present value	$(4,018)	

B. To value Very Berry, we can use the residual cash flow method. The acquisition is financed with equity, thus the required ROE is the discount rate. The residual cash flow valuation is shown as follows.

C. With this level of debt, Very Berry is a leveraged acquisition. We can join the residual cash flow valuation with the valuation of the debt tax shields in the adjusted present value. Note, with leverage declining over eight years, the required return on equity must be recalculated for each year for the residual cash flow valuation.

VERY BERRY
Residual Cash Flow Valuation—No Financing

	1	2	3	4	5	6	7	8	Normalized
EBIT	$ 145,000	$152,250	$159,863	$167,856	$176,248	$185,061	$194,314	$ 204,030	$208,110
Profit before taxes	$ 145,000	$152,250	$159,863	$167,856	$176,248	$185,061	$194,314	$ 204,030	$208,110
Taxes	(49,300)	(51,765)	(54,353)	(57,071)	(59,924)	(62,921)	(66,067)	(69,370)	(70,757)
Net profit	95,700	100,485	105,510	110,785	116,324	122,140	128,247	134,660	$137,353
Company price	(1,200,000)								
Terminal value								1,373,527	
Net cash flows	$(1,104,300)	$100,485	$105,510	$110,785	$116,324	$122,140	$128,247	$1,508,187	
Present values	$(985,982)	$80,106	$75,099	$70,406	$66,005	$61,880	$58,012	$609,131	
Net present value*	$34,658								

*Discount rate of 12 percent using the Very Berry beta.

(continued)

VERY BERRY
Adjusted Present Value with Financing

Assumptions:

Growth rate	5%	Risk premium	6%	Debt:
Terminal growth rate	2%	Unlevered beta	1.00	Term in years	8
Risk-free rate	6%			Interest rate	14.0%

Residual Valuation with Changing Required ROE

	1	2	3	4	5	6	7	8	9
EBIT	$ 125,000	$131,250	$137,813	$144,703	$151,938	$159,535	$167,512	$ 175,888	$179,405
Profit before taxes	$ 125,000	$131,250	$137,813	$144,703	$151,938	$159,535	$167,512	$ 175,888	$179,405
Taxes	(42,500)	(44,625)	(46,856)	(49,199)	(51,659)	(54,242)	(56,954)	(59,802)	(60,998)
Net profit	82,500	86,625	90,957	95,504	100,279	105,293	110,558	116,086	$118,407
Company price	(1,200,000)								
Terminal value								1,184,075	
Net cash flow	$(1,117,500)	$ 86,625	$ 90,957	$ 95,504	$100,279	$105,293	$110,558	$1,300,161	
Present values	$(756,909)	$50,011	$47,513	$46,213	$45,447	$44,942	$44,567	$95,621	
Net present value	$17,406								

CAPM-Based Required ROE Calculations

	1	2	3	4	5	6	7	8	9
Required ROE									
Unlevered beta	1.00								
Debt/total capital	90.0%	83.2%	75.4%	66.6%	56.5%	45.0%	31.9%	17.0%	0.0%
Debt/equity	900.0%	495.2%	307.3%	199.5%	130.0%	82.0%	46.9%	20.5%	0.0%
Levered beta	6.94	4.27	3.03	2.32	1.86	1.54	1.31	1.14	1.00
Risk free rate	6.0%								
Risk premium	6.0%								
Required ROE	47.6%	31.6%	24.2%	19.9%	17.1%	15.2%	13.9%	12.8%	12.0%

(continued)

Debt Repayment Schedule

	1	2	3	4	5	6	7	8
Beginning principal	$1,080,000	$998,385	$905,344	$799,276	$678,359	$540,513	$383,369	$204,225
Payment	232,815	232,815	232,816	232,816	232,816	232,816	232,816	232,816
Interest payment	151,200	139,774	126,748	111,899	94,970	75,672	53,672	28,591
Principal payment	81,615	93,041	106,068	120,917	137,846	157,144	179,144	204,225
Ending principal	$ 998,385	$905,344	$799,276	$678,359	$540,513	$383,369	$204,225	$ 0

Adjusted Present Value

	1	2	3	4	5	6	7	8
Interest payment	$151,200	$139,774	$126,748	$111,899	$94,970	$75,672	$53,672	$28,591
Tax shield	$51,408	$47,523	$43,094	$38,046	$32,290	$25,728	$18,248	$9,721
Present value (@ 14%)	$172,468							

Total Adjusted Present Value

Residual value	$17,406
Tax shield	$172,468
Adjusted present value	$189,874

Adjusted Present Value Tax Shields

	1	2	3	4	5	6	7	8
Interest payment	$151,200	$139,774	$126,748	$111,899	$94,970	$75,672	$53,672	$28,591
Tax shield	$51,408	$47,523	$43,094	$38,046	$32,290	$25,728	$18,248	$9,721
Present value (@ 14%)	$172,468							

Total Adjusted Present Value

Present value residual value	$ 34,658
Present value tax shield	172,468
Adjusted present value	$ 207,126

3. The following are the steps in determining the solution for Select Co.

Step 1. The dividend-discount model required return on equity is:

Required return on equity = (Dividend/Market price) + Dividend growth
$$= (\$0.40/\$6.90) + 0.057$$
$$= 0.058 + 0.057$$
$$= 0.115 \text{ or } 11.5\%$$

a. The dividend is 24 percent of net income of $504,000. With 300,000 shares outstanding, the dividend per share is $0.40.
b. The growth rate is 5.7 percent when calculated using:

Growth rate = (1 − Payout) × ROE
$$= (1 - 0.24) \times 0.075$$
$$= 0.057 \text{ or } 5.7\%$$

Step 2. The capital asset pricing model required return on equity is

Required return on equity = Risk-free rate + [Beta × (Risk premium)]

Given the data in the problem, the result is:

Required return on equity = 6.54% + [0.85 × (12.5% − 6.54%)]
$$= 6.54\% + 5.07\%$$
$$= 11.6\%$$

Step 3. For the embedded capital structure weights, in 2003 debt is $2.26 million, equity is $4.2 million, and total capital $6.46 million. Thus, debt is 35 percent of total capital, and equity is 65 percent. In 2004 the percentages change only slightly.

	2003		2004	
	Dollars	**Percentages**	**Dollars**	**Percentages**
Long-term debt	$2,261.50	35.0%	$2,487.7	35.0%
Common stock par value	1,500.00	23.2%	1,500.0	21.1%
Retained earnings	2,700.00	41.8%	3,120.0	43.9%
Long-term debt and equity	$6,461.50	100.0%	$7,107.7	100.0%

The market value capital structure is different. With a stock price of $6.90 and 300,000 shares outstanding, the value of the equity is below book value, $2.07 million. The debt yield to maturity is 9.96 percent and the coupon is 10 percent, thus the book and market values of the debt are virtually identical. The market value capital structure is:

	2003	
	Dollars	**Percentages**
Long-term debt	$2,261.50	52.2%
Equity market value*	2,070.00	47.8%
Long-term debt and equity	$4,331.50	100.0%

*Common stock and retained earnings

Step 4. The following shows the WACC for the two capital structures. Note, since the required ROE using the dividend-discount model and the CAPM were very similar, we averaged them and used 11.5 percent.

	Required Return	**After-Tax Cost**	**Capital Structure**	
			Embedded	**Market Value**
Debt cost	9.96%	6.6%	35.0%	52.2%
Equity cost	11.50%	11.5%	65.0%	47.8%
Weighted average cost of capital*			9.8%	8.9%

* After-tax cost times the capital structure weights

Index

487